YOUTH
DEVELOPMENT

Principles and Practices
in Out-of-School Time Settings

2nd Edition

Peter A. Witt and Linda L. Caldwell
Editors

SAGAMORE ◆◆ VENTURE

Publishers: Joseph J. Bannon and Peter L. Bannon
Sales and Marketing Manager: Misti Gilles
Sales and Marketing Assistant: Kimberly Vecchio
Director of Development and Production: Susan M. Davis
Production Coordinator: Amy S. Dagit
Graphic Designer: Marissa Willison

Library of Congress Catalog Card Number: 2018935303
ISBN print edition: 978-1-57167-915-4
ISBN ebook: 978-1-57167-916-1
ISBN extext: 978-1-57167-917-8

Printed in the United States.

SAGAMORE ◆◆ VENTURE

1807 N. Federal Dr.
Urbana, IL 61801
www.sagamorepublishing.com

Contents

Section 1

All About Youth

Section 2

Developing Youths' Potential

Section 3

Systematic Program Planning and Evaluation

Section 4

The Role of Adults in the Lives of Youth

Section 5

Diversity and Implications for Youth Development

Afterword

Acknowledgments

This book was a labor of love and professional commitment on the part of many people. First, thanks go to the authors who contributed chapters to this effort. Their expertise has enabled the book to go well beyond what it could have been if "we," Peter and Linda, had tried to write all of the chapters ourselves. We appreciate the flexibility and willingness of the authors to partner with us to make this second edition a reality. It was a sincere pleasure to work with so many interesting and talented individuals.

We would also like to thank a group of individuals who were willing to review the first edition of the book and provide us with critical feedback that helped shape the content and focus of this second edition: Jason Bocarro, Mat Duerden, Ann Gillard, Barry Garst, and Karen Melton.

The team at Sagamore–Venture has been nothing short of amazing for its work on producing this book. In particular, we would like to thank Peter Bannon, who agreed to let us undertake a second edition, and Susan Davis, Director of Development and Production, who guided the book through the production process. We would also like to thank Marissa Willison, graphic designer, and Misti Gilles, director of sales and marketing, who also contributed greatly to facilitating the development of a quality product. We would also like to thank Geof Godbey and the original crew at Venture Publishing who commissioned the first edition of this book.

We would also like to thank Peter's wife, Joyce Nies, who besides providing general support and encouragement, provided needed proofreading for all of the chapters. In addition, Linda thanks her husband, Ed Smith, for his support, understanding, patience, and encouragement. Being married to individuals who have shared academic backgrounds has made it much easier for us to justify the time and energy needed to complete this project.

Finally, we would like to thank all of the youth development professionals who have mentored and worked with us over the years, as well as all of those who make a difference in young people's lives. Linda particularly would like to acknowledge and thank Hildi Aspen, from the Monroeville, PA YMCA, who inspired and changed the lives of so many young people who were largely otherwise disenfranchised as they transitioned to adulthood. Peter would like to acknowledge the special contributions of Jerry Ringerman, a wonderful youth leader, who made such a meaningful difference in the lives of youth over his career.

We sincerely hope that you find yourself enriched by what you read in this volume, that you are encouraged to add to your existing arsenal of information that can inform practice, and that you extend your commitment to helping youth thrive.

Preface

If you are reading this book, you must have an interest in youth, and in particular, the principles and practices associated with offering youth development programs in out-of-school time (OST) settings. The purpose of this book is to increase the capacity of students and professionals working with youth in OST contexts to more fully contribute to their development. Thus, our goal is to facilitate increased knowledge about who youth are, why they do what they do, and how to facilitate their development through OST programs and services. This is the second edition of a project we began in 2005. The original volume was called *Recreation and Youth Development*. Changes in the field and our own thinking led to the retitled and updated book you are reading today.

We hope you are challenged and inspired by what you read so that you undertake efforts to help youth thrive as they make their way through adolescence and, hopefully, move on successfully to young adulthood. Perhaps you will be confronted with new ideas and perspectives. We hope so. We also hope you will discuss and debate these ideas, perspectives, and issues with others. To facilitate these discussions, authors have included at the end of each chapter a set set of discussion questions and assignments that should enhance your learning experience.

Guiding Beliefs for this Book

We want to share some of the basic beliefs that guided the development of this book and its 2005 predecessor. These basic beliefs should be evident as you move through the book. Fundamentally, we believe the following:

- It necessary to take an ecological approach to conceptualizing and developing youth services.
- OST settings are powerful contexts for youth development.
- The diversity in the racial, ethnic, and cultural backgrounds and experiences, as well as ability levels, of young people must be understood and honored when developing programs and services.
- Adults can be powerful contributors to youth development.
- Youth can and must be meaningful contributors to their own development.
- A strategy based on promoting positive experiences through OST activities is more effective than an approach solely focused on reducing problems.
- Deliberate, well-planned programs based on achieving healthy developmental outcomes are essential.
- Youth need to be educated and guided in order to reap healthy developmental benefits through OST programs.
- We must move beyond simply counting the number of participants in programs to a fuller understanding of why programs work (or not), for whom they work, and under what conditions they work.

Who and Context

One of the challenges with a book where chapters are supplied by different authors is to try to bring coherence to the overall work. For example, authors used a variety of terms to refer to young people, including adolescents, youth and young people. You will also notice that there are several different labels that the authors used when referring to professionals who work with young people, including youth worker, recreation professional, youth development specialist or professional, and program specialist. In the end, we decided that the diversity of terms referring to "youth" and "professionals" reflects the reality of the different contexts through which supports, opportunities, programs, and services are available to youth. Thus, these various terms are used throughout the book.

Flow and Progression of Book

This book has a deliberate flow to it. In addition, we tried to relate the material in a chapter to ideas in other chapters. Because of this, there are at times some redundancies of basic ideas across chapters. In our editing, we worked to eliminate unnecessary redundancies, but left instances where we felt they might help the reader link ideas together and avoid the book becoming simply a series of disparate chapters written by different authors. Although we think that most readers will want to read the book in the current order of the chapters, some may choose to read only specific chapters of special interest. We would like to suggest, however, that the material in the first section of the book is essential groundwork and provides a context for grasping some of the nuances of information presented later in the book.

The book is divided into five sections:

- All About Youth
- Developing Youths' Potential
- Systematic Program Planning and Evaluation
- The Role of Adults in the Lives of Youth
- Diversity: Implications for Youth Development

Chapters in the first section combine to paint a picture of what youth development means, who youth are today, and the evolution and current status of youth organizations.

The second section contains chapters that describe some of the basic theoretical frameworks that examine youth development, the role of recreation as a context for youth development, and the specific role of youth sport, nature-based activities, and arts and creative activities as settings for youth development.

In the third section, authors present information about systematic programming and evaluation, including the importance of intentional programming and the use of logic models and program assessment and evaluation. Approaches to structuring what are called deep and impactful experiences for youth are also presented.

The chapters in the fourth section discuss the crucial role played by adults in the lives of youth, including families, youth leaders, and mentors.

In the fifth section, chapters include discussions of the necessity to consider the diversity of youth and the importance of context in the development of youth's potential. Issues of race and ethnicity are discussed, along with issues related to providing programs for immigrant youth and lesbian, gay, bisexual, and transgender youth. The final chapter in this section deals with the philosophy behind and design of programs for youth with differing abilities.

Finally, we end the book with a chapter about the knowledge, skills, and behaviors necessary to become a skilled youth professional. Whether you are a student or a youth professional already in the field, we hope you will find the information enlightening and helpful as you create a plan for professional advancement. Even if you are already working in the field, we hope you find this material useful to your thought processes and for thinking about how the content might inform practice.

The Voices in the Book

When you read the bios of the authors, you will see that we were fortunate that individuals with a broad set of backgrounds and experiences were willing to contribute chapters or work with us as co-authors on chapters for the book. Thus, the material is enriched by the involvement of a number of different "voices." We owe a debt of gratitude to all of our partners who made this book possible, including the following: Lynn Anderson, Cheryl Baldwin, Jason Bocarro, Aishia Brown, Laurie Browne, Leslie Nicole Camarillo, Rachel Chamberlain, Mary Ann Devine, Michael Edwards, Gary Ellis, Andrea Ettekal, Patti Freeman, M. Gayle Gabriel, Barry Garst, Ann Gillard, Camilla Hodge, Gareth Jones, Andrew Lacanienta, Reed Larson, Nicole McAninch, Karen Melton, Denise Montgomery, Erika Olschewski, Corliss Outley, Daniel Perkins, Rebecca Saito, Sandra Simpkins, Monika Stodolska, Alex Sullins, Theresa Sullivan, Daniel Theriault, Kathrin Walker, and Elizabeth Weybright.

We worked with each of the chapter authors in an effort to create material that related to the overall themes of the book. Thus, all of the chapters were edited and underwent several rounds of revisions, including the ones we were involved in as authors. We hope this improved the readability of the overall book.

You will notice in the book that when it is necessary to refer to the authors, the term "we" was used. The use of "we" made it easier for the book to have a common voice. This does not mean, however, that all authors are collectively responsible for any failings of the book. It would be fair to say that all the individual strengths of the book are due to the expertise of our contributors and all of the areas needing improvement or clarification are on us, Peter and Linda.

Peter A. Witt
Texas A&M University

Linda L. Caldwell
The Pennsylvania State University

About the Authors

Editors

Linda L. Caldwell

Linda L. Caldwell is a distinguished professor emerita in the Departments of Recreation, Park and Tourism Management and Human Development and Family Studies at The Pennsylvania State University. Linda also serves as an "extraordinary professor" at the University of the Western Cape and North West University, both in South Africa, and as a guest professor at the University of Iceland. Her research focuses on interventions that develop youth competencies, promote healthy lifestyles, and reduce risky leisure behavior. She is the co-developer of two interventions that focus on preventing adolescent risk behavior through the positive use of free time: *TimeWise: Taking Charge of Leisure Time*, and *HealthWise South Africa: Life Skills for Young Adults*.

Peter A. Witt

Peter A. Witt is a professor emeritus and former Bradberry Recreation and Youth Development Chair in the Department of Recreation, Park and Tourism Sciences at Texas A&M University. His major interests are in youth program evaluation and the design of sustainable youth programs. He has undertaken evaluations of numerous after-school and youth programs in Texas and other parts of the U.S. He is the recipient of the Roosevelt Research Award from the National Recreation and Park Association and the Crawford Youth Prize from the National Recreation Foundation. He has also received the Bush Faculty Excellence in Community Service Award and several community awards (along with his wife, Joyce Nies) for contributions to local nonprofit organizations.

Contributors

Lynn S. Anderson is a distinguished service professor at State University of New York at Cortland, where she teaches primarily in the graduate program. She is also director of the Inclusive Recreation Resource Center headquartered at SUNY Cortland.

Cheryl K. Baldwin is a faculty member in Administrative Leadership at the University of Wisconsin-Milwaukee. Her work focuses on instructional, evaluation, and leadership strategies for enhancing practitioner learning in youth program quality initiatives and social innovation partnerships.

Jason N. Bocarro is an alumni distinguished undergraduate professor and university faculty scholar in the Department of Parks, Recreation & Tourism Management at North Carolina State University. He has spent the last 20 years examining how sport, park and recreation programs, and environments can influence child and adolescent health.

Aishia Brown is a postdoctoral research associate at the University of Louisville in the School of Public Health and Information Sciences Commonwealth Institute of Kentucky. Her work examines the intersections of youth development, social justice, and community engagement.

Laurie Browne is the director of research at the American Camp Association, where her work focuses on engaging camp professionals in sustainable evaluation that is used to improve programs, train staff, and advocate for the value of camp experiences.

Leslie N. Camarillo is a master's student in the Department of Recreation, Sport and Tourism at the University of Illinois at Urbana-Champaign. Her research focuses on family dynamics and leisure behavior among second-generation Mexican-American youth.

Rachel Chamberlain is a research assistant at Search Institute and uses her experience as a practitioner in K-12 education and community youth development to inform her work. Her research interests include school culture and the ways in which relationships produce positive outcomes for adults and youth.

Mary Ann Devine is a professor at Kent State University in the Recreation, Park, & Tourism Management and Disability Studies programs. Her areas of teaching and research interests are in the inclusion of people with disabilities in leisure contexts and best inclusion practices.

Michael B. Edwards is an associate professor in the Department of Parks, Recreation & Tourism Management at NC State University. His research focuses on understanding how sport and recreation facilities and programs can be managed to promote active lifestyles, reduce health disparities, and provide tools for sustainable community development

Gary D. Ellis is professor and Bradberry Chair in the Department of Recreation, Park and Tourism Sciences at Texas A&M University and Texas A&M AgriLife Research. His research agenda is directed at understanding how immediate, point-of-service experiences may be structured to enhance experience quality.

Andrea Vest Ettekal is an assistant professor in the Department of Recreation, Park and Tourism Sciences at Texas A&M University. She does research on youth programs; conducts evaluations of youth programs; and teaches classes on youth development concepts, programs, and practices.

Patti A. Freeman is a professor in the Experience Design and Management Department and associate dean of General Education at Brigham Young University. Her research focuses on understanding the impact of structured experiences on guest experiences and she enjoys studying experience provision around the world.

M. Gayle Gabriel earned her Ph.D. with a focus on youth development in Recreation, Park and Tourism Sciences at Texas A&M University. She is interested in equitable research and programming for Asian American youth populations.

Barry A. Garst is an associate professor of Youth Development Leadership at Clemson University whose applied research focuses on factors that influence youth program outcomes in summer camps and other out-of-school time youth programs. Previously Barry served as the director of Program Development and Research Application with the American Camp Association.

Ann Gillard is the director of Research and Evaluation at The Hole in the Wall Gang Camp and an independent program evaluation consultant. Her work focuses on youth development, youth with serious illnesses, and social justice.

Camilla J. Hodge has worked with adolescents in substance abuse treatment, after-school sports, and religious programs and is currently an assistant professor of Health, Kinesiology, and Recreation at the University of Utah. She teaches courses on management, positive youth development, and research methods, and studies family leisure among parents and adolescents, emerging adults, and siblings.

Gareth J. Jones is an assistant professor of Sport of Recreation Management at Temple University. His research focuses on sport-based youth development (SBYD) as well as the overarching policies and management structures guiding youth sport delivery systems.

Andrew Lacanienta is a doctoral candidate in the Department of Recreation, Park and Tourism Sciences at Texas A&M University. He is an experience wizard who designs, stages, and researches extraordinary, memorable experiences.

Reed W. Larson is a professor of Human Development and Family Studies, Psychology, and Educational Psychology at the University of Illinois, Urbana-Champaign. His research is aimed at understanding the developmental experiences youth have in after-school programs and how staff facilitate these experiences.

Nicole McAninch is a senior lecturer of Child & Family Studies at Baylor University, bringing to the classroom over 10 years of practical experience working with children and families in school and ministry settings. She teaches courses on family relationship development and managing resources for quality family functioning and studies how families manage their resources effectively in order to achieve their goals.

Karen K. Melton has worked with adolescents for over a decade in a variety of out-of-school settings such as camp, after-school, religion, wilderness, welfare, and residential. She is currently an assistant professor of Child & Family Studies at Baylor University, teaches courses on adolescent development, program design, and evaluation; and conducts research on positive family experiences.

Denise Montgomery is founder and principal of CultureThrive, a consulting practice providing research, program development, and organizational development services for arts and cultural organizations and for youth organizations. Denise has led development of the *National Blueprint to Advance Creative Youth Development*, and written several reports and publications, including *The Rise of Creative Youth Development; Something to Say: Success Principles for Afterschool Arts Programs from Urban Youth and Other Experts*; and *Partnering with Community Arts Organizations: A Pathway to a High-Quality Club Experience*.

Ericka J. Olschewski has worked with youth in various capacities and settings for over 20 years. She is currently working as the primary therapist on an inpatient pediatric behavioral health unit for Intermountain Healthcare in Utah.

Corliss Outley is associate department head and associate professor for the Recreation, Park and Tourism Sciences Department at Texas A&M University. Her research focuses on youth development, race and ethnicity, and urban parks.

Daniel F. Perkins is a professor of Family and Youth Resiliency and Policy at The Pennsylvania State University. He is principal scientist and founder of the Clearinghouse for Military Family Readiness at Penn State and has designed and evaluated strengths-based family and youth development programs in 4-H and Cooperative Extension.

Rebecca (Beki) N. Saito is a senior research associate at Rainbow Research with over 30 years of experience evaluating nonprofits, with a particular focus on youth development. Saito is best known for her work in underrepresented communities and utilizing the strengths of young people as agents of change through creative, participatory methods.

Sandra D. Simpkins is a professor in the School of Education at the University of California at Irvine. Her research examines how youth development unfolds over time and how families, friendships, and social position factors (such as ethnicity and culture) shape adolescents' organized after-school activities and motivation.

Monika Stodolska is a professor in the Department of Recreation, Sport and Tourism at the University of Illinois at Urbana-Champaign. Her research focuses on issues of race, ethnicity, immigration, and leisure.

Alex Sullins is a doctoral student studying youth development in the Recreation, Park and Tourism Sciences department at Texas A&M University. He is a certified Park and Recreation Professional with nearly a decade of professional experience programming youth and adult sports.

Theresa (Terri) K. Sullivan is director of Applied Qualitative Research and Community Mobilization at Search Institute, where she works with field partners to employ qualitative research to inform youth development goals, policy, practice, and measures. A core area of interest and expertise is engaging marginalized youth as agents of change in policies, programs, and practices that affect them.

Daniel Theriault is an assistant professor of Recreation and Leisure Services at Benedict College. His research seeks social justice in and through recreation.

Kathrin C. Walker is an associate extension professor and specialist at the University of Minnesota Extension Center for Youth Development. She studies the role of youth workers and leads professional development programs to support youth work practice.

Elizabeth H. Weybright is an assistant professor of Human Development and adolescent extension specialist at Washington State University. Using a prevention science perspective, her research focuses on adolescent development and how leisure serves to promote healthy development or engagement in risk behavior.

Chapter 1

Ten Principles of Youth Development

Linda L. Caldwell and Peter A. Witt

This book was written to help you (a) understand how youth develop through their out-of-school time (OST) experiences and (b) structure and provide the necessary supports, opportunities, programs, and services (SOPS) to promote optimal youth development in OST settings. The goal of this chapter is to set the stage for the rest of the chapters in this book by providing a set of general principles to guide youth development. These principles have evolved over the last 45-plus years as practitioners, researchers, and young people have defined the basic SOPS necessary to enable youth to develop fully from childhood through adolescence into adulthood. All of the chapters in the book relate in some way to these principles.

Simply speaking, a youth development approach is "rooted in a commitment to enabling all young people to thrive" (Hamilton, Hamilton, & Pittman, 2004, p. 3). Note the use of the word *all*. Thus, one overarching ideal of a youth development approach is universality or inclusiveness; no matter the background and circumstances, all youth are in need of SOPS that promote positive youth development. A second overarching ideal is youth development work focuses on providing SOPS so that youth can thrive. The 10 principles in this chapter are based on these two ideals.

Thriving

Thriving is an exciting concept for youth workers interested in the value of OST activities. There are numerous facets to the concept, but essentially,

> Thriving entails the *engagement of one's unique talents, interests, and/or aspirations.* In this lies the assumption of one's self-awareness of his or her uniquenesses and the opportunities to purposefully manifest them. Through such engagement, one might be thought of as actively working toward fulfilling his or her full potential. (Bundick, Yeager, King, & Damon, 2010, p. 892)

Unpacking this statement is important to understanding the role youth workers in OST contexts play in promoting thriving among youth. Thriving happens when young people work with purpose to achieve their full potential. All young people can thrive, but those who have the requisite SOPS are more likely to *fully* thrive. Thriving is forward momentum that, over time, contributes to youth realizing their optimal development. Thus, thriving is not just being "okay" or avoiding negative outcomes, but rather a trajectory toward achieving one's full potential.

Benson and Scales (2009) coined the term *sparks* to describe the reciprocal interaction between youth and SOPS that enable youth to (a) recognize their talents and interests and (b) develop strong intrinsic motivation to develop the knowledge and skills necessary to pursue their passions. Passions can include anything. For one person it may be pursuing a favorite activity (e.g., art, sports, outdoor activities); for someone else it may be wanting to grow up and make a difference in the lives of others; and for someone else it may be a passion for new knowledge. In all of these endeavors, having a strong sense of purpose and a mind-set focused on personal growth are key.

Sparks are facilitated by having caring adults in one's life to support and guide one's choices and help identify resources and pathways to achieve desired outcomes (Search Institute, 2017). That is, youth workers have strong potential to ignite sparks through OST programs. Furthermore, as you will read in Chapter 4, youths' brains are particularly amenable to being sparked!

Supports, Opportunities, Programs, and Services

Understanding the terms *supports, opportunities,* and *programs* will help you articulate and better grasp the essential nature of youth development goals and practices (Pittman, Irby, Tolman, Yohalem, & Ferber, 2003). These SOPS are discussed below.

Supports

Supports provide affirmation that youth matter and are valued. Supports also facilitate youth setting and accomplishing goals. Supports can take many different forms, including those that are motivational, emotional, and strategic. According to Pittman and colleagues (2003), supports include the following:

- Healthy relationships through nurturance and friendship
- Role models, resources, and networks that provide planning skills, help access resources (e.g., financial, social)
- High expectations and clear standards through guidance and monitoring

All people need supports that are affirming, respectful, and ongoing in order to succeed in life. Supports are most powerful when offered by a variety of people who are involved in the lives of youth, such as parents and close relatives, community social networks, teachers, youth workers, employers, health providers, and peers.

Opportunities

Young people need opportunities to learn how to act in the world around them, and to explore, express, learn, belong, and contribute. Opportunities give young people the chance to test ideas and behaviors and to experiment with different roles. It is important to stress that young people, just like adults, learn best through active participation and that learning occurs in all types of settings and situations. Opportunities include the following:

- Quality instruction and opportunities for informal learning through skill building, exploration and reflection, expression and creativity, and leisure and play
- Challenging roles and responsibilities through employment and earned income, opportunities for having influence and being an advocate, and opportunities for belonging to something larger than oneself (e.g., membership)

Programs and Services

Programs and services offered by a variety of organizations are essential to promoting positive youth development. These organizations or agencies provide access to human services in a wide variety of domains, including education, recreation, physical and mental health, employment, social networking, and juvenile justice. They should also provide access to the following:

- Appropriate and maintained infrastructure such as transportation, roads, housing, and retail and healthy food choices
- Stable places such as homes, neighborhoods, and community meeting places

Programs and services should adhere to a set of standards in areas of administration, management, and service delivery (Council on Accreditation, n.d.). These programs and services should be available to all youth (inclusive of race, ethnicity, gender, socioeconomic status, etc.) and not just those with problems. In other words, all youth benefit from the chance to be involved in youth development opportunities. Agencies and organizations, including those that are publicly funded; privately funded; and provided by nonprofit, quasi-public organizations, offer a wide range of programs and services.

Historically, SOPS stemmed from an underlying philosophy that youth had many problems and that adolescence was a period of "storm and stress." Initially, therefore, SOPS were often geared toward fixing problems or providing opportunities so that youth could avoid trouble or negative behaviors (read more in Chapters 5 and 6). Fortunately, a new perspective evolved that considers youth to be largely responsible, caring, and concerned individuals who are learning to navigate the world, trying to figure out who they are, and learning how they fit into society. SOPS are means for helping young people thrive as they make their way through adolescence into young adulthood and beyond. Based on this perspective, we present and discuss a set of 10 principles for enabling youth to thrive as they progress through adolescence into adulthood.

Ten Principles of Youth Development

Based on a review of literature, we developed a set of 10 principles for providing the necessary supports, opportunities, programs, and services in OST contexts that will enable youth to thrive. The principles are not mutually exclusive from one another, nor is the list exhaustive, but we hope they offer a good foundation for providing the SOPS necessary to promote youth development. The list of principles follows.

1. Adopt a positive perspective to promote thriving
2. Thriving emerges from a foundation of strengths-based models
3. Thriving requires knowledge, skills, and behaviors
4. Thriving is a journey, and it is complex
5. It takes a village to foster thriving
6. Youth voice and choice promote thriving
7. One size may not fit all—but sometimes it does
8. It's not magic: Youth development by design and evaluation
9. Consider fit, quality, and dosage of SOPS
10. Work toward sustainability

Principle 1. Adopt a Positive Perspective to Promote Thriving

When reading, viewing, or listening to the news, it is easy to get the impression that many young people are problems in their homes, at their schools, and in their communities. "Teen Arrested for Convenience Store Robbery," "Boy Carrying Gun Detained at School," and "Teen Pregnancy a Local Issue" are examples of headlines that appear in local media outlets, very often on the front page. These headlines lead many adults to assume there is a crisis among young people, that the behavior of adolescents is out of control, and that swift remedial and punitive actions are necessary to eliminate negative behaviors and protect society. Stories about the good things that adolescents are doing (e.g., going to and doing well in school, volunteering in their communities, participating in community activities, and starting nonprofit efforts to contribute to identified societal needs) are less often told. Consequently, young people are too often seen as liabilities to be controlled rather than assets to be nurtured.

Clearly, some youth do get in trouble. Caldwell and Weybright note in Chapter 4 that part of the reason youth get into trouble is due to changes in the teen brain. The combination of impulsivity and sensation seeking lead some youth to engage in risky behaviors. These youth require extra attention and remedial intervention to help them navigate adolescence and thrive. However, it is important to emphasize that the vast majority of young people are able to steer a smooth course through adolescence with the assistance and support of parents, schools, community members, and organizations. In addition, even adolescents who get into trouble have strengths and positive attributes that need to be recognized, nurtured, and rewarded.

Even adolescents who get into trouble have strengths and positive attributes that need to be recognized, nurtured, and rewarded.

Understanding the current and future potential of adolescents is essential to developing appropriate SOPS to facilitate their positive development. As suggested previously, "When supports and opportunities are plentiful, young people can and do *thrive*; when their environments are deficient or depleted, youth tend not to grow and progress" (Gambone & Arbreton, 1997, pp. 1–2). Thus, working from a positive perspective provides youth workers with the openness and perspective to recognize youths' strengths, helps reduce the likelihood or impact of negative life experiences, and promotes healthy development and well-being (often called resiliency, see Chapter 8). Principle 1 leads directly to Principle 2.

Principle 2. Thriving Emerges from a Foundation of Strengths-Based Models

Using and/or developing asset-based (strengths-based) models, rather than deficit-based models, is essential to the enhancement of SOPS to support the development of young people. Deficit-based models assume that the main goal of youth work is to help young people be problem free. For example, some people might consider the goal of youth work is to provide the SOPS necessary to enable young people to avoid using drugs, become involved in a gang, drop out of school, and/or become pregnant. Although young people definitely need programs that serve to prevent problem behaviors or minimize their effects, these programs should be combined with approaches that focus on maximizing a young person's strengths and assets. Historically, preventing risky behaviors usually focused on teaching youth about the consequences of negative behaviors and encouraging them to "just say no." The contemporary view of what are currently referred to as *prevention programs* includes an orientation toward promoting healthy behaviors that build on each youth's strengths, interests, passions, and sparks, as well as available personal and community resources (e.g., OST programs).

This expanded view of prevention stems from the understanding that even when young people are *problem free* they may not necessarily develop the knowledge, values, attitudes, skills, and behaviors necessary to be fully prepared to successfully function as adults. Thus, enabling a young person to be problem free is only part of the story. Efforts also are needed to promote development beyond problem reduction. Pittman and colleagues (Pittman, Irby, & Ferber, 2000) encapsulated these ideas in their seminal statement: *Problem free is not fully prepared.* This perspective "emphasizes the manifest potentialities rather than the supposed incapacities of young people" (Damon, 2004, p. 15). Furthermore, youth respond more positively to programs that focus on their strengths and take a positive approach than to programs that focus on problems (as explained in Chapter 4).

> Problem free is not fully prepared. And fully prepared is not fully engaged (Pittman et al., 2000).

Moreover, even if young people develop the requisite knowledge, values, attitudes, skills, and behaviors, they might not choose to put them into action. Thus, Pittman further argued that: *Fully prepared is not fully engaged.* Young people can be fully prepared but not have the motivation or resources to use their knowledge and skills to practice pro-social and productive behaviors. Thus, it is possible to be problem free and still not grow up to thrive as an adult; it is also possible to be fully prepared and not use the skills and abilities one has in a positive manner. Thus, OST programs are important vehicles for providing SOPS for youth to be engaged in a variety of positive activities and reap developmental benefits.

This formulation of the need for both preparation and engagement is similar to the evolution of the health field after World War II. Prior to 1948, the World Health Organization (WHO) defined health as the "absence of illness or disease." In 1948, WHO adopted the perspective that health is "a state of complete physical, mental, and social well-being and not merely the absence of disease or infirmity" (WHO, 1958). This shift in perspective eventually ushered in the health promotion perspective in the 1980s. During this time, WHO again revised the definition of health to be "the extent to which an individual or group is able to realize aspirations and satisfy needs and to change or cope with the environment. Health is a resource for everyday life, not the objective of living; it is a positive concept, emphasizing social and personal resources, as well as physical capacities" (WHO, 1984). The evolving perspective on health spawned the field of prevention science, which has twin goals of preventing health risk behaviors and promoting healthy lifestyles. Chapter 2 provides a number of health related statistics on various indicators of the health of youth, some of which are goals of the Office of Disease Prevention and Health Promotion's *Healthy People: 2020*.

Positive youth development and the notion of thriving clearly fit into this lifestyle and strengths-based perspective. Efforts such as America's Promise (www.americaspromise. org) and the Search Institute's Development Assets Model (www.search-institute. org) have emerged from the desire to move beyond deficit reduction and identify the competences one must develop to fully function and thrive in society.

America's Promise proposes a series of five promises that society should make to young people. According to America's Promise, society should provide the following:

- Opportunities for ongoing relationships with caring adults—parents, mentors, tutors, or coaches—to support, care about, and guide youth
- Safe places with structured activities during non-school hours for both physical and emotional safety for youth
- Adequate nutrition, exercise, and health care to pave the way for healthy bodies, healthy minds, and smart habits for adulthood
- Marketable skills through effective education to help youth navigate the transition from school to work successfully
- Opportunities to give back through community service to enhance self-esteem, boost confidence, and heighten a sense of responsibility to the community

Keeping these promises is critical to positive youth development; consequently, families, schools, and community organizations need to define their role in meeting the five promises.

The Developmental Assets model, championed by the Search Institute, provides a powerful tool for identifying and building 40 assets (20 internal and 20 external) deemed necessary for youth to move along the pathway to thriving and adulthood. The assets model is based on research about both protective factors that inhibit high-risk behaviors and resilience factors that increase young people's ability to function positively and even perhaps thrive in the face of adversity. For example, a strong, positive adult role model in a youth program may help the individual be resilient even though positive adult role models are lacking in the home. In addition, learning yoga, mindfulness, and/or stress reduction skills can provide a resilience mechanism for an individual who is living in poverty in an area fraught with gang activity. In Chapter 8, you will learn more about the concept of resilience.

In the Developmental Assets model, the 20 external assets are grouped into four areas:

- Support from family, neighborhood, schools, and other adults
- Actions to empower youth
- Establishment of boundaries and expectations
- Provision of opportunities for the constructive use of time

The 20 internal assets (the attitudes and behaviors that are necessary for youth to grow up to navigate their adolescent years and function successfully as adults) are grouped into four areas:

- Making a commitment to learning
- Developing positive values
- Developing social competencies
- Creating a positive identity

You may also wish to go to the Search Institute website (www.search-institute.org/content/40-developmental-assets-adolescents-ages-12-18). This website contains a detailed description of each asset and offers an interactive table that shows the reader how to take action on each asset.

Studies undertaken by the Search Institute provide evidence of the relationship between the number of assets young people have and their problem or positive behaviors and attitudes. For example, 44% of young people who indicate they have 0 to 10 of the 40 assets are likely to engage in problem alcohol use, as opposed to only 2% of young people with 31 to 40 assets. The same relationship holds true for being involved in violence, illicit drug use, and sexual activity (Figure 1.1). Conversely, 59% of young people with 31 to 40 assets succeed in school, while only 8% of those with 0 to 10 assets do so (Figure 1.2). Similar percentages are found for other positive or thriving behavior attitudes such as exhibiting leadership, maintaining good health, and valuing diversity (Benson, Scales, & Roehlkepartain, 2011).

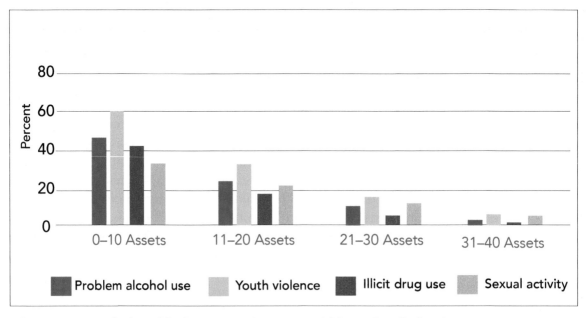

Figure 1.1. Relationship between Assets and Negative Behaviors

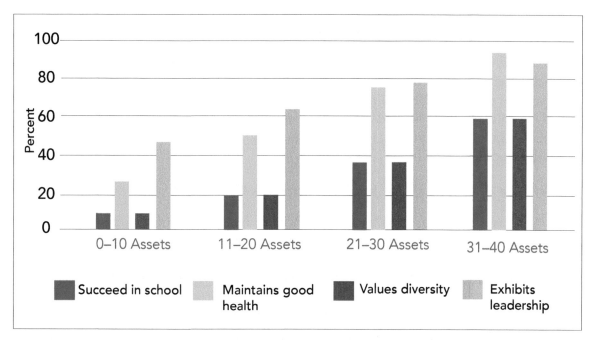

Figure 1.2. Relationship between Assets and Negative Behaviors

Principle 3. Thriving Requires Knowledge, Skills, and Behaviors

The goal of providing SOPS for young people should be more than simply providing ways to keep youth off the streets, entertained, and out of trouble. This means moving beyond simply supplying "fun and games" to a purposeful strategy of helping young people develop the foundation they will need to thrive during their adolescent years and have a chance to achieve positive characteristics as adults. This includes enabling individuals to maximize their educational potential; helping individuals develop a positive identity, personal sense of well-being and self-efficacy; and enabling individuals to develop habits associated with good citizenship (e.g., making positive contributions to one's community). SOPS must be available to develop the full range of knowledge, skills, and behaviors necessary for youth to successfully thrive and transition to adulthood. Young people need to achieve vocational, physical, emotional, civic, social, cultural, and spiritual competence.

As noted in Chapter 4, understanding the developing brain helps youth workers provide SOPS that promote self-regulation and social-emotional competence. SOPS that provide opportunities for experiential learning, in both structured and unstructured programs with the right mix of adult guidance and youth leadership, are important. Participation in experiential activities will promote learning across several domains such as personal (e.g., identity development), social (e.g., developing close relationships with peers, as well as relationships with caring adults), and behavioral (e.g., developing initiative and persistence). Chapters 9 through 12 contain a wealth of information about specific programs that promote development of knowledge, skills, and behaviors in OST activities such as sports, nature, and the arts. Chapter 15 focuses on structuring these and other activities so that youth will experience deep engagement in what they do.

Learning is rewarding for adolescents if the learning sparks passions and interests. Developing feelings of competence is also rewarding for adolescents. People tend to take action when they believe they have some level of competence. Youth development practitioners need to promote opportunities for youth to learn to take actions that lead to positive outcomes. Becoming competent in different skills, as well as being able to self-regulate emotions, depends not only on opportunities, but on adults who are able to challenge growth by expecting the best and holding youth accountable, but also helping youth reflect on failure.

Principle 4. Thriving is a Journey, and it is Complex

The Search Institute (2017) suggests thriving is not a destination but a journey. According to the bioecological systems theory (e.g., Bronfenbrenner, 2001), the journey is influenced by reciprocal interactions among a multitude of factors that influence behavior and individual development. The work of Benson and Saito (2000) and Lerner (e.g., Lerner, 2006), among others, points to the importance of understanding the dynamic nature of the interactions between individuals and the contexts within which they live, learn, and interact with others. Specifically, according to the bioecological systems theory, personal characteristics (e.g., biological and psychological), the social environment (e.g., family, friends, teachers, etc.), "things" in the environment (e.g., a school system or social service system), and cultural context (e.g., resource rich or resource poor) are important factors that influence, and are influenced by individuals' behavior.

From a developmental perspective, these reciprocal interactions occur across time and result in numerous changes and growth in individuals and communities. As noted by Lerner (2006):

> A competent, confident, and caring adolescent, who is positively connected to other people, and who interacts with them with character and integrity, will become an adult who is morally, spiritually, and civically engaged with his or her world. Our adolescents will become adults who contribute to themselves, to their families, to their communities, and ultimately to social justice and civil society. (p. 3)

Lerner and colleagues (Lerner, Lerner, Bowers, & Geldhof, 2015) proposed a relational, developmental systems model of the individual →← context relations involved in PYD. At the core of this model is a set of *five Cs* achieved by youth that result when individual and contextual elements interact positively. These five Cs are competence, confidence, connection, character, and caring. When a youth manifests the first five Cs, a 6th C, contribution, emerges (Geldhof et al., 2014; Lerner et al., 2005). See The Six Cs sidebar for a definition of each of the Cs. Combined, these six Cs provide a foundation for a long-term view for how to help youth develop an orientation toward thriving. Development and maintenance of the six Cs takes time and sustained energy on the part of youth and youth workers.

THE SIX Cs

- **Competence** is a "positive view of one's actions in specific areas, including social, academic, cognitive, health, and vocational" (Lerner & Lerner, 2011, p. 6).
- **Confidence** is a "sense of self-worth and mastery; having a sense of self-efficacy (belief in one's capacity to succeed)" (Act Youth Center of Excellence, 2016, p. 1).
- **Connection** refers to "positive bonds with people and institutions," including family, school, peers, and community (Conway, Heary, & Michael, 2015, p. 2).
- **Character** is an "indication of an individual's respect for societal and cultural rules" (Conway, Heary, & Michael, 2015, p. 2).
- **Caring/Compassion** is an "indication of a person's sense of sympathy and empathy for others" (Conway, Heary, & Hogan, 2015, p. 2).
- **Contribution** refers to being involved as an active participant in decision making in services, organizations, and community (Lerner & Lerner, 2011).

Figure 1.3 is adapted from Lerner and colleagues' relational, developmental systems model (2015). The figure shows the relationship between assets, the six Cs, and thriving and risk reduction. Other chapters in this book will delve into many issues and processes related to the thriving journey.

Principle 5. It Takes a Village to Foster Thriving

An African proverb reminds us that "It takes a village to raise a child." In keeping with the proverb, it takes a community of adults, families, agencies, and organizations to provide SOPS to youth. The bioecological systems theory, along with work by many other researchers, suggests that the development of internal and external assets requires the meaningful involvement of adults. In addition, there is substantial evidence that "resilient children, the ones who thrive despite obstacles, typically have caring adults present and active in their lives" (Walker & White, 1998, p. 14).

Adults play critical roles in youth development through supporting young people in their efforts to navigate the pathways to adulthood, while still enabling youth to have real voice, choice, and power in planning, organizing, and leading programs and activities. Caring adults can be youth program or school staff, volunteers from the community, and/or parents. In all cases, the adults are most effective when they "work in partnership with young people, who see themselves as supportive friends and advocates in contrast to adults motivated to save, reform, or rescue young people from their circumstances" (Walker & White, 1998, p. 15).

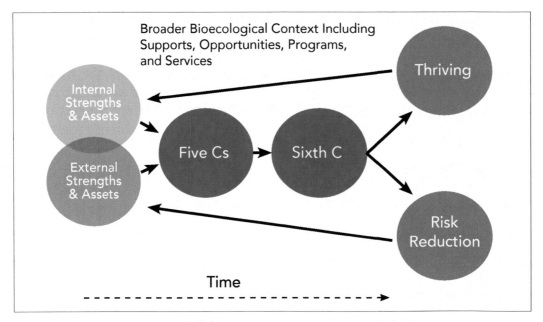

Figure 1.3. Systems model depicting journey toward thriving. Adapted from Lerner, Bowers, & Geldhof (2015)

Search Institute promotes a *relationships-first* approach to helping youth develop the knowledge and skills necessary to thrive. In addition to *challenging youth to grow*, this approach is based on adults who do the following:

- **Demonstrate caring** and are trustworthy
- **Provide support** by helping youth navigate challenges and complex situations, empower youth, and set boundaries
- **Share power** by respecting and collaborating with youth and letting them lead
- **Expand possibilities** by inspiring youth and connecting them to resources that expose youth to new ideas and possibilities

Chapter 16 expands on the importance of relationship-based programming.

One excellent example of building a relationships first approach is the development of youth-adult partnerships. Zeldin, Christens, and Powers (2013) define youth-adult partnerships (Y-APs) as:

The practice of (a) multiple youth and multiple adults deliberating and acting together; (b) in a collective [democratic] fashion; (c) over a sustained period of time; (d) through shared work; (e) intended to promote social justice, strengthen an organization, and/or affirmatively address a community issue. (p. 388)

Y-APs have four core elements:

- **Authentic decision-making** refers to the idea that more important than just being heard (such as a token voice), youth should be involved in making meaningful decisions and their participation is sought, valued and listened to.
- **Natural mentoring** includes the notion that youth develop different types of relationships with non-familial adults. Natural mentors more typically occur outside of structured programs; therefore, they tend to be more neutral and can offer independent observations and guidance. Youth see these mentors as very helpful in developing social networks and visioning their future.
- **Reciprocity** is central to the idea of a partnership in which both adults and youth have mutual influence on each other and the activity or environment. Reciprocity is built on the notions of co-learning and co-creation.
- **Community connectedness** fosters feelings of meaning and belonging to something bigger than themselves. Participating in authentic decision-making with reciprocity, and being supported by natural mentors, promotes community connectedness.

Another way adults across a variety of settings contribute to youth development is by setting boundaries and high expectations. Adults in youth-serving organizations must clearly define rules, monitor youths' behavior, and set consequences for not following the rules. A relationships-first approach facilitates the ability of adults to set high expectations and ability of youth to be receptive toward and strive to meet those expectations.

In addition to adults youth encounter in OST settings, parents are critical in helping guide their children in making appropriate choices, providing opportunities for family activities, and modeling appropriate behaviors. Chapter 17 focuses on families as sources of youth development.

Principle 6. Youth Voice and Choice Promote Thriving

Too often youth feel that adults plan *for* them, rather than *with* them. When this happens, the result is often that the programming is not relevant because what adults think youth want or need is not based on the realities as seen by youth. This is illustrated by another African proverb that suggests if the lion told the story, it would be very different from the one told by the hunter. That is, the lion's perspective would no doubt interpret the hunt differently. Although unlikely, imagine if the lion and hunter cooperated on the story. Supporting youth in telling their own stories refers to the notion that youth should have voice in their own development and that adults should not "do development" to them. Thus, Principle 6 suggests that when possible, adults should work *with* young people, as opposed to always initiating, planning, and directing youth activities.

A related issue is youth sometimes feel that even though adults seek their opinions, they do not authentically consider their input, leaving youth feeling the process was only an exercise. Youth workers often forget that genuinely involving youth and honoring their opinions and input is just as important and rewarding as participation in the activity itself. Thus, in many youth development programs, adult leaders are undertaking considerable efforts to empower youth to take ownership and responsibility for developing and sustaining programs, in addition to moving away from centralized top-down decision-making by youth professionals to more decentralized, youth-centered decision-making, with the support of adults (see Chapter 18).

Young people have a basic need for *autonomy, agency,* and *self-determination.* Consequently, preserving choice and initiative is critical to helping youth fully engage in their surroundings. On the other hand, when individuals are over-regulated or opportunities to self-determine behavior are thwarted (i.e., doing *for* them rather than *with* them), young people may have a tendency to become externally rather than internally motivated, resulting in a lack of interest and full engagement, dependency, and apathy (Deci & Ryan, 2000; Ryan & Deci, 2000).

The key to adult involvement in promoting decision-making and leadership development is to provide young people with the *scaffolding* necessary to enable growth and development (Pittman, Irby, & Ferber, 2000). Youth, like an emerging building, need support ("training wheels") during their development (i.e., "construction."). Scaffolding refers to the framework of temporary supports provided by adults as youth develop new knowledge, skills, and behaviors. As skill development increases, the scaffolding is gradually reduced (called fading) until youth no longer need the scaffolding. Providing the right level of scaffolding, however, is critical. Adults should not stifle youth by too much support or offer too little support, which may contribute to failure. Scaffolding is a dynamic process where the adult assesses youths' ability to get to the next rung,

the help needed to get there, and when to discontinue help when youth have already mastered or gained a particular level of knowledge, skill, or behavior.

An example of the right level of scaffolding focuses on the benefits of, and difference between, adult-driven versus youth-driven programs. As an example, Larson, Walker, and Pearce (2005) interviewed high-school youth and adult advisors who participated in four different high-quality programs, such as planning a day camp for younger children (a youth-driven program) and putting on a play (an adult-driven program). They observed the programs in action to discern any differences in youths' experiences. The researchers' conclusion was that both types of programs have merit in terms of skill and talent development, as well as boosting self-confidence of the high school students. However, they also concluded that it was important for adults to find the right balance of letting youth make their own mistakes and perhaps getting off track, while also adopting a more directive approach when it is necessary to keep things task oriented and keep youth from floundering due to inexperience and lack of knowledge.

Principle 7. One Size May Not Fit All—But Sometimes it Does

One of the themes in a number of chapters in the book is "For whom and under what conditions?" does something apply. For example, understanding the way social media affect adolescents depends on their access to social media (see Chapter 3). On the other hand, chapters also provide information about some general commonalities that are applicable to the majority of adolescents (e.g., similarities due to having a generational perspective). The principle of inclusivity requires that youth workers be sensitive to asking "for whom and under what conditions" will program X or service Z be applicable, while also recognizing that there are general principles that are universally effective in most instances. Confused? It is complex.

Chapters 2 and 3 provide some background regarding this complexity. For example, as noted in Chapter 2, the sociodemographic profile of youth in the U.S. is becoming more diverse, a trend that will continue into the near future. The material in Chapters 2 and 3 also suggests that access to many of society's SOPS depends on race and ethnicity, ability, social class, and gender. Differences in access means that when youth workers are providing SOPS to adolescents they should understand not only how to make sure all youth have equal access, but also when, and if, differential services are needed based on race/ethnicity, ability, social class, and gender (or other distinguishing characteristics). Some questions that might arise are as follows:

- Should youth workers provide gender segregated programs (including transgender youth)? That is, will some programs be more powerful if they are just for girls, or just for boys, or just for gender fluid, transgender, or questioning youth?
- Does the race, ethnicity, or gender of a leader need to be matched to the characteristics of the youth being served?
- Is it better to segregate youth who have exhibited a proclivity to negative risk behaviors or integrate them with those who do not?
- Is it better to provide inclusive or separate services to youth with differing abilities?

Not surprisingly, there are no clear answers to these questions, and determining the right course of action for a given situation becomes a critical challenge for youth workers. Several chapters in this book should help youth workers meet these challenges. For example, Chapter 19 suggests that ethnic and racial minority youth who are dealing with aspects of racism or struggling with their identity as a member of a racial or ethnic minority group may need tailored services and programs. Chapter 3 suggests that males who exhibit strong traits associated with the "Boy Code or Man Box" may need tailored services. Chapters 20–23 continue these discussions as well.

In Principle 2, we introduced the idea that a prevention approach includes both a focus on reducing deficits (e.g., substance abuse) and on promoting developmental assets. The prevention approach avoids the "either/or" trap that many SOPS fall into, and suggests that the answers to the above questions are not either/or but should include approaches built on the principles of *problem free* and *fully prepared*. In this way, youth development practices fall on a continuum, with positive youth development services at one end and social control or incarceration at the other (Quinn, 1999).

Pittman and her colleagues at the Forum for Youth Investment provide other examples of where the *and* approach is needed and superior. Each of these can be applied to the issue of inclusivity. Thus, there is a need for the following:

- Quickly turning around negative behaviors *and* developing long-term supports for positive development
- Promoting both basic services targeted to a single issue or area of the community *and* at the same time promoting efforts to strategically plan a system of services in our communities
- Utilizing youth professionals to lead and plan activities *and* ensuring that youth, their parents, and other stakeholders in the community are fully engaged and involved
- Developing new ideas into pilot programs *and* making concerted efforts to develop long-term programs with solid funding streams (Pittman et al., 2000)

The *and* approach is important for OST providers to adopt from a bioecological perspective because it suggests that models of collaboration with a variety of services such as health agencies, schools, and quasi-public agencies (e.g., YM/YWCA) are important in working toward the ideal of inclusivity. In addition, adopting an *and* approach reduces territoriality and promotes keeping the focus on youths' needs and positive development.

The *and* approach also suggests the need for providers to partner with other organizations that offer complementary services. For example, youth professionals are often skilled at the *promotive* aspect of services (e.g., skill development, competence, and fun), but might not focus on overcoming deficits. Thus, if youth workers partner with other organizations who might be more focused on risk reduction, an ideal situation is created for overall youth development to occur.

Principle 8. It's not Magic: Youth Development by Design and Evaluation

In the past, the main goal of most OST programs for children and youth was to provide fun opportunities to keep youth busy and off the streets (see Chapter 5). Thus, youth program providers mainly provided a place for young people to go and things to do when they got there. However, in concert with the youth development movement and the related quest to promote thriving, it is increasingly critical for programmers and service providers to move beyond causal approaches focused on how many youth showed up at a program (i.e., attendance counts) to deliberate approaches that emphasize planning and leading on an *intentional* basis (McLaughlin, 2000; Walker, 2006). Employing intentionality requires answering the questions: "What do we want to happen?," "How are we going to make it happen?," and "How will we know if it actually happened due to our program or service?" Consciously planning and implementing programs leads to creating effective SOPS for development. Furthermore, youth workers who follow good programming design principles (see Chapter 13) also follow good evaluation principles (see Chapter 14).

To practice intentionality, youth workers utilize a comprehensive planning model—one that moves from assessing needs, to setting goals, to developing programs to meet goals, to assessing whether goals have been met, to identifying needed changes in future program development. In some cases, this planning process needs to occur at the micro-level and focus on the needs of a particular group of youth in a particular setting (e.g., immigrant youth from Pakistan attending an after-school program offered by a local nonprofit organization). In other cases, the process is at the macro-level, which might include efforts to think broadly about community needs and the kinds of actions required to meet those needs (e.g., developing a community-wide approach to addressing the needs of all immigrant youth).

Practicing intentional programming requires an understanding of basic developmental processes (see Chapter 7) as well as the dimensions of activities that can help youth thrive and make the transition to adulthood more likely to succeed. Two major reports on youth development by the National Academy of Sciences (2001) and the National Research Council and Institute of Medicine (2002) list basic elements that characterize quality youth programs (see Table 1.1). These elements are the building blocks of quality youth development programs. Changing the way we think about the design and delivery of programs can help achieve development beyond problem prevention.

Table 1.1
Characteristics of Environments that Promote Positive Youth Development

- Physical and psychological safety
- Structure that is developmentally appropriate
- Supportive relationships
- Opportunities to belong and be valued
- Positive social norms
- Support for efficacy and mattering
- Opportunities for skill building and mastery
- Integration of family, school, and community efforts
- Opportunities to make a contribution to one's community

Adapted from National Academy of Sciences (2001) and National Research Council and Institute of Medicine (2002)

Another resource that addresses the issue of youth development by design is Communities that Care (CTC). CTC (www.communitiesthatcarecoalition.org/) is a prevention system that gives communities tools to address adolescent health and behavior problems using a risk and protective factors framework. CTC provides a structure that guides community stakeholders (youth, parents, schools, community agencies, and local government) in establishing a shared community vision, setting measurable goals, and deciding on appropriate evidence-based programs through a menu of choices.

Principle 9. Consider Fit, Quality, and Dosage of SOPS

Organizations need to offer SOPS at an appropriate level of scale and saturation to make an impact on young people's lives. Creating SOPS at appropriate levels of scale and saturation means that SOPS have to be appropriate for the target audience, be delivered with a level of *quality*, and in enough *dosage* to have the desired short-term and longer-term effects.

As noted in the discussion of Principle 8, Communities that Care (CTC) is a system that helps community leaders work together to form a vision of a comprehensive approach to community-wide youth development programs to reach appropriate target audiences. CTC works on the premise that *evidence-based programs* (EBPs) are superior to ones that lack evidence regarding their effectiveness. EBPs have been evaluated using rigorous research methods, are based on theory, and have demonstrated effectiveness in addressing a desired outcome (e.g., reducing substance use or promoting autonomy development). Youth workers who wish to implement EBPs can consult websites/ organizations such as The Afterschool Alliance (2014; www.afterschoolalliance. org/documents/Deeper_Dive_into_Afterschool.pdf), Blueprints for Healthy Youth Development (www.blueprintsprograms.com/), or CTC for guidance.

Unfortunately, it is very difficult to demonstrate program effectiveness on a large scale (i.e., for programs that have reached many youth across time). For example, Blueprints reviewed over 1,400 youth development programs, with only about 5% meeting their criteria for designation as an EBP. Programs that have been evaluated and shown positive results, but have not met criteria to be called evidence-based, are often called *promising practices*.

When choosing programs, youth workers understand that not all evidence-based or promising practices fit their needs. Likewise, all EBPs and promising programs have limitations. Thus, program selection depends on careful consideration of the needs of the community, the target audience of youth to be served, and the ease of implementation. All of these factors influence the likelihood that the program will be implemented as intended. For further information, you may wish to consult a document created by The Family and Youth Services Bureau (2012a) that provides guidance for selecting evidence-based programs.

EBPs and promising programs have strong logic models that demonstrate intentional programming linked with inputs, desired outcomes, and evaluation (see Chapters 13 and 14). In particular, EBPs and promising programs have the following traits:

- Appropriate content, such as addressing knowledge, attitudes, and skills
- A strong pedagogical foundation, including active participation and engagement of youth and appropriate sequencing of material
- Good implementation, which includes fidelity, adaptation, appropriate dosage, quality staff, and effective community partners

When providing any program, and in particular evidence-based and promising practice-based programs, consideration of implementation issues is critical. *Fidelity* means that the program was delivered the way the developers intended for the program to be delivered. In order for youth workers to achieve the same outcomes as reported by the research associated with a program, the program has to use the same content in the same sequence, and the same methods. It also has to be delivered with the same level of dosage.

Dosage is concerned with how much of the planned SOPS youth need in order to make a difference in their development as well as how much of the SOPS youth actually get. This is a complex issue, especially for OST activities and programs that have fluid attendance, which makes it difficult to know how much of a particular program or service youth actually received. Youth workers measure dosage by metrics that measure intensity, duration, and breadth (Dietel, 2009). *Intensity* is the amount of time youth attend a program, such as number of hours or number of lessons. Youth workers measure intensity by percentage of lessons delivered (e.g., five out of six lessons were given, or 75% of lesson two was given). *Duration* of the program is the amount of time in weeks, months, or years the program was offered (e.g., program is six lessons over six weeks). *Breadth* refers to the variety of activities to which youth are exposed (e.g., sports, the arts, and leisure education programs).

Often youth workers feel the need to adapt a program. Adaptations may be necessary if the program will be delivered to youth who have different ethnic/racial, ability, or other characteristics than those for whom the original SOPS was developed. For example, many programs are school-based and often provided in majority White schools. If these programs are offered for immigrant youth, they may need to be adapted. Although adaptations are important to make sure programs fit the needs of the target group of youth, youth workers should not necessarily expect the same outcomes to be derived when program elements are changed. On the other hand, often youth workers are able to make adaptations that do not compromise the fidelity and integrity of the program. The Family and Youth Services Bureau (2012b) provides a helpful guide on adapting evidence-based programs.

Another dosage-related issue is *saturation*. Saturation involves finding ways to offer a critical mass of services to a critical mass of young people. Thus, efforts are needed to ensure that a sufficient quantity of quality SOPS are provided so that more young people in more neighborhoods can be served more of the time (Pittman et al., 2000). Even when an appropriate community-wide system is designed, however, SOPS often serve only a limited number of the young people who

> Saturation involves finding ways to offer a critical mass of services to a critical mass of young people.

could benefit from involvement. For example, sometimes youth living in the highest risk environments are targeted for services, ignoring other youth who could have also benefited from attention. Unfortunately, agencies are often so poorly under-resourced that choices about whom to serve are necessary. Another issue is that some parents who are better off financially suggest that services for their children are lacking because providers assume either parents can take care of their youth's needs, or that services are not necessary for youth from higher income households. In either case, needed SOPS may be limited in their application.

Despite the benefits of using EBPs and promising programs, it is unlikely that all SOPS provided by an organization or agency will be evidence-based or promising. For a variety of reasons, youth workers often create their own programs for use at the local level. While there is nothing wrong with this approach, and locally developed programs can be powerful, programs should still be intentionally developed and evaluated (Chapters 13 and 14).

Principle 10. Work Toward Sustainability

The preceding principles all serve to promote program sustainability, which is critical to program success and gaining the trust and involvement of youth. Discontinuing a successful program after a few months, or even one or two years, can be unsettling for youth, parents, and staff. At the same time, failure to terminate ineffective programs can be equally damaging. Program discontinuation often happens. In addition, sporadic funding from foundation and government grants can lead to an ever-rotating series of service system components. For example, pilot project and short-term grant funds are only available for a specified time period. Furthermore, grants often come with the expectation that the receiving organization will make efforts to raise the necessary funds from other sources to continue programs after the initial grant period ends. Although staff are sometimes successful in finding the funds to maintain programs, it is a challenging task that most personnel are not trained to do, and in some cases funds for sustaining programs may not be available.

In addition to issues with funding, there are a number of reasons to avoid one-shot or short-term programs. First, achieving a quality program in the first few months or even the first year can be difficult. It usually takes at least a complete program cycle for program staff to identify appropriate personnel and stabilize their service model. For young people, this may mean that the service system designed to meet their needs is a matrix of ever-changing programs and personnel. Thus, young people may find it difficult to commit to being involved if they have had past experience with programs and staff they have grown to trust but who have moved on to the next funded priority when current funding ends.

Another reason short-term programs should be avoided is that youth development is ongoing. Continued involvement in a program allows youth to develop skills and competence and leads to initiative. One-shot/short-term programs can generate participants but not necessarily meaningful youth development. Finally, it is almost impossible to evaluate properly the effectiveness of short-term programs, especially if the goal is to achieve longer-term objectives.

Sustainability issues also apply to personnel. To realize the full power of adults in the lives of youth, organizations must hire, train, reward, and retain quality adult leaders. However, this is not always easy to accomplish. Many youth-serving organizations hire individuals who are too young and/or have too many issues themselves to be strong resources in the lives of youth. In addition, too often organizations hire leaders for a short period based on programming needs, thus undermining the value of creating longer-term, meaningful relationships and/or partnerships between adults and youth. In many cases, a system is not in place to develop leaders who understand the principles of youth development and know how to translate these principles into meaningful practice. Finally, low wages may prevent youth workers from applying for jobs, let alone remaining in them. These situations result in entrusting responsibility for youth development to low paid individuals who turnover far too quickly (Chapter 24 focuses on the skills required for those seeking to become a youth professional.)

One of the results of hiring "short-timers" is that youth miss the advantages of developing longer-term, sustainable relationships with adults. Young people often have difficulty investing in a relationship they know is only temporary. For young people from families where divorce has taken place, leading to limited access of a parent, or where they cannot depend on adults to "be there" for them, transient relationships can lead to a lack of involvement of caring adults in their lives. Developing trust and respect takes time and requires some stability in adult–youth relationships. In some cases, young people develop relationships with adults who by leaving might be perceived as breaking their promise to be there for the young person, thus undermining the future willingness of the young person to invest in developing meaningful relationships.

In sum, to be most effective, youth development efforts must begin early, be sustained throughout the adolescent years, and allow for skill development through participation in various levels of challenge. Programs should be comprehensive, addressing many aspects of youth development. Youth workers need to be adequately trained, compensated, and retained. Finally, it is important to develop a system of services that are ongoing and inclusive of the variety of services necessary to meet youths' needs.

Final Thoughts

Youth development advocates maintain that efforts are needed to create organizations and communities that enable youth to thrive and move along the pathways to adulthood by supplying the supports, opportunities, programs, and services (SOPS) beyond simple problem prevention. These approaches do not eliminate the need to target specific individuals with high risk factors for attention, but clearly, efforts should not be restricted only to youth from high-risk environments or only focus on problem remediation. Central to this thinking is the idea that development for young people is dependent on a range of SOPS coming from their families, the community, and other institutions that have the potential to influence them positively. When SOPS are plentiful, young people can and do thrive; when their environments are deficient or depleted, youth tend not to grow and progress.

The principles and understandings discussed in this chapter represent exciting changes in the evolution of the philosophy of youth development. Unfortunately, in a number of cases, youth-serving agencies have adopted "the youth development language," but have in reality made few changes in their service priorities and approaches. Thus, the purpose of this book is to help provide the necessary information about how to not only "talk the talk" but also "walk the walk" of youth development.

Possibly the most exciting takeaway from these principles is the fact that youth workers who provide OST-related SOPS have enormous power and responsibility to provide opportunities for sparks that will ignite youth on the pathway to thriving, not only in adolescence but throughout adulthood. Each of the subsequent chapters in this book addresses one or more of these principles in more detail and provides information that will prepare you for well-grounded work with young people using a youth development approach.

Discussion Questions

1. Discuss which of the 10 principles you think will be most difficult to follow or implement, and why.
2. The following questions were raised in the discussion of Principle 7. Please discuss them.
   a. Should youth workers provide gender-segregated programs (including transgender youth)? That is, will some programs be more powerful if they are just for girls; just for boys; or just for gender fluid, transgender, or questioning youth? What do you think, and why?
   b. Does the race, ethnicity, and/or gender of a leader need to be matched to the characteristics of the youth being served? Again, what has been your own experience with the background of youth leaders compared to the groups they are leading? How important do you think this matching process is to the success of youth development programs? Explain your response.
   c. Is it better to segregate youth who have exhibited a proclivity to negative risk behaviors or integrate them with those who do not? Why or why not?
   d. Is it better to provide inclusive or separate services to youth with differing abilities? Again, why or why not?

Assignments

1. Write about one of your sparks. How did you develop that spark? What SOPS enabled you to become exposed to, interested in, and participate in your spark? What other SOPS would have further enhanced your pursuit of your spark?
2. Go to Search Institute's page describing the 40 Developmental Assets: www. search-institute.org/content/40-developmental-assets-adolescents-ages-12-18.

Identify the assets you found to be most helpful in your own life. Write a paragraph about specific ways five of the assets on your list helped you thrive.

3. Write a poem, compose a song, or develop a piece of art depicting the concept of youth thriving.

References

Act Youth Center of Excellence. (2016). Positive youth development outcomes. Retrieved from http://www.actforyouth.net/youth_development/development/outcomes.cfm

America's Promise. (2003). America's Promise Alliance. Retrieved from http://www.americaspromise.org/

Benson, P. L., & Saito, R. (2000). The scientific foundation of youth development. In N. Jaffe (Ed.), *Youth development: Issues, challenges, and directions* (pp. 124–148). Philadelphia, PA: Public Private Ventures.

Benson, P. L. & Scales, P. C. (2009). The definition and preliminary measurement of thriving in adolescence. *The Journal of Positive Psychology, 4*, 85–104.

Benson, P. L., Scales, P. C., & Roehlkepartain, E. C. (2011). *A fragile foundation: The state of developmental assets among American youth* (2nd ed). Retrieved from https://www.searchinstitutestore.org/product_p/e533-w.htm.

Bronfenbrenner, U. (2001). The bioecological theory of human development. In N. J. Smelser & P. B. Baltes (Eds.), *International encyclopedia of the social and behavioral sciences* (Vol. 10, pp. 6963–6970). New York, NY: Elsevier.

Bundick, M. J., Yeager, D. S., King, P. E, & Damon, W. (2010). Thriving across the life span. In R. M. Lerner & W. F. Overton (Eds.), *The handbook of life-span development, Volume 1: Cognition, biology, and methods* (pp. 882–923). Hoboken, NJ: John S. Wiley & Sons.

Conway, R. J., Heary, C., & Hogan, M. J. (2015). An evaluation of the measurement properties of the five Cs model of positive youth development. *Frontiers in Psychology, 6*. doi: 10.3389/fpsyg.2015.01941

Council on Accreditation. (n.d.). Standards for child and youth development (CYD) programs. Retrieved from http://coanet.org/standards/standards-for-child-and-youth-development-programs/

Damon, W. (2004). What is positive youth development? *Annals of the American Academy of Political and Social Science, 59*(11), 13–24.

Deci, E. L., & Ryan, R. M. (2000). The "what" and "why" of goal pursuits: Human needs and the self-determination of behavior. *Psychological Inquiry, 11*, 227–268.

Dietel, R. (November, 2009). After-school programs: Find the right dose. *Phi Delta Kappan, 91*, 62–64.

Family and Youth Services Bureau. (2012a). Selecting an evidence-based program that fits tip sheet. Retrieved from https://www.acf.hhs.gov/sites/default/files/fysb/prep-program-fit-ts.pdf

Family and Youth Services Bureau. (2012b). Making adaptations tip sheet. Retrieved from https://www.acf.hhs.gov/sites/default/files/fysb/prep-making-adaptations-ts.pdf

Gambone, M. A., & Arbreton, A. J. A. (1997). *Safe havens: The contributions of youth organizations to healthy adolescent development.* Philadelphia, PA: Public/Private Ventures.

Geldhof, G. J., Bowers, E. P., Boyd, M. J., Mueller, M. K., Napolitano, C. M., Schmid, K. L., Lerner, J. V., & Lerner, R. M. (2014). Creation of short and very short measures of the five Cs of positive youth development. *Journal of Research on Adolescence, 24*(1), 163–176.

Hamilton, S. F., Hamilton, M. A., & Pittman, K. (2004). Principles for youth development. In S. F. Hamilton & M. A. Hamilton (Eds.), *The youth development handbook: Coming of age in American communities* (pp. 3–22). Thousand Oaks, CA: Sage Publications, Inc.

Larson, R., Walker, K., & Pearce, N. (2005). A comparison of youth-driven and adult-driven youth programs: Balancing inputs from youth and adults. *Journal of Community Psychology, 33,* 57–74.

Lerner, R. M. (2006). Thriving: A Mark Twain Primer. p. 3. Retrieved from http://www.thrivefoundation.org/wp-content/uploads/2014/11/Thriving-A-Mark-Twain-Primer.pdf

Lerner, R. M., & Lerner, J. V. (2011). The positive development of youth report of the findings from the first seven years of the 4-h study of positive youth development. Retrieved from ase.tufts.edu/iaryd/documents/4HPYDStudyWave7.pdf

Lerner, R. M., Lerner, J. V., Almerigi, J., Theokas, C., Phelps, E., Gestsdottir, S…& von Eye, A. (2005). Positive youth development, participation in community youth development programs, and community contributions of fifth grade adolescents: Findings from the first wave of the 4-H Study of Positive Youth Development. *Journal of Early Adolescence, 25*(1), 17–27.

Lerner, R. M., Lerner, J. V., Bowers, E., & Geldhof, G. J. (2015) Positive youth development and relational developmental systems. In W. F. Overton & P. C. Molenaar (Eds.), *Theory and method. Volume 1 of the handbook of child psychology and developmental science* (7th ed., pp. 607–651). Hoboken, NJ: Wiley.

McLaughlin, M. W. (2000). *Community counts: How youth organizations matter for youth development.* Washington, DC: Public Education Network.

National Academy of Sciences. (2001). *Community programs to promote youth development.* Washington, DC: National Research Council, National Academy of Sciences.

National Research Council and Institute of Medicine. (2002). *Promoting positive youth development in New York State: Moving from dialogue to action.* Albany, NY. Retrieved from http://www.nyspartnersforchildren.org/teen.htm

Office of Disease Prevention and Health Promotion (ODPHP). *Healthy People 2020.* Retrieved from https://www.healthypeople.gov/2020

Pittman, K., Irby, M., & Ferber, T. (2000). Unfinished business: Further reflections on a decade of promoting youth development. Takoma Park, MD: The Forum for Youth Development. Available at http://forumfyi.org/files/UnfinishedBusiness.pdf

Pittman, K. J., Irby, M., Tolman, J., Yohalem, N., Ferber, T. (2003). *Preventing problems or promoting development: Competing priorities or inseparable goals?* Washington, DC: Forum for Youth Investment.

Quinn, J. (1999). Where need meets opportunity: Youth development programs for early teens. *The Future of Children: When School is Out, 9*(2), 96–116.

Ryan, R. M., & Deci, E. L. (2000). Self-determination theory and the facilitation of intrinsic motivation, social development, and well-being. *American Psychologist, 55*, 68–78.

Search Institute. (2018). 40 Developmental Assets Model. Retrieved fromhttp://www.search-institute.org/research/developmental-assets

Search Institute. (2017). Sparks: A gateway to developmental relationships. Retrieved from http://www.search-institute.org/research/developmental-relationships-and-sparks

Walker, J. A. (2006). Intentional youth programs: Taking theory to practice. *New Directions for Youth Development, 112*, 75–92.

Walker, J., & White, L. (1998). Caring adults support the healthy development of youth. *The Center,* pp. 14–19.

World Health Organization. (1958). *The first ten years of the World Health Organization.* Geneva, Switzerland: World Health Organization.

World Health Organization. (1984). *Health promotion: A discussion document on the concept and principles: Summary report of the Working Group on Concept and Principles of Health Promotion, Copenhagen, 9-13 July 1984.* (ICP/HSR 602(m01), 5 pp. Copenhagen: WHO Regional Office for Europe.

Zeldin, S., Christens, B. D., & Powers, J. L. (2013). The psychology and practice of youth-adult partnership: Bridging generations for youth development and community change. *American Journal of Community Psychology, 51*, 385–397.

Chapter 2

The Big Picture
Youth Today and Tomorrow

Linda L. Caldwell

When were you born? Where did you grow up? What color is your skin? What is your native language? What is your gender? What is the background of your parents?

Why do the answers to these questions matter? More specifically, why is it important for providers of out-of-school time (OST) programs and services to know these things about the young people they serve? Despite the fact that we are all human beings with more similarities than differences, this chapter will address why questions like the above matter in terms of the provision of supports, opportunities, programs, and services for youth. The chapter provides an overview of the status and characteristics of adolescents in the United States, including statistics reflecting the number of people under 18, their demographic profiles, descriptions of their living conditions, considerations of their health status, and general information about their educational attainment.

Youth development professionals who understand youths' backgrounds and what they experience in their daily lives will be able to provide targeted and more effective services to help youth thrive. Recognizing and understanding the trends, issues, strengths, problems, and challenges faced by today's adolescents will maximize youth development professionals' ability to plan for the future as well as offer appropriate services and programs in the present.

Many people wonder whether youth are worse off today than they were a decade or two ago. Despite some of the sensationalism and negativity often seen on the news reports about young people, the majority of youth in the United

States are relatively happy, well adjusted, healthy, and are making good developmental progress toward adulthood. For example, data from *America's Children: Key National Indicators of Well-Being, 2017* suggests that fewer children are living in poverty than in previous years. From 2005 to 2010, poverty rates of children from birth to age 17 increased from 18% to 22%, but by 2015 had dropped to 20%. Similarly, the percentage of children without health insurance in 1993 was 14%, but decreased to 5% in 2015.

Despite the fact that youth may not have as many problems as society perceives, it is still important to recognize that as youth mature and go through adolescence they must deal with a number of physical and emotional changes that provide challenges during their transition to adulthood. Youth also must navigate the lure of using drugs, cigarettes, and alcohol, or engaging in early and/or risky sexual behavior. Research has shown that youth who have the basic skills, knowledge, and characteristics necessary to navigate this period in their lives make the transition from childhood to adolescence to adulthood more easily than their less prepared peers do. Most youth need help from adults in acquiring skills, knowledge, and characteristics. Essentially that is the focus of youth development: providing supports, opportunities, programs, and services to help youth develop into well-adjusted, happy, and thriving adults.

You will maximize what you learn from this chapter if you continually ask yourself the following question: *In what ways can providers of OST programs and services contribute to enhancing some of the highlighted youth strengths and mitigating some of the problems and issues faced by adolescents?* Keeping this question in mind will provide a way of assessing the applicability of the information and not becoming overwhelmed by the statistics. Other questions to ask yourself as you read the statistics in this chapter are as follows:

- For whom and under what conditions do the statistics apply?
- Do the statistics apply to all youth regardless of gender, race or ethnicity, or income level?
- Are there differences among different sub-groups?

This chapter will walk you through some examples of this kind of targeted thinking, and ask you to continue to think about how differences and similarities among youth apply to how to deliver appropriate programs and services.

Beyond the material in this chapter, a considerable amount of additional information about adolescents is available. To assist you in finding additional information about youth, a list of selected websites with a brief description of each is included in Appendix A. Two types of websites are included: (1) websites for agencies and organizations (private and public) whose activities and services make a major contribution to improving the life possibilities for youth, and (2) websites containing major national studies that focus on life choices and health behaviors of youth.

Current Social and Demographic Profiles and Future Trends

Let's begin by reviewing some relevant demographic data. Much of the following information comes from the Child Trends website (www.Childtrends.org). Child Trends is a nonprofit, nonpartisan research organization that promotes and engages in scientific research aimed at improving the lives of children and youth. The Child Trends website brings together data on the status of youth from a variety of state and national sources. In cases where the chapter includes information that does not come from the Child Trends website, the source is noted.

Information is also included from *Healthy People 2020* (www.healthypeople. gov/2020), which comes from the Office of Disease Prevention and Health Promotion (ODPHP). The Healthy People initiative is based on a set of aspirational goals developed and updated each decade to benchmark progress toward improving the development, education, health, and well-being of U.S. citizens. Several of those goals are discussed in this chapter. In addition, you are encouraged to visit the website and view all of the goals and the related statistics. When data do not come from one of these two sources, the appropriate citation is included.

How Many Youth Are There?

Understanding current and future population trends is critical to effective strategic planning for supports, opportunities, programs, and services that can help adolescents thrive as they make the transition to adulthood. For example, in 2014, there were about 42 million adolescents between the ages of 10 and 19 in the United States. Projections suggest the number of adolescents will grow to about 45 million by 2050. Although the number of adolescents will increase by 2050, adolescents will represent a smaller proportion of the total U.S. population, falling from about 13% to 11%. OST professionals will have to factor that basic population shift into planning future services and activities.

Currently, 51% of adolescents are males, and 49% females. Additionally, adolescents can be divided into younger adolescents (aged 10–14) and older adolescents (aged 15–19), with about 50% of adolescents in each group. Grouping adolescents into age-related categories is important because younger adolescents have different developmental needs and health risk behaviors than older adolescents.

Race and Ethnicity

It is also important to break down youth numbers by race and ethnicity because children from different racial and ethnic backgrounds often show differences in well-being, including health, mortality, school performance and attainment, and access to family and community resources. For example, generally members of racial and ethnic minorities have less access to education, health, and human services, among other things. Understanding these differences will enable youth professionals to provide more culturally appropriate services. (See Chapters 19, 20, and 21 for in-depth examinations of issues related to race and ethnicity).

One of the major population shifts in the U.S. is that the demographic profile of youth is becoming more diverse. For example, between 2000 and 2010, the Hispanic population in the U.S. grew at four times the rate of the total population, according to the Census Bureau (Ennis, Rio-Vargas, & Albert, 2010). In particular, from 1980 to 2016, the percentage of children who are Hispanic increased from 9% to 25% of the population. In addition, the number of Americans self-identifying as mixed white-and-black biracial rose 134%. Likewise, the number of Americans of mixed white and Asian descent grew by 87%.

Projections for the year 2050 suggest that 32% of U.S. children will be Hispanic, 39% White, non-Hispanic, 13% Black, non-Hispanic, 7% Asian, non-Hispanic, and 9% non-Hispanic, "all other races" (Federal Interagency Forum on Child and Family Statistics, 2017). Thus, by 2050, the combined number of minority group members will actually comprise approximately 61% of the U.S. population. Furthermore, from 1994 to 2016, the percentage of children living in the U.S. with at least one foreign-born parent rose from 15% to 25%.

Given these statistics, the ethnic and racial composition of middle and high schools will be much different in the future. The Pew Research Center projects that the public high school graduating class of 2025 will be barely majority white (see Figure 2.1; Fry, 2015).

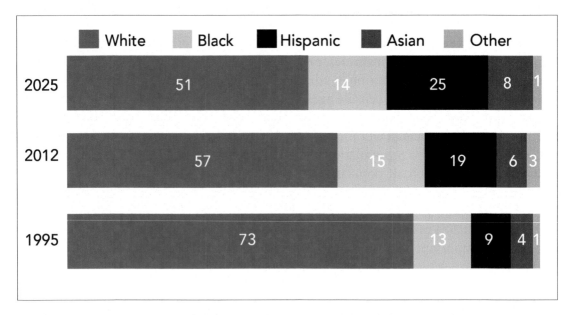

Figure 2.1. Diversity of Future High School Graduating Classes, 1995 to 2025: Percentage of Public High School Graduates by Race/Ethnicity. Source: National Center for Education Statistics, Western Interstate Commission for Higher Education

Where Do Youth Live?

Most adolescents live in or just outside an urban area (see Figure 2.2). Adolescents living in urban, impoverished areas typically lack access to good health care and are more likely to be exposed to higher levels of environmental toxins, violent crime, gangs, and limited availability and higher costs for healthy foods (with these areas sometimes referred to as food deserts).

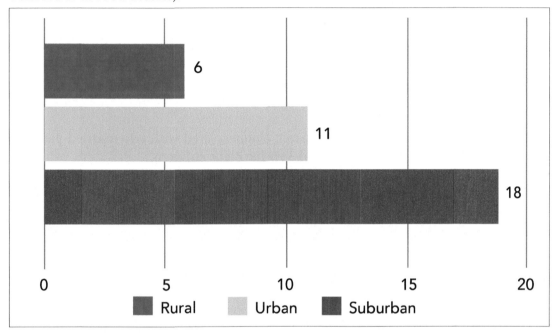

Figure 2.2. Areas Where Youth Live, in Millions. Source: U.S. Census Bureau. (2014). Current Population Survey, Annual Social and Economic Supplement, Retrieved from www.census.gov/cps/data/cpstablecreator.html

On the other hand, youth who live in rural areas are less likely to have access to community or recreation centers, parks, or playgrounds, and therefore have limited opportunities for organized recreation and sports activities. Youth in rural areas also tend to come from poorer families than urban youth. Transportation barriers for rural youth are higher than for youth in urban or suburban areas. They are more likely to be overweight or obese, spend more time watching TV or other media, and live with someone who smokes cigarettes. At the same time, they are more likely to share a family meal every day of the week and attend religious services at least weekly (Office of Adolescent Health, n.d.).

Under What Conditions Do Youth Live?

Youth live in a variety of situations. Where youth live and with whom, and whether or not they are living in poverty, have major implications for youths' access to OST programs and the types of OST programs and activities that are most appropriate for and successful in helping youth develop their full potential. The following data provide a snapshot of some of the important situational differences among youth.

Household living arrangements. Because parents play important roles in the growth and development of children, both the number and the type of parents (e.g., biological, step, single, grandparents, foreign-born, gay, or lesbian) in a child's household influences his/her well-being. Family composition has changed over the years (see Figure 2.3), with single-parent households becoming more common and two-parent households in decline (Stepler, 2015). The following are some pertinent statistics related to household living arrangements:

- The number of children from birth to age 17 living with two married parents fell from 77% in 1980 to 65% in 2016. One reason this is important is that children in married-couple families are much less likely to be living in poverty.
- In 2016, 23% of children lived with their mothers only, 4% with their fathers only, and 4% with neither parent (the majority of whom lived with grandparents or other family members).
- In 2016, 74% of White, non-Hispanic children lived with two married parents, compared to 60% for Hispanic and 34% for Black children.
- In 2016 about 83% of native-born children with a foreign-born parent lived with two parents compared to 68% of native-born children with two native-born parents. Typically, foreign-born first-generation parents have less education than children whose parents were born in the U.S.

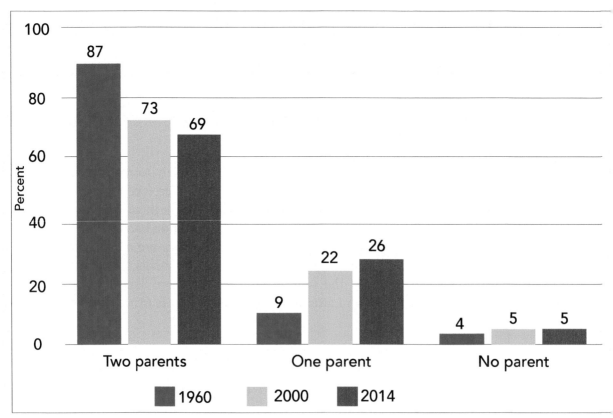

Figure 2.3. Decline in Two-Parent Households: 1960 to 2014. Source: Pew Research Center analysis of 1960-2014 Decennial Census and 2010 and 2014 Community Survey

Housing problems and homelessness. Households with children in the U.S. face three main types of housing problems: physically inadequate housing, crowded housing, and/or a housing cost burden greater than 30% of household income. In 2015, 39% of households with children reported at least one of these housing problems. Housing problems represent serious risks to children's ability to thrive. For example, housing problems can lead to increased levels of homelessness, poorer nutrition, more frequent moving, lack of parental supervision, and lower academic achievement.

Being homeless means that students "lack a fixed, regular, and adequate nighttime residence" (Balden, 2017). National estimates of youth homelessness are limited because no government or philanthropic organization has invested adequately in research to accurately estimate prevalence of homelessness. The most reliable estimates come from those youth who remain in school and thus can be assessed through U.S. Department of Education or organizations like the Center for Public Education.

There were 1.2 million homeless youth in pre-K through Grade 12 during the 2014-15 school year. That number represents a 34% increase in homelessness since the recession ended in 2009. Twenty-one states reported at least a 10% increase in the prevalence of homelessness between 2012 and 2014 (Baldari, 2017). According to a report on Homeless Children and Youth in Public Schools (2017, https://nces.ed.gov/programs/coe/pdf/coe_tgh.pdf) the largest numbers of homeless students in 2014–2015 resided in city districts (3.7% of students), compared to 2% in suburban areas, 2.4% in rural areas, and 2.6% in town areas.

These are staggering numbers. The Homeless Children and Youth Act of 2017 (H.R. 1511/S. 611) is under consideration at the time of writing this chapter. Proponents of the act provide a fact sheet that gives some further insight into why youth development professionals should care about homelessness (The Homeless Children and Youth Act of 2017, 2017). Some of these include the following. You are encouraged to download the fact sheet to better understand the effects of homelessness and efforts by U.S. Housing and Urban Development to address this public health and human development issue.

- Youth and family homelessness is different than adult homelessness.
    - Homeless families with children and unaccompanied youth stay wherever they can, move frequently between living situations, and often hide their situation due to fear of child welfare involvement.
    - Often, families and youth must stay in motels, or with others temporarily, because there is no family or youth shelter in the community, shelters are full, or shelter policies exclude them.
    - These living situations are precarious, crowded, unstable, and often unsafe, putting youth and families at high risk of harm, abuse, and neglect.
- Homeless youth are at high risk for trafficking and other abuse.
    - According to the National Human Trafficking Hotline, runaway/homeless youth and unstable housing situations statuses are among the top five risk factors for human trafficking.
    - One in four homeless youth in recent studies either were victims of sex trafficking or felt like they had no choice but to trade sex for something of value, including food and shelter, or engage in commercial sex out of desperation.

  – Forty-one percent of homeless youth surveyed in Louisville and Southern Indiana said they had been victims of sex trafficking at least once.

Poverty. In 2017, a four-person household with an annual income of less than $24,600 was below the federal poverty level. Consider the following U.S. statistics for 2015 (Federal Interagency Forum on Child and Family Statistics, 2017):

- Twenty percent of children aged birth to 17 lived in poverty.
- Poverty levels differed by race and ethnicity, with the poverty level much higher for Black, non-Hispanic (34% lived in poverty), and Hispanic children (29% lived in poverty), than for White, non-Hispanic children (12% lived in poverty).
- About 43% of children in female-headed families were living in poverty compared to 10% of children in married-couple families.
- Eighteen percent of children lived in households that were classified as food insecure (i.e., not having reliable access to sufficient quantities of affordable, nutritious food). Not surprisingly, 44% of those living below the poverty level had food insecurity.

Being raised in poverty puts youth at increased risk for a wide range of problems. For young children, growing up in poverty is associated with lower cognitive abilities, lower school achievement, and impaired health and development. For adolescents, growing up

in poverty is associated with factors such as a lower probability of graduating from high school. Poor children are also more likely to have behavioral and emotional problems. Finally, growing up in poverty is associated with a lower earning potential as an adult, more years of unemployment, and lower occupational status. Being raised in severe poverty (less than 50% of the poverty threshold) makes all of the indicators worse.

What Is the Educational Attainment of Youth?

Higher levels of education are associated with economic success. Over an adult's working life, individuals with only a high school education can expect to earn about $1.2 million, while those with a bachelor's or master's degree can expect earnings of about $2.1 million and $2.5 million, respectively (U.S. Department of Commerce, 2002). In addition, completing more years of education protects against unemployment as well the possibility of more opportunities for advancement. A higher level of educational attainment is also associated with better health and higher levels of socioemotional well-being.

> Higher levels of education are associated with economic success.

In 1984, 84% of young adults aged 18-24 completed high school with a diploma or alternative credential (e.g., GED). In 2015, 93% had reached this level of educational achievement.

High school completion rates rose from 75% in 1980 to 92% in 2015 among non-Hispanic Blacks aged 25 to 29. For Hispanic youth, high school completion rates increased from 57% in 1980 to 88% in 2015. In addition, 97% of Asian youth completed high school in 2015.

What About the Health Status of Youth?

This section addresses five of the most important indicators of health status among youth: sexual health, violence, feeling sad or hopeless, physical health and activity, and substance use. Before reviewing these data, please note that national statistics on these and other health and developmental indicators are collected via surveys conducted by a variety of organizations, (e.g., Youth Risk Behavior Surveillance System [YRBS] conducted by the Centers for Disease Control and Prevention [CDC]). Often these data sets contain not only nationally representative data but also statewide data. Thus, you are encouraged to consult these data sets for statistics pertinent to your geographic locality. In many cases, you can get a better indication of needs in your own community and provide better service responses if you know facts about your state and local context.

As you read the following information, also note the time frame encompassed by each statistic. Survey questions typically ask a respondent to report on a behavior over a specific time period, such as the past month or over the past 12 months. Keep these time periods in mind as you view the results, as it makes a difference in interpretation. Students reporting consuming five drinks of alcohol in a period of two hours twice over the past month suggests a very different picture than students who report doing so twice over the past 12 months. When no time frame is given, it is usually safe to assume the period covered is during the previous 12 months from when the survey was given.

Sexual health. Nationally, the number of high school students who have reported having sexual intercourse has decreased significantly (from a statistical perspective) from 47% sexually active in 2013 to 41% in 2015 (Kann et al., 2016). Also, based on 2015 data among high school students (grades 9-12):

- Forty-one percent of all students reported they had sexual intercourse (43% for males and 39% for females).
- Seven percent of all students reported they had experienced forced sex (3% for males, 10% for females).
- About 10% of all students reported they had experienced dating violence, which could include being hit, slammed into something, or injured with an object or weapon on purpose by someone they were dating or going out with (7% for males, 12% for females).

Violence. Nationally, about 4% to 6% of all students reported violence at school (Kann et al., 2016). Additionally, the following statistics were also reported:

- Carrying a weapon on at least one day over the past 30 days (e.g., gun, knife, or club) on school property (6% for males, 2% for females).
- Not going to school out of fear for safety at least one day out of the past 30 (5% for males, 6% for females).
- Being threatened or injured on school property one or more times during the past 12 months (7% for males, 5% for females).

Unfortunately, national rates of violence during out-of-school time are much higher than for violence reported at school (Kann, et al., 2016):

- Carrying a weapon over the past 30 days (e.g., gun, knife, or club; 16% overall; 6% for males, 2% for females). Nine percent of males reported they carried a gun.
- About 23% of all students reported being in a physical fight one or more times over the past 12 months (28% for males, 16% for females).

Twenty percent of students reported they were bullied on school property.

Bullying has become a great concern in today's society. CDC data indicate that 20% of students reported they were bullied on school property during the past 12 months (16% for males and 25% for females), with 16% reporting they were bullied electronically during the same time period (10% for males and 22% for females; Kann et al., 2016).

Harassment based on a student's sexual orientation or gender identity is a growing problem in today's society. Therefore, one of the *Healthy People 2020* goals is to "increase the proportion of middle and high schools that prohibit harassment based on a student's sexual orientation or gender identity," with a target goal of having 92.2% of high schools meeting that goal in 2020. In 2014, 89.8% of schools met that goal. To check your state to see if it has met the goal, go to www.healthypeople. gov/2020/topics-objectives/topic/Adolescent-Health/objectives.

Feeling sad or hopeless. Surveys have measured the degree to which adolescents feel sad or hopeless because feeling sad or hopeless over the long term are predictors of depression (though not necessarily sufficient for a diagnosis). Furthermore, depressed youth are at higher risk for poor health outcomes as adults. Depressed youth are also more likely to use drugs or alcohol, drop out of school, or engage in promiscuous sex than those who are not depressed (Child Trends Data Bank, 2016). Feeling sad or hopeless is defined as "felt sad or hopeless almost every day for two or more weeks in a row so that they stopped doing some usual activities during the 12 months before the survey" (Centers for Disease Control and Prevention, 2016a).

Trends related to the prevalence of "sad or hopeless" feelings are not promising. The prevalence of feeling sad or hopeless remained steady at 29% between 1999 and 2007 and decreased to 26% by 2009, over the next five years (until 2015). Since then, prevalence increased to 30%, with the increase mainly driven by these feelings among females (i.e., 40% of females reported feeling sad or hopeless during the past 12 months; Centers for Disease Control and Prevention, 2016). These rates were highest among Hispanic females (47%), with Black, non-Hispanic youth of both sexes having the lowest prevalence of reporting feeling sad or hopeless. See Figure 2.4 for a comparison of youth who felt sad or hopeless by race and family status. You may wish to consult http://www. cdc.gov/mmwr/volumes/65/ss/ss6506a1.htm#T24_down for 2015 estimates of feeling sad or hopeless among 9-12 graders for select states and cities. Likewise, http://www. samhsa.gov/data/sites/default/files/NSDUH-DetTabs-2015/NSDUH-DetTabs-2015/ NSDUH-DetTabs-2015.pdf has 2015 data on major depressive episodes for youth aged 12 to 17.

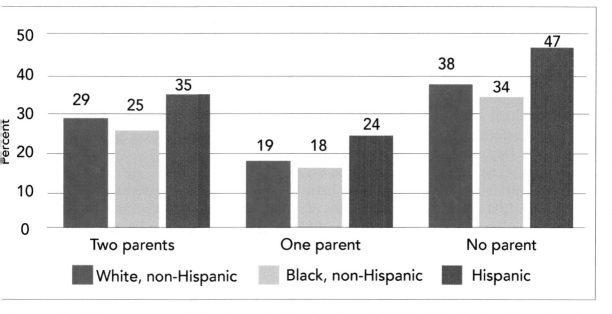

Figure 2.4. Percentage of Students in Grades 9 to 12 Who Felt Sad or Hopeless by Race and Family Status, 2015. Source: Centers of Disease Control and Prevention (2016). 1991-2015 High School Youth Risk Behavior Survey Data

Closely related to depression is suicide.

- Eighteen percent of all students reported that they seriously considered attempting suicide over the past 12 months (12% for males, 23% for females).
- Nine percent of all students reported an actual attempted suicide one or more times over the past 12 months (6% for males, 12% for females).

You have probably noticed that negative indicators of mental health are generally twice as high for females as males. This may suggest that there are reasons to have gender-specific programming that addresses the unique mental health challenges of adolescent females.

One of the *Healthy People 2020* goals is to reduce the proportion of adolescents who experience a major depressive episode from 8.3% in 2008 to 7.5% in 2020. More information is available at www.healthypeople.gov/2020/topicsobjectives2020/objectiveslist.aspx?topicId=28. Clearly, given the preceding statistics, there is room for improved supports and opportunities to meet this goal.

Physical health and activity. Among youth aged 12 to 17, about 82% in 2015 reported that they were in excellent to very good physical health (National Center for Health Statistics, CDC, https://www.cdc.gov/nchs/fastats/adolescent-health.htm). Only 2.5% of youth reported being in fair or poor health. However, health status varies by race and ethnicity, with Asian-American, White, non-Hispanic students having the highest levels of physical health.

Despite positive health indicators overall, as of 2015, fewer than three in 10 high school students met the current recommendations for level of physical activity (PA; Child Trends Data Bank, 2017). Regular PA is important for both short and long-term outcomes. PA helps control weight and has positive psychological benefits, such as increased self-esteem. PA is also related to decreased likelihood of engaging in risky behavior such as violence and drug use. The importance of physical activity for youth is further emphasized since youth who are active tend to become adults who are active.

The YRBS defines physical activity as "doing any kind of physical activity that increased their heart rate and made them breathe hard some of the time during the 7 days before the survey" (CDC, 2016b). The U.S. Department of Health and Human Services recommends that youth aged 6-17

> ... youth who are active tend to become adults who are active.

engage 60 minutes daily in a level of PA that increases heart rate and causes hard breathing. Between 2011 and 2015, fewer than 30% of students met that recommendation. As you can see in Figure 2.5, White males have the highest levels of vigorous PA, and Hispanic females have the lowest.

Other pertinent physical activity statistics according to the YRBS (CDC, 2016) include the following:

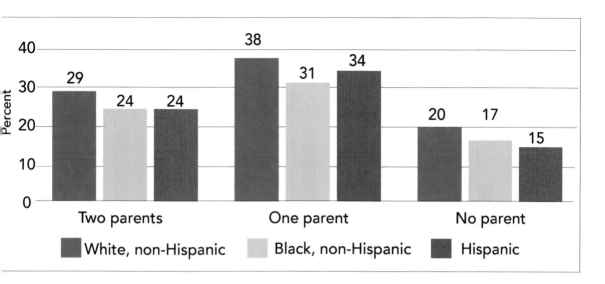

Figure 2.5. Percentage of Students in Grades 9 to 12 Who Participated in Vigorous Physical Activity by Race and Hispanic Origin, 2015. Source: Centers of Disease Control and Prevention (2016). 1991-2015 High School Youth Risk Behavior Survey Data

- Just about half of males and females reported that they had attended a physical education class on average of one or more days during the school year.
- Fifty-eight percent of all students reported they played on at least one sports team for fun operated by their school or community group during the past 12 months (62% for males, 52% for females).
- Twenty-five percent of high school students reported watching television three or more hours per day on an average school day, and 42% reported using computers three or more hours per day for non-school-related activities (e.g., video games) on an average school day. (The proportion of males and females were roughly the same.)

In 2015, self-reported height and weight data for students in grades 9–12 (CDC, 2016b) indicated that 14% of all students were considered obese (17% for males and 11% for females). Obesity is defined as "greater than or equal to the 95th percentile for body mass index (BMI) based on sex- and age-specific reference data from the 2000 CDC Growth Charts." Thirty-two percent of all students reported that they described themselves as slightly or very overweight (25% for males and 38% for females). Looking at Figure 2.6, there is an overall increase over time in the percentage of children aged 6–19 who are obese (Child Trends Data Bank, 2014).

Another *Healthy People 2020* goal is to increase the number of adolescents who meet current federal physical activity guidelines for aerobic physical activity from the 2011 level of 29%, to 32% by 2020. Additional goals are to increase the proportion of public and private schools that require daily physical education for all students and that require or recommend recess. More information is available at www.healthypeople. gov/2020/topics-objectives/topic/physical-activity/objectives.

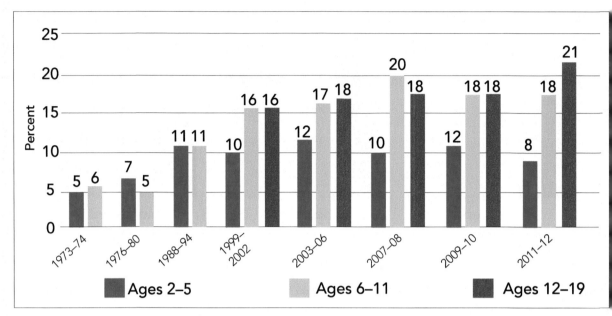

Figure 2.6. Percentage of Children Ages 2-19 who are Obese by Age, for Selected Years 1971-2012. Source: Child Trends Data Bank

Substance use. With regard to substance use, there is good news. Youth in grades 8–12 are reporting less use of cigarettes and alcohol, and a greater percentage report being substance-free over the past 30 days (see Figure 2.7) than in previous years. Likewise, rates of abstaining from using illicit drugs other than marijuana (e.g., hallucinogens, cocaine, heroin and other narcotics, amphetamines, and barbiturates)

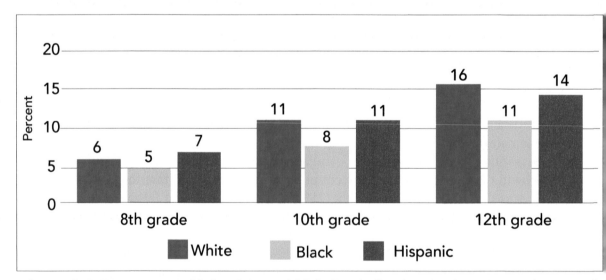

Figure 2.7. Percentage of 8th, 10th, and 12th Grade Students Who Report They Used any Illicit Drugs other than Marijuana in the Past Year, by Race and Hispanic Origin: 2014-15. Source: Miech, R. A., Johnson, L.D., O'Maley, P. M., Bachman, I. G., & Schulenberg, J. E. (2016). *Monitoring the future national survey results on drug use, 1975-2015: Volume 1-Secondary school students.* Ann Arbor, MI: Institute for Social Research.

among 8th through 12th grade students are increasing (see Figure 2.8). The use of cigarette products, alcohol, marijuana, and other illicit drugs among young people are highly predictive of risky short and long-term outcomes. For example, use of cigarettes is strongly associated with cancer and cardiovascular disease. Use of alcohol, marijuana, and other illicit drugs are predictive of risky sexual behavior, delinquency, crime, and increased risk for depression. In addition, public health officials are concerned about the impact of substance use because of the effect on the adolescent brain.

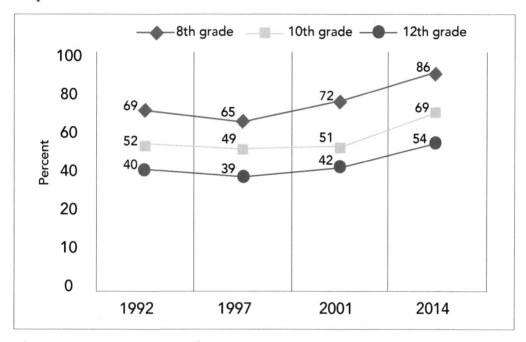

Figure 2.8. Percentage of Students who Reported being Substance-free in the Past 30 Days by Selected Years, 1990-2014. Source: Adapted from original analysis by Child Trends of Monitoring the Future Data.

More specifically, in 2017 among youth in grades 9–12 (Federal Interagency Forum on Child and Family Statistics, 2017):

- Sixty-eight percent of all students reported that they had never tried cigarette smoking; not even one or two puffs (66% for males, 69% for females). In 2013, 59% of all students reported never having tried cigarette smoking.
- Eleven percent of all students reported they smoked cigarettes on at least one day during the past 30 days; in 2013, the rate was 16%.
- One-third of all students reported drinking at least one drink of alcohol on at least one day during the past 30 days; this rate was about equal for males and females.
- Eighteen percent of all adolescents reported binge drinking on at least one day over the past 30 days (19% male, 17% female). The overall rate in 2013 was 21%. For males, binge drinking is defined as five or more drinks of alcohol in a row (four for females) within a couple of hours.
- Although 8% of all youth reported they did not drink and drive one or more times over the past 30 days (10% male, 6% female), 20% of both males and females

reported they rode in a car or other vehicle one or more times during the past 30 days with a driver who had been drinking alcohol.

- About 39% of males and females reported using marijuana, and 7% reported using inhalants at least once in their lives.

The concerning news is that students are using electronic vapor products (although data from previous years are not available since electronic products are relatively new). In 2015, 24% of all students reported using electronic vapor products (e.g., e-cigarettes, e-cigars, vape pipes, vaping pens, e-hookahs and hookah pens) on at least 1 day during the past 30 days (26% for males 23% for females).

The 2015 Youth Risk Behavior Survey (http://nccd.cdc.gov/YouthOnline/App/Default.aspx) and the National Household Survey on Drug Abuse (2013-14; www.samhsa.gov/data/) both provide data broken down by state, U.S. Census Bureau region (www.census.gov/prod/cen2010/briefs/c2010br-04.pdf), and metro region. You might consider looking at these websites for statistics relevant to your local area.

In October 2017, the U.S. Department of Health and Human Services declared the opioid crisis as a public health emergency. Opioids are a class of drugs that include heroin as well as prescription pain relievers (e.g., oxycodone, hydrocodone, codeine, morphine, fentanyl, as well as others). During 2015, there were an average of 91 opioid overdose deaths each day (CNN Library, 2017). It is important to consider that the prescribing rates for prescription opioids among adolescents and young adults nearly doubled from 1994 to 2007 (American Society of Addiction Medicine, 2016). That rate, however, seems to have declined since then (McCabe et al., 2017), as it became clear to physicians that these medications were highly addictive. Nevertheless, use of prescription opioids still occurs, and roughly 25% of patients prescribed opioids for chronic pain misuse them. Using prescribed opioids is associated with later non-prescription opioid use; about 80% of heroin users first misused prescription opioids (National Institute on Drug Abuse, 2017).

Although the overall percentage of youth using opioids is small (estimates are about 1% of the adolescent population currently use opioids) there is cause for concern. Unintentional opioid overdose rates for youth aged 15–19 tripled from 1999 through 2007, declined through 2014 for males only, and have increased for all adolescents since then (Curtin, Tejada-Vera, & Warner, 2017). Heroin overdoses were the highest. Death by suicide was twice as likely for females than for males. It will be important to monitor adolescent opioid use as time goes on.

How Do Youth Spend Their Time?

This next section focuses on general time use data; screen time, including television viewing, and use of computers and hand-held devices; and participation in extra-curricular and OST activities, including sport participation and volunteering. The U.S. Bureau of Labor Statistics conducts the American Time Use Survey (www.bls.gov/tus/), which provides a profile of a day in the life of a high school teen, by comparing time use on a typical school day to time use on a weekend day during the school year. (Note that additional information about sport, nature-based, and arts activities is contained in separate chapters later in the book).

How much sleep do youth get? According to the Office of Adolescent Health (n.d.), on average adolescents get 8.6 hours of sleep per weekday (males 9.2, females 8.2) and both males and females report getting 10.9 hours per weekend day. Other reports indicate that youth get much less sleep, and in fact get less than the 8 to 10 hours needed to function best. The National Sleep Foundation (n.d.) calls sleep "food for the brain." Consequences of not getting enough sleep include poorer mood (e.g., being aggressive, getting frustrated or upset more easily), engaging in more risk-taking behaviors, drowsy driving, poor cognitive ability and academic performance, eating too much, being more stressed, and being more prone to pimples and other skin conditions. As youth development professionals, it is important to be attuned to

> Sleep is "food for the brain."

how much sleep youth are getting and discuss with them ways to get more sleep. The National Sleep Foundation website has suggestions for how to help teens get more sleep.

When not in school and not sleeping, with whom do high school students spend their time (from U.S. Bureau of Labor Statistics, 2016)?

- **Time with family.** On average, both females and males spend more time with their families on weekend days than weekdays (an average of 2.6 more hours for males and 2.3 hours more for females). High school males and females spend a similar amount of time with family on weekend days (5.7 hours per day), but high school females spend more time with their families than males on weekdays (3.8 vs. 2.9 hours per day).

- **Time with friends.** Males and females spend similar amounts of time with friends (1.8 to 2.5 hours per day on weekdays and 2.1 to 2.2 hours per day on weekends).
- **Time alone.** High school males spend more time alone than females on weekdays (an average of 3.5 hours per day compared with 2.7 hours), but they spend a similar amount of time alone on weekend days (3.0 to 3.5 hours).

Table 2.1 provides a 2013 snapshot of the average amount of time youth spent per day in particular leisure and sport activities by age (U.S. Bureau of Labor Statistics, 2016). From this table, you can see that young people aged 15 to 19 spent about 5 hours a day, on average, on all activities considered "leisure and sport." The greatest amount of time spent is on watching TV at almost two hours per day. Playing games and computer use for leisure is next, at almost one hour per day. Taken together, this means that youth spent about three hours a day in front of screens on a weekday and closer to four and a half hours on weekend days.

Table 2.1

Average Hours per Day in 2016 Spent in Leisure and Sport Activities, All Days of the Week, By Selected Characteristics

Characteristic	Total, all leisure and sports activities	Participating in sports, exercise, and recreation	Socializing & communicating	Watching TV	Reading	Relaxing/ thinking	Playing games and computer	Other leisure/ sports activities/ travel
Sex								
Men	5.51	0.39	0.64	2.94	0.25	0.34	0.49	0.46
Women	4.77	0.25	0.67	2.52	0.33	0.30	0.34	0.37
Age								
Total, 15 Years and over	5.13	0.32	0.65	2.73	0.29	0.32	0.41	0.41
15–19 years	5.20	0.67	0.72	1.94	0.12	0.20	0.92	0.62
20–24 years	4.80	0.36	0.73	2.12	0.14	0.24	0.67	0.53
25–34 years	4.13	0.32	0.67	1.95	0.15	0.21	0.46	0.38

Source: U.S. Bureau of Labor Statistics

Screen time: Television and media. Although 2013 is not that long ago for some statistics, data from The American Time Use Study is probably already outdated due to the rapidity with which technology changes. For example, if you are a college student, think about how your television viewing habits have changed since you were in middle or high school, given the expansion of available video-based media options. Although conventional TV viewing has declined over the past 20 years, if you include viewing TV content on computers and hand-held media devices, as well as conventional TV, screen viewing has actually increased by 38 minutes per day from 1999 to 2009, and is probably much higher today. Almost 100% of children have access to television, with 71% having a television set in their bedroom (in 2009).

Recent data reported by Common Sense Media (Rideout, 2015), for example, has tweens (children 8 to 12) spending about six hours consuming media and teenagers 12 years and older spending nine hours a day. Those statistics are similar to other reports of media use via hand-held devices, although estimates of use may vary by plus or minus an hour. There is a great deal of controversy about young people's use of screens at such a high rate. Parents and researchers worry about what the constant need for stimulation does to one's ability to focus and concentrate. Others worry about restorative sleep, sensory overload, and what the blue light that smartphones emit does to the growing adolescent brain (Kim, 2014).

There is a digital divide due to economic resources of families and teens. Only 54% of teens in households making less than $35,000 a year have a laptop in their home, versus 92% of teens living in households making $100,000 a year (Wallace, 2015). Although there is controversy about use of screen time in today's digital landscape, youth use media for both educational and social networking purposes. Therefore, the digital inequality is a public-policy issue, which includes bringing Internet services/cell phone coverage to digital desert areas (e.g., geographic areas with limited or no cell phone coverage).

The *Healthy People 2020* initiative set a goal to decrease screen time (i.e., "Increase the percentage of children and adolescents who view television, videos, or play video games no more than two hours a day.") Data from the YRBS indicate that 75.1% meet this goal to date, and the target is set at 82.6% (Office of Disease Prevention and Health Promotion, n.d.). Considering that media/screen use is so high, this may be a difficult goal to reach. In Chapter 2, we will discuss the role of media and technology in adolescents' lives in detail.

Extracurricular and out-of-school activities. Another one of the *Healthy People 2020* goals is to "Increase the proportion of adolescents who participate in extracurricular and/or out-of-school activities." In 2011–12, 82.7% of 12- to 17-year-olds were participating in extracurricular and OST activities. The 2020 target goal set by ODPHP is to increase that percentage to 91%. However, here is another case where it is important to look beyond national statistics and break down the data by demographic characteristics such as race and ethnicity, income, and where one lives. For example, considering race and ethnicity, 90.3% of the Asian population participate in some type of extracurricular and/or OST program, but only 60.9% of the American Indian or Alaska native population are similarly involved. Not surprisingly, the lower the income, the less likely it is that youth participate in extracurricular and/or OST programs. Figure 2.9 provides data for how income level is related to parents' ability to find after-school programs for their children (Stepler, 2015).

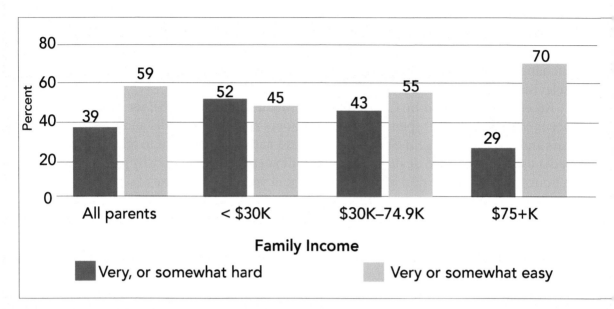

Figure 2.9. Percentage of Parents with Children Aged 7-17 Saying it is [harder or easier] to Find After-School Activities or Programs that are Affordable and High Quality by Family Income. Source: Pew Research Center (2015) survey of parents with children under 18, Sept. 15-Oct. 13.

Examining these statistics at the state level, we find that Connecticut and South Dakota are close to the 2020 goal (90.5% and 90.1% rates of participation, respectively) while Kentucky and Florida, for example, are a long way off (75.9% and 74.8%, respectively). Using the *Healthy People 2020* website, what are the statistics for your state?

Two related *Healthy People 2020* goals are important for youth development professionals to know about. One goal is to "Increase the proportion of parents who attend events and activities in which their adolescents participate." In 2012, 82.6% of parents reported attending such an event or activity; the goal is for 90.3% to attend. White parents are more likely to attend these events or activities (86.7%) than Asian and Native Hawaiian or other Pacific Islander parents (66.4 % for both groups). Once again, income plays a factor, with those with lower incomes less likely to attend.

The second goal is "An increase in the proportion of adolescents who have an adult in their lives with whom they can talk about serious problems." In 2014, 79.3% of 12- to 17-year-old adolescents reported they did have an adult with whom they could talk (81.5% for males, 76.9% for females); the 2020 target is 83.2%. Consider what you might do to help realize these goals. Adults working in OST programs can play an important role in increasing the availability of adults to interact positively with adolescents.

School athletics. Participation in high school athletics is associated with healthier eating habits, higher levels of cardiovascular fitness, academic achievement, lower absentee levels, and decreased anxiety and depression (Child Trends, 2015). Sports participation is also related to greater overall psychological well-being. The evidence is mixed regarding participating on a sport team and substance use; some research has indicated that student-athletes are less likely to use substances and other research shows that student-athletes are more likely to use substance. Chapter 10 provides more information on youth sports participation.

Figure 2.10 shows youth sports participation rates by gender, grade, and year, comparing 1991 and 2014. You can immediately see that males have higher participation rates than females across all years and grades. Before the introduction of Title IX, these discrepancies were much greater. Notice also that participation in grades 8 and 10 are greater than in grade 12.

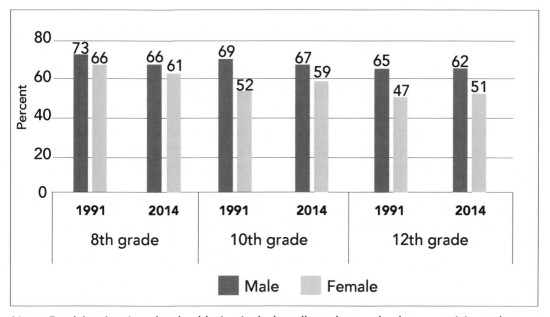

Note: Participation in school athletics includes all students who have participated to any degree on school athletic teams during the current year. *Source:* Original analysis by Child Trends of Monitoring the Future data 1993-2014.

Figure 2.10. Percentage of Students in Grades 8, 10, and 12 Who Participate in School Athletics by Gender, from 1991 to 2014.

The *Healthy People 2020* initiative includes three goals directly related to increasing physical exercise among children and adolescents, as well as several related goals such as increasing the number of schools that offer daily recess and increasing the proportion of schools and adolescents that have daily physical education. Additional information is available at www.healthypeople.gov/2020/topics-objectives/topic/physical-activity/objectives?topicId=33.

Volunteering. More than a third of high school seniors report that they volunteer at least once a month (Child Trends, 2015). Further, between 2010 and 2014 volunteering among 10th and 12th graders increased, from 33% to 39%. Why is volunteering important? Adolescents who are involved in community service or who volunteer in political activities are more likely to have a strong work ethic as adults and are more likely to volunteer and vote in the future. Youth who volunteer are less likely to become pregnant or to use drugs, and volunteering in adolescence is related to overall positive academic, psychological, and occupational outcomes.

Most teenagers (aged 16–19) volunteer with either education, youth-service, or religious organizations. What prompts a young person to volunteer? Thirty-nine percent of youth volunteers reported that they initiated the contact with their organization. On the other hand, 22% report that someone in the organization approached them, and 15% report that a relative or friend suggested they volunteer. Girls are more likely than boys to volunteer, especially as they get older (43% of 12th grade girls vs. 35% of boys).

Concluding Remarks

We hope this chapter has raised your awareness of some the living situations and experiences of young people and stimulated you to think about circumstances in your community. After reading this chapter, if someone asked you to paint a picture of a typical child or adolescent, could you? Probably not, because there is no such person. Yet, these statistics do provide a broad picture of some of the current social and demographic characteristics of youth and issues that youth face as they grow up. These statistics also provide further evidence that race, ethnicity, and gender play important roles in understanding youth and promoting PYD. Later chapters in this book address some of these issues in more detail.

As youth face the challenges of adolescence, those who have the highest degree of access to supports, opportunities, programs, and services that facilitate the acquisition of appropriate knowledge, values, skills, and behaviors will be most likely to thrive and succeed. Clearly, some youth are growing up in less than ideal circumstances, faced with poverty or low-income environments and a concomitant lack of social and other services. As you continue through this book, you will become more aware of how OST activities can contribute to the mitigation of risk factors and promotion of protective factors, leading to risk reduction and healthy development of youth.

It is also important to note that while this chapter has provided a great deal of information, data were not provided for *all* of the various statistics that can help us understand the current status of young people. Thus, I challenge you to do some of your own research about some of these other topics, or at least keep in mind that there are other important issues facing youth in their daily lives, such as the following:

- It important to know who joins gangs. What family and community factors make it more likely that someone will join a gang? What are the consequences of gang membership?

- It is important to understand differing opportunities available to youth in urban, suburban, and rural living environments. What is the effect of growing up in suburbia vs. a rural area? Are there settings that make it easier for youth to make connections with other youth and participate in organized recreation?
- How local, state, and federal government policies and programs affect the prospects of youth transitioning to adulthood and thriving is an important consideration. For example, how does where one lives create more or less access to supports, opportunities, programs, and services that enable adolescents to thrive?
- In what ways do religion and religious institutions play a significant role in youths' lives? How do these institutions provide support not available through other means?

Keeping in mind the conditions and circumstances in which youth are growing up and how these factors influence each other (e.g., poverty, poor health, and poor academic achievement are all linked), will enhance the ability of youth development professionals to purposefully plan and deliver programs that enhance youth development in the particular community and setting they are working. In other words, what might be helpful to youth in a low-income, Hispanic neighborhood may not work as well in a suburban, non-Hispanic white neighborhood, and of course, vice versa. In the following chapter, we dig a little deeper into a few selected topics that will provide you with an expanded picture of the current context of adolescent development.

Discussion Questions

1. Data in Figure 2.1 project that high schools will become increasingly more diverse from between the time you read this book and 2025. Discuss specific implications for what this means for educators and policy makers in terms of how they will address education in the future. Are changes necessary from how things are done today? Why or why not? How will youth development professionals be affected by projections of increased diversity?
2. What are the implications for OST programs, considering the fact that the percentage of children living in two-parent households is declining?
3. What are the various roles OST programs and youth development professionals could play in the lives of youth who are homeless? Identify pros and cons of each role.

Assignment

You are a newly hired youth development professional in your community. Identify the main sociodemographic characteristics you would consider first when analyzing what type of programs and services might be most appropriate. Justify your answer by first describing your community in terms of issues discussed in this chapter, such as various health status indicators or household living arrangements. Next, select which characteristics are most salient to your job and describe why and how you would address the issues in your youth programs. You will need to consult the various websites provided throughout this chapter in order to get state-level or local statistics.

References

American Society of Addiction Medicine. (2016). Opioid addiction: 2016 facts and figures. Retrieved from https://www.asam.org/docs/default-source/advocacy/opioid-addiction-disease-facts-figures.pdf

America's Children. (2017). Key national indicators of well-being, 2017. Retrieved from https://www.childstats.gov/americaschildren/press_release.asp

Baldari, C. (2017). Fact sheet: The Homeless Children and Youth Act of 2017. First Focus Campaign for Children. Retrieved from https://campaignforchildren.org/resources/fact-sheet/fact-sheet-the-homeless-children-and-youth-act-of-2017/

Balden, C. (2017). Fact sheet: The Homeless Children and Youth Act of 2017. Retrieved from https://www.nn4youth.org/learn/how-many-homeless/

Centers for Disease Control and Prevention (CDC). (2016a). 1991-2015 High School Youth Risk Behavior Surveillance System Data. Retrieved from http://nccd.cdc.gov/Youthonline/App/Default.aspx

Centers for Disease Control and Prevention (CDC). (2016b). 1991-2015 High School Risk Behavior Surveillance System Data. Retrieved from http://nccd.cdc.gov/youthonline/

Child Trends. (2016). http://www.Childtrends.org. Child Trends Data Bank. (2014). Overweight children and youth: Indicators of child and youth well-being. Retrieved from https://www.childtrends.org/indicators/overweight-children-and-youth

Child Trends Data Bank. (2015). Participation in school athletics: Indicators of child and youth well-being. Retrieved from https://www.childtrends.org/indicators/participation-in-school-athletics

Child Trends Data Bank. (2016). Adolescents who felt sad or hopeless: Indicators of child and youth well-being. Retrieved from https://www.childtrends.org/wp-content/uploads/2016/09/30_Felt_Sad_or_Hopeless.pdf

Child Trends Data Bank. (2017). Vigorous physical activity by youth: Indicators of child and youth well-being. Retrieved from https://www.childtrends.org/wp-content/uploads/2017/03/16_Vigorous_Physical_Activity_Youth.pdf

CNN Library. (October. 29, 2017). Opioid crisis fast facts. Retrieved from http://www.cnn.com/2017/09/18/health/opioid-crisis-fast-facts/index.html

Curtin, S. C., Tejada-Vera, B., & Warner, M. (August 2017). Drug overdose deaths among adolescents aged 15–19 in the United States: 1999-2015. NCHS Data Brief No. 282. Retrieved from https://www.cdc.gov/nchs/products/databriefs/db282.htm

Ennis, S. R., Rios-Vargas, M., & Albert, N. G. (May, 2011). The Hispanic population: 2010. 2010 Census Briefs. U. S. Department of Commerce, Economics and Statistics Administration. Retrieved from https://www.census.gov/prod/cen2010/briefs/c2010br-04.pdf

Federal Interagency Forum on Child and Family Statistics. (2017). *America's children: Key national indicators of well-being.* Washington, DC: U.S. Government Printing Office.

Fry, R. (2015). Class of 2025 expected to be the biggest, most diverse ever. Retrieved from http://www.pewresearch.org/fact-tank/2015/09/11/class-of-2025-expected-to-be-the-biggest-most-diverse-ever

Homeless Children and Youth Act of 2017. (2017). Retrieved from https://campaignforchildren.org/wp-content/uploads/sites/2/2017/03/HCYA-Fact-Sheet-March-2017-FINAL-.pdf

Kann, L., McManus, T., Harris, W. A., Shanklin, S. L., Flint, K. H., Hawkins, M., ... Zaza, S. (2016). Youth risk behavior surveillance—United States, 2015. *MMWR Surveillance Summaries 2016, 65*, (No. 6), 1-180.

Kim, M. (Sept. 1, 2014). Blue light from electronics disturbs sleep, especially for teenagers. *The Washington Post.* Retrieved from https://www.washingtonpost.com/national/health-science/blue-light-from-electronics-disturbs-sleep-especially-for-teenagers/2014/08/29/3edd2726-27a7-11e4-958c-268a320a60ce_story.html?utm_term=.0febc6d19117

McCabe, S. E., West, B. T., Veliz, P., McCabe, V.V., Stoddard, S. A., & Boyd, C. J. (2017). Trends in medical and non-medical use of prescription opioids among U.S. adolescents: 1976-2015. *Pediatrics, 139*, doi: 10.1542/pred.2016-2387

National Household Survey on Drug Abuse. (2013-14). Retrieved from https://www.samhsa.gov/data

National Institute on Drug Abuse. (2017). Opioid crisis. Retrieved from https://www.drugabuse.gov/drugs-abuse/opioids/opioid-crisis

National Sleep Foundation. (n.d.). Teens and sleep. Retrieved from https://sleepfoundation.org/sleep-topics/teens-and-sleep

Office of Adolescent Health. (n.d.a). The changing face of America's adolescents. Retrieved from https://www.hhs.gov/ash/oah/facts-and-stats/changing-face-of-americas-adolescents/index.html

Office of Adolescent Health. (n.d.b). A day in the life. Retrieved from https://www.hhs.gov/ash/oah/facts-and-stats/day-in-the-life/index.html

Office of Disease Prevention and Health Promotion (ODPHP). *Healthy People 2020.* Retrieved from https://www.healthypeople.gov/2020

Pew Research Center, www.pewresearch.org

Rideout, V. (2015). The common sense consensus: Media use by tweens and teens. *Common Sense.* Retrieved from https://www.commonsensemedia.org/sites/default/files/uploads/research/census_researchreport.pdf

Stepler, R. (2015). 5 key takeaways about parenting in changing times. Retrieved from http://www.pewresearch.org/fact-tank/2015/12/17/key-takeaways-about-parenting

The Hispanic Population 2010. (2011). U.S. Census Bureau. Retrieved from https://www.census.gov/prod/cen2010/briefs/c2010br-04.pdf

U.S. Bureau of Labor Statistics. (2016). Time spent in leisure and sports activities for civilian population by selected characteristics, averages per day, 2016 annual averages. Retrieved from https://www.bls.gov/news.release/atus.t11a.htm

U.S. Department of Commerce. (2002). The big payoff: Educational attainment and synthetic estimates of work-life earnings. Economics and Statistics Administration. Retrieved from https://www.census.gov/prod/2002pubs/p23-210.pdf

Wallace, K. (November 3, 2015). Teens spend a 'mind-boggling' 9 hours a day using media, report says. CNN. Retrieved from http://www.cnn.com/2015/11/03/health/teens-tweens-media-screen-use-report/index.html.

Youth Risk Behavior Survey. (2015). Retrieved from http://nccd.cdc.gov/YouthOnline/App/Default.aspx

Appendix A

Major Sources of Information and Major Studies of Youth

Centers for Disease Control and Prevention (CDC) (www.cdc.gov/nchs/fastats/ado-lescent-health.htm) and **National Center for Health Statistics** (https://www.cdc.gov/healthyyouth/data/index.htm) monitors the U.S. national health indicators and provides public reports, datasets for researchers, research aids for students and librarians, and media resources, among others.

Child Trends (www.childtrends.org/) is a nonprofit, nonpartisan children's research organization. They collect and analyze data; conduct, synthesize, and disseminate research; design and evaluate programs; and develop and test promising approaches to research in the field. Child Trends has achieved a reputation as one of the nation's leading sources of credible data and high-quality research on children.

ChildStats (www.childstats.gov/) offers easy access to federal and state statistics and reports on children and their families, including population and family characteristics, economic security, health, behavior and social environment, and education. Reports of the Federal Interagency Forum on Child and Family Statistics include *America's Children: Key National Indicators of Well-Being*, the annual federal monitoring report on the status of the Nation's children.

Monitoring the Future (www.monitoringthefuture.org/) is an ongoing study of the behaviors, attitudes, and values of American secondary school students, college students, and young adults. Each year, a total of approximately 50,000 8th, 10th and 12th grade students are surveyed (12th graders since 1975, and 8th and 10th graders since 1991). In addition, annual follow-up questionnaires are mailed to a sample of each graduating class for a number of years after their initial participation. The Monitoring the Future Study has been funded under a series of investigator-initiated competing research grants from the National Institute on Drug Abuse, a part of the National Institutes of Health. MTF is conducted at the Survey Research Center in the Institute for Social Research at the University of Michigan.

Office of Disease Prevention and Health Promotion (www.healthypeople.gov/) is the site for access to *Healthy People 2020* and past *Healthy People* initiatives. This site includes leading health indicators, provides the ability to search state level data, and provides tools and resources for the public. It also provides searchable databases to better understand health disparities and interactive infographics.

The Innovation Center for Community and Youth Development (www.theinnovationcenter.org/) unleashes the potential of youth, adults, organizations, and communities to engage together in creating a just and equitable society. The center connects thinkers and leaders of all ages to develop fresh ideas, forge new partnerships, and design strategies that engage young people and their communities. The center helps innovative programs become strong, sustainable ventures. The website provides information on youth leadership, civic engagement, youth development, program evaluation, and community building.

The International Youth Foundation (www.iyfnet.org/) is working in nearly 60 countries and territories to improve the conditions and prospects for young people where they live, learn, work, and play. Established in 1990 to bring worldwide resources to young people in need, IYF works with hundreds of companies, foundations, and civil society organizations to strengthen and "scale up" existing programs that are making a positive and lasting difference in young lives.

The National Longitudinal Study of Adolescent Health (www.cpc.unc.edu/projects/addhealth) is a longitudinal study of a nationally representative sample of adolescents in grades 7-12 in the United States during the 1994-95 school year. The Add Health cohort has been followed into young adulthood with four in-home interviews, the most recent in 2008, when the sample was aged 24-32. Add Health is re-interviewing cohort members in a Wave V follow-up from 2016-2018 to collect social, environmental, behavioral, and biological data with which to track the emergence of chronic disease as the cohort moves through their fourth decade of life. Add Health combines longitudinal survey data on respondents' social, economic, psychological, and physical well-being with contextual data on the family, neighborhood, community, school, friendships, peer groups, and romantic relationships, providing unique opportunities to study how social environments and behaviors in adolescence are linked to health and achievement outcomes in young adulthood. The fourth wave of interviews expanded the collection of biological data in Add Health to understand the social, behavioral, and biological linkages in health trajectories as the Add Health cohort ages through adulthood, and the fifth wave of data collection continues this biological data expansion.

The Youth Risk Behavior Surveillance System (www.cdc.gov/healthyyouth/data/yrbs/index.htm) of the Center for Disease Control was developed in 1990 to monitor priority health risk behaviors that contribute markedly to the leading causes of death, disability, and social problems among youth and adults in the United States. The YRBSS monitors six types of health-risk behaviors that contribute to the leading causes of death and disability among youth and adults, including: behaviors that contribute to unintentional injuries and violence; sexual behaviors related to unintended pregnancy and sexually transmitted diseases, including HIV infection; alcohol and other drug use; tobacco use; unhealthy dietary behaviors; and inadequate physical activity. YRBSS also measures the prevalence of obesity and asthma and other priority health-related behaviors plus sexual identity and sex of sexual contacts. YRBSS includes a national school-based survey conducted by CDC and state, territorial, tribal, and local surveys conducted by state, territorial, and local education and health agencies and tribal governments.

The Search Institute (www.search-institute.org/) is an independent nonprofit organization whose mission is to provide leadership, knowledge, and resources to promote healthy children, youth, and communities. To accomplish this mission, the institute generates and communicates new knowledge, and brings together community, state, and national leaders. At the heart of the Institute's work is the framework of 40 developmental assets, which are positive experiences and personal qualities that young people need to grow up healthy, caring, and responsible.

Youth.gov (https://youth.gov/) offers one-stop access to government resources that support after-school programs. You can find information to help you understand the issues that face kids and teens or fund, start, and operate an after-school program. Research studies, news, and publications are added as they are released to keep you up to date on what is happening in the field of after-school programs.

Chapter 3

Growing Up Slower With Fast-Forward and Like Buttons

Linda L. Caldwell

> *"Generation Z has grown up with a fast-forward button and a like button. They use their multiple-screen view of the world to get peer-reviewed (most social media likes) content and they won't pay attention to anything that isn't as good as something they can find online."*
>
> **Tom Richmond,** executive director of enrollment marketing at
> Bradley University in Peoria, Illinois, as cited in Loveland, E. (Winter, 2017), p. 37.

Having read the previous chapter, you may have concluded that "the typical" adolescent does not exist; each person is unique, in part due to sociodemographic and economic factors. On the other hand, you have no doubt seen headlines such as the following:

- "Millennials are the Most Likely Generation of Americans to Use Public Libraries" (Geiger, 2017)
- "It's Becoming More Common for Young Adults to Live at Home—and for Longer Stretches" (Fry, 2017)

As implied in these headlines, society often treats groups of people in a homogeneous fashion; that is, it lumps people together and makes broad statements and generalizations about their characteristics and behavior. Although this practice is fraught with problems, there are some benefits to being able to make broad statements about groups of people.

One of the more common approaches is grouping people who grow up during the same time period, with the same general political, technological, economic, and other factors exerting influence on their lives—even if they were not directly aware of the influences and events going on around them. Because of these common experiences, people who grow up during the same period tend to exhibit some common characteristics, despite the fact that they are all unique individuals. It is similar to noting that students who attend the same university have a common bond because of the constellation of their shared experiences, despite their individuality. One grouping that has proven useful when assessing societal trends has been to look at people who grow up during the same historical period or *generation* (e.g., Baby Boomers and Millennials).

Understanding shifts in behaviors and trends between and among generations is important for planning and program development on a broad societal level. Understanding population level or generational characteristics is also important for youth workers in order to avoid carrying over ideas, principles, and practices used to provide programs and services to one generation that may not be applicable to the next. In addition, these understandings are important, because often adolescents and the youth workers who provide them with programs and services come from different generations.

This chapter addresses the common experiences of young people who were born roughly between the mid-1990s and mid-2000s, the generation being termed iGen, Gen Z, or Generation Z, Homeland Generation, or post-Millennial (among other terms). I will refer to them as Gen Z in this chapter. Specifically, the chapter covers the concept of a generation, describes the influence of digital media on Gen Z and adolescent development, and explores the issue of gender as it relates to growing up as a member of Gen Z.

A Generational Approach

What constitutes a generation? As noted, although there are many intrapersonal, interpersonal, sociopolitical, and cultural factors that combine and interact to shape and support people's behavior, it is common to ascribe certain attributes to people based on the generation to which they belong. People growing up during the same historical and cultural events and contexts (such as the Great Depression, Vietnam War, War with Iraq, 9/11, digital media) are shaped in similar ways by broad cultural and economic perspectives. For example, as a Baby Boomer, I have often been asked, "Do you remember where you were when President John F. Kennedy, Dr. Martin Luther King, or Senator Robert Kennedy were shot?" or "Were you at Woodstock?" Questions that might resonate more with today's readers are "Do you remember where you were when 9/11 happened?" or "Do you remember when you got your first smartphone?"

Most of you are probably members of Gen Z, although some may be members of the Millennial generation, which includes those born roughly from the late 1970s to 1995. Generations usually cover about a 20-year span, but there is no hard and fast rule and no clear delineations between generations, unless a significant, defining event clearly shaped the perceptions, outlook, and perspectives of those defined during a given time period. Examples are the Great Depression in 1929, the Civil Rights movement of the late 1950s and early 1960s, the Vietnam War, 9/11, or the Great Recession of 2008. Some researchers and policy makers think in terms of age cohorts rather than generations, but they are in essence the same thing, and provide insight into how each age group uniquely views and behaves regarding communication, leadership, technology, and work. Table 3.1 provides a brief description of different American generations and selected characteristics.

Table 3.1
Generations: Defining Moments and Basic Characteristics

Generation	Defining Moments and Characteristics
Silent or Greatest Generation, Traditionalists • Born before 1945 • ~28 million in generation	• Great depression, WWII, Korean War • Raised with structure, discipline, role models • Solid, industry-based economy • Labor unions • Respect authority • Hard work • New Deal
Baby Boomer • Born between 1945 to about 1964 • ~78 million in generation	• Hippies turned Yuppies • Vietnam War • Civil rights • Environmental justice • Challenging status quo • Cold war • Sexual revolution • Space travel
Generation X, Latchkey, or MTV Generation • Born between early to mid-1960s to early 1980s • ~50 million in generation	• Latchkey (both parents working) • Single-parent households • Dotcoms, rise of technology • Increasing divorce rates • Hip-hop music • Work-life balance important • Want structure and direction • Watergate • Energy crisis
Millennials, Generation Y, or Generation Me • Born early 1980s–early 2000s • ~77 million in generation	• Technology and Internet • 9/11, Columbine • Diversity • Extracurricular activities • Great Recession • HIV/AIDS • Child-focused world and sheltered • Children and youth scheduled

To complicate matters even further, individuals who belong to the same generation do not necessarily share the same characteristics or view world events in a similar manner. In part, this depends on when someone was born within the 20 or so years of the generation. In part, this is also depends on individual, regional, and sociodemographic characteristics of people generally.

As an example, the music and culture of the late 1960s and early 1970s was the backdrop to my life, while my husband, five years older and also a Boomer, had a different musical backdrop. During this period, five years made a significant difference in terms of who performed and what we listened to. I grew up listening to groups like Jimi Hendrix (e.g., "Purple Haze") and The Who (e.g., "Tommy"); he loved groups like Jackie Wilson (e.g., "Lonely Teardrops") and Dion & the Belmonts ("A Teenager in Love"). Nevertheless, we both grew up during a time when our generation was challenging the mores and attitudes of the previous generation (i.e., our parents, sometimes known as the Silent Generation). The Vietnam war, Black Power, and racial tensions/Civil Rights, and environmental responsibility (think Earth Day) gave us an overarching commonality. Therefore, the fact that he was born in Brooklyn and I was born in small-town Punxsutawney, and he was a jock and I was a hippie, matters less than our overall cultural, political, and social experiences.

If generational boundaries are fuzzy and not all people of a generation fit into a mold, why is it important to consider the role played by the generation to which one belongs? Categorizing people into generations is important for a number of reasons. One reason, for example, is economics. Marketers rely on the ability to classify groups of people, not only to influence their purchasing decisions, but also to plan for future product lines and marketing strategies. Gen Z is of particular interest for businesses because it is the largest generation in terms of number of people, encompassing almost 2.6 billion people worldwide by 2020 (Smith, 2017); thus it has a wide appeal to marketers and businesses. Gen Z holds more than $44 billion in annual purchasing power in the U.S. alone.

Another reason for categorizing people into generations is to understand the role of generational differences in the workplace. Understanding generational differences and similarities also helps people understand others' behaviors and perspectives. This knowledge helps managers understand the behavior of younger and older employees, and helps employees working on teams comprised of individuals from different generations understand each other. For example, some members of the Baby Boomer generation may prefer face-to-face conversations, members of Gen X might prefer email or cell phone calls, and Millennials might prefer texts or tweets.

Using a generational approach can provide insight into the values, attitudes, and behaviors of people from a similar age cohort.

Overall, using a generational approach can provide insight into the values, attitudes, and behaviors of people from a similar age cohort. However, it is important to keep in mind that a generational approach does not provide a prescriptive approach to treating all people from a given generation in exactly the same way, or expecting people of one generation to act or think a certain way. Individual differences and unique characteristics and perspectives will always influence the way people think and act.

Gen Z

People often use the phrase "sex, drugs, and rock and roll" to characterize the Baby Boomer generation; the "MTV generation" for Generation X; and the "me generation" for Millennials. How do, and will, we characterize Gen Z? Table 3.2 provides some terms applied to Gen Z at the time this chapter was written.

Table 3.2
Common Terms Applied to Gen Z

Ableism	Activism	Change the world
Collaborative	Compassionate	Digital native
Educated	Entrepreneurial	Gender neutrality
iEverything	Open-minded	Pragmatic
Risk averse	Selective attention span	Slow life strategy
Social responsibility	Sustainability	Thoughtful world view
Transgeneration	Transglobal	Transracial

A few events and factors in particular have shaped Gen Z. One event, the Great Recession from 2007 to 2009, resulted in unemployment skyrocketing from 5% to 9.5%. Household and nonprofit organization net worth plummeted by $14 trillion (Rich, 2013). As a consequence, one of the general characteristics of Gen Z is that they tend to be more cautious, particularly with regard to spending. Another influential context for those in Gen Z is that the specter of terrorism has been a prominent backdrop to their lives. This generation has never lived during a time when the U.S. was not at war. Growing up in the shadows of the Great Recession and terrorism has resulted in many members of Gen Z experiencing feelings of being unsettled and insecure.

Another hallmark of Gen Z is the rapidly growing diversity among American youth. Pew Research identified Gen Z as the generation with the largest number of multiracial households. As an example, Pew Research reported that almost half of Asian cohabiters have a partner of a different race or ethnicity, with 18% of all cohabiters reporting having a partner of a different race or ethnicity (Livingston, 2017).

Some researchers think that Gen Z is growing up more slowly than previous generations (Twenge & Park, 2017). That means that Gen Z members are slower to adopt activities associated with adulthood such as dating, having sex, and drinking alcohol. This slowness to adopt adult-like activities seems to have led to participation in less risky behaviors at an early age. Members of Gen Z are also slower to start driving, working for pay, and going out without one's parents, which could place additional burdens on parents.

Despite these influences on Gen Z, many researchers and popular media suggest that the most influential factor shaping Gen Z is instant access to digital media. In fact, using the term "online" may not even make sense, because for Gen Z there is no offline (Trifecta, 2015). Gen Z has never known the world without the Internet, and thus are true digital natives. The iPhone was introduced in 2007, and since that time, Gen Zers have had ever-present, instant media in the palm of their hands or on a digital tablet. The remainder of this chapter provides some perspective on what it might be like to be growing up as a member of Gen Z, with a particular focus on technology and gender.

Digital Media and Technology

Before discussing media and technology use by Gen Z members, several caveats are worth noting. First, there are conflicting data about the role of digital media and its effect on health and well-being of young people. For example, studies on the effect of technology use and psychological adjustment are mixed (Nesi & Prinstein, 2015). This is not surprising because digital media have not been around long enough for researchers to agree on definitions surrounding media use (e.g., the definition of excessive or problematic media use) as well as tools to measure these phenomena. Therefore, there is a lack of rigorous research in this area (Bányai et al., 2017). Despite these challenges,

there is some consensus in the current literature about some of the trends and issues around digital media and growing up in Gen Z.

Second, I would like to highlight several sources, in addition to research journal articles, that were useful in writing this portion of the chapter. One source was Common Sense Media (Rideout, 2015) that collected survey data from a large sample ($n = 2,600$) of 8- to 18-year-olds. Another source was *iGen: Why Today's Super-Connected Kids are Growing Up Less Rebellious, More Tolerant, Less Happy—and Completely Unprepared for Adulthood—and What that Means for the Rest of Us* (Twenge, 2017a), which focuses on the alarming role of digital media in the lives of youth. Twenge (2017b) asserts that in particular, the nature of young people's social interactions has dramatically shifted due to smartphones and other hand-held devices. Finally, I referred to a number of rigorous studies conducted by The Pew Research Center (http://www.pewresearch.org/), which provided excellent data regarding media and technology use of Gen Z.

> "I think we like our phones more than people." –13-year-old girl, (Twenge, 2017b)

The following sections point out where there are conflicting opinions or data regarding Gen Z's media and technology use. Thus, readers are encouraged to view this information through a critical lens, while also considering the implications of this information for working with youth in OST programs and activities.

Gen Z Media Use

Recall that the previous chapter reported that young people spend about six to nine hours a day using media. Most research suggests that they spend most of their digital lives on smartphone screens, although it is most common for youth to use multiple screens (Patel, 2017). In addition, 71% of teen social media users access more than one social media, and 24% report being "almost constantly" online (Lenhart, 2015). Teens spend some of that media time listening to music while doing other activities. Given the amount of time spent on media, it is little wonder that media are having such a profound effect on young people.

Figure 3.1 shows the number of hours spent on media per day from the Common Sense Media Study. You can see that 28% of tweens (8- to 12-year-olds) use two or less hours of media per day, and only 11% use media for more than eight hours. On the other hand, 31% of teenagers (13- to 18-year-olds) report using media four to eight hours per day, and 26% report spending more than eight hours on media (Shapiro, 2015). The same study indicates that 37% of girls report listening to music during the time they are using media, and 27% of boys report playing video games while listening to music. Most concerning is that half or more of teens report multitasking (watching TV, 51%; texting, 60%; and listening to music, 76%) while doing homework. Of those who report multitasking, almost two-thirds do not think it interferes with the quality of their work.

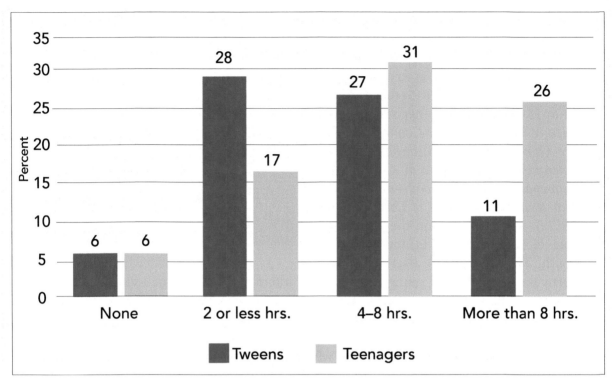

Figure 3.1. Hours Spent on Media Per Day, by Tweens and Teenagers
Source: Common Sense Media

The Common Sense Media (Rideout, 2015) study offers a set of conclusions that provides a picture of media use among young people in 2015:

- Tweens' and teens' patterns and preferences of media use are very diverse. This diversity is observed between boys and girls; younger and older; richer and poorer; and Black, White, and Hispanic teens.
- Despite that diversity, young people gravitate to two media activities: watching TV and listening to music.
- Young people use media passively and consumptively, with very little use devoted to creation (3% or less).
- Socioeconomic and racial and ethnic differences in media use patterns are concerning. Children from lower income homes and Black and Hispanic children spend far more time with media, especially screen media, than White children and children from higher- and middle-income homes.

Media and Adolescent Development of Gen Z

Adolescent development is clearly influenced through social media (see sidebar quote by Barth on the following page). As noted in other chapters in this book, identity development is a major issue for adolescents, and particularly among youth aged 14–17. The goal for adolescents is to emerge from the identity development process with a clear and stable sense of who they are as persons and how they fit into society. This process is extremely important because adolescents who have a strong identity are more likely to thrive and experience positive life outcomes and psychological well-being (Phinney, Horenczyk, Liebkind, & Vedder, 2001). This is particularly true for those from minority ethnic and racial groups (e.g., Ellithorpe & Bleakley, 2016). During the process of identity development, young people compare themselves with, and seek feedback from, others in their immediate environment (e.g., family and peers), as well others with whom they have contact, either in person or online. As young people get older, social comparisons become increasingly important. Social comparison facilitates answering questions about gender identity, sexuality, religious and political beliefs, and what it means to be part of a family, social group, and/or ethnic or racial group, among other things.

> What is clear is that no matter what one thinks about these new forms of communication, normal developmental dynamics, conflicts, and stages of contemporary adolescence are often experienced through social media and cyber technology (Barth, 2015, p. 201).

Throughout generations, adolescents have compared themselves to others in an attempt to come to a comprehensive understanding of how they are similar to, and different from, others—parents, siblings, peers, and the world. This process is called *separation-individuation* (Barth, 2015). The goal is not to become a wholly detached and independent person (i.e., separation-individuation) but rather to become an attached-individuated person, which is built on a concept of mutuality. Mutuality is a relationship based on shared feelings or actions that benefit both or all parties, including peers and adults. Attached-individuated persons feel close connections to others but also have a sense of how they are unique. How does social media use help or hinder identity development and the attached-individuation process? Does social media use foster mutuality? Let's explore these questions.

Social media offer adolescents a powerful means of comparison and a platform for seeking feedback about themselves and their status. However, there is considerable concern about the ability of members of Gen Z to construct and manage their online social identity. Consider this quotation: "Don't laugh at youth for his affectations; he is only trying on one face after another to find a face of his own." Although this statement is gendered and could describe Gen Z youth today, it may surprise you that the author was Logan Pearsall Smith (an American-born British essayist and critic), writing nearly 100 years ago. The process of trying out different identities and "faces" is something that all humans have gone through; Gen Z just has different tools to use.

Today's teens seem to feel that they must develop their own brands and have an audience; many are driven by getting enough "likes" or "followers" and suffer emotionally when they do not. Although this may be an example of mutuality, it is only a very superficial interaction with others. One young women I'll call K told me about the time she posted the same photo on three different occasions within a couple of hours of each other. The first time she did not get enough likes so she removed the photo and caption, uploaded the photo again with a different caption. She still did not get enough attention, so she tried the same photo a third time with another caption. It appeared to me that by altering the labels, she was trying to develop or try out different identities. Either that or she was trying to appear to others as being "liked" and popular.

K's story begs the question of whether one's self-presentation online distorts the process of social comparison. Did K really care about what her 300 "friends" thought of her, or was it more important to her that her 12 most important and close friends liked what she posted? Or maybe she was trying to attract new friends. Whatever the motivation, it seemed that K was driven by establishing her online identity as a popular, fun-loving person. Nesi and Prinstein (2015) observe that many times one's online presentations of self do not reflect stable personality traits but rather reflect situational factors, such as who one is with physically at the time. Thus, social comparisons may be distorted reflections of reality, especially since many online connections really are not close friends in real life.

Consider again the concept of mutuality. In K's situation, I doubt that there was authentic mutuality because her initial post was not authentic, given that she tried various captions to manage her identity. Nevertheless, teens are eager to be liked by their audience and will try various ways to get positive evaluative comments or likes. K's story also begs the question of how adolescents go about developing a coherent, stable identity of themselves when they are simultaneously managing an online identity.

> … how [do] adolescents go about developing a coherent, stable identity of themselves when they are simultaneously managing an online identify?

The constant need to manage one's identity and actions and respond in timely ways to postings of others is anxiety producing for many teens. Twenge (2017) calls this the *psychic tax* of social media. It is almost as if teens are creating and starring in their own reality shows. Like K, once teens post something, they then become concerned about the response to the post. Will they be ridiculed, liked, or ignored? Will they be cyberbullied? A survey cited by Twenge (2017) found that between 2010 and 2015, the percentage of girls and boys feeling "often left out" based on their social media activity increased by 48% and 24%, respectively. These findings may help explain data from Common Sense Media (Rideout, 2015) that only 10% of teens choose social media as their favorite media activity.

At the same time, it is more common for adolescents from Gen Z to be concerned about privacy, prompting many to prefer Instagram and other apps that feature rapidly vanishing posts rather than ones such as Facebook and Twitter that leave a digital trail about one's life. It is easy to see why teens like having two types of Instagram accounts:

finstas (fake) and *rinstas* (real). In order to reduce social anxiety, teens use finstas when they want to share with others their "real" self and not have to be worried about showing themselves as perfect. Finstas are private accounts only for close friends. These accounts also allow teens to hide from parents and other adults postings that might contain risky or socially unacceptable behavior. On the other hand, teens carefully manage their rinstas by carefully choosing photos and captions for wider public scrutiny and evaluation. Presenting a different self, depending on one's audience, is a contemporary example of *code shifting*, which is a linguistic term meaning to alternate between two or more languages, depending on the context.

Another consequence of the way young people use social media is the "fear of missing out" (FOMO). Although it appears that teenagers are hanging out with each other in person less than in the past two generations, when they do connect in person, the whole world knows because they continuously document their activities and emotions online. As a result, often those who were not there or invited to be there feel left out, isolated, and/or lonely.

Twenge (2017) links use of smartphones to a decline in young people's mental health status. She asserts that these changes have affected all young people in the U.S., regardless of race, ethnicity, gender, socioeconomic status, and geographic location. However, recall the previous caution to reflect critically on *for whom and under what conditions* a certain phenomenon might occur. Contrary to Twenge's findings, Common

Sense Media (Rideout, 2015) found in a 2012 survey that adolescents report benefits to social networking, including feeling less shy and more outgoing (about 29%), more popular (19%), more sympathetic to others (19%), and better about themselves (55%). Common Sense Media also found that half of all teen social media users feel it helps their relationships with friends and helps them keep in touch with friends they could not see regularly (88%). This study suggests that only about 4% to 5% of the respondents report negative outcomes such as feeling worse about themselves. Similarly, Pew Research (Lenhart, 2015) found that 65% of teenage boys and 52% of teenage girls who use social media reported that social media platforms such as Facebook and Instagram made them feel more connected with what was happening in their significant other's life. Finally, some members of Gen Z report that their closest relationships are made via Tumblr, Instagram, and Facebook (Williams, 2015).

There is one last developmental issue to consider for the purposes of this chapter. Barth (2015) considers Gen Z members to be the most articulate generation, with young people holding many sophisticated worldviews and having knowledge on a wide range of topics. She notes, however, that this generation seems unable to put their emotional intelligence to use in daily communications. She suggests that although they can name their emotions, they do not really understand what they are feeling or how to describe it. (I wonder if the increased use of emojis has had anything to do with this observation?) In a similar vein, Twenge (2017) suggests that some teens are beginning to become frustrated with their friends because even in one-on-one conversations, friends interact with their phones and rarely establish eye contact or really seem to be paying attention. It might not be surprising, then, that findings from Common Sense Media (Rideout, 2012) indicate that about half of teens who use social media report that their favorite way to communicate with each other is in person; texting is the next preferred (33%). Forty-four percent of the teens in the same study reported that social media often distracts them from the people they are with in person.

As previously noted, there are often conflicting reports and conclusions about how social media use is connected to adolescent development and well-being. To date, reports suggest both very positive and very concerning outcomes associated with media use among Gen Zers. As more research is conducted and Gen Zers grow up, youth workers and other professionals may have a better picture of the role of social media in adolescent development.

Media Use and Its Effect on the Brain

To date, there is little research about how use of technology affects adolescent cognitive development, such as working memory capacity, attentional control, and social cognition (Mills, 2016). There is growing evidence, however, that use of screens at bedtime has serious consequences. A meta-analysis on the association between portable screen-based media and sleep reveals some startling conclusions. Combining data from studies of over 125,000 children (mean age 14.5), researchers found clear and consistent evidence that use of a media device at or near bedtime was associated with the following (Carter, Rees, Hale, Bhattacharjee, & Paradkar, 2016):

- Inadequate sleep quality
- Poor sleep quality
- Excessive daytime sleepiness

Specifically, young people who used media before bedtime were about twice as likely not to get enough sleep. Having access to a media device in the sleeping environment, not just active use, is also associated with an inadequate amount of sleep. Another large study of almost 10,000 teens found that four hours or more of screen time during the day, not just at bedtime, resulted in needing more than one hour to fall asleep, called *sleep latency* (Hysing et al., 2015).

The National Sleep Foundation (2014), an advocacy organization, sponsored a 2014 national survey about sleep practices in families. The survey asked parents to respond to questions about their own and their children's (aged 6 to 17) sleep patterns. Results indicate that 68% of parents and 51% of children had two or more devices in their bedroom at night, and 89% of youth between the ages of 15–17 had one device in their bedroom at night. Their results also indicate that the sleep quality of youth is diminished if devices are left on at night.

> Young people who used media before bedtime were about twice as likely not to get enough sleep.

There are many reasons why screen time can be problematic to adequate and restful sleep, as well as the brain in general. Regarding sleep, the culprit is blue light. Smartphones, laptops, and most other electronic screens emit blue LED light. This blue light has increased in strength over recent years, as has its effect on the brain and sleep. In particular, blue light prevents the release of melatonin, a hormone that signals sleep (Kim, 2014).

Besides sleep, there is growing, but not conclusive, evidence that young people are especially susceptible to having their brains "rewired" due to screen time, especially excessive screen time. However, there is controversy as to what constitutes "excessive" screen time. The American Academy of Pediatrics (AAP) suggests that for children over 6 years of age, parents should monitor and place limits on what children view and how much time they spend on media so that media use does not interfere with adequate sleep and physical well-being (AAP, 2016). Dating to 1999, the AAP recommended no screen time for children under 2 years of age. However, in October 2016, they revised that recommendation and suggest that no screens are best for babies under 18 months except for live video chat, but that screen time after 18 months may not be as bad as previously thought in order to give young children as many sensory experiences as possible. Various researchers, however, have debated that notion (Hamilton, 2016), with numerous writings joining the debate and raising concerns (see box on the next page for a partial list of publications about concerns with media use and the brain). Clearly, there is a societal curiosity and concern about screen time and in particular for children and adolescents.

Resources for Further Reading about Media Use and Brain Impacts

- *The Shallows: What the Internet is Doing to our Brains* (Carr, 2011)
- *The Distracted Mind: Ancient Brains in a High-Tech World* (Gazzaley & Rosen, 2016)
- *Wired Child: Reclaiming Childhood in a Digital Age* (Freed, 2015)
- *Glow Kids: How Screen Addiction is Hijacking Our Kids—And How to Break the Trance* (Kardaras, 2016)
- *Reset Your Child's Brain: A Four-Week Plan to End Meltdowns* (Kunckley, 2015)
- *Screens and Teens: Connecting with Our Kids in a Wireless World* (Koch, 2015)
- *iDisorder: Understanding our Obsession with Technology and Overcoming its Hold on Us* (Rosen, 2013)
- *iBrain: Surviving the Technological Alteration of the Modern Mind* (Small, 2009)

Another perspective suggests that smartphones may have a drug-like effect on the brain. Recall that the last chapter provided data showing that for 2016 use of illicit drugs (other than marijuana) among 8th, 10th, and 12th grade students was at the lowest level in the last 40 years, corroborating Twenge and Park's (2017) perspective that members of Gen Z are growing up more slowly. In addition, use of marijuana was also down over the past decade for 8th and 10th graders. Reflecting on these data, the director of the National Institute on Drug Abuse, Dr. Nora Volkow, wondered if interactive media is "an alternative reinforcer" to drugs. Similarly, others have wondered if smartphones were like a portable dopamine pump (Richtel, 2017). Although there is little research on this possibility at the time this chapter was written, there is support for the idea and that future research is needed.

Social Justice, Media Use, and Entrepreneurship

Most people who write about Gen Z suggest that this is a generation concerned with social justice issues and making a difference in the world. For example, Meehan (2016) observes one prominent social justice issue is a feminist agenda that ultimately empowers all people through the support of women. Social media play a role in supporting the agenda. For example, recall Mattel's Barbie campaign, "Imagine the Possibilities," which was designed to empower young girls as an example of this agenda.

Gen Z members are also characterized as entrepreneurs, even at a young age. Many members of this generation have been through primary school programs that focus on social-emotional learning, recognizing and eliminating bullying, and understanding that "all lives matter." As previously noted, Gen Z is not only the most ethnically and racially diverse generation in U.S. history, but it has the most mixed-race members. It is no wonder that Meehan (2016) has highlighted Gen Z interests in social justice (see pull quote below).

There is a great deal of evidence that Gen Z uses social media platforms in entrepreneurial ways to contribute to the social good. Nonprofit Tech for Good (2017) reports that 60% of millennials give around $481 to nonprofits each year, 26% of Gen Z has raised money for a cause, and 32% have donated their own money. The Compassionate Crowdfunding Blog (https://www.youcaring.com/blog) provides tips and ideas for how teenagers can raise money to help causes like raising awareness of mental health issues, supporting creative endeavors, animal well-being, challenging a health care crisis such as pediatric cancer, and combating youth homelessness.

> They fight for themselves, their friends, their classmates, and others they see treated unfairly, whether due to issues of gender, sexuality, pay, or environment (Meehan, 2016).

To document the power of social media, 59% of Gen Z members report being inspired by a message or image on social media to donate to charity (Nonprofit Tech for Good, 2017). Another example is how the World Wildlife Foundation (WWF) used Snapchat for a campaign titled *The Last Selfie*. In this campaign, WWF staff photographed the top five endangered animals in the world and sent the photos to social media users with the caption "Don't Let this be my #LastSelfie" or "better take a screenshot this could be my #lastSelfie." In just three days, WWF reached their donation target for the month (http://www.justforthis.com/).

A new term has emerged for the youngest entrepreneurs, *kidrepreneurs* (DeBose, 2017). As an example, using the hashtag #FlexinInHerComplexion, 10-year-old Kheris Rogers launched her fashion t-shirt line in an effort to end colorism or discrimination based on skin tone. She received over 30,000 retweets and 80,000 likes (DeBose, 2017). J. Walter Thompson Intelligence reports on several other trend-setting kidrepreneurs at https://www.jwtintelligence.com/2017/07/gen-z-kidrepreneurs/. For example, a presentation by sparks & honey (2015) included a quote by a 12-year-old girl who wrote, "I want to be a doctor, a business person, an entrepreneur, and an engineer. Right now, I'm working at my parents' office to get a little money on the side. Sometimes it's boring, but that's how jobs are. I also have a job selling jewelry."

Independent, Instant, and Information Savvy

There are a few other phenomena to consider in understanding the role of technology and social media on Gen Z. As noted in Chapter 7 and elsewhere in this book, one of the major tasks during adolescence is developing autonomy and becoming self-determined. In previous generations, youth gained autonomy from parents largely through acquiring a driver's license and getting a job. Physically being out of a parent's house was a badge of freedom and allowed for a great deal of independent action, exploration, and experiencing the consequences of one's decision-making; parents had no way of contacting their children instantly as with Gen Z and the Millennials. Thus, youth were free to explore "sex, drugs, and rock and roll" on their own. The main ways youth could be social was to see friends at school and church, have phone conversations via a landline telephone, and physically hanging out with friends (usually with a curfew).

> The age at which you get your first smartphone is more important than the age at which you get your driver's license (Dorsey, 2016, p. 6).

Technology, and in particular being a digital native, has changed things dramatically. In many ways, Gen Z does not experience physical boundaries. They exert their independence via smartphones and other digital devices and do not have to leave home to spend time with their friends. Digital access is no doubt one of the reasons Gen Z members are waiting longer to get a driver's license and why getting a smartphone is considered so important. Barth (2015) offers a similar perspective; she suggests that technology has allowed adolescents to develop more independence, but ironically, at the same time, they are also tethered to their parents. Similarly, Shapiro (2015) wonders if smartphones have actually provided a means to curtail teens' feelings of independence. The advent of the smartphone and texting, he observes, requires teens to be reachable instantly. Thus, he wonders if, since "…kids have lost some of their basic freedoms, they have necessarily moved to a virtual landscape" (p. 3), meaning that adolescents are living their lives virtually in many ways, rather than physically.

Another characteristic of Gen Z that stems from being a digital native is the way, and the ease with which, they access information. Williams (2015) quoted an 18-year-old UCLA student who said, "I can

> "They live their lives on-demand" Helen (2017).

almost simultaneously create a document, edit it, post a photo on Instagram and talk on the phone, all from the user-friendly interface of my iPhone. … Generation Z takes in information instantaneously and loses interest just as fast." Gen Z is very adept at seeking and analyzing information as to whether it instantly meets their needs or not. Marketers are very interested in this generation, as they will account for 40% of all consumers by the year 2020 (Patel, 2017). Thus, marketers pay attention to how to get, and keep, the attention of this generation. As such, many write about this generation's eight-second attention span. As Patel (2017) wrote, "If you want them to click on your blog post, watch your video, or like your Instagram photo, you need to help them understand what the content is about, why they should care, and how it will help or entertain them."

sparks & honey, a cultural research group, believes that Gen Z does pay attention to blog posts and advertisements, but sorts through information very quickly to find what interests them. Thus, they can stay focused and either learn what they set out to learn (e.g., how to build a birdhouse via YouTube videos) or get the information they seek on a product or the news. sparks & honey also reports that in order to help Gen Z members manage all products, options, and customizations available to them, many rely on curated knowledge. Many Gen Zers subscribe to and/or follow their peers who have blogs or YouTube videos that discuss fashion, the news, and popular culture. They rely on those peers to sort through information and provide a summary of things in which they are interested.

Finally, Gen Z seems to be taking a different approach to education. According to sparks & honey (2015), most Gen Zs (75%) believe there are many pathways to learning and that college is not necessarily the best way to get an education, although at this point, 66% still intend to go to college. Consistent with being entrepreneurial, 63% of Gen Z wants colleges to offer courses in founding or running businesses, and 42% intend to work for themselves (sparks & honey, 2015).

Digital Divide

In the previous chapter, we highlighted the digital divide in the U.S. between those who have access to laptops and other means of accessing technology and those who do not. Imagine not having access to social media or a laptop or computer. Despite some of the challenges noted in this chapter, social media are one of the major characteristics shaping and defining Gen Z. It must be challenging being a member of Gen Z without having access to social media. An adolescent without access to social media, not to mention the educational value of access to the Internet, is certainly at a loss from a popular culture and social perspective.

The Internet is not a luxury (CBS News, 2017).

A U.S. Federal court defined the Internet as a basic utility like running water or electricity (CBS News, 2017). Only 3% of people in urban areas lack access to broadband services, but 35% of those living in rural America lack access (CBS News, 2017). Shapiro notes, "In the U.S., privileged access to brand new technologies has always been the pink elephant of teen culture" (2015, p. 3). He cites statistics from Common Sense Media that only 54% of teens in low-income families (<$35,000 per year) have laptops in the home, and only 51% have smartphones, compared to 92% and 78%, respectively, for teens in families with over $100,000 per year of income. Smartphones seem to be important sources of Internet access particularly among Hispanics and Blacks with household incomes under $30,000 a year (Perrin, 2017).

Libraries are also important sources of Internet access. In a survey conducted in 2015, 52% of Americans living in households with annual incomes of $30,000 or less have visited the library in the past year. Of those, 42% of Blacks and 35% of those with annual household incomes of \$30,000 or less report using library computers and Internet connections (Horrigan, 2016). Not only are libraries important physical places for accessing the Internet, they also provide free digital media for those who have smartphone or computer access to the Internet. One innovative effort is Open eBooks, which is a coalition of literacy, library, publishing, and technology partners, and was part of the White House ConnectED Initiative (under President Barack Obama) that began in 2013. Open eBooks is an app that contains thousands of titles of books for children in lower income households. Access is free and requires no checkouts or holds. The goal is to inspire a love of reading.

The Gender Revolution (Is There One?)

In January 2017, *National Geographic* magazine ran a special issue on the Gender Revolution. This revolution challenges the norm about what gender means from biological, social, and psychological perspectives. For example, about half of Millennials reported that they believed gender is a continuum and not a binary (male-female) construct (Rivas, 2015), and the popular press indicates that Gen Z will be even more accepting of gender diversity than past generations.

What is the normative view of gender? Read Hofstede's (2001) definitions of masculinity and femininity in the box below. Does anything surprise you about these definitions? How would you define masculinity and femininity? Are all boys masculine and all girls feminine? These are complex questions.

> **Masculinity** stands for a society in which social gender roles are clearly distinct: Men are supposed to be assertive, tough, and focused on material success; women are supposed to be more modest, tender, and concerned with the quality of life. **Femininity** stands for a society in which social gender roles overlap: Both men and women are supposed to be modest, tender, and concerned with the quality of life (Hofstede, 2001, p. 297).

First, consider the difference between biological sex and gender. When a baby is born, it is assigned a sex based on its sex organs. Gender, however, is based both on an individual and social construction. *Gender identity* is one's personal experience of one's own gender. It can be consistent with the sex one is assigned at birth or can be completely different. Social norms and environments also contribute to feelings about one's gender. Society expects males and females to act and dress in certain ways. Sometimes these two perspectives conflict with each other. This is when a perception about who one is as a person does not match with the assigned sex given at birth; *transgender* is the term used to describe individuals who fall into this category.

Hofstede's definitions of masculinity and femininity are based on large-scale, cross-national research. In the past, other researchers have defined femininity as being concerned with one's physical appearance, beauty, and thinness; being modest, deferential, and dependent; being a caretaker, and being emotionally sensitive (Ward & Aubrey, 2017). These researchers further characterize traditional masculinity by emotional restrictiveness, self-reliance, aggression, risk taking, heterosexual presentation, status seeking, competitive, anti-femininity, and having power.

The *binary perspective* has been the traditional view of gender. According to this perspective, one is either male/masculine or female/feminine. However, this perspective is not as prevalent today as in previous years. For example, since the 1990s, many women see themselves

> "Sexuality is who you go to bed with, and gender identity is who you go to bed as." –Brendan Jordan, quoted in Adams (2017)

as more androgynous, a blend of masculinity and femininity, than feminine (Donnelly & Twenge, 2016), although the vast majority of people consider themselves to be at one end of the gender spectrum or the other (Henzig, 2017). While the predominant majority of people consider themselves strictly male or female (cisgender), there are a growing number of young people who consider themselves to be genderfluid, gender expansive, androgynous, or some other term.

What if one does not fit into the typical norms associated with masculinity and femininity associated with one's assigned sex, or consider oneself transgender? The J. Walter Thompson Intelligence unit conducted a small study of 300 young people and found that 56% of 13- to 20-year-olds reported knowing someone who went by gender neutral pronouns such as "they," "them," or "ze" (Laughlin, 2016). A couple of high school teachers I know report that some of their students refer to themselves as "they" and it is usually accepted by their peers, but not always. In general, society is making strides in being more accepting, or at least recognizing, different gender identities. For example, Target Corp removed gender-based signage in some of their stores in 2016 and stated it would allow customers to use the bathroom of their choosing, a decision that was met with much resistance in some parts of the country.

Other marketing efforts that target Gen Z consumers also favor gender-neutral advertising. Some brands create products and fashion to appeal to any gender. For example, Zara has an ungendered line to appeal to those who identify with androgyny and gender fluidity. These attitudes and actions, as well as the controversies and media discussion surrounding them, all set the context for the way Gen Z is growing up.

What does gender identity and assigned sex have to do with sexual orientation? Sexual orientation and gender are two very different things, although it is easy to see how they are confused. Being lesbian, gay, or bisexual is not the same as being transgender or some other gender than male or female. Sexual orientation is whom one feels drawn to emotionally, sexually, and romantically. From a sexual orientation standpoint, one can be gay, lesbian, straight, bisexual, or asexual. Chapter 22 provides further discussion about issues related to lesbian, gay, bisexual, and transgender youth; the remainder of this chapter will address gender and adolescent development.

Selected Issues Regarding Gender and Adolescent Development

This next section will focus on two questions:

1. What is the role of media in shaping gender, gender identity, gender roles, and gender equality?
2. What pressures do boys and girls experience growing up in a world that is transforming its perspective on gender, gender identity, gender roles, and gender equality?

Based on an extensive review of research papers and popular press, a research brief by Ward and Aubrey (2017) concludes that media (television and movies) perpetuate the belief that boys have more value than girls, and that gender inequality is deeply ingrained and insidious. Furthermore, the authors suggest that most people do not even recognize this bias. Ward and Aubrey, and many others, believe that gender inequality has vast consequences for all genders. For example, the Organization for Economic Co-operation and Development (OECD) estimated that gender discrimination costs the global economy up to $12 trillion annually in wasted potential (Ward & Aubrey, 2017). Gender inequality results in unequal access to resources, power, education, and discriminatory sociocultural practices (Kågesten et al., 2016). Further, gender-biased media are linked to girls' avoidance of thinking about careers in STEM (i.e., science, technology, engineering, and mathematics) fields, unhealthy body image concerns of both boys and girls, emotional regulation problems, dating and sexual violence, and risk-taking behaviors. Girls report less self-confidence and are dropping out of sports at an earlier age (Ward & Aubrey, 2017) and boys trail girls in levels of school engagement, have lower grades in all subjects (including math and science), and are more likely to drop out of school (Rogers, Updegraff, Santos, & Martin, 2017).

> Gender attitudes that endorse norms that perpetuate gender inequality are thought to be harmful to both boys and girls (Kågesten et al., 2016, p. 3).

Media too often portray boys and girls and men and women in gender-restrictive ways, although there is evidence that things might be shifting. That is, media, and especially mainstream media, portray men as the providers and deciders and women as the nurturers and purchasers. Not only do television and movies depict males and females in gender-restrictive roles, females are also underrepresented (Ward & Aubrey, 2017). There is growing evidence, however, that cable and other streaming companies like Netflix are moving out of that mold.

Hegemonic Masculinity, Policing of Masculinity, the Man Box, Alpha Girls, and the Woman Box

Cultivation theory is a prominent perspective in communications research (Giaccardi, Ward, Seabrook, Manago, & Lippman, 2016). Cultivation theory posits that frequent viewing of media messages that present a homogeneous perspective (e.g., all females are caring and nurturing, and all males are stoic) creates in viewers a consistent worldview. How do gender inequality and gender-restrictive identities portrayed in the media affect Gen Z's identity development? What are the pressures associated with media portrayal of gender? Do social media (as opposed to television and movies) provide a different type of experience with regard to exploration of or construction of a gender identity?

Previously in this section, the concepts of femininity and masculinity were introduced. One term used to depict the traditional view of how males are supposed to act is *hegemonic masculinity*—some might say "boys will be boys," but hegemonic masculinity is more than that. The term hegemonic masculinity characterizes White, heterosexual, Western men's dominance over women and racial, ethnic, and sexual minorities (Levant & Richmond, 2017). This traditional masculinity, however, is associated with and predicts lower levels of well-being across behavioral, psychological, emotional, and social indicators of adjustment (Rogers et al., 2017). Rogers and colleagues further speculate that for boys especially, adherence to aspects of traditional masculinity, such as emotional stoicism and physical toughness, are negatively associated with school adjustment. In their study of middle school youth, they found that boys more strongly associated with notions of emotional stoicism and physical toughness than did girls. Latin adolescents even more strongly endorsed physical toughness than did their White counterparts. Furthermore, the researchers found that emotional stoicism predicted lower levels of school engagement and school liking, and higher levels of school avoidance.

Of course, media are not the only conduits of socialization regarding gender. Many aspects of adolescents' social environments contribute to the way members of Gen Z "learn gender." Parents, significant adults, and institutional rituals embedded in places such as schools and churches model gender roles and gender identity to young people. Coupled with media and social media, these influences create a pressure for young people to behave in a certain way given their gender.

Much of what is written about being a young male has to do with *Boy Code* (Pollack, 1998), which has to do with emotional stoicism. The four pillars of the Boy Code include the following:

1. **Being a sturdy oak:** Boys must be stable, stoic, and independent, never showing weakness.
2. **Give 'em hell:** Boys engage in competitive and risky physical behavior because it is part of their biological imperative.
3. **Being a big wheel:** Boys strive to achieve status and avoid shame at all costs; they wear a mask of coolness that everything is all right in order to repress feelings of failure or unhappiness.

4. **No sissy stuff:** Pollack calls this a gender straitjacket because this part of the code forbids any action that seems feminine.

In order to enforce the Boy Code, boys exert pressure on each other to abide by it through what has been termed *policing of masculinity* (POM; Reigeluth & Addis, 2016). POM functions at both the macro and micro levels of society and is defined as "any action that serves to prevent or punish individual or group behavior perceived as insufficiently masculine" (Reigeluth & Addis, p. 75). Based on interviews with 14- to 19-year-old boys, Reigeluth and Addis found that the most common form of POM were misogynistic and homophobic insults such as "fag," "pussy," "girlie," and "homo." Anti-femininity and homophobia are the hallmarks of hegemonic masculinity. POM serves two functions in addition to masculine norm enforcement. One is that if a boy enacts POM strategies, it serves to preserve or even elevate his status in the eyes of his peers. A related function of POM is that boys report that their friendship with others in their group is enhanced when they police their masculinity.

Barker is president and CEO of Promundo, whose mission is to engage men and boys in gender equality and prevention of violence by trying to help men and boys break out of the *Man Box*. The Man Box "refers to a set of beliefs, communicated by parents, families, the media, peers, and other members of society, that place pressure on men to be a certain way" (Heilman, Barker, & Harrison, 2017, p. 7). There are seven pillars to the Man Box: self-sufficiency, acting tough, physical attractiveness, rigid masculine gender roles, heterosexuality and homophobia, hypersexuality, aggression, and control. Barker and colleagues conducted a representative, random sample survey of more than 3,600 young men in the U.S., Mexico, and the United Kingdom. Findings indicated that males who felt pressured by the Boy Code or Man Box were over two times more likely to have had suicidal thoughts, over six times more likely to have bullied someone, and six times more likely to have reported sexually harassing women. However, Barker remains optimistic that since media have played a role in creating the Man Box, it can play a critical role in changing the way society perceives what it means to be masculine.

In other words, we're feeding young men and boys a media diet that has the potential to cause great harm— to themselves and to others around them (Barker, 2017).

What about the girls? Is there a growing, nontraditional perspective about what it means to be a female and feminine? The *New York Times* ran a piece with the headline "From Sex Object to Gritty Woman: The Evolution of Women in Stock Photos" (Miller, September 7, 2017). The article notes that if someone in 2017 searched the Getty [stock] Image Library using the term "woman" an image of a woman hiking alone along a rugged, rock-laden path with a lake and mountains in the background would appear. This symbol of woman as powerful represents a societal change, especially since in 2007 the top-selling image was a stock photograph of a dreamy-eyed, naked woman in bed with a soft towel draped over her bottom. Miller credits some of this shift in perception of what it is like to be a female on Sheryl Sandberg's nonprofit (Leanin.org) efforts to make sure more contemporary, powerful, diverse, and empowering images of women were available. Miller notes that the collection of over 14,000 empowering images come with an unofficial tagline of "You can't be what you can't see."

Feminism, including Title IX and the girl empowerment movement of the 1990s, served to create an environment where "gritty women" were possible narratives to be included in concepts of femininity (Bettis, Ferry, & Roe, 2016). Kindlon (2006) coined the name *alpha girl* to represent this new type of girlhood. The alpha girl focuses on a future perspective and career and is less concerned with traditional aspects of femininity.

> "The ideal girl is...like strong. Doesn't take crap from anybody. Athletic. Kind person to everyone and has her own aura about them. They're likable and interesting" (Serena, from Bettis et al., 2016, p. 174).

Alpha girls embrace some aspects of masculinity such as risk taking, and being confident, assertive, and competitive. They also embrace traditional aspects of femininity such as being collaborative and relationship oriented (Bettis et al., 2016).

Bettis and colleagues (2016) conducted a study using formal interviews and observations to gather information about how the day-to-day realities of eighth grade girls connect with the narrative of the alpha girl. The researchers note that the girls in their study eschewed the concept of an ideal girl and stressed the importance of authenticity and confidence (see pull-out quote for an example). This quotation is in line with how other researchers and the popular press view Gen Z.

The conclusions drawn by Bettis and colleagues (2016) are both optimistic and cautionary. Optimism is reflected in that the girls in their study offered opinions and beliefs about themselves as being independent and wanting and expecting their voices to be heard. However, there is a backlash to the alpha girl construct that hinges on the notion that this perspective creates a new type of gender-restrictive identity that one might call the *Woman Box* to mirror the Man Box. Thus, the caution refers to the realization that the political, social, and economic context within which all girls are growing up largely perpetuates hegemonic masculinity and gender inequality. In fact, Bettis and colleagues noted that the girls' comments reflected masculine hierarchies and gender binaries. They were "also concerned that the alpha girl rhetoric shifts the conversation about girlhood away from an intersectional analysis that examines the constraints that race, ethnicity, sexual orientation, ability, and social class play in the construction of girlhood" (p. 179). The fear is neoconservative perspectives that feminist concerns are no longer valid (because they have been addressed), and gender and racial inequality have been overcome will dominate if the alpha girl perspective is the monolithic view of the world today. Nevertheless, Bettis and colleagues reflect forward movement in the way society views femininity and masculinity providing teachers, researchers, and youth can carefully construct the new girlhood, avoid the pitfalls, and overcome the privileges that are linked with race and socioeconomic status.

The subtitle of this section asks whether there is a gender revolution. Although there is no answer to this rhetorical question, it does provide food for thought regarding the way members of Gen Z might be viewing the world and developing their own identities. Millennials use social media to try out who they might be if they were a different gender or not binary (Hamel, 2017), and there is no reason to think Gen Z is any different. As part of this process of creating and exploring gender online, Hamel addressed the question of whether or not this activity served to fragment one's identity or served to facilitate a multifaceted identity. Although he never was able to answer the question, it seems an interesting one to consider. What is clear from the material in this chapter is that members of Gen Z are growing up at a time when gender, feminism, and masculinity are viewed differently from previous generations.

Final Thoughts

To date, Gen Z seems to be a generation of paradoxes (e.g., girls are more confident, yet girls are less confident, depending on the situation). Social media play a detrimental role in some aspects of adolescent development (e.g., feelings of anxiety and lack of authentic communication), but on the other hand, social media provide many benefits and contribute to some positive developmental outcomes (e.g., freedom to explore identity and being in touch with friends). In many ways, members of Gen Z are healthier (e.g., lower rates of substance use and early sex) than previous generations, but also less healthy (e.g., higher rates, especially among girls, of mental health issues).

Some of these paradoxes are due to the many racial, ethnic, gender, economic, and regional factors, among others, that contribute to the way members of Gen Z experience things. This is one reason readers are cautioned to keep in mind that although Gen Z has an overall common experience growing up, they still have unique personal experiences. Because Gen Z is still "a work in progress," it will be interesting to see what future research tells us about this complex generation. Keep in mind that Gen Z is a "product" of the values and experiences of Gen X and the Millennials. By extension, therefore, they will influence the next generation.

The material in this chapter may be daunting in terms of how to take the information and apply it to developing and offering OST programs for Gen Z. The discussion questions and assignments that follow may help you think about how to apply some of this material. I hope this chapter has given you another perspective about the lives of young people growing up as we approach the end of the second decade of the 21st century.

Discussion Questions

1. What are the best and/or most appropriate ways to communicate with members of Gen Z? Discuss the merits and drawbacks of various communication methods. For example, should you be Facebook friends or Snapchat with the young people to whom you provide programs? Should you share your cell phone number? How do you go about making this decision? What other factors should you consider?

2. How will Gen Z's reliance on social media in general, and social media platforms, affect how youth workers interact with them? How will it affect program offerings?

3. The American Academy of Pediatrics (AAP) suggests that for children over 6 years of age, parents should place consistent limits on the time spent using media, the types of media used, and make sure media do not take the place of adequate sleep, physical activity, and other behaviors essential to health. Is this adequate? What can youth workers do to contribute to decreasing excessive screen time? What personal behaviors might youth workers adopt?

4. Consider what it is like being a teenager without access to a smartphone or a cell tower. What are the implications to providing programs and services? What are the implications of how they interact with their peers who do have access?

5. As an OST provider, how would you make use of the entrepreneurial spirit and social justice attitudes held by Gen Z?

6. Discuss and debate the developmental implications of autonomy development via social media.

7. How do young people access and use news? What does it matter to youth workers? Consider these infographics: https://www.commonsensemedia.org/research/news-and-americas-kids-infographic.

8. Youth workers can help Gen Z become wiser and more self-reflective in using social media so that they can be as real in cyber-space as they are in real life, and to manage how they portray themselves. What are ways you could help Gen Z be better and wiser consumers of social media?

Assignments

1. Suppose you were going to conduct a training workshop on how to best serve and work with Gen Z. Identify seven to 10 main points that you would cover in your training protocol. For each point, note specific items to cover (in bullet points).

2. Escape boxes are a growing form of entertainment. Suppose you were to create a game with two parts based on this growing phenomenon. Create a game where players have to escape the Man Box as well as the Woman Box. What clues would

you give players? What would you expect them to do to escape the boxes? Would you have different expectations of males and females? Adults and adolescents?

3. Write up a summary of this chapter and present it verbally to a young person (or a few) between the ages of 14 and 17. Ask that person/persons whether or not the material reflects their life and those of their peers.

References

Adams, C. (March 24, 2017). The difference between sexual orientation and gender identity. CBS News. Retrieved from https://www.cbsnews.com/news/the-difference-between-sexual-orientation-and-gender-identity/

American Academy of Pediatrics. (October 21, 2016). American Academy of Pediatrics announces new recommendations for children's media use. Retrieved from https://www.aap.org/en-us/about-the-aap/aap-press-room/pages/american-academy-of-pediatrics-announces-new-recommendations-for-childrens-media-use.aspx

Bányai, F., Zsila, Á., Király, O., Maraz, A, Elekes, Z., Griffiths, M. D., Andressen, C. S. & Demetrovics, Z. (2017). Problematic social media use: Results from a large-scale nationally representative adolescent sample. *PLoS ONE, 12,* 1–13, doi:10.1371/journal.pone.0169839

Barth, F. D. (2015). Social media and adolescent development: Hazards, pitfalls, and opportunities for growth. *Clinical Social Work Journal, 43,* 201–208.

Bettis, P., Ferry, N. C., & Roe, M. (2016). Lord of the guys: Alpha girls and the post-feminist landscape of the American education. *Gender Issues, 33,* 163–181.

Carter, B., Rees, P., Hale, L., Bhattacharjee, D., & Paradkar, M. S. (2016). Association between portable screen-based media device access or use and sleep outcomes. *JAMA Pediatrics, 170,* 1202–1208.

CBS News. (August 4, 2017). The digital divide between rural and urban America's access to Internet. Retrieved from https://www.cbsnews.com/news/rural-areas-internet-access-dawsonville-georgia

DeBose, K. (20 July 2017). Gen Z kidpreneurs. J. Walther Thompson Intelligence. Retrieved from https://www.jwtintelligence.com/2017/07/gen-z-kidpreneurs/

Donnelly, K., & Twenge, J. M. (2016). Masculine and feminine traits on the Bem Sex-Role Inventory, 1993–2012: A cross-temporal meta-analysis. *Sex Roles, 76*(9–10), 556–565. Retrieved from http://dx.doi.org/10.1007/s11199-016-0625-y

Ellithorpe, M. E., & Bleakley, A. (2016). Wanting to see people like me? Racial and gender diversity in popular adolescent television. *Journal of Youth and Adolescence, 45,* 1426–1437.

Fry, R. (May 5, 2017). It's becoming more common for young adults to live at home-and for longer stretches. Pew Research Center. Retrieved from http://www.pewresearch.org/fact-tank/2017/05/05/its-becoming-more-common-for-young-adults-to-live-at-home-and-for-longer-stretches/

Geiger, A. (June 21, 2017). Millennials are the most likely generation of Americans to use public libraries. Pew Research Center. Retrieved from http://www.pewresearch.

org/fact-tank/2017/06/21/millennials-are-the-most-likely-generation-of-americans-to-use-public-libraries/

Giaccardi, S., Ward, L. M., Seabrook, R. C., Manago, A., & Lippman, J. (2016). Media and modern manhood: Testing associations between media consumption and young men's acceptance of traditional gender ideologies. *Sex Roles, 75,* 151–163. doi: 10.1007/s111-99-016-0588-z

Hamel, C. W. (2017). Facebook, Twitter, gender: How social media allows for fragmentation of self in the digitally native Millennial. Bard Undergraduate Senior Projects Spring 2017. Retrieved from http://digitalcommons.bard.edu/senproj_s2017/369

Hamilton, J. (November 19, 2016). Heavy screen time rewires young brains, for better and worse. National Public Radio Weekend Edition Saturday. Retrieved from http://www.npr.org/sections/health-shots/2016/11/19/502610055/heavy-screen-time-rewires-young-brains-for-better-and-worse

Heilman, B., Barker, G., & Harrison, A. (2017). The man box: A study on being a young man in the US, UK and Mexico: Key Findings. Washington, DC and London: Promundo-U.S. and Unilever. Retrieved from https://promundoglobal.org/wp-content/uploads/2017/03/TheManBox-KeyFindings-EN-Final-29.03.2017-POSTPRINT.v2.pdf

Helen, C. (January 5, 2017). Adapting your brand for an attention span of 8 seconds. Say hello to Generation Z. Retrieved from https://www.cucumbermarketing.com/adapting-your-brand-for-an-attention-span-of-8-seconds-say-hello-to-generation-z/

Henzig, R. M. (January 2017). How science is helping us understand gender. *National Geographic.*

Hofstede, G. (2001). *Culture's consequences: Comparing values, behaviors, institutions, and organizations across nations* (2nd ed.). Thousand Oaks, CA: Sage.

Horrigan, J. B. (2016). Library usage and engagement. Pew Research Center, Internet & Technology. Retrieved from http://www.pewinternet.org/2016/09/09/library-usage-and-engagement

Hysing, M., Pallesen, S., Stormark, K. M., Jakobsen, R., Lundervold, A. J., & Siversten, B. (2015). Sleep and use of electronic devices in adolescence: Results from a large population-based study. *BMJ Open, 5,* e006748. doi: 10.1136/bmjopen-2014-006748

Kågesten, A., Gibbs, S., Blum, R. W., Moreau, C., Candra-Moul, V., Herbert, A., & Amin, A. (2016). Understanding factors that shape gender attitudes in early adolescence globally: A mixed-methods systematic review. *PLoS ONE, 6:* e0157805. doi:10.137/journal.pone.0157805

Kim, M. (Sept. 1, 2014). Blue light from electronics disturbs sleep, especially for teenagers. *The Washington Post.* Retrieved from https://www.washingtonpost.com/national/health-science/blue-light-from-electronics-disturbs-sleep-especially-for-teenagers/2014/08/29/3edd2726-27a7-11e4-958c-268a320a60ce_story.html?utm_term=.0febc6d19117

Kindlon, D. (2006). *Alpha girls: Understanding the new American girl and how she is changing the world.* New York, NY: Rodale.

Laughlin, S. (March 11, 2016). Gen Z goes beyond gender binaries in new Innovation Group data. Retrieved from https://www.jwtintelligence.com/2016/03/gen-z-goes-beyond-gender-binaries-in-new-innovation-group-data/

Lenhart, A. (April 9, 2015). Teens, social media and technology overview 2015. Pew Research Center. Retrieved from http://www.pewinternet.org/2015/04/09/teens-social-media-technology-2015/

Levant, R. F, & Richmond, K. (Spring, 2017). A review of research on masculinity ideologies using the male role norms inventory. *Journal of Men's Studies, 15*(2), 130.

Livingston, G. (June 8, 2017). Among U.S. cohabiters, 18% have a partner of a different race or ethnicity. FactTank: News in the Numbers. Pew Research Center. Retrieved from http://www.pewresearch.org/fact-tank/2017/06/08/among-u-s-cohabiters-18-have-a-partner-of-a-different-race-or-ethnicity

Loveland, E. (Winter, 2017). Instant generation. *The Journal of College Admission, 235,* 35–38.

Meehan, M. (August 11, 2016). The next generation: What matters to Gen We. *Forbes.* Retrieved from https://www.forbes.com/sites/marymeehan/2016/08/11/the-next-generation-what-matters-to-gen-we/#5f23a6dc7350

Miller, C. C. (September 7, 2017). From sex object to gritty woman: The evolution of women in stock photos. *The New York Times.*

Mills, K. L. (2016). Possible effects of Internet use on cognitive development in adolescence. *Media and Communication, 4,* 4–12.

National Sleep Foundation. (March, 2014). 2014 Sleep in America Poll: Sleep in the Modern Family. Washington (DC): The Foundation. Retrieved from http://www.sleepfoundation.org/sleep-polls-data/sleep-in-americapoll/2014-sleep-in-the-modern-family

Nesi, J., & Prinstein, M. J. (2015). Using social media for social comparison and feedback-seeking: Gender and popularity moderate associations with depressive symptoms. *Journal of Abnormal Psychology, 43,* 1427–1438.

Nonprofit Tech for Good. (June 26, 2017). What your nonprofit needs to know about Gen Z. Retrieved from http://www.nptechforgood.com/2017/06/26/what-your-nonprofit-needs-to-know-about-gen-z

Patel, D. (Aug. 8, 2017). 10 Tips for marketing to Gen Z on social media. *Forbes.* Retrieved from https://www.forbes.com/sites/deeppatel/2017/08/08/10-tips-for-marketing-to-gen-z-on-social-media/#64df5d7e2718

Perrin, A. (August 31, 2017). Smartphones help blacks, Hispanics bridge some—but not all—digital gaps with whites. Pew Research Center. Retrieved from http://www.pewresearch.org/fact-tank/2017/08/31/smartphones-help-blacks-hispanics-bridge-some-but-not-all-digital-gaps-with-whites

Phinney, J. S., Horenczyk, G., Liebkind, K., & Vedder, P. (2001). Ethnic identity, immigration, and well-being: An interactional perspective. *Journal of Social Issues, 57,* 493–510. doi:10.1111/0022-4537.00225

Reigeluth, C. S., & Addis, M. E. (2016). Adolescent boys' experiences with policing of masculinity: Forms, functions and consequences. *Psychology of Men & Masculinity, 17*(1), 74–83.

Rich, R. (2013). The Great Recession. Federal Reserve History. Retrieved from https://www.federalreservehistory.org/essays/great_recession_of_200709

Richtel, M. (March 13, 2017). Are teenagers replacing drugs with smartphones? *The New York Times*. Retrieved from https://www.nytimes.com/2017/03/13/health/teenagers-drugs-smartphones.html?mcubz=0&_r=0

Rideout, V. (2012). Social media, social life: How teens view their digital lives. Common Sense Media. Retrieved from https://www.commonsensemedia.org/research/social-media-social-life-how-teens-view-their-digital-lives

Rideout, V. (2015). The common sense census: Media use by tweens and teens. Common Sense. Retrieved from https://www.commonsensemedia.org/research

Rivas, J. (2015, February 3). Massive millennial poll: Half of young people believe gender isn't limited to male and female. Retrieved from http://fusion.net/story/42216/half-of-young-people-believegender-isnt-limited-to-male-and-female/

Rogers, A. A., Updegraff, K. A., Santos, C. E., & Martin, C. L. (2017). Masculinity and school adjustment in middle school. *Psychology of Men & Masculinity, 18*, 50–61.

Shapiro, J. (Nov. 3, 2015). Teenagers in the U.S. spend about nine hours a day in front of a screen. *Forbes*. Retrieved from http://onforb.es/1WtESSz

Smith, A. S. (January 12, 2017). Despite living a digital life, 98 percent of Generation Z still shop in-store. National Retail Federation. Retrieved from https://nrf.com/media/press-releases/despite-living-digital-life-98-percent-of-generation-z-still-shop-store

sparks & honey. (2015.) Gen Z 2025: The final generation. sparks & honey culture forecast. Retrieved from https://www.slideshare.net/sparksandhoney/gen-z-2025-the-final-generation-preview

Trifecta Research. (2015). Generation Z media consumption habits: True digital natives. Retrieved from http://trifectaresearch.com/wp-content/uploads/2015/09/Generation-Z-Sample-Trifecta-Research-Deliverable.pdf

Twenge, J. M. (2017a). *iGen: Why today's super-connected kids are growing up less rebellious, more tolerant, less happy—and completely unprepared for adulthood—and what that means for the rest of us.* New York, NY: Simon and Schuster.

Twenge, J. M. (2017b). Have smartphones destroyed a generation? *The Atlantic*, p. 2. Retrieved from https://www.theatlantic.com/magazine/archive/2017/09/has-the-smartphone-destroyed-a-generation/534198/

Twenge, J. M., & Park, H. (2017). The decline in adult activities among U.S. adolescents, 1976-2016. *Child Development.* doi: 10.1111/cdev.12930

Ward, L. M., & Aubrey, J. S. (2017). *Watching gender: How stereotypes in movies and on TV impact kids' development.* San Francisco, CA: Common Sense. Retrieved from https://www.commonsensemedia.org/research/watching-gender

Williams, A. (Sept. 18, 2015). Move over millennials, here comes Generation Z. *The New York Times*. Retrieved from https://www.nytimes.com/2015/09/20/fashion/move-over-millennials-here-comes-generation-z.html?_r=0

Chapter 4

It's a No-Brainer

Understanding the Adolescent Brain Is Important

Linda L. Caldwell and Elizabeth H. Weybright

Introduction

"Learning what one wants and how to mobilize internal and external resources to achieve it can perhaps be appreciated as the 'what' of adolescence—the lifespan development task to be accomplished" (Luciana, 2016, p. 340). What about the "how" of adolescence?

As you have read thus far, youth are co-producers of their own development. Vygotsky (e.g., 1978) suggested youth develop by exerting influence on, and being influenced by, other people and their environments. Other chapters in this book describe various ways youth are active in their own development, for example, through having voice or when youth workers provide scaffolding for youth to learn new things or accomplish tasks, and through making mistakes and learning from them. This chapter will focus on how youth are co-producers of their own development through the lens of a bioecological perspective. This perspective focuses on how changes in the brain during *puberty* and adolescence, or neurobiology, interact with adolescent personality and environmental factors to influence behavior and experience. All of these factors combine to form the unique person who emerges as an adult.

Vygotsky's dialectic perspective paved the way for a meta-theoretical perspective, the *bioecological model* (formerly ecological systems theory), which provided an expanded foundation for understanding the reciprocal and multi-layered influences on human development (see Bronfenbrenner & Morris, 2006). The bioecological model was borne out of the recognition of the biological factors that influence behavior in addition to the individual, social, community, and cultural factors that influence (and are influenced by) individuals.

Why is it important for someone who works with youth to understand adolescence from a bioecological perspective? Research suggests there is a profound change in neural development in the brain during adolescence that affects processes such as motivation, social-emotional learning, creativity, development of strong and enduring interests, and aspects of cognition such as executive intelligence. These changes also affect social interaction and risk-taking. Understanding what goes on from this bioecological perspective will help youth workers better understand why adolescents do what they do and how to better support their development through out-of-school time (OST) activities.

From a *neurobiological* perspective, adolescence begins when a young person enters puberty, which is where we will begin our exploration of the adolescent brain in relation to the "how" of adolescent development.

Puberty

Puberty marks the biological transition into becoming a sexually mature adult who can reproduce. This biological transition includes a cascade of hormonal, physical, physiological, and emotional changes. Girls and boys both experience puberty but typically at different rates and times. Girls usually enter puberty between the ages of 8 and 14 (average age of 11) and boys between the ages of 9 and 15 (average age of 12; Blakemore, Burnett, & Dahl, 2010). Puberty lasts about 2 to 5 years, but the length of time it lasts is different for every individual.

Essentially, going through adolescence and going through puberty mean the same thing, but specialists define puberty as the process of sexual maturation, specifically the activation of the *hypothalamic-pituitary-gonadal axis* that ends in *gonadal* maturation (Sisk & Foster, 2004). Adolescence typically refers to the period of psychological and social transition between childhood and adulthood and focuses on the social-emotional and behavioral aspects of adolescent development, many of which are discussed in this book. From an evolutionary biological perspective, these two aspects of adolescent development assure the continuation of humanity—developing sex hormones that allow for reproduction and development of the social and behavioral desires and skills to form romantic and sexual relationships to facilitate reproduction. Of course, not all romantic couples are comprised of a male and female, and not all couples reproduce, but in general, this explains the evolutionary purpose of the changes experienced during puberty and adolescents.

General Brain Neurobiology

Before we delve into details about the workings of the adolescent brain, a number of caveats are in order. It is critical to underscore that developmental psychologists and neurobiologists do not consider the brain to be the only driver of adolescent behavior. That is why the bioecological model is important; the brain is just one factor that helps explain and predict behavior. As you will read later in the chapter, other factors such as peers and the context in which an adolescent lives also help to explain behavior. A second caveat is that although there is growing consensus among researchers about the various roles and functions of the brain, as well as internal processes and networks, new research provides greater detail on how these processes work (e.g., the role of synaptic pruning in gray matter density; Steinberg, 2010a). Finally, and related to the second caveat, much of what has been learned about the human brain, including the adolescent brain, is based on laboratory experiments. Thus, there is a possible lack of generalizability from laboratory settings to the real-world environment. However, despite these concerns or caveats, there is considerable support and consensus for the material presented in this chapter.

Maturing adolescent brains undergo rapid and vast changes. From a simplistic perspective, the brain is rewiring itself. Some neurological pathways are strengthened, while other networks and connections are pruned by eliminating unused pathways. Specifically, areas in the brain that control movement, problem-solving, memory, spontaneity, language, motivation, judgment, impulse control, decision-making, and social and sexual behavior undergo dramatic changes (Arain et al., 2013).

As the adolescent brain begins to mature, beginning at about age 12, there are two developing networks that govern behavior: *cognitive-control* and *socioemotional networks*.

> From a simplistic perspective, the brain is rewiring itself.

Steinberg (2010b) and others have named this the *dual systems model*. These two systems develop at different times and at different rates. The slower maturing cognitive control network paired with the earlier maturing socioemotional network creates an imbalance between these two systems. This temporal gap in the brain's development is linked to *impulsivity* and *risk-taking*, which we will explore subsequently. Figure 4.1 displays a simplistic model of the brain.

The socioemotional network is located in the *paralimbic areas* of the brain and is driven by affective (emotional) processing and reward circuits of the *ventral striatum* (e.g., *nucleus accumbens*) and *amygdala*. These areas of the brain are responsive to emotion and novelty. They are the command center for reward processing, which has to do with associative learning (e.g., if I do this action, I will get something I desire in return or avoid punishment), motivation, and desire, among others. From early to middle adolescence, this network becomes increasingly activated, resulting in a heightened sensitivity to social and emotional stimuli and a greater need for and propensity to seek

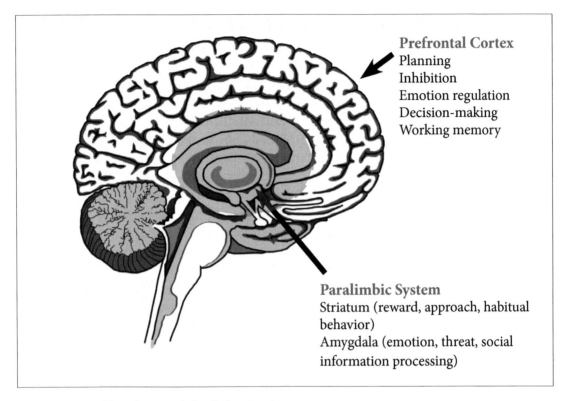

Prefrontal Cortex
Planning
Inhibition
Emotion regulation
Decision-making
Working memory

Paralimbic System
Striatum (reward, approach, habitual
behavior)
Amygdala (emotion, threat, social
information processing)

Figure 4.1. Simple Model of the Brain

out excitement and crave intense feelings. This system matures in early adolescence and is associated with seeking novel and adult-like activities (Romer, 2010).

The cognitive-control network, in the *prefrontal cortex*, controls *executive functions* such as planning, future orientation, and self-regulation. This system matures gradually, reaching maturation during later adolescence, and is independent of puberty. It is associated with impulsivity, which we will address later in the chapter. Executive functions in the human brain include the following (Arain et al., 2013):

- Focusing attention
- Considering the future and making predictions
- Balancing short-term rewards with long-term goals
- Delaying gratification and impulse control
- Modulating intense emotions
- Shifting/adjusting behavior when situations change
- Foreseeing and weighing possible consequences of behavior
- Considering multiple streams of information when simultaneously faced with complex and challenging information
- Inhibiting inappropriate behavior and initiating appropriate behavior
- Forming strategies and planning
- Organizing thoughts and problem-solving

The inability to regulate one's emotional intensity is an indication of either poor cognitive control or an underdeveloped, immature cognitive control system. Regulation refers to the ability to regulate one's emotions and motivational drives (i.e., seeking rewards). Psychologists term severe cases of the inability to regulate one's emotions as emotional dysregulation. It is also known as lability or mood swings (e.g., Ernst, 2014). We will return to this when we discuss *risk-taking*.

Pruning and the Importance of Out-of-School Time Activities

The processes by which the two neurobiological networks develop and interact provide insight into why OST activities are important. It is also an example of how youth are co-producers of their own development. Initial cell proliferation of gray matter results in the overproduction of *neurons* and their interconnections or synapses. This proliferation results in *synaptic pruning* and selective elimination of infrequently used cells and connections; approximately 50% of neurons are eliminated during the pruning process (Low & Cheng, 2006).

A related process is *myelination*, which is the development of myelin (a fatty coating) that insulates nerve fibers and speeds neural processing between regions of the brain's gray matter. Myelination is slower in the frontal lobes that connect the cognitive-control and socioemotional networks, which may result in the cognitive-control system being unable to handle the socioemotional system under emotionally laden and/or social conditions.

The process of pruning is associated with learning and with establishing precursors to adult behavior. It is during pruning and myelination that the brain may be tailored by experiences. Thus, the early activation of emotions combined with the plasticity due to pruning and myelination of the brain make adolescence an ideal time to intervene and promote positive youth development. Furthermore, pruning combined with intensified emotions sets the stage for igniting passions and developing interests (sparks) in activities such as music, art, and hobbies as well as goal-setting behavior (Dahl, 2004). Consequently, adolescent brains are primed to become hard wired for developing OST activity preferences, skills, and behaviors, thus setting the stage for continued participation throughout adulthood.

Motivation, Emotion, and Reward Seeking

Changes in the developing adolescent brain affect a number of phenomena related to motivation, emotions, and reward seeking. This section will address motivation for short-term rewards, goal seeking, sensitivity to positive feedback, ability for brain flexibility and learning, and responsiveness to social cues.

From a neurobiological perspective, motivation is the amount of effort one exerts for attaining a goal (Ernst, 2014). Adolescents who are more motivated expend more effort to reach their goals or rewards (as goals are often called in the literature). These incentive-based goals motivate actions to satisfy curiosity, needs, or desires, accomplish something, and avoid unpleasant or negative situations. Motivation can be a seeking or

Motivation can be a seeking or an avoiding behavior; each originates from a different part of the brain.

an avoiding behavior; each originates from a different part of the brain (Luciana, 2016). Seeking behaviors occur when adolescents pursue rewards, enhance the effect of rewards, and for older adolescents, anticipate rewards (e.g., Hoogendam, Kahn, Hillegers, van Burren, & Vink, 2013; Suleiman, Galvàn, Harden, & Dahl, 2017). Reward seeking is closely tied to learning new things, committing to causes one believes in, and creativity. This behavior contributes to the development of interests and passions mentioned earlier.

Younger adolescents have less patience for waiting for a reward and need more immediate gratification. The *dopaminergic* and *striatal networks* are involved in reward seeking, which is linked to positive emotions. For example, consider Rhoda, a 13-year-old girl who loves horseback riding. The manager of a local riding academy offered Rhoda 10 free riding lessons if she mucked the stalls for a month. Rhoda's mom dropped her off the first day and Rhoda mucked five stalls, and then her mom picked her up and she went home. Two days later the same scenario occurred. Rhoda "really, really" wanted those 10 free riding lessons because neither she nor her family could afford to pay—so she was very motivated. But after a few days of mucking stalls, she told her mom she was too tired and did not want to continue. What was the problem? The reward was not immediate enough, even though getting free lessons was potentially very motivating. Thus, she did not get the immediate boost from dopamine and other chemicals in the brain that signaled happiness, and from an executive function perspective, she could not link her actions with the reward that would happen some weeks in the future.

Negative emotions are linked to motivation that stems from avoidance (Ernst, 2014). The amygdala is the part of the brain from which avoidance-seeking motivation arises. Avoidance-seeking occurs when someone anticipates negative emotions to occur as a result of doing something, so they avoid that something. Sixteen-year-old Shareef, for example, had been going to the local YMCA and was involved in a drama production, something he had enjoyed in the past. When he stopped going to rehearsal, the leader of the production called him to inquire why. Shareef indicated that he never felt as though he was getting his lines right and felt embarrassed (obviously a negative emotion) in front of his peers, who were unfortunately teasing him. In this case, Shareef was motivated by avoiding a negative situation rather than seeking a reward.

Most research indicates that the adolescent brain is more sensitive to positive feedback than avoiding negative experiences. Therefore, adolescents are more motivated by experiences that provide them with rewards (Davidow, Foerde, Galvàn, & Shohamy, 2016). In a laboratory study, Davidow et al. found that compared to adults, adolescents learned to complete a task with more accuracy than adults when they experienced positive reinforcement rather than neutral or negative feedback. The researchers concluded this was because the adolescent brain, compared to adults, was "biased" toward seeking positive reinforcement, and this bias facilitated more rapid responses and learning than was found in the adults who participated in the experiment. The researchers further speculated this was because the adolescents had previously formed

positive memories from receiving similar rewards in the past. Due to the brain's bias in seeking positive reinforcement, the brain accessed those memories (e.g., *working memory*, see subsequent discussion on this), therefore causing the adolescents to learn more from positive reinforcement rather than neutral or negative reinforcement. The researchers suggested their findings have implications for what types of memories are formed in adolescence, because these memories may be important drivers of future behavior.

Learning is Rewarding

One of the ways adolescents are co-producers of their own development can be seen in the reciprocal influence between the parts of the brain that influence motivation, emotion, and the choices and experiences adolescents seek based on prior experience, personality, and situational influences. In short, the brain during this period has *neuroplasticity* (Suleiman et al., 2017), meaning it is not only receptive to cues and factors in the environment, but it adapts based on those cues. Therefore, the brain is flexible, particularly during adolescence.

Suleiman et al. and others call this process *adaptive learning* and suggest it contributes to forming *wisdom*. More specifically, Murty, Calabro, and Luna (2016) call the process of *experience-driven adaptive learning*. Stimulated by chemical reactions (i.e., dopaminergic activation) in the brain, adolescents are motivated to seek and explore novel experiences from which to learn. In this way, adolescents learn from feedback from both their errors and successes. Seeking experiences helps an adolescent develop individual preferences, passions, and identity. Seeking experiences is an important developmental process because it helps build memories that use experience to develop adaptive decision-making (Luciana, 2016) and learn to engage in adult-like behavior (Murty et al., 2016). Thus, adolescence is a unique period of brain plasticity "...for the establishment of contextually relevant responses [in the prefrontal cortex] to guide and optimize goal-oriented behaviors" (Murty et al., 2016, p. 54).

A host of situational and stable factors comes into play in adaptive learning (Ernst, 2014), as with all other behaviors connected to the brain. Situational factors include adolescents' mental state (e.g., depressed or stressed), physical state (e.g., impaired or sleepy), and the behavioral context (e.g., school, home, or social setting). Stable factors include personality (e.g., sensation seeking or cautious), maturation level (e.g., age, pubertal development), genetic make-up, past experiences (e.g., early deprivation or parental attachment), and gender. For example, as one gets older and more experienced in the world, one's identity development progresses. Therefore, goals become increasingly longer-range and are based on a more salient and curated set of interests and preference based on one's past experiences. As well, the executive capabilities based in the prefrontal cortex become more sophisticated, thus allowing for and supporting better decision-making and cognitive control (Luciana, 2016).

Previously, we stated that adaptive learning contributes to wisdom. However, it is a bit more complicated than that. Wisdom can be thought of as gaining insight from the accumulation of what one learns from experiences, plus the ability to apply those insights in current and future situations. For example, although older adolescents' brains have greater cognitive control than younger adolescents do, it does not mean they have gained wisdom from those experiences. Learning from experiences and creating memories from those experiences enable abstract thinking, which Goldberg (2006) calls *executive intelligence*. Abstract thinking allows adolescents to make better decisions in situations where rules for how to behave are not clear.

> ## Abstract thinking allows adolescents to make better decisions in situations where rules for how to behave are not clear.

Executive intelligence is particularly important for interpreting when a situation might turn risky, for example, when young people are hanging out and bored. Using executive intelligence might help an adolescent realize that boredom is linked with substance use and vandalism and therefore leave either the situation or attempt to change it to alleviate the boredom in positive ways. Adding to the complexity of developing wisdom is that as adolescents are learning to work with their accumulated memories and experiences, they may have difficulty thinking rationally about complex decisions and/or environments, especially in emotionally charged situations (Arain et al., 2013). Therefore, in the boredom example, it might be more difficult for any of the young people to assess that the situation might turn risky if some in the group are also experiencing intense emotions, such as jealousy or anger.

Social Reorientation and Social Rewards

One of the primary rewards for adolescents emanates from the brain's social reorientation (Ernst, 2014). During puberty, the maturing adolescent brain is more sensitive to social cues, particularly related to peers, and responds with greater emotional and motivational intensity. This is known as the *social-information processing network*. Achieving and maintaining a desired level of social status within the hierarchy of one's peers is very rewarding for adolescents (Op de Macks, Bunge, Bell, Kriegsfeld, Kayser, & Dahl, 2017). Clearly, the social-information processing network is closely connected to the way adolescents use social media (see Chapter 3). For example, the search for validation of one's social status through "likes" or "followers" is directly related to the social reorientation in the brain. Research has found greater brain activity in reward regions when viewing "likes" on one's own photos (Sherman, Payton, Hernandez, Greenfield, & Dapretto, 2016).

Changes in *gonadal hormones* contribute to an increased motivation to pursue social goals and particularly social status (Luciana, 2016). *Testosterone* levels increase in both boys and girls during puberty. Testosterone is related to aggression levels and sexual motivations. It is also related to status-seeking and status maintenance, as well as risk-taking. Testosterone may also influence an adolescent's ability to weigh the risk/reward consequences of an action, particularly given salient social contexts when peers are present (Chick, 2015). *Estradiol* and *progesterone* levels also increase in both males and females and play a role in sexual, social, and risk-taking behavior (Suleiman et al., 2017).

The way adolescents respond to the pull for social rewards has implications for impulsivity and sensation seeking, but research is inconclusive regarding how seeking social rewards influences risk-taking (Op de Macks et al., 2017). Therefore, there is much to learn about how peers influence the reward system. It is not as simple, for example, to state that peer pressure can lead to negative risky behavior, although it can and does. Because the maturing adolescent brain directs one's attention to social cues, a number of researchers suggest that adolescents learn better when in socially relevant situations such as when peers are present (e.g., Paul, 2015).

Think back to Shareef's situation. Being in the presence of peers and experiencing negative emotions was too much for him to handle at the time. On the other hand, think how rewarding and emotionally positive his situation would have been if the adult leader had been proactive in addressing the situation. Research studies consistently find the presence of an adult and/or adult regulation helps to mitigate the influence of peer pressure (Luciana, 2016). Discussion question number two (at the end of the chapter) asks you to put yourself in the shoes of the leader of the drama production in which Shareef was involved and problem solve what strategies could have been used to prevent Shareef's embarrassment and perception that his social status among his peers was falling.

Remember, however, hormonal changes and peer influences by themselves are only two sets of factors in the interrelated environment-behavior-development feedback loop system to consider. The temporary and stable factors (e.g., personality, mental state) described previously apply here as well.

So far, we have touched on the issues of risk-taking, impulsivity, and sensation seeking. Now let's take a deeper dive into these complex issues.

Risk-Taking: Impulsivity and Sensation Seeking

Impulsivity and *sensation seeking* are two personality traits stimulated by brain development in adolescence. They are distinct concepts and processes within the brain (Romer, 2010). Impulsivity is "...the tendency to act on behavioral impulsiveness without planning or considering potential consequences" (Harden & Tucker-Drob, 2011, p. 739). It stems from a failure to exert cognitive control and is associated with poor decision-making. On the other hand, researchers suggest that sensation seeking, or "...the tendency to seek out experiences that are novel, exciting, or rewarding" (Harden & Tucker-Drob, p. 739), stems from the way the brain is motivated by seeking novel and stimulating rewards (Steinberg, 2008). Sensation seeking peaks around age 19 in males and 16 in females (Romer et al., 2017) and is motivated by recognition and anticipation of reward, which is a marker of dopaminergic activation. The rewards are part of the *behavioral activation system* (BAS), which is a personality cluster that includes fun seeking (related to sensation seeking) and achievement motivation (Romer et al., 2017).

Before proceeding with this section, it is important to note that up to 80% of adolescents have little or no problems coping with stress or avoiding risk-taking behavior as they mature (Dahl, 2004), despite increased attraction to risky sensation-seeking behaviors (Romer, Reyna, & Satterthwaite, 2017). Compared to other age groups, adolescents are characterized by vitality and resilience. Unfortunately, news reports contain examples of adolescent impulsivity and propensity to engage in risk-taking behaviors such as substance use, unprotected sex, and vandalism; little is reported about the 80% of adolescents who are thriving and having few problems with stress or risk-taking behaviors.

... rates of death by injury between ages 15 and 19 are about six times that of the rate between ages 10 and 14.

Despite the fact that the vast majority of adolescents are healthy and thriving, there is still cause for concern about adolescent health. That is because this period is also characterized by an increased level of morbidity and mortality (Dahl, 2004). For example, rates of death by injury between ages 15 and 19 are about six times that of the rate between ages 10 and 14 (National Institute of Mental Health, 2011). Therefore, it is important to understand better what contributes to adolescent risk-taking.

The dual systems model represents the imbalance between the "accelerating" socioemotional network in early adolescence without a corresponding increase in the "brakes" from an advanced cognitive control ability from the prefrontal cortex, which develops in later adolescence. This imbalance means adolescents may make decisions without fully considering the risks involved and elevates the possibility for some adolescents of engaging in risk-taking behavior in the name of reward-seeking behavior

(Steinberg, 2016). Figure 4.2 contains a diagram depicting the idea of equilibrium and disequilibrium. It is important to note that Figure 4.2 contains situational and stable processes that serve to change the calculus of the balance for each person.

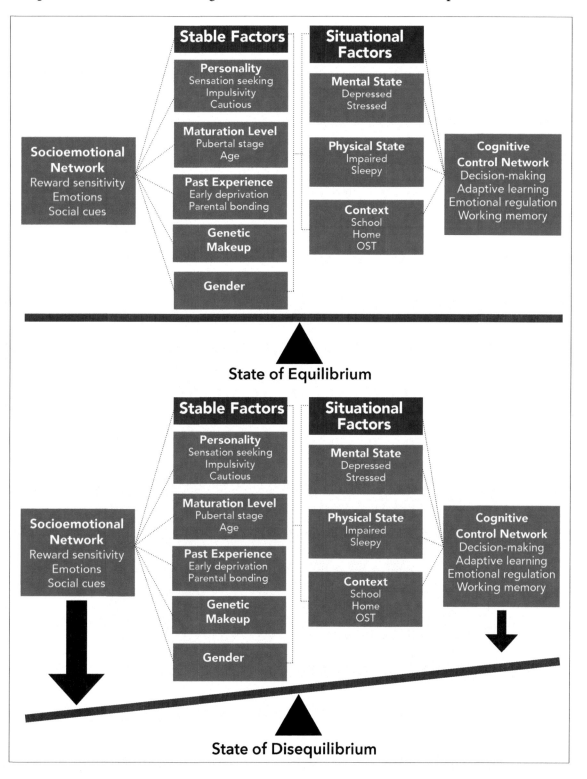

Figure 4.2. Dual Systems Model and Stable and Situational Factors

This dual systems model provides a way to understand how the adolescent brain influences behavior. It is important to emphasize that the model does not suggest adolescents are inherently reckless and incompetent decision makers. In fact, there is growing empirical evidence that there are no age differences in being aware of and assessing risk and one's vulnerability to such risk (Steinberg, 2007). Steinberg and his colleagues suggest that under conditions that minimize arousal of the socioemotional system, adolescents, particularly from mid-adolescence on, make adult-like judgments. They suggest, however, that it is when adolescents are in emotionally charged situations and have the potential to gain an immediate reward, such as novelty or excitement, they are more likely to engage in risky behavior.

Impulsivity: What's Really Going On?

It is important to consider the differences between sensation seeking and impulsivity when examining the role of cognitive control (Romer et al., 2017). Romer and colleagues suggest risk-taking is not necessarily the result of an imbalance between the cognitive control systems and the socioemotional systems but rather a result of a failure during

childhood to learn to control impulses. They also suggest that when adolescents start experimenting with adult-like behavior, the behavior is so novel they may not have the appropriate level of experience to navigate or avoid risky behaviors. For example, these adolescents have either not learned from experience-driven adaptive behaviors or have not even had experiences that approximate the adult-like behavior in question.

Romer and colleagues (2017) consider impulsivity to be "…a form of decision-making that is overly sensitive to immediate urges (e.g., desired and anticipated rewards, such as a belief that one's social status has been affirmed) without adequate consideration of consequences" (p. 22). They suggest there are two forms of impulsivity: *impulsive action* and *impulsive choice*. Impulsive action is acting without thinking. It also peaks during adolescence and is associated with sensation seeking and BAS rewards (i.e., fun seeking and achievement motivation).

> Adolescents who make impulsive choices are not able to identify alternatives and make alternative selections of action.

Working memory is one factor that distinguishes impulsivity from sensation seeking (Romer et al., 2017). Adolescents who act on impulse have low levels of working memory, or at least do not use working memory, and thus they lack the ability to focus on the situation and consider alternative actions to the strong impulses they have for the anticipated reward. Working memory is a psychological term that describes an immediate, attention-related type of memory to plan and carry out behavior (Cowan, 2008). It is the ability to recognize visual and auditory cues in the environment and keep them in one's head for immediate use. In addition, it is the ability to learn someone's name at a party and be able to remember that name matched with a face or keep numbers in one's head as they are added together.

Impulsive choice, or impatience, happens when adolescents typically choose smaller and immediate rewards over larger but delayed rewards (Romer et al., 2017). Impulsive choice does not seem to be related to sensation seeking, but instead is negatively related to working memory. Adolescents who make impulsive choices are not able to identify alternatives and make alternative selections of action. In contrast to sensation seeking and acting without thinking, impatience declines slowly from childhood to adolescence and therefore does not peak in adolescence.

In addition to impulsivity and sensation seeking operating differently in the brain, they also have different consequences (Romer et al., 2017). Sensation-seeking youth who act thoughtfully (and therefore avoid impulsive action) have fewer negative risk or health consequences than those who act impulsively. In this case, the cognitive control system seems to dampen the possibility of problematic risk behaviors, such as becoming addicted to drugs or problem gambling.

Younger adolescents who make impulsive *choices* are the ones who continue to make those choices during later adolescence. That is, early problematic risk takers are more likely to be impulsive than sensation seekers. Romer et al. (2017) summarized, "…the increase in sensation seeking that characterizes adolescence does not necessarily lead to maladaptive behavior unless it is accompanied by weak executive function [cognitive control], such as exhibited by acting without thinking or the desire for immediate reward" (p. 22).

Research looking at the association between cognitive control and sensation seeking finds no difference in cognitive control between adolescents and adults. In fact, by age 16 and 17, adolescents perform as well as adults. Despite the finding that executive functioning and working memory generally increase with age, late adolescents, not middle adolescents, exhibit greater levels of impulsive action and sensation-seeking impatience. Part of the reason is due to greater social controls on younger and middle adolescents than on older adolescents. For example, older adolescents have greater access to alcohol and cars (Shulman et al., 2016). Thus, despite the fact that younger adolescents have more imbalance between the cognitive control system and the socioemotional system, older adolescents have more freedom and opportunity to engage in impulsive and/or sensation-seeking behaviors with fewer structural constraints placed on them.

The inability to inhibit impulsivity to act emotionally is heightened in a social context (Albert, Chein, & Steinberg, 2013). For example, research finds when adolescents are with friends, they more positively evaluate risk behavior and tend to take more risks than when they are alone (Gardner & Steinberg, 2005). On the other hand, when there is less emotionality, the cognitive-control system can provide regulatory control and the two systems are in balance. In this case, adolescents, in the absence of intense psychosocial factors, are as competent as adults as decision makers. The differential influence these two systems have in the face of emotionally laden contexts diminishes as adolescents mature.

Summary and Concluding Remarks

Research on adolescents' brain plasticity, early propensity toward sensation seeking and passion, and the later evolution of the cognitive-control and goal-setting system, provides a foundation for youth workers to understand better the role of activities, experiences, and contexts in promoting healthy growth and development during adolescence. In simple terms, OST contexts are uniquely situated to help youth develop enduring interests, learn socioemotional regulation in a social context, and prevent unsafe risky behavior. Youth workers can take advantage of the developing brain as well as contribute to its maturation.

Adolescents are motivated by seeking rewards and gaining positive emotions.

The early activation of emotions and passions can be applied to a wide range of activities, in particular those that have a social component. Adolescents are motivated by seeking rewards and gaining positive emotions. Goal-directed behavior intensifies during this time and is manifested by developing passions (sparks) in music, art, sports, nature and other recreational activities and hobbies. Because of the pruning that takes place in the brain, youth workers can help youth enhance their abilities to control impulses and hone skills. Spear (2009) calls this customizing the maturing brain as connections among neurons are strengthened while less used ones are pruned.

By virtue of the ways adolescents' brains are developing, as well as other stable and situational factors, they are particularly vulnerable to intense emotions and misinterpretation of others' intentions and emotions. In addition, they have not yet developed the capacity to critically reflect and problem-solve. On the other hand, the brain's plasticity during this period means that experience-driven adaptive learning takes place through experience, memory making, and self-reflection. Thus, this is a period of vulnerabilities and opportunities, particularly because trajectories that are set during this period have a major impact on adult life.

> OST contexts are uniquely situated to help youth develop enduring interests, learn socioemotional regulation in a social context, and prevent unsafe, risky behavior.

One area that we have not touched on in this chapter deserves mention. As we have described, researchers believe that many of the "risk" behaviors in which adolescents engage are actually important to their development by supporting exploration and learning and are normative behaviors in the process of becoming an adult (Romer, 2010; Romer et al., 2017; Suleiman et al., 2017). From an evolutionary perspective, some researchers suggest that adolescents engage in sensation seeking to learn how to gain independence from parents; thus, it is an adaptive behavior (Cservenka et al., 2013). If one considers that perspective more closely, one may wonder when adolescents should initiate sexual behaviors such as intercourse or experiment with substances such as marijuana and alcohol. When are these types of behaviors developmentally helpful and when are they not? When are these behaviors, which are normative in an individual's developmental trajectory, risky or adaptive? Of course these are complex question that are also related to religious and cultural belief systems, as well as a host of other factors (e.g., the stable and situational factors previously discussed). There is no firm or right answer to when is a good time, but we hope that these issues will stimulate further thought as you consider adolescent development and risk-taking from a bioecological perspective.

Adolescents, and especially early adolescents, have a heightened sensitivity and drive to explore their environments. They are open to new ideas. This is an incredibly important time for learning through adult scaffolding. Consider Luciana's comment: "… the exuberance of incentive motivation leads to experiential learning…" (2016, p. 340). Armed with the information in this chapter, youth workers may be better equipped to develop the supports and opportunities that youth need to engage in experience driven adaptive learning, engage in developmentally helpful risk-taking, and help youth navigate their desire for positive social interaction and sensation seeking in ways that help them become unique and capable adults.

Practical Implications

The following list provides a number of practical considerations when applying your newly gained understanding of the adolescent brain in OST settings.

- **Use adolescents' reward sensitivity in the service of prosocial goals.** One way to incentivize adolescents is to provide them with roles and activities in which they can adaptively learn (e.g., planning and implementing a special event). Another example is to enable them to learn new social roles, because "all things social" are motivating to adolescents if the experience is positive. Keep in mind that adolescents are much more motivated when they receive positive rewards rather than by avoiding negative situations. In addition, younger adolescents are typically more driven by immediate rewards than by anticipating rewards.
- **Find ways to provide experiences that satisfy the need for sensation seeking and opportunities to learn from them.** Novel, exciting, and rewarding risk-taking experiences within a protective, supervised environment contribute to adaptive learning.
- **Use OST activities as effective vehicles to help adolescents understand what their brains are doing** and how to deal with their experiences, emotions, and lack of ability to self-regulate in certain situations. One helpful website to facilitate these types of activities is www.mindful.org/how-to-teach-your-kids-about-the-brain/.
- **Help adolescents constructively learn to interpret cues in the environment.** This is why debriefing is important, to help with the process of adaptive learning and building executive intelligence. Similar to the previous point, youth workers should help youth learn about how they learn. This means that programs for youth should help them develop means of cognitive control, particularly when they are seeking certain rewards. They should learn to understand what rewards they are seeking and how to manage those feelings.
- **Use contextual salience to your advantage.** If adolescents are given socially or emotionally salient information, it is more likely that they will remember and internalize messages and act on them in the future, lessening the chance they will engage in harmful behavior. Prevention or other efforts to mitigate risk-taking with negative outcomes should not focus on primarily cognitive messages because risk activity is more social and emotionally instigated. Efforts should focus on the context under which risky behavior takes place, thereby implicating the need for an experiential component that will help youth take lessons learned during the experience and apply them to real world challenges and problems.

Discussion Questions

1. Refer back to the example of Rhoda's situation (mucking stalls for a reward of free riding lessons), and change the story in two different ways so that she would receive rewards that would keep her motivated.

2. How could you help Shareef learn from his situation and gain rewards in order to become re-motivated? Put yourself in the shoes of the leader of the drama production in which Shareef was involved and problem-solve strategies that could have been taken to prevent Shareef's embarrassment and perception that his social status among his peers was falling.

3. Consider this statement based on the work of Suleiman et al. (2017): *Adolescents have the cognitive capacity to navigate early romantic and sexual experiences safely, and yet they need appropriate support to do so successfully.*
   What are appropriate roles for youth workers in OST contexts to facilitate healthy, developmental "high-intensity" (Suleiman et al., 2017, p. 212) learning experiences around feelings of sexual desire, attraction, and arousal? How should youth workers minimize risky sexual activity or substance use?

4. What are the major risk factors in adolescents' lives from a bioecological perspective?

5. How can youth workers maximize the positive power of peers in social learning and positive risk-taking, versus negative risk-taking?

Assignments

1. Design a program that would teach youth how their brains work.

2. You have just assumed the position of the director of youth services at a local agency. You inherited staff who have not been trained in youth development and do not seem to understand how young people mature. Develop a set of training materials based on this chapter that will help the youth workers understand the adolescent developing brain.

3. Design a set of positive sensation seeking activities that will provide youth with positive risks. What would you take into consideration based on the material from this chapter?

References

Albert, D., Chein, J., & Steinberg, L. (2013). The teenage brain: Peer influences on adolescent decision making. *Current Directions in Psychological Science, 22,* 114–120.

Arain, M., Haque, M., Johal, L., Mathur, P., Nel, W., Rais, A., Sandu, R., & Sharma, S. (2013). Maturation of the adolescent brain. *Neuropsychiatric Disease and Treatment, 9,* 449–461.

Blakemore, S., Burnett, S., & Dahl, R. E. (2010). The role of puberty in the developing adolescent brain. *Human Brain Mapping, 31,* 926–933.

Bronfenbrenner, U., & Morris, P. A. (2006). The bioecological model of human development. *Handbook of Child Psychology, 1,* 793–828.

Chick, C. F. (2015). Reward processing in the adolescent brain: Individual differences and relation to risk taking. *The Journal of Neuroscience, 35,* 13539–13541.

Cowan, N. (2008). What are the differences between long-term, short-term, and working memory? *Progress in Brain Research, 169,* 323–338. doi:10.1016/S0079-6123(07)00020-9

Cservenka, A., Herting, M. M., Mackiewicz Seghete, K. L., Hudson, K. A., & Nagel, B. J. (2013). High and low sensation-seeking adolescents show distinct patterns of brain activity during reward processing. *Neuroimage,* 184–193. doi:1-.1016/j.neuroimage.2012.11.003

Dahl, R. (2004). Adolescent brain developoment: A period of vulnerabilities and opportunities. *Annals of New York Academies of Science, 1021,* 1–22.

Davidow, J. Y., Foerde, K, Galvàn, A., Shohamy, D. (2016). An upside to reward sensitivity: The hippocampus supports enhanced reinforcement learning in adolescence. *Neuron, 92,* 93–99.

Ernst, M. (2014). The triadic model perspective for the study of adolescent motivated behavior. *Brain Cognition, 89,* 104–111. doi: 10.1016/j.bandc.2015.01.006

Gardner, M., & Steinberg, L. (2005). Peer influence on risk taking, risk preference, and risky decision-making in adolescence and adulthood: An experimental study. *Developmental Psychology, 41*(4), 625–635.

Goldberg, E. (2006). *The wisdom paradox.* New York, NY: Gotham Books.

Harden, K. P., & Tucker-Drob, E. M. (2011). Individual differences in the development of sensation seeking and impulsivity during adolescence: Further evidence for a dual systems model. *Developmental Psychology, 47,* 739–746.

Hoogendam, J. M., Kahn, R. S., Hillegers, M.H. J., van Burren, M., & Vink, M. (2013). Different development trajectories for anticipation and receipt of reward during adolescence. *Developmental Cognitive Neuroscience, 6,* 113–124.

Low, L., K., & Chen, H. J. (2006). Axon pruning: An essential step underlying the developmental plasticity of neuronal connections. *Philosophical Transactions of the Royal Society B: Biological Sciences, 361,* pp. 1531–1544.

Luciana, M. (2016). Commentary on the special issue on the adolescent brain: Incentive-based striving and the adolescent brain. *Neuroscience and Biobehavioral Reviews, 70,* 339–342.

Murty, V. P., Calabro, F., & Luna, B. (2016). The role of experience in adolescent cognitive development: integration of executive, memory, and mesolimbic systems. *Neuroscience and Biobehavioral Review, 70,* 46–58. Retrieved from http://dx.doi.org/10.1016/j.neubiorev.2016.07.034

National Institute of Mental Health. (2011). The teen brain: Still under construction. Retrieved from http://www.nimh.nih.gov/health/publications/the-teen-brain-still-under-construction/index.shtml

Op de Macks, Z. A., Bunge, S. A., Bell, O. N., Kriegsfeld, L. J., Kayser, A. S., & Dahl, R. E. (2017). The effect of social rank feedback on risk taking and associated reward processes in adolescent girls. *Social Cognitive and Affective Neuroscience, xx,* 240–250. doi: 10.1093/scan/nsw125

Paul, A. M. (November 1, 2015). Peer pressure has a positive side. *Scientific American.* Retrieved from https://www.scientificamerican.com/article/peer-pressure-has-a-positive-side/

Romer, D. (2010). Adolescent risk taking, impulsivity, and brain development: Implications for prevention. *Developmental Psychobiology, 52,* 263–276. doi:10.1002/dev.20442

Romer, D., Reyna, V. F., & Satterthwaite, T. D. (2017). Beyond stereotypes of adolescent risk taking: Placing the adolescent brain in developmental context. *Developmental Cognitive Neuroscience, 27,* 19–34.

Sherman, L. E., Payton, A. A., Hernandez, L. M., Greenfield, P. M., & Dapretto, M. (2016). The power of the like in adolescence: Effects of peer influence on neural and behavioral responses to social media. *Psychological Science, 27*(7), 1027–1035.

Shulman, E. P., Smith, A. R., Silva, K., Icenogle, G., Duell, N., Chein, J. & Steinberg, L. (2016). The dual systems model: Review, reappraisal, and reaffirmation. *Developmental Cognitive Neuroscience, 17,* 103–117.

Sisk, C. L., & Foster, D. L. (2004). The neural basis of puberty and adolescence. *Nature Neuroscience, 7,* 1040–1047.

Spear, L. P. (2009). *The behavioral neuroscience of adolescence.* New York, NY: W. W. Norton & Co.

Steinberg, L. (2007). Risk taking in adolescence: New perspectives from brain and behavioral science. *Current Directions in Psychological Science, 16,* 55–59.

Steinberg, L. (2008). A social neuroscience perspective on adolescent risk-taking. *Developmental Review, 28,* 78–106. doi:10.1016/j.dr.2007.08.002

Steinberg, L. (2010a). A behavioral scientist looks at the science of adolescent brain development. *Brain and Cognition, 72,* 160–164.

Steinberg, L. (2010b). A dual systems model of adolescent risk-taking. *Developmental Psychobiology, 52,* 216–224.

Steinberg, L. (2016). Commentary on special issue on the adolescent brain: Redefining adolescence. *Neuroscience and Biobehavioral Reviews, 70,* 343–346.

Suleiman, A. B., Galvàn, A., Harden, K. P., & Dahl, R. E. (2017). Becoming a sexual being: The 'elephant in the room" of adolescent brain development. *Developmental Cognitive Neuroscience, 25,* 209–220.

Vygotsky, L. S. (1978). *Mind and society.* Cambridge, MA: Harvard Press.

Chapter 5

Why and How Youth Services Were Developed

Peter A. Witt

Many of us were members of some kind of youth-serving organization when we were growing up. Maybe you belonged to the Boys & Girls Clubs of America, Boy Scouts, Girl Scouts, YMCA, YWCA, 4-H, or attended programs at your local parks and recreation department community center. Each of these organizations has a distinguished history, a history that shares common roots in societal forces and events that took place in the second half of the 1800s and the first several decades of the 1900s. In this chapter, we will discuss these forces and events in general, and then in Chapter 6 we will discuss the specific history of some of the major youth-servicing organizations and describe some of the programs they currently offer.

To begin, let's discuss some of the forces and events that led people to conclude that youth-serving organizations should be created. From the mid-1800s through the early 1900s, a period of rapid transformation occurred in which an agrarian and rural society was replaced by a society characterized by urbanization and industrialization. To better understand the impact of these changes on children and youth, this chapter will discuss the following:

- The creation of a distinct period between childhood and adult status that was labeled *adolescence*

- The subsequent development of youth-serving organizations to serve the developmental needs of this newly created group of young people

Understanding the origin of these organizations in historical context will help us understand the origin of many of the current societal attitudes about young people and the way supports, opportunities, programs, and services (SOPS) have been developed to meet their needs.

Societal Forces Leading to a Different Way of Viewing Young People

From the mid-1800s through the early 1900s, the United States underwent dramatic structural and economic changes, including rapid industrialization, massive immigration and migration of rural populations to urban settings, and increased urbanization. These factors influenced the way youth were viewed and treated by society and laid the groundwork for the development of a variety of organizational responses to youth needs.

Industrialization

The Industrial Revolution began in England in the late 1700s and quickly spread to other parts of the world, including the United States. As it spread, it fundamentally changed the way goods were produced. Before the Industrial Revolution, goods were made laboriously with hand tools, but after the revolution, factories increasingly turned out identical products crafted by machines. These factories thrived on increased division of labor and specialization of job responsibilities. Workers became more productive, and because more items were manufactured, prices dropped, making exclusive and hard-to-make items available to the masses and not just the rich and elite. As will be discussed later, young people were central to supplying the labor that made the industrial revolution possible; however, their involvement in the production process eventually drew public attention and calls for reforms.

Immigration and Migration

In the 1800s, and particularly after the Civil War, a flood of immigrants from Europe and Eastern Europe began to arrive in the United States and settle mainly in the major cities along the Eastern seaboard near their point of entry. Many people originally immigrated because of crop failures (e.g., the potato famine in Ireland), poor economic conditions, and/or religious prejudice in their home countries. Most immigrants arrived willing to work but without the education or skills to enable them to pursue more than working-class jobs.

Between 1820 and 1880, almost 3.5 million Irish and 3 million Germans entered the United States. At the same time, many families, but more particularly many young people from rural settings in the United States, migrated to the cities. Due to increases in industrialization, young people were more able to find work in the cities than they were in rural and smaller communities. In fact, the migration of rural residents was so extensive that between 1880 and 1890, almost 40% of the townships in the United States lost population to the urban centers (Library of Congress, 2004).

Urbanization

As a result of immigration and migration, the population of urban centers grew rapidly. For example, New York's population grew from 33,131 in 1790 to 312,710 in 1840, 1,206,299 in 1880, and 3,437,202 in 1900. Chicago grew from 503,185 in 1880 to 1,698,575 in 1900, and Boston grew from 362,839 in 1880 to 589,141 in 1900 (Gibson, 1998).

Increases in the population of the major cities had a number of significant impacts on urban residents, particularly members of the lower class. For one thing, cities lacked the infrastructure to deal with the rapid population increases. Housing, roads and transportation systems, and sewage treatment were inadequate. Noise and pollution increased. Working conditions were often dangerous, but due to the need for labor, increasing numbers of women and young children were employed, often working long hours at monotonous and repetitive jobs. Cities also lacked public spaces for lower class children, adults, and families to recreate during their non-work hours, therefore:

> The children played on the streets because there was nowhere else for them. Urban space was a commodity, an item bought and sold like any other. As the population of the cities expanded, land became more and more valuable... undeveloped land was wasteland. With space at a premium, even the backyards were too valuable to be given over to children...and were used for raising animals, vegetable gardens, and storage. Indoor space was also not available for play, with what there was given over to sleeping and eating. (Nasaw, 1985, pp. 17–18)

Commercial recreation locations (e.g., dance halls, saloons, small theaters, and other forms of "pleasure seeking") opened to serve the needs of workers who sought things to do during their non-work time; however, many of these establishments encouraged prostitution and drunkenness. Unfortunately, children had ready access to these locations and their associated vices.

Middle-class children were also impacted by urban and small-town life. As middle-class incomes rose, parents were able to "forego the labor or earnings of their teenagers and invest instead in preparing them for success as adults" (Mcleod, 1983, p. 9). Thus, the number of years children were expected to go to school was lengthened.

> Although some youth involved themselves beyond school in chores or part-time work, there was still plenty of free time, creating the need for outlets to occupy time and safeguard parents' investment [in their children] by strengthening their sons' morality and ambition... (Mcleod, 1983, p. 9)

The main goal of parents was to help their children better themselves and lead lives that preserved middle-class values and standing. City life and the activities of lower-class youth were seen as a threat to achieving these goals.

One of the reformers was Jane Addams, a founder of Hull House, a major settlement house in Chicago that offered community-based services for both children and adults. Addams argued that many of the problems associated with young people were not the result of their faults or internal deficits, but were due instead to the lack of constructive outlets or opportunities. Through her work at Hull House, Addams saw firsthand the need for positive contact between youth and adults. Speaking up for the needs of immigrants and what we would now call inner-city children, Addams worried about the impacts of city life on young people and persons from the working class (Figure 5.1).

Jane Addams (1969) noted:

The social organism has broken down through large districts of our great cities. Many of the people living there are very poor, the majority of them without leisure or energy for anything but the gain of subsistence. They move often from one wretched lodging to another. They live for the moment side by side, many of them without knowledge of each other, without fellowship, without local tradition or public spirit, without social organization of any kind. Practically nothing is done to remedy this. The people who might do it, who have the social tact and training, the large houses, and the traditions and custom of hospitality, live in other parts of the city. The club-houses, libraries, galleries, and semi-public conveniences for social life are blocks away.

We find working men organized into armies of producers because men of executive ability and business sagacity have found it to their interest thus to organize them. But these working men are not organized socially; although living in crowded tenement houses, they are living without corresponding social contact. The chaos is as great as it would be were they working in huge factories without foreman or superintendent. Their ideas  and resources are cramped. The desire for higher social pleasure is extinct. They have no share in the traditions and social energy which make for progress. Too often their only place of meeting is a saloon, their only host a bartender; a local demagogue forms their public opinion. Men of ability and refinement, of social power and university cultivation, stay away from them. Personally, I believe the men who lose most are those who thus stay away. But the paradox is here: when cultivated people do stay away from a certain portion of the population, when all social advantages are persistently withheld, it may be for years, the result itself is pointed at as a reason, is used as an argument, for the continued withholding (pp. 4–5).

Figure 5.1. It's Broke, We Must Fix It

The Age of Reform

In response to the negative consequences of these rapid structural and social changes, a social reform movement began after the Civil War and gained momentum near the end of the 19th century and into the early 20th century. The reform movement was instigated and promoted by members of the middle class who worried about the activities and morals of their own children, and were concerned about the impact of lower-class children's activities on middle-class children. The efforts of these reformers were aimed at improving working conditions, making cities more livable, and ensuring that children had appropriate places to play. Their efforts led to the promulgation of child labor laws, extension of the age for compulsory schooling, and the development of curfews. A number of youth-serving organizations were also created to provide character development and/or safe environments for children and youth and to serve the needs of either middle-class or working-class children in urban and rural communities. Many of these organizations are still prominent today.

Many of the reform efforts were based on changing attitudes toward children. Before the early to mid-1800s, childhood led almost directly into adulthood. If children went to school, they usually dropped out by the sixth grade, and even during the school year, they only attended if there was a slack period in the work they were required to do. Whether in rural settings or the cities, children in poorer families went to work as soon as they were strong enough to do physical labor, which was usually well before puberty. By the time these children were teenagers, those living in rural settings were expected to achieve a level of semi-independence through either working on the farm or being "farmed out" to other nearby farms or businesses in the city. Children of families living in the cities were also expected to begin working at an early age. In other cases, children needed to seek work because one or both of their parents were no longer living (Kett, 1977).

> Before the early to mid-1800s, childhood led almost directly into adulthood.

The presence of large numbers of working youth in the cities, both those who recently immigrated and those who came from rural settings, was not without its consequences. In factory settings, children were exposed to and potentially influenced by adults and their behavior. In addition, during their non-work hours, youth, especially boys, were exposed to street life and to adults who were engaged in drinking, gambling, and other licentious behaviors. Girls employed in the factories often spent their evenings at the dance halls, which many believed would lead to prostitution and out-of-wedlock child bearing.

Many lower class parents condoned their children's life on the streets as a means of supplementing family income. In New York, for example, boys might be involved in huckstering, scavenging, peddling, errand running, bootblacking (shoe shining), horseholding, and newspaper selling (Stansell, 1987). Most of these endeavors had the potential to lead children into contact with adults of questionable character. In addition, some children had no choice but to take on these jobs as the streets were often the only refuge for youth whose parents had died or they were on their own because they had moved alone from the country to the city (Halpren, 2002).

Addams felt that the widespread availability of urban pleasures was having a particularly negative impact on youth. In *The Spirit of Youth and the City Streets*, Addams (1972) wrote that for boys:

> It is nothing short of cruelty to over-stimulate his senses as does the modern city. This period is difficult everywhere but it seems at times as if the great city almost deliberately increases it perils. The newly awakened senses are appealed to by all that is gaudy and sensual. (p. 27)

The increased involvement of youth in immoral and illegal behaviors led to efforts by social reformers to deal with the "boy and/or girl problem," although most of the initial efforts were aimed at boys.

> Lads from fourteen to twenty-one are the busiest instigators, the most active abettors, and the most daring perpetrators of offenses against the peace and good order of society. In tumults, street fights, and riotous assemblies, in resistance to authority and contempt for law, they generally take the lead. (Brace, 1852, p. 812)

While many middle-class girls became teachers and tenders of shops, unmarried working-class girls, especially immigrants, were usually employed in the factories. Reformers expressed concern with the increased frequency of out-of-wedlock births, divorce, venereal disease, illegitimacy, and prostitution among this segment of the youth population. They attributed these increases to girls having their own money and to girls' involvement in non-work discretionary-time activities in the community. They also felt that work environments subjected young women to the untoward advances of fellow workers and supervisors (what today we might call sexual harassment). Dance halls, movies, and other forms of free-time outlets were also seen as contributing to girls' sexual awakening and misconduct (sometimes leading to pregnancy). Adolescent females who had migrated from rural areas were thought to be particularly at risk due to their sheltered upbringing and lack of prior exposure to city life. As noted by Addams (1972): "As farmers' daughters, they were strong and capable of taking care of themselves in an environment they understood," but once a part of city life, she was "in constant danger…as every effort is made to demoralize her completely" (p. 150).

Reformers such as Rev. Joseph Tukerman (a Unitarian minister who worked with the poor in Boston), Robert M. Hartley (founder of the New York Association for Improving the Condition of the Poor), Charles Loring Brace (founder of the New York Children's Aid Society), and Josephine Shaw Lowell (a leader in the New York Charity Organization Society) adopted the Victorian view of street life as the antithesis of home and family being valued as the central institutions leading to a moral life (Schwartz, 2000). Middle-class families viewed children on the streets as a sign of parental neglect or lack of adult supervision, and a failure to promote virtuous behavior (including

diligence, sobriety, and thrift vs. indolence, intemperance, and improvidence). Thus, they felt that bettering oneself and one's children and leading a virtuous life was a matter of personal responsibility.

Other reformers blamed urban problems on structural issues, including lack of opportunity, low wages, inadequate housing, and language difficulties (Schwartz, 2000). True (1914) studied the lives of 65 teens and placed much of the responsibility for youthful indiscretions with the community. His comments regarding a group of working-class girls, aged 14 to 18, from the tenements on the West Side of New York are representative of the views of many of the reformers (True, 1914):

> They have been brought up from babyhood in these blocks. Born in the crowded, dark tenement house they had had for a nursery the crowded sidewalk, and for a playground, the street. They had gone to the nearest school and from there to work in the nearest factory. They had seen the West Side, breathed the West Side, fed on the West Side for fourteen years or more, and had built up their adolescent ideals of the same forlorn material. That they had succumbed to unwholesome influences does not prove them to have been peculiarly weak or susceptible. Nor does it prove that their parents had been culpably delinquent in their duties. Conditions of living in the crowded city have tended to loosen the family bond, and the powerful force of neighborhood influence cannot be adequately combated by parental authority alone. The community must assume the responsibility for the environment of its least protected members. (p. 16)

The reformers argued that the failure to demonstrate virtuous behavior was not the primary reason that individuals were and remained poor. They noted that for the poor, the laissez-faire market did not appear to reward virtuous behavior (and among the rich, nonvirtuous behavior did not often lead to poverty). They saw the poor as already essentially virtuous, but still poor. They also recognized that the vast majority of the poor wanted to improve their lot (Schwartz, 2000).

Nevertheless, most members of the working class were not looking for a handout or a free ride. Despite applying themselves to work and avoiding vice, there was little economic reward for their hard work and good behavior. Thus, virtuous behavior was threatened by societal conditions and poverty. Much of the poverty could be ascribed to "unemployment, overwork, old age, or industrial accidents" (Schwartz, 2000, p. 102).

Addams (1972) even argued that structural reforms would increase virtuous behavior. For example, women involved in prostitution were viewed as virtuous having no other way to make money if unemployed or employed at wages below a reasonable level of subsistence. Social reformers' goals were to keep lower-class children from working in unsafe factories or being involved in street life, by substituting compulsory school attendance and involvement in wholesome non-school and non-work time activities.

Middle-class families were also worried about the structural changes taking place in the cities. In the larger cities, the middle class sought to make boys strong and virtuous to prepare them for business and professional success. In the smaller towns, the middle class also felt threatened by what was occurring in the larger cities and sought to preserve small-town values. As a result, middle-class parents undertook efforts to protect their children from working-class and urban influences by creating separate youth-serving organizations and focusing attention on character building to ensure that their children would grow up with the right values

> ## Virtuous behavior was threatened by societal conditions and poverty.

and thus preserve their middle-class standing (Macleod, 1983, p. xvi). Most of the early efforts were drop-in centers where children could come and go as they wished and "any youngster who refrained from tearing up the place was welcome" (MacLeod, 1983, p. 66).

The Creation of Adolescence

The reformers' efforts resulted in the "creation" of a period of called "adolescence" that would come between childhood and adulthood. They saw this period as an opportunity for young people to avoid some of the negative influences of city life and develop the skills necessary to become fully functioning adults (Kett, 1977). For educators, psychologists, and leading thinkers of the time, extending dependence or semi-independence further into the teenage (adolescent) years was thought to be necessary to develop fully the capacity of children to grow into fully functioning adults.

The word *adolescence* was used infrequently until the late 1800s, but became institutionalized with the publication in 1904 of G. Stanley Hall's two-volume, *Adolescence, its Psychology and its Relations to Physiology, Anthropology, Sociology, Sex, Crime, Religion and Education*. The creation of a distinct stage of adolescence recognized that by age 11 or 12, children had moved beyond childhood but had not yet achieved adult status. Hall saw adolescence as "a new birth, a wiping clean of the slate of childhood" (Kett, 1977, p. 217), but also a time of "storm and stress" due to the onset of puberty and young people being suspended between the worlds of childhood and adulthood. In marking adolescence as a separate stage, Hall and the reformers identified a period that would be dominated by school dependence rather than independence and work.

Experiencing adolescence was increasingly seen as a necessity to enable young people to make the transition to adulthood. Interestingly, Hall believed that if children did not naturally go through this stage, they should be forced through it. Hall, like many others of his time, saw urban life and industrialization as hostile to an adolescent's normal course of development, since it encouraged precocity (i.e., children being exposed to circumstances that forced or enabled them to grow up too quickly).

Hall advocated a balance of "freedom and control," recognizing that adolescents needed the time and opportunity to develop their full potential and the necessity of helping channel youth through this difficult period by avoiding deviant and antisocial behavior. Hall also advocated making the city more like the country, with the inclusion of nature trips, playgrounds, and sports as distractions from the negative opportunities available on the streets (Kett, 1977, p. 219).

> Experiencing adolescence was increasingly seen as a necessity to enable young people to make the transition to adulthood.

Controlling boys' time was deemed particularly necessary as they were seen as vulnerable, awkward, and easily misguided. In general, "young people stood less in need of earnest advice than of the artful manipulation of their environment" (Kett, 1977, p. 6). This led to an "ideology of protection," which included state and other organizational interventions to encourage the appropriate growth of adolescents into socially acceptable adults (Acland, 1995), including the following:

- Removing children from the workplace by implementing child labor laws designed to decrease the types of work children could do and the hours they could be employed
- Reforming education and extending the period over which it would be compulsory
- Undertaking efforts to keep children off the streets and at home late in the evening
- Creating a juvenile court system
- Organizing the spare-time activities of middle-class boys and girls through adult-sponsored youth organizations

In the following sections we will discuss each of these interventions.

Removing Children from the Workplace

Efforts began in the late 1800s to institute child labor laws designed both to increase the age at which children could begin working and to control the kinds of work that young people could do. Prior to the institution of these laws, it was not uncommon for children to be employed for long hours in repetitive factory jobs under poor working conditions. At night, children often served as newsies, bootblacks, peddlers, and messengers (for both legal and illegal enterprises). Night work led to boys (mainly) spending their evenings without adult supervision, but with a ready source of earned funds available to partake of "urban pleasures." Middle-class parents worried that their children would learn about sex, smoking, gambling, swearing, and drinking if they had too much interaction with lower- or working-class boys (Baldwin, 2002).

These concerns led to laws regulating the permissible hours for boys and girls to engage in the street trades, controlled the types of work children could undertake in the factories, and removed many children and young adolescents from the labor market altogether. However, it was not enough to keep children and adolescents from unacceptable work and unsavory contact with adults; other activities for them to do needed to be provided.

Extending Education

Efforts were made to extend the period of education beyond grades 6 or 8, although for many poorer and immigrant youth, they were lucky if they stayed in school that long. Extended schooling was intended to produce a more educated person, but also served to delay when youth could enter the workforce.

High school was created to extend educational opportunities beyond grade 8, and over time, the educational structure became more like the one we see today: six years of elementary school, three years of middle school, and three years of high school. This structure institutionalized the separation of children into different groups based on their stage of development. Attending school also was considered a way to Americanize and control immigrant children, and decrease the amount of time available for them to get into trouble (Sommerville, 1982, p. 196).

Attending school was considered a way to Americanize and control immigrant children …

Compulsory education laws were developed in Massachusetts as early as 1852, followed by Nevada (1873), Kansas (1874), and New York (1874). Laws usually required school attendance beginning from age 6 or 7 through age 16 (State Compulsory School Attendance Laws, 2004). Compulsory education laws worked in tandem with child labor laws to curtail the uncontrolled hours available for youth to work or be involved in "unacceptable" activities. In accordance with this, school non-attendance was increasingly seen as deviant and habitual truants could be sent to reform schools to keep them off the streets.

Implementing Juvenile Curfews

Efforts were also made to implement juvenile curfews as a means of controlling the street time of adolescents. These efforts began mainly in smaller cities in Canada and then spread to smaller then larger cities in the United States. Curfews were designed to prevent children, under 15 in most cases, from loitering on the street late at night without adult supervision. Alexander Hogeland (1884) was one of the leaders of this movement and made a case for curfews in his book, *Ten Years Among the Newsboys*. Newsies were primarily boys, usually between ages 8 and 15, who lived on the streets, maybe going to school during the day, but making their living selling newspapers for a penny a piece. They were mostly immigrants from impoverished families. As many as 30,000 deserted kids, many of whom became newsies, were thought to be living on the streets of New York in the late 1800s, in most cases because their parents had died or their parents could not afford to care for them at home. Efforts were begun as early as 1853 to help the newsies when Charles Loring Brace set up a newsboys' lodging home in New York City (Adoption History Project, 2004). He also developed a program, the orphan trains, which exported boys and girls to live in the country (See Figure 5.2).

One solution to the street problem was the institution of "placing-out" programs, which involved moving wayward lower-class children to foster homes in rural areas. This movement was instigated by the Children's Aid Society of New York, under the leadership of Rev. Charles Brace. The New York Foundling Hospital also sent children west.

The orphan trains were also intended to supplement the labor pool in rural areas while removing some of the pressures for employment in the cities. However, they were mainly aimed at removing children from the streets and away from what were perceived as inadequate home environments to more stable homes with more caring adults.

Between 1854 and 1930, between 150,000 and 200,000 children were sent by train from New York to be adopted or placed in families in states as far away as Nebraska and Kansas. True orphans were sent on the trains, but children who had been "turned loose" by parents who could not care for them due to poverty were also sent. Most were children from families who were struggling to make a living in New York after having immigrated to the United States in the mid-to-late nineteenth century (Stansell, 1987, p. 313).

Two methods were used to adopt children. One method used by the Children's Aid society put children (some as old as 14) on trains with placing agents. Advance notices of "Homes Wanted for Orphans" were placed in newspapers in towns along the route. When the children arrived, prospective families inspected them, and if a local organizing committee and the placement agent agreed, children were "adopted" by the local family. Siblings did not have to be adopted by the

Figure 5.2. The Orphan Trains: Exporting Children and Youth to the Country (cont.)

same family. The agent usually made return visits to the towns to check on the welfare of the children. It was expected that children would be treated like any other member of the family and not as indentured servants.

The other method of placing children involved Catholic families applying in advance to the New York Foundling Hospital for a particular kind of child (e.g., a 2-year-old, blue-eyed, blond-haired girl). The Sisters of Charity of St. Vincent de Paul then matched requests with available children, some of whom had been abandoned in a cradle on the front porch of the Hospital. Local priests in the Midwest and the South served as the liaisons between the Hospital and the prospective families.

With the start of the Great Depression, the orphan trains ended. Prospective families found it more difficult to add another child, and other means, such as foster home placement, were developed to deal with orphaned or abandoned children (DiPasquale, 2002).

Figure 5.2. (cont.) **The Orphan Trains**

Curfews were more popular in smaller cities; however, they were not supported unanimously in any setting. An 1898 *New York Times* editorial ridiculed those who advocated curfews:

> Much literature from the "curfew" cranks has reached this office, and enough of it was read to justify its wholesale disposition in—or around—convenient waste baskets. The documents sent gave enough evidence that by shutting children up in the house at nightfall juvenile crimes and misdemeanors had been made less numerous in several towns, but what of the effect? Even more effect in this direction would be produced by cutting the throats of everybody under age. (Untitled Editorial, *New York Times,* July 10, 1898)

Curfews were mostly implemented when a link could be made between adopting a curfew and decreased crime. The legacy of these efforts in the 1990s is that 80% of American cities with a population greater than 30,000 now have some form of juvenile curfew law (Baldwin, 2002, p. 605).

Creating Juvenile Courts

Over time, there also was movement away from treating youth as adults when they committed a crime. Thus, juvenile courts were developed, beginning with Illinois in 1899 (Center on Juvenile and Criminal Justice, n.d.). In addition, youth were often prohibited from enjoying some of the same rights as adults (e.g., the establishment of a legal drinking age). Adolescence thus became a legal as well as a social category (Kett, 1977).

Reformers wrestled with many of the age-related status issues we still struggle with today, including the appropriate age when a young person can drink, drive, vote, register for the military, run for office, leave public school, or be tried as an adult. Decisions about the appropriate age to permit involvement in each of these activities reflect the need to balance the tension between youths' responsibilities for their own actions and society's responsibility to protect young people.

Instead of encouraging the popular attitude that "boys will be boys," wayward boys' activities, in particular, were more likely to be treated as delinquent acts that needed to be punished (Breckinridge & Abbott, 1912). Interestingly, juvenile courts treated "wayward" girls more harshly and differently than misbehaving boys. "Girls who transgressed were much more likely to be removed from their homes, given stricter sentences, and longer probationary periods. The courts frequently sentenced young women to reformatories or training schools. These institutions sought to reform wayward females through resocialization in traditional female codes of conduct and often detained girls until they were of a marriageable age of 21 or older" (Abrams, 2000, p. 440).

> Girls who transgressed were much more likely to be removed from their homes, given stricter sentences, and longer probationary periods.

In the 1840s, the courts began to experiment with probation for young offenders in an effort to keep them out of jail. However, in some cases, even minor offenders were brought under the control or supervision of the courts, thus extending control over their behavior. For example, beginning in the early 1800s, efforts were made to segregate juvenile offenders and potential juvenile offenders from adults. The New

York House of Refuge, founded as early as 1825, was among the first juvenile facilities. Besides removing children from the streets, these institutions attempted to rehabilitate them and eventually return them to city life (Sommerville, 1982).

Reform schools were developed beginning in the mid-1800s for both boys and girls. These were usually in the country, state supported, and aimed at the reformation of juvenile offenders as opposed to being places of refuge for street children. Unfortunately, reform schools became dumping grounds for teenage troublemakers and felons and those characterized by "vagrancy and stubbornness" (Kett, 1977, p. 132).

This chapter focused on the forces at work in society from the mid- to late 1800s and into the early 1900s that set the stage for the development of a number of the prominent youth-serving organizations that still exist today. Although some of these organizations have altered their missions in keeping with current national youth development practices, most have remained true to their original goals, but may go about meeting these goals in different ways than they did when originally created. The next chapter outlines specific details regarding the founding and current status of some of these organizations.

Discussion Questions

1. What was the role of industrialization, immigration and migration, and urbanization on the way that society viewed young people? What are the major forces in society today that are changing the way society views young people?
2. The chapter makes the case that adolescence is an artificial time period between childhood and adulthood. What forces do you see operating in society today that continue to reinforce the existence of the time period we call adolescence?
3. In order to reinforce and perpetuate adolescence, the reformers at the end of the 19th century undertook particular actions regarding schooling and social control of adolescent behavior. Think of laws, rules, and societal perspectives operative today that have been put in place that help keep young people from assuming adult roles. (Hint, think about all of the laws related to what young people can do or not do before they turn 18 or 21). Are there any of these laws you think should be changed? Why or why not?
4. How was your life advantaged or disadvantaged by the laws and rules that define when adolescents are considered adults?

Assignment

The reformers of the late 19th and early 20th century played an important role in bringing about social change. From the following list, pick an individual and describe in one page his or her contribution to improving living and working conditions for children, youth, and families. There are other individuals who could be added to this list. Feel free to pick one...but make sure to clear the choice with your instructor first.

Jane Addams, Alexander Hodeland, Jacob Riis, Charles Loring Brace, Sojourner Truth, Dorothy Dix, Horace Mann, Elizabeth Cady Stanton, Susan B. Anthony, W. E. B. Du Bois, John Muir, Ida B. Wells, Florence Kelley, Lewis Hine, Booker T. Washington.

References

Abrams, L. S. (2000). Guardians of virtue: The social reformers and the "girl problem," 1890-1920. *Social Service Review, 74*(3), 436–452.

Acland, C. R. (1995). *Youth, murder, spectacle: The cultural politics of "youth in crisis."* Boulder, CO: Westview Press.

Addams, J. (1969). *Philanthropy and social progress: Seven essays.* Freeport, NY: Books for Libraries Press.

Addams, J. (1972). *The spirit of youth and the city streets.* Reprint of the 1909 ed. Urbana, IL: University of Illinois Press.

Baldwin, P. C. (2002). "Nocturnal habits and dark wisdom": The American response to children in the streets at night, 1880-1930. *Journal of Social History, 35*(3), 593–611.

Brace, C. L. (October 15, 1852). Youthful depravity, home influences. *Common School Journal, 4*(20), 812–814.

Breckinridge, J., & Abbott, E. (1912). *The delinquent child and the home.* New York, NY: Russell Sage Foundation Charities Publication Committee.

Center on Juvenile and Criminal Justice (n.d.). Juvenile justice history. Retrieved from http://www.cjcj.org/education1/juvenile-justice-history.html

DiPasquale, C. (2002). A history of the Orphan Train. Retrieved from http://www.kancoll.org/articles/orphans/or_hist.htm

Gibson, C. (1998). *Population of the 100 largest cities and other urban places in the United States: 1790 to 1990.* Working Paper No. 27. Washington, DC: Population Division, U.S. Bureau of the Census. Retrieved from https://www.census.gov/population/www/documentation/twps0027/twps0027.html

Hall, G. S. (1904). Adolescence, its psychology and its relations to physiology, anthropology, sociology, sex, crime, religion and education. New York, NY: D. Appleton and Company.

Halpren, R. (2002). A different kind of child development institution: The history of after-school programs for low-income children. *Teachers College Record, 104*(2), 178–211.

Hogeland, A. (1884). *Ten years among the newsboys* (5th ed.). Louisville, KY: Norton and Co.

Infoplease (n.d.). State compulsory school attendance laws. Retrieved from http://www.infoplease.com/ipa/A0112617.html

Kett, J. F. (1977). *Rites of passage: adolescence in America 1790 to the present.* New York, NY: Basic Books.

Library of Congress. (n.d.). Rise of industrial America, 1876-1900: City life in the late 19th century. Retrieved from http://www.loc.gov/teachers/classroommaterials/presentationsandactivities/presentations/timeline/riseind/city/

Macleod, D. I. (1983). *Building character in the American boy: The Boy Scouts, YMCA, and their forerunners, 1870-1900.* Madison, WI: Wisconsin University Press.

Nasaw, D. (1985). *Children of the city: At work and at play.* Garden City, NY: Anchor/Doubleday.

Schwartz, J. (2000). *Fighting poverty with virtue: Moral reform and America's poor, 1825–2000.* Bloomington, IN: Indiana University Press.

Sommerville, C. J. (1982). *The rise and fall of childhood.* Volume 140, Sage Library of Social Research. Beverly Hills, CA: Sage Publications.

Stansell, C. (1987). *City of women: Sex and class in New York: 1789-1860.* Urbana, IL: University of Illinois Press.

The Adoption History Project. (n.d.). Charles Loring Brace. Retrieved from http://darkwing.uoregon.edu/~adoption/people/brace.html

True, R. S. (1914). *Boyhood and lawlessness: The neglected girl.* New York, NY: Survey Associates.

Untitled Editorial. (July 10, 1898). *New York Times*, p. 16.

Chapter 6

Youth-Serving Organizations

Then and Now

Peter A. Witt

In this chapter, you will read about some of the prominent youth-serving organizations, including why each was created and the programs and services they currently offer. This chapter will enable you to understand more fully the current philosophies and practices of these organizations and some of their contributions to youth development.

The Need for Youth Organizations

Based on the critical social issues that existed at the end of the 19th and early 20th centuries, a number of organizations designed to organize young people's out-of-school time were developed. Different organizations were created to serve individuals from different social classes and different locations (e.g., urban, small town, farm communities), including the following:

- **Boys Clubs,** and eventually playgrounds, were developed to serve the needs of lower-class and immigrant children as well as adolescents in large urban centers. Reformers could have tried to either rid the city of its vices and dangers or "quarantine" the young by shielding and protecting them from the negative influences of the city. They chose the latter, since the former seemed virtually impossible (Nasaw, 1985). Therefore, efforts were often aimed at serving large numbers in a single building or space. Due to the high volume of youth served, Boys Clubs were labeled as "mass clubs."

- **The YWCA, YMCA, Camp Fire Girls, and Girl Guides** (the precursor to the Girl Scouts) were developed to serve middle-class youth. Their primary goals were to create and/or reinforce middle-class values by keeping middle-class youth separate from those of the lower class. These organizations also existed to help develop young people's physical and moral fitness.
- **Settlement houses** were created in poor or immigrant neighborhoods and were usually staffed by college students. The goal was to create a community that could improve the economic prospects of community residents. In the United States, settlement houses were active in immigrant communities in efforts to create legislation providing for juvenile courts, mothers' pensions, workers' compensation, and the regulation of child labor.
- **4-H** began due to the interest of farm families to reinforce rural family values, attachment to the land, and the agricultural skills that characterized their own lives by providing activities for children in farm and rural settings. Organized as part of the Land Grant University system, 4-H Clubs were developed in every state, first for boys, then for girls.
- **Playgrounds** were established in densely populated urban areas to provide places for children to play, but just as importantly to keep them from being on the streets. Most cities lacked safe places for children to play, and being on the street was often dangerous and subjected children to potentially negative influences.

In the following sections, you will read about some of these youth-serving organizations. To facilitate understanding, organizations are divided into those originally intended to serve boys, those intended to serve girls, and those designed to serve both.

Boys Work

Boys Clubs (Now Boys & Girls Clubs of America)

In 1860, a Boys Club was created by female volunteers at a Congregational church in the slums of Hartford, Connecticut. The first official Boys Club, however, opened in New York in 1876, and featured both meeting spaces and a gymnasium. Then in 1906, the Federated Boys Clubs was formed with the purpose of bringing together 74 individual Boys Clubs, the majority of which were in New England or the Middle Atlantic states.

The first Boys Clubs attempted to keep male children and young adolescents from entering a life of crime, but over time the organization evolved to serve older adolescents as well. Many of the early clubs served street orphans and doubled as homeless shelters. Wealthy philanthropists, such as railroad magnet E. H. Harriman, supported the development of clubs because they saw their potential to control the behavior of lower class and street boys. They also saw the club's potential to create good citizens and to Americanize participants, while also increasing working-class productivity in the work place. While proselytizing was a feature of the early Boys Clubs, this was quickly dropped not only because boys tended to shy away from clubs with too much religious content but also because children came from a variety of religious backgrounds (Macleod, 1983).

Attendance at the clubs was voluntary and usually on a drop-in basis, with most clubs designed to serve large numbers of boys. Some of the "mass clubs" were so large that their primary emphasis was keeping children off the streets rather than providing meaningful contact with adults. However, even with this goal, clubs still only served a small proportion of youth in a given area of the city. The mass clubs contrasted to the group clubs often run by settlement houses. According to one Boys Club worker,

> ...any boy in the city could be admitted to the club. The workers consisted of a doorkeeper, librarian, and superintendent. During the club session, the superintendent was obliged to walk about the rooms as a moral policeman. Occasionally visitors from the various churches came to assist by playing games with the boys. Later, a few industrial classes, such as carpentry, clay-modeling, word-carving, cobbling, typesetting, and other trades, were added. A penny savings bank was a leading feature of this sort of club, and occasional entertainments. Finally, with this plan, it is possible to have an exceedingly large membership. This itself is a strong feature in the minds of many. Large figures look prosperous in a report. (quoted in Forbush, 1913, p. 68)

Efforts were made to enroll boys before their teens, to keep them busy, and build habits and interests that might later prevent them from getting into trouble on the streets (Macleod, 1983, p. 66). In a word, prevention was the major purpose of the early clubs, as opposed to the character-building agendas of organizations such as the Boy Scouts and YMCA. Over time, however, the Boys Club mission shifted to attracting working-class and working boys instead of mainly street boys.

Leaders in the clubs put emphasis on activities that had the potential to attract boys as long as they obeyed the rules. The leader of a club acted only as a moral police officer and mainly was responsible for breaking up fights and preventing equipment thefts. Thus, positive contacts with adults were often lacking. This problem was compounded because in many cases boys preferred to be on their own without having adults telling them what to do, and therefore clubs were constantly fighting to keep attendance numbers up (Nasaw, 1985).

> In a word, prevention was the major purpose of the early clubs ...

By 1911, there were 110 Boys Clubs in the United States with a combined enrollment of 108,063 youth. Most clubs rented the space they occupied, but some, with funds donated from local businessmen, bought or built their own buildings. For example, a five-story building built for the exclusive use of the Albany Boys Club in 1911 was funded by a wealthy local businessman (Nasaw, 1985).

Boys and Girls Clubs Today

Since its inception in the late 1800s, the role of Boys Clubs has changed considerably, as they now embrace a greater focus on the positive youth development of both boys and girls of all socioeconomic classes. However, some things have remained consistent with the clubs. For example, most are still located in poorer neighborhoods, many still strive to keep children off the streets, and clubs still tend to serve large numbers of individuals.

In 1956, the Boys Clubs of America celebrated its 50th anniversary and received a United States Congressional Charter. In 1990, to recognize the fact that girls also participated in programs, the national organization's name was changed to Boys & Girls Clubs of America (BGCA). In 2017, the organization served over 4 million boys and girls at over 4,300 club locations in all 50 states, Puerto Rico, the Virgin Islands, and domestic and international military bases.

Boys & Girls Clubs provide the following:

- Safe places to play, laugh, discover, and learn during out-of-school time, including the summer
- Life-changing programs that help youth advance in three key outcome areas: academic success, good character and citizenship, and healthy lifestyles
- Opportunities to build new skills so that kids can succeed and receive recognition for personal accomplishments
- Ongoing, supportive relationships with caring adults and friends that foster a sense of belonging, responsibility, civility, and civic engagement (Boys & Girls Clubs of America, 2015)

Besides offering opportunities for open recreation, the clubs also offer opportunities for youth to participate in a variety of youth development programs. The organization has been successful in getting a number of these programs sponsored by major national companies. The following are four examples of Boys & Girls Clubs national programs (Boys & Girls Clubs of America, 2004a):

- **Keystone Clubs** are the Boys & Girls Club movement's ultimate teen program for youth ages 14 to 18. This unique program provides leadership development opportunities for youth to participate in activities, both in and out of the Club, in three focus areas: academic success, career preparation, and community service. With the guidance of an adult advisor, Keystone Clubs aim to impact teens, their Club, and local communities in a positive manner. BGCA hosts an annual National Keystone Conference for Boys & Girls Club teens that brings together members from all across the globe.

- **Power Hour: Making Minutes Count** is a comprehensive homework help and tutoring program that provides Club professionals with the strategies, activities, resources, and information to create an engaging homework help and tutoring program designed to raise the academic proficiency of Club members aged 6 to 18.

- **SMART Moves (Skills Mastery and Resistance Training)** is a prevention/education program that addresses the problems of drug and alcohol use and premature sexual activity among youth. The program uses a team approach that involves Club staff, peer leaders, parents, and community representatives. Young people aged 6 to 15 engage in discussion and role-playing, practicing resilience and refusal skills, developing assertiveness, strengthening decision-making skills, and analyzing media and peer influence. The ultimate goal is to promote abstinence from substance abuse and adolescent sexual involvement through the practice of responsible behavior.

- **Fitness Authority** promotes fitness in all youth through fun, engaging weekly activities and an annual competition with local, regional and national levels. The program features 12 weekly sessions for each of three age groups. Club members play games and try new sports, and their fitness levels are measured with simple tests of endurance, flexibility, and strength.

Boy Scouts

Lord Robert Baden-Powell, a British general who served in India and later in South Africa, founded the Boy Scouts in England in 1908. Baden-Powell was dismayed that many of his soldiers did not have basic first aid or elementary survival skills. Therefore, he developed scouting as a "remedy to Britain's moral, physical, and military weakness," a problem considered to be a threat to the British Empire.

Using small group instruction, competition, and games, Baden-Powell began training his men in the skills necessary for scouting (e.g., following a trail, giving directions, recognizing danger signs, finding food and water). He wrote *Aids to Scouting*

The Boy Scouts sought to be a "character factory" and an instrument of "social control" ...

(1899), which outlined the instructional methods he used. He eventually rewrote this book to make it more appealing to boys and scout patrols (*Scouting for Boys*, 1908); and because of these promotional efforts, Boy Scout troops sprang up all over England. Then, because of interest among girls, Baden-Powell's sister, Agnes, formed the Girl Guides.

The Boy Scouts was promoted by the middle class and quickly became popular in England. The organization did not adopt any specific church affiliation, but sought to be a "character factory" and an instrument of "social control" by inculcating the habits of obedience, cleanliness, temperance, and loyalty that would best guarantee the perpetuation of the middle class, masculinity, economic efficiency, and ultimately the survival of the British Empire (Rosenthal, 1986, pp. 6–7).

In 1910, William D. Boyce, a Chicago entrepreneur and philanthropist, imported the scouting concept to the United States (see The Unknown Boy Scout). Although there were already several other loosely structured outdoor-oriented youth organizations in the United States, (some using the name "Boy Scout" and some using other names, e.g., Woodcraft Indians created by Ernest Thompson Seton; Sons of Daniel Boone founded by Daniel Beard), Boyce provided needed structure and organization to these

The Unknown Boy Scout (Boy Scouts of America, 2017)

William D. Boyce, a Chicago newspaper publisher, was said to be visiting London when he became lost in the fog. Out of the fog a boy appeared who offered to lead him to his destination. Successfully arriving where he wanted to go, Boyce offered to tip the boy, but he refused, saying that he could accept no money for his good deed. Intrigued, Boyce asked the boy about scouting and eventually the boy took him to Baden-Powell's office and disappeared into the fog. Boyce's conversations with Baden-Powell led him to promote scouting in the United States. The boy was never identified, but a statue is erected in honor of the "Unknown Scout" in London. In the British Scout Training Center at Gilwell Park, England, Scouts from the United States erected a statue of an American Buffalo in honor of this unknown scout.

Source: Scoutingnewsroom.org

endeavors, and recruited key youth professionals to design and operate the programs. He also provided much of the start-up funding.

On February 8, 1910, Boyce filed incorporation papers for the Boy Scouts of America (BSA) in the District of Columbia. Seton merged his Woodcraft Indians with the new organization and became the BSA's first Chief Scout (1910 to 1916). The purpose of the organization was

> …to promote, through organization, and cooperation with other agencies, the ability of boys to do things for themselves and others, to train them in Scoutcraft, and patriotism, courage, self-reliance, and kindred virtues, using the methods which are in common use by Boy Scouts. (Boy Scouts of America, 2015, p. 3)

The Boy Scouts tried to extend boyhood and to distract youth from the problems of adolescence. For example, Boy Scouts intended to short circuit young boys' sexual urges by encouraging them to participate in vigorous exercise and by keeping them working toward goals (e.g., merit badges, which mostly dealt with rural-oriented skills and interests). However, as the original efforts were aimed at young adolescents, it was often hard to keep them involved as they got older. In addition, it was thought that involving younger boys would drive out the older ones (Robinson, 1902).

Boy Scouts had its greatest presence in the North and Midwest. However, the term "Boy" Scouts was problematic in the South. Even in the North and Midwest, many older adolescents were not attracted to the scouts due to the uniforms.

Boy Scouts Today

Today, BSA provides young people with character-building programs that foster ethical decision-making skills while engaging in fun outdoor activities with friends and adult leaders. More than 100,000 Scouting units are owned and operated by chartered organizations. Of these, approximately 70% are chartered to faith-based organizations (e.g., Catholic Church, United Methodist Church), 22% of all units are chartered to civic organizations (e.g., Elks Lodges, Kiwanis International), and nearly 8% of all units are chartered to educational organizations (Boy Scouts of America, 2017a).

> **The Boy Scout Pledge**
> On my honor I will do my best
> To do my duty to God and my country
> and to obey the Scout Law;
> To help other people at all times;
> To keep myself physically strong, mentally awake, and morally straight.

BSA offers five areas of programming:

- **Cub Scouts** serves boys 7 to 10 years old. Boys are organized into packs and dens. Volunteer leaders help teach activities that promote citizenship and develop physical fitness.
- **Boy Scouts** is for boys 11 to 17 years old. Activities are designed to build character, citizenship, and personal fitness through activities that emphasize learning by doing. The highest award possible is becoming an Eagle Scout. A Scoutmaster leads each troop.
- **Venturing** serves youth from 14 to 21 years old. The program provides positive youth-led experiences with an emphasis on adventure, leadership, personal growth, and service to prepare young people to become responsible and caring adults.
- **Sea Scouts** serves both boys and girls from 14 to 21 years old. The program seeks to build character through high-adventure military and maritime career exploration. Activities promote water safety, boating skills, outdoor activities, and social interactions.
- **Exploring** provides males and females aged 10 to 20 the opportunity to learn about career fields, network with business leaders, and gain hands-on experience. (Boy Scouts of America, 2017b)

In the first decade of the 21st century, the Boy Scouts faced considerable internal turmoil over policies that banned openly gay individuals from being members. After considerable debate, on May 23, 2013, the voting members of the National Council lifted the ban and openly gay individuals were allowed to join the Boy Scouts. It is highly probable that gay individuals had been members before 2013, but the vote lifted the veil of secrecy.

In 2015, the Boy Scouts took the further step of removing all restrictions on sexual orientation for adult leaders and association employees. However, the new policy states:

Chartered organizations continue to select their adult leaders and religious chartered organizations may continue to use religious beliefs as criteria for selecting adult leaders, including matters of sexuality. This change allows Scouting's members and parents to select local units, chartered to organizations with similar beliefs, that best meet the needs of their families. This change also allows religious chartered organizations to choose adult volunteer leaders whose beliefs are consistent with their own. (Boy Scouts of America, 2015a)

In 2017, the Scouts went even further when the Boy Scouts began accepting members based on the gender listed on their application. This change paved the way for transgender boys to join the organization (Chokshi, 2017). In addition, in October 2017, the Boy Scouts announced plans to admit girls to full membership at all levels of Scouting. This step was taken for two reasons. First, there appears to be interest among girls to have full access to working their way through the different levels of Scouting and achieve Eagle Scout status. In addition, like most youth organizations, the Boy Scouts have experienced a decline in enrollment, and giving girls full status in the organization is one way to stem the decline. Of course, organizations like the Girls Scouts have reacted negatively to efforts by the Boy Scouts to recruit more girls. It will be interesting to see how all of this plays out over the coming years.

YMCA

In response to the unhealthy social conditions arising in the big cities due to the Industrial Revolution, the Young Men's Christian Association (YMCA) was founded in London, England, on June 6, 1844. The growth of the railroads and the centralization of commerce and industry brought many young rural men who needed jobs into cities such as London. George Williams and a group of fellow drapers (i.e., garment workers) organized the first YMCA with the goal of substituting Bible study and prayer for life on the streets (Marshfield Area YMCA, 2017).

By 1851, there were 24 YMCAs (also known as Ys) in Great Britain, with a combined membership of 2,700. The first YMCAs in North America were established in 1852, first in Montreal and then in Boston. In 1854, the first international convention was held in Paris. At that time, there were 397 Ys in seven nations.

> The Y's purpose (1866): "The improvement of the spiritual, mental, social, and physical condition of young men."

In the United States during the Civil War, YMCA membership shrunk to one third its size. Fifteen of the remaining northern Ys formed the U.S. Christian Commission to assist the troops and prisoners of war. Among other accomplishments, the YMCA gave more than one million Bibles to soldiers, and in doing so began a commitment to working with soldiers and sailors that continues to this day through the Armed Services YMCAs.

Four years after the end of the Civil War, there were over 600 Ys. The focus of these centers was on "saving souls" by spreading the Christian religion through saloon and street-corner preaching, distributing lists of Christian boarding houses, and providing lectures, libraries, and meeting halls. In 1866, the influential New York YMCA adopted a fourfold purpose: "The improvement of the spiritual, mental, social, and physical condition of young men" (Marshfield Area YMCA, 2017).

Many of the branches imposed an upper age limit on participation, usually around 40, but not an official lower age limit. However, up until the 1880s, younger boys (those less than 14 or 15 years) were generally excluded. Nevertheless, the YMCAs eventually started working with boys younger than 15, both because there was significant interest among younger boys and to help recruit boys to eventual membership in the YMCA as adults. This change led to the creation of Junior Departments, designed to work with younger boys and to act as a feeder system for programs for young men.

The focus of the YMCA shifted over time to exclusively meeting the needs of young working- and middle-class boys and men, rather than focusing on the poor like the Boys Clubs (MacLeod, 1983). In doing so, the goals of the YMCA became character formation and prevention of negative behaviors, rather than rescue and reformation. YMCA officials were worried that involving working-class and street boys would expose middle-class boys to negative influences (Macleod, 1983). Therefore, most programs charged a fee to discourage working-class and street boys from attending. They also sought to keep numbers smaller than the "mass" Boys Clubs to provide more individualized attention.

In response to growing concerns about the range of opportunities available for boys, Ys began offering exercise classes and organizing summer camps. Sports were increasingly seen as a means to promote middle-class values, such as the willingness to follow rules and strive for rewards. Thus, basketball was invented, along with other team activities such as volleyball (see Figure 6.1). Physical training became the main YMCA activity during the 1890s; while the religious training emphasis of the YMCAs remained, the main initial attraction for many boys was the opportunity to participate in recreation and physical activities. Together these elements (i.e., sports, religion, and recreation) formed the spirit, mind, and body triangle that is the symbol of YMCAs today.

At the request of Luther Gulick, James Naismith invented the game of **basketball** at the International YMCA Training School in December 1891. Gulick needed a game to occupy a class of incorrigibles—18 future YMCA directors who were more interested in rugby and football, and did not care for leapfrog, tumbling, and other activities they were forced to do during the winter. Gulick, obviously out of patience with the group, gave Naismith two weeks to come up with a game to occupy them.

William Morgan, an instructor at the Y who felt that basketball was too strenuous for businessmen, invented **volleyball** at the Holyoke YMCA (Massachusetts) in 1895.

Professional football began at a YMCA. In 1895, in Latrobe, Pennsylvania, John Brailer was paid $10 plus expenses by the local YMCA to replace the injured quarterback on their team. Years later, however, Pudge Heffelfinger claimed that he was secretly paid to play for the Allegheny Athletic Association in 1892. The NFL elected to go with Pudge's version of events.

Softball was given its name by Walter Hakanson of the Denver YMCA in 1926 at a meeting of the Colorado Amateur Softball Association (CASA), itself a result of YMCA staff efforts. Softball had been played for many years prior to 1926, under such names as kittenball and even sissyball.

Racquetball was invented in 1950 at the Greenwich, Connecticut, YMCA by Joe Sobek, a member who could not find other squash players of his caliber and who did not like handball. He tried paddleball and platform tennis and came up with the idea of using a strung racquet similar to a platform tennis paddle (not a sawed-off tennis racquet, as some say) to allow a greater variety of shots.

Figure 6.1. Sports Invented by the YMCA

YMCA Today

Today's YMCAs still pay considerable attention to the needs of children and youth; however, few Ys exist in poorer communities, and many Y programs charge a fee, although scholarships and financial assistance programs are available. There are approximately 2,700 YMCAs in about 10,000 communities across the United States. Together these organizations have about 20,000 full-time staff and utilize approximately 600,000 volunteers. The YMCA engages approximately nine million youth each year in the United States. (YMCA, 2017d).

YMCA youth programs work to nurture development from birth to career through programming, experiences and supports. Much of the Y's work is based on adoption of character development and assets-based approaches. The Y is active in providing youth programming in four areas (YMCA, 2016):

- **Child Care**—Safe, nurturing environments for children to learn, grow, and develop social skills, so parents can go to work knowing their kids are still with people who care about their development and well-being
- **Education and Leadership**—Knowledge, character development, guidance, and encouragement to help children learn and realize their potential
- **Swim, Sports, and Play**—Positive, fun activities that build physical and social skills, so children develop a lifetime appreciation for active living
- **Camp**—Exciting, safe communities for young people to explore the outdoors, build confidence, develop skills, and make lasting friendships and memories, so they can grow as individuals and leaders

Girls Work

Among the reformers, girls aroused less alarm than did boys, and thus work with girls began after clubs started working with boys, and was initially much less extensive. It was generally thought that girls made an easier transition from childhood to fulfilling adult expectations than boys. According to MacLeod (1983),

> They stayed a little longer in high school and a good deal longer in Sunday school. After classes each day, they mostly went straight home, whereas boys hung about on the streets. Consequently, by one contemporary tabulation, there were twenty times as many groups doing boys' work as girls' in 1910. (p. 51)

Girls work was heavily influenced by boys work, but differing expectations for each gender led to some differences in the way services were conceptualized and organized. Until about 1909, YWCAs did little work with girls under 16, but subsequently developed programs of athletics, outdoor life, literary studies, and domestic skills to meet the needs of older girls. Luther Gulick, who along with his wife founded the Camp Fire Girls, thought it was necessary to maintain sex differences because it would be "fundamentally evil" to copy Boy Scouting. Because girls must learn "to be womanly," the "domestic fire" became the group's symbol (MacLeod, 1983, p. 51).

Both boys and girls workers wanted all youth to be more physically active and both saw the value of achievement awards (e.g., merit badges). However, Girl Scouts and Camp Fire Girls (and the girls'-related elements of 4-H to be discussed later in this chapter) emphasized involvement in activities consistent with homemaking and volunteerism. According to one early writer,

> in adapting Boy Scouting to the psychology of the young girl, it had been recognized that boys like to be boys, while girls do not like to be girls. They are fundamentally little women, and the surest way to win their interest is to open to them the pursuits of women so modified as to insure to them the rewards of achievement. (Price, 1918, p. 367)

Girl Scouts

Juliette Gordon Low founded the Girl Scouts in United States in 1912. Low used her own funds to underwrite the development of the organization. (Low may have had the longest name in youth work: Juliette "Daisy" Magill Kinzie Gordon Low; extra points if you can remember this for an exam!). Juliette had married William Low, an Englishman, and lived in England and Scotland for a time. After William Low's death, Juliette traveled and settled in Paris, where she planned to study sculpture (Girl Scouts of the USA, 2004).

Based on the interest in scouting among girls in England, Sir Robert Baden-Powell's sister, Agnes, formed the Girl Guides in 1910. "Daisy," as Low was known, became involved in this new organization and moved back to Scotland to lead a Girl Guides troop. Soon after, she returned to her birthplace in Georgia to begin a troop in the carriage house behind her home. Daisy became a strong advocate of the Girl Scouts, and her promotional efforts led to the establishment of troops in many other cities. A national organization called the Girl Scouts was incorporated in 1915. The organization initially copied the uniform, handbook, and other basic principles from the British Girl Guides, but later changed these to fit the American character of the organization (Girl Scouts of the USA, 2004a).

Girl Scout Promise
On my honor, I will try to serve God and my country, to help people at all times, and to live by the Girl Scout Law.

Daisy was a firm believer in letting the girls run their own troops. Adults involved in the troops were advisers, not leaders. Over time, the Girl Scouts offered national training schools for leaders, and colleges and universities offered Girl Scout leadership training courses, with some universities offering scholarships for students who were Girl Scouts.

Girl Scouts Today

Today there are nearly 2.6 million Girl Scouts—1.8 million youth, members and 800,000 adult members. Girl scouting includes the following five levels:

- Daisies, grades K-1
- Brownies, grades 2-3
- Juniors, grades 4-5
- Cadettes, grades 6-8
- Seniors, grades 9-10
- Ambassadors, grades 11-12 (Girls Scouts of America, 2017a)

Daisies, Brownies, and Juniors earn petals and badges, join troops, hike and camp, and participate in the cookie-selling program. Beginning with the Cadette program, girls can also explore careers in science and technology, travel the world, discover nature, and take on projects that transform their communities (Girls Scouts of America, 2017b).

Girl scouting is a values-based organization, not a religious one, although the Girl Scout Promise includes the word God. However, on the adult membership form, it says, "When making the Girl Scout Promise, individual members may substitute wording appropriate to their own spiritual beliefs for the word 'God'" (Girl Scouts of America, 2017c).

> When making the Girl Scout Promise, individual members may substitute wording appropriate to their own spiritual beliefs for the word "God."

While the most visible program run by the Girl Scouts is the annual cookie sale fund-raiser (love those Thin Mints!), other programs are offered that help girls to develop leadership, financial literacy, and math, science, and technology skills. Girl Scout activities also include health, fitness, and sports; environmental education; the arts; and programs that promote global awareness. Programs are designed to help girls to do the following:

- **Discover:** by finding out who they are, what they care about, and what their talents are
- **Connect:** by collaborating with other people, both locally and globally, learning from one another, and expanding one's horizons
- **Take Action:** by doing something to make the world a better place (Girl Scouts of America, 2017d)

Camp Fire Girls of America

The Camp Fire Girls of America was created in the United States just after the founding of the Boy Scouts. From its beginnings, it was intended to provide for girls what the Boy Scouts provided for boys. It was founded by many of the same people who played a prominent role in developing Boy Scouting in the United States.

Luther Gulick, MD, and his wife, Charlotte Vetter Gulick, founded the organization in 1910 as the first nonsectarian organization for girls in the United States. Dr. Gulick was also a leader in the YMCA movement. His wife, Charlotte, developed a girls summer camp in Maine, based on Indian lore and ceremonies influenced by Ernest Thomas Seton. The camp was called "WoHeLo," the first two letters of the words work, health, and love.

Dr. Gulick chose the name "Camp Fire" for the new organization because camp fires were the origin of the first communities and domestic life. He felt that once people learned to make and control fire, they could develop and nurture a sense of community (Camp Fire USA, 2017a).

Camp Fire USA Today

Beginning in 1975, Camp Fire Girls became coeducational. By 2001, as the number of boy members of the organization grew, the organization changed its name from Camp Fire Girls to Camp Fire USA. In 1993, Camp Fire added sexual orientation to its inclusion policy.

In 2016, Camp Fire reported 128,000 participants from 57 Camp Fire councils. Forty-six percent of the participants were male and 54% were female (Camp Fire USA, 2016). In recent years, Camp Fire has adopted a Thrive(ology) framework. This approach helps youth "build positive sustained relationships and learn life skills that include self-reflection and goal management, while practicing these skills in valued home, school and community activities" (Camp Fire, 2017a). The Thrive approach seeks to enable youth to achieve their full potential through four components:

1. Identifying and growing Sparks (See Chapter 1)
2. Adopting a growth mind-set—the belief that one can learn new skills at any time
3. Building goal management skills
4. Creating the opportunity to reflect on activities and outcomes

Organizers believe that if participants are equipped with these skills, and have the support of trained, caring adults, participants will be more likely to do the following:

- Stay in school
- Demonstrate social competence
- Lead a healthy lifestyle
- Be environmentally conscious
- Have a sense of purpose
- Achieve their full potential (Camp Fire, 2017c)

Camp Fire operates through a variety of program structures:

- Before- and after-school programs (partnering with communities and schools to support children's education and help them become leaders in their daily lives)
- School-day programs (working with teachers to integrate Camp Fire programs and materials into lesson plans)
- Camp Fire club programs (using trained, volunteer leaders to implement Camp Fire curricula with a small group of children in a community)

- Teens in Action (involving teens in youth-led, youth-driven service activities guided by trained adults)
- Camp programs (enabling children and youth to experience residential camp, day camp, and environmental education experiences) (Camp Fire, 2017b)

YWCA

The YWCA began as a movement; its name came later. The movement began in England in 1855, and then in the United States in 1858. In each country, a small group of women was drawn together to make life better for other women. They sensed the anxiety of young women who came to cities from a supportive home base in rural areas in search of work so they could become self-supporting. Leaders of the movement recognized the unsanitary conditions, long work hours, lack of rest periods, and poor ventilation in the factory workplace. Recreation opportunities for these women were limited (YWCA, 2017a).

> The YWCA is dedicated to the elimination of racism; empowering women; and promoting peace, justice, freedom, and dignity for all.

The first association in New York City provided a boarding house for young girls as early as 1860, and in Boston in 1868, a residence was opened for students and young workers under age 25. On college campuses in the late 1800s, young women needed meeting rooms where students could exchange ideas, conduct Bible classes, and hold parties.

Boston was the first to use YWCA as the name for its association in 1859. The first student association began its work in 1873 at Illinois State Normal University (now Illinois State University). YWCAs quickly sprang up on other college campuses and other communities. By 1875, there were 28 YWCAs, and by 1890, the total student associations reached 106. As the number of associations increased, the need for centralization to share information on issues and program, and to handle reports, records, and other aspects of administration, also increased. As a result, in 1907 the National Board of the YWCA of the USA was incorporated in the state of New York (YWCA, 2004a).

The YWCA Today

The YWCA is dedicated to the elimination of racism; empowering women; and promoting peace, justice, freedom, and dignity for all (YMCA, 2017b). Although the individual programs found at various local associations take different approaches to these issues according to the specific situation of the communities they serve, the goals remain the same. Local associations also address other issues, such as women's health and prevention of violence, based on locally identified needs.

Currently, the YWCA serves approximately two million women, girls, and their families in the United States and 25 million women worldwide. In the United States, the YWCA movement provides a variety of services.

- The YWCA is the largest provider of shelters and services for women and their families in the country, serving over 500,000 women and children annually through their safety services.
- The organization is a provider of women's health programs.
- The YWCA advocates at the local and national level on racial justice and economic equality issues and offers extensive programming to address these topics at their local associations.
- The organization is one the country's largest nonprofit providers of child care services, with 200,000 children participating in child care and after-school programs annually.
- The YWCA offers a program called TechGYRLS to address the significant gender gap in girls' development of interest and skills in science, technology, engineering and math (STEM; YWCA, 2004c).

Girls Inc.

The Girls Inc. movement started in New England during the Industrial Revolution in response to the needs of working-class young women who had migrated from rural communities in search of newly available job opportunities in textile mills and factories (Girls Inc., 2004a). The oldest Girls Inc. affiliate, formed in 1864 in Waterbury, Connecticut, provided programs not only for young working women but also for younger daughters of mill families who had no place to gather beyond the city streets.

During the Depression, Dora Dodge, executive director of the Worcester affiliate, published an article in a national magazine that pointed out the growing needs of girls in the congested areas of American cities. As a result, a number of people responded with concerns about the problems of girls in their own communities. Dodge invited other directors of similar organizations in Pittsfield and Springfield to talk over

> Girls Inc. programs are designed to help girls develop strategies for leading successful, independent, and complete lives.

common problems, to discuss ways of bringing about better programs and facilities, and to create publicity that could strengthen all girls' organizations. For 10 years, these three organizations maintained their informal association. Finally, in 1945, representatives of 19 organizations met in Springfield to form Girls Clubs of America. The fledgling organization had two concerns: to exchange information on programs relevant to girls and to help communities establish new centers (Girls Inc., 2004a).

Programming in the early days was focused on recreation and preparing girls for their future roles as wives and homemakers. Every local organization had courses in cooking, sewing, and knitting; some offered dramatics and swimming. By the 1970s, Girls Inc. began examining its original mission in terms of the realities of a new era. Leaders of the organization felt it was time to move the organization beyond its original role of preparing girls as wives and homemakers, considering the powerful challenges of the civil rights movement, the women's movement, the increase in women entering the workforce, and the adolescent turbulence of the time. With changing women's roles, girls needed to prepare for very different

adulthoods. Concerned by the lack of knowledge about girls' issues and the inequity in funding, Girls Inc. took on responsibility for increasing knowledge among policy makers and government officials about the needs of girls, which in turn contributed to lowering some of the legal barriers to women's full involvement in the workforce and community life. The next step was to create programs that could affect the way thousands of girls and young women made decisions about their careers, their sex lives, and their identities as adult women (Girls Inc., 2004a).

Girls Inc. Today

In many instances, Girls Inc. currently operates through local centers that girls attend after school. In other instances, Girls Inc. collaborates with schools or other youth-serving organizations and uses their facilities to offer Girls Inc. programs. Programs are designed to help girls develop strategies for leading successful, independent, and complete lives. The organization also undertakes research to identify pressing issues girls face and to advocate for equitable opportunities for girls. Girls Inc. organizers believe "in a society that still delivers subtle, often unintentional messages that girls are weaker, softer, and not as bright as boys. Girls Inc. helps girls become strong, smart, and bold" (Girls Inc., 2004a).

Girls Inc. programs help to foster a girl's self-sufficiency by exposing her to a range of possibilities and helping her avoid obstacles that could stand in the way of success. The organization reaches over 140,000 girls aged 6–18 at over 1,200 sites in 350 cities across the United States and Canada. Sixty-four percent of the girls are either African American or Hispanic, 56% come from families with incomes below $20,000, and 53% come from single-parent families.

Current programs offered by Girls Inc. include the following:

- **Economic Literacy** helps girls learn about money and the economy, including how to manage, invest, and save money and how to help others through philanthropy.

- **Friendly PEERsuasion** helps girls develop skills to resist pressure to use harmful substances, such as drugs, alcohol, tobacco, and household chemicals. Girls also learn to become peer educators for younger girls.
- **Media Literacy** encourages girls to think critically about media messages and fosters their awareness of the scope and power of the media and its effects on girls and women. Girls gain media literacy skills that enhance their ability to critically examine and advocate for change in entertainment, news, and advertising media.
- **Operation SMART** helps girls develop skills in science, technology, engineering, and mathematics (STEM)
- **Girls Inc. Project Bold** strengthens girls' abilities to lead safer lives. Girls develop strategies for self-defense, including physical techniques, for seeking out and talking with caring adults about personal violence, and for advocating about violence issues for girls and young women. Age-appropriate components include Kid-Ability! (Kid Jr.), Action for Safety, and Taking Action (Girls Inc., 2004b).

Organizations Designed to Serve Both Boys and Girls

4-H

Character building was considered as necessary by people living in rural settings as it was for urban families. Farm families were worried by their children's increasing attraction to city life. They also were concerned that public school education did not meet the applied learning and agricultural education needs of farm youth (Reck, 1950; Wessel & Wessel, 1982). Therefore, beginning around the early 1900s, 4-H clubs became the major vehicle for organizing the free-time activities of rural youth. While youth in smaller communities were involved with the Boy Scouts and YMCA, these programs generally failed to attract youth from farm families (Kett, 1977, p. 246).

4-H activities were more likely to involve a philosophy of producing something useful, compared to city youth groups that might attempt a "simulation of life on a long-dead frontier" (Kett, 1977, p. 246). The movement did not have a single charismatic leader like some of the other youth movements of the time, but a number of different educators at university and public school levels began in the late 1890s and early 1900s to develop youth clubs focused on learning agricultural skills. "Corn Clubs" began in Illinois and quickly spread to other states to involve boys in contests to determine who could grow the most and highest quality corn. "Canning Clubs" were soon developed for girls, followed by other clubs dealing with aspects of the domestic sciences. Girls also became involved in clubs dealing with agricultural production.

In most cases, young people developed a project around a particular commodity (e.g., seed selection criteria, milk testing, road improvement), or the domestic sciences (e.g., baking, sewing, basketry). Some United States Department of Agriculture (USDA) workers realized that technology and new methods could be introduced more quickly and easily by involving farm children, who would subsequently influence their parents. The Smith-Lever Act of 1914 provided federal funds for the emerging Cooperative Extension Service, which included Extension efforts by Land Grant Universities in cooperation with their respective state and county governments. This system provided an administrative and developmental home for 4-H clubs and activities.

By 1915, there were 4-H clubs in 47 states. Leadership for 4-H clubs was provided by volunteers, often a parent of one of the participants or a local school teacher. During World War I, the energies of 4-H members were devoted to raising food to support the war effort (Wessel & Wessel, 1982). The term 4-H was first used in a federal publication written in 1918.

When Congress created the Cooperative Extension Service at USDA in 1914, it included boys and girls club work. This soon became known as 4-H clubs—Head, Heart, Hands, and Health. The pledge was adopted in 1927. By 1960, more than half of 4-H participants were nonfarm youth (National 4-H Headquarters, 2017).

4-H Pledge

I pledge my head to clearer thinking, my heart to greater loyalty, my hands to larger service, and my health to better living, for my family, my club, my community, my country, and my world.

4-H Today

Currently, 4-H serves youth in rural, urban, and suburban communities in every state. 4-H'ers tackle the nation's top issues, including global food security, climate change, sustainable energy, childhood obesity, and food safety. Out-of-school programming, in-school enrichment programs, clubs, and camps also offer a wide variety of STEM opportunities, including agricultural and animal sciences, rocketry, robotics, environmental protection, and computer science (National 4-H Headquarters, 2017a).

4-H reaches almost six million young people through 100 public universities. An estimated 3,500 4-H professionals and 500,000 volunteers deliver programs. Young people experience 4-H through school and community clubs, in-school and after-school programs and 4-H camps. A significant portion of 4-H participation occurs through youth completing projects (e.g., raising a particular animal and showing it at a local or state fair). In 2016, 4-H participants completed 3 million projects related to agriculture, 2.5 million related to citizenship, and 2.5 million related to healthy living.

Some of the programs offered by 4-H include the following:

- **4-H Tech Wizards** is an after-school youth mentoring program for underserved youth grades 4-12, designed to spark interest in STEM fields.
- **Juntos 4-H** is a program that helps Latino youth (grades 8–12) and their families gain the knowledge and skills they need to bridge the gap between high school and higher education. Program goals include helping more Latino youth to benefit from 4-H programming, building relationships with Latino communities, and empowering Latino families with the resources needed to achieve their educational goals for their youth.
- **Food Smart Families** targets families eligible for or receiving SNAP and/or WIC benefits and teaches them how to plan, shop, and prepare healthy meals on a budget. Instructors teach participants cooking skills and basic nutrition facts using a variety of commonly available foods.
- **Youth Choice** supports communities across the nation to promote healthy living among youth and their families. Through this innovative and culturally relevant program, youth are mobilized to take action around three healthy living priorities—nutrition, physical fitness, and safety—and to develop action plans that improve the health and well-being of their communities.
- **Communication and Expressive Arts** (filmmaking to photography) programs and curricula emphasize artistic expression and communication. 4-H's visual arts programs include both print and digital media so youth have the opportunity to use the latest technology. The theater programs teach communication skills, creative thinking, improvisation, and writing.
- **Citizenship Washington** brings thousands of high school youth from all across the country to Washington, DC each summer to partake in the preeminent 4-H citizenship and leadership experience. (National 4-H Council, 2017b)

4-H has adopted the positive youth development model in designing programs and training volunteers. 4-H has also been involved in an extensive research program to better understand the impacts associated with participation in 4-H and other youth programs (National 4-H Council, 2017c).

Parks and Recreation Movement

Creating play spaces and recreation programs was another approach to working with lower class and immigrant boys that grew out of the 1880's progressive movement. In most cases, these programs were developed to help remove youth from the dangers and attractions of using the streets as play spaces. According to Goldmark (1914), the street was

...the earliest, latest, and greatest influence in [a child's] life. Long before he knew his alphabet, it began to educate him, and before he could toddle it was his nursery. Every possible minute from babyhood to early manhood is spent in it. Every day, winter and summer, he is here off and on from early morning till 10 o'clock at night. It gives him a training in which school is merely a repressive interlude. From the quiet of the classroom he hears its voice, and when lessons are over, it shouts a welcome at the door. The attractions that it offers ever vary. Now a funeral, now a fire; "craps" on the sidewalk; a stolen ride on one of Death Avenue's freight trains; a raid on a fruit staff; a fight, an accident, a game of "cat"—always fresh incident and excitement, always nerve-racking, kaleidoscopic confusing. (p. 11)

Nasaw (1985) had this to say about the danger of the streets:

While the children played, policemen walked their beats, prostitutes solicited "johns," peddlers shouted their wares, delivery, wagons squeezed down the block to neighborhood shops, and men and women clustered in small groups on the comers, in front of the shops, at the threshold of the saloons, and on their front stoops. (p. 20)

The allure of street life and the lack of suitable places for children to play prompted settlement house workers and reformers to campaign in the newspapers, magazines, city halls, and legislative lobbies for parks, playgrounds, and after-school programs. The reformers were, no doubt, hoping to use such supervised play programs as vehicles for socialization and Americanization, but they were also genuinely concerned for the future of children who had no place but the street to play. (p. 22)

Adults present on the streets and looking out tenement windows could protect children from predators or dangerous situations, but they could not protect children from the many negative influences of street life. Therefore, the reformers envisioned the creation of play spaces that had adult leaders who could provide leadership and guidance. They saw the importance of getting playgrounds funded by municipal

> Reformers envisioned the creation of play spaces that had adult leaders who could provide leadership and guidance.

government and making the control of play a state responsibility. City governments were targeted as the major source of funding (Cavello, 1976).

Reformers saw the following three specific benefits of play in an urban-industrial society:

1. Play provided opportunities to recapitulate the necessary stages of development, as laid out by Hall (1904).

2. Play developed moral ideals and social interactions necessary for modern economic and political life, including the reduction of individualism and development of an orientation toward group, means-ends activities. The team was seen as the primary vehicle for immigrant acculturation and as substitute for the lack of authority of the traditional socializing agencies: family, church, schools (Cavello, 1976, pp. 518-519).

3. Play encouraged physical activity, fitness, and moral and social development.

Recapitulation theory. Interest in developing play opportunities for children in part grew out of an interest in recapitulation theory put forth by G. Stanley Hall. Henry Curtis, one of the founders of the Playground Association of America, completed his doctoral dissertation under Hall at Clark University in 1898. In his 1915 book, *Education through Play*, Curtis stated play was a production of recapitulation and that almost every play-form consisted of the same physical activities that had enabled primitive men and women to survive a hostile milieu (e.g., running, chasing, and hurling objects at targets). Thus, play, while fun, was an instinctual act necessary for the healthy development of the child (Cavello, 1976, p. 510).

Another view expressed by Joseph Lee (1916), who served as the president of the Playground Association for 27 years, was the necessity of prolonging childhood for children to go through all of the necessary stages of development. These stages, according to Lee, included the following:

- **Babyhood (birth to age 3):** Manipulation of objects and reaching out (bonding) to mother
- **Dramatic (up to age 6):** A period of imitative play, belonging, and social solidarity
- **Big Injun (up to age 11):** Self-assertive period of individualism, including rampaging and anarchistic impulses, adventure, curiosity, egoistic activity
- **Age of Loyalty (up to about age 20):** Period of adolescence, desire for social cooperation, sexual urges, and moving away from parental influence, which in turn leads to bonding with peers in organized group settings, referred to as a *belonging instinct*, could lead to membership in gangs as well as teams, which is seen as the modern counterpart of the tribe

Development of group loyalties. The last stage advocated by Lee was of particular interest to play advocates. Through recreation activities, efforts were made to direct youth away from loyalty to gangs and encourage loyalty to a sport team (Cavello, 1976). The group was seen as a way to subordinate individualism in favor of group efforts, which in turn would help participants to acculturate to the collectivist demands of work settings created by industrialization (Cavello, 1976). The team experience could also help balance what they called "the feminine" (e.g., passive, domestic, emotional, intuitive, and self-sacrificing) with "the masculine" (e.g., aggressive, worldly, rational, empirically oriented, and self-interested) to create the ideal team player (Cavello, 1976). The group was also a way to further democratic ideals through integration and acceptance of others across ethnic lines.

Forming groups (e.g., gangs, clubs) was seen as part of the "gang instinct," a necessary stage in the recapitulation of the history of the race, and a result of social Darwinism (i.e., the survival of the fittest). Thus, according to Gulick (1911),

Forming groups (e.g., gangs, clubs) was seen as part of the "gang instinct," a necessary stage ...

> this tendency to sympathize, cooperate, and hang together would form a large factor in survival in times of famine, since the, group would always be able to rob and kill the individual, and protect their respective families from external harm. Those possessed of these social feelings would be better fitted to survive than those who were purely selfish, and so, gradually, the egoistic man would be eliminated from the race. Through the steady elimination of the more egoistic, and the survival of the more altruistic, the children would inherit social capacity, and be more and more cooperative in their tendencies and actions. (p. 87)

The team experience was also thought of as creating a balance between independence and dependence:

> To an extent, peer-group direction was designed as a substitute for family supervision, which play organizers thought an inept agency of discipline and social control. Advocates of play generally saw the plight of the urban ghetto youth in the darkest terms: "He ran wild in the streets while his overworked, ignorant, or negligent parents sat in dark tenements unaware of his activities. For this reason play advocates perceived the peer group as a community-controlled institution providing adolescents with values and skills that were not being transmitted by the urban, especially ethnic family." (Cavello, 1976, p. 7)

Thus, peer interactions were to be managed by adult playground directors. As a result, a cadre of "professional playground leaders" was trained to organize and manage activities. Courses were offered at a number of universities, which emphasized child development and included the social and psychological sciences. A civil service test was devised and cities were encouraged to hire only play directors who passed the test (Cavello, 1976, pp. 41-42).

By 1908, over 200 cities had playgrounds, with two thirds supported by public funds. By 1917, 481 cities operated 3,940 playgrounds (Cavello, 1976, p. 45).

Fitness and social development. With the passage of child labor laws and mandatory extended school attendance, the amount of available idle time for children also increased. Work, if undertaken, did not promote physical fitness, as had often been the case in rural, agrarian settings. For young children, there were few places to play beyond the crowded tenement houses they lived in or the neighboring streets. For older children, reformers were concerned about exposure to dance halls, poolrooms, gambling, street life, alcohol, and the vagaries of adult free-time involvements, which impinged on the opportunities for social and moral development. Play advocates felt that play:

>...was a vital factor in the development of the moral faculty because it was the agency through which motor coordinations were established, perceptions sharpened, and social habits formed, and all these were related to will functioning. To avoid a fatigued will; that is, one susceptible to the numerous temptations inherent in city life, one had to avoid a fatigued or inadequate musculature. (Cavello, 1976, p. 517)

Reformers also expressed concern that because of declining physical fitness, fewer individuals qualified for military service. A perceived increase in nervous disorders, which they felt was related to the congestion and pace of city life, might be overcome through participation in play (Curtis, 1917).

In 1885, the first children's designated sandlot was created in Boston. The space consisted of a pile of sand surrounded by boards to demark the area. A number of efforts to promote children's play quickly followed. On April 12, 1906, the Playground Association of America (changed to the Playground and Recreation Association of America [PRAA] in 1910) was organized through the efforts of Luther Gulick (president) and Henry Curtis (secretary and treasurer), Jane Addams (vice-president), Theodore Roosevelt (honorary president), and Jacob Riis (honorary vice-president). Joseph Lee, a Boston philanthropist and play advocate, took over as president in 1909 and served for 27 years. (Lee was a member of an anti-immigration movement, but the organizers felt that he was the right person to lead the PRAA because Lee felt strongly about providing acculturation and recreation opportunities for immigrants once they were in the country). PRAA was the forerunner of today's National Recreation and Park Association (NRPA).

In 1917, Curtis summed up the five components of the play movement as follows:

1. Provision of places for play where children can go during leisure time, be off the streets and away from the evil influences which they might encounter, and enable contact with trained adults
2. Promotion of opportunities for play in schools, given play's critical role in development
3. Development of outdoor play spaces for preschool children
4. Development of public recreation opportunities
5. Promotion of the rebirth of the spirit of play, balance between work and play, shortening of the workday, inclusion of vacations, and an increase in attendance at cultural events

Addams argued strongly for the necessity of public recreation opportunities for children and youth. She saw the value of parks and recreation amenities in helping to reduce delinquency and teaching citizenship. Addams stated:

In 1908, the first traditional playground with equipment was installed in Boston, on Tremont Street. *Source:* APC Play (2017)

The fifteen Small Parks in Chicago, equipped with clubrooms, poolrooms, drawing-rooms, refectories, reading-rooms, gymnasiums, swimming-pools, and much other social paraphernalia, are, we believe, centers in which a higher type of citizenship is being nursed. Certainly the number of arrests among juvenile delinquents falls off surprisingly in a neighborhood where such a park has been established—a negative measure, possibly, but one which cannot be disregarded. As the temple of the Greeks inspired the youth's patriotism, and as the city walls conserved but at the same time limited his imagination, so, we hope, these centers of public recreation, simply because they stand for high comradeship and intercourse, will inspire American youth to a sense of political obligation, while at the same time they teach him that the kingdom of the mind is without boundary and that he may find patriotic relationship with the youth of all nations. (Addams, 1912, p. 619)

Their 1910 statement of purpose statement summed up the approach taken by the Playground Association of America:

Dependence is reduced by giving men more for which to live. Delinquency is reduced by providing a wholesome outlet for youthful energy. Industrial efficiency is increased by giving individuals a play life which will develop greater resourcefulness and adaptability. Good citizenship is promoted by forming habits of cooperation in play. People who play together find it easier to live together and are more loyal as well as more efficient citizens. Democracy rests on the most firm basis when a community has formed the habit of playing together. (p. 73)

Parks and Recreation Today

Today parks and recreation departments (PARDs) can be found in all major cities and the vast majority of smaller communities in the United States. Depending on the community, PARDs operate parks, community centers that house programs for young children to older adults, playgrounds, swimming pools, skateboard parks, and special event facilities (e.g., amphitheaters). In many communities, PARDs have more facilities and operate more programs than any other organization. Their funding comes from city, county, or sometimes regional sources. On occasion, departments have been able to secure grant funds to operate special programs.

PARDs have continued their historic mission to provide open space, neighborhood activities, and opportunities for young people to engage in a range of out-of-school-time involvements. In many inner-city neighborhoods, community centers may be the only safe place for young people to participate after school, at night, on the weekend, and during the summer.

> Park and recreation departments have continued their historic mission to provide open-space neighborhood activities and opportunities for young people to engage in a range of out-of-school-time involvements.

Many PARDs provide supports, opportunities, programs, and services (SOPS) that make meaningful contributions to the lives of young people. A number are using the Search Institute's (2017) 40 developmental assets model as the basis for program conceptualization and design. In some instances, communities have realized that not all young people who could benefit by program involvement attend community center programs. Thus, these departments have created outreach or Roving Leader programs to enable contact with nonparticipants and to encourage their participation in community center activities. A number of cities have established comprehensive approaches to conceptualizing and developing youth programs.

The following are examples of programs offered by parks and recreation departments around the United States.

- Austin Parks and Recreation's long-standing *Totally Cool Totally Art* program emphasizes the importance of the process of creation, values a hands-on learning approach, and encourages all teens to participate and explore their creative side regardless of their experience level. An important part of the program is exhibition opportunities of participants' work at various venues throughout the year.
- The City of Phoenix Parks and Recreation Department has a long-standing *after-school program* that offers a fun, supportive, and educational place for children aged 6 to 13 to spend crucial after-school hours. The program is available at 38 school sites throughout Phoenix. Program components include homework help; educational enrichment activities; book blast, which provides books for all level readers to enjoy once homework is complete; reading assistance programs; STEM activities; and physical, social, and arts activities.

- Arlington County (Virginia) offers a *Hang Out After School* program where teens can have fun, make new friends, and develop skills at center-based programs, held September to mid-June. Programs include opportunities for music, dance, games, cooking, art, sport games, and activities chosen by teen participants.
- San Jose (California) offers *teen centers* through its Parks, Recreation and Neighborhood Services department. Programs focus on helping teenagers navigate the challenges and social pressures of growing up by offering a safe place for teens to socialize as well as take part in field trips, sports leagues, mentoring programs, and volunteer opportunities.
- The Minneapolis Park and Recreation Board offers *Nite Owlz*, which provides extended teen programming at various recreation centers from 8–11 p.m. on Friday and Saturday nights. Activities include open gym, cooking, computer labs, and other activities.
- Portland Parks & Recreation's (Oregon) *Youth Conservation Crew* provides summer employment opportunities for youth, aged 14–18. Crews protect, restore, and manage Portland's parks and natural areas while developing essential job skills and exploring environmental career paths.

City budget restrictions have diminished some of the creative approaches to youth programming that was observed in the 1990s and early 2000s. However, park and recreation departments still play a vital role in the provision of out-of-school time recreation opportunities.

Summary/Closing Thoughts

Many of the issues surrounding the development of youth services in the late 1800s and early 1900s still exist today. As modern child-saving agencies and professions have developed, they have intensified their foci on treating children and families as problems, abandoning social action, and letting go of social and economic understandings of the causes of children's problems (Macleod, 1983). Professionals are still debating whether the focus of our attention should be on intervention programs for youth who are considered at-risk of undertaking negative behaviors or development of the potential of all youth.

Professionals are still wrestling with the degree of protection society should afford young people and the values that should form the foundation for youth-serving programs. In many cases, the child-saving reforms of 100-plus years ago were there to preserve childhood and to promote child welfare, even though others saw it as a form of social control (e.g., preserve and promote middle-class values and Americanize immigrants). Adults and the middle class still feel threatened by immigrants, people with different value systems than their own, and those growing up in different circumstances than they did (Levine & Levine, 1970).

A challenge to those reading this book: Think about youth-serving organizations today. To what extent do these organizations continue to play a significant role in separating young people by class, neighborhood, and race? How do membership and hiring policies of these organizations impact inter-group and community understanding and tolerance?

Society is also still debating the degree of professionalization necessary to deal with the needs of youth. Thus, current statements about the need to credential and otherwise authenticate youth workers reflect the same issues and concerns of over 100 years ago. For example, while speaking about the developmental period of youth services, Sommerville (1982) observed,

> For the first time in history, the child's image became a matter of professional concern. Those who worked with wayward or neglected children had to keep them before the public's attention. Only thus could they guarantee the funding needed to continue their work and their jobs. Naturally, they wanted to create sympathy for these children. This would ensure that the public's help was given in a good spirit and would tend to raise their status as well. But they could not give the impression that children were too noble, for fear that their job would seem too easy. Above all, they could not claim to be solving the problem, for then there would be a question whether they could be needed much longer. Their agencies would be threatened with closure and their staff with dismissal. On the other hand, if they could not claim some success, people would wonder if all their efforts had been wasted. (p. 201)

Thus, rather than claim that efforts to work with youth were being successful, professionals could claim that the problem of juvenile misbehavior was growing. In others words, despite some success, the public would need to make an even greater commitment to efforts to work with young people. Thus, permanent organizations and bureaucracies could be created and sustained. Youth-serving agencies encouraged the message that children were a growing problem, whether this conclusion was justified or not. However justified, the rising figures on juvenile delinquency became a major concern at the turn of the 20th century and a variety of youth-serving organizations and institutional responses emerged.

Today, youth agencies work to balance the justification for their programs between preventing negative behaviors and increasing positive, adaptive values, attitudes, knowledge, skills, and behaviors. Funding may be more easily justified based on overcoming the negative, but the lives of youth are better served by building the abilities of youth to thrive in an increasingly complex society.

Discussion Questions

1. The landscape of youth organizations is changing. What impact do you think the decision to admit girls by a traditionally all-male organization like the Boy Scouts will have on membership, quality of programs, and program experience?
2. What youth organizations did you belong to while growing up? Why did you join? What did you gain through membership in the organization(s)? What negative experiences did you have?

3. What youth organizations did your parents belong to while they were growing up? Why did they join? What did they gain through membership in the organization(s)? What negative experiences did they have?
4. Now, compare the experiences of you and your parents in terms of youth organizations experiences during childhood and adolescence. How did differences in the time period of these experiences make a difference in what you and your parents experienced and gained through your contact with these organizations?

Assignment

Choose a youth organization in your community not included in this chapter. Interview someone who works for the organization to learn about their history, organizational structure, funding, enrollment history, activities, staff qualifications, and studies they have undertaken regarding program impact. Also determine major issues and challenges faced by the organization.

References

Addams, J. (1912, March). Recreation as a public function in urban communities. *American Journal of Sociology, 17*(5), 615–619.

Baden-Powell, R. S. S. (1899). *Aids to Scouting for NCOs and men.* Aldershot, England: Gale and Polden.

Baden-Powell, R. S. S. (1908). *Scouting for boys.* London, UK: Horace Cox.

Boys & Girls Clubs of America. (2015). 2015 Annual Report. Atlanta, GA: Boys & Girls Clubs of America. Retrieved from https://www.bgca.org/-/media/Documents/AboutUs/2015-AnnualReport.pdf?la=en&hash=7B4336B3E66BC-5C395910CE8B6244076FD57BCED

Boys & Girls Clubs of America. (2017). About our programs. Retrieved from http://www.bgca.org/programs

Boy Scouts of America. (2015a). Boy Scouts of America amends adult leadership policy. Retrieved from https://web.archive.org/web/20160902071556/http://scoutingnewsroom.org/blog/boy-scouts-of-america-amends-adult-leadership-policy/

Boy Scouts of America. (2015b). Charter and Bylaws of the Boy Scouts of America. Retrieved from www.scouting.org/filestore/pdf/bsa_charter_and_bylaws.pdf

Boy Scouts of America. (2017a). Chartered organizations. Retrieved from http://www.scoutingnewsroom.org/about-the-bsa/fact-sheets/chartered-organizations-and-the-boy-scouts-of-america/

Boy Scouts of America (2017b). Programs. Retrieved from http://www.scoutingnewsroom.org/about-the-bsa/fact-sheets/overview-of-boy-scouts-of-america/

Boy Scouts of America National Council. (2017). History of Cub Scouting. Retrieved from http://www.scouting.org/Home/CubScouts/Parents/About/history.aspx

Camp Fire USA. (2016). Campfire National Headquarters Annual Report. Retrieved from http://campfire.org/financials

Camp Fire USA. (2017a). History. Retrieved from http://campfire.org/about/history

Camp Fire USA. (2017b). Camp Fire's Thrive(ology). Retrieved from http://campfire.org/experience/thrive

Camp Fire USA. (2017c). The Camp Fire experience. Retrieved from http://campfire.org/experience/

Cavello, D. (1976). Social reform and the movement to organize children's play during the progressive era. *History of Childhood Quarterly, 3*(4), 509–522.

Chokshi, N. (2017, January 30). Boy Scouts, reversing century-old stance, will allow transgender boys. *New York Times.* Retrieved from https://www.nytimes.com/2017/01/30/us/boy-scouts-reversing-century-old-stance-will-allow-transgender-boys.html?_r=0

Curtis, H. (1915). *Education through play.* New York, NY: MacMillan.

Curtis, H. S. (1917). *The play movement and its significance.* New York, NY: Macmillan.

Forbush, W. B. (1913). *The boy problem.* Boston, MA: Pilgrim Press.

Girl Scouts of America. (2017a). About Girl Scouts. Retrieved from http://www.girlscouts.org/en/about-girl-scouts/who-we-are.html

Girl Scouts of America (2017b). Grade levels. Retrieved from http://www.girlscouts.org/en/our-program/grade-levels.html

Girl Scouts of America. (2017c). Adult membership form. Retrieved from http://www.usagso.org/content/dam/usagso/documents/usagso/USAGSO%20Adult%20Membership%20Form%20-%202016-17.pdf

Girl Scouts of America. (2017d). Our program. Retrieved from http://www.girlscouts.org/en/our-program/our-program.html

Girls, Inc. (2017a). History. Retrieved from http://www.girlsinc.org/about/history/girls-inc-history.html

Girls, Inc. (2017b). Programs. Retrieved from http://www.girlsinc.org/resources/programs/girls-inc-programs.html

Goldmark, R. D. (1914). *West Side studies.* New York, NY: Survey Associates.

Gulick, L. (1911, July). Games and gangs. *Lippincott's Monthly Magazine, 88,* 87–89.

Hall, G. S. (1904). *Adolescence: Its psychology and its relations to physiology, anthropology, sociology, sex, crime, religion, and education* (2 vols.). New York, NY: Appleton.

Kett, J. F. (1977). *Rites of passage: Adolescence in America 1790 to the present.* New York, NY: Basic Books.

Lee, J. (1916). *Play in education.* New York, NY: McMillan Co.

Levine, M., & Levine, A. (1970). *Social history of the helping services: Clinic, court, school, and community.* New York, NY: Appleton Century Croft.

Macleod, D. I. (1983). *Building character in the American boy: The Boy Scouts, YMCA, and their forerunners, 1870-1920.* Madison, WI: The University of Wisconsin Press.

Marshfield Area YMCA. (2017). Our history: A brief history of the YMCA movement. Retrieved from http://www.mfldymca.org/about_us/history_national.php

Nasaw, D. (1985). *Children of the city.* Garden City, NY: Anchor Press.

National 4-H Council. (2017a). 4-H history. Retrieved from http://4-h.org/about/history/

National 4-H Council. (2017b). What is 4-H? Retrieved from http://4-h.org/about/what-is-4-h/

National 4-H Council. (2017c). Research. Retrieved from http://4-h.org/about/research/

Playground Association of America. (1910). Purpose. *Playground, 4,* 73.

Price, T. H. (1918). Girl Scouts. *Outlook, 118,* 367.

Reck, F. M. (1950). *The 4-H story: A history of 4-H club work.* Chicago, IL: National Committee on Boys and Girls Club Work.

Robinson, E. M. (1902). Age grouping of younger association members. *Association Boys, 1,* 35.

Rosenthal, M. (1986). *The character factory: Baden-Powell and the origins of the Boy Scouts.* New York, NY: Pantheon Books.

Search Institute. (2017). 40 developmental assets. Retrieved from http://www.search-institute.org/research/developmental-assets

Sommerville, C. J. (1982). *The rise and fall of childhood.* Volume 140, Sage Library of Social Research. Beverly Hills, CA: Sage Publications.

Wessel, T., & Wessel, M. (1982). *4-H, an American idea, 1900-1980: A history of 4-H.* Chevy Chase, MD: National 4-H Council.

Witt, P. A., & Crompton, J. L. (2002). *Best practices in youth development in public park and recreation settings.* Ashburn, VA: National Recreation and Park Association.

YMCA. (2016). Overview of the Y in the United States: For every person and the common good. Retrieved from http://www.ymca.net/sites/default/files/organizational-profile/ymca-national-impact-report.pdf

YWCA. (2017a). History. Retrieved from http://www.ywca.org/site/c.cuIRJ7NTKrLaG/b.7515891/k.C524/History.htm

YWCA. (2017b). Mission and vision. Retrieved from http://www.ywca.org/site/c.cuIRJ7NTKrLaG/b.7515887/k.9633/Mission__Vision.htm

YMCA. (2017c). Services at YWCA local associations. Retrieved from http://www.ywca.org/site/c.cuIRJ7NTKrLaG/b.8481993/k.4AE9/Services_at_YWCA_Local_Associations.htm

YMCA. (2017d). Organizational profile. Retrieved from http://www.ymca.net/organizational-profile/

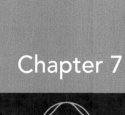

Chapter 7

Processes of Positive Development

Classic Theories

Reed W. Larson and Kathrin C. Walker

The youth had a great time at the Lawndale after-school recreation program. They were writing and producing a play, did other fun activities, and shared a great deal of hilarity. The young adult running the program, Julia Escobar, was skilled at organizing activities. She also had a special knack for making them enjoyable, and she instinctively felt that the smiles and laughter from the youth validated that she was doing things right. However, Julia occasionally stopped herself and asked, is having fun enough? Is she making a long-term difference in these youths' lives? Are the youth growing from their experiences; are they developing?

But what is development—or "positive development"—and how does it occur? The process of human change is not something any of us can readily observe, as when watching a sweater being woven or a plant growing from a seed. It is an abstract process, unfolding over long periods of time, and partly occurring within the private thoughts and feelings of youth. We only catch glimpses, and sometimes we do not know what we are looking for. We are often only aware of development when a youth suddenly surprises us with a display of skill, wisdom, or maturity that we had not expected. In order for someone like Julia to facilitate development, however, it is helpful to have ideas about how it occurs. You need what is often called a "theory of change."

The academic field of human development has drawn on research to formulate theories of how children and adolescents grow. These theories provide concepts for thinking about the processes of developmental change: What happens inside youth, or in their interactions with others, that leads to this change? Each also suggests different ways of thinking about the role of program leaders, like Julia, in facilitating these processes. We are going to describe five of the most prominent "classic" theories and theoretical perspectives on human development (Table 7.1). Each provides a useful set of ideas about how development takes place and how it can be fostered. For each theory, we will present an example from our research that illustrates the applicability of the theory to what happens in youth development programs.

Table 7.1

Five Theories and Perspectives on Human Development

Developmental Theory	How Youth Learn and Develop
Social Learning Theory	Rewards, Reinforcement, Modeling
Constructivist Theory	Experimentation, Discovery, Reasoning
Collaborative Learning	Social Interactions, Scaffolding
Relationship Theories	Caring Relationships, Emotional Support
Sociological Theories	Learning Norms, Social Connections

One of the messages across these theories is that young people have tremendous potential for growth. Humans, especially children and adolescents, are highly motivated to develop. They have natural dispositions to learn and grow from challenging activities (Csikszentmihalyi, 1990). In fact, the enjoyment that Julia was so skilled at bringing out in the youth is related to these dispositions. Nearly all of the theories we cover present development as a process in which these dispositions are activated. They describe the natural, positive dynamics of growth in young people. Indeed, the reason people working in youth development sometimes add the word "positive" to development is to emphasize the goal of mobilizing these natural processes in youth; these are processes in which youth actively engage in their own development (Larson, 2000).

> Humans, especially children and adolescents, are highly motivated to develop.

Learning Theory: Teaching and Shaping

Many early ideas about human development, however, did not take this positive perspective. They saw development as something that adults do to young people. Adults have knowledge, which they teach to youth. Youth develop by faithfully learning what they are taught. When young people make mistakes, the teacher, parent, or coach steers them back on track. Learning is directed by a knowledgeable authority.

The scientific foundation for this first theoretical perspective is called "learning theory," and early researchers who took this approach developed a robust science of how to shape behavior (Fester & Skinner, 1957; Hilgard & Bower, 1966). Much of this research was based on experiments with rats and pigeons, but the basic principles were found to work with humans as well. The key to learning in this model is the "reinforcements" that the teacher or trainer uses to shape behavior. If, in a specific situation, an experimental subject's behavior was followed by a reward, researchers found that the subject was likely to repeat that behavior again. If this connection between behavior and reward occurs over and over, the behavior becomes habituated—it becomes automatic in that situation.

A number of important and consistent findings emerged from this research. First, rewards are much more effective than punishment in shaping behavior. Sometimes punishment works, but other times it has unintended effects. A second finding is that progressive use of reinforcement along a sequence of steps permits the shaping of complex patterns of behavior. In the first step, the learner is reinforced for performing one small component of the desired behavior, but through gradual rewards of additional components, more complete behavioral sequences can be shaped. Third, the teacher or trainer has to be alert that undesired behavior is not reinforced. For example, when a youth gets peers to laugh by doing exactly the opposite of what an adult leader wants the youth to do, that youth may be experiencing positive reinforcement for this behavior from peers' laughter.

Early proponents of learning theory, such as B.F. Skinner, saw learning as a mechanistic process that occurs the same across humans and other animals. However, more recent advocates of "Social Learning Theory," such as Albert Bandura (1986), recognized that humans are conscious beings, and their conscious awareness of this process is important. For example, the reason punishment is not very effective is that it can make people feel inept—that "I can't do anything right"—so they stop trying. Alternatively, it can make them angry and resentful, so they start thinking about how unfair the situation is, rather than about how they can perform the desired behavior. Bandura also showed that some of the most effective reinforcement occurs through modeling and watching others. When youth see someone else being rewarded for a behavior, they may say to themselves, "I'm going to do the same thing so that I can get that reward."

We observed this developmental approach being used by a choral director, Diane, as she taught her show choir a new song. She gathers the youth at the piano and has them start singing. The group is tentative and lifeless. Diane interrupts to ask, "What'd you forget?" One youth offers, "Take a breath?" Diane has something else in mind. Several other youth offer incorrect guesses. Unable to reward someone for the right answer, Diane finally exclaims, "TO ACT!" They go through the song again, this time with more animation and arm movement. Diane praises their improvement. Then she sings a line, "Go tell it on the mountain," and nods to the youth to repeat. Diane continues, "Over the hills and everywhere," and the youth repeat again. Diane has the youth sing the two lines together, and this time youth sway to the music, and Diane praises them again. A few moments later she interrupts and instructs them not to lock their knees, and that to avoid fainting they should stand slightly bent with their feet shoulder's length apart. They continue until Diane calls out two girls who are talking and sternly says their names, then "Hi!" in a sarcastic tone as if to say, "Pay attention!" The girls get back on track, and in the end, all the youth are dancing, clapping, and strolling with arms linked while singing with spirit.

This rehearsal is successful in that the youth were engaged and learning from the instruction. In a short period of time they were singing and expressing themselves much more effectively. They had also gained valuable technical knowledge from Diane, such as how to stand. Learning theory suggests that Diane was successful because she made learning rewarding. She corrected mistakes; but she used praise rather than punishment to influence the youths' behavior. The one exception was her sarcastic reproach of the two girls, which may or may not have helped them pay attention. All in all, the youth appeared to have been reinforced by the satisfaction of pleasing Diane, as well as by the enjoyment they experienced in mastering the song.

Learning theory is useful for youth development because it helps us think about what rewards youth are getting and the influence of these rewards. This approach can be a valuable means for adults to pass on knowledge and shape youth's behavior. But it also has limits. Regardless of how positive adults are, youth are reliant on them for direction. The noted Brazilian educator, Paulo Freire (1970), argued that learners in this situation are in a passive and dependent role. They do not have ownership of the learning process, which can make them alienated and unmotivated—as happens all too often in schools. Further, they are not learning to learn on their own; they are not learning to be reflective and make decisions for themselves. By just trying to mimic or produce what Diane wanted, these youth had limited opportunity to develop their creativity and a broad range of other skills for self-direction. Across his career, Bandura became more appreciative of the importance of the active role of learners in their own development. To best understand this active process it is helpful to turn to other theories of human development.

Constructivist Theory: Youth as Producers of Their Own Development

At the same time that Skinner and Bandura were developing their theories, other scholars were developing theories that saw young people not as passive clay to be molded, but as active clay that molded itself. Some of these scholars based their ideas on basic biology, and their theoretical approach is sometimes called the "organismic model." They observed that organisms creatively adapt to their environment, and that humans are particularly good at this. Humans are able to adapt by actively learning and figuring things out. Learning is as fundamental to our species as eating and breathing (Mayr, 2001). In other words, you do not need to make young people learn, they are highly motivated to do it.

Humans are able to adapt by actively learning and figuring things out.

The most influential of these theorists, Jean Piaget, provided extensive observations showing how intelligent, creative, and motivated young people are as learners. Piaget believed that infants start with no knowledge at all. They do not even understand that an object exists when it is out of sight. They learn through an active process of experimentation and making deductions from what they experience. Thus, by 6–8 months, most infants figure out that objects continue to exist, even when hidden from view (Piaget, 1936). As this process of experimentation and discovery continues through childhood, they gradually develop a complex understanding of themselves and the world. In adolescence, they develop abstract concepts such as density, mass, the self, and how social groups function (Piaget, 1965; Piaget & Inhelder, 1969).

Piaget is sometimes called a "constructivist," because in his theory, children and youth mentally "construct" these concepts through this process of active experimentation and reasoning. He saw humans as highly motivated to organize the experiences they have into concepts and theories of how the world works. One of the implications of Piaget's ideas is that young people learn best on their own or with peers—knowledge that is taught to them lacks the depth of understanding that comes from this process of figuring things out. This implies that perhaps adults should get out of the way!

This was exactly the philosophy of Mr. Baker, one of the adult advisors at an FFA agricultural education program that we studied. He believed that youth learn by doing, including learning from their mistakes. During our research, the youth planned a day camp for fourth graders, and the mantra of Mr. Baker and his colleague, Mr. Jensen, was, "It's their day camp." So, they turned all the planning over to the youth. The adults provided support, but the youth ran the meetings, generated ideas for activities, and did the grunt work. After an initial idea-generating stage, we observed the youth were often disorganized and struggled quite a bit. They spun their wheels and sometimes locked horns with each other. "They're driving me nuts," one girl said of her peers. But, by the end, the youth reported having developed some powerful concepts about how to work on a project like this. These included insights on organizing effort, managing one's emotions, and working as a group (Larson, Hansen, & Walker, 2005).

Piaget would say that this type of development is superior because it was derived from active experience. The concepts were not simply taught and mindlessly memorized. Consistent with Piaget's theory, our analysis suggested that the FFA youths' new concepts emerged directly from the challenges they had struggled with in their work (Larson et al., 2005). Thus, the conflicts they experienced with other group members appeared to prime them for fundamental insights about working as a group: that you cannot always have it your way; you need to pay attention to others. One girl reported learning that "everybody's gotta give and everybody's just gotta hold back a little bit." The youths' statements reflect a significant developmental change—a shift from an egocentric way of viewing the group to one that takes into account the perspective of other members and the dynamics of group functioning.

Constructivist theories, then, help us think about the powerful natural tendencies of youth to develop—to organize their experiences into understanding. Research using this approach can also help us think about what level of concepts youth are ready for at different developmental stages. Nevertheless, there are also limits to this theory. Youth in the FFA program struggled in their work because they had little experience planning and running activities for children. In fact, the day camp was successful in the end only because the adults began to take a more active role in providing structure; and Mr. Baker had to step in and run one of the

> Constructivist theories, then, help us think about the powerful natural tendencies of youth to devleop—to organize their experiences into understanding.

camp activities because a youth was not able to hold the children's attention (Larson et al., 2005). Research shows that when people lack expertise in a domain, they easily get stuck or flounder (Rogoff, 1998), as happened here. It is possible that giving youth a lot of freedom may be helpful for learning concepts related to working with others. But it is likely to be less effective for learning, say, athletic, artistic, or other skills. You might have to wait a long time for them to discover these skills on their own.

So, if a shortcoming of learning theory was that it put learners in a passive dependent role, a risk of the constructivist model is that when learning is turned over to youth, they may flounder and spin their wheels. Is there a middle ground, a theory that allows knowledgeable leaders to help guide youth in an active process of learning? Lev Vygotsky and his successors conceived of developmental processes in ways that conceptualizes adults and youth as partners, working together.

Collaborative Learning: Guided Participation

A key idea for Vygotsky was that we should stop thinking of development as something that happens inside a young person's mind. While Piaget pictured development as coming from the child, Vygotsky (1962, 1978) saw it as coming from interactions between a child and other people. To understand development, he argued, our focus should not be the solitary individual, but rather on this shared interaction. Yes, children and adolescents gradually internalize what they gain from these interactions, but learning starts with the interactions, not the individual. Development is a collaborative process.

In this theoretical perspective, youth are still active producers of their development; we are not headed back to the mechanistic adult-driven theories like Skinner's. But they are active in cooperation with others. In some cases, these others are peers at the same level of knowledge and experience. Although a youth may work with peers to solve a problem and learn, we are going to concentrate on the situation where the other is an adult or an older, more experienced peer—someone who is in a position to provide guidance. Adherents of this theoretical approach often describe this guidance as taking the form of "scaffolding." Thus, while Piaget saw young people as "constructing" development on their own, this model recognizes that this construction process often benefits from scaffolds. It is important to keep in mind, however, that this is not fixed and rigid scaffolding; it is creatively adapted in response to the learner.

An experienced adult or guide can provide scaffolding for a youth's learning in multiple ways (Wood, Bruner, & Ross, 1976). The guide may direct the youth's attention to important clues or help to simplify a task. The guide may model a behavior for a youth to learn or provide words that help lead the youth to key concepts. The guide may also provide motivational support by offering encouragement, challenging youth to stretch, or steering them away from situations that will create high frustration. This interaction between the learner and guide is a mutual process. The guide talks with the learner and uses cues from the learner to determine what scaffolding (if any) is needed. It also includes youth requesting help from the guide when he or she wants it.

We observed this process of collaborative learning in a media arts program when the youth were starting to film their first videos. Each youth has developed a storyboard and recruited others to be the camera person and actors as they direct their piece. Hector is first, and has planned an animated scene in which two actors will quarrel, leaving one in tears. The youth have a lot of energy, but on the first take, the filming is chaotic and actors are confused. Janna, the adult leader, steps in and asks Hector to explain the scene. When the camera person is confused, she refocuses him in order to correctly capture the progression of events. She also positions Hector next to the camera person so that he can see how the picture will appear in the film. For the second take, Hector is able to better direct the actors and crew on his own. When the next youth have their turns directing their videos, Janna continues to provide occasional input, but it is clear that they have learned from watching Hector and Janna's interactions. They demonstrate progressively greater abilities to think about camera angles, sound, and how to instruct the actors and crew. The youth had internalized the guidance they received from Janna.

Janna provided multiple forms of scaffolding in this and other interactions with the youth. She sometimes broke a complex problem down into simpler pieces that were easier for youth to solve. Often her scaffolding took the form of posing questions. For example, she would ask, "Do you want her voice to be heard?" When the answer was yes, she said, "The mic is not going to pick up from this far away. So what's the solution?" This questioning led the youth to trouble shoot: zooming in and out, moving the camera closer and further, and trying to determine what combination of lens angle and distance would optimize the desired visual and audio effects. She also provided motivational scaffolding; as one youth said, she "gives us a little inspiration."

What is notable is that Janna supported the youth's active process of learning at the same time that she intervened to keep the filming and the learning process on track. Unlike the show choir conductor, she was not trying to shape the youth, indeed the youth described the process as one of giving them "freedom." Unlike the FFA advisors, she intervened in ways that kept the youths' learning from being stalled.

> Maintaining the right balance of supporting youth ownership and intervention, we have found, is by no means easy.

Maintaining the right balance of supporting youth ownership and intervention, we have found, is by no means easy (Larson et al., 2005; Larson, Walker, & Pearce, 2005). When do you stand back, when do you provide scaffolding? The right balance may differ according to the situation, the age of youth, and the subject matter. Research suggests that in some domains, like moral development, youth appear to grasp concepts more effectively through interactions with peers, without adults (Rogoff, 1998). Perhaps that is what we observed with the FFA's youth learning about teamwork. But for other domains of learning and development, adult assistance can facilitate youths' learning (Rogoff, 1998). We suspect that some measured degree of scaffolding from adults is helpful for most domains, especially with younger youth.

When we are talking about youth-adult relationship as a vehicle of learning, there is an additional theoretical perspective that it is critical to include. Theories of collaborative learning conceptualize support as mainly an instrumental and cognitive process. If takes the form of technical assistance for solving a problem or learning a procedure. But the feelings and emotions that occur in these relationships are also important to the process of human development.

Relationship Theories: Caring Connections as a Base for Development

Humans are needy and emotional creatures. Behind our public faces, we harbor strong drives, longings, and insecurities. It often takes little to make humans— especially children and youth—feel distressed, angry, or crushed. This portrait of the human condition is the starting point for attachment theory and object relations theory (Bowlby, 1969; Winnicott, 1975).

These theories see close relationships with caring adults as essential to human development. Starting in infancy, the child who is fortunate has a stable parent figure (or figures) who helps her or him manage this internal cauldron of strong drives and feelings. The stability these children get from this caring relationship—called by some a "secure attachment relationship"—helps them feel safe enough to take on new challenges. The relationship provides a secure base for development (Mahler, Pine, & Bergman, 1975). In addition, these children develop through the process of experiencing need or distress and being helped to address it. Over the course of many, many cycles of distress followed by patient assistance from parent figures, these youth gradually develop greater self-confidence and greater ability to regulate internal states. These children learn to do on their own what their parent figures have been doing for them. They internalize a "working model" of the caring they received.

Some children, however, do not have this type of secure caring relationship with a parent figure. They do not get this consistent emotional support, or get it only sporadically. Because they cannot count on support, these children are more vulnerable to panic and careening emotions. They do not have a trusted safe base to fall back on. Furthermore, without experiencing the cycles of distress followed by comforting support, they are less likely to develop healthy means to regulate their internal drives and feelings (Sroufe, 1989). They are likely to have a less effective working model that helps them regulate emotions, or they have a dysfunctional model. For these youth and even for those who did get this consistent support in childhood, early adolescence can be a time of new emotional challenges and threats to self-esteem. It is often also a time of greater autonomy from parents, which increases the value for adolescents to have this type of caring, safe, and stable relationship outside the family.

Youth development programs are one place where young people form connections with caring adults who serve this function. Mentoring programs that pair youth with mature adults are often designed to specifically provide this kind of supportive relationship. Research suggests that a long-term relationship with a mentor can help youth—especially younger adolescents—by providing empathy, acceptance, and help with learning to regulate emotions and threats to self-esteem (Rhodes, 2002). In other types of youth development and recreational programs, adults cannot have this type of close one-on-one relationship with all youth. However, they can provide a stable and caring environment that serves some of the same functions. They can cultivate an emotionally safe setting that provides youth the security to take on new challenges and grow (Griffith & Larson, 2016).

The role of program leaders in providing this supportive environment is most apparent when something happens that triggers youths' emotional insecurities. In a girls basketball team that we studied, the girls became upset and fearful when they learned that one of their members had been briefly taken in by the police for assaulting another youth. Melissa, the co-captain, was a close friend of this girl, but said that she was afraid that the girl would become angry and "beat me up." Melissa reported that rumors were flying and people's fears were getting "cranked up." No one could focus at their next practice.

The coach, Sara, responded by canceling everything else on her schedule so she could deal with this situation. She talked with the assailant's mother and decided that the girl should not be excluded from team practices. Sara, who many described as like a second mother, also made herself available to team members. Melissa had a long talk with her in which she was able to express her fears and get support. This talk, Melissa said, had a "huge" role in helping her get a hold on her fear: "I was like, 'Hello, news flash, there is no reason to be afraid of her.'" When the assailant—her friend—came to the next practice, Melissa walked up to her and gave her a hug, then, "I just let her talk to me and spill her guts out and tell me her side of the story." Melissa said it still took days to fully get control of her feelings: to stop "pretending it didn't happen, accept it, and move on." But she described it as a valuable learning experience, "a taste of what real life is going to be like." She reported that the experience, including the support she received from her coach, had helped her "mature as a person."

The coach, Sara, had developed strong trusting relationships with the girls that facilitated their capacity to manage and learn about emotions. Over the course of the season, the youth praised her patience and commented that "she's really here for us." We were repeatedly impressed by Sara's abilities to create a caring, stable environment that minimized the rivalries and strong negative emotions that frequently emerge in competitive activities. Because of this environment, the youth often seemed able to handle potentially threatening situations in very mature ways. They reported learning about their own and others' emotions. They came to recognize emotions as part of human relationships and learned to conceal, express, or "vent" them according to the situation.

The importance of these relationship theories for youth development is in helping us think about how important relationships can be for young people. Many adherents to these theories believe that a child's core patterns of emotional regulation are laid down in the first five years of life, and one cannot expect relationships in adolescence to easily reshape them. Nonetheless, secure relationships with adults outside the family can make a significant difference in youths' development, including leading to improvements in their relationships with their parents (Rhodes, 2002).

We are also not suggesting that every program leader has to be as emotionally attuned as Sara. Indeed, some researchers have downplayed this emotional dimension of program leaders' relationships, especially for older youth (Darling, Hamilton, & Shaver, 2003). But even if this relationship is matter-of-fact—focused on the work youth are doing—adults' ways of relating to youth are critical to creating an environment of trust and psychological safety that facilitates youths' engagement in positive development (Griffith & Larson, 2016).

> Adults' ways of relating to youth are critical to creating an environment of trust and psychological safety that facilitates youths' engagement in positive development.

We shift now from thinking about a broader level of human relationships. Theories of human development are not solely the provenance of the psychologists we have covered thus far. Sociologists have useful ideas about young people coming of age within a wider interpersonal arena.

Sociological Theories: Learning Norms and Building Social Connections

Sociologists see humans as social creatures. Development for sociologists is a process of coming to take your place within social groups and society. Thus, development includes learning the general rules, meanings, and ways of acting for being, for example, an American or a Filipino. It can also include figuring out how to act and think as a member of a given religious faith, a member of a specific profession, or a participant in a particular youth program. Whether the social group is the entire society, a community of some type, or a small group, development takes the form of learning to follow and navigate the "norms" of that group. As part of this process, one also develops a social identity as a member of that group.

These norms and identities are acquired through social interactions. Early sociological theories saw young people as passive learners of these norms, who are "socialized" into society. Young people learn from watching others, being reinforced for following norms, and sometimes from being sanctioned for doing something wrong. Sociological theories now stress that people are often active in this socialization process (Berger & Luckmann, 1966). Of course, when a young person enters society, many rules, norms, and ways of thinking are already in place. However, youth may create new meanings for old norms, or create new norms. As youth come to accept norms, new or old, they also become active in enforcing those norms.

These sociological processes happen within youth programs. Although adults may try to set the norms for the program, youth do not automatically follow them. They may modify them, adhere to them selectively, as well as creating some of their own norms. Youth also have norms from the worlds of their peers, their families, and their families' cultures that they bring into a youth program. For example, youth from different cultural backgrounds have different frameworks for how youth and adults relate (Serpell & Hatano, 1997), which can shape their expectations for relationships with adult leaders (Deutsch & Jones, 2008).

In an urban arts program, Art-First, we saw a process in which youth were socialized into the world of adult artists. Many of the teachers in this program were practicing artists, and through their teaching they invited the youth into their way of thinking and doing art. One youth, Marco, explained that artists "like looking at things at a deeper perspective," and he described having adopted that way of looking at himself, along with a colorful style of dressing. Marco was learning and coming to follow the iconoclastic norms of artists. Other youth mentioned the openness they had discovered in the arts world. Several said that participation in Art-First had "opened me up" or brought "me out of my shell." In fact, they were sometimes now impatient with peers at school whom they perceived as having a closed way of thinking. This process of development and change was an active process in which youth acquired insider knowledge about the art world and began to find a place for themselves inside this world. Through their classes, youth were also developing their own artistic styles, which started to give them distinct artistic identities.

Usually the norms youth learn in a program are positive. Youth acquire norms to function effectively within a community, and they develop group norms for mutual respect and responsibility. Youth at Art-First developed skills to function in the art world and learned about viable career paths in the arts. But sometimes youth bring negative norms into a program from elsewhere in their lives, and these can propagate within the program. Researchers found that Swedish youth centers were a context in which the antisocial behavior of some youth was being reinforced and passed on to other youth (Mahoney, Stattin, & Magnusson, 2001). Several studies have suggested that teen boys in sports programs get socialized by other youth into alcohol use (Eccles & Barber, 1999). In neither instance is it likely that the adults in these recreational contexts directly supported these negative norms, but the ineffectiveness of the adults in promoting alternative norms may have been a factor. Although adult leaders cannot force positive norms onto a group, they can play major role in cultivating an organizational culture that supports pro-social behavior (Eccles & Gootman, 2002).

Another useful idea from sociology is that taking one's place in society involves not just learning things, but also forming relationships of exchange. To successfully enter society, you need not just the competencies stressed by psychologists, but a social network. It is helpful to know people! Connections to people provide information, assistance, and connections to yet other people: what is sometimes called "social capital" (Bourdieu, 1985). For older youth, knowing the right people can help them get a job, learn about different college choices, or chose a career.

> Although adult leaders cannot force positive norms onto a group, they can play a major role in cultivating an organizational culture that supports pro-social behavior.

Urban youth, like those at Art-First, often know few people who provide this type of social capital (Wilson, 1987). At Art-First, the adult leaders were very deliberate about connecting youth with adults who could provide it through special events and an internship program. Indeed, as the youth had ideas about going to college or pursuing arts careers, they actively drew on adults they had met through the program for advice and connections (Jarrett, Sullivan, & Watkins, 2005).

Conclusion: Theories as Tools

It should be clear by now that no one of these theories is the "right one." Rather each is useful for different youth, situations, and developmental goals. The purpose of developmental theories is to help us think creatively about how young people develop (Garbarino & Abramowitz, 1992). These theories (and others we have not covered) provide tools for understanding the processes of growth and our role in facilitating these processes. Of course, theory alone is not enough to make you a good practitioner. Your toolbox needs to include the type of knowledge, intuition, and rules of thumb that come only from experience. But theory plays an important role in helping you think about the abstract, hard-to-see processes of change in youth.

A common theme across these theories (except early learning theory) is that development occurs through a process in which youth are active agents of their own growth. They drive development. They are not pigeons or rats who can easily be shaped by others. Rather they think, feel, and react. They pay attention to what the rewards are in a situation and they learn behaviors that help them obtain rewards that they want (Bandura, Social Learning Theory). They actively try to figure things out by experimenting, observing, and drawing conclusions (Piaget, Constructivist Theory). They willingly enter into partnership with adults who can help guide their learning (Vygotsky, Collaborative Learning) and who provide a safe environment that allows them to take on challenges (Relationship Theories). They are also active members of social groups who contribute to the creation and reinforcement of social norms (Sociological Theories). Human growth is a natural positive process.

Our primary message, then, is that development is not something that proceeds one way from adults to youth. Adults will rarely be successful if they do not think about what youth are thinking and feeling and how they are relating to others. In order to unlock youths' natural processes of development, program designers and leaders need to listen and be attentive. They need to think about mobilizing young people's natural dispositions for growth, such as their eagerness to figure things out and their motivation to participate in relationships and social groups. When someone like Julia Escobar is able to facilitate youths' enjoyment of challenging activities, she is going a long way toward activating young people's potential for development.

Youth practitioners also need to think about creating a fit between what happens in the program and young people's developmental levels and needs (Eccles & Gootman, 2002). For example, some youth—particularly younger ones—may have greater need for emotional support from adults, whereas older youth may place more importance on access to adults who can provide social capital or the type of technical guidance that we described Janna providing in the media arts program. In optimal situations, skilled practitioners are able to help adapt a program to an individual youth's motivations and developmental levels. They may help find a "hook" that motivates a youth, or help the youth shape goals that allow him or her to excel.

> In order to unlock youths' natural processes of development, program designers and leaders need to listen and be attentive.

A second message, however, is that this active process of development is not easy and automatic. Piaget had a very optimistic view of young people as organisms who are highly motivated and able to grow. However, other theories draw our attention to obstacles that can stand in the way of these natural processes. The collaborative learning model recognizes that youth do not have X-ray vision. They are not always able to figure out what they need to learn and how best to learn it. They can easily get off track or have their motivation stalled. Relationship theories describe how strong emotions and insecurities can easily shut down the developmental process. Sociological theories call our attention to the norms, identities, and cultural orientations that youth bring into the program from other parts of their lives, which can be opportunities or obstacles for development.

Knowledge of these obstacles helps us think about the roles that practitioners can play. Most of the theories suggest ways in which adults can help youth navigate this obstacle course. In collaborative learning, adults are guides who provide scaffolding in the form of clues, breaking down tasks, or supporting motivation. In relationship theories, adults can provide a caring, safe, and stable emotional base that quells youths' insecurities and allows them to explore. In sociological theories, adults might play a role in cultivating norms and helping youth develop social capital. Across all these theories, adults need to find a balance between providing guidance around obstacles and keeping the experience of agency in the hands of youth. When youth are engaged, experience ownership, and can see an unobstructed path ahead, their tremendous potential for positive development becomes mobilized.

Discussion Questions

1. Which theory most resonates with you, and why?
2. Describe a time when you have experienced each of these teaching techniques as learner or used them as an educator: modeling (social learning), scaffolding (collaborative learning), providing consistent emotional support (relationships theory), cultivating norms (sociological theory), or getting out of the way (or giving someone freedom to learn) (constructivist theory)?
3. How can these theories be tools to inform your work with young people?

Assignment

It's not easy for program staff to strike the right balance between letting youth learn on their own and providing structure and guidance. The chapter described how Mr. Baker took a constructivist approach, letting youth plan a day camp and "learn by doing, including learning from their mistakes." The youth gained important skills, but they also struggled. Their lack of experience with planning and running activities for children was a handicap. Pretend you are Mr. Baker and you choose to take a more collaborative learning approach next year. Describe what kinds of scaffolding you would provide to support youth as they plan and execute the day camp.

Acknowledgment: The research described in this paper was carried out with support from the W. T. Grant Foundation.

References

Bandura, A. (1986). *The social foundations of thought and action: A social cognitive theory.* Englewood Cliffs, NJ: Prentice-Hall.

Berger, P., & Luckmann, T. (1966). *The social construction of reality.* New York, NY: Anchor.

Bourdieu, P. (1985). The forms of capital. In J. G. Richardson (Ed.), *Handbook of theory and research for the sociology of education* (pp. 241–258). New York, NY: Greenwood.

Bowlby, J. (1969). *Attachment.* New York, NY: Basic Books.

Csikszentmihalyi, M. (1990). *Flow: The psychology of optimal experience.* New York, NY: Harper & Row.

Darling, N., Hamilton, S. E., & Shaver, K. H. (2003). Relationships outside the family: Unrelated Adults. In G. R. Adams & M. D. Berzonsky (Eds.), *Blackwell handbook of adolescence* (pp. 349–370). Malden, MA: Blackwell Publishing.

Deutsch, N., & Jones, J. (2008). "Show me an ounce of respect": Respect and authority in adult-youth relationships in after-school programs. *Journal of Adolescent Research, 23,* 667–688.

Eccles, J. S., & Barber, B. L. (1999). Student council, volunteering, basketball, or marching band: What kind of extracurricular involvement matters? *Journal of Adolescent Research, 14,* 10–43.

Eccles, J., & Gootman, J. (2002). *Community programs to promote youth development.* National Research Council Institute of Medicine. Washington, D. C.: National Academy Press.

Fester, C., & Skinner, B. F. (1957). *Schedules of reinforcement.* New York, NY: Appleton-Century-Crofts.

Freire, P. (1970). *Pedagogy of the oppressed.* Translated by M. B. Ramos. New York, NY: Continuum.

Garbarino, J. A., & Abramowitz, R. H. (1992). The ecology of human development. J. Garbarino (Ed.). *Children and families in the social environment.* (pp. 11–33). New York, NY: Aldine de Gruyter.

Griffith, A. N., & Larson, R. W. (2016). Why trust matters: How confidence in leaders transforms what adolescents gain from youth programs. *Journal of Research on Adolescence. 26*(4), 790–804.

Hilgard, E., & Bower, C. (1966). *Theories of learning.* New York, NY: Appleton-Century.

Jarrett, R. L., Sullivan, P. J., & Watkins, N. D. (2005). Developing social capital through participation in organized youth programs: Qualitative insights from three programs. *Journal of Community Psychology, 33*(1), 41–55.

Larson, R. (2000). Toward a psychology of positive youth development. *American Psychologist, 55,* 170–183.

Larson, R., Hansen, D., & Walker, K. (2005). Everybody's gotta give: Adolescents' development of initiative and teamwork within a youth program. In J. Mahoney, R. Larson, & J. Eccles (Eds.), *Organized activities as contexts of development: Extracurricular activities, after-school and community programs* (pp. 159–183). Hillsdale, NJ: Erlbaum.

Larson, R., Walker, K., & Pearce, N. (2005). Youth-driven and adult-driven youth development programs: Contrasting models of youth-adult relationships. *Journal of Community Psychology, 33*(1), 57–74.

Mahler, M. S., Pine, F., Bergman, A. (1975). *The psychological birth of the human infant: Symbiosis and individuation.* New York, NY: Basic Books.

Mahoney, J. L., Stattin, H., and Magnusson, D. (2001). Youth recreation centre participation and criminal offending: A 20-year longitudinal study of Swedish boys." *International Journal of Behavioral Development,* 509–520.

Mayr, E. (2001). *What evolution is.* New York, NY: Basic Books.

Piaget, J. (1936). *The origins of intelligence in children.* New York, NY: International Universities Press, Inc.

Piaget, J. (1965). *The moral judgement of the child.* Translated by T. A. Brown & C. E. Kaegi. Palo Alto, CA: Annual Reviews.

Piaget, J., & Inhelder, B. (1969). *The growth of logical thinking: From childhood to adolescence.* New York, NY: Basic Books.

Rhodes, J. (2002). *Stand by me: The risks and rewards of mentoring programs.* Cambridge, MA: Harvard Press.

Rogoff, B. (1998). Cognition as a collaborative process. In W. Damon, D. Kuhn, & R. Siegler (Eds.), *Handbook of child psychology, Vol. 2* (5th ed., pp. 679–744). New York, NY: Wiley.

Serpell, R., & Hatano, G. (1997). Education, schooling, and literacy. In J. W. Berry, P. R. Dasen, & T. S. Saraswathi (Eds.), *Handbook of cross-cultural psychology: Vol. 2. Basic processes and human development* (2nd ed., 339–376). Boston, MA: Allyn & Bacon.

Sroufe, L. A. (1989). Relationships, self, and individual adaptation. In A. Sameroff & R. Emde (Eds.), *Relationship disturbances in early childhood* (pp. 70–94). New York, NY: Basic Books.

Vygotsky, L. S. (1962). *Thought and language.* Cambridge, MA: MIT Press.

Vygotsky, L. S. (1978). *Mind and society.* Cambridge, MA: Harvard Press.

Wilson, W. J. (1987). *The truly disadvantaged: The inner city, the underclass, and public policy.* Chicago, IL: University of Chicago Press.

Winnicott, D. W. (1975). *Through paediatrics to psycho-analysis.* New York, NY: Basic Books.

Wood, D., Bruner, J. & Ross, G. (1976). The role of tutoring in problem-solving. *Journal of Child Psychology and Psychiatry, 17,* 89–100.

Chapter 8

Resiliency, Protective Processes, Promotion, and Community Youth Development

Daniel F. Perkins, Linda L. Caldwell, and Peter A. Witt

In Chapter 1 we identified a shift in the way youth development has been conceptualized—from thinking of youth as problems to be fixed to thinking of them as resources to be nourished and engaged in community life. This shift has spawned a great deal of thought and attention about how to prevent problem behaviors, while at the same time thinking about how to promote positive development, a perspective evident in many of the chapters in this book.

One question we have not addressed so far is "How do some youth who live and develop in less than ideal circumstances mature into responsible, thriving adolescents and adults, while others succumb to the pressures in their high-risk environments and get into trouble with the police or participate regularly in unhealthy and unproductive behaviors?" The purpose of this chapter is to examine more closely some important concepts related to understanding how youth are affected by and respond to their everyday life situations.

The main concepts important to this chapter are *resiliency, protective factors, prevention,* and *promotion.* After introducing these concepts, we turn to a discussion of how youth development programs can contribute to prevention and promotion efforts through an overall framework called *community youth development.*

Resiliency

In the last 35 years, service providers and social scientists have increasingly explored the concept of youth resiliency and reduced their focus on vulnerability and maladjustment. Several scholars, Werner and Smith (1992), Rutter (1985), Masten (2001), and Luthar and her colleagues (e.g., Luthar, Cicchetti, & Becker, 2000), have championed this approach and devoted considerable attention to the study of resiliency. This shift in focus means that although it is still important to conduct programs and research that focus on negative developmental outcomes (e.g., risk behaviors), a critical emphasis now includes (a) understanding how youth adapt successfully to challenging life conditions and adversity and (b) providing programs that promote positive development. Recall that this was one of the principles of youth development presented in Chapter 1 (not "either/or," but "and"). Clearly, out-of-school time (OST) programs fall more heavily into the positive and promotive category.

Along with the shift in focus to include the positive, researchers and practitioners have increasingly focused on the ways youth and their environments shape each other. People and settings are not just acting on youth, but youth also actively shape and influence things in their environment. In other words, there is reciprocal interaction among elements in a youth's life (e.g., parents, teachers, peers, coaches, ministers, and neighborhoods). Several chapters in this book are premised on the principle of reciprocal interaction because it is a critical component of understanding youth development, including resiliency.

Definition of Resiliency

Consider Jacinda, who is 15. She was born and raised on a farm in a rural area in Pennsylvania. Her parents make less than $30,000 per year, and she has two younger brothers. The closest town (population 1,300) is five miles away, and she is bussed for 45 minutes to school. Her parents smoke heavily even though they cannot afford to, and her mother is obese. Her mother really loves her children, but verges on depression and does not exhibit good parenting skills. Often, Jacinda's dad drinks too much and becomes violent toward the family dog, although he has not yet hurt Jacinda or her mother. Lately, her 14-year-old brother has been experimenting with drugs. It is summer and she feels there is absolutely nothing for her to do on the farm except the expectation that she help with the milking at 4:30 every morning and afternoon. Many people would consider Jacinda to be at high risk, in particular because of the many *risk factors* to which she is subjected (e.g., consistent poverty, mother's apathy, parental smoking, and her father's consistent drinking and violence). We will discuss all of these things in more depth, but let us first look at Jacinda's resilience despite the presence of these risk factors.

According to Masten (2001), resiliency involves *competence and adaptability in the face of adversity*. In addition, resiliency requires a young person to assess if the adaptation is "good" or "helpful." To make that assessment, youth use criteria to assess their behavior and their situation based on specific societal and cultural norms within their contexts. For example, if Jacinda was resilient, what characteristics would she have drawn from herself and her environment? What markers would we use to assess her competence and adaptiveness in the face of her adversity?

Jacinda demonstrates her resilience in several ways. She has set life goals for herself, which include finishing high school and going on to post-secondary education (e.g., college or a two-year trade school). She has teachers and other caring adults who are supportive and facilitative of her goals. Jacinda also has set a goal that she would not become pregnant at a young age. She has learned how to make meaningful use of her free

Resiliency involves competence and adaptability in the face of adversity.

time by developing a low-cost hobby (e.g., making sculpture out of old farm materials), which helps her cope with daily stressors. She has also learned how to cope with her father's outbursts by calling and talking to a friend or leaving the room. In addition, Jacinda has had to learn to assess whether the way she has adapted and dealt with her situation is positive.

Each of the things Jacinda has chosen to do appear to be appropriate for her "farm context" and age. She might decide at some point, however, that talking with her friend does more harm than good; for example, if her friend is in a similar situation and their conversations start a downward spiral of depression. Or, she might realize that getting up and leaving the room when her father has an outburst only makes her father angrier when she returns.

While there are many definitions of resiliency, the one we employ is borrowed from Masten (2001): Resiliency is defined "as a class of phenomena characterized by good outcomes in spite of serious threats to adaptation or development" (p. 228). Resiliency focuses on how people succeed despite challenges in their environments, thus programs that promote resiliency provide skills and supports that will help youth navigate and succeed when subjected to challenging circumstances.

Let us fast-forward 10 years and look at Jacinda in her mid-20s. We see she has met her goals and in fact exceeded them. She attended veterinary school and joined a seasoned vet in her practice in rural Pennsylvania, not far from her family. Given the above definition, we would conclude that Jacinda is resilient; she has achieved good outcomes in spite of serious threats to her development. She has thrived.

Resiliency sounds like a wonderful concept, but there are many common myths associated with it. In order to understand what resiliency really means, let us explore those myths.

Myth 1: All People Who Survive Their Childhood and Adolescence Are Resilient

All children and youth have to cope with stress and adverse situations in their lives; thus, in some ways all people who survive their childhood and adolescence are resilient. However, not all stress or adverse situations are alike or are of the same magnitude, and some youth are at greater risk for failure than others; thus, some people display more resiliency than others. Examining individuals who are most at risk or vulnerable is the hallmark of resiliency research. Biological risk factors, contextual risk factors, and stressful life events are what place a person at risk of succumbing to stress or not succeeding. In sum, youth display resiliency through their responses to serious adversity, whether it is a stressful life event or a situation of continuous stress (e.g., war, death of a parent, abuse, poverty).

Originally, investigators emphasized the association between a single risk variable, such as low IQ or a stressful life event (e.g., loss of parent), and negative developmental outcomes (e.g., alcohol abuse, holding down a job, forming long-term relationships). Now, resiliency researchers have learned from epidemiologists and have shifted from looking at these single variables to models that involve multiple stressors that typically co-occur. For example, the literature suggests that violence (e.g., parental abuse, neighborhood killings) and poverty often co-occur (Werner & Smith, 1992), as happened in Jacinda's case.

Myth 2: Resilient Individuals are Completely Successful in Every Area of Their Lives

Resiliency is multidimensional in nature. Thus, one may be resilient in one domain (such as school) but not exhibit resiliency in another domain (work or leisure). For example, Kaufman, Cook, Arny, Jones, and Pittinsky (1994) found that approximately two-thirds of children with histories of maltreatment were academically resilient; however, when examining the social competence of these same children, only 21% exhibited resiliency. In fact, Luthar and her colleagues (2000) suggest that not only might one exhibit competence in one area and not another, but also one might actually exhibit incompetence or problem behaviors in other areas.

Jacinda was lucky because she exhibited competence in her academic work and went on to become a veterinarian. However, suppose she became a veterinarian because she really preferred being around animals more than people. Perhaps it was even difficult for her to communicate well with the animal's humans. To make matters worse, suppose Jacinda was unable to sustain a mature, loving relationship with another person. In this case, should we consider Jacinda resilient? It would appear that Jacinda displayed competence and resilience in certain aspects of her life; however, in forming a sustained loving relationship, Jacinda did not display competence and needed to seek psychological counseling.

Myth 3: Resilience Stems from an Internal Personality Trait

Resiliency itself is not a personality trait, although there are personality traits that promote resiliency (e.g., humor and flexibility). Despite the contribution of these important traits, characteristics of the person's environment seem to be more important for resiliency. For example, Jacinda was in a very stressful economic and emotional situation, but she also had personal motivation and intelligence. However, without a teacher who took a vested interest in her over a sustained time period, it is unlikely she would have fared so well. Perhaps she would have continued on to further education, but a teacher helped direct her attention to veterinary sciences and supported her choices and decisions. Thus, it took both personal and environmental factors to create resiliency in Jacinda's case.

> Indeed, no human is invulnerable or unbreakable, or able to conquer any level of stress.

The degree of resistance to stress varies over time according to one's circumstances (e.g., Luthar et al., 2000; Masten, 2001; Rutter, 1985). Furthermore, resistance to stress in an individual is relative, not absolute. Indeed, no human is invulnerable or unbreakable, or able to conquer any level of stress. If we fast-forward 10 more years in Jacinda's life, we see that she is clinically depressed. Although she did get help with her relationship issues, got married, and was happy for about five years, it did not work out because her husband became an alcoholic, and they are in the process of a divorce. Even though she had done very well for a while, circumstances in her life in her mid-30s were too much for her to handle. Unfortunately, this circumstance is a common phenomenon, and researchers have come to realize that the definition of resilience must acknowledge a history of success while also implying the possibility of succumbing to future stressors (e.g., Masten & Garmezy, 1985; Rutter 1985; Werner & Smith, 1992).

Myth 4: Resiliency is Rare

Most children and youth are resilient in the face of adversity. For example, in most studies, approximately 70% of children who were living in extremely adverse situations were resilient. These included children and youth who were sexually abused (Wilkes, 2002), were placed in foster care (Festinger, 1984), were in gangs (Vigil, 1990), lived in families where mental illness was present (Beardslee & Prodoresfky, 1988; Werner & Smith, 2001), were born to teen mothers (Furstenberg, Cook, Eccles, Elder, & Sameroff, 1998), and grew up in poverty (Vaillant, 2002). In a study designed to learn about how resilience lasts over time, Werner and Smith followed nearly 700 at-risk individuals (one-third of whom had multiple risk factors) from birth to adulthood, and found that the children grew increasingly like their counterparts who did not have risk factors. Moreover, in adulthood (age 32 and again at age 40), only 20% of these children who were high risk previously (i.e., possessing multiple risk factors) were doing poorly (e.g., chronic financial problems, domestic conflict, violence, substance abuse).

In another study, Romanian children reared under severe deprivation in an institution were able to catch up developmentally in terms of physical and cognitive abilities once they were adopted into families (Ames, 1997; Rutter & ERA Study Team, 1998). As noted by Masten, "the capacity for developmental recovery when normative childrearing conditions are restored is amazing" (Masten, 2001, p. 233). Indeed, Werner and Smith (1992) have noted that resiliency research results are evidence of the self-righting tendencies that move youth toward normal adult development under all but the most persistent adverse circumstances.

> "The capacity for developmental recovery when normative childrearing conditions are restored is amazing."

Nevertheless, while resiliency is not rare, it is not guaranteed. That is, a substantial minority of youth (about 30%) do not recover from adversity and therefore are not considered resilient. Indeed Masten (2001) stated, "Resiliency does not come from rare and special qualities, but from the everyday magic of ordinary, normative human resources in the minds, brains, and bodies of children, in their families and relationships, and in their communities" (p. 9). Those individuals who do bounce back from adversity have connected to parts of their environment that provide support, encouragement, and opportunities that nurture their development.

In Summary: A Model of Resiliency

As we have described, understanding resiliency involves an examination of the link between the person and the demands and challenges of the context, and understanding the factors and processes that will either promote or subvert adaptation. Resilient individuals are well adapted in spite of serious stressors in their lives. They have the environmental supports to help them cope with these stressors. The balance between a person's own traits that support adaptability, environmental supports, and the level or severity of stress are what are important in detracting from or promoting resiliency. Figure 8.1 displays a representation of this balance.

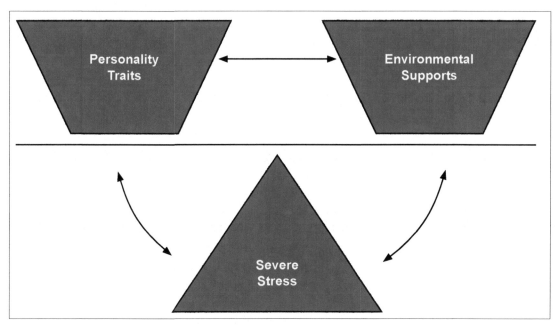

Figure 8.1. Resiliency: A Balancing Act Over Time with Reciprocal Influences

There is a time element involved in resiliency as well. That is, resiliency is a process that occurs over time, and the cumulative effects of life events and situations are important. Time is also important, because although adversity may exist in a youth's life initially, other challenges or supports might happen over time that either adds to or reduces the stress. These challenges and supports include things such as being placed in foster care, moving to a new neighborhood, or having a mentoring relationship. The arrows in Figure 8.1 represent the multiple interactions among stressors in the environment, environmental supports, and personality traits. Thus to understand or promote resiliency means we cannot focus on a single aspect of a youth's life—a holistic approach must be taken. One must look at the multiple contexts that comprise a youth's world.

There are many implications of this model for youth professionals, because they offer important services under the *environmental supports* component of the model. Coordination among agencies and services (e.g., YMCAs, 4-H Youth Development

Programs, schools, community park and recreation departments, and human services agencies) and working with parents are means by which the holistic approach to service provision are achieved. This coordination, coupled with adopting a risk prevention and community youth development perspective, help create a context for resiliency. We will discuss what youth-service and community-service providers can do to promote resilience in more detail later in this chapter, but next we will turn our attention to understanding what constitutes both risk and protective factors in a young person's life.

Risk and Protective Factors and Processes

What factors (e.g., events or situations) and processes (e.g., becoming educated or playing on a summer basketball league) contribute to or thwart an individual becoming resilient? Researchers have broken these factors and processes into two categories: (a) risk factors and processes and (b) protective factors and processes.

Risk factors and processes are defined as *individual or environmental hazards that increase an individual's vulnerability to negative developmental behaviors, events, or outcomes such as alcohol and drug abuse, early unprotected sexual activity, delinquency and violence, and school failure* (e.g., Masten, 2001; Werner & Smith, 1992). Examples of risk factors include poverty, violent neighborhood, parental style characterized by inconsistent discipline and lack of warmth, extreme shyness, and lack of socio-emotional control. Jacinda's situation was filled with risk factors and processes. However, it is important to understand that the presence of risk factors and processes does not guarantee that negative outcomes will occur; rather, they simply increase the probability of their occurrence (e.g., Masten, 2001; Werner & Smith, 1992).

> The presence of risk factors and processes does not guarantee that negative outcomes will occur; rather, they simply increase the probability of their occurrence.

The probability of negative outcomes varies as a consequence of the presence of protective factors and processes. Protective factors and processes buffer, modify, or ameliorate an individual's reaction to an adverse situation that, in ordinary circumstances, would lead to maladaptive outcomes (Kumpfer, 1999; Werner & Smith, 1992). Protective processes are incorporated into the multiple levels of adolescents' contexts and enable them to overcome adversity. They are the processes that occur in the *personality characteristics* and *environmental supports* blocks of Figure 8.1. According to our definition, a protective process is *primarily* evident in combination with a risk factor. Some protective processes and factors do not have a strong effect on resiliency in low-risk populations, since for these individuals, resilience is not an issue in the first place. They do contribute, however, to youth development, which we will discuss in more detail subsequently. The main point here is that the effect of protective factors and processes is magnified in the presence of risk (Rutter, 1987; Werner & Smith, 1992).

Types of Protective Factors and Processes

What factors and processes in life are protective and promote resiliency? A couple notable studies help to answer this question. In their longitudinal study of a cohort of children from the island of Kauai, Hawaii, Werner and Smith (1992) described three types of protective processes that emerge from analyses of the developmental course of high-risk children from infancy to adulthood:

1. **Dispositional attributes** of the individual, such as activity level and sociability, at least average intelligence, competence in communication skills (e.g., language and reading), and an internal locus of control
2. **Affectional ties** within the family that provide emotional supports in times of stress, whether from a parent, sibling, spouse, or mate
3. **External support systems,** whether in school, at a youth program, at work, or at church, that reward the individual's competencies and determination, and provide a belief system by which to live

Finally, the researchers found that an individual's hopefulness that the odds could be surmounted was a central positive factor in his or her life.

Using the Ecological Model (Bronfenbrenner, 1979) as her framework, Bogenschneider (1998) concluded that there are protective factors and processes in each level of a youth's environment (or ecosystem):

1. **Individual level**—such as well-developed problem-solving skills and intellectual abilities
2. **Familial level**—for example, a close relationship with one parent
3. **Peer level**—a close friend
4. **School level**—positive school climate
5. **Community level**—required helpfulness (e.g., as it occurs when the adolescent is needed to bring in extra income or help manage the home), and a positive relationship with a non-parental adult (e.g., neighbor and teacher)

What protective factors and processes did Jacinda have in her environment? She knew her mother loved her very much, she had at least one good friend she could confide in, she was creative and had developed a hobby, and she had strong support and assistance from her teachers. Imagine if none of these factors had existed for Jacinda. Would she have been resilient? Probably not. A question you might be asking now is how many of these protective factors and processes are necessary, and are some better than others? These are excellent questions, but there is not a good answer yet; more research is needed to better understand how risk and protective factors and processes influence each other.

Protective Processes and Factors for All Youth

In this book, we are interested in promoting the development of all youth. Therefore, although we noted earlier that a specific protective factor or process is most often apparent in combination with a specific risk variable (e.g., Jacinda's physical and/ or emotional withdrawal from negative situations) some protective processes have universally positive influences on all youth. Thus, some protective processes have a direct effect in enhancing adolescents' positive development regardless of their risk level. Therefore, even if a youth is facing little adversity, these protective processes enable him or her to thrive or do even better. In her comprehensive review, Bernard noted (2004) three environmental protective processes, in particular, that significantly promote and foster the positive development of all youth. These universal protective processes include (1) caring relationships with nonparental adults; (2) high expectations; and (3) opportunities for participation, contribution, and recognition. These three protective factors and processes can be exhibited at multiple levels of the youth's context (e.g., family, school, youth programs, and neighborhood). The more contexts that provide or facilitate these processes the more likely it is that the youth is going to succeed. This relationship is just as valid for youth with many risk factors as for those without risk factors.

Caring Relationships with Adults

Since resiliency research began, caring relationships with nonparental adults has been found to be essential for youth overcoming adversity (Perkins & Borden, 2003; see Chapter 16 for more discussion about these relationships). Of course, the role of parent(s) is critical to the positive development of youth; however, the socially toxic and chaotic environment that surrounds some youth, like Jacinda, cannot be addressed within families alone. Caring relationships with nonparental adults provide a frame of reference and a model for how one is supposed to act. Nonjudgmental love and mentoring are the characteristics of these caring relationships. Rhodes (2002) found in her analysis of the Big Brothers/Big Sisters program that duration of the relationship is also an important factor to consider. One of the alarming findings from the study by Rhodes was that relationships between mentor and youth mentee that were less than six months in length tended to inflict more damage than good on the youth and contributed to a lack of continuity and stability in the youth's life. Moreover, Masten (2001) found that these relationships seem to be needed most during times of transition such as the transition into high school, which is exactly when we first were introduced to Jacinda.

> Caring relationships with nonparental adults are important for all youth and provide an environment of reinforcement, good modeling, and constructive feedback for physical, intellectual, psychological, and emotional and social growth.

Caring relationships with nonparental adults are important for all youth and, according to the report from National Research Council and the Institute of Medicine provide, "an environment of reinforcement, good modeling and constructive feedback for physical, intellectual, psychological [and emotional], and social growth (Eccles & Gootman, 2002, p. 96). However, youth development professionals must understand that the relationships must be long term to be effective, and that harm can be done if relationships are not of sufficient duration.

High Expectations

High expectations from parents and nonparental adults and within youths' environments (e.g., school, youth programs, and neighborhood) provide a consistent, predictable message and address the sense of safety and structure that all youth require —all of which are important protective factors and processes. In order for these high expectations to be absorbed by youth, they must be coupled with the warmth and responsiveness found in caring relationships as previously noted. For example, Blum and Mann Rinehart (1998) found that when parents have high expectations of their youths' academic success, this lowered youths' level of emotional distress and the likelihood of their using cigarettes or engaging in violent behavior.

Rutter and colleagues' classic examination of student outcomes in different types of school contexts in some of the most impoverished areas of London provides another example that is described thoroughly in their book *Fifteen Thousand Hours* (Rutter, Maughan, Mortimore, Ouston, & Smith, 1979). The researchers found significant differences in students' rates of academic attainment, delinquency, and behavioral disturbance (even after statistically controlling for family risk factors), which they attributed to differences in school context. Teachers in successful schools (in comparison to nonsuccessful schools) emphasized academics; established clear expectations and regulations; encouraged high levels of student participation; and provided alternative resources such as library facilities, vocational work opportunities, art, music, and extracurricular activities. Moreover, the National Research Council and Institute of Medicine report on youth programs (Eccles & Gootman, 2002) highlights the importance of clear rules about acceptable behavior while in the program and monitoring of behavior by staff, even when youth are elsewhere. Thus, youth program staff who are communicating with a youth's school to monitor behavior as well as establish a clear message of expectations across settings should have a positive impact on that youth.

Opportunities for Participation, Contribution, and Recognition

Opportunities for participation, contribution, and recognition are critical universal protective processes for youth living in high-risk environments, as well as for youth not facing extreme adversity. Youth gain many developmental benefits through participation in and engagement with their environment. In terms of protective factors and processes, opportunities for participation, contribution, and recognition enable youth to address several of their needs, including the ability to have a sense of belonging, sense of mastery, and sense of generosity and mattering (Brendtro, Brokenleg, & van Bockern, 1990; Eccles & Gootman, 2002). A sense of mattering is created when a youth is efficacious; that is, a youth has an opportunity and feels competent to do things that make a real difference in his or her social world (Eccles & Gootman, 2002). For example, youths' participation in family activities, school extracurricular activities, out-of-school (OST) youth programs, and other group activities provide a thread of connectedness that addresses youths' need for belonging and recognition. For youth with challenging home lives to be resilient, it is important that they have a place, if not multiple places, where they can go to feel comfortable, can fully engage, and can be recognized for their skills and talents (Werner & Smith, 1992).

Moreover, through these activities and experiences, youth are tied to positive social norms (Eccles & Gootman, 2002) that assist them in understanding society's expectations. A sense of mastery is developed through participation in autonomy-granting activities or experiences that are engaging, challenging, and interesting and promote a range of competencies and skills. As we will discuss in greater detail in Chapter 9, these experiences, labeled *flow* experiences (Csikszentmihalyi, 1997), involve high levels of goal-directedness, concentration, and intrinsic motivation. Through participation in these experiences, youth engage in discovery process about their skills, talents, and interests because they have opportunities to problem-solve, make decisions, and work with others. The power of these activities comes from the *voice* and *choice* that youth are afforded within the school, youth program, and community contexts. Indeed, according to Larson (2000), structured, voluntary youth activities provide a rich context for flow activities to occur, which ultimately can foster the development of initiative.

Finally, both resiliency research and youth development research have found that opportunities to contribute or to *matter* within one's context are linked with successful outcomes in adolescence (Eccles & Gootman, 2002; Villarruel, Perkins, Borden, & Keith, 2003). For example, Werner and Smith (1992) found that resilient youth were often required to look after younger siblings or take over tasks usually done by an adult. They called this phenomenon *required helpfulness.* The key is that these chores are not just to help around the house (chores), but they are necessary for household (if not human) functioning. By engaging in acts to help others, youth gain a sense of generosity and self-worth, as well as an opportunity to overcome the egocentric thinking so prevalent in adolescence. Youth involved in contributing are reframing their self-perceptions as well as other adults' perceptions of them from being a problem to be solved and a receiver of services to being a resource and provider of services (Bernard, 2004).

> Structured, voluntary youth activities provide a rich context for flow activities to occur, which ultimately can foster the development of initiative.

In addition, youth have so few opportunities for recognition, especially youth in risky environments, that youth service providers should structure ways for their peers and the community to recognize youth for their contributions. Recognition is very powerful and motivating to youth. Providing them with opportunities to contribute is explicitly demonstrating the concept that individuals are producers of their own development (Silbereisen & Eyferth, 1986) and shapers of their communities. According to the Carnegie Council on Adolescence (1995) report, one of the most powerful strategies for enriching the lives of youth is to enlist their energies in improving their own homes and communities.

Promotion and Prevention through Community Youth Development

The results of numerous longitudinal studies and other resiliency studies have provided critical information to the field of youth development. Specifically, by identifying universal protective processes, researchers and practitioners have gained important information for understanding what youth need in terms of opportunities and supports from different levels of the youths' context, including designing and implementing programming for youth development.

Society expects young people will grow up to be adults who are healthy, contributing members, as outlined in the vision of a thriving adult (see Chapter 1). In order for youth to become competent, contributing adult members of society, they need opportunities and support from their communities to develop important personal and social assets (see Table 8.1). These assets can also be thought of as protective factors, and can be grouped into the *five Cs* identified by Lerner and his colleagues (Lerner, 2004; 2002; Lerner, Fisher, & Weinberg, 2000). These include the following:

1. **Competence** in academic, social, emotional, and vocational areas
2. **Confidence** in whom one is becoming (identity)
3. **Connection** to self and others
4. **Character** that comes from positive values, integrity, and strong sense of morals
5. **Caring** and **compassion**

However, from a community youth development perspective, there is a sixth C, **Contribution** (Pittman, 2000; Lerner, 2004). By contributing to their families, neighborhoods, and communities, youth are afforded practical opportunities to make use of the other five Cs. These six Cs help clarify and provide some guidance to the positive youth development framework.

More recently, practitioners (Hughes & Curnan, 2000; Pittman, 2000) and researchers (Villarruel, Perkins, Borden, & Kieth, 2003) have advanced the field of youth development by integrating positive youth development and community development to address the need for a broader, more holistic approach to increasing protective factors and thereby helping to promote resiliency. *Community youth development* is defined as

> Purposely creating environments that provide constructive, affirmative, and encouraging relationships that are sustained over time with adults and peers, while concurrently providing an array of opportunities that enable youth to build their competencies and become engaged as partners in their own development as well as the development of their communities. (Perkins, Borden, & Villarruel, 2001, p. 41)

Clearly youth-serving agencies that create and promote recreation opportunities are an important part of community youth development.

Community youth development means promoting processes that provide *all* youth with the critical elements needed for successful development and engagement in their communities, regardless of their level of risk.

> Youth-serving agencies that create and promote recreation opportunities are an important part of community youth development.

Therefore, while resiliency focuses on youth that are at high risk or in adverse situations, community youth development focuses on what all youth need to thrive and become engaged partners in their own development and the development of their communities.

The community youth development framework involves a two-prong strategy for providing an atmosphere that fosters fully functioning youth. The first and most explicit strategy involves the promotion of universal protective processes and the six Cs. These processes and the six Cs address the personal and environmental assets needed by youth as outlined in the seminal book commissioned by the National Research Council and the Institute of Medicine (see Table 8.1).

Table 8.1

Personal and Social Assets that Facilitate Positive Youth Development Aligned with Six Cs of Positive Youth Development

Assets Category (Cs of Positive Youth Development)	Individual Assets
Physical Development (Competence)	• Good health habits • Good health risk management skills
Individual Development (Competence)	• Knowledge of essential life skills • Knowledge of essential vocational skills • School success • Rational habits of the mind—critical thinking and reasoning skills • In-depth knowledge of more than one culture • Good decision-making skills • Knowledge of skills needed to navigate through multiple cultural contexts
Psychological and Emotional Development (Competence, Confidence, Character, Caring/Compassion)	• Good mental health, including positive self-regard • Good emotional self-regulation skills • Good coping skills • Good conflict resolution skills • Mastery motivation and positive achievement motivation • Confidence in one's personal efficacy • Planfulness—planning for the future • Sense of personal autonomy and responsibility for self • Optimism coupled with realism • Coherent and positive personal and social identity • Prosocial and culturally sensitive values • Spirituality or a sense of a "larger" purpose in life • Strong moral character • A commitment to good use of time

(cont.)

Table 8.1 (cont.)

Assets Category (Cs of Positive Youth Development)	Individual Assets
Social Development (Connection, Caring/ Compassion, Contribution)	• Connectedness—perceived good relationships and trust with parents, peers, and some other adults • Sense of social place/integration—being connected and valued by larger social networks • Attachment to prosocial/conventional institutions, such as school, church, and non-school programs • Ability to navigate in multiple cultural contexts • Commitment to civic engagement

The second strategy involves an implicit understanding and goal within the community youth development framework that prevention of risk behaviors among youth and decreasing risk factors or processes in their environment are necessary if youth are to thrive. The second strategy is important and necessary; however, it is insufficient without simultaneously addressing the first strategy.

Concluding Remarks

Youth programs have a critical role to play in the promotion of resiliency, creating universal protective factors and processes, the six Cs, and ultimately in the promotion of personal and environmental assets (see Table 8.1). They also have an important role in preventing youths' engagement in risk behaviors and mitigating or eliminating risk factors and processes. As discussed throughout this book, OST contexts and experiences provide excellent settings for developmental experiences to occur, if programmers and service providers are deliberate in how they go about providing these opportunities and services.

Ironically, however, while the need for structured environments to help guide children's development has been a major focus of public attention, policy, and research over the last decade (Eccles & Gootman, 2002; Roth & Brooks-Gunn, 2003; Tolman & Pittman, 2002), public commitment to supporting youth development tends to weaken as youth grow older and their needs grow more complex. The "developmental imperative" for youth, addresses this state of affairs by suggesting that young people need and deserve the following:

• Early and sustained investments throughout the first two decades of life
• Supports throughout their waking hours

- Investments that help them achieve a broad range of outcomes (Tolman & Pittman, 2002, p. 21–22)

The developmental imperative calls on us to consider the full range of youths' time, particularly time spent out of school, as crucial to ensuring positive youth development.

Discussion Questions

1. Do you know individuals who have been resilient? If yes, what skills and protective factors have they drawn on?
2. In what ways did Jacinda demonstrate resiliency? We painted a rather depressing, but possible, picture of Jacinda's life. What are other possible scenarios of Jacinda's life? What would have needed to happen? What supports would have helped her achieve different and more positive outcomes?
3. Can resiliency be taught? Why or why not?
4. Discuss risk and protective factors associated with adolescents' use of social media. Are certain ones more powerful than others? Justify your argument.
5. Explain how the six Cs fit within the risk and protective factors concept of resiliency.

Assignments

1. Write a blog post about a famous person in history who demonstrated resiliency but also had one area in his/her life where he/she did not demonstrate competency.
2. Think about your own life. Identify the risk and protective factors that have been operative in your life to date. What additional protective factors do you think it would be worthwhile developing to ensure that you thrive over the next phase of your life?

References

Ames, E. W. (1997). *The development of Romanian orphanage children adopted to Canada*. Final report to the National Welfare Grants Program: Human Resource Development Canada. Burnaby, British Columbia, Canada: Simon Fraser University.

Beardslee, W., & Podorefsky, D. (1988). Resilient adolescents whose parent have serious affective and other psychiatric disorders: The importance of self-understanding and relationships. *American Journal of Psychiatry, 145*, 63–69.

Bernard, B. (2004). *Resiliency: What have we learned?* San Francisco, CA: WestEd.

Blum, R. W., & Mann Rinehart, P. (1998). *Reducing the risk: Connections that make a difference in the lives of youth.* Minneapolis, MN: Division of General Pediatrics and Adolescent Health, Department of Pediatrics, University of Minnesota.

Bogenschneider, K. (1998). What youth need to succeed: The roots of resiliency. In *Wisconsin family impact seminars briefing report: Building resiliency and reducing risk: What youth need from families and communities to succeed* (p. 1–16). Center for Excellence in Family Studies, School of Human Ecology, University of Wisconsin. Madison, Wisconsin.

Brendtro, L. K., Brokenleg, M., & Van Bockern, S. (1990). *Reclaiming youth at risk: Our hope for the future.* Bloomington, IN: National Education Service.

Bronfenbrenner, U. (1979). *The ecology of human development: Experiments by nature and design.* New York, NY: Cambridge University Press.

Carnegie Council on Adolescent Development. (1995). *Great transitions: Preparing adolescents for a new century.* New York, NY: Carnegie Corporation.

Csikszentmihalyi, M. (1997). *Finding flow: The psychology of engagement with everyday life. The masterminds series.* New York, NY: Basic Books.

Eccles, J., & Gootman, J. A. (2002). *Community programs to promote youth development.* Committee on Community-Level Programs for Youth. Board on Children, Youth, and Families, Commission on Behavioral and Social Sciences Education, National Research Council and Institute of Medicine. Washington, DC: Sage.

Festinger, T. (1984). *No one ever asked us: A postscript to the foster care system.* New York, NY: Columbia University Press.

Furstenberg, F., Cook, T., Eccles, J., Elder, G., & Sameroff, A. (1998). *Managing to make it: Urban families and adolescent success.* Chicago, IL: University of Chicago Press.

Hughes, D. M., & Curnan, S. P. (2000, Winter). Community youth development: A framework for action. *CYD Journal, 1,* 7–13.

Kaufman, J., Cook, A., Arny, L., Jones, B., & Pittinsky, T. (1994). Problems defining resiliency: Illustrations from the study of maltreated children. *Development and Psychopathology, 6,* 215–229.

Kumpfer, K. L. (1999). Factors and processes contributing to resilience: The resilience framework. In M. D. Glantz & J. L. Johnson (Eds.), *Resiliency and development: Positive life adaptations* (pp. 179–224). New York, NY: Kluwer Academic/Plenum Publishers.

Larson, R. W. (2000). Toward a psychology of positive youth development. *American Psychologist, 55,* 170–183.

Lerner, R. M. (1995). *America's youth in crisis: Challenges and options for programs and policies.* Thousand Oaks, CA: Sage.

Lerner, R. M. (2002). *Adolescence: Development, diversity, context, and application.* Upper Saddle River, NJ: Prentice-Hall.

Lerner, R. M. (2004). *Liberty: Thriving and civic engagement among America's youth.* Thousand Oaks, CA: Sage Publications.

Lerner, R. M., Fisher, C., & Weinberg, R. (2000). Toward a science for and of the people. Promoting civil society through the application of developmental science. *Child Development, 71,* 11–20.

Luthar, S. S., Cicchetti, D., & Becker, B. (2000). The construct of resilience: A critical evaluation and guidelines for future work. *Child Development, 71,* 543–562.

Masten, A. S. (2001). Ordinary magic: Resilience processes in development. *American Psychologist, 56,* 227–238.

Masten, A. S., Garmezy, N. (1985). Risk vulnerability and protective factors in developmental psychopathology. In B. B. Lahey & A. E. Kazidin (Eds.), *Advances in clinical child psychology* (Vol. 8, pp. 1–52). New York, NY: Plenum Press.

Perkins, D. F., & Borden, L. M. (2003). Risk factors, risk behaviors, and resiliency in adolescence. In R. M. Lerner, M. A. Easterbrooks, & J. Mistry (Eds.), *Handbook of psychology: Vol. 6 Developmental psychology* (pp. 373–394). New York, NY: Wiley.

Perkins, D. F., Borden, L. M., & Villarruel, F. A. (2001). Community youth development: A partnership for action. *School Community Journal, 11*(2), 39–46.

Pittman, K. J. (2000, March). *Grantmaker strategies for assessing the quality of unevaluated programs and the impact of unevaluated grantmaking.* Paper presented at Evaluation of Youth Programs symposium at the Biennial Meeting of the Society for Research on Adolescence, Chicago.

Rhodes, J. E. (2002). *Stand by me: The risks and rewards of mentoring today's youth.* Cambridge, MA: Harvard University Press.

Roth, J., & Brooks-Gunn, J. (2003). What exactly is a youth development program? Answers from research and practice. *Applied Developmental Science, 7,* 94–111.

Rutter, M. (1985). Resilience in the face of adversity: Protective factors and resistance to psychiatric disorder. *British Journal of Psychiatry, 147,* 598–611.

Rutter, M. (1987). Psychosocial resilience and protective factors. *American Journal of Orthopsychiatry, 57,* 316–331.

Rutter, M., Maughan, B., Mortimore, P., Ouston, J., & Smith, A. (1979). *Fifteen thousand hours.* Cambridge, MA: Harvard University.

Rutter, M., & The English and Romanian Adoptees (ERA) Study Team. (1998). Developmental catch-up and deficit, following adoption after severe global early deprivation. *Journal of Clinical Psychology and Psychiatry, 39,* 465–476.

Silbereisen, R. K., & Eyferth, K. (1986). Development as action in context. In R. K. Silbereisen et al. (Eds.), *Development as action in context* (pp. 3–16). Berlin, Heidelberg: Springer-Verlag.

Tolman, J., & Pittman, K. (2002). *Toward a common vision: Naming and framing the developmental imperative.* Washington, DC: Academy for Educational Development.

Werner, E., & Smith, R. (1992). *Overcoming the odds: High-risk children from birth to adulthood.* Ithaca, NY: Cornell University.

Werner, E., & Smith, R. (2001). *Journeys from childhood to midlife: Risk, resiliency, and recovery.* Ithaca, NY: Cornell University Press.

Wilkes, G. (2002). Abused child to nonabusive parent: Resilience and conceptual change. *Journal of Clinical Psychology, 58,* 261–278.

Vaillant, G. (2002). *Aging well: Surprising guideposts to a happier life from the landmark Harvard study of adult development.* Boston, MA: Little, Brown, and Company.

Vigil, J. D. (1990). Cholos and gangs: Culture change and street youth in Los Angeles. In R. Huff (Ed.), *Gangs in America: Diffusion, diversity, and public policy* (pp. 146–162). Thousand Oaks, CA: Sage.

Villarruel, F. A., Perkins, D. F., Borden, L. M., & Keith, J. G. (2003). *Community youth development: Practice, policy, and research.* Thousand Oaks, CA: Sage.

Chapter 9

The Importance of Leisure and Recreation as Contexts for Youth Development

Linda L. Caldwell and Peter A. Witt

The chapters in this book make a collective rationale for the importance of, and need for, positive, organized out-of-school time (OST) programs that contribute to youth development. Two common themes run throughout the chapters; one is obvious, and the other more subtle. The obvious theme is a focus on helping youth develop their potential and thrive by engaging in meaningful, organized activities. The more subtle theme provides the focus of the current chapter—when youth engage in these organized programs, they usually are *choosing* to do so voluntarily, and their participation occurs during their *free time*. Therefore, in this chapter, we explore the notion of free time in more detail and focus specifically on the concepts of *recreation* and *leisure*, which are the umbrella terms under which OST programs fall.

We focus on recreation and leisure because there are particular elements of activities (such as sports, nature, and the arts, as addressed in several chapters in this book), settings, and experiences that make these activities and contexts ripe for fostering youth development. As touched on in Chapters 5 and 6, many organized youth programs are housed in recreation and leisure-based public, quasi-public/nonprofit, other nonprofit (e.g., church groups), and commercial organizations and agencies. Therefore, in this chapter we will address the general question: "Why are recreation and leisure important in promoting youth development?"

Setting the Stage for Understanding the Power of Recreation and Leisure Contexts

Let us begin by clarifying the way the terms *free time, recreation,* and *leisure* are used in this chapter. The general population often uses these terms interchangeably, but for practitioners and researchers, it is useful to make a distinction among them. For our purposes, *free time* is considered unobligated time in a youth's life; it is usually time other than school and doing chores. Often free time is filled with recreation and leisure activities, but not always.

The concept of *leisure* embodies the perspective that engagement is enjoyable, interesting, personally meaningful, self-expressive, self-endorsed, and intrinsically motivated. Leisure may also be considered a state of disengagement or relaxation, but even then it is still self-endorsed, freely chosen, and intrinsically motivated.

Recreation is done in leisure, and most people consider it to be activity-based. Some draw attention to the notion that recreation is *re-creation*, because participating in recreation refreshes one for other aspects of life. For the purposes of this chapter, we will use the word recreation generally to refer to *recreational activities* and *leisure* as the overarching umbrella term.

When free time is used for meaningful leisure, it is more likely that positive development will take place. Conversely, positive development is less likely when free time is empty of meaningful activity (i.e., when one is just filling time). Thus, free time may lead to less than positive development, and at times unhealthy behavior. For example, boredom in leisure, substance use, and feeling stress in leisure are examples of potentially unhealthy and problematic experiences that may lead to unhealthy developmental outcomes. Our focus in this chapter is on the positive developmental opportunities gained through leisure and organized recreational activities, although we will briefly address unhealthy experiences and emotions that can occur in these contexts as well.

To help set the stage for this chapter, imagine Kaylia, age 16, in four different contexts. She is solving a problem in each one.

- At her after-school part-time job: Kaylia is trying to figure out how to maximize space on shelves so she can display more magazines at the bookstore where she works.
- At school: Kaylia is working on a math word problem.
- At home: Kaylia is trying to figure out how to get rid of some of the clutter in her bedroom because her mother is going to paint it.
- At leisure: Kaylia is a youth leader and co-director of a play a drama group she belongs to is working on; she needs to decide the most effective lighting for a certain musical scene.

Each of these situations represents a place or context where youth development can take place: work, school, home/family, and after school. Think about the inherent qualities in each situation…what elements in each environment are likely to contribute to youth development? In which context does Kaylia:

- Have the greatest opportunity to choose the activity she is doing?
- Have the greatest degree of relative freedom to make choices and decide on actions within the activity?
- Have the opportunity to learn from mistakes and successes?
- Feel most like her true self?
- Have the most adult support and guidance to help her learn?
- Experience the most pleasant emotions?
- Experience the greatest degree of challenge and risk from which she can learn?
- Have the opportunity to make authentic connections with her friends?

Kaylia's Story

From an early age, Kaylia loved to sing and dance. However, she was a shy child, and became shyer as she got older. Although she took singing and dancing lessons starting at age 12, she became extremely anxious when performing in front of anyone. Still, she loved watching videos on YouTube and elsewhere that showed young people performing. When she was 16, she saw an advertisement for a new drama group. The local YWCA just hired a new staff member, Manuel, who had spent some time on a Broadway production. Manuel loved working with youth and developing their potential through creative arts. He was also very skilled at intentionally developing projects in which youth developed leadership skills and were able to take ownership of their activities.

Kaylia was intrigued by the ad. She stopped by the Y one day and talked to Manuel, explaining her passion but also her extreme anxiety about performing. Manuel explained his process of working with youth and convinced Kaylia that with his support and the support of her peers, she would be safe and would succeed. He suggested that she start by working behind the scenes and developing her confidence. Kaylia was overjoyed, joined the group, and developed many skills; her confidence improved as well. In addition, she started performing small parts in a play. After a year with the group, she became a co-director of a play. Even though she was a talented performer and overcame her anxiety, she discovered that her true passion was directing.

Some researchers have called leisure as the fourth developmental context (Silbereisen, Noack, & Eyferth, 1986), in addition to home, school, and work. Considering Kaylia's activities might help you see why leisure is held in such high esteem. Regardless of who sponsored Kaylia's drama group (e.g., a public recreation and park department, a YM/YWCA, Boys & Girls Club of America, a 4-H club, a nature camp, or some other

OST program), she was experiencing an activity in a leisure context that can lead to development. You can see by reading about Kaylia's participation with her drama group why her participation in this leisure activity was so important (see Kaylia's story on previous page).

Figure 9.1 is a general summary of how recreation activities contribute to adolescent development and longer-term health and academic outcomes. It implies a chain of events that occur based on intentional programming (as discussed in Chapter 13). The left-hand block in Figure 9.1 provides just some examples of the kinds of things that happen, just as in Kaylia's situation, within a recreational OST program. Intentionally programmed activities that provide these experiences are likely to contribute to developmental outcomes, as suggested in the middle block of the figure. You might recognize that Kaylia achieved many of those outcomes through her participation over time in her drama group. These outcomes are then likely to contribute to longer term health and academic outcomes, ultimately contributing to thriving adolescents and adults. For example, one study found strong evidence that adolescents who participate in organized activities are less likely to engage in criminal and delinquent acts, less likely to be violent and aggressive, less likely to misuse alcohol and marijuana, and less likely to drop out of school (Bohnert, Richards, Kolmodin, & Lakin, 2009). We might speculate that Kaylia will achieve these longer-term outcomes as well.

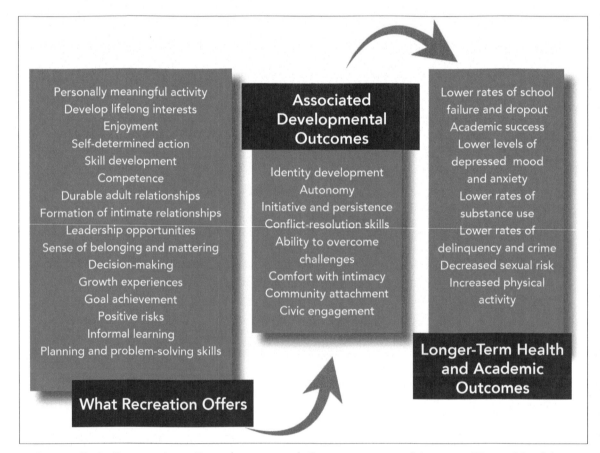

Figure 9.1. Recreation, Developmental Outcomes, and Longer-Term Health and Academic Outcomes

Therefore, leisure (compared with school, family, and work) is important to development because it affords many unique opportunities to gain developmental outcomes. Think back to Kaylia solving problems in different contexts. Although she would reap developmental outcomes in each context, in the leisure context, Kaylia was engaging in intrinsically motivating and self-determined behavior. She wanted to be part of her drama group because she enjoyed it. It is this intrinsic interest coupled with the ability to be self-determined that many researchers think is most motivating to people, thereby contributing to healthy development. Situations rich in the ability to be self-determined and intrinsically interested foster skill development, competence and self-efficacy, positive identity formation, and a sense of belonging (among other things). The leisure context is the most likely context for these experiences to occur.

Elements of Recreation and Leisure: A Closer Look at the LACE Model

To understand how recreation and leisure contribute to youth development, it is essential to appreciate that recreation *is more than just participating in an activity*, although as we will discuss, the *activity* itself is important. It is also necessary also to understand the *experiences* (e.g., emotions and attitudes) that accompany doing the activity and the *context* or *container* in which the activity takes place. Figure 9.2 provides the Leisure Activity, Context, and Experience (LACE) model that contains the basic elements of a leisure/recreational activity. You can see that these elements are intertwined and interdependent. This model suggests that *leisure contributes to youth development when the right elements of context, activity, and experience exist*. Although all of these elements influence each other and are interdependent, we will discuss each of them separately in the following sections.

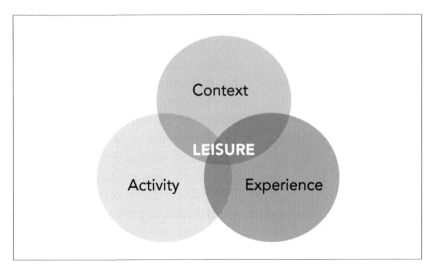

Figure 9.2. Leisure, Activity, Context, and Experience Model (LACE). Adapted from Caldwell (2011)

Activity

Activity implies that there is action and behavior taking place. One can *do* an activity (such as kayaking) or *observe* an activity (such as attending a soccer match). Activities take place in context, and thus the elements of an activity and the elements in the context mutually influence each other. Not all activities are equal in terms of youth development; some are better than others at producing positive affect and healthy outcomes. A Carnegie Council on Adolescent Development (1992) report about the risk and opportunities of free time for youth label *better* activities as *high-yield activities*. Characteristics of high-yield activities include the following:

- Are goal-oriented and/or creative and expressive in nature
- Require discipline and focused attention
- Offer challenges to overcome
- Build skills and increase one's level of competence
- Require persistence, commitment, and continuity to participation over time

Overall, activities that have these characteristics tend to produce the best experiences for youth and contribute to their long-term health and development, although in some instances, high-yield activities can also be associated with stress and anxiety and possibly eventual boredom. Many of the conditions we have just discussed contribute to a condition that Csikszentmihalyi (1990) labels *flow*, which is discussed in detail under *experience*. High-yield activities are more likely to be associated with feelings of competence and positive affect, while low-yield activities are more likely to produce feelings of boredom and apathy.

A related perspective to high-yield leisure comes from the work of sociologist Robert Stebbins. Stebbins coined the terms *serious* and *casual leisure* (see www.seriousleisure.net for a complete list of his works). Serious leisure is the systematic pursuit of an amateur, hobbyist, or volunteer activity that participants find so meaningful and interesting that typically they launch themselves on what Stebbins calls a *career* centered on acquiring and expressing its special skills, knowledge, and experience over time (e.g., birding, stamp collecting, community theater involvement, or volunteering at a local hospital). On the other hand, casual leisure is an immediately intrinsically rewarding, relatively short-lived pleasurable activity often requiring little or no special training to enjoy it. It is fundamentally hedonic, pursued for its significant level of pure enjoyment or pleasure. Stebbins suggested that humans need both serious and casual leisure, but that greater benefits accrue to those engaged in serious leisure.

> **Humans need both serious and casual leisure, but greater benefits accrue to those engaged in serious leisure.**

There are several important developmental outcomes associated with high-yield activities to consider. First, these high-yield activities tend to be self-determined and intrinsically interesting to youth. Larson (2000) links being self-determined with *initiative,* which he calls a "core quality of positive youth development" (p. 170). Initiative essentially means that youth are motivated to engage in activities and maintain interest. In turn, this increases voluntary, self-generated attention, which not only fosters intrinsic motivation and persistence in interesting activities but also can help cultivate a sense of mastery and responsibility over one's life. Similarly, Stebbins suggests that serious leisure requires perseverance and sustained personal effort and skill development across time. It also helps one develop the ability to overcome constraints and challenges in systematic pursuit of the activity.

A second developmental outcome related to high-yield activities and serious leisure is that of goal-setting and positive perspectives about the future. High-yield activities tend to require realistic goal setting. Research has shown that youth who set goals in a recreation and leisure context are more likely to report having a positive future perspective (i.e., a positive outlook on one's future prospects), which is critical to making the transition to adulthood. Although we focus a great deal in this chapter on the importance of intrinsic motivation, we make the somewhat nuanced point here that goal-oriented activities, sometimes called *identified* motivation (Ryan & Deci, 2000), may not be entirely intrinsically motivated. That is, although the activities may be inherently interesting, youth engage in these activities for some type of purpose or goal beyond "just being really interested" or "just doing it because it is fun." These *self-endorsed* activities also promote many healthy developmental outcomes. Youth participate in most recreational OST activities out of pure intrinsic motivation or because they identify the activity with a goal they wish to pursue.

Other durable and tangible benefits associated with high-yield and serious leisure include fun, self-fulfillment, and personal satisfaction. Those engaged in serious leisure find themselves part of a social world with a unique culture. Finally, a strong personal identity is typically a product of serious leisure and high-yield activities.

Figure 9.3 presents a *leisure pyramid* (just like the food pyramid with which you are probably familiar). The pyramid suggests that a healthy *leisure diet or repertoire* should be built on active and/or creative engagement with one's environment. High-yield activities that allow youth to manipulate or construct their own experiences, such as participating in sports, singing in a choir, playing a musical instrument in a band, or

Figure 9.3. Activity Pyramid

creating an art project, should be the foundation of one's leisure repertoire. This bottom rung is where serious leisure pursuits fit. Volunteering and community service also fit into this bottom category of activities. Giving back and making one's community better can not only be powerful endeavors for youth and contribute to one's personal sense of accomplishment, but also can contribute to a larger *sense of community* and belonging to something *bigger than myself*. Activities on the bottom rung can be done alone or with others, but they have the highest probably of containing the elements of high-yield activities identified above.

The next rung of the pyramid contains computer and other games. These are closely related to creative and engaged activities, but typically do not contain quite the degree of high-yield elements as the activities on the first rung of the pyramid. These activities and those in higher rungs of the pyramid are examples of casual leisure, particularly the top rung.

As we move up the pyramid, activities become less absorbing. Spectating at sports or cultural arts, while exciting and temporarily engaging, does not require the viewer to be fully engaged or to use as many skills as activities represented on the first two rungs of the pyramid. The level of challenge to the spectator is usually minimal. In addition, one's personal level of challenge and skill does not appear to increase over time.

A steady diet of socializing and media does not fully contribute to meaning and engagement in one's life.

Several of the most common leisure activities among adolescents are media based. In most cases, these are *low-yield* activities. Just hanging out also appears on the least developmentally productive rung of the pyramid. As discussed in Chapter 3, although use of media, and in particular social media, have many benefits, there are numerous downsides to too much use. Furthermore, too much use takes away opportunities and time for participating in more engaging activities. Connecting with peers is an important social aspect of life, even over social media, but a steady diet of socializing and media does not fully contribute to meaning and engagement in one's life.

Context

All activities and behaviors take place within specific contexts. Contexts include all of the elements or things within the environment that surround and can influence behaviors in a particular setting. These things contribute to how adolescents experience the activity. A few groups of researchers have conducted studies about contextual elements that lead to the most positive outcomes (e.g., Reed Larson and his colleagues [http://youthdev.illinois.edu/]; Richard Lerner and his colleagues [https://ase.tufts.edu/iaryd/aboutPeopleLernerR.htm]; and Jacquelynne Eccles and her colleagues [e.g., Eccles, Fredricks, & Baay, 2015]). Their work provides insight into why, how, and for

whom various contextual elements contribute to development. The following sections summarize those aspects of structured or organized activities that research has identified as most effective in promoting youth development.

Leisure contexts should provide opportunities. Opportunities refer to aspects embedded in the leisure context or setting that contribute to the acquisition of positive developmental outcomes. In order to achieve these outcomes, contexts should include opportunities for the following:

- Youth voices to be heard
- Autonomous and intrinsically motivated actions
- Authentic decision-making and the ability to work with a degree of independence (i.e., agentically)
- Being recognized as being valued and important
- Skill building
- Exploring one's identity and gender roles
- Being challenged and developing competence
- Forming durable relationships with adults
- Opportunities to develop social capital

The experiences in this list are discussed in detail throughout the book. However, it is important to note that, unfortunately, lack of opportunity to access leisure resources is a big problem for many youth in the U.S., as well as other parts of the world. In addition, even when opportunities are available, some youth cannot afford the associated costs of participation. Living in poverty and/or living in rural and even urban settings are among the biggest causes of lack of opportunity to use leisure resources in North America. According to Lerner and his colleagues (2001), it is very important in resource-restricted contexts to help youth learn to develop leisure interests and goals that are in the realm of the possible. That is, recreation staff (and other adults) should help youth cultivate interests that they can pursue within the parameters (limitations and opportunities) of their immediate environment. For example, teaching youth how to snow shoe in central North Carolina would not make a lot of sense.

The role of adults in leisure contexts. The amount of supervision provided by adults is also an important contextual element of recreation and leisure. Depending on the circumstances, adults may supply too much, too little or just the right amount of supervision. Following are some specific points regarding adult involvement in OST activities:

- Leadership, guidance, and facilitation from competent and caring adults are critical.
- Adults should provide specific feedback in order to improve performance and create learning.
- Adults should appropriately scaffold opportunities for youth to learn, be challenged, and be supported through success and failure.
- Adults provide support for efficacy and mattering (autonomy, growth, and improvement).
- Youth need adults who will hold them accountable and instill a sense of responsibility.
- The degree of structure and supervision needs to be balanced with the ability of adolescents to make their own decisions and learn from mistakes.
- Both structured and unstructured/unorganized activities are very important.
- Adult guidance and support should also include shared fun. Adults should not always just sit on the sidelines, watch, and coach; having fun with adults is an important protective factor for youth.

Providing the right mix of guidance, structure, and support depends in part on the age of the youth—that is, guidance and support need to be developmentally appropriate. In general, older youth require less supervision. However, if they are participating in risky leisure activities, such as river kayaking in whitewater, or are learning skill-based activities that require coaching, the level of supervision should go up. Thus, in addition to age, the type and level of guidance also relate to the activity. Although skill-based and/ or risky activities will require the right mix of coaching, high expectations, and relevant feedback to youth, older youth will still need more opportunity to make decisions in these contexts.

One of the reasons the right mix of guidance, structure, supervision, and support is important is because too much of those things can hamper developmental outcomes from being realized. Imagine a pick-up game of softball, for example. Suppose one of the youth hit a fly ball that went into a sewage drain and the players could not immediately reach it. How might the absence of adult supervision be beneficial to their development? With no adults around, the youth would have to work together and problem-solve themselves. Maybe one of the youth would take a leadership role, or maybe they would share leadership. No doubt they would have to learn how to work together and cooperate, not to mention how to retrieve the ball.

On the other hand, consider the consequences if an adult coach had completely structured and organized the game with no input from the youth. Under these circumstances, the context might have inhibited opportunities to try out skills and could have spoiled the youths' ability to exercise control over the environment. The coach may have told the youth how to go about getting the ball, gotten it herself, or ignored the issue and just used another ball. Each of those options would thwart the youths' opportunity to develop intrinsic interest and problem-solving skills.

> The right mix of guidance, structure, supervision, and support is important because if there is too much guidance and adult control, there is the danger that youth will become extrinsically motivated.

Another reason that the right mix of guidance, structure, supervision, and support is important is because if there is too much guidance and adult control, there is the danger that youth will become extrinsically motivated; that is, they may begin to focus on the external rewards for participation (trophies and popularity) or feel that participation is obligatory. Extrinsically motivated youth typically become apathetic toward their recreation involvements, and therefore their interest and participation are unlikely to be sustained. This may explain why there is such a drop off in participation in formal sports and other recreational activities as youth get older (e.g., Caspersen, Pereira, & Curran, 2000; see also Chapters 10 and 15 for more discussion on this issue). Over time, young people's need for choice and voice grows dramatically, and adult-led sports or other activities usually do not have opportunities for youth to express these needs. If there is too much adult control, the activity is no longer fun and rewarding.

What youth do need as they mature are adults who can facilitate, encourage, and support their efforts, help them process their failures, and celebrate their successes. All of these supports will contribute to youths' ability to *establish emotional and behavioral autonomy* from parents and other adults as part of the developmental process. Becoming close to adults who lead OST programs affirms to youth that they matter. Youth who feel that they are important and worthy of attention are in a much better position to reap the developmental benefits of leisure. As youth try to figure out who they are (identity development), the supportive feeling that they matter to someone removes some of the need to constantly prove themselves in unauthentic ways (e.g., posturing violence when that is not really an option one cares to exercise).

Finally, youth also need adults who will keep them accountable for their actions and instill a sense of responsibility into leisure choices and engagement. Similarly, adults who set high but realistic standards and work with youth to achieve those standards contribute to youth development. One way adults can work with youth to develop responsibility and reach high standards is through high-quality instruction and coaching. This provides youth the opportunity to gain skills and develop competence. Without proper guidance, youth may choose to participate in activities that provide little challenge and less opportunity for initiative development or meaning.

The role of peers in leisure contexts. Peers are a very powerful contextual force in youths' lives and can exert both positive and negative influences on behavior (e.g., trying a new skill or smoking cigarettes) or experience (e.g., feeling competent or lonely). On the positive side, peers who support another youth's attempts to try out a new activity can promote confidence and self-efficacy. For example, in a study by Culp (1998), girls described how their friends (and family) supported their attempts at new outdoor activities, and that helped them develop confidence and competence. On the other hand, peers can also have a negative influence. Some girls in Culp's study reported being inhibited from choosing to participate in outdoor recreation activities because they were concerned their peers would react negatively (e.g., they might be ridiculed).

Zaff and Moore (2002) suggest that regardless of having a negative or positive influence, peers tend to self-select groups to hang out with, and these groups are self-perpetuating. Thus, youth whose friends drink and smoke are more likely to do so than if their friends do not drink and smoke, regardless of the partying context. Learning ways to deal with peers in a social leisure setting is therefore an important developmental skill for youth to practice and learn.

Youths' leisure, because it is predominantly social, is a critical context for developing social competence and emotional regulation. Peers have the ability to act as excellent role models to each other through modeling social and emotional competence as well as new skills (Zaff & Moore, 2002). In these cases, peers promote positive social norms and feelings of belonging, which are important to positive youth development. For example, interacting with others may require youth to learn how to lead and how to follow. They also learn basic social skills and the necessity of paying attention to other people's feelings and interests. In fact, in a study by Dworkin, Larson, and Hansen (2003), one of the benefits of interacting with peers in more structured activities was the ability to control anger and anxiety and stay focused on the activity at hand.

Leisure is also a fertile context for youth to interact with others who are "different" from themselves and learn to understand and appreciate those differences. Dworkin et al. (2003) found that adolescents reported that interacting

> Youths' leisure, because it is predominantly social, is a critical context for developing social competence and emotional regulation.

with peers who would normally be outside their existing network was one of the most important benefits to participating in structured, formal, youth-based activities. Youth who participate in these types of activities tend to have broader types of friends than youth who do not (Dworkin et al., 2003).

There are three main takeaway messages to consider when thinking about the role of peers in a leisure context:

1. Peers should develop a culture of positive social norms and take opportunities to recognize and celebrate these norms.
2. Peers should hold each other accountable and should be supported in doing so.
3. Peers should support each other in taking positive risks and exploring new things.

Physical and psychological attributes of leisure contexts. A final aspect of a recreation and leisure context that contributes to developmental outcomes is the *physical environment* in which activity takes place. OST activities take place in many environments. Built environments such as schools, rooms, malls, and churches, for example, offer opportunities and also constraints to certain types of experiences and activities. An obvious constraint, for example, is that it is difficult if not impossible to play field hockey in a mall. More natural and outdoor environments, such as wilderness areas or state parks, offer other types of opportunities and constraints. (Chapter 11 explores the important role of nature in youth development.) Likewise, empty lots, ball fields, and urban parks also offer a certain set of opportunities and constraints. Studies from the work of many researchers (e.g., Reed Larson and his colleagues, Richard Lerner and his colleagues, and Jacquelynne Eccles and her colleagues) suggest that environments where OST activities take place should do the following:

- Provide adolescents with perceptions of physical and psychological safety
- Be aesthetically pleasing
- Afford the opportunity to experience the appropriate level of physical challenges

As an example of the importance of physical aspects of the context, and particularly an activity taking place in the out-of-doors, imagine the youth in the pick-up softball scenario described earlier as a severe thunderstorm approached. The challenge of retrieving the ball would have been increased and perhaps higher-level problem-solving skills would have been required, including an assessment of safety issues. Mahoney, Cairns, and Farmer (2003) suggest that as skills increase by overcoming one type of challenge, individuals set new and more challenging goals. They believe that this process may carry over from recreational activities to other settings, such as work or school.

Aesthetics of the context is also an important consideration. Environments and spaces that are youth-focused and designed are particularly compelling to youth and provide safe places to experiment with developmental issues such as competence, identity, and gender roles. On the other hand, environments that are unsafe, run-down, sterile, or "school-like," are not likely to encourage youth participation and engagement, thus preventing potential development.

A few more remarks about context. These contextual elements just described are crucial because they shape the experiential qualities of engagement that can contribute to positive developmental outcomes. No magic formula exists that determines how much and what combination of elements needs to be present to promote healthy development. A person's age, gender, culture, race/ethnicity, and experience all influence the impact and importance of these contextual elements.

Throughout this book you will find examples of the importance of context. The related concepts of *stage-environment fit* (also known as person-environment fit; e.g., Booth & Gerard, 2014; Eccles, 2013) and *restorative niches* (Roe & Aspinall, 2012) suggest that people are optimally motivated when they perceive the environment they are in provides a good fit for their needs and desires to be met. As discussed in Chapter 4, adolescents are primed for exploration and learning new things, particularly in social situations. Environments that have the elements listed above in the right mix for the right persons provide that "fit" where exploration and positive experiences that are developmentally productive can occur.

As we have noted, leisure in particular is an important context for youth development because it promotes self-determined behavior and the development of intrinsic interest. In leisure, with appropriate structure and supervision, relationships can be formed with caring adults and peers, and opportunities to learn skills and develop competence are available. In a leisure context, youth are likely to feel that they matter and belong. Now we shift our focus to look more closely at the experiential aspects of leisure engagement.

Experience and Emotion

Engagement in leisure and recreational activities and in various contexts evokes emotional responses that can be positive (e.g., being interested, enjoying oneself, and feeling competent) or negative (e.g., feeling bored, anxious, and stressed). Those activities that produce joy or stress release are far more likely to produce positive benefits than those that produce anger, stress, or boredom. Joy, fun, interest, and happiness are emotional hallmarks of leisure. These emotions are a direct result of how youth experience their involvement in activities.

...people are optimally motivated when they perceive the environment they are in provides a good fit for their needs and desires to be met.

The way youth typically experience their leisure is more important than an occasional response to an activity. If, for example, one is bored occasionally, there is usually little cause for alarm. However, being in a constant state of negative emotion such as boredom suggests a problem and can be a risk factor for substance use and other risky behaviors. Therefore, it is important in OST activities that youth workers structure activities to *maximize sustained positive experiences* and emotions and mitigate sustained negative ones. Of course, experiencing both types of emotions is important to development, as is learning how to self-regulate these emotional responses, which are quite strong in adolescence (see Chapter 4) and help to develop social emotional competence and psychological health (Johnson & Johnson, 2004).

We highlight three experiences that occur in leisure that are important to youth development: interest, intrinsic motivation, and flow. *Interest* is the opposite of boredom and is important for cognitive growth. Having to focus one's attention on a task promotes brain activity. Interest is also associated with physical benefits such as a decreased heart rate (Hunter & Csikszentmihalyi, 2003). Finally, interest fosters *intrinsic motivation* by serving as an internal source of compulsion to engage in activity because "it feels good!" Being interested is linked with joy, competence, and tension release (Izard, 1991). Chapter 4 describes how the brain is primed to explore and engage in interests.

Intrinsic motivation, as previously noted, is associated with the degree to which youth act out of internal or external compulsion to engage in the activity. Adolescents who engage in an activity purely for their own enjoyment and/or to achieve a personally meaningful and self-endorsed goal (such as co-directing a theater performance) are intrinsic in nature.

Youth with higher levels of internal motivation for after-school activities set more goals for themselves (Beiswenger & Grolnick, 2009). Research also suggests that intrinsically motivated activities are related to health and well-being (Csikszentmihalyi & Hunter, 2003; Larson, 2000). For example, having higher levels of intrinsic motivation is associated with lower levels of substance use (Caldwell, Bradley, & Coffman, 2009). Furthermore, participation in internally driven activities is linked with promoting self-reflection about how they are unique and at the same time part of something bigger than themselves (Dworkin, Larson, & Hansen, 2003), thus contributing to identity development.

As we saw with Kaylia, leisure is the context in adolescents' lives where they have the most opportunity to exercise free choice and self-determination (and therefore intrinsic motivation), which is one of the reasons leisure is an important developmental context. Leisure, and by extension OST activities, that are intrinsically motivated lead to the development of initiative, which is important in terms of navigating the transition to adulthood. When internally motivated, adolescents are more likely to remain focused and stick to a personally desired activity even when faced with challenges (for example, transportation difficulties or lack of initial skill).

Interest and intrinsic motivation are also linked with the experience of *flow* (e.g., Csikszentmihalyi, 1990), which is a state of consciousness in which one loses track of time and becomes completely engrossed in the activity. Flow contributes to positive youth development outcomes such as initiative, self-efficacy, and competence. Research has suggested that the happiest adolescents tend to be more often engaged in flow-producing situations (Csikszentmihalyi & Hunter, 2003).

Flow has nine main elements that are easily achieved in leisure or a recreation activity:

1. Clear goals
2. Immediate feedback
3. Optimal balance between skill and challenge
4. Merging of action and awareness
5. Being unaware of surroundings
6. No worry of failure
7. Experience of time is distorted
8. Lack of self-consciousness
9. The activity becomes self-guiding

Activities on the first two rungs of the leisure pyramid in Figure 9.3 are more likely to produce the conditions under which flow can occur than those at the top.

One of the important things about flow, as well as other positive leisure experiences, is since these types of experiences are *internally rewarding* (e.g., one feels competent, interested, excited, and so on) they have the potential to generate future participation. That is, when these rewards are regularly derived from an activity, youth strive to continue participating (Delle Fave, & Bassi, 2000) in order to get more of these rewards—and the more rewards, the more one is motivated to sustain participation. This sets up a chain of developmentally positive outcomes and processes. For example, the more that flow-producing activities are sought and experienced, the more youth will have to problem-solve and overcome challenges to continue their participation. Youth will also have to learn to increase both skill level and challenge in an appropriate ratio such that the optimal experience of flow is maintained—that is, they learn to self-regulate, a critical developmental process.

> When rewards are regularly derived from an activity, youth strive to continue participating.

Many other positive experiences and emotions are associated with recreation and leisure, such as love, excitement, joy, serenity, and peacefulness. Of course, there are also negative emotions such as stress, anxiety, and hate that adolescents experience in leisure. For example, boredom in leisure is a common complaint among adolescents. Being bored during leisure is particularly troubling because leisure is *supposed* to be intrinsically motivating, self-directed, fun, and enjoyable. If an adolescent is bored during leisure, it should trigger the need to identify the sources of boredom and deal with that. Think back to the pick-up softball game. If the youth were starting to get bored, they could change aspects of the game (e.g., changing rules to make it more fun) or find something more interesting to do. If they were unable to come up with ideas to decrease their boredom, they might turn their attention to other, more exciting activities.

Thus, boredom can be a staging area for creative action; unfortunately, many times boredom leads to risky or deviant behavior. Youth who experience consistently high rates of boredom and disengagement during their leisure time or report just hanging out in their leisure are at greater risk for engaging in substance use and delinquency behaviors (Mahoney Larson, & Eccles, 2005; Osgood, Anderson, & Shaffer, 2005). For example, the National Center on Addictions and Substance Abuse (2003) surveyed close to 2,000 12- to 17-year-olds and found that high stress, boredom, and/or disposable income were associated with higher risk of substance use. Some recent longitudinal work also suggests that high school youth who experience high levels of leisure boredom are more likely to engage in risky sexual behaviors (Miller et al., 2014).

Fortunately, most youth do not regularly experience boredom or other negative emotions in leisure. The nature of the leisure context (e.g., providing opportunities for self-determination and intrinsic motivation) as well as the nature of the activity (e.g., need for focused attention and appropriate challenges) promotes many positive experiences. There is a need, however, to understand that negative emotions can occur, and it is just as important to understand the causes of these negative experiences (e.g., low-yield activities or too much adult structure and guidance). As we noted previously, appropriate guidance and support from parents and other adults can help youth avoid negative experiences and gain positive ones.

Summary and Concluding Remarks

From a developmental perspective, recreation and leisure facilitate acquisition of a number of positive benefits, and as noted, high-yield leisure is more likely to occur with the right mix of contextual elements, activity, and experience. If the appropriate opportunities, context, and activities do not exist or are not developmentally appropriate, youth will either be unable to reap the developmental benefits of leisure, or they will disengage from their leisure activities. Thus, youth workers in OST programs are encouraged to understand the developmental underpinnings of their programs from a leisure perspective. Vandell, Pierce, and Dadisman (2005) caution that a substantial number of after-school programs are becoming more school-like, and thus mitigate acquisition of possible developmental outcomes. They are proponents of understanding youths' experiences associated with contextual opportunities, adult structure and supervision, and person-environment fit. They conclude that research findings about the power of youths' participation in structured activities in which they participate voluntarily are fairly conclusive. They state, "What appears to be key is that the activities are voluntary, are characterized by sustained engagement and effort, and provide opportunities to build or develop skills" (Vandell et al., p. 43).

We hope this chapter has helped you use a leisure lens to better examine how and why OST programs might be effective. As you continue through the book, we hope that you will keep in mind how and why leisure is important for positive youth development. By becoming engaged with peers, family, and community through recreation and leisure, youth can reap enormous developmental benefits. In sum, leisure is an extremely fertile context for development because it has the traits listed below:

- Provides opportunities for self-determined behavior
- Supports intrinsic motivation, interest development, and persistence of interests
- Increases the ability to experience positive emotions and self-regulate emotions
- Facilitates decision-making and planning skills
- Increases interaction with peers, adults, and the community in meaningful ways
- Contributes to identity development

Discussion Questions

1. In a small group, each person should describe one leisure experience or recreational activity that was extremely important to him or her in middle school or high school. Identify specifically why those experiences were important using the LACE model.
2. When are you typically bored? Why does this boredom occur? What do you do when you are bored? Are there better ways to overcome boredom?
3. We presented the Activity Pyramid in Figure 9.3. Discuss whether or not you agree with the notion that different types of activities are better than other types from a developmental perspective, and why.

Assignments

1. Think about when you get into a flow experience. Write a blog post that describes in detail when you experience flow, what happens, how long it lasts, what happens to end the flow experience, and how you feel after you have had the experience.
2. Suppose someone from your local newspaper is writing a story about a recreation professional who has made significant contributions in young people's lives. This person was very special and important to you when you were a teenager. Who was that person? To help the reporter develop the story, write about 500 words describing why this person was meaningful in your life.

References

Beiswenger, K. L., & Grolnick, W. S. (2009). Interpersonal and intrapersonal actors associated with autonomous motivation in adolescents' after-school activities. *Journal of Early Adolescence, 30,* 369–394.

Bohnert, A. M., Richards, M. H., Kolmodin, K. E., & Lakin, B. L. (2009). Young urban African American adolescents' experience of discretionary time activities. *Journal of Research on Adolescence, 18,* 517–539.

Booth, M. Z., & Gerard, J. M. (2014). Adolescents' stage-environment fit in middle and high school: The relationship between students' perceptions of their schools and themselves. *Youth and Society, 46,* 735-755. doi:10.1177/0044118X12451276

Caldwell, L. L. (2011). Leisure. In B. Bradford Brown & M. J. Prinstein, (Eds.), *Encyclopedia of adolescence* (pp. 169–177). San Diego, CA: Academic Press.

Caldwell, L. L., Bradley, S., & Coffman, D. (2009). A person-centered approach to individualizing a school-based universal prevention intervention. *American Journal of Alcohol and Drug Addictions, 35,* 214–219.

Carnegie Council on Adolescent Development. (1992). *Task force on youth development and community programs. A matter of time: Risk and opportunity in the nonschool hours.* Washington, DC: Author.

Caspersen, C. J., Pereira, M. A., & Curran, K. M. (2000). Changes in physical activity patterns in the United States, by sex and cross-sectional age. *Medicine and Science in Sport and Exercise, 32,* 1601–1609.

Csikszentmihalyi, M. (1990). *Flow: The psychology of optimal experience.* New York, NY: Harper and Row.

Csikszentmihalyi, M., & Hunter, J. (2003). Happiness in everyday life: The uses of experience sampling. *Journal of Happiness Studies, 4,* 185–199.

Culp, R. H. (1998). Adolescent girls and outdoor recreation: A case study examining constraints and effective programming. *Journal of Leisure Research, 30,* 356–379.

Delle Fave, A., & Bassi, M. (2000). The quality of experience in adolescents' daily lives: Developmental perspectives. *Genetic, Social, and General Psychology Monographs, 126,* 347–367.

Dworkin, J. B., Larson, R., & Hansen, D. (2003). Adolescents' accounts of growth experiences in youth activities. *Journal of Youth and Adolescence, 32,* 17–26.

Eccles, J. S. (2013). Schools, academic motivation, and stage-environment fit. In R. M. Lerner & L. Steinberg (Eds.), *Handbook of adolescent psychology* (2nd ed.). Retrieved from http://onlinelibrary.wiley.com/book/10.1002/9780471726746

Eccles, J. S., Fredricks, A., & Baay, P. (2015). Expectancies, values, identities, and self-regulation. In G. Oettinger & P. M. Gollwitzer (Eds.), *Self-regulation in adolescence* (pp. 30–56). Cambridge, MA: Cambridge University Press.

Hunter, J. P., & Csikszentmihalyi, M. (2003). The positive psychology of interested adolescents. *Journal of Youth and Adolescence, 32,* 27–35.

Johnson, D. W., & Johnson, R. T. (2004). The three Cs of promoting social and emotional learning. In J. E. Zins, R. P. Weissberg, M. C. Wang, & H. J. Walberg

(Eds.), *Building academic success on social and emotional learning* (pp. 40–58). New York, NY: Teachers College Press.

Larson, R. W. (2000). Toward a psychology of positive youth development. *American Psychologist, 55,* 170–183.

Lerner, R. M., Freund, A. M., De Stefanis, I., & Habermas, T. (2001). Understanding developmental regulation in adolescence: The use of the selection, optimization, and compensation model. *Human Development, 44,* 29–50.

Mahoney, J. L., Cairns, B., & Farmer, T. (2003). Promoting interpersonal competence and educational success through extracurricular activity participation. *Journal of Educational Psychology 95,* 409–418.

Mahoney, J., Larson, R., & Eccles, J. (Eds.). (2005). *Organized activities as contexts of development: Extracurricular activities, after-school and community programs* (pp. 45–64). Mahwah, NJ: Lawrence Erlbaum Associates, Publishers.

Miller, J. A., Weybright, E. H., Caldwell, L. L., Smith, E. A., Vergnani, T., & Wegner, L. (2014). Was Bob Seger right? Relation between free time boredom and [Risky] sex. *Leisure Sciences, 36,* 52–67. doi: 10.1080/01490400.2014.860789

National Center on Addiction and Substance Abuse. (2003). *National survey of American attitudes on substance abuse VIII: Teens and Parents.* National Center on Addiction and Substance Abuse at Columbia University.

Osgood, D. W., Anderson, A. L., & Shaffer, J. N. (2005). Unstructured leisure in the after-school hours. In J. Mahoney, R. Larson, & J. Eccles (Eds.), *Organized activities as contexts of development: Extracurricular activities, after-school and community programs* (pp. 45–64). Mahwah, NJ: Lawrence Erlbaum Associates.

Roe, J. J., & Aspinall, P. A. (2012). Adolescents' daily activities and the restorative niches that support them. *International Journal of Environmental Research and Public Health, 9,* 3227–3244. doi:10.3390/ijerph9093327

Ryan, R. M., & Deci, E. (2000). Self-determination theory and the facilitation of intrinsic motivation, social development, and well-being. *American Psychologist, 55,* 68–78.

Silbereisen, R. K., Noack, P. N., & Eyferth, K. (1986). Adolescents, leisure settings, and developmental tasks. In R. K. Silbereisen et al. (Eds.), *Development as action in context* (pp. 87–108). Berlin, Heidelberg: Springer-Verlag.

Vandell, D. L., Pierce, K. M., & Dadisman, K. (2005). Out-of-school settings as a developmental context for children and youth. *Advances in Child Development and Behavior, 33,* 43–77.

Zaff, J. F., & Moore, K. A. (2002). *Promoting well-being among American's teens.* An executive summary of adolescent development research reviews completed for the John S. and James L. Knight Foundation. Child Trends.

Chapter 10

The Status of Youth Sport in American Society

Gareth J. Jones, Jason N. Bocarro, and Michael B. Edwards

This chapter is about youth sport and the potential impact that participation can have on youth development. Before we begin, however, here are two examples of youth sport experiences, as told by the second author, Bocarro.

Meet Hannah

One of my undergraduate students recounted this story about the first game of her senior varsity soccer season in high school. Hannah was a top girls' soccer prospect and had already accepted a scholarship to a major college soccer powerhouse. Early in her first game, she suffered a horrific broken leg that ultimately prevented her from playing high-level competitive soccer again. She reflected on that moment:

> As I lay on the field that day, I knew my leg was broken; I heard it and I felt it. I didn't even try to get up, and I heard my Dad yelling from the sideline, "Come on, Hannah; you're fine. Get up!" My mind raced. I thought about my parents and how much time, money, and emotion they had invested in my soccer career since I was little. I thought about my coaches and teammates and how much they were counting on me. Our team had a

great chance to win the state championship that year. Then I thought about how much of my life had been consumed by soccer since I was six years old. At that moment, I realized that I wouldn't have to play soccer anymore. It was the happiest day of my life.

When I met Hannah, it was three years after the injury. She said that she had just started playing soccer again with our university's club soccer team. She mentioned how much she loved getting the chance to bond with teammates and participate again in a less formal and pressurized environment. Without coaches and parents on the sideline, she said, playing had really become fun again.

Anybody Can Participate

I once did some fieldwork with a mobile recreation program. During my observations, I noticed that some of the youth workers recognized that there were certain kids who for various reasons rarely got to participate in sports. The workers identified the reason(s) behind the kids' nonparticipation and developed strategies grounded in youth development principles to engage them with sports. For example, one youth worker was determined to promote female athletics in a predominately Hispanic area of the community where many of the girls did not compete in sports. Thus, she set up different female-only sport teams. Two other youth workers decided to recruit kids who did not usually play sports but had an interest. As one pointed out:

> I don't want to knock the kids or anything, but our teams are always made up of scrubs, the kids who are never going to win a league, they may never even win a game but we make sure that when we lose a game our kids aren't upset. They are just happy that they got to play. It's about having fun, getting a chance to participate, and teaching them teamwork and sportsmanship. And we achieved that.

While umpiring a softball game in which his team was playing, I got to see this youth worker's philosophy in practice. Despite being outscored by a much more athletic team in a local league, his team continually sang songs, cheered for each other in the dugout, and seemed to have more fun than the team who beat them. Over the course of the season, their interest never waned, and they slowly got better (Bocarro, 2001).

What these two stories highlight is that sport is not an inherently positive or negative experience for youth. The outcomes and impacts depend on how youth sport experiences are designed, coached, and delivered. Our goal in this chapter is to discuss sport's potential for impacting youth in a positive manner and how to avoid youth having negative experiences as much as possible. We first outline the scope of youth sport and highlight both positive and negative ways it can influence youth development. We then provide a historical background of youth sport delivery systems in the United States (U.S.), and describe how such systems have influenced sport-based youth development and participation. We end the chapter with a discussion of future trends related to youth sport and key considerations for youth sport managers.

Scope of Youth Sport

Participation in sport remains among the most popular activities for young people. The National Council of Youth Sports estimates that 60 million U.S. children aged 6–18 participate in some form of organized athletics, with 44 million participating in more than one sport. Moreover, the Aspen Institute estimates that 40% of U.S. youth aged 6–17 participate in sports on a regular basis, defined as engaging in high-calorie activities for a minimum of 151 times during the year. Sport participation is associated with myriad individual and community youth development benefits, including psychological and emotional development (e.g., Eime et al., 2013), engaged citizenship and social capital (e.g., Kay & Bradbury, 2009), improved self-esteem, decreased stress (e.g., National Center for Education Statistics, 2005), friendship (e.g., Neely & Holt, 2014), and improved physical fitness (Barnett et al., 2008). However, as the stories at the start of this chapter highlight, youth sport can also lead to risk of injury and burnout (e.g., DiFiori et al., 2014), psychosocial problems (e.g., Merkel et al., 2013), and negative family dynamics (e.g., Hyman, 2012). Although this list of positive and negative impacts is extensive, we have chosen to summarize three key outcomes from each side that have been especially influential in youth sport policy, practice, and management.

Potential of Youth Sport to Promote Positive Youth Development Outcomes

Physical Activity, Health, and Youth Sport

One of the most important benefits of sport for young people is the potential for increased levels of physical activity. Sport's potential to promote physical activity has been highlighted amid growing concerns regarding childhood obesity, as levels of free-time physical activity have been directly linked to decreased obesity and improved health outcomes among children (Janssen, 2014). Beyond decreasing obesity, increased physical activity can also promote a variety of other positive youth health outcomes (Floyd, Bocarro, & Thompson, 2008). For example, regular physical activity has been shown to improve cardiovascular and bone health, increase brain development, reduce risk of cancer, and provide positive mental health benefits (Eime et al., 2013). Compared to other leisure-time activities, sport is often regarded as a more enjoyable way for children to meet

Physically active children are more likely to grow up to be physically active adults.

the need for appropriate levels of physical activity (Right to Play International, 2008). Additionally, physically active children are more likely to grow up to be physically active adults (Green, Smith, & Roberts, 2005), so getting involved in a variety of sports during childhood is considered essential to sustaining participation into adulthood.

Although physical activity is often considered the primary health benefit associated with sport participation for youth, there are also multiple secondary health benefits as well. Compared to nonparticipants, youth sport participants report healthier eating habits (Pate et al., 2000) and lower use of tobacco (Wichstrøm & Wichstrøm, 2009) and drugs (Kwan, Bobko, Faulkner, Donnelly, & Cairney, 2014). Sport participants also report lower levels of depression and anxiety, as well as higher levels of self-esteem and social competence (Babiss & Gangwisch, 2009). Adolescent girls who play sports are also less likely to engage in sex or experience an unwanted pregnancy (Miller Farrell, Barnes, Melnick, & Sabo, 2005). These studies highlight the potential of sport to not only influence various aspects of physical health, but also the related dimensions of social, emotional, and mental health as well.

Academic Benefits and Youth Sport

Although evidence remains mixed, participation in organized sport has been linked with positive academic outcomes (Bradley, Keane, & Crawford, 2013). In particular, sport participation has been associated with increased school belongingness or the connection youth feel to the school social environment. This relationship is thought to be especially important for students who struggle academically. Sport also provides opportunities for youth to connect with the school in ways that may be more difficult in classroom settings. By developing strong social ties between players, coaches, and school officials, students who participate in sport have opportunities to develop a sense of school belongingness that is not as contingent upon academic or social status. Importantly, promoting and maintaining these connections is especially critical during adolescence, when the incidence of school disengagement, truancy, and dropout become more prevalent.

In addition to facilitating a greater sense of school belongingness, sport participation has also been linked with greater academic performance. Compared to nonparticipants, sport participants often receive higher grades in school (Darling, Caldwell, & Smith, 2005). Although this trend cannot be directly attributed to sport participation, many of the positive benefits associated with sport participation have been similarly linked with academic performance (Eitle & Eitle, 2002). For example, youth who participate in sport often exhibit stronger social ties to other students, teachers, and parents, which has been associated with higher academic

> Youth who participate in sport often exhibit stronger social ties to other students, teachers, and parents, which has been associated with higher academic achievement.

achievement (Broh, 2002). Moreover, many of these benefits have been shown to last into adulthood, as youth who participate in sport often have higher academic and career aspirations than non sport participants, and are also more likely to attend college and earn degrees (U.S. Department of Education, 2005). While these outcomes have been associated with many different types of community-based youth sport activities (e.g., Holt, Kingsley, Tink, & Scherer, 2011), school-sponsored sport is considered the most effective context for promoting academic benefits because their association with educational institutions provides opportunities to build direct connections with the school environment, which is not always possible in external programs (Trudeau & Shephard, 2005).

Psychological, Emotional, and Social Outcomes and Youth Sport

Youth sport can induce positive psychological, emotional and social outcomes for youth and their families. Much of the research in this area has focused on the individual-level benefits of sport participation. Youth can develop important traits such as self-esteem, character, and confidence that contribute positively to youth development. In addition, sport can help youth enhance important life skills such as goal-setting, time management, and commitment that similarly reinforce positive outcomes. Although many of these skills are developed and refined in the sport context, youth can transfer and apply what they have learned to their everyday lives (Turnnidge, Côté, & Hancock, 2014).

In addition, sport activities provide settings for youth to develop social competence and key social relationships. In fact, some youth sport programmers intentionally design programs to facilitate positive social relationships between youth from diverse backgrounds. By ensuring equality among participants and providing opportunities to work toward common goals, these programs help alleviate social tensions between youth from different cultural, racial, and religious groups. Social benefits are not exclusive to peer-to-peer relationships either, as strong youth-adult relationships can also form during youth sport participation. Positive relationships with adults is an essential element of youth development, and sport programs provide opportunities for youth to establish these connections with coaches, volunteers, and parents. In addition, regular participation in organized sport can provide opportunities for families to form closer bonds through their collective engagement in both on- and off-field activities (Trussell, 2009).

Negative Issues Affecting the Potential to Promote Positive Youth Development Outcomes

Physical Activity, Health, and Youth Sport

The health benefits of increased physical activity have been central to advocacy for expenditures on, and promotion of, youth sport. However, youth sport, particularly in North America, increasingly emphasizes competition, specialization, athlete development, and talent identification (Coakley, 2017). Although the physical activity required of sport training is beneficial, this may not be an intentional outcome of participation in competitive sport, nor may it promote healthy physical activity outcomes. Organized, competitive sport may not always encourage recommended

levels of physical activity for enough participants in comparison to unstructured, non-competitive physical activities. For example, baseball and softball may provide fewer opportunities for physical activity among participants than other sports due to these games' sedentary dimensions (e.g., sitting in the dugout waiting to bat or standing in the field). Additionally, the nature of some sports may discourage healthy lifestyles. To maximize performance at some positions, for example, American football players may be motivated to gain unhealthy weight levels (Head & Iannarino, 2017).

Even in sports that require continual physical activity (e.g., basketball), roster restrictions and coaches' decisions regarding playing time, which often favor better athletes, may keep many interested participants off the team or on the bench instead of actively participating. With an interest in retaining elite-level athletes to perform in upper-level competitions, many coaches allow some participants to "sit on the bench" for long periods of game time. In fact, the contentious nature of playing time decisions has led to multiple lawsuits involving youth sport leagues/coaches and the parents of players who were benched (e.g., Cameron, 2017; Jouvenal, 2015). In the short-term, benched participants remain sedentary during games and are less likely to meet appropriate physical activity standards. In the long-term, chronic lack of playing time can decrease youth enjoyment with sport and ultimately contribute to them dropping out (Crane & Temple, 2015), which may negatively influence future health outcomes.

Injuries, Burnout, and Youth Sport

In addition to questions about whether sport can deliver recommended levels of physical activity, many critics suggest that not only are there too many sport-related injuries, but also the prevalence of injuries is increasing. According to the CDC, more than 3.1 million children 5–14 years old receive medical treatment for sport injuries each year, with many of these injuries considered preventable musculoskeletal injuries attributed to increased and repeated specialized training regimens, or so-called "overuse injuries" (Sheu, Chen, & Hedegaard, 2016). The repetitive nature of many drill-based practice regimens, and the physiological motions they require, often place recurrent stress on the muscles, tendons, and bones of youth. Without adequate time to recover between sessions, or extended periods of rest between seasons, youth are susceptible to a range of ailments, especially to joints and growth plates.

Perhaps most alarmingly, recent research has uncovered a relatively high incidence of concussions among high school athletes. Youth athletes aged 19 and under accounted for roughly 2.5 million sports and recreation-related traumatic brain injuries treated in emergency departments in the U.S. from 2001–2012, which is almost two-thirds of the total amount during that period (Coronado et al., 2015). Although states and youth sport associations have put policies in place to improve the diagnosis, treatment, and return-to-play protocols for concussions, issues related to implementation still exist.

Burnout is a term used to describe youth who stop participating in a previously enjoyable activity due to chronic stress. This stress can be physically induced through overtraining and specialization, or psychologically induced through rigorous training schedules and hyper-competitive sport environments. In youth, the psychological aspects of burnout appear to be especially prevalent in adult-supervised activities (DiFiori et al., 2014). This is particularly true for youth who are involved in high performance sport and those who specialize in single sports at too early an age. It should be noted that not all youth who drop out of sport are "burned out," as time, resources, and changes in interest can also lead youth to discontinue sport participation. However, burnout remains a significant concern because it can have lasting physical and mental health effects that influence future prospects for youth development.

> In youth, the psychological aspects of burnout appear to be especially prevalent in adult-supervised activities.

Psychological, Emotional, and Social Outcomes and Youth Sport

Too often in competitive youth sport, the focus on winning and elite athlete development changes the meaning of sport, and many youth stop playing sport due to low perceptions of athletic competence. In other words, once youth perceive that they are less skilled than their peers, and that skill and winning are paramount, they experience lower self-esteem and confidence and are more likely to stop participating (Hedstrom & Gould, 2004). This can be exacerbated by substantial financial investments and parental pressure (Dunn, Dorsch, King, & Rothlisberger, 2016), a lack of developmentally focused coaching (Vella, Oades, & Crowe, 2013), and the overall societal and cultural emphasis often placed on winning (Coakley, 2017). In addition, the pressures of elite sport and high-performance environments can provoke negative behaviors such as the use of alcohol (Kwan et al., 2014) and performance-enhancing drugs (Woolf, Rimal, & Sripad, 2014), which are often influenced by social norms perhaps associated with the stress of competition.

In terms of psychological and social development, most research has found that evidence supporting this connection is largely mixed, with positive outcomes often contingent upon a variety of factors (Coakley, 2011). For example, the coach relationship is an essential component of the youth sport experience that can either positively or negatively influence psychological and social development (Camiré & Kendellen, 2016). Although a variety of coaching models have been developed to help guide this process, not all coaches draw on such models to inform their philosophy. Instead, many youth sport coaches and administrators are driven by an inherent belief in the "power of sport" to promote youth development (Coakley, 2011). In order to effectively promote youth development through sport, activities and environments must be delivered in a way that intentionally targets key outcomes. This highlights the importance of understanding how and why sport might contribute to youth development, and intentionally designing activities in ways that maximize this benefit.

The coach relationship is an essential component of the youth sport experience that can either positively or negatively influence psychological and social development.

Critics have also questioned sport's role in promoting healthy social interactions among participants and families. For example, competition with peers for specific positions on teams can create rivalries among youth that mitigate opportunities for positive social interactions (Fraser-Thomas & Côté, 2009). This can also manifest itself at the team level, as ideals of sportsmanship and social camaraderie can often disintegrate in contests involving intense rivalries between opposing teams. In addition, it is easy to find examples in the media about aggressive and even violent interactions at youth sporting events, particularly confrontations by parents toward coaches, officials, and even youth sport participants (Heinzmann, 2002). Levels of emotional stress and anxiety may interfere with healthy social functioning when the stakes of winning and elite performance expectations increase. Given the aforementioned importance of positive youth-adult relationships, adults modeling inappropriate behaviors in sport environments is clearly antithetical to youth development efforts.

How Youth Sport Delivery Systems Have Changed Over Time

To understand fully how youth sport facilitates or constrains youth development, it is important to understand how the delivery system has changed over time. The management and delivery of youth sport has undergone drastic changes in the U.S. over the last 70 years. This has not only influenced the association between sport and youth development but also affected rates of participation. For example, a recent U.S. study (Aspen Institute, 2016) showed that participation in youth sport has been declining since about 2008. However, participation has declined in some segments of the youth population more than others have. For example, girls, especially those from racial and ethnic minority groups, drop out of sport at higher rates than boys (Phillips & Young, 2009) and youth with disabilities have more difficulty finding opportunities to participate in sport (Fitzgerald, 2009). However, the strongest predictor of sport participation is family income. Children from lower economic backgrounds are not only less likely to participate in sport, but are also more likely to drop out when they do participate. This highlights the growing economic barriers to youth sport participation.

In this section, we summarize four key shifts that have significantly altered the management and delivery of youth sport in the last 70 years, and use them to inform our discussion of the current state of youth sport. While not inclusive of all events, the summary provides a useful framework for understanding key youth sport delivery structures, their evolution over time, and their role in shaping the current system.

Pre-1970s: Growth of Adult-Organized Leagues and Associations

In the first half of the 20th century, youth service workers offered sport programs primarily to occupy "idle" time (Alston, 2007). Many fathers had joined the military during the World Wars, and mothers were entering the labor force in increasing numbers, so a large proportion of youth were left unsupervised during out-of-school time hours (Alston, 2007). Similar to other youth-based programs at the time, the public viewed sport as an effective tool for "keeping youth out of trouble," while also instilling values such as obedience, discipline, and respect for authority. These values were important aspects of the youth sport experience because they helped preserve the prevailing social order (Eitzen, 2000).

At this time, most organized youth sport experiences were delivered through social agencies (e.g., YMCAs, Boys & Girls Clubs, Boy Scouts, and Girl Scouts), and to a lesser extent, parks and recreation departments and schools. In agency-sponsored settings, it was common for youth to organize "pick-up" or "open" games themselves. It was also common for adults to take a supervisory role and integrate sport activities as components of broader curricula (Seefeldt & Ewing, 1997). Comparatively, sport activities offered by parks and recreation departments and schools typically aligned with the institutional values of those settings. In parks and recreation departments, the primary focus was on providing activities for all youth within communities and promoting healthy lifestyles. In schools, sport was an integral part of physical education curricula, and an important mechanism to engage youth with the school environment (Finn, 1989).

This landscape shifted in the 1950s as adult-organized leagues and associations took a more prominent role in the delivery of youth sport services (Seefeldt & Ewing, 1997), a trend epitomized by the rapid growth of organizations such as Pop Warner Football and Little League Baseball. Pop Warner was created in 1929 when Joseph Tomlin, a

Philadelphia stockbroker, formed an athletic program intended to curb the incidence of vandalism among youth in a Northeast Philadelphia neighborhood. With the support of local factory owners, many of whom owned the buildings affected by recurring vandalism, Tomlin formed a four-team league to keep kids occupied and out of trouble. With the support of Glenn Scobie "Pop" Warner, who at the time was coaching at nearby Temple University, and other notable individuals and organizations, Pop Warner grew to over 3,000 teams by the 1960s, serving over 90,000 youth.

Similarly, Carl Stotz founded Little League Baseball in 1938 to provide younger children with an opportunity to play baseball in his hometown of Williamsport, Pennsylvania. The league started with two teams in 1938 and doubled the following year, thanks to support from local business executives who were friends of Stotz's (Frederick, 1965). By 1963, Little League Baseball had grown to over 5,000 leagues across the U.S. and Canada, providing baseball for over one million boys.

The rapid growth of these leagues signaled the rising influence of adults in the management, organization, and delivery of youth sport services. As seen in the Little League and Pop Warner examples, business contacts of parents and other volunteers were often leveraged to enhance the youth sport delivery process. Drawing on the extensive human and social capital of adults, youth sport leagues were able to legitimize, and to a certain extent professionalize, the youth sport experience (Brower, 1979). In fact, the parallel growth and commercialization of professional and youth sport during this period was in many ways intentional, as adults wanted to provide youth with opportunities to "play like the pros" and use youth sport as the ultimate feeder system for developing pro athletes. Upgrades in youth sport facilities, equipment, and organizational structures became more aligned with the professional leagues, and many youth sport environments began to transform into scaled-down replications of their "big league" counterparts (Brower, 1979). This surge led to a dramatic increase in the number of youth sport opportunities, with the potential individual benefits of sport participation often used to spur additional social, political, and financial support (Brower, 1979). Yet at this stage, the connection between sport and youth development still remained largely substantiated by a "deficit-reduction" perspective, whereby youth simply being present in a supervised environment meant they were not engaging in the type of deviant activities often associated with unsupervised "idle" time.

1970s: Privatization of Parks and Recreation

This evolution was a precursor to the next dramatic shift in the mid-1970s, when public service sectors such as parks and recreation began implementing more "businesslike" management models to improve efficiency. Traditionally, public parks and recreation departments unilaterally controlled community-based youth sport programs through direct service delivery models (Crompton, 1998). They constructed and maintained facilities and equipment, provided administrative oversight, and recruited coaches and volunteers to run programs. Under this model, leaders organized community-based youth sport activities into different seasons, and residents selected from various options at the beginning of each season (Crompton, 1998).

This changed when agencies began to integrate more privatization and reduced government oversight at the national, state, and local levels. Driven by a belief in the efficiency of free markets and small government, budgets for many parks and recreation departments were reduced significantly during this period. As a result, managers were compelled to adopt commercial principles in their delivery of youth sport. Agency-sponsored organizations such as Little League and Pop Warner had established corporate governance structures, and a growing number of private sport clubs and associations were offering specialized pay-for-service programs. These nonprofit and commercial entities were not subject to the same administrative and legal constraints as parks and recreation departments, which allowed them to create much more streamlined service delivery processes. Thus, when faced with difficult decisions regarding budget allocations, parks and recreation departments often reduced funding for "in-house" youth sport programs and instead relied upon the services of a burgeoning nonprofit and private sector to meet the demands of their stakeholders.

This evolution of the youth sport delivery system led to an increasingly complex system of public-private partnerships (PPPs) between parks and recreation departments and a host of external youth sport providers. PPPs range from formalized agreements ratified through memorandums of understanding (MOUs) or contracts, to less formal relationships bound simply by permits for use. In many instances, PPPs arose simply from the need to coalesce divergent resources. For example, while funding for youth sport programming was reduced in parks and recreation departments, most agencies still owned and managed the facilities used for youth sport. Consequently, parks and recreation departments needed external providers to deliver youth sport services more efficiently, and nonprofit and private providers needed parks and recreation facilities to operate their programs. As a result, parks and recreation managers often managed their remaining inventory of programs and balanced the logistical and infrastructural obligations of youth sport programs that had been "contracted out." Of course, the degree to which departments contracted out youth sport services varied across communities, yet the general trend toward utilizing PPPs has certainly remained salient in public parks and recreation departments (Pitas, Mowen, Liechty, & Trauntvein, 2015).

It is important to note that this reconfiguration did not necessarily alter assumptions regarding the connection between sport and youth development. In fact, the late 1980s and early 1990s were characterized by a rapid growth in the number of sport programs

> This evolution of the youth sport delivery system led to an increasingly complex system of public-private partnerships (PPPs) between parks and recreation departments and a host of external youth sport providers.

directed toward "at-risk" youth (Hartmann, 2001). These programs specifically targeted young adolescent males in mostly minority, inner-city neighborhoods, and championed sport as a catalyst for preventing issues such as substance abuse, gang affiliation, and juvenile delinquency (Hartmann, 2001). Such programs have been described as the start of the "social problems industry" in sport and recreation, whereby the widening gap in public services was increasingly filled by philanthropic and nongovernmental agencies seeking to leverage the "power of sport" to alleviate key social problems (Pitter & Andrews, 1997). Once again, many of these programs were organized around deficit-reduction or problem-based models of youth development, with sport often viewed as a mechanism for occupying youth and keeping them out of trouble in the face of difficult family and community circumstances.

2000s: Downsizing School Sport

The next shift influencing the structure of youth sport delivery systems started around the turn of the 21st century, and involved the increasing role of organized sport in both in- and out-of-school student experiences. As youth progress into middle and high school, physical education takes the place of recess as the primary form of in-school physical activity, which is offered typically only from pre-kindergarten through elementary school (Miracle, 1987). In addition, organized sport teams become important mechanisms for promoting positive social and emotional outcomes and improving academic engagement and performance during out-of-school hours (Finn, 1989). They also create the pipeline for producing athletes for high school sport teams.

During the late 1990s and early 2000s, national requirements for other core subjects, such as reading and mathematics, became increasingly tied to federal funding appropriations, and many school administrators responded by reducing physical education hours to accommodate more instruction in these areas (Institute of Medicine, 2013). At the same time, the amount of school funding dedicated to out-of-school sport programs, such as extracurricular teams and activities, began to decrease. When faced with difficult budgetary decisions, school administrators were often forced to prioritize activities considered more academically focused, and in many cases this precluded sport.

It is important to note two underlying trends that influenced this shift in thinking. First, the philosophical and altruistic foundation of school-based athletics was beginning to change during this time (Eitzen, 2000). Historically, school sport was seen as a way to promote school values and above all, enhance the educational experience of students (Finn, 1989). However, the rapid growth of major collegiate athletics was underway and middle and high school athletics became increasingly intertwined with this competitive model. The "win-at-all-costs" mentality presented ethical dilemmas for school administrators as issues related to injury, substance abuse, and burnout became more prevalent. Although the presumed developmental benefits of sport were still being espoused in public rhetoric, many questioned whether middle and high school athletics were appropriate contexts for youth development or just "training grounds" for the next wave of collegiate athletes (McEwin & Dickinson, 1996).

Second, schools generally offered two types of sport activities. Interscholastic sport comprised competitive athletic teams that competed with other schools and imposed roster restrictions that often require "cuts" for both junior varsity and varsity teams. Conversely, intramural and club sports comprised athletic activities that were generally self-contained within schools and promote participation over competition, with no roster restrictions. Due to the growing emphasis on competitive sport in schools, the balance between interscholastic and intramural activities started to shift during this period (Stewart et al., 2005). When faced with difficult funding decisions, intramural and club sports were more likely budget casualties than interscholastic sport teams. Moreover, considerable investments in facilities and equipment to support the competitive success of interscholastic teams were often made at the expense of other extracurricular programs, with a 2007 study finding that opportunities for intramural and club sports had declined across the U.S. (Lee et al., 2007).

> The "win-at-all-costs" mentality presented ethical dilemmas for school administrators as issues related to injury, substance abuse, and burnout became more prevalent.

These trends have continued into the 21st century, with an estimated $3.5 billion being cut from school sport budgets from 2009 to 2011 (Up2Us Sports, 2011). In an effort to make up for this shortfall, many athletic directors and school administrators either implemented "pay-to-play" policies that charge students fees to participate in sports, or discontinued school sport altogether. As of 2010, at least 40% of public schools charged "pay-to-play" fees for sport participation, and recent estimates suggest that by 2020, 27% of public high schools will no longer have sport teams of any kind.

2018 and Beyond

These shifts have contributed to the current structure of youth sport delivery systems in the U.S., characterized by a diverse mix of multi-sector providers. As funding for youth sport in public parks and recreation departments and schools has declined, the number of private for-profit and nonprofit agencies providing youth sport has continued to grow. In particular, the number of travel teams, private clubs, and commercial youth sport programs has increased dramatically. Unlike the seasonal and multi-sport programs traditionally offered by parks and recreation departments and other agencies, many of these organizations are year-round and specialize in just one sport. As the youth sport "market" has become more commercialized, these organizations have sought ways to extend the length and breadth of their services. Instead of having youth participate and pay for just one season, it makes more commercial sense to encourage youth to participate year-round. However, year-round participation also reduces the likelihood that youth will join, and pay, for other sport programs and requires "selling" parents on the benefits of year-round and exclusive participation. The allure of athletic success,

college scholarships, and even professional careers has thus become a driving force behind many youth sport programs, rather than the broader goals of youth development.

As a result, youth are entering competitive sport environments and specializing in single sports at earlier ages than ever before. A recent study by the National Collegiate Athletic Association (NCAA) found that many college athletes began specializing in their sport by the age of 12 (NCAA, 2016). Moreover, the same study found that many athletes reported high parental/family expectations of playing college and/or professional sport, and wish they had spent more time sampling other sports during their youth. The impact of these developments on youth development is profound. Early sport specialization has been linked with a host of issues, including social isolation, psychological stress, overuse injuries, and burnout (Myer et al., 2015), and competitive sport does not appear to be as conducive to promoting youth development.

Moreover, this has contributed to a drastic rise in the costs associated with youth sport participation, with parents regularly spending thousands of dollars to fund equipment and coaches' salaries, and the youth sport industry now estimated at more than $15 billion (Gregory, 2017). In addition to pricing out lower-income families, this trend has also compelled many municipalities to invest significant sums of public money into constructing youth sport mega-complexes to attract regional and national tournaments. The rationale for these investments is the potential influx of "new money" that will flow in from hosting these events. However, large-scale investments often divert money from other locally focused youth sport programs that would serve a broader and more diverse segment of the population. Similarly, many schools have invested millions in public funding for state-of-the-art sport facilities, yet the functional use of these facilities is often limited to student-athletes who participate on varsity teams and freeze out use by intramural participants or youth sport programs in the broader community.

Another area of notable growth has been in the nonprofit sector, where deficit-reduction perspectives have gradually been replaced by the positive youth development (PYD) paradigm. Rather than focusing on problems believed to be inherent in youth, PYD models emphasize positive aspects of youth development that should be cultivated and enhanced. This philosophy has filtered into the youth sport space, as many PYD-based organizations have emerged, particularly in low-income areas. Yet while these organizations provide important programs for youth, the extent to which PYD principles have actually been integrated into sport activities varies considerably (Coalter, 2011). Despite the positive rhetoric espoused in mission statements and objectives, many organizations still rely on the "power of sport" to induce positive change, with less attention to more purposeful and theory-based strategies (Coakley, 2011). In addition, many sport-based PYD programs have been criticized for focusing narrowly on the individual outcomes of sport participation, and falling short of addressing community-level issues that influence youth development.

The confluence of these trends has led to an interesting mix of public, nonprofit, and commercial youth sport providers that operate rather independently of one another, with very little strategic coordination (Jones, Edwards, Bocarro, Bunds, & Smith, 2017). In fact, the contest over limited space and facilities, funders and sponsors, and perhaps most importantly, participants, has actually created intense competition among youth sport providers. This has led to questions regarding the purpose and intended population of youth sport programs, particularly in the burgeoning nonprofit sector. For example, many travel and club teams are registered as 501(c)3 nonprofit organizations, meaning they are exempt from federal, state, and local income and property tax, and are not bound by the same employment regulations as commercial/public entities (e.g., unemployment compensation). However, some have questioned the degree to which these organizations actually deliver charitable services to groups in need. Rigorous travel and practice schedules and high user fees often exclude participation from lower income families, while many elite performance teams only target a relatively small segment of the population. Similarly, many larger nonprofit agencies, such as YMCAs, have evolved from primarily targeting low-income youth and underserved communities, to serving middle- and upper-class communities through more modern and contemporary facilities. How are these structural changes influencing the availability and accessibility

The confluence of these trends has led to an interesting mix of public, nonprofit, and commercial youth sport providers that operate rather independently of one another, with very little strategic coordination.

of youth sport across different communities? Are these changes contributing to the disproportionate rates of sport participation of people of different genders, races/ethnicities, and income groups? These are key questions that will only become more salient for contemporary youth sport managers.

Where Are We Going?

Sport participation has the potential to contribute positively to youth development, but, as noted earlier, has also been linked with a variety of negative youth development outcomes. Over the last 70 years, youth sport delivery systems have changed dramatically, and are now characterized by a diverse mix of public, nonprofit, and commercial providers. Much of the change has been directed toward making the youth sport delivery process more efficient and creating elite player pathways for talent development. The increased role of parents in organizing and managing youth sport has helped legitimize teams and leagues, and the subsequent growth of nonprofit and commercial providers is indicative of a system-wide effort to make the delivery process more cost effective and judicious. However, there remains a critical need to assess the values of youth sport in the U.S. and how they align with youth development principles. This assessment requires moving beyond a singular classification of *youth sport* to a deeper recognition of how sport is being organized, managed, and delivered.

> There remains a critical need to assess the values of youth sport in the U.S. and how they align with youth development principles.

In his insightful discussion of the sport-for-development movement, Coalter (2010) distinguishes between three modes of sport that are differentiated by the relative emphasis they give to achieving certain objectives. Coalter (2010, p. 298) summarizes these three modes as described below.

Traditional Sport

Traditional or "mainstream" forms of sport, are based on the assumption that sport has inherent developmental benefits for participants. For example, youth sport organizers that operate under this model assume that just by participating in youth sport, participants derive positive developmental benefits.

Sport Plus

Sports are adapted and often combined with other youth development programs in order to maximize their potential to achieve developmental objectives. For example, the NHL's "Hockey is for Everyone" (http://www.usahockey.com/page/show/2062713-

hockey-is-for-everyone) is a sport-based youth development program designed to integrate a life skills curriculum alongside the regular hockey program.

Plus Sport

Sport's popularity is used as a type of "fly paper" to attract young people to education and training programs, with the systematic development of sport rarely the primary goal. For example, the goal of the Football Foundation of South Africa's "Food for Sport" program (https://www.youtube.com/watch?v=AqqqjBPQo3s) is to educate local children about organic food production, nutrition, and life skills. Sport is used as a "hook" to get children to sign up for the program.

When we carefully review the growth of youth sports in the U.S., particularly over the last 20 years, it is clear that *traditional* sport systems have undergone the most significant changes. In particular, high-performance and elite sport systems have received a tremendous amount of resources to professionalize youth sport experiences and create specialized player pathways. Although youth development is often seen as a byproduct of these experiences, this connection is typically substantiated by an assumption that sport possesses the inherent qualities necessary to promote developmental objectives. This perspective is not limited to competitive youth sports, as many youth sport programs operate under the premise that youth who are exposed to the "power of sport," regardless of its form or substance, will receive positive developmental benefits. Yet as the two stories at the beginning of this chapter indicate, sport participation does not automatically lead to positive youth development outcomes, and can actually have the reverse effect. Thus, there is a need to look more critically at how *sport plus* and *plus sport* systems may be integrated into the current system.

As the PYD movement has gained traction within the youth sport context, managers and researchers have developed a range of useful strategies and models for strategically promoting positive PYD through sport activities. For example, Hellison's (2011) Teaching Personal and Social Responsibility (TPSR) model has been adopted in a variety of settings to promote accountability and action in youth, and the Developmental Model of Sport Participation (DMSP) (Côté & Vierimaa, 2014) offers a viable framework for promoting performance, participation, and personal development in youth. In addition, Lerner and colleagues' (2005) 5 Cs model and the Search Institute's developmental assets model (Benson, 1997) have also been adapted to guide the design and implementation of many sport-based youth development initiatives.

However, although the components of these models provide a useful starting point to design youth sport experiences, they alone cannot be relied upon to promote youth development. Youth development requires the integration of local norms, beliefs, and values that reflect what "development" means in a particular setting or community. Since these qualities vary across different communities, standardized approaches to sport-based youth development are not likely to be effective. Thus, managers should consider adapting these models and strategies to reflect the unique needs of the youth and communities they serve.

One technique that can help facilitate this process is logic modeling. Logic models are used to articulate a program's "theory of change," which describes the components, mechanisms, and activities of a program that lead to desired outcomes and impacts (see Chapter 13). This process should be informed by a mix of youth development theory, practice-based insight, and local knowledge, and go beyond assumptions regarding the inherent *power of sport*. Developing a theory of change can help identify and critically examine underlying assumptions, and allow youth sport managers to establish an informed approach to sport-based youth development that is tailored to their specific context. In addition, it provides a useful tool for designing monitoring and evaluation strategies that help sport managers understand if their program is reaching their intended audience, enhancing the intended outcomes, and having the intended impact.

As youth sport managers proceed through developing more systematic program design and delivery processes, they are likely to be confronted by the uncomfortable reality that many youth development principles do not mesh with the current sport value systems in the U.S. For example, although competitive sport can provide valuable opportunities for youth to challenge themselves and develop stronger perceptions of personal competence, sport, particularly competitive high-stakes sports, is not an appropriate context for many youth. An overemphasis on competitive sport can alienate youth from participating in sport, causing youth who do participate to only associate positive feelings with winning, and inducing negative outcomes for those who are not competitively successful.

> As youth sport managers proceed through developing more systematic program design and delivery processes, they are likely to be confronted by the uncomfortable reality that many youth development principles do not mesh with the current sport value systems in the U.S.

In addition, many *sport plus* and *plus sport* programs require modifications to traditional sport settings and rules that accommodate more diverse curricula and participation. Yet modified sports (e.g., flag football, indoor golf, and more play-based activities that emphasize physical activity over skill development) are often phased out during adolescent and teenage years to make way for competitive athletics. Although competitive options have an important place in the overall mix of youth sports, their presence should not usurp resources at the expense of other noncompetitive sport options that are likely to attract a broader and more diverse segment of the population.

Perhaps most importantly, there is a pressing need to consider the sport value system of the general public. The rapid privatization and commercialization of youth sport has been accelerated by a cultural emphasis on competitive and elite sport that is fueled by professional leagues, large-scale equipment suppliers, and the continued interest of parents in this form of sport involvement for their children. Even if youth sport managers design effective programs based around youth development principles, will there be enough interest to sustain these types of programs? Professional and even college athletes represent powerful social figures who represent the pinnacle of sport in the U.S. These individuals are often lauded for their athletic prowess, strict training regimens, and win-at-all-costs attitudes. Such characteristics represent a very specific form of sport participation that is not necessarily compatible with youth development, yet nevertheless filters down into many forms of youth sport. For example, much of the recent investment in youth sport delivery structures has gone toward facilities and equipment that cater to youth who fit these high-performance standards and exclude those who do not. How do these decisions influence the social status of different sport activities, and how does this status influence participation? If youth are unable to "make the cut" for the team that plays in sponsored uniforms under the bright lights of a multimillion-dollar sport facility in front of 20,000 fans, will they still be interested in playing in a pick-up league at the local recreation facility? Is this form of sport participation still valued, or do youth/parents feel that the only type of sport participation worth pursuing is the kind glorified in mainstream news, television, and media?

These are key issues that must be addressed through a system-level assessment of youth sport structures and values. The reduction of public funding and trends toward privatization are not unique to youth sport and actually characterize the delivery of most public and social services today. However, rather than focusing on the boundaries between public, for-profit, and nonprofit sectors, contemporary youth sport managers must embrace the amalgamated nature of the industry and acknowledge the multiple youth sport providers that comprise it. This "system" cannot afford to work at cross-purposes or be hampered by issues of competition over facilities, funding, and participants. Multi-sector collaboration and strategic coordination are needed to ensure that all providers are working together to collectively provide youth with opportunities to participate in sport. More importantly, youth sport managers must ensure that in addition to traditional sport options, a comprehensive system of *sport plus* and *plus sport* options that specifically target youth development outcomes are also provided. These programs must be appropriately resourced so that they are presented and managed as legitimate sport options for youth and families and not perceived as just alternative options for those who are "not good enough" to play competitive sport.

A lot is at stake here. At the national level, there is little evidence that the social, mental, and physical health outcomes typically associated with sport participation are improving among youth. The incidence of school dropout has remained fundamentally the same since the 1990s (Chapman, Laird, Ifill, & KewalRamani, 2011), as has illicit drug use (Banken, 2006), alcohol use (Center on Alcohol Marketing and Youth, 2006), and juvenile delinquency (Snyder & Sickmund, 2006). Youth are now twice as likely to suffer from anxiety compared to 30 years ago (Hagell, 2012), and the Centers for Disease Control and Prevention (CDC) (2013) estimates that as many as one out of every five American children under the age of 18 suffers from some form of mental disorder (e.g., depression). Further, recent studies show that more than one-third of children aged 6–19 are obese or overweight (Ogden, Carroll, Kit, & Flegal, 2012), a rate that has remained consistent for over a decade (Ogden, Carroll, Kit, & Flegal, 2016). Most alarmingly, each of these outcomes is significantly linked with social, economic, and racial disadvantages that are actually becoming more pronounced (Omi & Winant, 2014).

> Moreover, the continued professionalization, commercialization, and commodification of youth sport is indicative of a sport value system increasingly rooted in competition rather than key youth development principles.

While sport alone does not account for all of these problems, the role sport has played in perpetuating these trends should be recognized. Although sport remains one of the most popular activities among youth, recent studies indicate participation is decreasing. This trend is particularly evident among disadvantaged youth (e.g., minority, low-income, rural), indicating barriers to sport participation are becoming even more restrictive for certain populations. Moreover, the continued professionalization, commercialization, and commodification of youth sport is indicative of a sport value system increasingly rooted in competition rather than key youth development principles. While sport remains the most popular leisure activity among youth, and one of most influential social, economic, and political industries in the world, its potential utility in promoting youth development remains drastically underdeveloped. By improving the coordination of youth sport providers, and integrating more developmentally focused and strategically designed sport plus and plus sport programs into the current system, sport can play a vital role in promoting youth development in the U.S.

Discussion Questions

1. What are some of the ways that sport can facilitate youth development principles?
2. What are some of the ways in which sport may negatively impact youth development?
3. There are three main modes of youth sport. How do these different modes impact the way that sport contributes (or does not contribute) to youth development?

Case Studies and Exercises

Case Study/Exercise 1

Overall, the ability of sport participation to provide positive benefits may be dependent on how sport programs are organized and managed. One critical dimension of managing a positive sport experience for youth is a well-trained coach. Effective coaches have the knowledge to improve young athletes' competence, confidence, connection, and character in the sporting context. Unfortunately, according to Project Play, few youth coaches receive any type of training. Additionally, if training occurs, the training focuses on skill development, rather than communicating with young people, promoting positive youth development outcomes through sport, or encouraging youth's long-term participation in sport.

Think back to some of the youth development principles outlined in Chapter 1 as you move through the following questions.

Throughout your life, you have played soccer. You now have a 6-year-old who wants to begin playing in a recreation soccer league primarily made up of volunteer youth coaches. You decide to volunteer to be the head coach of the team. The season is 12 weeks long; you meet twice a week with the kids. All the parents will be present at practices and games. Take some time to think about why you want to coach this team. In addition, what do you want participants to get out of the experience? Use these two questions to write out a coaching philosophy statement. After you have written out your statement, think about what PYD principles your philosophy contains.

As you think about putting these PYD principles into action, what specific action steps would you implement to ensure that your players get the benefits of participating in sport (think about schedules, communicating with parents, athletes, other coaches, problems and issues that may arise, equity issues, cultural issues)?

Case Study/Exercise 2

You are a youth sport coordinator at a sport-based youth development organization. For years, your organization has provided a parent-child flag football program in the spring season that allows adults and youth to participate together. Following PYD principles, the program is primarily designed to build positive social relationships between parents and their children and strengthen the social ties among families. The scores of games are not recorded, and many games are followed by some sort of social activity (e.g., barbecue).

However, recently the interest in this program has decreased considerably. Fewer parents are interested in flag football and more are asking for the spring season to be utilized as a training camp for youth to learn "real" football skills (e.g., running, throwing, catching) that may be deployed during the competitive tackle season, which is in the fall. Similar to other organizations, approximately 80% of your total budget comes from registration fees, so keeping parents happy is vital to the future of your organization.

- Is it possible to promote the youth development values targeted during the flag football program with a competitively focused training camp?
- What type of message would you convey to the parents in order to resolve this issue?
- Would you continue to run the flag football program? What if participants begin to leave the program? How might that influence your decision?

Case Study/Exercise 3

You are starting a sport-based youth development organization targeting youth in a low-income community. To begin, you need to develop specific ideas that will guide the management, delivery, and assessment of your program. To help guide this process, answer the following questions related to the activities, outcomes, and impacts of your program.

- Write out a mission statement that will guide your program. This should be a broad statement that summarizes your organization, activities, and intended impact on youth development.
- Write out three to five objectives that, if achieved, will specifically contribute to the youth development impact you highlighted in the mission statement.
- Think about the sport or sports you intended to utilize. What are some activities that specifically contribute to each of the objectives listed in question two? These should go beyond just providing sport opportunities to include particular aspects of the setting, rules, and coaching/instruction.

References

Aspen Institute. (2016). State of Play 2016: Trends and Developments. Retrieved from http://www.aspenprojectplay.org/sites/default/files/StateofPlay_2016_FINAL.pdf

Babiss, L. A., & Gangwisch, J. E. (2009). Sports participation as a protective factor against depression and suicidal ideation in adolescents as mediated by self-esteem and social support. *Journal of Developmental and Behavioral Pediatrics, 30*(5), 376–384.

Banken, J. A. (2006). Drug abuse trends among youth in the United States. *Annals of the New York Academy of Sciences, 1025*(1), 465–471.

Benson, P. L. (1997). *All kids are our kids: What communities must do to raise caring and responsible children and adolescents.* San Francisco, CA: Jossey-Bass.

Bocarro, J. N. (2001). Mobile beacons: Roving leaders and the communities they serve. Unpublished doctoral dissertation, Texas A&M University, College Station.

Bradley, J., Keane, F., & Crawford, S. (2013). School sport and academic achievement. *Journal of School Health, 83*(1), 8–13.

Broh, B. A. (2002). Linking extracurricular programming to academic achievement: Who benefits and why? *Sociology of Education, 75*(1), 69–95.

Brower, J. J. (1979). The professionalization of organized youth sport: Social psychological impacts and outcomes. *The ANNALS of the American Academy of Political and Social Science, 445*(1), 39–46.

Cameron, C. (August, 2017). Former baseball player sues coach for benching him. *Athletic Business.* Retrieved from http://www.athleticbusiness.com/civil-actions/former-baseball-player-sues-coach-for-benching-him.html

Camiré, M., & Kendellen, K. (2016). Coaching for positive youth development in high school sport. In N. L. Holt (Ed.), *Positive youth development through sport* (2nd ed., pp. 126–136). New York, NY: Routledge.

Center on Alcohol Marketing and Youth. (2006). *Underage drinking in the United States: A status report, 2005.* Washington, DC: Georgetown University.

Chapman, C., Laird, J., Ifill, N., & KewalRamani, A. (2011). *Trends in high school dropout and completion rates in the United States: 1972–2009* (NCES 2012-006). U.S. Department of Education. Washington, DC: National Center for Education Statistics. Retrieved from http://nces.ed.gov/pubsearch.

Coakley, J. (2011). Youth sports: What counts as positive development? *Journal of Sport & Social Issues, 35*(3), 306–324.

Coakley, J. (2016). Positive youth development through sport: Myths, beliefs, and realities. In N. L. Holt (Ed.), *Positive youth development through sport* (2nd ed., pp. 22–33). New York, NY: Routledge.

Coakley, J. (2017). *Sports in society: Issues and controversies* (12th ed.). New York, NY: McGraw Hill.

Conrad, D. (2016). The Stanford Sports to Prevent Obesity Randomized Trial (SPORT). In D. Conrad & A. White (Eds.), *Sports-based health interventions* (pp. 261–267). New York, NY: Springer.

Coronado, V. G., Haileyesus, T., Cheng, T. A., Bell, J. M., Haarbauer-Krupa, J., Lionbarger, M. R., Flores-Herrera, J., McGuire, L. C., & Gilchrist, J. (2015). Trends in sports- and recreation-related traumatic brain injuries treated in U.S. emergency departments: The National Electronic Injury Surveillance System-All Injury Program (NEISS-AIP) 2001-2012. *Journal of Head Trauma Rehabilitation, 30*(3), 185–197.

Côté, J., & Vierimaa, M. (2014). The developmental model of sport participation: 15 years after its first conceptualization. *Science and Sports, 29*(Suppl), S63–S69.

Crane, J., & Temple, V. (2015). A systematic review of dropout from organized sport among children and youth. *European Physical Education Review, 21*(1), 114–131.

Crompton, J. L. (1998). Forces underlying the emergence of privatization in parks and recreation. *Journal of Park and Recreation Administration, 16*(2), 88–101.

Crompton, J. L. (1999). Emergence of the unfair competition issue in United States' recreation. *Managing Leisure, 3*(2), 47–70.

Darling, N., Caldwell, L. L., & Smith, R. (2005). Participation in school-based extracurricular activities and adolescent adjustment. *Journal of Leisure Research, 37*(1), 51–56.

DiFiori, J. P., Benjamin, H. J., Brenner, J. S., Gregory, A., Jayanthi, N., Landry, G. L., & Luke, A. (2014). Overuse injuries and burnout in youth sports: A position statement from the American Medical Society for Sports Medicine. *British Journal of Sports Medicine, 48*(4), 287–288.

Dunn, C. R., Dorsch, T. E., King, M. Q., & Rothlisberger, K. J. (2016). The impact of family financial investment on perceived parent pressure and child enjoyment and commitment in organized youth sport. *Family Relations, 65*(2), 287–299.

Eime, R. M., Young, J. A., Harvey, J. T., Charity, M. J., & Payne, W. R. (2013). A systematic review of the psychological and social benefits of participation in sport for children and adolescents: Informing development of a conceptual model of health through sport. *International Journal of Behavioral Nutrition and Physical Activity, 10*(1), 98.

Eitle, T. M., & Eitle, D. J. (2002). Race, cultural capital, and the educational effects of participation in sports. *Sociology of Education, 75*(April), 123–146.

Eitzen, D. S. (2000). Social control and sport. In J. J. Coakley & E. Dunning (Eds.), *Handbook of sports studies* (pp. 370–381). London, UK: Sage.

Finn, J. D. (1989). Withdrawing from school. *Review of Educational Research, 59*(2), 117–142.

Fitzgerald, H. (2009). *Disability and youth sport.* London, UK: Routledge.

Floyd, M., Bocarro, J., & Thompson, T. (2008). Research on race and ethnicity in leisure studies: A review of five major journals. *Journal of Leisure Research, 40*(1), 1–22.

Fraser-Thomas, J., & Côté, J. (2009). Understanding adolescents' positive and negative developmental experiences in sport. *The Sport Psychologist, 23*(1), 3–23.

Frederick, G. C. (1965). Little league baseball. Master's Theses. Central Washington University ScholarWorks@CWU (Paper 446). Retrieved from from http://digitalcommons.cwu.edu/cgi/viewcontent.cgi?article=1460&context=etd

Green, K., Smith, A., & Roberts, K. (2005). Young people and lifelong participation in sport and physical activity: A sociological perspective on contemporary physical education programs in England and Wales. *Leisure Studies, 24*(1), 27–43.

Gregory, S. (2017, August 24). How kids' sports became a $15 billion industry. TIME Sports. Retrieved from http://time.com/4913687/how-kids-sports-became-15-billion-industry/

Hagell, A. (2012). *Changing adolescence: Social trends and mental health.* Bristol, UK: Policy Press.

Hartmann, D. (2001). Notes on midnight basketball and the cultural politics of recreation, race, and at-risk urban youth. *Journal of Sport and Social Issues, 25*(4), 339–371.

Head, K. J., & Iannarino, N. T. (2017). Understanding the psychosocial influences on high school football players' weight-gaining behaviors. *Western Journal of Communication, 81*(1), 127–147.

Hedstrom, R., & Gould, D. (2004). Research in youth sports: Critical issues status. Retrieved from http://edweb3.educ.msu.edu/ysi/articles/CTSAWhitePapers.pdf

Heinzmann, G. S. (2002). Parental violence in youth sports: Facts, myths, and videotape. *Parks & Recreation, 37,* 66–75.

Hellison, D. (2011). *Teaching responsibility through physical activity* (2nd ed.). Champaign, IL: Human Kinetics.

Holt, N. L., Kingsley, B. C., Tink, L. N., & Scherer, J. (2011). Benefits and challenges associated with sport participation by children and parents from low-income families. *Psychology of Sport and Exercise, 12,* 490–499.

Hyman, M. (2012). *The most expensive game in town: The rising cost of youth sports and the toll on today's family.* Boston, MA: Beacon Press.

Janssen, I. (2014). Active play: An important physical activity strategy in the fight against childhood obesity. *Canadian Journal of Public Health, 105*(1), 22–27.

Jones, G. J., Edwards, M. B., Bocarro, J. N., Bunds, K. S., & Smith, J. W. (2017). A structural perspective of cross-sector partnerships involving youth sport non-profit organizations. *European Sport Management Quarterly.* doi.org/10.1080/161 84742.2017.1322625

Jouvenal, J. (2015, July). When being benched in youth sports means a lawsuit. *Daily Herald.* Retrieved from http://www.dailyherald.com/article/20150404/ news/150409561/

Kay, T., & Bradbury, S. (2009). Youth sport volunteering: Developing social capital? *Sport, Education and Society, 14*(1), 121–140.

Kwan, M., Bobko, S., Faulkner, G., Donnelly, P., & Cairney, J. (2014). Sport participation and alcohol and illicit drug use in adolescents and young adults: A systematic review of longitudinal studies. *Addictive Behaviors, 39*(3), 497–506.

Lerner, R. M., Lerner, J. V., Almerigi, J., Theokas, C., Phelps, E., Gestsdottir, S., & von Eye, A. (2005). Positive youth development, participation in community youth development programs, and community contributions of fifth-grade adolescents: Findings from the first wave of the 4-H Study of Positive Youth Development. *Journal of Early Adolescence, 25*(1), 17–71.

McEwin, C. K., & Dickinson, T. S. (1996). Placing young adolescents at risk in interscholastic sports programs. *The Clearing House, 69*(4), 217–221.

Merkel, D. L. (2013). Youth sport: Positive and negative impact on young athletes. *Open Access Journal of Sports Medicine, 4,* 151.

Miller, K. E., Farrell, M. P., Barnes, G. M., Melnick, M. J., & Sabo, D. (2005). Gender/racial differences in jock identity, dating, and adolescent sexual risk. *Journal of Youth and Adolescence, 34*(2), 123–136.

Myer, G. D., Jayanthi, N. DiFiori, J. P., Faigenbaum, A. D., Kiefer, A. W., Logerstedt, D., & Mitcheli, L. J. (2015). Sport specialization part II: Alternative solutions to early sport specialization in youth athletes. *Sports Health: A Multidisciplinary Approach, 8*(1), 65–73.

National Collegiate Athletic Association (NCAA). (2016, January). NCAA GOALS study of the student-athlete experience: Initial summary of findings. Retrieved from http://www.ncaa.org/sites/default/files/GOALS_2015_summary_jan2016_final_20160627.pdf

Neely, K. C., & Holt, N. L. (2014). Parents' perspectives on the benefits of sport participation for young children. *The Sport Psychologist, 28*(3), 255–268.

Ogden, C. L., Carroll, M. D., Kit, B. K., & Flegal, K. M., (2012). Prevalence of obesity and trends in body mass index among U.S. children and adolescents, 1999-2010. *Journal of the American Medical Association, 307*(5), 483–490.

Ogden, C. L., Carroll, M. D., Lawman, H. G., Fryar, C. D., Kruszon-Moran, D., Kit, B. K., & Flegal, K. M. (2016). Trends in obesity prevalence among children and adolescents in the United States, 1988-1994 through 2013-2014. *Journal of the American Medical Association, 315*(21), 2292–2299.

Omi, M., & Winant, H. (2014). *Racial formation in the United States.* New York, NY: Routledge.

Pate, R. R., Trost, S. G., Levin, S., & Dowda, M. (2000). Sports participation and health-related behaviors among U.S. youth. *Archives of Pediatrics and Adolescent Medicine, 154*(9), 904–911.

Phillips, J. A., & Young, D. R. (2009). Past-year sports participation, current physical activity, and fitness in urban adolescent girls. *Journal of Physical Activity and Health, 6*(1), 105–111.

Pitas, N. A., Mowen, A. J., Liechty, T., & Trauntvein, N. (2015). "Proceed with caution:" Public perceptions regarding corporate sponsorship of park and recreation services. *Journal of Park and Recreation Administration, 33*(4), 1–15.

Pitter, R., & Andrews, D. L. (1997). Serving America's underserved youth: Reflections on sport and recreation in an emerging social problems industry. *Quest, 49,* 85–99.

Seefeldt, V. D., & Ewing, M. E. (1997). Youths ports in America: An overview. *President's Council on Physical Fitness and Sports Research Digest; Series 2, No. 11.* Sep 1997. Washington, DC. ED 413 324 SP 037 635. (pp. 3–14).

Sheu, Y., Chen, L., & Hedegaard, H. (2016). *Sports- and recreation-related injury episodes in the United States, 2011-2014.* National Health Statistics Reports; No. 99. Hyattsville, MD: National Center for Health Statistics.

Snyder, H. N., & Sickmund, M. (2006). *Juvenile offenders and victims: 2006 national report.* Washington, DC: U.S. Department of Justice, Office of Justice Programs, Office of Juvenile Justice and Delinquency Prevention.

Stewart, C., Warhol, J., Overton, K., Wiet, C. E., Freeman, C., Bourbeau, J., Moon, S., & Crawford, S. A. G. M. (2005). Has the decline of intramural sports contributed to the youth obesity epidemic? *Journal of Physical Education, Recreation & Dance (JOPERD), 76*(11), 11–14.

Trudeau, F., & Shephard, R. (2005). Contribution of school programmes to physical activity levels and attitudes in children and adults. *Sports Medicine, 35*(2), 89–105.

Turnnidge, J., Côté, J., & Hancock, D. J. (2014). Positive youth development from sport to life: Explicit or implicit transfer. *Quest, 66*(20), 203–217.

Up2Us Sports. (2011). Going, going, gone: The decline in youth sports. Retrieved from   https://s3-us-west-2.amazonaws.com/up2us/uploads/center_resource/document/561/GoingGoingGone_Up2UsReport.pdf

Vella, S. A., Oades, L. G., & Crowe, T. P. (2013). The relationship between coach leadership, the coach-athlete relationship, team success, and the developmental experiences of young athletes. *Physical Education and Sport Pedagogy, 18,* 549–561.

Wichstrøm, T., & Wichstrøm, L. (2009). Does sports participation during adolescence prevent later alcohol, tobacco and cannabis use? *Addiction, 104*(1), 138–149.

Woolf, J., Rimal, R. N., & Sripad, P. (2014). Understanding the influence of proximal networks on high school athletes' intentions to use androgenic anabolic steroids. *Journal of Sport Management, 28*(1), 8–20.

Chapter 11

Nature and Youth Development

Barry A. Garst

Engaging youth in nature is not always an easy task. Today's parents as well as youth leaders face a generation of adolescents raised on technology and new media, who often have a range of activity options (often indoors) to occupy their time and attention. Moreover, this generation of adolescents (see Chapters 2 and 3) is also surrounded too often by peers and adults who choose recreation and leisure options not involving nature. In addition, 80% of youth say that bugs and heat make the outdoors too uncomfortable (The Nature Conservancy, 2011). Without engaging opportunities, positive role models, and sufficient encouragement, many youth simply make the choice to spend time in settings other than nature. As parents of 14- and 9-year-old girls, my wife and I stress the importance of balance between non-nature time (e.g., playing on an iPad, reading, watching television) and time outdoors (e.g., hiking, exploring, spending time at the lake). We supplement our family outdoor trips with regular reminders to our girls, "You've had enough time on devices, now find something to do outside." But striving for such balance takes time, commitment, and a willingness among parents to intervene when children may prefer to be doing something indoors.

Connecting youth and nature has not always been such a challenge. Across most of human history, nature and childhood have been synonymous and often inseparable, with nature as the center of the culture of childhood. Describing children in the 19th century, Pyle (2002) noted that "when children were left to their own devices, their first choice [was] often to flee to the nearest wild place…" (p. 311). This natural preference for nature is supported by research documenting that people—across cultures, populations, and environments—have a strong preference for nature (Kaplan, Kaplan, & Ryan, 1998). This predilection has its roots in evolutionary biology and the preference that living organisms have for settings that will help them stay alive and thrive (Wells & Evans, 2003). In fact, children and adolescents have a developmental need to spend time in nature, engaged in settings and experiences that place them in direct, active contact with the natural, non-human-made world. Interacting with nature provides a range of developmental, health, and well-being benefits, including enhanced concentration, reduced stress, improved mood, and increased creativity (Kellert, 2012; Wells, 2014). Experiences in nature can also shape youths' values, their understanding of their world, and their perceptions of themselves (Kahn, 2002).

Research suggests that youth are engaging in fewer and fewer nature-based experiences (The Nature Conservancy, 2011), with the greatest declines among the youngest age groups (see Figure 11.1; The Outdoor Foundation, 2016a). At the same time, passive forms of entertainment are increasing among youth, particularly use of media and screens (i.e., technology-enabled activity). As highlighted by Pew Family Research Center (Lenhart & Page, 2015), 92% of teens aged 13–17 now go online daily,

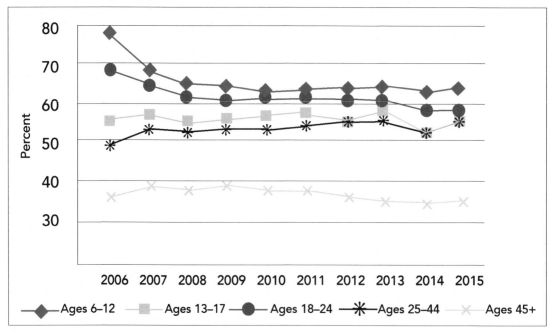

Figure 11.1. Outdoor Activity Participation by Age
(Outdoor Foundation, 2016a)

with 24% of teens going online "almost constantly" because of their ubiquitous access to mobile devices. Furthermore, most teens have daily access to four to five different devices (e.g., computer, smartphone, basic phone, tablet, and a game console. Also see Chapter 3).

In addition to the increased access to and use of technology, the decline of nature-based experiences and rise of media use is impacted, in part, by a range of barriers that some youth face in accessing the outdoors. Scholars also note that youth are experiencing "a more supervised, planned, and organized childhood" (Karsten & van Vliet, 2006, p. 79). This trend is reflected in notable changes in contemporary parenting approaches that reflect enhanced monitoring and protection (Garst & Gagnon, 2015) as well as increased parental anxiety associated with the outdoors (Prezza, Alparone, Cristallo, & Luigi, 2005). Whether real or imagined, if parents believe that their children will be harmed or become injured while spending time outdoors, then they are less likely to allow their children to participate in nature-based experiences.

> ... youth are experiencing "a more supervised, planned, and organized childhood.

Because of concerns about youth detachment from nature, several states have adopted a "children's outdoor bill of rights." The California Roundtable on Recreation, Parks and Tourism (2017) was one of the first organizations to adopt this bill of rights, creating a fundamental list of experiences every child in California should have prior to high school. The outdoor bill of rights includes 10 experiences to which children should have access:

- Learn to swim
- Play on a team
- Follow a trail
- Catch a fish
- Celebrate their heritage
- Discover the past
- Splash in the water
- Play in a safe place
- Camp under the stars
- Explore nature

This chapter will explore the relationship between youth development and nature by examining how nature contributes to youth growth, development, and well-being. Barriers that limit youths' contact with nature will be identified, as well as promising programs for nature-based youth development. Such an examination is inherently multidisciplinary, including perspectives from environmental and cognitive psychology, human development, public health, recreation/leisure science, natural resources, urban studies, interior design, environmental education, geography, and evolutionary biology. The following sections will integrate elements of this diverse literature through the lens of youth development to empower students, scholars, and practitioners to better recognize nature as a positive youth development (PYD) setting.

A guiding assumption of this chapter is that participation in high-quality activities, such as nature-based experiences, is an ecological/contextual asset for promoting positive youth outcomes (Eccles & Gootman, 2002). Context is a critical component of PYD, and emphasizes the reciprocal relationship between a young person and his or her environment (Benson, Scales, & Syvertsen, 2011). Such a relationship suggests that contexts—in this case nature—can influence the assets that youth have access to and can take advantage of, and also that youth can influence the context they are in (e.g., nature) based on their choices and behaviors. Thus, this chapter examines nature as a contextual asset that may serve as a resource for positive development.

Defining Nature-Based Experiences

Nature-based environments and experiences are commonly described based on the degree of human influence present. For example, Ives et al. (2017) suggested that nature reflects "places, landscapes, and ecosystems that are not completely dominated by people, but also included non-human organisms, species, and habitats" (p. 106). This definition helps us differentiate a nature-based experience from simply doing something outdoors (e.g., playing a sport in an outdoor field).

Youth contact with nature differs from person to person and takes many forms. In fact, the ways in which young people experience and perceive nature are unique across individuals (Nisbet & Zelenski, 2013) and may even contrast with the ways adults interact with and perceive nature (Nabhan & Trimble, 1995). For example, some research has suggested that adults pay attention to the broader landscape, while children focus on smaller niches within nature (Nabhan & Trimble, 1995).

Youth contact with nature can be described in three different ways: *direct, indirect,* and *vicarious* (Kellert, 2002). *Direct* experiences provide real physical contact with nature that is often unplanned and unconstrained. Within the context of youth development programs, examples might include nature-based leisure or play in a park, forest, creek, or similar setting. *Indirect* experiences involve real physical contact with nature that is structured, managed or programmed in some way through human planning, programming, or intervention. Examples include encounters with nature through a nature center, gardens, zoos, or museums, or even through activities like gardening

> Some youth development programs may provide a combination of direct, indirect, and vicarious forms of nature contact, which is important because developmental outcomes of nature are supported through varied and sustained outdoor experiences.

and raising livestock. *Vicarious* (i.e., symbolic) experiences involve no real nature contact. In vicarious experiences, youth experience representations of nature instead of real physical contact most often through books and media (e.g., watching a YouTube video about nature). Some youth development programs may provide a combination of direct, indirect, and vicarious forms of nature contact, which is important because developmental outcomes of nature are supported through varied and sustained outdoor experiences. Kellert (2012) proposed that such experiences:

> can be satisfied through a broad matrix of direct, indirect, and vicarious encounters with nature in settings and circumstances from early childhood through adolescence. This contact produces the greatest maturational benefits when it occurs in stable, accessible, and culturally relevant social and physical environments. (p. 88)

Scholars have noted the significant growth in youth involvement in vicarious nature-based experiences, described as artificial (Kellert, 2012) or mediated nature (Chawla, 1994). These artificial and mediated nature experiences include activities such as interacting with a nature app on a mobile device or reading a nature-related book. Although these fictional or fantasy-based depictions of nature can provide benefits, they fail to provide youth with a "strong and lasting emotional responses, such as wonder, joy, surprise, challenge, and discovery" when compared to a direct experience (Kellert, 2012, p. 74).

The timing of nature-based experiences is relevant, as time spent in nature during some periods of a young person's life may be particularly impactful. Middle childhood between the ages of 6–12 has been identified as an important period for youth to experience nature. James, Bixler, and Vadala (2010) studied how adults ages 19–35—those in environmental-related careers as well as a comparison group of individuals generally disinterested in nature—remembered their childhood, teen, and early adult years. The researchers found that during middle-childhood many participants experienced a "crystalizing event" (p. 243), which represented their personal fascination with the natural world as well as a feeling of understanding and confidence later confirmed through social interaction and validated by peers and adults. Kellert (2002) stressed how this important moment can create an "imprint" that shapes how young people perceive nature across their lives. Because the moment that will become imprinted will vary across children and will occur at different ages across varying experiences in nature, youth should be provided with a range of nature-based experiences.

Research suggests youths' innate preferences for nature are strongest when they are younger. For example, when left to make a drawing of their choice, youth prefer to draw outdoor scenes and favor pictures of nature (Kaplan & Kaplan, 2002; Moore, 1986). However, these preferences for nature change during adolescence. Based on Kaplan and Kaplan's (2002) research, adolescents have less preference for nature and a greater preference for places that provide "action and activity" (p. 244). Similarly, James et al. (2010) found that people reported much less nature engagement during their teenage years compared with childhood and adulthood experiences. Many have attributed this change in preferences during adolescence to increases in teens' interest in

spending time with their friends in structured, action-oriented experiences and settings (Chawla, 2002). This period has been called a "time out" (Kaplan & Kaplan, 2002) from participation in the nature-based experiences that teenagers may have favored when they were younger. The researchers proposed that "youth at this state might thus be expected to be attracted to environments that afford opportunities for independent action, for testing alternative patterns, and for gaining respect from peers and/or the community" (p. 250). Others have suggested that this "time-out" period may be more reflective of adolescents' interest in shared outdoor experiences with peers rather than a lack of interest in nature (Kellert, 2012).

Mapping Youth Development Assets to Nature-Based Outcomes

Within youth development theory, personal and social assets refer to specific indicators of well-being (Benson, Scales, & Syvertsen, 2011). As highlighted by Eccles and Gootman (2002), "adolescents with more personal and social assets … have a greater chance of both current well-being and future success" (p. 42). While the assets do not ensure adolescent well-being, youth need access to contexts that facilitate their growth and development. Using the personal and social assets framework identified by the National Research Council and Institute of Medicine of the National Academy of Sciences (Eccles & Gootman, 2002), indicators of youth well-being can be mapped to outcomes of nature-based experiences based on the literature associated with nature's impact on human development.

Table 11.1 maps youth development assets with outcomes of nature-based experiences, providing empirical and conceptual support for the influence of nature-based experiences on the four youth development asset domains (e.g., physical, intellectual, psychological/emotional, and social development). This table provides a starting point in broadening awareness of the role of nature as a context promoting youth development.

Table 11.1

Nature-Based Youth Outcomes Associated with Youth Development Assets

Youth Development Domain*	Influence of Nature on this Domain	Author(s)
Physical development • Good health habits • Good health risk management skills	Increases physical activity	Godbey (2009); Sallis, Prochaska, & Taylor, (2000)
	Improves health-related quality of life	Gopinath, Hardy, Baur, Burlutsky, & Mitchell (2012)
	Boosts relaxation and revitalization	Coon et al. (2011); Song, Ikei, & Mityazaki (2016)
Intellectual development • Critical thinking and reasoning skills • Good decision-making skills • Knowledge of vocational skills	Reduces symptoms of attention deficit disorder in children	Faber Taylor, Kuo, & Sullivan (2001); Kuo & Faber Taylor (2004)
	Enhances creativity and problem-solving	Atchley, Strayer, & Atchley (2012)
	Increases academic performance	Lieberman & Hoody (1998)
	Enhances identity development about vocational and recreational interests	Clayton & Opotow (2003); James, Bixler, & Vadala (2010)
Psychological and emotional development • Positive self-regard • Emotional self-regulation • Resilience and coping skills • Autonomy/self-responsibility • Spirituality/sense of purpose in life	Improves mood and reduces negative emotions	Bowler, Buyung-Ali, Knight, & Pullin (2010)
	Boosts resilience and reduces stress	Corraliza, Collado, & Bethelmy (2012); Wells (2014)
	Promotes spiritual development	King (2008); Schein (2014)
Social development • Positive relationships • Connectedness • Sense of social place/integration • Ability to navigate cultural contexts • Commitment to civic engagement	Stimulates social interaction and serves as a source of social support	Coley, Kuo, & Sullivan (1997); Owens (1998); Chawla & Derr (2012)
	Promotes lifelong environmental attitudes and interest in environmentally responsible behaviors	Arnold, Cohen, & Warner (2009); Garner, Taft & Stevens, 2015; Kals, Schumacher, & Montada (1999); Schultz, Shriver, Tabanico, & Khazion (2004)

* Eccles & Gootman (2002)

Physical Development

The domain of physical development includes good health habits and health risk management skills central to youth well-being (Eccles & Gootman, 2002). The importance of the human health benefits of time spent in nature cannot be understated. Given the obesity epidemic, identifying experiences and settings that increase youth physical activity and enhance good health habits among youth is critical (Hill, Wyatt, Reed, & Peters, 2003). Put simply, youth who spend more time outdoors are more physically active (Sallis, Prochaska, & Taylor, 2000).

> Given the obesity epidemic, identifying experiences and settings that increase youth physical activity and enhance good health habits among youth is critical.

Nature also promotes adolescent health, and in the long-term, participation in outdoor experiences is associated with perceived health-related outcomes (Gopinath, Hardy, Baur, Burlutsky, & Mitchell, 2012). Not surprisingly, nature is relaxing for most people. Time spent in nature—such as forests and urban green spaces—provides the type of relaxation that impacts human physiology, from the central nervous system to the immune system, in many positive ways (Song, Ikei, & Mityazaki, 2016). In fact, when compared to spending time outdoors, active time in nature has been associated with "greater feelings of revitalization and positive engagement, decreases in tension…and increased energy" (Coon et al., p. 1761).

Intellectual Development

The intellectual development domain includes critical thinking and reasoning skills, decision-making skills, and the development of vocational interests and related skills (Eccles & Gootman, 2002). These cognitive skills are particularly important for adolescents to successfully transition to the workforce or higher education. In short, research suggests that nature provides youth with a cognitive advantage. Nature improves concentration, particularly for youth diagnosed with attention deficit hyperactivity disorder (ADHD). In fact, the same activities reduce ADHD symptoms even more when they take place outdoors (for example, walking outdoors improves concentration better than walking indoors; Kuo & Faber Taylor, 2004).

Time spent outdoors also enhances creativity and problem-solving. After extended time in nature, a person's creativity may be boosted as much as 50% (Atchely, Strayer, & Atchely, 2012). How does nature have this effect? Based on Attention Restoration Theory (Kaplan, 1995; Ohly et al., 2016), nature provides these types of benefits because it provides youth with a break from high-arousing stimuli (e.g., televisions, mobile devices, video games), while also providing exposure to gentle, fascinating natural features.

Nature can be a powerful context for learning, and a large body of evidence supports that learning is more effective when it takes place in a nature-based setting rather than within a traditional setting. In nature-based settings, youth perform better on standardized assessments of academic achievement (e.g., math, science, reading, writing, and social studies) and also show more enthusiasm toward learning (Lieberman & Hoody, 1998).

Finally, youth who spend time in nature develop a better understanding of their vocational and leisure interests. Direct experiences—because they involve greater amounts of exploration of nature—are most impactful on whether or not children and adolescents develop a personal identity related to the outdoors and whether or not they want to pursue a nature-related career or leisure pursuit (Clayton & Opotow, 2003). In other words, people who play in nature as children are more likely to work (or pursue a leisure interest) in nature as adults. The accumulation of nature-based experiences over the course of a young person's life is important for the development of a nature-vocation or nature-leisure interest, as well as the influence of mentors at different life stages (James, et al., 2010)

Psychological and Emotional Development

The psychological and emotional development domain includes outcomes related to youth positive self-regard, emotional self-regulation, resilience and coping skills, autonomy and self-responsibility, spirituality, and sense of purpose in life (Eccles & Gootman, 2002). At a time in which anxiety is the most common form of mental illness (e.g., 25% of teens aged 13–18 report a depressive episode in the past year; Merikangas et al., 2010), concerns about the potential risks associated with common childhood activities are ever present in the minds of adults (Backett-Milburn & Harden, 2004). In addition, overprotective parents solve problems for their children rather than allow them to accept failure or adversity (Locke, Campbell, & Kavanagh, 2012); experiences that help youth develop the right blend of resilience, coping skills, and independence are necessary to empower youth with the right tools for the transition to adulthood.

One way that nature influences a person's psychological and emotional state is through influence on mood and emotions. Specifically, outdoor time reduces anger, sadness, anxiety, as well as fatigue (Bowler, Buyung-Ali, Knight, & Pullin, 2010). In this way, nature is a protective factor through its ability to buffer negative factors in a young person's life. For example, time in nature might help a teenager recover from negative emotions associated with

> Experiences that help youth develop the right blend of resilience, coping skills, and independence are necessary to empower youth with the right tools for the transition to adulthood.

failing an exam or breaking up with a significant other. Researchers have suggested that nature's ability to boost resilience and increase coping skills in youth occurs because nature provides an opportunity for youth to build social relationships and stimulate executive functioning in the brain (the part that controls memory and self-control; Wells, 2014).

Finally, nature can catalyze spiritual development in youth. Nature evokes curiosity, awe, and wonder in children and facilitates the development of deeper connections with oneself and others that can lead to the emergence of pro-social dispositions (e.g., caring, empathy, and kindness; Schein, 2014). In this way, nature-based experiences encourage children to think about the world beyond themselves. Encouraging this type of growth during adolescence is important, as "spirituality provides an environment where youth can experience the self embedded within a larger context that simultaneously validates the inherent value of the self and promotes a sense of belonging and connectedness beyond the self" (King, 2008, p. 71). During a developmental stage in which adolescents often feel disconnected, feeling connectedness (through an evolving sense of spirituality) may provide needed comfort in times of stress and uncertainty.

Social Development

The social development domain represents positive relationships with peers, parents, and nonparental adults; good relationships and trust with parents; social and institutional connectedness; the ability to traverse cultural contexts; and being civically engaged in one's community (Eccles & Gootman, 2002). Relationships are fundamental to the human experience, and youth development models recognize the centrality of social development for fostering stable, healthy young people who are prepared for the next stage of life. Nature can play an important role in the social development of youth. First, nature stimulates social interaction and serves as a source of social support (Coley, Kuo, & Sullivan, 1997), and importantly, people socialize more when they have access to outdoor spaces. In fact, teens value nature because it provides a place where they can spend time with friends (Owens, 1998).

Nature also provides an opportunity for youth to get involved in their community. When asked how they became interested in environmental issues, young environmental leaders identify childhood experiences in nature as important for shaping their civic engagement (Arnold, Cohen, & Warner, 2009). In fact, affinity for nature (the emotional connection that a person can feel toward the outdoors), is a particularly good predictor of nature-protective behavior (Kals, Schumacher, & Montada, 1999). In other words, when young people are emotionally connected to nature and feel like they are a part of nature, they are more likely to protect nature. This interest in protecting nature encourages youth to get involved in their community to address environmental issues, which strengthens their connections with individuals, organizations, and institutions in their community and further broadens their social support.

By mapping the four youth development asset domains (i.e., physical, intellectual, psychological/emotional, and social development) to outcomes associated with exposure to nature, the role of nature as context for youth development becomes clear.

Although all youth may not experience growth in all areas through nature contact—human development is a complex process influenced by multiple individual, familial, and communal factors—there is compelling evidence that including nature experiences as an element of a young person's developmental ecology can advance positive outcomes in a number of ways beyond outcomes that would be achieved without nature contact.

A Model for Nature-Based Youth Development

By aligning the strengths of youth (e.g., physical, intellectual, psychological/emotional, and social assets described in Table 11.1) with the Big Three resources for positive growth found in youth development programs, young people will experience optimal healthy development (Lerner et al., 2014). The Big Three include the following:

- Positive and sustained youth-adult relationships
- Youth skill-building activities
- Youth involvement and leadership

Figure 11.2 displays a model for nature-based youth development that links the Big Three to characteristics of nature-based experiences. In the model, positive and sustained youth-adult relationships link to social interaction and social support for concerns/fears about nature. Youth skill-building activities link to opportunities for skill-building and demonstrating competence, direct experiences in nature that are repeated and accumulated, graduated access to nature, and exposure. Finally, youth involvement and leadership link to opportunities to learn through community action. Figure 11.2 also includes the context as an important element of youth development settings. Context is linked to critical characteristics of nature-based experiences (e.g., getting away, fascination, novelty, and awe). Although these contextual characteristics may be embedded in a given youth development program (e.g., camp, outdoor education/adventure program), they are made explicit in this model. Each characteristic is described below.

PYD Characteristics Important for Nature-Based Youth Development

Social interaction/Social support for nature apprehension. Social interaction during nature-based YD meets adolescents' developmental need for good social relationships with peers and caring adults (Eccles & Gootman, 2002; Gambone, Klem & Connell, 2002). Social interaction is also important for other outcomes such as increased resiliency (Wells, 2014) and validation of one's environmental identity (James et al., 2010), as well as care for the environment (Chawla & Derr, 2012). However, given that youth can have apprehensive or fearful reactions to the outdoors (Bixler & Floyd, 1997; Kellert, 2012) even though they generally enjoy action-oriented nature-based experiences with friends (Chawla 2002; Kellert, 2012), the provision of social support by caring adults is an important element of nature-based YD. Acknowledging and normalizing youth apprehension toward nature, while providing nature-based experiences that have both experiential as well as social elements, is key to creating effective youth development opportunities in outdoor settings.

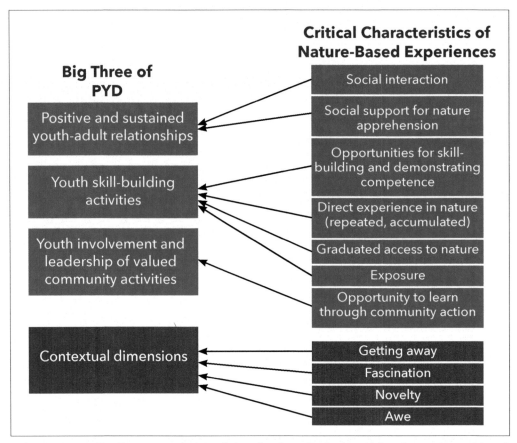

Figure 11.2. Proposed Model of the Relationship between Youth Development Features and Critical Characteristics of Nature-Based Experiences

Skill-building/Direct experiences/Graduated access/Exposure. Opportunities for youth skill building is broadly recognized as a critical component of PYD settings (Eccles & Gootman, 2002; Gambone et al., 2002). Within nature-based YD settings, such skill building is not only important for youth who need to demonstrate skill achievement and competence, but is often a result of direct experiences in nature. As described in this chapter, direct experiences can be the most impactful because they provide youth with greater level of exploration (Chawla & Derr, 2012; Kals & Ittner, 2003), which may also provide greater cognitive outcomes. Kellert (2012) observed, "for children, nature is the richest, most detailed, and most readily available informational context they are ever likely to encounter (p. 69). Repeated exposure to a developmental experience and context over time—an important concept within human development (Bronfenbrenner, 1995)—is related to both breadth (i.e., number of activities) and intensity (i.e., participation frequency) of nature contact (Rose-Krasnor, Busseri, Willoughby, & Chalmers, 2006).

Providing youth with opportunities to experience nature in ways that gradually build over time is also important. In addition, youth need "places of graduated risk, where challenges in the environment match children's developing capabilities to identify and negotiate" the environment (Chawla & Derr, 2012, p. 549). In this way, direct access to nature as well as repeated and accumulated nature-based experiences (Schultz & Tabanico, 2007) provide youth with the best opportunity for a positive nature-based experience.

The amount of time a young person spends in nature (i.e., exposure to nature) is important for nature-based youth development to be fully realized. Researchers propose that extended periods of exposure to nature-based experiences, ranging from at least three days (Williams, 2017) to five days (Stern, Powell, & Ardoin, 2008), can influence changes in a person's perspective, cognition, and awareness. Exposure may also have a social dimension, particularly if youth are participating with others, as it can take time to form supportive, warm relationships with other peers and adults (Eccles & Gootman, 2002).

> Researchers propose that extended periods of exposure to nature-based experiences, ranging from at least three days to five days can influence changes in a person's perspective, cognition, and awareness.

Opportunity to learn through community action. Youth engagement in community-based leadership increases their connection to nature as well as their community and enhances their pro-environmental behaviors (Chawla & Derr, 2012). Kellert (2012) has noted the appeal of nature-based programs that allow youth to learn and practice leadership, and research supports that leadership-focused nature-based programs can be effective in building independence, problem-solving, affinity for nature, and empowerment (Browne, Garst, & Bialeschki, 2011).

Other Contextual Characteristics Important for Nature-Based Youth Development

Other critical characteristics not directly mapped to the Big Three of PYD in the model reflect the nature-based context, including getting away, fascination, novelty, and awe. Each of these contextual elements of nature-based youth development is described below.

Getting away. This characteristic, often described as escape, being way, or going to a restorative place (Kaplan, 1995), can reflect a change in setting [for example, travel from a person's neighborhood to a nearby (or far away) nature-based place] or a conceptual change that allows a young person to see an old setting in a new way. The concept of getting away has also been identified an important element of adolescents' most valued outdoor places (Owens, 1998).

Fascination. Another characteristic of nature-based settings is fascination, described as a level of sensory stimulation in nature that draws a person's attention without

effort and does not require deep thinking (Kaplan, 1995). Noting the importance of experiencing fascination in nature, Atchley, Strayer, and Atchley (2012) pointed out that "modern society is filled with sudden events (sirens, horns, ringing phones, alarms, television, etc.) that hijack attention. By contrast, natural environments are associated with a gentle, soft fascination, allowing the executive attentional system to replenish" (p. 1). The benefits of soft fascination available through nature-based experiences may be particularly important for adolescents, whose regular use of digital technologies has introduced them to a number of health and well-being risks (Howard-Jones, 2011).

Novelty. Defined as being new, unique, or unfamiliar, novelty is an impactful characteristic of nature-based recreation (Garst, Williams, & Roggenbuck, 2010), therapy (Berman & Davis-Berman, 1995), and education (Orion & Hofstein, 1994). Others have recognized novelty as important for youth engagement (Gambone & Arbreton, 1997) as well as a motivation for youth curiosity (Bishop & Jeanrenaud, 1995). Orion and Hofstein (1994) discussed three aspects of novelty (i.e., cognitive, geographical, and psychological) that are important when engaging youth in meaningful outdoor experiences. This view of novelty recognizes that nature-related novelty (e.g., unfamiliarity with a physical area or gap between what a young person expects from the experience and what actually happens) can be a barrier if not appropriately planned.

Awe. Awe has been proposed as an important element of a nature-based experiences (Kellert, 2012). Awe has been defined as a "feeling a deep emotional, spiritual, or transcendental connection to…the specialness of an experience" (Adler & Fagley, 2005, p. 82). Awe is an emotion that people feel when they experience something different from anything they have experienced before, something that transcends the person's current frame of reference and cannot be easily understood or categorized (Piff, Dietze, Feinberg, Stancato, & Keltner, 2015). Awe also has a social dimension important to adolescents, as it encourages youth to be curious, to ask questions, and to seek information from others.

Barriers to Nature-Based Youth Development

Research has examined barriers that youth face in accessing the outdoors and participating in nature-based experiences and programs. Table 11.2 summarizes findings from four studies that examined trends in youth participation in outdoor recreation (Larson, Green, & Cordell, 2011; Nature Conservancy, 2011; The Outdoor Foundations, 2016a, 2016b). Although the methodologies and targeted populations

Table 11.2
Barriers Affecting Youth Participation in Nature

Barrier	The Nature Conservancy (2011)	Larson, Green, & Cordell (2011)	The Outdoor Foundation (2016a)	The Outdoor Foundation (2016b)
	Youth aged 13–18	Youth aged 6–19	Youth aged 13–17	Youth aged 13–30
Lack of transportation	✓	✓		✓
Lack of access to/availability of a natural area	✓	✓		
Being uncomfortable in nature (e.g., bugs, heat)	✓			✓
Lack of interest	✓		✓	
Lack of time	✓	✓	✓	✓
Safety concerns	✓	✓		✓
People are not welcoming	✓			
Health issues prevent participation	✓			
Too expensive			✓	✓
Parent/family influence				✓
Lack of skills			✓	
No one to participate with			✓	
Interested in other activities		✓		✓

differed, consistent themes emerged across these studies regarding barriers to youth participation in nature-based experiences. Each of the studies identified lack of time as a major barrier, and three out of the four studies identified lack of transportation as a barrier. Other barriers identified in at least two of the four studies included lack of access, lack of interest, being uncomfortable, lack of safety, health issues, too expensive, lack of skills, and lack of someone with whom to participate.

As suggested by Table 11.2, not all youth prefer outdoor nature experiences. While some youth may actively seek time in nature, others may avoid such experiences (Bixler & Floyd, 1997; Kellert, 2002) due to real or perceived barriers or because they prefer other experiences. In addition to positive feelings, studies have suggested that nature can also elicit uncertainty, disgust, anxiety, fear, or pain, for both rural and urban youth populations (Bixler & Floyd, 1997; Kellert, 2012). These feelings often arise in youth with limited positive, ongoing exposure to nature (Bixler, Carlisle, Hammitt, & Floyd, 1994). As noted by Kellert (2012), "the emotional power of nature to inspire and instruct depends on sentiments ranging from pleasure and satisfaction to vulnerability, foreboding, and a feeling of danger" (p. 73–74). As independent, self-directed individuals, youth can often choose how they will spend their discretionary time.

Negative feelings regarding nature often arise in youth with limited positive, ongoing exposure to nature.

The findings summarized in Table 11.2 suggest a range of constraints (i.e., "intervening factors between leisure preferences and participation;" Crawford & Godbey, 1987, p. 124) that impact involvement in nature-based experiences. Most of these identified constraints reflect structural barriers such as lack of time, transportation, access, or financial resources, which may be more common because people are more aware of them. However, constraints may also be interpersonal (e.g., lack of someone to participate with and the influence of parents/ family members) or intrapersonal (e.g., being uncomfortable in nature), and thus may reflect the influence of societal norms and expectations on participation in nature-based experiences (Crawford & Godbey, 1987). Finally, the influence of a young person's choices (e.g., not going outside because he or she wants to avoid being uncomfortable) or feelings of friends and/or family that nature is dangerous due to strangers or natural hazards (Backett-Milburn & Harden, 2004; Prezza et al., 2005), can contribute to a lack of youth engagement in nature.

Promising Nature-Based Programs and Initiatives

A wide variety of nature-based programs exists, from community gardening and nature-education programs to wilderness expeditions and naturalized play opportunities. The following programs offer examples of promising models for engaging youth (as well as their families) in nature-based experiences.

Role of Camps in Providing Nature-Based Youth Development

Nature has been a vital part of the camp experience since their establishment in the 1870s and 1880s (Paris, 2008). Camp experiences provide youth with exposure to nature through a combination of direct and indirect experiences that are unique in four ways: youth are unplugged from technology and social media, they have time for unstructured play, they can be physically active in a novel setting, and they can connect with something greater than themselves (American Camp Association, 2015).

Researchers have examined the influence of camp participation on nature-related outcomes, including the role of camp in positively impacting changes in physical activity (Hickerson & Henderson, 2013), environmental stewardship (Browne, Garst, & Bialeschki, 2011), emotional affinity toward nature (Collado, Staats, & Corriliza, 2013; Schmillen & Jacobs, 2011), pro-environment behaviors (Collado, Staats, & Corriliza, 2013), and spiritual development (Henderson & Bialeschki (2008).

The American Camp Association (2012) has established accreditation standards for the camp industry, which outline practices that support the provision of high-quality programs and services. Camps are required to use the natural environment on a regular basis for structured activities that "help campers feel comfortable in the natural environment," "build appreciation for and knowledge of ecological principles," and help youth "develop an awareness of and responsibility for practices that have minimal impact on the environment" (p. 154).

Camp provides youth with diverse and sustained exposure to nature. In one study, camp directors reported that 96% of resident campers spent five hours or more outdoors, and 68% spent more than eight hours outdoors daily (American Camp Association, 2008). In addition, 32% of day campers spent five to six hours outdoors daily. In a follow-up, 46% of ACA resident camps and 38% of day camps operated a nature center for nature-based and environmental education-related programs and activities (American Camp Association, 2011). Additionally, a wide variety of nature-based activities is offered at ACA camps, including fire-building, environmental ethics/Leave No Trace, recycling/composting, conservation, night hiking, and orienteering/GPS, wilderness safety/survival, and forest ecology. One example of a camp offering innovative nature-based opportunities for youth is the Green River Preserve.

Residential Summer Camp (Green River Preserve)

The mission of Green River Preserve (GRP) is "to provide a challenging and nurturing learning experience and to inspire a deep appreciation of interconnectedness, ecological respect, and the joy of living" (A. Izard, personal communication, July 6, 2017). GRP provides a noncompetitive, co-ed summer camp connecting children to nature. Located on a 3,400-acre wildlife preserve in the Blue Ridge Mountains of Western North Carolina, GRP "inspires campers to have a greater understanding of themselves, their environment, and those around them. GRP's program, designed with the help of a child psychologist, encourages bright, curious, and creative children to unplug from computers, television, video games, and cell phones, and to connect with nature, learn their own strengths, and find their inner voice" (A. Izard, personal communication, July 6, 2017). GRP's curriculum is a combination of inquiry and placed-based learning. Camp staff provide the setting and an open-ended discussion forum for learning, but youth drive the experience. In this way, daily hikes become a classroom where young people share new information and encourage their peers to do the same.

GRP offers one-, two-, and three-week summer camp sessions. As youth progress from being "base campers" in their first years at camp to being *expeditioners* in their teenage years, the curriculum strategy takes a more *hands-off approach*. Camp staff act more as facilitators and enable the expeditioners to make choices and have a voice in the decision-making process. This approach promotes responsibility, a healthy balance of teamwork and independence, and resiliency. According to the camp directors, these strategies have proven invaluable for reflecting on individual values and relationships with nature.

Connecting Communities to Nature Initiative (Mecklenburg County Parks and Recreation)

Mecklenburg County Park and Recreation (MCPR; A. Chambers, personal communication, June 29, 2017) includes nature as a part of recreational programming to promote conservation, health and wellness, and social equity. Through cooperation among Community Recreation Center Services (CRCS), Nature Preserves and Natural Resources (NPNR) and Cooperative Extension, the "Connecting Communities to Nature" (CC2N) initiative was developed. CC2N brings nature fully into the Recreation Centers by training staff to facilitate nature programming for youth (preschool through high school) at a level at which they are comfortable. Nature Center naturalists mentor recreation center staff and recreation specialists by providing a resource guide of lesson plans and vocabulary, and offering opportunities for external training in national curriculums like Project WILD and Project Learning Tree. Staff are guided through three tiers (reflecting a gradual progression in the introduction of nature) based on participants' comfort level with the outdoors: (1) *seed,* in which staff take traditional indoor recreation programs outside; (2) *sapling,* which includes altering an activity to include a nature focus; and (3) *sweetgum,* a nature-based education program.

To address barriers associated with youth access to nature (e.g., the urban parks near their homes) as well as to provide youth with the opportunity to get outside and experience new places and activities, MCPR developed a four-week Urban Outdoor Adventures Camp (UOC) day camp. Underserved youth aged 7–12 are picked up from the county recreation center and provided with a wide range of outdoor experiences (e.g., kayaking, tree-climbing, stream stomping, swimming, and mountain biking).

Mecklenburg County also offers the Bringing Accessible Agriculture Recreationally Now program (BAARN). BAARN is a creative approach for utilizing recreation centers to address childhood obesity rates by educating teens aged 15–18 about the benefits of eating fresh fruits and vegetables while also providing youth with access to agriculture entrepreneurship and mentoring opportunities with local farmers. Mentors are paired with recreation specialists and a farmer who assist teens in preparing and selling fresh fruit and vegetables at the farmers market. Youth learn agricultural methodology through these tasks, including soil composition, seed selection, integrated pest management, harvesting techniques, and calculating market value to sell their wares. Successful mentees become mentors when a new group of youth join BAARN the following year.

Community-Based Outdoor Recreation (Outdoor Afro)

Started as a blog by Rue Mapp in 2009, Outdoor Afro (OA) is a national nonprofit organization that celebrates and inspires African American connections and leadership in nature through a national network of volunteers who lead a wide range of nature-based recreational activities. The goals of OA are to "disrupt the false perception that black people do not have a relationship with nature, shift the visual representation of who can connect with and lead in the outdoors, and work to restore outdoor leadership back to the home" (Outdoor Afro, 2017). OA is a national leader in helping people, particularly African Americans, to successfully reconnect with nature through outdoor recreation. As of 2017, OA estimates that through planned activities, the organization reaches 20,000 people, yet through coordinated social media as well as traditional media efforts, they reach millions. Through their efforts, OA is "changing the visual narrative and inspiring access to the most pristine nature as well as urban nature, including local parks, trails, and open spaces. These activities promote not only a healthy lifestyle, they also help communities find healing, connect to black history found in many natural areas, and inspire an increased desire to protect vulnerable public lands for all to enjoy" (Outdoor Afro, 2017).

Family Nature Clubs (Children and Nature Network)

Richard Louv (2008; 2014) founded the Children and Nature Network (C&NN) to encourage and support individuals and organizations working to reconnect children with nature. The mission of the Children & Nature Network (C&NN) is "to connect all children, their families, and communities to nature through innovative ideas, evidence-based resources and tools, broad-based collaboration and support of grassroots leadership" (Children & Nature Network, 2017b). C&NN also provides access to the latest news and research in the field, creates and manages networks of leaders, families, and teachers for promoting children and nature, hosts annual conferences, and focuses the energy of the children and nature movement toward positive outcomes.

One strategy C&NN implements for achieving its mission is through Family Nature Clubs (FNC; Children & Nature Network, 2017a). FNCs are community-based clubs that bring families together throughout the year to enjoy the benefits of time spent in nature. Key features of the FNCs include no fees, little organization, and a design that is easy for busy families. C&NN developed the Nature Club Toolkit for Families (Children & Nature Network, 2009), which provides a simple template for starting a FNC. Research has examined the role of FNCs in fostering pro-environmental behavior as well as individual, familial, and community well-being (D'Amore, 2015). Data were collected from participants at 47 FNCs. Twenty outcomes of FNC participation were identified, including enhanced knowledge of and connection with nature, increased time spent in nature, heightened sense of individual and familial well-being, stronger social connections, and enriched environmental and social action.

Conclusion

The purpose of this chapter was to examine the role of nature in promoting positive youth development (PYD). Continued examination of nature as a significant context within an adolescent's ecology (along with families, schools, peer groups, and out-of-school programs as described by Lerner et al., 2014) is important. As Williams (2017) reflected, "we don't experience natural environments enough to realize how restored they can make us feel, nor are we aware that studies also show they make us healthier, more creative, more empathetic and more apt to engage with the world and with each other. Nature, it turns out, is good for civilization" (p. 4). Increased research is needed to more fully understand the developmental benefits of nature as a setting that can contribute to positive youth development outcomes and create increased opportunities for young people to undertake nature-based experiences.

"Nature, it turns out, is good for civilization."

Discussion Questions

1. Think about the time you spent in nature as a child or adolescent. What do you remember most about those nature experiences? How do you think your experiences in nature as a child/adolescent have influenced your perception of nature now?
2. What impact does nature contact have on developmental outcomes for youth, and what are the characteristics of the most impactful nature spaces for children and youth?
3. How much nature contact is necessary for positive youth development? Are certain forms of nature contact better than other forms? What evidence do we have? What do we still need to better understand?
4. Think about the classification of nature-based experiences as direct, indirect, and symbolic. How would you classify nature-based experiences available to youth in your community? What are the implications of reduced direct contact with nature and increased indirect and vicarious contact with nature?
5. Who participates in nature-based recreation? Who does (and does not) have access to nature? What are the disparities in nature access and exposure?
6. What can youth program providers do to better integrate elements of positive youth development into nature-based programs and experiences? What program enhancements or adaptations would be relatively easy and require fewer resources, and which would take more time or resources?

7. When you learned about the youth development outcomes of nature contact, which findings were new or surprising to you? If you were asked how nature is important for children, what would you say? What evidence would you cite for support?

8. What role should youth development organizations play in connecting youth and families to nature? What barriers or limitations do youth development organizations face in this regard, and what organizational opportunities or strengths might be leveraged for success?

9. How should youth development organizations partner with each other or other organizations to achieve greater outcomes related to youth development and nature? What do these partnerships look like in practice?

10. What consequences, if any, may result if youth become emotionally and/ or physically disconnected from nature due to limited access or resource degradation where they live and recreate? What role can youth development organizations play in reducing these barriers?

11. What resources are needed to engage more people in nature? What is the role of schools, families, PYD program providers, faith-based organizations, and so on?

12. Which type of nature-based experiences should be valued, protected, encouraged and why?

Activities and Resources

Multiple strategies exist for individuals and groups to explore nature in a more impactful way. Provided below are several ideas and resources to help you get started.

1. **Connect with nearby nature.** Focus on natural elements around you. Spend time in local natural places and spaces. Remember that nature can be a garden, park, greenway, or backyard. If you work with youth, teach them they can experience nature at home (planting a garden, creating a composting area, identifying trees in their yard, and drawing pictures of things in nature that live around their house/ community).

2. **Join the Natural Leaders Network.** The Natural Leaders Network, an initiative of the Children and Nature Network, empowers a worldwide youth movement to strengthen the bond between children and nature (www.facebook.com/ NaturalLeadersNetwork/).

3. **Take the "Green Spoken Here!" pledge.** Incorporate this pledge into your youth development programs, or use this pledge with your family or friends (www. acacamps.org/members/nature/green_spoken_here.php).

4. **Organize a nature-focused group.** Establish a social group that regularly meets to spend time outdoors. Groups can be organized around a host of activities, from

hiking and birdwatching to trail-running and snowboarding. If you have a family, then the Children and Nature Network's Nature-Club Toolkit for Families is a great resource to help you get started (www.childrenandnature.org/wp-content/uploads/2015/04/NCFF_En_2014.pdf).

5. **Volunteer at a local summer camp or nature center.** Contact a local summer camp or nature center and find out how you can get involved. Many camps and nature centers have volunteer opportunities, experiences like working with youth, beautifying the landscape, building trails, restoring habitat, and many more. The American Camp Association's "Find a Camp" is an easy-to-use resource (http://find.acacamps.org/).

6. **Attend the Children and Nature Network's National Conference.** Attending this conference will enable you to network with students, practitioners, researchers, and other professionals interested in the importance of nature for youth and adults (www.childrenandnature.org/).

7. **Check out the educational resources of Nature Works Everywhere.** Developed by The Nature Conservancy, Nature Works gives teachers, students, and families everything they need to start exploring and understanding nature around the globe alongside Nature Conservancy scientists. Interactive lesson plans align to standards that can be customized for specific teaching applications (www.natureworkseverywhere.org/resources/).

8. **Become a member of the American Camp Association for free!** ACA offers a one-year free membership, which comes with a range of benefits, including access to member-only content and discounts on books, online courses, and webinars. Many of these resources target nature and environmental education (www.acacamps.org/membership/free-one-year-membership).

9. **Learn the seven Leave No Trace principles.** Incorporate the principles into your nature-based experiences (or the experiences of youth you take in the outdoors). The principles include (1) Plan ahead and prepare, (2) Travel and camp on durable surfaces, (3) Dispose of waste properly, (4) Leave what you find, (5) Minimize campfire impacts (be careful with fire), (6) Respect wildlife, and (7) Be considerate of other visitors (https://lnt.org/learn/7-principles).

10. **Promote the Children's Outdoor Bill of Rights.** Encourage others to recognize the ways in which nature is beneficial for youth. Adopt this list of rights to fit your youth organization or group (www.calroundtable.org/files/COBR_Edit.pdf).

11. **Use the Affinity for Nature Scale.** Designed to measure a person's emotional connections a young person (aged 10–17 years old) might make to nature as a result of a program. This tool can help you identify if nature-based experiences are having an impact on youth you work with (https://www.acacamps.org/resource-library/research/aca-youth-outcomes-battery).

References

Adler, M. G., & Fagley, N. S. (2005). Appreciation: Individual differences in finding value and meaning as a unique predictor of subjective well-being. *Journal of Personality, 73*(1), 79–114.

American Camp Association. (2008). *Camp sites, facilities, and programs report.* Martinsville, IN: Author.

American Camp Association. (2011). *Camp sites, facilities, and programs report.* Martinsville, IN: Author.

American Camp Association. (2012). *Accreditation process guide.* Healthy Learning/ Martinsville, IN: Author.

American Camp Association. (2015). *Director-CAQ (nature and environment lesson).* Martinsville, IN: Author.

Arnold, H. E., Cohen, F. G., & Warner, A. (2009). Youth and environmental action: Perspectives of young environmental leaders on their formative influences. *Journal of Environmental Education, 40*(3), 27–36.

Atchley, R. A., Strayer, D. L., & Atchley, P. (2012). Creativity in the wild: Improving creative reasoning through immersion in natural settings. *PloS one, 7*(12), e51474.

Backett-Milburn, K., & Harden, J. (2004). How children and their families construct and negotiate risk, safety, and danger. *Childhood: A Global Journal of Child Research, 11*(4), 429–447.

Benson, P. L., Scales, P. C., & Syvertsen, A. K. (2011). The contribution of the developmental assets framework to positive youth development theory and practice. In M. Lerner, J. Lerner, & J. Benson (Eds.), *Advances in child development and behavior* (pp. 197–230). Minneapolis, MN: Search Institute.

Berman, D. S., & Davis-Berman, J. (1995). Outdoor education and troubled youth. ERIC Clearinghouse on Rural Education and Small Schools. Retrieved from http://files.eric.ed.gov/fulltext/ED385425.pdf

Bishop, D., & Jeanrenaud, C. (1995). Creative growth through play and its implications for recreation practice. In P. A. Witt & T. L. Goodale (Eds.), *Recreation and leisure: Issues in an era of change* (pp. 87–104). State College, PA: Venture.

Bixler, R., Carlisle, C., Hammitt, W., & Floyd, M. (1994). Observed fears and discomforts among urban students on field trips to wildland areas. *Journal of Environmental Education, 26*(1), 24–33.

Bixler, R. D., & Floyd, M. E. (1997). Nature is scary, disgusting, and uncomfortable. *Environment and Behavior, 29,* 443–467.

Bixler, R. D., James, J. J., & Vadala, C. E. (2011). Environmental socialization incidents with implications for the expanded role of interpretive naturalists in providing natural history experiences. *Journal of Interpretation Research, 16*(1), 35–64.

Bowler, D. E., Buyung-Ali, L. M., Knight, T. M., & Pullin, A. S. (2010). A systematic review of evidence for the added benefits to health of exposure to natural environments. *BMC Public Health,* 10. Retrieved from http://bmcpublichealth. biomedcentral.com/articles/10.1186/1471-2458-10-456

Bronfenbrenner, U. (1995). Developmental ecology through space and time: A future perspective. In P. Moen, G. Elder, Jr., & K. Lüscher (Eds.), *Examining lives in context: Perspectives on the ecology of human development* (pp. 619–647). Washington, DC: American Psychological Association.

Browne, L., Garst, B., & Bialeschki, M. D. (2011). Engaging youth in environmental sustainability: Impact of the Camp2Grow program. *Journal of Park and Recreation Administration, 29*(3), 70–85.

California Roundtable on Recreation, Parks, and Tourism. (2017). Children's outdoors bill of rights. Retrieved from http://calroundtable.org/Copy_of_cobor.htm

Chawla, L. (1994). Editors' note. *Children's Environments, 11*(3), 175–176.

Chawla, L. (2002). *Growing up in an urbanising world.* London, UK: Earthscan Publications.

Chawla, L., & Derr, V. (2012). The development of conservation behaviors in childhood and youth. In S. Clayton (Ed.), *The Oxford handbook of environmental and conservation psychology* (pp. 537–555). New York, NY: Oxford University Press.

Children & Nature Network. (2009). Nature clubs for families toolkit. Retrieved from http://www.childrenandnature.org/wp-content/uploads/2015/04/NCFF_En_2014.pdf

Children & Nature Network. (2017a). Natural families. Retrieved from http://www.childrenandnature.org/initiatives/families/

Children & Nature Network. (2017b). Vision and mission. Retrieved from https://www.childrenandnature.org/about/

Clayton, S., & Opotow, S. (2003). Introduction: Identity and the natural environment. In S. Clayton & S. Opotow (Eds.), *Identity and the natural environment: The psychological significance of nature* (pp. 1–24). Cambridge, MA: MIT Press.

Coley, R. L., Kuo, F. E., & Sullivan, W.C. (1997). Where does community grow? The social context created by nature in urban public housing. *Environment and Behavior, 29*(4), 468–494.

Collado, S., Staats, H., & Corraliza, J. A. (2013). Experiencing nature in children's summer camps: Affective, cognitive, and behavioural consequences. *Journal of Environmental Psychology, 33*, 37–44.

Coon, J., Boddy, K., Stein, K., Whear, R., Barton, J., & Depledge, M. H. (2011). Does participating in physical activity in outdoor natural environments have a greater effect on physical and mental well-being than physical activity indoors? A systematic review. *Environmental Science Technology, 45*, 1761–1772.

Corraliza, J. A., Collado, S., & Bethelmy, L. (2012). Nature as a moderator of stress in urban children. *Procedia-Social and Behavioral Sciences, 38*, 253–263.

Crawford, D. W., & Godbey, G. (1987). Reconceptualizing barriers to family leisure. *Leisure Sciences, 9*, 119–127.

D'Amore, C. (2015). Family nature clubs: Creating the conditions for social and environmental connection and care. Doctoral dissertation, Prescott College. Retrieved from http://gradworks.umi.com/37/07/3707605.html

Eccles, J. S., & Gootman, J. A. (2002). *Community programs to promote youth development: Committee on community-level programs for youth.* Washington, DC: National Academy Press.

Faber Taylor, A., Kuo, F. E., & Sullivan, W. C. (2001). Coping with ADD: The surprising connection to green play settings. *Environment & Behavior, 33,* 54–77.

Gambone, M. A., & Arbreton, A. (1997). *Safe havens: The contributions of youth organizations to healthy adolescent development.* Philadelphia, PA: Public/Private Ventures.

Gambone, M. A., Klem, A. M., & Connell, J. P. (2002). *Finding out what matters for youth: Testing key links in a community action framework for youth development.* Philadelphia, PA: Youth Development Strategies, Inc. and Institute for Research and Reform in Education.

Garner, M. A., Taft, E. D., & Stevens, C. L. (2015). Do children increase their environmental consciousness during summer camp? A comparison of two programs. *Journal of Outdoor Recreation, Education, and Leadership, 7*(1), 20–34.

Garst, B., & Gagnon, R.J. (2015). Exploring overparenting within the context of youth development programs. *Journal of Youth Development, 10*(1), 6–18. Retrieved from https://jyd.pitt.edu/ojs/jyd/article/view/416

Garst, B., Williams, D., & Roggenbuck, J. (2010). Exploring early 21st century developed forest camping experiences and meanings. *Leisure Sciences, 32,* 90–107.

Godbey, G. (2009). *Outdoor recreation, health, and wellness: Understanding and enhancing the relationship.* RFF Discussion Paper No. 09-21. Washington DC: Resources for the Future. Retrieved from http://dx.doi.org/10.2139/ssrn.1408694

Gopinath, B., Hardy, L. L., Baur, L. A., Burlutsky, G., & Mitchell, P. (2012). Physical activity and sedentary behaviors and health-related quality of life in adolescents. *Pediatrics, 130*(1), e167.

Henderson, K. A., & Bialeschki, M. D. (2008). Spiritual development and camp experiences. *New Directions for Youth Development, 118,* 107–110.

Hickerson, B. D., & Henderson, K. A. (2014). Opportunities for promoting youth physical activity: An examination of youth summer camps. *Journal of Physical Activity and Health, 11*(1), 199–205.

Hill, J. O., Wyatt, H. R., Reed, G. W., & Peters, J. C. (2003). Obesity and the environment: Where do we go from here? *Science, 299*(5608), 853–855.

Howard-Jones, P. (2011). The impact of digital technologies on human well-being: Evidence from the sciences of mind and brain. Nominet Trust. Retrieved from https://static.lgfl.net/LgflNet/downloads/online-safety/LGfL-OS-Research-Archive-2011-Nominet-Impact-on-Wellbeing.pdf

Ives, C. D., Giusti, M., Fischer, J., Abson, D. J., Klaniecki, K., Dorninger, C., ... & Raymond, C. M. (2017). Human–nature connection: a multidisciplinary review. *Current Opinion in Environmental Sustainability, 26,* 106–113.

James, J. J., Bixler, R. D., & Vadala, C. (2010). From play in nature, to recreation then vocation: A developmental model for natural history-oriented environmental professionals. *Children, Youth and Environments, 20*(1), 231–256.

Kahn, P. H. (2002). Children's affiliation with nature: Structure, development, and the problem of environmental generational amnesia. In P. Kahn, Jr. & S. Kellert (Eds.), *Children and nature: Psychological, sociocultural, and evolutionary investigations* (pp. 93–116), Cambridge, MA: MIT Press.

Kals, E., & Ittner, H. (2003). Children's environmental identity: Indicators and behavioral impacts. In S. Clayton & S. Opotow (Eds.), *Identity and the natural environment: The psychological significance of nature* (pp. 135–157). Cambridge, MA: MIT Press.

Kals, E., Schumacher, D., & Montada, L. (1999). Emotional affinity toward nature as a motivational basis to protect nature. *Environment & Behavior, 31*(2), 178–202.

Kaplan, S. (1995). The restorative benefits of nature: Toward an integrative framework. *Journal of Environmental Psychology, 15*, 169–182.

Kaplan, R., & Kaplan, S. (2002). Adolescents and the natural environment: A time out? In P. Kahn, Jr. & S. Kellert (Eds.), *Children and nature: Psychological, sociocultural, and evolutionary investigations* (pp. 227–258). Cambridge, MA: MIT Press.

Kaplan, R., Kaplan, S., & Ryan, R. (1998). *With people in mind: Design and management of everyday nature.* Washington, DC: Island Press.

Karsten, L., & van Vliet, W. (2006). Increasing children's freedom of movement: Introduction. *Children Youth and Environments, 16*(1), 69–73.

Kellert, S. (2002). Experiencing nature: Affective, cognitive, and evaluative development in children. In P. H. Kahn & S. R. Kellert (Eds.), *Children and nature: Psychological, sociocultural, and evolutionary investigations* (pp. 117–151). Cambridge, MA: MIT Press.

Kellert, S. R. (2012). *Building for life: Designing and understanding the human-nature connection.* Washington, DC: Island Press.

King, P. E. (2008). Spirituality as fertile ground for positive youth development. In R. Lerner, R. Roesner, & E. Phelps (Eds.), *Positive youth development and spirituality: From theory to research* (pp. 55–73). West Conshohocken, PA: Templeton Press.

Kuo, F. E., & Faber Taylor, A. (2004). A potential natural treatment for attention-deficit/hyperactivity disorder: Evidence from a national study. *American Journal of Public Health, 94*(9), 1580–1586.

Larson, L. R., Green, G. T., & Cordell, H. K. (2011). Children's time outdoors: Results and implications of the national kids' survey. *Journal of Park and Recreation Administration, 29*(1), 1–20.

Lerner, R. M., Wang, J., Chase, P. A., Gutierrez, A. S., Harris, E. M., Rubin, R. O., & Yalin, C. (2014). Using relational developmental systems theory to link program goals, activities, and outcomes: The sample case of the 4-H Study of Positive Youth Development. *New Directions for Youth Development, 144*, 17–30.

Lieberman, G. A., & Hoody, L. L. (1998). *Closing the achievement gap: Using the environment as an integrating context for learning.* Poway, CA: SEER.

Lenhart, L., & Page, D. (2015). Teens, social media, & technology overview 2015: Smartphones facilitate shifts in communication landscape for teens. Pew Family Research Center. Retrieved from http://assets.pewresearch.org/wp-content/uploads/sites/14/2015/04/PI_TeensandTech_Update2015_0409151.pdf

Locke, J. Y., Campbell, M. A., & Kavanagh, D. (2012). Can a parent do too much for their child? An examination by parenting professionals of the concept of overparenting. *Australian Journal of Guidance and Counselling, 22*(2), 249–265.

Louv, R. (2008). *Last child in the woods: Saving our children from nature-deficit disorder.* Chapel Hill, NC: Algonquin Books.

Louv, R. (2012). *The nature principle: Human restoration and the end of nature-deficit disorder.* Chapel Hill, NC: Algonquin Books.

Merikangas, K. R., He, J. P., Burstein, M., Swanson, S. A., Avenevoli, S., Cui, L., ... & Moore, R. C. (1986). *Childhood's domain: Place and play in child development.* London, UK: Croom Helm.

Nabhan, G. P., & Trimble, S. (1995). *The geography of childhood: Why children need wild places.* Boston, MA: Beacon Press.

Nisbet, E. K., & Zelenski, J. M. (2013). The NR-6: a new brief measure of nature relatedness. *Frontiers in psychology, 4.* Retrieved from https://www.ncbi.nlm.nih.gov/pmc/articles/PMC3814587/

Ohly, H., White, M. P., Wheeler, B. W., Bethel, A., Ukoumunne, O. C., Nikolaou, V., & Garside, R. (2016). Attention restoration theory: A systematic review of the attention restoration potential of exposure to natural environments. *Journal of Toxicology and Environmental Health, 19*(7), 305–343.

Orion, N., & Hofstein, A. (1994). Factors that influence learning during scientific field trips in a natural environment. *Journal of Research in Science Teaching, 31,* 1097–1119.

Outdoor Afro. (2017). Our impact. Retrieved from http://outdoorafro.com/impact/

Owens, P. E. (1988). Natural landscapes, gathering places, and prospect refuges: Characteristics of outdoor places valued by teens. *Children's Environments Quarterly, 5*(2), 17–24.

Paris, L. (2008). *Children's nature: The rise of the American summer camp.* New York, NY: NYU Press.

Piff, P. K., Dietze, P., Feinberg, M., Stancato, D. M., & Keltner, D. (2015). Awe, the small self, and prosocial behavior. *Journal of Personality and Social Psychology, 108*(6), 883.

Prezza, M., Alparone, F. R., Cristallo, C., & Luigi, S. (2005). Parental perception of social risk and of positive potentiality of outdoor autonomy for children: The development of two instruments. *Journal of Environmental Psychology, 25*(4), 437–453.

Pyle, R. (2002). Eden in a vacant lot: Special places, species and kids in community of life. In P. H. Kahn & S. R. Kellert (Eds.), *Children and nature: Psychological, sociocultural and evolutionary investigations* (pp. 305–327). Cambridge, MA: MIT Press.

Rose-Krasnor, L., Busseri, M. A., Willoughby, T., & Chalmers, H. (2006). Breadth and intensity of youth activity involvement as contexts for positive development. *Journal of Youth and Adolescence, 35,* 385–499.

Sallis, J., Prochaska, J. & Taylor, W. (2000). A review of correlates of physical activity of children and adolescents. *Medicine and Science in Sports and Exercise, 32*(5), 963–975.

Schein, D. (2014). Nature's role in children's spiritual development. *Children, Youth, and Environments, 24*(2), 78–101.

Schultz, P. W., Shriver, C., Tabanico, J. J., & Khazian, A. M. (2004). Implicit connections with nature. *Journal of Environmental Psychology, 24,* 31–42.

Schultz, P. W., & Tabanico, J. (2007). Self, identity, and the natural environment: Exploring implicit connections to nature. *Journal of Applied Social Psychology, 37*(6), 1219–1247.

Schmillen, J., & Jacobs, J. (2011, July). Campers' affinity for nature in environmental education programs. *Camping Magazine, 8*(4), 8.

Song, C., Ikei, H., & Miyazaki, Y. (2016). Physiological effects of nature therapy: A review of the research in Japan. *International Journal of Environmental Research and Public Health, 13*(8). Retrieved from https://www.ncbi.nlm.nih.gov/pubmed/27527193

Stern, M., Powell, R., & Ardoin, N. (2008). What difference does it make? Assessing outcomes from participation in a residential environmental education program. *Journal of Environmental Education, 39*(4), 31–43.

Swendsen, J. (2010). Lifetime prevalence of mental disorders in US adolescents: results from the National Comorbidity Survey Replication–Adolescent Supplement (NCS-A). *Journal of the American Academy of Child & Adolescent Psychiatry, 49*(10), 980–989.

The Nature Conservancy. (2011). Connecting America's youth to nature. Retrieved fromhttps://www.nature.org/newsfeatures/kids-in-nature/youth-and-nature-poll-results.pdf

The Outdoor Foundation. (2016a). Outdoor participation report: 2016. Retrieved from http://www.outdoorfoundation.org/pdf/ResearchParticipation2016.pdf

The Outdoor Foundation. (2016b). Outdoor nation special report: Barriers to the outdoors. Retrieved from http://www.outdoorfoundation.org/research.outdoornation.barriers.html

Valentine, G. & J. McKendrick. (1997). Children's outdoor play: Exploring parental concerns about children's safety and the changing nature of childhood. *Geoforum, 28,* 219–235.

Wells, N. M. (2014). The role of nature in children's resilience: Cognitive and social processes. In K. G. Tidball & M. E. Krasny (Eds.), *Greening in the Red Zone* (pp. 95–109). Netherlands: Springer.

Wells, N. M., & Evans, G. W. (2003). Nearby nature: A buffer of life stress among rural children. *Environment and Behavior, 35*(3), 311–330.

Williams, F. (2017). *The nature fix: Why nature makes us happier, healthier, and more creative.* New York, NY: WW Norton & Company.

Chapter 12

The Arts and Creative Youth Development

Denise Montgomery

Before I came to RAW, I felt shy and nervous and angry. Now I feel creative and like I have a future and like I belong somewhere. I don't want to leave because RAW makes me feel better about myself. (Karl age 15, participant, Boyz Lync Group at Raw Art Works)

I love knowing that when I perform, I am changing lives. (Asher, age 16, participant, Troupe, True Colors: Out Youth Theater, The Theater Offensive)

Across the United States and around the world, thousands of arts-based youth development programs combine principles of positive youth development, such as taking an assets-based approach and fostering caring relationships with peers and adults, with creative inquiry and hands-on skill building in the arts and humanities. Many of these programs refer to their work as *creative youth development* or *CYD*.

CYD programs can involve many different art forms or areas within the humanities. For example, programs are offered in the visual arts (painting, drawing, sculpture, print-making, photography, and subfields such as cartooning); media arts; graphic design; fashion design; dance (from street jazz to hip hop to ballet folklórico and many more genres of dance); music performance and music composition spanning the spectrum of music styles; theatre in its various forms; writing; history; and even game design.

There are several common characteristics of CYD programs including: setting high expectations for young people, encouraging positive risk taking, embracing youth leadership, and engaging young people in contributing to their communities and working for social justice. These creativity-based programs take place in a variety of settings and contexts, including the following:

- Nonprofit organizations dedicated to CYD
- Programs that are embedded within larger youth development organizations or arts organizations
- School-based programs both within school time and during out-of-school time (OST) programs
- Community recreation and park programs
- Other community contexts (e.g., juvenile detention facilities)

The basic formula of CYD is the combination of a holistic approach to positive youth development with hands-on creative inquiry in the arts or humanities. The following are several examples of organizations and programs from the diverse universe of CYD.

Choosing their own role models by interviewing and selecting their artist mentors is just one way that youth experience that their perspectives are valued at **New Urban Arts** (NUA, http://newurbanarts.org). NUA is a year-round community arts studio for high school students and emerging artists in Providence, Rhode Island. The program promotes long-term mentoring relationships between high school students and trained artist mentors. Participation is free. Students and mentors engage in positive risk-taking, collaboration, and self-directed learning. NUA directly shapes their experiences, and this high degree of influence proves to be engaging, as does their art making. Participation in the program cultivates young people's creative and independent thinking, provides a sense of belonging in a community of practicing artists, and validates and celebrates students' unique points of view.

True Colors: Out Youth Theater of Theater Offensive (http://www.thetheateroffensive.org) is the largest and longest-running lesbian, gay, bisexual, transgender, and queer (LGBTQ) youth theater program in the United States. Through playwriting, rehearsing, and performing, True Colors troupe members transform their life experiences of discrimination, fear, and isolation into powerful theatrical productions. At the same time, youth participants develop theatrical and life skills in a safe and caring environment. Through their art and social activism, these youth raise awareness and empathy among others and grow as leaders within their program and in the broader community. True Colors: Out Youth Theater is a vehicle for young people to convert often difficult personal experiences into fierce determination for the civil rights and well-being of LBGTQ youth and adults and other marginalized groups.

In **AjA Project's** (http://ajaproject.org) photography-based programs, youth document, reflect on, and share their personal and social landscapes. In the process, young people transform their own lives and their communities. More than about simply taking photographs, AjA Project works to ignite change, break cycles of marginalization, and build healthy communities. The 501(c)3 nonprofit organization is based in the City Heights neighborhood of San Diego, California, a diverse community with over 45 languages and 100 dialects spoken and significant immigrant and refugee populations. Programs take place in both out-of-school time and in-school and range from intensive short workshops to month-long programs. AjA Project's model puts youth at the heart of driving social justice efforts in their own communities. More than three million attendees have gained insight into the lives and viewpoints of young people by viewing their photography through AjA Project's large-scale public exhibitions.

Like high-quality youth development programs generally, many youth participants in arts- and humanities-based youth development programs say that their involvement changed the trajectory of their lives. In some cases, young people say that participation in a CYD program, in fact, saved their lives. In addition to the compelling testimonies of individual youth participants and program staff, a growing body of evidence documents outcomes such as youth acquiring life skills, confidence, resilience, sense of personal efficacy, and personal fulfillment (Gittelman, Mercado-Zizzo, & Swaback, 2016; Gutierrez & Spencer, 2008; Stevenson, 2013).

How interested are young people in the arts? The Search Institute (www.Search-Institute.org) has conducted substantial research in the area of young people's deep interests and passions, or their *sparks*.

A *spark* is an interest or skill. A person's spark is what they are really passionate about, an activity that energizes them and brings them joy, and one that may allow them to express their essence and bring their unique gifts to the world.

Every person has, or has the ability to have, at least one spark. Most people discover their spark over time, through experiences and opportunities. Young people often need caring adults to help them identify and develop their spark. This is an essential role for anyone who cares about young people: youth developers, family members, teachers, and community members (Benson, 2011).

A growing body of evidence documents outcomes [of CYD programs] such as youth acquiring life skills, confidence, resilience, sense of personal efficacy, and personal fulfillment.

When teens know their spark and have adults in their life who support them in their spark, they are more likely to:

- Possess a sense of purpose
- Be physically healthy and socially competent
- Volunteer in their community
- Have better attendance and higher grades in school

Additionally, young people who know their spark and have several adults who support their spark are also less likely to experience depression or to engage in acts of violence toward others (Tellet-Royce, 2012).

Among the top 10 spark categories named by American teenagers aged 12–17, the number one interest area cited was creative arts. Creative arts was named by 54% of teens, more than twice as often as the next most common category, athletics, which was cited by 25% of teens surveyed (Benson, 2008). As Peter Benson, Search Institute's founder, observed, "The creative arts also have the advantage of allowing a freedom of expression through which young people gain power or control over their world" (Benson, 2008, p. 59). Create a Spark Foundation (2018) also noted that

> …creative life…art, music, drama, dance, movement is the largest category in which sparks fall for America's kids.…That's the area in which the most kids say, I'm my best self. That's the arena in which [the] most kids will say, This is where life is the fullest and most hopeful. (p. 1)

Clearly young people are interested in the arts. So youth professionals who value supporting young people in identifying and cultivating their personal passions, or sparks, should provide opportunities for youth to participate in the arts. High-quality creative youth development programs are essential pathways for young people to experience and pursue their interests in the arts.

> High-quality creative youth development programs are essential pathways for young people to experience and pursue their interests in the arts.

Chapter Goals

Whatever path you take in your own professional and personal journey, awareness and knowledge of CYD will help prepare you to understand the full range of youth development opportunities for young people. As a practitioner, policy maker, funder, community leader, parent, or friend, this chapter can be a foundation or springboard to supporting positive outcomes for youth through CYD. Through this chapter you will do the following:

- Build understanding of the practice of creative youth development, including its key characteristics and principles of quality programs
- Discover the ways that the arts and creative inquiry support positive outcomes for youth
- Gain access to resources for further exploration

What Is Creative Youth Development?

Now that you have read descriptions of several CYD programs, it is time to get specific with a definition and characteristics of creative youth development programs.

Key Definition

Creative Youth Development is a theory of practice that intentionally integrates the arts and humanities with youth development principles sparking young people's creativity and building critical learning and life skills. (Creative Youth Development National Partnership, 2017)

Creative youth development is a recent term, coined in 2013 (Stevenson, 2013), for a longstanding community of practice that goes back several decades. This way of working with young people, by infusing skill building in the arts and the humanities with principles of positive youth development, has been taking place for many years, both informally, such as in people's living rooms and in community centers, and formally, in established nonprofit programs or as formal programs within other organizations. In the early 2010s, CYD practitioners and stakeholders started to unify as a field to strengthen awareness of and support for arts- and humanities-based youth development or creative youth development.

What is meant by *theory of practice* in the above definition? In this instance, theory of practice refers to a way of working and a set of characteristics but not a prescribed formula or rigid checklist. In this way, the definition recognizes that CYD can look different within different programs and acknowledges that different CYD programs are at varying points in their evolution and development. Some CYD practitioners and champions have used the analogy that creative youth development as a field of practice is in its adolescence, aware of its strengths, telling the world who and what it is, and finding its place in society.

It is important to note that not every program engaged in arts- or humanities-based youth development calls itself a CYD program. Some programs may not yet have encountered the term. Leaders at other programs may still be deciding what they are and how they want to refer to themselves. Yet, other program leaders may see themselves as part of long traditions rooted in a specific community and choose not to adopt the term creative youth development. The salient point is that creative

inquiry and hands-on involvement in the arts and humanities, coupled with principles of positive youth development, is a powerful and engaging combination. In the arts and humanities themselves, CYD enjoys immense diversity in practice. A set of key characteristics unifies the CYD field of practice and sets CYD apart from other types of arts or humanities learning experiences.

Key Characteristics of Creative Youth Development Programs

CYD programs nurture individual growth, youth leadership, and often, civic engagement. As young people create, they build skills that help them succeed in school, their careers, and life. One way to recognize CYD programs is the presence of core characteristics that differentiate CYD programs from other types of arts programs. Each of the six core characteristics is reviewed in the next section.

Key Characteristics of Effective Creative Youth Development Programs

1. Safe and Healthy Youth Spaces   4. Youth Driven
2. Assets-Based   5. High Expectations
3. Positive Relationships   6. Holistic and Inclusive

(Massachusetts Cultural Council, 2017)

1. CYD Programs Provide Safe and Healthy Youth Spaces

Going far beyond providing a safe haven that is free from violence or abuse, effective CYD programs cultivate environments that are emotionally and psychologically safe and nurturing for young people. CYD programs are places where youth feel accepted, protected, and secure.

> Shamir, a member of the Teen Arts Council at The Institute of Contemporary Art/Boston (ICA Boston), refers to ICA Boston, a contemporary art museum, as "my museum." Shamir's clear connection to the museum and his sense of being at home there are evident as he describes how comfortable and influential he feels in the Teen Arts Council program and in the physical space of the museum. The Teen Arts Council's emphasis on all participants and mentors valuing an atmosphere of trust and respect and clear ground rules and expectations help foster this sense of safety. (Remarks made during the Youth Fishbowl Conversation, Creative Youth Development National Stakeholder Meeting, Boston, MA, July 2017).

2. CYD Programs are Assets-Based

Rather than seeing young people as problems that need to be fixed or as the recipients of services, effective CYD programs view young people as partners in learning and as resources in the community. Operating from a core belief that all young people have strengths, these programs seek to help identify and build upon individual young people's strengths as a central part of supporting their healthy development. In practice, being assets-based involves engaging young people in activities designed to uncover their talents and expertise, skill-building projects, and community service.

Young people of all walks of life have a need to contribute to their communities, and each person, regardless of age, income, or any other factor, has something to give. CYD programs engage youth in community service, thereby flipping the script too often portrayed in the media and entertainment industries of young people causing trouble to one of young people actively making the world a better place.

How Ideas Manifest in Language

Taking an assets-based approach, as embraced in the broader field of youth development, has also resulted in less frequent use of language that highlights perceived deficiencies, such as *at risk*. Some programs say *at promise* or describe *opportunity youth*, and many programs simply say *youth*.

3. CYD Programs Foster the Development of Positive Relationships and Social Skills

CYD programs are intentional about prioritizing young people's development of supportive and stable relationships with caring adult mentors and with peers. The amount of time each week that young people spend in CYD programs (dosage) and the duration of their involvement support these relationships. Longer involvement and more hours of involvement have the potential to contribute to stronger relationships and create a virtuous cycle: stronger relationships result in young people choosing to spend more time at a CYD program, thus supporting a host of positive outcomes.

> Longer involvement and more hours of involvement have the potential to contribute to stronger relationships and create a virtuous cycle.

Rituals or customs are another way in which CYD programs create a sense of belonging. For example, CYD program participants may have a unique way of greeting one another at the start of a program session, or a program may establish a ritualized way of transitioning into the program space, such as coming together in a circle and all responding to a question of the day. In addition to daily rituals, many CYD programs also have annual rites of passage such as celebrations to mark youth graduating from a program.

Alchemy, Inc. is a CYD organization in Akron, Ohio, that employs mythological stories, journaling, and drumming in its work with urban adolescent males. Rituals are central to Alchemy's approach and help to create emotionally safe environments where youth involved in the program not only discuss and analyze myths but also share their personal experiences. Myths are told and group discussions occur within a *temenos*, or sacred space, and participants know that whatever they choose to share will remain within the temenos. Participants sit in a circle by age, from youngest to oldest, with the understanding that the older person provides care for the younger person. The circle and seating help to create a sense of order and safety.

Adult mentors and youth participants tell myths to the beat of an African *djembe* drum. Kwame Scruggs, Alchemy's founder and director states, "Drumming cultivates a sense of community, collaboration, oneness, and sacred space. The rhythm of the drumbeats reduces temporal distractions and creates a shared mental state. The longer we drum, the more connected our groups become" (Scruggs, 2017, p. 9). Within this safe and ritualistic space, emotions often arise and are welcomed. Alchemy takes care to discuss that crying is important as an indication for self and others that something is wrong. When a young man cries within the temenos, he rubs his tears into the head of the drum knowing that as the drum is hit going forward, his tears will reverberate into the universe (Scruggs, 2017).

CYD programs also can provide opportunities for young people to interact with supportive adults beyond a program's adult mentors, thus building young people's experiences and validating their efforts. For example, students at Riverzedge Arts in Woonsocket, Rhode Island, fulfill paid apprenticeships by providing goods and services such as silkscreened banners and graphic design to real-life clients. The organization's artist mentors coach young people about how to interact appropriately and professionally with the individuals and companies that commission them to do work. Through these successful interactions, the young artist apprentices are building valuable social and professional skills along with heightened confidence.

Creative Youth Development:
Distinct From Arts Exposure Programs or Arts Conservatory Programs

One way to understand creative youth development programs is to contrast them with other types of programs. Arts exposure programs, which students may experience through schools or youth development organizations, provide opportunities for youth to experience or participate in the arts on a short-term or sometimes one-time basis. For example, a local art museum may provide free tickets for a youth development organization to bring students to the museum one afternoon. Although students can have a meaningful experience in an arts exposure program, the experience, by nature of its one-time or short-term design, cannot involve substantive skill building or the establishment of caring relationships with adult mentors.

Conservatory programs, also in contrast to creative youth development programs, are intensive pre-professional programs with an emphasis on mastery of artistic technique. Although some conservatory programs are taking a more holistic approach to their work with young people, traditionally the sharp emphasis has been on skills mastery and not on positive youth development. Participating students generally intend to pursue a career in their art form, for example as a professional dancer or as a composer. Relationships with instructors may involve mentorship, but relationships with adults within a conservatory program may be distanced or sporadic.

Interestingly, most creative youth development programs do not include among their goals for young people the pursuit of professional careers in the arts or humanities. Rather, CYD programs commonly talk about supporting young people in realizing their potential, in leading satisfying and productive lives, in contributing to their communities, and in being prepared to succeed in whatever career they choose.

4. CYD Programs are Youth Driven

Youth know when they are being taken seriously through the culture and structures of CYD programs, such as a teen having a seat on the board of directors, and, importantly, when they see evidence of their influence on their CYD program or organization. In the most effective CYD programs, young people assume leadership roles and influence programming, administration, and evaluation, and in doing so deepen their sense of responsibility, initiative, ownership, and independence. When young people are able to determine what they want to do in a creative endeavor or community initiative, have the support of their adult mentors to pursue it, and exercise decision-making, they become agents of their own change and lead change in their communities.

> In school, teachers want it their way or the highway. You have an idea; they drop it. Here, they accept your ideas. They want you to have ideas; they want you to make up your own thing.—ARTLAB+ Student, Washington, DC (Stevenson, 2013).

One of the key ways in which CYD youth program participants differentiate their involvement in a CYD program from their experiences at school is the extent to which youth voice and youth leadership are embraced within a CYD program versus typical school cultures in which students have substantially fewer opportunities to be heard.

Many CYD programs are intentional about not saying that they *give* students voice in acknowledgment that students' voices are their own and young people determine how and when to use them. Rather, many programs use language such as *embrace*, *celebrate*, and *prioritize* youth voice. There is a nuance to the language that is conscious of power structures and that honors young people. Below is an excerpt from a 2017 blog post by Jamila Lyiscott that addresses language around youth development programs and youth voice.

If You Think You're Giving Students of Color a Voice, Get Over Yourself

Miss, miss! What the C.O. toldju about us?
They already gettin' in y'all heads right?
Miss, we human! I'm a human! We have families....
(Rikers Island [detention center] Youth Workshop Participant)

The walls on Rikers Island are the same as the walls in my high school. In a facility six security check-points deep, where it takes myself and my team of social justice educators over 1.5 hours to get from the first screening to the classroom where we run a workshop with a small group of incarcerated adolescent boys, the walls are the same style of brick as every inner-city school I have ever attended or visited. While I am struck by the visceral effects of this very concrete reality for these young men who have attended public schools across the five boroughs, I am not at all surprised. Still, within the physical, psychological, and emotional confines of this space that they navigate daily, I am the one who often feels the deep constraints of internalized social attitudes and perspectives about young Black and Brown men, who they are, what they need, and how they should be engaged within the context of the classroom. The possibilities of our time together are tethered to my internal work—the shedding of any savior complexes and constant collective reflection with the team to live in the tensions and questions of our work as critical educators.

So imagine my horror when on a recent phone call, a white educator who expressed interest in my youth development work, squealed with congratulations and awe for the way that we "give so many young people voice." Her words were deeply disturbing but hardly surprising. Grateful that in our last email I chose the phone call over the in-person or FaceTime option for our meeting, I rolled my eyes and promptly ended the call.

I should not have ended this call. I should have said to this woman, "If you think you're giving students of color a voice, get over yourself"… then hung up the phone. So what's the big deal? Why get caught up on words when you know that kind well-meaning woman only meant to celebrate the work that you are doing?

Some of the most deeply problematic issues of inequity within the field of education are sustained by well-meaning people embracing progressive politics without intentional frameworks of self-reflection to guide their praxis in a healthy direction.

Here's the problem:

1. **It's paternalistic.** Webster's defines paternalism as "the attitude or actions of a person, organization, etc., that protect people and give them what they need but does not give them any responsibility or freedom of choice." The idea of *giving* students voice, especially when it refers to students of color, only serves to reify the dynamic of paternalism that renders Black and Brown students voiceless until some salvific external force gifts them with the privilege to speak. Rather than acknowledge the systemic violences that attempt to silence the rich voices, cultures, and histories that students bring into classrooms, this orientation positions students, and by extension, the communities of students, as eternally in need of institutional sanctioning.

2. **Paternalism was a huge part of the rationale for slavery.** When we operate with the mind-set that we are *giving* students voice, we align ourselves with a deeply problematic and historic orientation. So much of the rationale for oppression through slavery, colonialism, and imperialism, had to do with

giving civilization to people who were *less fortunate*. Do not align your pedagogy with the ethos of slavery and colonialism.

3. **They woke up like that.** When the young men at Rikers share their work, I am fully intimidated by their uses of extended metaphors, similes, and other literary devices. But all we did was lend them an ear. They woke up like that. We did not give them a voice. What we gave them was space to be heard. Students navigate powerful spaces of learning every single day in their homes and communities. Especially when it comes to students of color, the skills, experiences, and rich knowledges that shape their voices are devalued in the classroom, but are still powerful and have absolutely nothing to do with our *salvation* (Lyiscott, 2017).

5. CYD Programs Set High Expectations for Effort, Growth, and Learning

Strong CYD programs convey to young people that they expect them to do their best and that youths' efforts are taken seriously. Adults working in CYD programs affirm young people's abilities in addressing them as artists, writers, dancers, filmmakers, etc., and they discuss young people's work with them in a manner that honors the ideas, effort, and person behind the work.

Rigorous skill-building is a cornerstone of CYD programs. In order to build skills, youth need to regularly attend programs and to elect to spend often 5–15 hours per week in program activities.

Professional artists are another key component of high expectations. Artists—who importantly also are skilled as educators and, increasingly, youth developers—know about holding themselves accountable to the same high expectations and deadlines that they expect of youth. They can also relate directly to the joy, exertion, and, at times, frustration, of the creative process.

Teaching Artists: An Essential Component of Quality CYD Programs

The artist mentors working with youth within effective CYD programs are practicing, professional artists who combine artistry and artistic technique with skills as educators and youth developers. They are teaching artists working in youth development settings. Teaching artists work in a variety of education and community settings, from schools to senior centers. The number of teaching artists is increasing nationwide, and the field of teaching artists has organized to advocate for their work and to share best practices and provide resources. (Teaching Artists Guild, 2017)

Many programs formally convey expectations, such as expected attendance, at the beginning of each program cycle. One way expectation setting occurs is by having youth participants, and sometimes their parent or guardian, sign a contract regarding attendance, conduct, and sometimes expected school grade point average while they are in the program. These contracts or compacts vary, with some even including a clause committing the young person to asking for help when it is needed, whether regarding a personal situation, academics, or help in the studio.

In addition to making a commitment and holding themselves accountable, CYD program participants also hold one another accountable. As their involvement in a program deepens, youth cherish the atmosphere of their CYD program, and many want to ensure that the space remains supportive. They may even call someone out, for example, should they behave in a manner that is perceived as disrespectful of another student or of an artist mentor. Youth participants are commonly empathetic and supportive of one another and, should a young person miss several program sessions in a row, reach out to peers in a caring way to see how they are doing and if anything is going on where they need help or support.

Youth also gain the skill of respectfully giving and receiving critique of their work, again within settings that are both supportive and demand that young people set high bars for themselves in their creative endeavors.

6. CYD Programs are Holistic and Address the Broader Context in which they Operate

Effective CYD programs are holistic. This means that CYD programs are concerned with all aspects of young people, including their physical, social, emotional, and intellectual needs and well-being. CYD programs take steps to support young people that extend beyond skills in the arts and humanities to include providing integrated, "wrap-around" services such as mental health counseling, coordinating referrals to agencies and organizations that can provide needed support, or offering services that support the college application process.

Trauma-Informed Practice at Youth Radio in Oakland, CA

CYD organizations are seeking to develop existing staff members' skills in restorative practice and trauma-informed practice and are also hiring staff with expertise in these areas as well as in counseling and other social services. Case in point: When Maeven McGovern joined the staff of Youth Radio, a CYD organization in Oakland, CA, as Director of Arts Pathway and Youth Outcomes, she began delivering extensive professional development in trauma-informed practice for community-based organizations, including CYD programs and educators around the Bay Area. McGovern uses and develops culturally relevant tools to support the implementation of trauma-informed artistic development programming within Youth Radio. When she started at the organization, McGovern started a poetry workshop that evolved into Youth Radio's Remix Your Life program, integrating music and poetry into the storytelling mediums available to youth participants.

CYD programs also respond to the larger context in which they function by engaging youth participants with local, national, global, and historic issues and events. Given the core value of equity within the field of CYD, these programs have a frequent bent toward examining issues of social justice through projects and civic engagement.

Note: a useful resource is the Teaching Artistry & Social Justice Resource Database, https://teachingartistsguild.org/social-justice-resource-database/. This ever-changing database is a crowd-sourced arts education and social justice repository featuring best practices with the purpose of providing inspiration and support for teaching artists engaged in social justice work.

CYD in Practice: *Stories Seldom Told*

Through the annual *Stories Seldom Told* exhibition, student-artists at SAY Sí, a CYD organization in San Antonio, Texas, are challenged to critically examine issues that they feel aren't being addressed in their everyday lives. After voting on a topic, the young artists spend three months researching and collaboratively creating multimedia art installations about their chosen topic, often relating to social justice. Students have explored issues of race, class, mental health, and poverty, as well as corporate America.

In one project, SAY Sí student-artists chose to use the exhibition to examine inequities in San Antonio's education system. One installation, titled "Human Geography," projected information on each Bexar County school districts' dropout rates onto a carved map of the districts. Projections on the 3-dimensional map showed student dropout statistics by district and median property values while the color-coded pencils represent the race of students who have dropped out of school. Engagement levels in projects such as this one are exceptionally strong, and participating students expand their awareness and connect with their community and the world in new ways.

Quality and CYD

We have established that CYD programs vary widely in program content or art form, geography, and size. CYD programs also vary in quality of experience, artistry and arts skill building, and degree of youth development that occurs. While many CYD programs are programs of excellence with years of reflective practice, program refinement, and commitment to embracing the most current information about positive

youth development, other programs are earlier in their evolution. Still other programs, in a misguided attempt to align themselves with the field of CYD, call themselves CYD programs but have large gaps to address before they could be considered to be of high quality.

How might practitioners who want to strengthen their programs go about doing so? What might a funder look for to evaluate which CYD programs are embodying the full breadth of CYD practice and are deserving of support? What could a prospective board member look for, if he or she were rigorous and resourceful, to understand the quality of experience that a CYD organization is providing to young people?

The Wallace Foundation commissioned research as part of its Youth Arts Initiative, the purpose of which is to increase equity and access for low-income youth to high-quality OST arts programs. The research examined barriers and motivations for young people with regard to how they make decisions about how to spend their free time. Another component of the research examined what constitutes quality within CYD programs (i.e., a common set of principles that might serve as a blueprint for high-quality OST arts programs). The resulting publication was *Something to Say: Success Principles for Afterschool Arts Programs from Urban Youth and Other Experts* (Montgomery, Rogovin, & Persaud, 2013).

> How might practitioners who want to strengthen their programs go about doing so?

The report discusses a common set of principles among the high-quality CYD programs studied. Strikingly, programs that had developed entirely independent of one another had evolved to embrace similar core ways of approaching their work. In addition, there was agreement between young people and experts in after-school programs about the need for professional artists to be involved in CYD programs.

The principles of high-quality OST arts programs from the *Something to Say* research are presented below. While these principles encompass the six key characteristics of effective CYD programs that were discussed previously in this chapter, the principles differ in three important ways:

1. In addition to the youth development principles that are presented in the key characteristics list, this set of principles addresses aspects of high-quality programs that are specific to the arts.
2. Taken in the aggregate, this set of principles provides a basic road map for developing a quality program.
3. Within the set of 10 principles, employing instructors who are professional, practicing artists is listed first to emphasize its foundational importance.

The 10 principles were validated further via a national survey of CYD practitioners conducted prior to a 2014 National Summit on Creative Youth Development. Survey respondents overwhelming agreed or strongly agreed that the set of quality principles were essential ingredients for effective CYD programs (Stevenson, 2014). This affirmation is meaningful since having shared awareness of the requirements of high quality programs is valuable as OST policymakers, researchers, and practitioners are increasingly focused on evaluating and ensuring quality in youth programs (Princiotta & Fortune, 2009; Smith et al., 2012).

The following are the 10 principles for effective, high-quality OST arts programs (Montgomery, Rogovin, & Persaud, 2013. p. 55):

1. Instructors are professional, practicing artists and are valued with compensation for their expertise and investment in their professional development.
2. Executive directors have a public commitment to high-quality arts programs that is supported by sustained action.
3. Arts programs take place in dedicated, inspiring, welcoming spaces and affirm the value of art and artists.
4. There is a culture of high expectations, respect for creative expression, and an affirmation of youth participants as artists.
5. Programs culminate in high-quality public events with real audiences.
6. Positive relationships with adult mentors and peers foster a sense of belonging and acceptance.
7. Youth participants actively shape programs and assume meaningful leadership roles.
8. Programs focus on hands-on skill building using current equipment and technology.
9. Programs strategically engage key stakeholders to create a network of support for both youth participants and the programs.
10. Programs provide a physically and emotionally safe place for youth.

Theory of Change

What positive outcomes occur for young people who participate in CYD programs? The Boston Youth Arts Evaluation Project (BYAEP), a partnership of practitioners, funders, and program evaluators, developed the following Framework for Outcomes in Youth Arts Programs (2012) or theory of change (Figure 12.1).

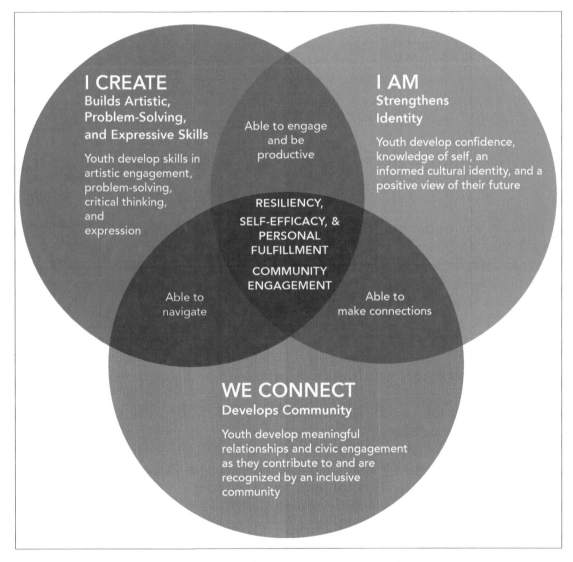

Figure 12.1. BYAEP's Framework for Outcomes in Youth Arts Programs. Reprinted with permission. Boston Youth Arts Evaluation Project (BYAEP). (2012). *Boston Youth Arts Handbook and Workbook*. Boston: MA.

The BYAEP theory of change states that:

- If youth participate in high-quality arts programs, they will develop specific skills and competencies (I Create, I Am, We Connect);
- which, in turn, lead to a set of intermediate outcomes (able to engage and be productive, to navigate, and to make connections with others);
- which in turn lead to a set of long-term outcomes (resiliency, self-efficacy and personal fulfillment, and community engagement) that together constitute life success.

The Creative Youth Development National Partnership has used the BYAEP framework in its efforts to support and strengthen the field of creative youth development. The BYAEP framework is consistent with other, independent efforts to create a theory of change for CYD (c.f., the model presented in Mosaic Youth Theatre of Detroit's *Excellence on Stage and in Life: The Mosaic Model for Youth Development Through the Arts*; Gutierrez, & Spencer, 2008).

Evidence of CYD as a Solution for Positive Outcomes for Youth

Creative youth development programs have conducted numerous independent research studies to document and understand the outcomes of participation for youth, such as social and emotional development. Findings demonstrate that CYD programs support young people in developing their creativity, perseverance, self-awareness, collaboration skills, and capacity for self-expression, cross-cultural understanding, and much more (Stevenson, 2013).

Many CYD programs also track statistics such as graduation rates, with dramatic findings such as SAY Sí's 100% graduation rate and 100% pursuit of higher education in a community with a 20% high school dropout rate. These findings not only illustrate the ways in which CYD programs support positive youth development, they are also valuable for making the case for the value of the program with funders, policymakers, parents, and other stakeholders.

While the scope of this chapter is too limited to examine in depth the research on CYD, more than 20 years of positive impact are documented through a longstanding and growing body of research-backed evidence. For example, Mosaic Youth Theatre of Detroit reports that a three-year University of Michigan study documented that 81% of Mosaic alumni indicated that they experienced more personal growth and transformation at Mosaic as compared to any other activity they participated in as a teenager. The same University of Michigan study tracked numerous indicators of academic success tied to participation in Mosaic, including increased grade point averages, a heightened sense of viewing themselves as capable of academic success, and increased educational aspirations. Additionally, Mosaic documented that 97% of its alumni thought their participation in Mosaic strengthened their ability to make positive decisions and 94% said that Mosaic helped them to develop and maintain a positive sense of self (Gutierrez & Spencer, 2008).

In a different study of a CYD program, an independent researcher found that youth participants at Destiny Arts Center in Oakland, CA related to the world with more awareness, confidence, and understanding. Additionally, these young people had positive effects on their families, schools, and communities stemming from their personal growth through participation at Destiny (Stevenson, Johnston Limón, & Reclosado, 2013).

To learn more, you can explore the resources presented in the Appendix at the end of this chapter, Touchstones and Resources for Creative Youth Development.

An International Movement

Creative youth development exists beyond North America in Africa, Asia, Australia, Europe, Central America, the Middle East, and South America, where arts programs focused on youth development goals are thriving. One of the most far-reaching in influence and participation is El Sistema, founded in Venezuela with a vision of providing high-quality and joyful music instruction to all youth throughout this South American country. El Sistema works with more than 800,000 students each year. The United States has a strong and growing network of El Sistema-inspired programs serving more than 250,000 students annually. More information is available through El Sistema USA (http://www.elsistemausa.org).

Some international CYD programs have been highly successful accessing funds outside of traditional arts or humanities funders, such as workforce investment funding. Creative Scotland has effectively advocated for government support that recognizes the contributions Scotland-based youth arts programs make to developing critical thinking, innovation, and other skills valued by employers.

Creative Youth Development in Collaboration with Allied Sectors

The arts allow young people to engage in a way that meets them where they are...the arts allow kids to get in touch with their feelings, whatever rage might be inside, whatever socioeconomic factors they might face. (Alex Johnson, Managing Director, Californians for Safety & Justice; Board Member, Arts for Incarcerated Youth Network)

As allied youth fields (e.g., juvenile justice, health and wellness, and workforce development) increasingly take a youth development approach, and as issues such as social justice and racial equity garner attention, energy, and resources, leaders in these sectors and movement are growing in their awareness and recognition of the ways in which CYD aligns with and can support mutual goals. CYD programs and organizations are forming cross-sector partnerships and alliances as strategies to connect with more young people, build engagement, and to expand funding sources.

One example is the Arts for Incarcerated Youth Network (AIYN; http://aiynetwork. org), based in Los Angeles. AIYN has successfully contracted with the Los Angeles

County's juvenile justice system to provide long-term arts programs for incarcerated youth. Through the Network, the interdisciplinary members strive to build resiliency and wellness, eliminate recidivism, and transform the juvenile justice system.

> ## The Arts Are Engaging in Youth Development
>
> "Our art programs are one of the clearest and most inspiring ways that we see our teenagers build skills and progress year to year. When we can point to an eighth grader who got into her preferred high school because of the arts, or when the arts are the reason that a high school senior is going to college, we understand that high-quality art instruction can be a very effective youth development tool."
> (Rob Connolly, President & CEO, Boys & Girls Clubs of San Francisco, 2017)

National youth development organizations, such as Boys & Girls Clubs of America, are increasingly providing programs in creative youth development, driven, in part, by young people's requests for more opportunities to create and by heightened awareness of how engaging high-quality CYD programs can be for young people. Some programs occur through partnerships with arts or humanities partners in the community, and other programs are supported with dedicated staff at the youth development organization. For example, the Walter Denney Youth Center of Boys & Girls Clubs of Dorchester in Dorchester, MA, has an extensive music program with offerings in drums, voice, guitar, beat making and more. The music director is a practicing, professional artist who is a graduate of the Berklee College of Music and is pursuing an advanced degree in youth development. The Club's Music Program includes a Music Council of youth leaders who are advisors to the program.

> Libraries, museums, and other community centers are additional venues where a growing number of CYD programs take place.

Libraries, museums, and other community centers are additional venues where a growing number of CYD programs take place. These varied entities are discovering that CYD programs can be highly successful in attracting and retaining youth. Cross-sector partnerships and the expansion of CYD within allied youth fields such as youth development and juvenile justice have the potential to connect more youth with CYD in order to support young people in discovering and nurturing their sparks in the creative arts and to help youth thrive.

> ### Changing Life Trajectories
>
> "The arts programs are the most popular programs among teens and young adults at our community centers funded by the City of Los Angeles. They are uniquely engaging…involvement in an arts program can open the door to the acceptance of other services by youth who have been disconnected, such as employment workshops or needed mental health services. All of this can change the fundamental trajectory of young people's lives…the arts can be a doorway or an on-ramp." (Robert Sainz, Assistant General Manager at City of Los Angeles and head of the City's Economic and Workforce Development Department)

Inadequate and Inequitable Opportunities to Participate in CYD

Unfortunately, access to arts education has been steadily declining for three decades (Rabkin & Hedberg, 2011). Deep gaps exist with regard to equity and access to arts learning opportunities. In a 2008 study, African American and Latino youth had less than half the access to arts education than did White students (Americans for the Arts, 2017). In addition to inequitable access to in-school arts education, students in low-income families are less likely to have opportunities to experience and pursue the arts outside of the school day, such as through private lessons or tuition-based programs or camps. Barriers for youth participation in CYD programs include program fees, transportation challenges, inadequate supply

> Equity is often a core value of CYD programs and organizations.

of quality CYD programs, and lack of awareness of or familiarity with the existence of OST arts programs and their benefits to young people. At the same time, the benefits of arts education can be the greatest for youth from low-income families (Catterall, Dumais, & Hampden-Thompson, 2012).

Equity is often a core value of CYD programs and organizations. Many CYD programs prioritize working with low-income youth and racially and ethnically diverse populations of youth and therefore working to improve equity in access to quality out-of-school time arts education (Montgomery, 2017). However, not enough CYD programs currently exist to meet the interest and needs of young people. We have more work to do as a society and as youth development leaders and practitioners to bridge gaps in opportunity to pursue the arts.

Conclusion

With more than two decades of changing young people's lives through arts- and humanities-based youth development, creative youth development organizations and stakeholders such as funders and allied sector leaders are unifying to organize nationally and to advance the field of creative youth development. In 2016 the Creative Youth Development National Partnership formed with a vision that:

> All young people will have equitable access to opportunities to develop their worldview and creative potential, to live richer, fuller lives and develop the critical learning and life skills they need to become active contributors to their communities. (Creative Youth Development National Partnership, 2017)

Young people stand to benefit as awareness grows of how CYD is a compelling path for positive outcomes for youth. As a youth ally and youth development leader of today or of the future, your awareness of CYD expands the range of approaches to positive youth development with which you are familiar. Youth and, increasingly, policymakers recognize the value and contribution of the arts.

The Universality of the Arts

"The arts are a response to our individuality and our nature, and help to shape our identity. What is there that can transcend deep difference and stubborn divisions? The arts. They have a wonderful universality. Art has the potential to unify. It can speak in many languages without a translator. The arts do not discriminate. The arts can lift us up." (Former Texas Congresswoman Barbara Jordan)

CYD Programs are LIFE CHANGING!

"I often find it hard to put the ICA's impact on my life into words. I want programs like this to get funding and recognition."

"Over the past 2 yrs, I've met practicing artists, interviewed them, worked with them, created art with them."

"I've shadowed ICA staff in multiple departments, learned how to make a resume that applies to me as a creative."

"I've learned how to plan large scale events, and work on a team."

"And most importantly, I've learned what it feels like to be loved, supported, and validated..."

(Sienna, participant in Institute of Contemporary Art/Boston's Teen Arts Council; Retrieved from Twitter August 18, 2017 https://twitter.com/siennakwami/status/898755089279574016)

Discussion Questions

1. How are creative youth development programs different from arts exposure programs? What do you perceive to be the strengths and weaknesses of CYD programs compared to arts exposure programs?

2. How are creative youth development programs different from conservatory programs in music, theatre, or dance? What do you understand to be the goals of CYD programs as compared to the goals of conservatory programs?

3. Imagine that you are the program director for a CYD program. You choose the art form—media arts, filmmaking, visual arts, dance, theatre, etc. What steps would you take to create an emotionally safe environment for student participants? What indicators would you use to determine how emotionally safe young people feel in your program? Give two examples of indicators that may tell you that you have more work to do to create an emotionally safe environment.

4. Consider your response to reading Jamila Lyiscott's blog post, "If You Think You're Giving Students of Color a Voice, Get Over Yourself." What do you think about Jamila's point of view regarding young people's voices? Does this blog post apply to any of your experiences at youth organizations? If so, in what ways? Discuss Jamila's reflection regarding her conversation with the *well-meaning* woman. Also, discuss the developmental issues surrounding adults *giving* voice versus embracing, celebrating, or prioritizing youth voice.

5. Why do you think that it is important that a practicing, professional artist lead a CYD program? What would a practicing professional bring to the experience for young people that an arts hobbyist or general youth worker would not be able to provide?

6. Corporations and businesses say that they need employees who can innovate, work in teams, effectively communicate, and problem-solve. These skills are often described as 21st century workforce skills. In what ways do you think that participation in creative youth development programs helps young people to develop 21st century workforce skills?

Assignment

Write a mission statement for an imaginary CYD program that conveys what you would want to achieve through your CYD program or what you are working toward (You choose the art form—media arts, filmmaking, visual arts, dance, theatre, creative writing, etc.). Following your mission statement, in 100–250 words, share why you included the components or language that you used. *Note:* You can look at the mission statements of existing CYD programs for inspiration and ideas, but make the mission statement your own. Craft a mission statement that speaks to your understanding of the ways that CYD programs can be beneficial to young people.

Now, email your mission statement to the executive director, program director, or program staff of a CYD program or organization. Ask them for feedback on the mission statement. What parts of the statement resonate with them and their understanding of CYD as practitioners who do this work? Do they see anything missing?

References

Americans for the Arts. (2017). *Arts facts: Access to arts education is not equitable.* Washington, DC: Americans for the Arts.

Benson, P. (2008). *Sparks: How parents can ignite the hidden strengths of teenagers.* San Francisco, CA: Jossey Bass.

Benson, P. (2011). Sparks: How youth thrive. TEDxTC. Retrieved from https://www.youtube.com/watch?v=TqzUHcW58Us

Boston Youth Arts Evaluation Project. (2012). Framework for outcomes in youth arts programs. Retrieved from http://www.byaep.com/1/BYAEP_Framework.html

Catterall, J. S., Dumais, S. A., & Hampden-Thompson, G. (2012). *The arts and achievement in at-risk youth: Findings from four longitudinal studies.* Washington, DC: National Endowment for the Arts.

Create a Spark Foundation. (2018). Spark - Learn, Create, Inspire. Retrieved from Hhttp://www.sparktx.org/about-us-2/

Creative Youth Development National Partnership. (2016). Our vision. Retrieved from http://creativeyouthdevelopment.org/

Gittelman, J., Mercado-Zizzo, R., & Swaback, K. (2016, November). Measuring youth arts impact. Presentation at the Conference for Community Arts Education, Chicago, IL.

Gutierrez, L. M., & Spencer, M. S. (2008). *Excellence on stage and in life: The Mosaic Model for youth development through the arts.* Detroit, MI: Mosaic Youth Theatre of Detroit.

Lyiscott, J. (2017). If you think you're giving students of color a voice, get over yourself. Retrieved from https://medium.com/@heinemann/if-you-think-youre-giving-students-of-color-a-voice-get-over-yourself-cc8a4a684f16

Massachusetts Cultural Council. (2017). Retrieved from Seen & Heard blog, http://seenandheard.massculturalcouncil.org/key-characteristics-of-youth-development-programs/

Montgomery, D. (2017). The rise of creative youth development. *Arts Education Policy Review Journal, 118*(1), 1–18.

Montgomery, D., & Rogovin, P. (2017). *Partnering with community arts organizations: A pathway to a high-quality club experience.* Atlanta, GA: Boys & Girls Clubs of America.

Montgomery, D., Rogovin, P., & Persaud, N. (2013.) Something to say: Success principles for afterschool arts programs from urban youth and other experts. The Wallace Foundation. Retrieved from http://www.wallacefoundation.org/knowledge-center/Documents/Something-to-Say-Success-Principles-for-Afterschool-Arts-Programs.pdf

Princiotta, D., & Fortune, A. (2009). *The quality imperative: A state guide to achieving the promise of extended learning opportunities.* Washington, DC: Council of Chief State School Officers.

Rabkin, N., & Hedberg, E. (2011). *Arts education in America: What the declines mean for arts participation.* Based on the 2008 Survey of Public Participation in the Arts. Research Report #52. Washington, DC: National Endowment for the Arts.

Scruggs, G. K. (2017). Temenos and the power of myth. Voices: The art and science of psychotherapy. *Journal of the American Academy of Psychotherapists, 53*(2), 7–16.

Smith, C., Akiva, T., Sugar, S., Devaney, T., Lo, Y., Frank, K., Peck, S. C., & Cortina, K. S. (2012). *Continuous quality improvement in afterschool settings: Impact findings from the youth program quality intervention study.* Ypsilanti, MI: David P. Weikart Center for Youth Program Quality.

Stevenson, L. (2014). *Setting the agenda.* Boston, MA: Massachusetts Cultural Council.

Stevenson, L., Johnston Limón, C., & Reclosado, T. (2013). Community-based afterschool and summer arts education programs: Positive impact on youth and community development. In T. K. Peterson (Ed.), *Expanding minds and opportunities: Leveraging the power of afterschool and summer learning for student success.* Retrieved from http://www.expandinglearning.org/expandingminds/article/community-based-afterschool-and-summer-arts-education-programs-positive

Teaching Artists Guild. (2017). Resource directory. Retrieved from https://teachingartistsguild.org/resources-new/

Tellet-Royce, N. (2012). *Sparks: Building deep and sustained relationships with young people.* Paper presented at BOOST (Best Out-of-School Time) Conference, Palm Springs, CA.

Appendix

Touchstones and Resources for Creative Youth Development*

Key pieces of research and developments that represent pivotal moments in time or big leaps forward for youth arts and creative youth development (*Source: National Guild for Community Arts Education Website. http://www.nationalguild.org/Programs/Key-Initiatives/Creative-Youth-Development/Fundamental-Resources.aspx

Theoretical Underpinnings

Dewey, J. (1934). *Art as experience.* New York, NY: Minton, Balch and Company.
Freire, P. (translated by Ramos, M.; 1970). *Pedagogy of the oppressed.* New York, NY: Bloomsbury.

1980s

Gardner, H. (2011). *Frames of mind: The theory of multiple intelligences.* New York, NY: Basic Books.

1990s

Brice Heath, S., & Smyth, L. (1999). *ArtShow: Youth and community development.* Washington, DC: Partners for Livable Communities.
Brice Heath, S., & Soep, E. (Spring, 1998). Youth development and arts in the nonschool hours. *Grantmakers in the Arts Newsletter, 9*(1). Retrieved from http://www.giarts.org/article/youth-development-and-arts-nonschool-hours
Brice Heath, S., Soep, E., & Roach, A. (1998). Living the arts through language-learning: A report on community-based youth organizations. *Americans for the Arts Monographs, 2.*
Fiske, E. B., Brice Heath, S., & Roach, A. (1999). *Imaginative actuality: Learning in the arts in the nonschool hours.* Washington, DC: Arts Education Partnership and President's Committee on the Arts and Humanities.
Weitz, J. H. (1996). *Coming Up taller: Arts and humanities for children and youth at risk.* Washington, DC: President's Committee for the Arts and Humanities
YouthArts Toolkit. (1998). Americans for the Arts. Retrieved from http://youtharts.artsusa.org/download.html

2000s

Gutierrez, L. M., & Spencer, M. S. (2008). *Excellence on stage and in life: The mosaic model for youth development through the arts.* Detroit, MI: Mosaic Youth Theatre of Detroit.

Levine, M. N. (2002). Powerful voices: Developing high-impact arts programs for teens. Surdna Foundation. Retrieved from http://www.surdna.org/what-we-fund/thriving-cultures/thriving-cultures-resources/38-powerful-voices.html

Peterson, T. K., & Fix, S. (2007). *Afterschool advantage: Powerful new learning opportunities.* Moorestown, NJ: Foundations, Inc.

Seidel, S., Tishman, S., Winner, E., Hetland, L., & Palmer, P. (2009). *Qualities of quality: Understanding excellence in arts education.* Project Zero, Harvard Graduate School of Education and The Wallace Foundation.

2010s

Boston Youth Arts Evaluation Project (BYAEP). (2012). *Framework for outcomes in youth arts programs, BYAEP Workbook,* and *BYAEP Handbook.* Boston Youth Arts Evaluation Project and Raw Art Works.

Creative Youth Development National Partnership. Retrieved from www.creativeyouthdevelopment.org.

Hirzy, E. (2011). *Engaging adolescents guidebook: Building youth participation in the arts.* New York, NY: The National Guild for Community Arts Education.

Montgomery, D. (2016). The rise of creative youth development. *Arts Education Policy Review Journal,* 118. Retrieved from http://dx.doi.org/10.1080/10632913.2015.1064051

Montgomery, D., Rogovin, P., & Persaud, P. (2013). *Something to say: Success principles for afterschool arts programs from urban youth and other experts.* Boston, MA: The Wallace Foundation.

Stevenson, L., Limón, C. J., & Reclosado, T. (2013). Community-based afterschool and summer arts education programs: Positive impact on youth and community development. In T. Peterson (Ed.), *Expanding minds and opportunities: Leveraging the power of afterschool and summer learning for student success.* Collaborative Communications Group, Inc. Retrieved from http://www.expandinglearning.org/expandingminds/article/community-based-afterschool-and-summer-arts-education-programs-positive

Chapter 13

Intentional Programming Using Logic Models

Linda L. Caldwell, Peter A. Witt, and Cheryl K. Baldwin

So far in this book we have identified a number of reasons out-of-school time (OST) activities and programs are important. The positive outcomes that accrue to youth through their participation in OST activities and programs are the "whys" behind what youth workers do. Examples of whys include providing opportunities for young people to enhance their skills, develop relationships, and decrease negative behaviors. However, desired outcomes do not occur simply because a young person attends a particular activity or program. To achieve desired outcomes, the programming must be intentionally designed to produce the desired outcomes. Thus, intentional programming happens when programmers make decisions about exactly what they desire to happen (the outcomes) as a result of youth participating in a particular program, and design the program to make those outcomes occur.

Unfortunately, being intentional about desired outcomes and program processes needed to achieve desired outcomes is a departure from the way many

OST staff conceive, plan, and deliver programs. Too often youth development workers operate from their hearts and not their heads. That is, they base their program design decisions on what they believe will work (the heart) and not on any scientific evidence or rationale (the head) that offering a program in a particular way will lead to the desired outcome(s). Imagine you are trying to explain to people in city government, a foundation, a school district, or a nonprofit agency why they should invest in your program. The heart explanation would be something like, "We are good people trying to provide quality programs to make a difference in the lives of youth." The head explanation would be, "These data suggest which outcomes young people will achieve as a result of participating in our program, and thus we have planned the program in the following ways to bring about those outcomes."

The purpose of this chapter is to introduce you to principles of theory-based programming that will enable you to use these principles to enhance program planning and design and to communicate to others the why, what, and how of your program. We will introduce you to a widely used tool in the youth development field called *logic models*. We hope that this information will inspire you to design supports, opportunities, programs, and services *intentionally* in order to achieve desired outcomes.

Heart and Head Whys

Let's return to the issue of the whys of youth programming, and in particular heart and head whys. Dealing with the whys helps youth workers do two important tasks. First, youth workers must identify the specific outcomes they hope their programs will achieve—that is, why they are doing the program in the first place. Second, youth workers must be able to explain the rationale for including particular activities or other components in the program (i.e., why they think the chosen components will produce the desired outcomes).

Identifying the whys, and articulating them to others, has long been important, but unfortunately has not always been done very well. OST professionals have a long history of needing to justify their programs as they compete for funding and other types of support. In Chapter 5, we discussed the origins of many of the youth-serving organizations that developed in the late 1800s and early 1900s to reduce crime, increase socialization, help young people grow effectively into adulthood, and be better citizens. The public and public officials viewed youth services as a means for dealing with critical social issues that had come about due to the industrial revolution, migration of people from rural environments to the cities, and the large influx of immigrants into the major cities. Most of the arguments for their beliefs about why programs were important to offer were based on heart whys, not head whys. Furthermore, many youth programs were offered

> Most of the arguments for their beliefs about why programs were important to offer were based on heart whys, not head whys.

without articulating clear outcomes beyond keeping youth off the streets and occupying their out-of-school time. Although many of these programs were no doubt successful, there was little effort to document their success through formal evidence.

In today's world, there are a multitude of programs and services competing for too few dollars. This makes it imperative that youth professionals know how to "tell their story" in a way that clearly convinces funders and other stakeholders (e.g., politicians, school personnel, parents, participants, etc.) that their programs are important and serve a social good (e.g., leading to needed and important outcomes). In addition, it is hard to call oneself a professional if one cannot explain how what one does leads to outcomes that society considers important. Unfortunately, however, most youth professionals are not trained in strategies that promote intentional programming. Thus, when youth workers only plan from the heart and not from the head, they are not able to successfully articulate the story of "the business they are in" in terms of issues that matter to funders, other stakeholders, and society generally.

In fact, both heart and head whys are essential in today's evidence-based management context. Figure 13.1 provides some examples of heart and head whys. Basing the story of a program on heart and head whys can lead to a blockbuster presentation. The heart whys provide the moral foundation and passion for the work one is doing. The head whys provide the scientific justification for how the program is designed to achieve the desired outcomes.

Following principles of intentional programming and using logic models, youth services workers can easily articulate why and how their programs address critical:

- **Social goals** (e.g., decreased crime, increased safety of children who otherwise might be on the streets or return to empty homes during the non-school hours)
- **Developmental goals** (e.g., autonomy and identity development)
- **Educational goals** (e.g., better test scores and graduation from high school)
- **Behavioral goals** (e.g., decrease risky behaviors, such as alcohol and drug use and involvement in early and/or unprotected sex)

Figure 13.1. Heart and Head Whys

Funders are usually only willing to support programs that provide a good return on their investment and thus are increasingly interested in information that demonstrates that programs do indeed achieve their intended outcomes (Reed & Brown, 2001). A National Recreation and Park Association white paper provides a rationale for and examples of outcomes associated with positive youth development (Witt & Caldwell, 2010).

There is scientific evidence of the effectiveness of well-designed youth programs leading to valued outcomes.

Luckily, there is scientific evidence of the effectiveness of well-designed youth programs leading to valued outcomes. Youth development researchers are increasingly exploring the impact of young people's involvement in school-based and community-based after-school, night and weekend programs, extracurricular activities, and informal involvements, including "hanging out" (Fredricks & Eccles, 2010; Sharp, Tucker, Baril, VanGundy, & Rebellon, 2015). Results from these types of studies are useful to youth workers as they seek to design intentional programs that focus on goals funders are willing to support. These goals are the outcomes of intentionally developed programs and are usually broken into short-term or immediate outcomes and longer-term or distal outcomes. We will discuss outcomes in detail as we move through the chapter.

The rest of this chapter will explore how a logic model is a useful conceptual and planning tool for intentionally articulating program goals and stipulating the processes that will lead to accomplishing these goals. First, let us discuss the role of theory in program development.

The Role of Theory in Program Development and Telling Your Story to Others

Basing programs on theory can help explain and link what happens in a program with specific outcomes (the whys). Programmers use two types of theory to construct a logic model (West & Aiken, 1997). One type is a *theory of explanation* that describes from a theoretical perspective why there are linkages between the short-term and longer-term outcomes. Theories of explanation are based on established social science theories and empirical evidence (i.e., scientifically based evidence as to why things happened as they did) as the basis for program decisions and statements made about program outcomes. Programmers use theories because they provide explanations or forecasts about how selected program activities and experiences will lead to particular participant outcomes.

As an example, a short-term outcome might be to teach young people how to develop interests in order to avoid situational boredom. Avoiding situational boredom is associated with reducing substance use, which is a longer-term outcome. The theory of explanation comes from empirical studies that demonstrate a link between situational boredom and substance use (e.g., Weybright, Caldwell, Ram, Smith, & Wegner, 2015).

Another type of theory is a *program theory* (sometimes called a *theory of intervention*). A program theory explains how program components and activities lead to program outcomes. Program theories provide a well-reasoned road map of what the programmer will offer in the program. Many programmers have vast experience designing and developing programs. They have developed strong beliefs and expectations about how the programs they offer affect participants. These program theories rely on a programmer's best professional judgment (in many ways, the heart why). Often the program theory is a combination of a theory of explanation and a programmer's professional judgment.

Combining a programmer's professional judgment with scientific theorizing is a powerful strategy for intentional programming. Through intentional programming, programmers can clearly identify the expected outcomes, articulate the processes by which those outcomes can be achieved, and develop an evaluation plan to determine whether the outcomes were actually achieved. We will provide an example of using theory in developing a logic model later in this chapter.

In sum, the ability to understand, assess, and apply theory is fundamental to quality programming. Ideally, theories should guide the design of programs, explain what one expects to occur as a result of a youth participating in a program, and serve as the basis for gathering evidence on whether program outcomes and expectations are achieved. Combined, head and heart theories identify *known linkages between program elements and desired outcomes*. These theories help youth service workers avoid "fuzzy thinking" about what they expect to happen as a result of youth program participation.

What Are Logic Models?

Logic models operationalize the theory of explanation and the program theory. That is, logic models provide a road map of where one is going and why (the program outcomes based on a theory of explanation) and how one is going to get there (the inputs that will be offered based on the program theory). More specifically, a logic model does the following:

- Provides a visual representation of the program design and theory
- Illustrates a chain of events that links inputs (e.g., staff, supplies) with outcomes
- Brings detail and clarity to fuzzy goals
- Identifies key elements of a program
- Clarifies differences among inputs, program activities, and outcomes

Logic models are the core of planning, program management, communications, and evaluation. They do the following:

- Provide a foundation for working with others around a common goal (communication)
- Assure the intervention is based on the why (theory)
- Provide a road map to evaluation

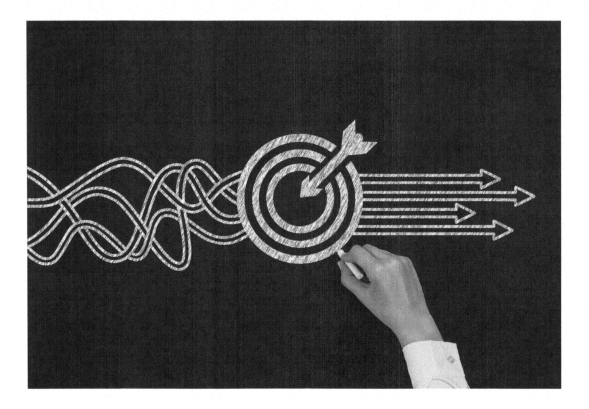

- Provide a useful grant writing tool, as funders often require a logic model as part of their application for funding

Figure 13.2 provides a diagram of the fundamental elements of a logic model. Logic model wisdom suggests that programmers plan from the right hand side in order to establish the outcomes that guide the program, and develop the program theory from the left. So right away, you can see that if you were designing your program intentionally, you would need to start with the outcomes, that is, what outcomes do you desire and expect to achieve by offering your program (e.g., reduce substance use)? As per the previous example, to achieve this goal, youth would need to learn to overcome situational boredom. Thus, you would plan your program to achieve this outcome.

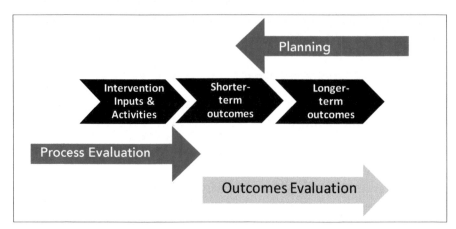

Figure 13.2. Logic Model Fundamentals

Once programmers decide which outcomes to target, they make decisions about the specific program activities to incorporate in order to make those outcomes happen. In addition, programmers need to identify all the resources and support activities (the inputs) necessary to conduct the program (e.g., staff, supplies, equipment). During and after the program, programmers would also conduct process and outcomes evaluation. The following chapter will address evaluation in detail.

Take a simple example from everyday life. Think about taking a spring break vacation. What are the outcomes you are seeking? Maybe you want to come back feeling rejuvenated so that you can do well on your school assignments during the rest of the semester (a longer-term outcome). Thus, you will need to create a spring break plan that includes activities that will create the feeling of having fun, yield stress release, and put school out of your mind for a while (all shorter-term outcomes).

Now that you have identified the whys of taking your vacation and the desired outcomes, what are the activities you need to do to achieve those outcomes, and how are you going to do them? Participating in yoga on the beach, trying your hand at sailboarding, reading a good book on the beach, and hanging out with friends—these are all good possible activities. So now you have to plan what you need to do to make those things happen (i.e., inputs). In this case, inputs would also include sufficient monetary resources to buy gas to drive to the beach and pitch in with friends to rent a condominium, pay for your food, make reservations to sailboard, and participate in yoga. Other resources could include bug spray, sunscreen, beach gear, and games. So, guess what, you have just completed an everyday logic model! If we diagrammed your logic model, it might look something like Table 13.1.

One important caveat: logic models come in all shapes and sizes. While the logic model presented in Table 13.1 is typical, Figure 13.3 contains the schematic for other representations of logic models. In the end, however, all models contain the same basic elements.

Table 13.1
Everyday Logic Model–Vacation Over Spring Break

Inputs	Activities	Shorter-Term Outcomes	Longer-Term Outcomes
Rent a condo	Read a book on the beach	Relaxation	Feel rejuvunated to finish spring semester
Drive to the beach	Goat yoga on on the beach	Stress release	
Make reservations	Sailboarding	Fun	
Money for gas and activities	Working together to prepare dinners	Bonding with friends	
Friends			

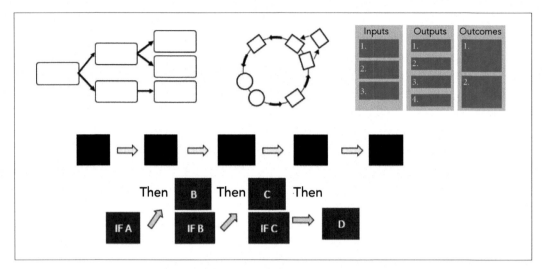

Figure 13.3. Types of Logic Models

Outcomes

As noted previously, outcomes have a temporal sequence. Some happen immediately after the program (shorter-term outcomes) and some take some time to develop (longer-term outcomes). Often programmers will plan for three levels of outcomes, short, medium, and long-term, in order to help them more specifically identify what is expected to happen as a result of youth participating in their program. Each outcome is dependent on (i.e., builds off) the previous outcomes, just as in the vacation example.

In the vacation example, short-term relaxation is expected to lead to slightly longer-term feelings of rejuvenation, which in the longer term is expected to produce better studying habits and completion of assignments, which in tern, after several months, is expected to lead to better end-of-course grades. Thus, the outcomes occur over time; they all do not happen at once. Now, look at Figure 13.3. The bottom figure does a good job of depicting a temporal sequence (i.e., if A happens, then B happens, and then if B happens, then C happens, and so on). This is a good way to think about how outcomes are linked in a temporal sequence.

One final caveat: In some instances, it is difficult to measure whether the longer-term outcomes actually occurred. For example, if the long-term goal of a sixth grade after-school program is to increase the odds that participants graduate from high school, you would have to wait six years to see if that actually happens. However, your funders may want more immediate evidence that your program is successful. Thus, it becomes important to show the known theoretical linkages between shorter term outcomes (e.g., participants express better bonding to school, attend school more often, and get better grades) and how these short-term outcomes are linked by theory and evidence to longer term outcomes like graduating from high school.

Figure 13.4 presents a four-level way to think about outcomes, staring with short-term (proximal) outcomes and proceeding to intermediate-term (medium), long-term (distal) and impact (way in the future or ultimate) outcomes. Figure 13.4 helps one understand the types of things that are most likely to occur in a temporal sequence. For example, it is unlikely someone's behavior will change after a six-week program. After six weeks, however, it is probable that if the program was intentionally designed, participants would learn something (knowledge and skills) and/or change their attitude about something. It is logical that if learning occurs, one's behavior might change and that would influence a more sustained condition in the longer-term.

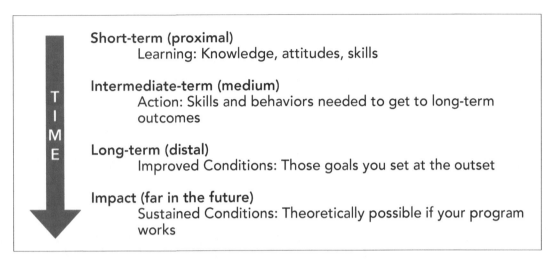

Short-term (proximal)
Learning: Knowledge, attitudes, skills

Intermediate-term (medium)
Action: Skills and behaviors needed to get to long-term outcomes

Long-term (distal)
Improved Conditions: Those goals you set at the outset

Impact (far in the future)
Sustained Conditions: Theoretically possible if your program works

Figure 13.4. Levels of Outcomes

Consider a five-week homework completion program in an after-school setting for youth transitioning into middle school. Using the levels of outcomes in Figure 13.4, programmers might have as an impact outcome that youth will thrive educationally, graduate college, and earn a productive living. Obviously, this is a long-term view of what might happen as a result of a program in middle school. Unless one had a lot of funding and the scientific expertise, it is unlikely that a programmer can demonstrate whether the program met this impact outcome. But, as noted previously, using theory based on previous research, the programmer has evidence that this is a viable "far in the future" outcome and provides a nice "end of the story" example to justify the program.

Working backwards in order to achieve this impact outcome, what long-term or distal outcomes might a programmer set? That is, in order for the impact outcome of graduating college and getting a job to be realized, what needs to happen first? You might immediately think that graduating high school with good grades is important. You might also think that being well adjusted and having a positive outlook, as well as having a healthy mix of extracurricular activities in high school, might also be important. These might be viable distal outcomes to consider, although you would have to verify that through published studies that have shown these connections.

Now, in order for these long-term (or distal) outcomes to happen, what has to happen before that? In other words, what intermediate or medium-term outcomes in conjunction with the short-term or immediate outcomes need to occur? Generally, the short-term outcomes that programs can most influence have to do with increased knowledge, improved attitudes, and skill development. In the homework completion example, programmers might designate the following short-term outcomes they expect youth to achieve as a result of participating in the five-week program:

- Youth will learn the importance of completing their homework in order to succeed in school and to value getting an education (attitude).
- Youth will achieve the learning outcomes, such as math, science, and language, as set forth in the curriculum (knowledge).
- Youth will improve their time management skills in order to increase the probability of them completing their homework in a timely manner (skills).
- Youth will turn their homework in on time (behavior).

Note that a programmer can evaluate whether these short-term outcomes have been achieved by measuring an increase in knowledge, a change in attitudes and/or skills, and whether homework assignments are actually turned in on time.

In addition, the programmer can expect that youth who achieve these short-term outcomes will see themselves as people more capable of being better students in the future (medium-term objective). By managing their time better, students can also engage in other extracurricular skills and acquire other benefits from participation in these types of programs, such as developing positive relationships with caring adults. These are all good examples of measurable intermediate or medium-term outcomes (i.e., something the programmer could see evidence of a month or so after the youth participated in the five-week program).

> Generally, the short-term outcomes that programs can most influence have to do with increased knowledge, improved attitudes, and skill development.

Figure 13.5 depicts the flow of the logic model outcomes. It shows the successive steps being "logically" time ordered, with the program leading in turn to short-term, intermediate-term, long-term, and impact outcomes. These successive steps depict how the program produced new knowledge, attitudes, and skills, which in turn led to longer-term behavioral outcomes, eventually leading to achieving the impact outcome.

Finally, note that in order to build a good logic model, and therefore a good program, the programmer will specify in advance the timeframe expected for each of the outcomes to happen (immediately, one month, six months, five years, etc.). This will aid in the development of specific program activities as well as in the development of the evaluation plan for the program.

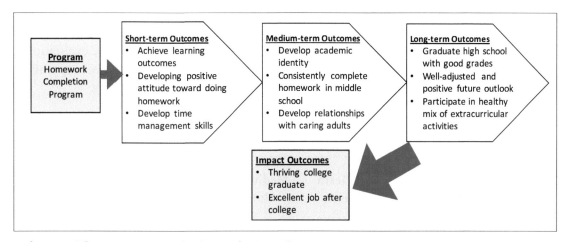

Figure 13.5. Homework Completion Outcomes

Although Figure 13.5 describes four outcome levels, programmers should choose the number of levels that make the most sense for their particular situation. At the very least, two levels will be included; one set of outcomes that the programmer expects to immediately happen as the result of participation in the program (shorter-tem), and the other set of outcomes related to longer-term outcomes that are expected as a result of youth participating in the particular program after some time has passed.

Theory of Explanation and the Program Theory: Linking Inputs and Program Components with Outcomes

Now that the programmer has developed a logic model, she or he must consider what goes into making the outcomes happen. That is, what program components and activities will achieve the outcomes? What resources and inputs does the programmer need to offer for the program to occur? For example, programmers would need to hire knowledgeable and caring staff to provide homework assistance to youth working on their homework. A quiet space with good tables or desks would also be necessary.

In the homework assistance program, the program theory represents how what happens in the program produces the desired short-term outcome. One important program component is to make sure time is set aside for students to complete their homework. In addition, tutoring or assistance by caring adults who have the ability to motivate students, answer questions, and provide positive rewards for successful homework completion must also be provided. These program activities will contribute to helping students develop time management skills, an academic identity, and motivation for continuing schooling. By providing the program components of time, assistance, and an appropriate space to work, students should be able to complete their homework.

Theories of explanation help us link the program to the various outcomes. In the case of the homework assistance program, research suggests that children who complete their homework are more likely to get higher grades and achieve higher standardized test scores. In turn, research also provides strong evidence that students with higher grades and test scores are more likely to graduate from high school and get better paying jobs.

Table 13.2 puts all the logic model components together, except for the evaluation plan. In this table, you can view the inputs, program activities, and outcomes. Hopefully this table helps you visualize the logical link among all of these components.

Table 13.2
Homework Completion Logic Model

Inputs	Program Activities	Short-Term Outcomes	Medium-Term Outcomes	Long-Term Outcomes	Impact Outcomes
Quiet room	Structured time to focus on homework	Developing positive attitude toward doing homework	Consistently complete homework in middle school	Graduate high school with good grades	Thriving college graduate
Dedicated and caring staff	One-on-one time with youth	Relationship with caring adult	Sustained relationship with caring adult	Well-adjusted and positive future outlook	Excellent job after college
Supplies (e.g., paper, pencils, computers)	Group discussion about future outlook	Learn importance of completing homework	Develop academic identity	Participate in healthy extracurricular activities in high school	
Salaries for staff	Lessons on time management	Develop and practice time management skills	Have more time for other activities		
Staff training					

Constructing a Theory-Based Program Using a Logic Model: An Example

Now let us look at one last example of a logic model and build it from the desired longer-term outcome back to the program components that will help achieve the outcomes. In this example, we highlight the role of theory. However, before we discuss our example, there are a few considerations to keep in mind. Remember, one can select any number of levels of outcomes as long as at least one shorter-term and one longer-term outcome are specified. Some programmers will not have an impact outcome in mind; that is perfectly okay, but one should think through in a general sense what impact their program might have on a youth in the longer run.

When considering which longer-term outcome(s) to choose, be realistic and not overly ambitious. In reality, what you choose will likely be related to characteristics of your community and agency. For example, is your community rural, urban, or suburban? Are community members concerned about the opioid epidemic and want programming that will act as a preventive measure? Is gang violence an issue? What are the skills and knowledge levels of the staff with whom you work, as well as your own knowledge base when it comes to offering programs that can deal with the central issues of interest in your community?

After you select one or more longer-term outcomes, you will need to review the literature to gain as much information as possible about these outcomes and theories explaining how you might achieve them. A good place to begin is to consult the literature for a *definition* of the desired outcome(s). A good definition helps in the measurement of the outcome and helps distinguish it from other behaviors with which it might be confused. For example, consider the outcome of developing youth autonomy, an important developmental task and protective factor identified in the literature. Without adequately defining autonomy and understanding its theoretical underpinnings, one could confuse autonomy with independence. Autonomy and independence are related, but they are not the same thing. If we are not clear about what we mean when we use the term *autonomy*, it will be much more difficult to influence its development and to evaluate the effectiveness of our program in developing autonomy for the program participants. In addition, a specific definition of autonomy allows us to state precisely what we mean when we talk with others about the program.

As an example of focusing on autonomy as an outcome, staff from a park district in a large, urban area observed that early in the summer youth coming to their summer programs seemed to lack any sense of taking responsibility for their own well-being or happiness. Staff believed that they needed to guide the youth into most activities. The youth also acted rather helpless, as if none of their decisions or actions really mattered or produced any results. The staff consulted with some youth development experts, did some preliminary reading, and realized that the youth lacked a sense of autonomy. Therefore, they decided to develop a program that over the long term (distal outcome) would promote the development of autonomy. They

> Without adequately defining autonomy and understanding its theoretical underpinnings, one could confuse autonomy with independence.

learned that development of autonomy is one of a number of important developmental tasks youth face during adolescence (e.g., Steinberg, 2002). Staff found evidence in the literature that youth who do not develop a healthy sense of autonomy during their adolescent years are more likely to exhibit depressive symptoms and social withdrawal as they get older (Chango, Allen, Szwedo, & Schad, 2015). With this knowledge, staff could have established an impact outcome of reducing depressive symptoms in early adulthood, but to keep this example as simple as possible, we will focus on fewer outcomes in order to demonstrate how theory is used to construct logic models. Therefore, we will use three levels of outcomes and not include an impact outcome.

As noted previously, the first step in developing the logic model is to better understand and define the concept related to the longest-term outcome in the model. According to Steinberg (2002), autonomy reflects self-governance, with governance conveying a personal sense of responsibility. Ryan and Deci (2000) view autonomy as a basic need central to a person's overall well-being. They conceptualize autonomy as the ability to act in a self-determined, volitional manner. An autonomous individual sees one's actions as motivated by one's own interests, beliefs, and values rather than things external to the self, like parental or school rules, rewards and pressures, or luck or chance (Deci & Ryan, 1985).

Some people consider adolescent autonomy as independence from one's parents, but based on the above definitions, this is only partially accurate. Although autonomy does encompass some behavioral independence from the supervision of parents or other adults in authority (Silverberg & Gondoli, 1996), it is not simply acting without direct adult supervision, nor is it rebelling against parent and adult authority. Rather, it involves depending on and staying connected with others while also maintaining one's own sense of individuality (Collins, Gleason, & Sesma, 1997). In contrast, non-autonomous individuals avoid acting in a purposeful manner, exercise irresponsible independence, over-rely on others, and view their actions as caused by forces external to themselves. Thus, it is necessary to define autonomy so we do not get it confused with independence.

> Based on the knowledge they gained, staff wanted to develop a program with activities that provided opportunities for and supported youth in making personal contributions to a program and making decisions about what happens in a program.

In our example, after the staff better understood what autonomy was and was not, they needed to find out what clues they could get from the literature that would help them design their program, and more specifically, what program elements should be included so that youth autonomy was increased. In their literature review, staff found that autonomy develops when those in authority such as parents, teachers, and coaches support self-initiated behaviors and give youth choices about what transpires in home, school, or OST program settings (Frederick & Ryan, 1995). Other adult actions that are supportive of autonomy are giving informational feedback in a non-controlling manner and being able to view things from the youth's perspective (Grolnick, Deci,

& Ryan, 1997). Youth demonstrate autonomy through their decision-making skills, including the ability to think ahead, seek support, assess outcomes associated with alternatives, and negotiate with peers as well as adults (Collins et al., 1997).

Based on the knowledge they gained, staff wanted to develop a program with activities that provided opportunities for and supported youth in making personal contributions to a program and making decisions about what happens in a program. The literature suggests that having a sense of choice is associated with seeing oneself as an important cause of what one does, as opposed to just responding to options provided by those in authority. Program staff also wanted to include opportunities for social interactions with peers and developing close relationships with program leaders. Based on autonomy theory, at least two aspects of adult leadership are important: (1) the degree to which leaders give informational rather than controlling feedback and (2) the degree to which leaders support youth-initiated ideas or points of view. When these leadership characteristics are present, research suggests that youth feel that they have a great deal of volition or choice in what they do. Therefore, staff realized that they needed training to provide appropriate, supportive, but nonjudgmental feedback to youth as they made decisions, realizing that failure was a possibility based on decisions the youth might make.

Given these theoretical and program requirements, staff formed a youth council and empowered youth who joined the council to develop a special event of their choosing. The goal was for members of the youth council to develop the special event and manage all aspects of the event, including its planning and implementation. In principle, the youth council program would be an opportunity for youth to develop autonomy. Youth workers would provide the necessary guidance during the process of developing the special event, but would make sure not to dictate how things should be done or take over the project.

Now that staff had a general idea of what they wanted to do, and why, they needed to dig deeper and identify short-term outcomes as well as intermediate outcomes that would lead to the longer-term development of autonomy. They also had to design specific program components and activities that would, theoretically, produce the outcomes. At this point, they began to create their logic model that showed the linkages among program components and outcomes. Although the logic model was challenging and took some time to develop, it ultimately simplified their programming efforts because it detailed why, what and how the program would be conducted. It also helped staff communicate to others what they were doing and why. The hard work up front would pay off in better program design and outcomes.

Figure 13.6 displays the final logic model developed by the staff. The proximal outcomes had to do with knowledge, skill development, and attitudes. Therefore, they designed their program activities to produce these outcomes. In addition, staff developed a set of intermediate outcomes that they felt would accrue once youth had developed the knowledge, skills, and attitudes, and that all of these outcomes would then lead to the distal outcome of autonomy development.

When reviewing Figure 13.6, notice the arrows. Although it is impossible to identify and/or even show all of the linkages (based on the program theory and theory of explanation), it is helpful to identify in the logic model what linkages seem to be the most salient. For example, it makes sense that if staff offered a session to teach planning and decision-making skills, youth would learn those skills and practice them, which, in turn, would develop confidence in their abilities, which in part would lead to autonomy development. This chain of events is most likely to happen when staff provide non-controlling input and support the youth in making decisions.

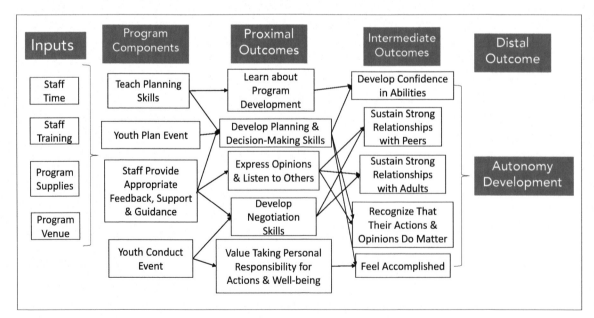

Figure 13.6. Youth Council Autonomy Development Program

You can see that by using a logic model how much easier it would be to describe the purpose and outcomes of this program to others, as well as to evaluate whether it was effective. For example, if staff were seeking funds to support their program, they would have a solid way to sell the program based on both head and heart whys. Staff could describe why they wanted to do the program in the first place and recount how the youth they served seemed listless, without direction, and were failing to take personal responsibility for their actions (i.e., the youth lacked autonomy). Here is where the staff could emphasize their passion for making a difference in lives of these youth. However, remember that passion alone would not be enough to convince the funder to grant support to the program. Using the logic model, staff also would be able to explain from a more scientific perspective how important autonomy development is for the healthy transition to adulthood and how they were going to help youth develop autonomy.

In addition, staff would be able to tell the funder that they designed their program to support youth by empowering them to make decisions, expressing their opinions to others, learning to listen to others' opinions, and developing negotiation skills. These outcomes would be facilitated through program staff providing appropriate feedback, support, and guidance, and by doing so, they would be enabling youth to develop confidence in their abilities, develop a sense of accomplishment, recognize that their opinions and actions do matter, and develop sustained relationships with peers and adults. Thus, through their explanation the program staff could help funders see how leadership, planning, and managing an activity would influence youths' perceptions of autonomy through how leaders interact with youth (e.g., nature of feedback) and how the program elements encourage behaviors such as expressing personal ideas.

Other Thoughts Regarding the Autonomy Example

Deduction (also known as professional judgment) is sometimes necessary if there is insufficient information in the literature to justify completely a particular link. For example, it is a logical premise that being able to exercise and express one's ideas and beliefs is a prerequisite skill to feeling a sense of choice/volition. As a result, staff included this link in Figure 13.6. Although it would be optimal if programmers primarily could base logic models on theory and empirical evidence, and less on deduction, theory, and research may not yet have clearly addressed all aspects of desired outcomes and what it would take to bring them about. However, this should not stop programmers from offering programs based on heart whys. If this is the case, programmers will need to be extra cautious to detail why they are doing what they are doing and then conduct an evaluation to see if their professional judgment was correct, or identify changes they need to make in the future.

Another consideration is that although the connections among the outcomes are driven by explanatory theory, the links between the program components and proximal outcomes are sometimes less evident and require an analysis of "the processes and elements" of the program components and activities. The links between the program components and the proximal outcomes are based in part on an understanding of the kinds of activities or program features that affect the short-term and longer-term outcomes. In the autonomy example, the program components included the leaders (e.g., leadership style), planning, and conducting the event (e.g., activities). When designing this program, staff determined which elements they thought would influence the proximal outcomes. Although the explanatory theory indicated that all of the proximal and intermediate outcomes influenced autonomy, knowing how and whether the program components affected the proximal outcomes was another matter. As you can see, it is important that programmers commit to a logic model approach before they design a program so these connections are built into a program deliberately.

> It is important that programmers commit to a logic model approach before they design a program so these connections are built into a program deliberately.

The program logic model illustrated in the autonomy example also provides an opportunity to discuss several issues regarding theory-based programming and the construction of logic models. When you reflect on all the activities and experiences that are a part of developing and running a special event, why were only four program components included in the model? This question illustrates the challenge of representing a program in a relatively easy to understand model. It may be necessary at times to depict a conceptual logic model where there is some degree of abstraction between the model and the inputs needed to carry out a program. This may happen when programmers explain a complex program to the public. In this case, leaving out some details may make the model easier to comprehend. For "in-house" planning purposes, however, creating a more detailed logic model is important.

Other Issues in the Development of Theory-Based Programming

If you are in a situation where you are working with an existing program that does not have a logic model, the process of developing a program logic model will help identify the implicit beliefs that program staff have about what the program is intended to accomplish and the design of the program to achieve those outcomes (Rogers, 2000). Reviewing these implicit beliefs may reveal that different staff members have different interpretations of a program's purpose and benefits and how planned activities lead to achieving the desired outcomes. Constructing a logic model can strengthen the quality of a program by making sure all stakeholders share a common understanding of the program and its impacts. Thus, constructing a logic model helps staff move from implicit beliefs to shared explicit understandings about the relationship between program design and outcomes.

Weiss (2000) suggested that when constructing a program logic model, staff should focus on the most salient (important) and enduring (lasting) aspects of the program experience. In the autonomy development example, the salient features were dictated in part by the nature of autonomy, the distal outcome. It is completely plausible that the same special event management experience could produce other important outcomes (e.g., community attachment) and in that case, an alternative model would describe the relationship between the outcome and other aspects of the program experience (e.g., levels of bonding to peers and nonparental adults).

Also, note that there is a tendency for youth program planners to think about everything that happens in the course of a program and create long lists of benefits. However, focusing on the most important and most enduring benefits should help focus attention on those deemed most important and most connected to the program activities.

Finally, youth program directors often focus on schedule, program details, and logistics when supervising existing programs. They may have difficulty summarizing the program in a conceptual logic model and may be tempted to create a flow chart of what happens when. With practice, programmers can develop the theory-based programming skills described in this chapter and find natural ways to conceptually divide the program experience into distinct components and corresponding outcomes.

When constructing a program logic model, staff should focus on the most salient (important) and enduring (lasting) aspects of the program experience.

The Role of a Program Logic Model in Program Evaluation

A logic model also serves as the basis for systematic program evaluation by specifying expected outcomes, as well as the pathways for achieving those effects. However, in most cases, to conduct an in-depth evaluation, it is necessary to have considerable resources, individuals with research methods expertise, and a large number of program participants (Donaldson, 2001; West & Aiken, 1997). The goal of these large-scale evaluation studies is both to demonstrate that a program produced outcomes and examine how the program produced those effects. Some examples of these types of evaluation of OST programs exist, but lack of funding and understanding among professionals of their value and necessity still limit their being undertaken.

In the early stages of establishing theory-based programs and outcome evaluations, programmers should focus on the underlying assumptions and theory linking the program components and proximal outcomes. Recall that in theory-based programming, theory and research evidence are used to represent a program as a series of successive and linked steps. Because the logic model supplies predictions about what happens in a program, it may be useful to begin the evaluation process by assessing these steps and assumptions. For example, are the participants reporting and describing their experience in a manner consistent with the outcomes specified in the model? This is an example of a process evaluation, as noted in Figure 13.2.

For our autonomy development example, staff hypothesized that the way they provided leadership and then implemented the program activities would affect the short-term (proximal) outcomes. Thus, it is appropriate to ask the participating youth to rate the leaders' feedback styles and support of youth-initiated ideas and comments. Additionally, systematic observations of the staff by qualified individuals not associated with the program could help evaluate whether staff demonstrate these behaviors. If leaders do not receive high scores on their feedback styles and support, it would challenge the basic assumption underlying the program logic model and would suggest a need for staff training or rethinking the importance of these characteristics for this particular program.

Youth could also report or describe their experience in the program. In this case, it would be important to analyze the extent to which youth felt that the program activities required the kinds of features represented in the proximal outcomes. For example, youth could report the extent to which the program experience provided or required them to use their personal ideas. Note that the focus here is not on the youths' level of ability to express their ideas, but rather whether they felt the ability to express opinions characterized their experience. Programmers could ask the same types of questions regarding peer-to-peer coordination and collaboration, as well as planning. This evaluation strategy would facilitate determining whether the programmers' beliefs about the salient features of the program match the experience that youth actually have in the program.

Programmers could gather additional information by asking youth to complete open-ended questions about their experiences and the elements of the experiences they thought were important. Program staff may be surprised to find that youth identify program components they had not considered. For example, Fetterman and Bowman (2002) evaluated an experiential science education program for high school youth and found that the youth reported "fun" as an important element of the program, while the staff had not considered this in their program model. An additional benefit of analyzing the program components is to ensure that claims about outcomes are consistent with the types of experiences that youth have in the program.

A program evaluation can also help staff understand if participants received "enough" of the program to influence a change in outcomes. This is called "program dosage." Programmers may realize that they need one or more additional sessions to influence participants' attitudes or knowledge, for example.

To summarize, program staff need to develop a data collection strategy based on the program logic model that systematically measures both outcomes and program processes. The examples described here

> Program staff need to develop a data collection strategy based on the program logic model that systematically measures both outcomes and program processes.

illustrate information that would help programmers make decisions about a program. Rather than asking the youth if the program was beneficial, the evaluation strategy proposed here is to examine closely fundamental beliefs about how the program works. While a more sophisticated outcome evaluation process may require some outside support, program staff can and should gather important information about the key hypotheses underlying the program logic model. Chapter 14 provides further information about program evaluation.

The Future of Theory-Based Programming

As societal interest in the value of OST activities continues to grow, the need for quality programming also increases. Based on the information provided in this chapter, whether parents, policy makers, funders, and youth will judge a program to be of high quality will depend on whether the program produces valued outcomes. As this chapter has illustrated, theory-based programming and evaluation are fundamental aspects of designing programs that positively affect youth. The quality of programs depends upon a programmer's ability to effectively construct and manage programs based on theory and evidence of program outcomes. Adopting theory-based programming strategies will help youth development programmers position their supports, opportunities, porgrams, and services as important.

The challenge that confronts OST program planners is to determine what kinds of program activities (components) actually affect specific types of valued short- and longer-term outcomes. For example, which type of activity might do a better job of increasing a youth's level of autonomy: planning and leading a recreation special event or volunteering to lead children's games at special events? Planning and leading a special event would no doubt increase feelings of autonomy as compared to volunteering because a greater level of responsibility and decision-making is needed to plan and lead.

Additionally, we must begin to better understand whether program activities work well for both girls and boys; youth of sexual minorities; urban, suburban, and rural youth; youth of various racial, ethnic, and cultural backgrounds; and so on. As the number of theory-based programs and outcome evaluations increases, programmers will need to continue to keep abreast of the growing body of knowledge in OST programming. We hope this chapter has provided you with the tools to begin to effectively address these challenges.

Chapters 14 and 15 provide additional perspectives regarding intentional programming. Chapter 14 provides tools to evaluate whether or not programmers achieved the outcomes specified in a logic model. Chapter 15 describes a more specific example of programming based on the Theory of Structured Experience (Ellis, Freeman, Jamal, & Jiang, 2017) that facilitate "deep structured experiences."

Discussion Questions

1. Debate whether all of the programs offered by OST settings have to have outcomes. Don't some youth choose to participate in activities simply because they value being on a team or doing a recreational activity such as swimming or skateboarding?
2. Can all outcomes be predicted? Consider the autonomy example. What additional, unexpected, or unintentional outcomes might have occurred due to the autonomy program? Are unintentional outcomes always positive? Explain your response.
3. Discuss head and heart reasons for a program with which you are familiar.
4. Discuss which type of activity might do a better job of increasing a youth's level of autonomy and why: planning and leading a recreation special event or volunteering to lead children's games at a special event.

Assignment

1. Identify a set of longer-term outcomes that you would like to work toward if you were running an OST program.
   a. Find a theory that would help you develop a logic model and describe it.
   b. Develop a set of short-term outcomes that might be more easily achieved and make a list of short-term outcomes that might be more difficult to achieve based on that theory. Organize the list by outcomes associated with knowledge, skills, and attitudes. Decide on two or three short-term outcomes to focus on.
   c. Decide how you would go about designing a program to achieve the outcomes. How long would the program be? What inputs would you need?

References

Chango, J. M., Allen, J. P., Szwedo, D., & Schad, M. M. (2015). Early adolescent peer foundations of late adolescent and young adult psychological adjustment. *Journal of Research on Adolescence, 25*(4), 685–699.

Collins, W. A., Gleason, T., & Sesma, A. (1997). Internalization, autonomy, and relationships: Development during adolescence. In J. E. Gursec & L. Kuczynski (Eds.), *Parenting and children's internalization of values: A handbook of contemporary theory* (pp. 78–99). New York, NY: John Wiley & Sons.

Deci, E. L., & Ryan, R. M. (1985). *Intrinsic motivation and self-determination in human behavior.* New York, NY: Plenum Press.

Donaldson, S. I. (2001). Mediator and moderator analysis in program development. In S. Sussman (Ed.), *Handbook of program development for health behavior research and practice* (pp. 470–496). Thousand Oaks, CA: Sage.

Ellis, G. D., Freeman, P. A., Jamal, T., & Jiang, J. (2017). A theory of structured experience. *Annals of Leisure Research*, 1–22. Retrieved from http://dx.doi.org/10.1080/11745398.2017.1312468

Fetterman, D., & Bowman, C. (2002). Experiential education and empowerment evaluation: Mars rover educational program case example. *Journal of Experiential Education, 25*, 286–295.

Frederick, C. M., & Ryan, R. M. (1995). Self-determination in sport: A review using cognitive evaluation theory. *International Journal of Sport Psychology, 26*, 5–23.

Fredricks, J. A., & Eccles, J. S. (2010). Breadth of extracurricular participation and adolescent adjustment among African-American and European-American youth. *Journal of Research on Adolescence, 20*, 307–333.

Grolnick, W. S., Deci, E., L., & Ryan, R. M. (1997). Internalization within the family: The self-determination theory perspective. In J. E. Gursec & L. Kuczynski (Eds.), *Parenting and children's internalization of values: A handbook of contemporary theory* (pp. 135–161). New York, NY: John Wiley & Sons.

Reed, C. S., & Brown, R. E. (2001). Outcome-asset impact model: Linking outcomes and assets. *Evaluation and Program Planning, 24*, 287–295.

Rogers, P. J. (2000). Program theory: Not whether programs work but how they work. In D. L. Stufflebeam, G. F. Madaus, & T. Kellaghan (Eds.), *Evaluation models: Viewpoints on educational and human services evaluation* (2nd ed., pp. 209–232). Boston, MA: Kluwer Academic.

Ryan, R., & Deci, E. L. (2000). Self-determination theory and the facilitation of intrinsic motivation, social development, and well-being. *American Psychologist, 55*, 68–78.

Sharp, E. H, Tucker, C. J., Baril, M. E., VanGundy, K. T., & Rebellon, C. J. (2015). Breadth of participation in organized and unstructured leisure activities over time and rural adolescents' functioning. *Journal of Youth and Adolescence, 44*, 62–76.

Silverberg, S. B., & Gondoli, D. M. (1996). Autonomy in adolescence: A contextualized perspective. In G. R. Adams, R. Montemayor, & T. P. Gullotta (Eds.), *Psychosocial development during adolescence* (pp. 12–61). Thousand Oaks, CA: Sage.

Steinberg, L. (2002). *Adolescence* (6th ed.). Boston, MA: McGraw-Hill.

Weiss, C. H. (2000). Which links in which theories shall we evaluate? In P. J. Rogers, T. A. Hacsi, A. Petrosino, & T. A. Huebner (Eds.), *Program theory in evaluation: Challenges and opportunities* (pp. 35–45). San Francisco, CA: Jossey-Bass.

West, S. G., & Aiken, L. S. (1997). Toward understanding individual effects in multicomponent prevention programs: Design and analysis strategies. In K. J. Bryant, M. Windle, & S. G. West (Eds.), *The science of prevention: Methodological advances from alcohol and substance abuse research* (pp. 167–209). Washington, DC: American Psychological Association.

Witt, P. A., & Caldwell, L. L. (2010). *The rationale for recreation services for youth: An evidenced-based approach.* Ashburn, VA: National Recreation and Park Association. Retrieved from http://www.nrpa.org/uploadedFiles/nrpa.org/Publications_and_Research/Research/Papers/Witt-Caldwell-Full-Research-Paper.pdf

Weybright, E. H., Caldwell, L. L., Ram, N., Smith, E. A., & Wegner, L. (2015). Boredom prone or nothing to do? Distinguishing between state and trait leisure boredom and its association with substance use in South African adolescents. *Leisure Sciences, 37*, 311–331. doi: 10.1080/01490400.2015.1014530.

Chapter 14

Program Assessment and Evaluation

Ann Gillard and Laurie Browne

Why Evaluate?

- Does our program make a difference in the lives of participants? If it doesn't, what can we do to improve it?
- I think something is missing from what we are doing in our program, but I don't know what.
- Parents are not sending their children to our program any more. Why? What changes can we make to prevent attrition?
- The teens seem to love this program; I wonder what it is that they love about it?
- I have been here for 20 years, and I know what works; I don't need to evaluate anything!

Do any of these queries or statements sound familiar to you? They are all focused on program evaluation and assessing what works, what does not, and what needs improvement. In addition to the questions and statements above, programmers and managers evaluate their youth programs because many funders require evaluation on a regular basis. Other reasons for evaluation include demonstrating to policy makers and the public that youth programs are important and should be sustained.

The main goal underlying all evaluation in out-of-school time (OST) programs, however, is for programmers and managers to find out if their programs are actually affecting the desired positive youth development (PYD) outcomes. For example, one might ask, did the program we offered result in positive changes in participants' knowledge, values, attitudes, skills, or behaviors?

Thus, program assessment and evaluation is an essential activity for youth-serving organizations. In this chapter, we will discuss evaluation-related definitions, purposes, topics, techniques, and planning.

What is Program Evaluation?

We evaluate things all the time by watching, reading, listening, and sensing what is going on in a situation, and then making some kind of judgment based on what we see, feel, and hear. This ongoing, informal evaluation is a powerful source of information to which people turn to guide their decisions. We call this *anecdotal evidence*, which results from ongoing and informal evaluation. While evidence from informal evaluations is plentiful, it is also prone to bias, which makes it difficult to use when making programmatic decisions or advocating for funding.

Evidence gathered systematically, on the other hand, is more objective. The American Evaluation Association defines evaluation as "a systematic process to determine merit, worth, value, or significance" (http://www.eval.org/p/bl/et/blogid=2&blogaid=4). Systematic implies that you are gathering evidence using a planned, intentional strategy. It also implies that the evidence is gathered and recorded in way that minimizes individual bias so the information is believable and can be used to inform decision-making.

> While evidence from informal evaluations is plentiful, it is also prone to bias, which makes it difficult to use when making programmatic decisions or advocating for funding.

Let's look at how evaluation fits into a youth-serving organization. Evaluation is not something that comes only at the end of a program. Good programming moves from program design, to implementation, to evaluation…with evaluation results leading to improvements in program design which leads to program implementation, and so on (Figure 14.1).

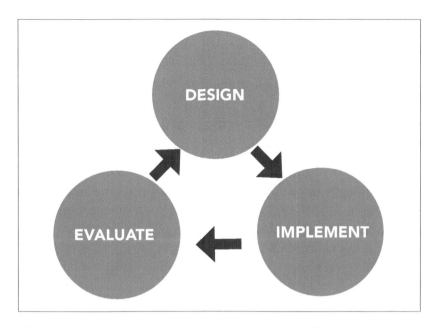

Figure 14.1. Design-Implement-Evaluate Cycle

To help illustrate these reciprocal relationships, consider how The Hole in the Wall Gang Camp used evaluation to design a new program. Each summer, The Hole in the Wall Gang Camp serves about 1,000 children aged 7–15 with serious illnesses such as cancer, sickle cell disease, hemophilia, HIV/AIDS, and metabolic diseases in its residential camp program. After a period of time, camp staff found they had a "good" problem to solve: many campers who had "aged out" of camp wanted to stay involved. Therefore, staff conducted a needs assessment to find out more about what types of programming these adolescents and emerging adults wanted to see implemented to further serve their needs. The needs assessment revealed that most campers wanted both technical and social support for transitioning into adulthood. To meet this need, staff designed a conference with learning opportunities related to technical and social support. After implementation of the conference, participants completed surveys to evaluate their experience so the program planners could see if participants felt their participation had increased their level of technical and social support. The evaluation results were used to design future conferences.

As a side benefit, the results from the program evaluation were also shared with stakeholders to showcase the value of the conference. Evaluators also used the results in future grant applications to show how the camp was systematically evaluating its programs. Most importantly, after reviewing the evaluation results, staff used the information to implement improvements in the program, which included adding more interactive activities and opportunities for participants to share contact information and network with each other.

In this example, evaluation was conducted so that program staff could better understand the needs of a group they wanted to serve, and then to see if the participants' needs were being met by the program. There were actually two forms of evaluation in this example: needs assessment and post-program information collection. The results of the needs assessment led to the conference. The results from the post-program evaluation, based on the logic model's outcomes, led to program improvements.

Purposes for Evaluations

Purposes for evaluation fall into two major categories:

1. Program improvement, which entails making programmatic changes and staff training about needed changes in leading and presenting programs.
2. Communication with stakeholders. For example:
   a. *Youth* want to know what the program does for kids like them.
   b. *Parents/caregivers* want to know if sending their kids to the program is worthwhile.
   c. *Funders* want to know if program outcomes are consistent with their investments.
   d. *The public* wants to know if its community investment is worthwhile.

Choosing What to Evaluate

As you read in Chapter 13, a logic model is an important tool to explain linkages in a program and demonstrate how program components lead to intentional outcomes. Youth program evaluators can focus on what to evaluate by considering how inputs relate to program outputs, and how outputs lead to program activities and components, which lead to short-, medium-, and long-term outcomes for participants. Let's look at different possible areas for evaluation through the lens of a logic model.

Process Evaluation

In order to evaluate a program's inputs or outputs, one can use process or formative evaluation. Sabatelli, Anderson, and LaMonte (2005) note that "A process evaluation determines whether the program is being carried out as planned. It is intended to answer the basic question, "Who is being served and what has actually happened in this program?" (p. 5). The process evaluation focuses on the left side of the logic model—the program operations or processes that lead to participant outcomes.

Who is being served and what has actually happened in this program?

Thinking about the logic of a logic model, when staff add something to the left side of a logic model such as staff or money or program supplies, there should be an improvement in outcomes on the right side of the logic model. Most evaluations of inputs involve simple counting: for example, how many hours of staff time are devoted to the program, how many activities are offered, and how much money is spent? The same applies to evaluations of outputs: how many people were served and what were their characteristics? As noted in the previous chapter, many programmers stop after reporting about inputs and outputs and do not think about how participants were influenced or what participants gained over the short-, medium-, and long-term from their participation in the program. Although it is important to document the scope of the program by assessing the inputs and outputs (e.g., the resources used and number of sessions offered and people served), these areas alone are not enough to gain information necessary for program improvement or attract support to sustain the program; evaluation of outcomes is also vital.

Outcome Evaluation

Outcome evaluation is defined as changes, influences, effects, or impacts of a program on participants. Basically, outcome evaluation focuses on the right side of the logic model, or the changes that are believed to occur if participants experience the left side of the logic model (inputs, outputs, and program activities and components). Outcomes—sometimes called key performance indicators or metrics—relate to changes in participants' knowledge, skills, attitudes, beliefs, or behaviors. Outcome evaluation focuses on assessing how well the program influenced each level of outcome as specified by the logic model.

To illustrate the concept of outcome evaluation, we will use the example of Camp Sunshine (a fictitious camp) that operates summer programs in conjunction with a school district aimed to target skills considered critical in the 21st century, such as teamwork, creativity, and problem-solving skills. The camp serves middle-school students from the school district.

Let's suppose Camp Sunshine's desired long-term outcome is for youth to thrive in college or other postgraduate training or employment opportunities. What might be the short- and medium-term outcomes that would lead to this long-term outcome? Short-term outcomes (e.g., knowledge, attitudes, and skills) related to this long-term outcome might focus on youth learning how to work in teams, be creative, and use effective problem-solving strategies. A medium-term outcome might be that participants reported using their teamwork, creativity, and problem-solving skills during the traditional school year. Remember that medium-term outcomes are those that reflect some change in actions or decision-making as a result of improved knowledge, skills, or attitudes.

In general, conducting an outcome evaluation on the effectiveness of Camp Sunshine's programs would mean finding out whether the program activities produced the desired outcomes. The trick is to design a strategy for determining whether it was actually Camp Sunshine's programs that resulted in the outcomes, or whether it was something else that resulted in the outcomes (such as another school program). There are various methods that are useful in this endeavor, all of which aim to reduce bias and provide an objective means of collecting data about program experiences and effects. For example, surveys, interviews, focus groups, and systematic observations could

all provide useful information in assessing campers' perceptions of their teamwork, creativity, and problem-solving skills. Staff could use any of these methods immediately after the summer program to determine whether the short-term outcomes were met.

Medium-term outcomes are trickier to assess because they occur later in time, perhaps months after the program has taken place, and often in a different setting (e.g., school). However, evaluators can also use the same methods as used to assess short-term outcomes. For example, staff could design a survey focused on whether and how participants used problem-solving skills at school, or interview parents or teachers about their observations of participants' use of these skills outside of camp.

Long-term outcomes are the hardest outcomes to evaluate because it is difficult to attribute changes in people to a program they attended in the past without implementing a rigorous research design. For example, if youth programmers think their program will, in the long run, successfully prepare participants to thrive in college or in their careers, they would need to design a study that would provide solid evidence that it was their program, and not other factors, that led program participants to thrive compared to a similar group of youth who did not participate in the program. Strategies to measure long-term outcomes may involve longitudinal approaches and would typically use an experimental and control or comparison group of participants, such as using a group of youth from a wait list of youth who did not participate in your program. In these situations, youth program professionals might decide to work with academic researchers or outside evaluators to measure long-term outcomes.

Measurement of Outcomes

In order to assess whether the program has met its goals, evaluators need to measure outcomes. By measuring we mean determining how much an outcome has been changed over the course of the program. Measurement is challenging, particularly in the social sciences, because it is difficult to measure abstract characteristics, such as a person's attitude. How would you measure degree of creativity, for example? It is much easier to measure someone's height and weight because these are objective measures. When there are no objective measures of something, evaluators have to determine the most accurate and unbiased way to measure the phenomenon of interest.

> Measurement is challenging, particularly in the social sciences, because it is difficult to measure abstract characteristics, such as a person's attitude.

Take the long-term outcome example just presented. There are various ways to measure college and career preparedness, and each way has its pros and cons that have to do with accuracy, validity, and ease of use. Asking participants to self-report on their academic progress is one way to measure college and career preparedness, but this is a less accurate measure than other direct measures, such as grades or academic growth over time. Of course, not only do these vary in accuracy, but they also vary in expense and accessibility.

Measuring if and how a participant uses teamwork, creativity, and problem-solving skills can also be challenging. How do you measure degree of teamwork? Self-report measures, such as asking someone how many times they worked on a team, can provide some information, but it does not really address the quality of their contributions and the effectiveness of the team. Direct measures such as performance on a task that involved teamwork or teacher observations are a preferred way to measure teamwork skills over self-report measures because they do not rely on self-perception. When asked to report on their own behavior, people will typically respond in a biased way, whether intentional or not. Observational measures of a behavior such as teamwork are considered less biased, but are often more difficult to access for out-of-school or summer program planners. An example of an observational measure might be counting of a specific set of behaviors (e.g., using "we language") during a specified period (e.g., a 30-minute duration). Often there are published measurement tools that assist in developing an appropriate evaluation. For example, pre-designed problem-solving assessment tools administered weeks after the program has ended may be a more accurate way of assessing this medium-term outcome.

Finding previously developed measurement tools and assessments requires careful review of the literature and an understanding of how and by whom the assessment was developed. Therefore, not enough can be said about the importance of learning about previous research and evaluations that have been conducted about the youth outcomes you are targeting. Reading reports and attending conferences that teach and share methods of measuring youth outcomes is vital for youth program staff to begin to identify which youth outcomes to evaluate. Many youth outcomes already have established, validated, and reliable ways to evaluate them. Since thinking about methods and measures of outcomes can be overwhelming at first, we suggest you consider using some of the following resources:

- **The What Works Clearinghouse (https://ies.ed.gov/ncee/wwc/).** The What Works Clearinghouse reviews research on different programs, products, practices, and policies in education. The goal is to provide educators with information they need to make evidence-based decisions. They focus on the results from high-quality research to answer the question, "What works in education?"
- **American Camp Association (https://www.acacamps.org/about/who-we-are/ research).** The site contains briefing papers, research blogs, research reports, and more.
- **My Environmental Education Evaluation Resource Assistant (MEERA; http://meera.snre.umich.edu/).** The site contains articles and how-to guides for evaluating outdoor programs for youth and a searchable database of evaluation projects and tools.
- **United Way Out-of-School Time Tools (https://www.unitedway.org/our-impact/focus/education/out-of-school-time/tools).** This site contains articles and learning modules related to a variety of evaluation topics and evaluation tools organized by topic.

Evaluation Planning

How do you go about making an evaluation plan? Here are nine steps to think through before you start undertaking an evaluation of your program. Planning your evaluation in advance, in conjunction with your logic model, will help you manage time and make sure you have the right resources and people to successfully carry out a quality evaluation. It is important to remember that the step-by-step approach presented here might happen differently, or in a different order, in real life. The fictitious example of Camp Sunshine is included to suggest some ways these steps might realistically occur.

Step 1: Establish Evaluation Questions

The first step is to develop good questions that relate to the outcomes of your program, the mission of your organization, and relevant and timely matters for your participants. Remember: what gets measured, gets done! Look to your logic model to decide which processes and/or outcomes to evaluate. To plan an outcomes evaluation, you might choose two or three outcomes to measure rather than evaluate every single possible outcome of your program, and the same applies to a process evaluation. Start small and build up. Talk with key stakeholders in your organization about what they want to know about and why they want to know it. Key stakeholders might include managers or directors, frontline staff, board members, advisory group members, and most importantly, youth and their parents and caregivers. Think about how the results of your evaluation questions will help each of your stakeholder groups.

To reiterate, outcome evaluation questions might relate to short-term changes in participants, such as increased knowledge, change in attitude, or improved skill development. Medium-term outcomes could relate to changes in participants' decisions or behaviors, such as staying in school or reducing drug use. Long-term outcome questions might relate to college completion or adult physical activity. Remember, evaluations that focus on short-term outcomes are the easiest outcomes to logically and empirically attribute to the program.

For example, the evaluation team at Camp Sunshine recognizes that they are new to evaluation and already have a lot to do to prepare for and run camp, so they decided to explore three short-term outcomes, teamwork, creativity, and problem-solving skills, during just one session of camp. Their evaluation question is: Do participants practice at least one 21st century learning skill (teamwork, creativity, or problem-solving) during their time at camp?

What if your evaluation questions suggest methods for which you are not trained or equipped? Consider involving an outside evaluation consultant or researchers from a nearby university. The American Evaluation Association offers a searchable "Find an Evaluator" function at http://www.eval.org/p/cm/ld/fid=108. Here, you can sort by location or key word. To find a researcher from a university, reach out to the university's office of community relations or applied research, or to specific departments such as education, recreation, adolescent psychology, sociology, exercise science, or other areas related to your evaluation questions.

> Evaluations will focus on short-term outcomes because these are the easiest outcomes to logically and empirically attribute to the program.

Step 2: Identify Evaluation Methods

Once you determine the evaluation questions, decide on the best way to answer them. For questions related to medium- or long-term outcomes, consider working with an outside evaluation consultant or university professor to help you determine evaluation methods that will answer your questions with high levels of credibility and trustworthiness. In this section, we focus on evaluating short-term outcomes. Decisions about evaluation methods involve the following:

- Who will be in the sample
- Methods of data collection, including decisions on whether to collect qualitative or quantitative data
- Design of the evaluation

The sample. The first problem is to figure out how many participants will be "enough" to include in your sample and which particular participants to include so that their data will adequately represent the entire group of participants. For example, do you want to evaluate every participant or a sample with an equal number of participants from your service areas or of different ages? Will you collect information from the youth participants, and/or their parents/caregivers, and/or program staff? Although youth are experts at representing their own reality, parents/caregivers, teachers, or program staff may be able to provide assessments of behaviors that are more objective.

Avoiding bias in the sample is a basic tenet of evaluation. This means the evaluator has to make sure the sample is representative of the people for whom conclusions will apply. It means the evaluator cannot choose who is in the sample because they might be more prone to provide positive responses, for example. There are many ways to determine an appropriate sample. All participants of the program could be surveyed, or a random sample could be chosen, where everyone has an equal probability of being selected. These are two common ways to avoid sample bias.

Methods of data collection. As we noted previously, three common methods of collecting data are surveys, interviews, and observations. Just what are data? Data are pieces of numerical, textual, photographic, videographic, or musical information that when combined and analyzed provide knowledge about a phenomenon. Data are empirical evidence of the existence of some phenomenon. Evaluators must decide on what type of data to collect and what it means for how they will analyze the data once collected.

Surveys. Qualitative data are typically words, pictures, or other nonnumerical pieces of information. *Quantitative data* are typically numbers. Many evaluations have a mix of qualitative and quantitative data. For example, a survey might ask participants to respond to a question, "How satisfied were you with the program?" using a response option of 1 = not at all satisfied, 2 = neither satisfied nor unsatisfied, and 3 = very satisfied. These questions might be followed up with an open-ended question asking, "What were you most and least satisfied with?" In this scenario, you could count how many people were satisfied, neutral, and unsatisfied. For each of those responses, you could share two to three representative quotations to highlight each group.

Many surveys will have several quantitative questions with two or three open-ended questions at the end to get at ideas not otherwise represented by the quantitative questions. However, because qualitative data can take a long time to read and analyze, be careful not to ask too many open-ended questions. On the other hand, quantitative data might not be able to measure all aspects of the phenomenon you are evaluating, so consider including at least one open-ended question to elicit other ideas from youth.

Qualitative data typically come from interviews, focus groups, or open-ended survey questions. Quantitative data typically come from closed-ended survey questions. Observations can yield quantitative or qualitative data. Let us look at methods of data collection in more detail.

Surveys can be administered in paper form, verbally, or using computers or mobile devices. Surveys contain some combination of closed-ended questions where respondents are given a set of responses to choose from (e.g., response formats of 1 = strongly disagree to 5 = strongly agree or 1 = yes and 2 =no) and open-ended questions that generate qualitative data (comments and narratives). Evaluators can give surveys directly to participants or they can survey other people such as parents about their youth's experiences in a program. Some benefits and drawbacks of surveys are listed in Table 14.1.

Table 14.1
Survey Benefits and Drawbacks

Benefits
- Can be done quickly and can collect data from large numbers of people
- Are familiar to most people from whom you wish to collect data
- Can be anonymous

Drawbacks
- Might miss information important to your participants
- Can feel to youth like taking a test
- Can be difficult to design
- Relies on people's willingness and ability to accurately report about themselves

---

Some tips on writing good survey questions include the following:

- Use as few questions as possible to get at the essence of your evaluation purpose.
- Consider the cognitive needs and developmental stages of your respondents and adapt reading level and instructions accordingly.
- Test the survey with a small group of people similar to your potential respondents to make sure the questions make sense and give you the type of information you are looking for.
- Place easy questions at the beginning, harder or sensitive questions in the middle, and demographic questions at the end, unless demographic information is crucial to your evaluation purpose.
- Be careful about biasing respondents' answers, such as frontloading your question with something like, "People love this program! Tell us how much you love it!" because that leads the respondent into wanting to please you by aligning their answers to "loving the program."
- Do not use double-barreled questions by including the words "and" or "or" because you will not know which part is being answered by the respondent. An example

is "How satisfied were you with the program and the staff?" If a respondent was satisfied with the staff but not the program; how would the respondent answer?

- Make sure all possible answers are covered but that they do not overlap. For example, if you ask, "How many times did you come to the program this month?" and offer answers for "once, twice, 2-4 times, 6-7 times," the answers for people who came twice overlapped, and there are no options for people who did not come or who came 8 or more times.
- Include open-ended questions only if you have the time and understanding of how to analyze qualitative data.
- Thank the respondents for their time and effort.
- Consider using SurveyMonkey or SurveyGizmo or other online survey companies. They typically provide you with suggestions and advice for survey creation.

The following are useful resources for writing good survey questions:

- http://www.quickanddirtytips.com/education/grammar/how-to-write-good-survey-questions
- https://www.qualtrics.com/blog/good-survey-questions/
- https://www.surveymonkey.com/mp/writing-survey-questions/
- https://www.surveygizmo.com/survey-blog/10-tips-for-crafting-good-survey-questions/

Interviews. Interviews are verbal, structured, semi-structured, or unstructured discussions with youth. Interviews can also include interviews in which a group of 4–10 youth respond to questions and play off each other's answers (called a focus group). You should develop interview questions to align with your evaluation purpose and consider the developmental levels of your participants. Like surveys, think about how you will select participants, how many interviews you need, and how they will be representative of your program participants. Some benefits and drawbacks of interview questions are listed in Table 14.2.

Table 14.2
Interview Benefits and Drawbacks

Benefits
- Can feel like conversations
- Are useful for youth who might have a hard time reading or completing a survey
- Can provide rich insights
- Can be recorded to listen to later

Drawbacks
- Need for care in designing interview questions
- Takes a lot of time to analyze responses
- Lack of anonymity
- Time needed to build rapport with participants or avoid bias from preexisting relationships with participants

---

Interview tips include the following:

- If you do not know participants, build in time to develop rapport with them so they get to know you and feel comfortable answering questions. You might also train someone else such as a frontline staff member or former participant to facilitate the interview if they are more familiar to participants.
- If you do know participants, encourage them to answer honestly and assure them that their responses will not be tied back to their names.
- Avoid questions that can be answered by a simple yes or no.
- Use questions that start with "what" or "where" or "when" to elicit descriptive information.
- Use questions that start with "why" or "how" or "does anyone have an opinion that is different?" to elicit deeper answers.
- Avoid saying things like "good" or "that makes sense" in response to participants' comments. These types of comments may make the participants feel you are judging their responses and respondents may start to form their answers to please you. Thus, keep your responses as neutral as possible, such as "I see," or "uh huh," or "thank you for sharing your thoughts."
- Ask easy or less personal questions at the beginning and more sensitive questions later.
- Include probing or follow-up questions such as, "What else can you say about that?," or "Please say more," or "Why is that important to you?"
- A good final question is "What else would you like to share?"

Observations. Observations are formal or informal ways of evaluating a setting or people's behaviors. For formal or structured observations, a checklist or guide is typically used. For informal observations, the evaluator typically considers the evaluation question and looks for evidence related to the phenomenon being evaluated. Some of the benefits and drawbacks of observations are listed in Table 14.3. Examples of youth program aspects to observe include structured and informal activities, administrative practices, the learning and activity climates, physical space, the degree to which the program is implemented as planned (fidelity), and the degree of youth engagement.

Tips for observations include the following:

- Be specific about what you are looking for in youths' behaviors or in a youth setting.
- Consider analyzing program documents, materials, archives, or artifacts.
- Plan for a lot of time for analysis and report writing of your findings.
- Explain the purpose of your observations to youth and program staff if appropriate. While you want people to act naturally, it is also important that they are aware of your purpose and consent to being observed.
- If you are using other people to conduct the observations, training is essential. Training should include how to conduct the observation. Practice sessions should occur before the actual data collection.

- If there is more than one observer, observers should calibrate how to rate or code behaviors so they are coding or rating the same behavior in the same way (termed *reliability*).

Table 14.3
Observation Benefits and Drawbacks

Benefits
- Can gather a lot of information about program quality and use it for program improvement processes
- Does not rely on self-report
- Does not require youth participants to do anything (which can be helpful for youth who might find difficulty in completing a survey or interview)
- Does not take away from regularly scheduled program time

Drawbacks
- The need to train observers
- Making sure the observers have a high degree of reliability in their rating or coding
- Managing the relationship between the observer and participants
- The lack of participants' perspectives

Other data collection methods. Other methods include photovoice, most significant change, and creative approaches such as using art, improvisation, or games to collect data. If your program serves older youth, consider asking them to be the evaluators. "Participatory" approaches give youth a sense of voice and might even yield more insights than traditional surveys. Youth participants can help identify the evaluation question, brainstorm methods, administer surveys or facilitate focus groups, and analyze data—all of which can give them a great learning opportunity while providing useful evaluation information.

In planning the way data will be collected, it is necessary to be realistic about your financial, time, and resource constraints. Always start small and allow plenty of time to practice and learn from your mistakes. That way, you can build comfort and capacity for evaluation in your program over time, and you can experience some successes that will help motivate people in your program to continue to evaluate. In most cases, it will be necessary to pilot test your data collection procedures to work out logistical, comprehension, or other unexpected issues.

> In planning the way data will be collected, it is necessary to be realistic about your financial, time, and resource constraints.

Evaluation design. Choosing the method of data collection goes hand in hand with choosing an evaluation design. A design for collecting data includes considering the

timing of the data collection and ways to avoid bias so that if changes in outcomes are found, they can be attributed directly to the program. Entire courses are offered on evaluation design, and we will focus on two designs in particular that relate to collecting quantitative data via surveys. Recall that in this section we focus on evaluating only short-term outcomes.

Pre-post evaluation method. A pre-post evaluation method is a common and useful way to demonstrate that participants changed their knowledge, attitudes, skills, or behavior over time and that those changes might have had something to do with the program. A pre- and post-test design is where participants of a program complete a survey prior to the program and again after the program is finished. The strength of this design is that evaluators can assess changes that occur during the program. The challenge with this design is that anything could have caused the change in knowledge, attitudes, or skills. An even stronger way to attribute changes to your program is to use a comparison group, such as assessing youth from a waitlist for the program being evaluated. Doing so can help control for other factors that might have influenced the changes, such as new teachers at school or the natural growth and maturation of the participants. If the evaluator randomly assigned participants to the "treatment" or "control" group, the design would be a lot stronger, but this type of design is logistically more difficult to carry out in the real world. Many evaluators use pre- and post-tests to provide some information about whether or not outcomes were achieved. Coupled with process evaluation, this is a reasonable way to assess program success and ideas for strengthening the program.

Retrospective pre-test. Another type of design that is useful is a retrospective pre-test, which is helpful when program participants enter a program at different times during the course of the program (see box below). Camp Sunshine has limited resources available for evaluating 21st century learning outcomes, so staff decide to use a survey to explore their evaluation question. Because the camp session is short, and their campers are 11 years old and above, they feel a retrospective pre-test is a good option. They select an existing tool and add some open-ended questions that ask campers to describe a specific time at camp when they practiced teamwork, creativity, or problem solving. To pilot test the survey, camp staff give the survey to a small group of campers the session prior to their targeted evaluation session and fix the wording in the surveys that campers found confusing.

> ## Retrospective Pre-Test
>
> Hold on! In our program, we have kids who enter at different times, so it would be hard for us to do pre- and post-tests because we do not have someone to administer the surveys to youth all the time, and it would be awkward because we want youth to engage in the program right away, not take a test.

In a retrospective pre-test, participants reflect on their knowledge, attitudes, beliefs, behaviors, or skills before the program compared to after the program. Table 14.4 provides a list of benefits and drawbacks to using retrospective pre-testing.

Examples of retrospective pre-test questions include the following:

> How much, if any, has your experience as a camper in this camp changed you in each of the following ways?
> a) Getting to know people who I might want to become friends with
> b) Finding ways to meet people who I want to be friends with

Response options included "decreased," "did not increase or decrease," "increased a little," "increased some," and "increased a lot."

Another way to ask retrospective pre-test questions is to ask participants to answer two separate but related questions. This requires a little bit more complex thinking than the previous example, so it is generally not recommended for young children or youth with cognitive disabilities. Here is an example from American Camp Association's Youth Outcomes Battery (2011) to illustrate this line of questioning.

> a) I am good at getting to know people who I might want to become friends with (response options included false, somewhat false, a little false, a little true, somewhat true, and true).

b) Is the above statement more or less true today than before camp? (response options included a lot less, somewhat less, a little less, a little more, somewhat more, and a lot more).

Table 14.4
Retrospective Pre-Test Survey Benefits and Drawbacks

Benefits
- Better than not doing evaluation at all or doing only post-tests
- Can be administered just once
- Can be used when traditional pre-tests are not possible
- Provides data that, with other supporting data, can be used to evaluate the effectiveness of a professional development intervention
- Less likely to bother participants who do not like being put in the role of students or research subjects required to complete both pre-tests and post-tests
- Unlike traditional pre-tests, does not risk negatively impacting intervention effectiveness by possibly introducing terms and concepts before participants are ready for them
- Can be used for most youth aged 10 and older because they have more of an ability to reflect on themselves in the past
- Avoids the response shift bias (e.g., Pre-test: How much do you know about sex? A lot! Post-test: How much do you know about sex? Not much!)

Drawbacks
- Desire by participants to show positive change
- Responses can be biased by errors in self-report and memory recall
- Possibility of fabricated and biased responses
- Challenges traditional methodological logic because both pre-data and post-data are collected after the intervention
- Can be perceived as less rigorous, and therefore less convincing, than other approaches
- Not good for youth under age 10 or with cognitive issues that affect their ability to think about themselves in the past

Adapted from http://www.hfrp.org/evaluation/the-evaluation-exchange/issue-archive/evaluation-methodology/the-retrospective-pretest-an-imperfect-but-useful-tool

Step 3: Engage Staff

In many youth program evaluations, frontline staff carry out the evaluation, especially administering surveys. So how can staff get motivated and enthusiastic about evaluation? Youth development professionals would benefit by knowing if they are actually making a difference and so evaluation may be of interest to them. Senior staff can help younger colleagues ignite their passions by helping them articulate their questions about the program and its potential effects on youth.

An "evaluation champion" can also help with evaluation efforts in terms of getting it done, and getting it done well. An evaluation champion can be a staff member who is excited about evaluation and is motivated to be a contact person or take the lead. Institutional rewards are particularly helpful in developing and sustaining champions. For example, management might give the evaluation champion special recognition, or a pay increase or some other form of appreciation. In addition, if responsibilities for evaluation are written into the job description, it is also more likely to get done. Of course, training for the evaluation will take time, so plan for evaluation champions to spend time reviewing the materials or tools and planning data collection. Engaging in evaluation is one of several professional competencies for youth development professionals. Engaging staff in evaluation can provide staff with transferable skills necessary for proficiency in the field of youth development.

> To engage the cabin counselors who will be administering the survey, the Camp Sunshine evaluation team dedicates time during staff training to discuss 21st century learning and why it is important at camp. Staff then brainstorm what 21st century learning looks like, plan activities that encourage campers to use teamwork, creativity, and problem-solving, and plan the survey process.

Step 4: Plan Data Collection

Planning data collection for specific youth programs involves much care and thought before actually collecting the data. Following are some logistical tips for planning data collection.

- Schedule data collection
- Plan for a pilot test of your data collection
- Order/prepare supplies
- Test anything involving technology, such as recording devices
- Ensure space conducive to data collection prior to data collection
- Train staff (all staff, even those not directly administering, so they are aware of the evaluation activities)
- Plan for youth not participating (due to random sampling selection or youth who do not have parent/caregiver permission to participate in evaluation activities), such as offering games or crafts in another space at the youth program
- Plan for special accommodations such as reading or listening support
- Plan ways to make it fun
- Plan incentives (if appropriate)

Ethics. One important part of planning an evaluation is thinking through ethical issues involving collecting data from human study participants. Ethics affect many parts of an evaluation, from the choice of participants in the sample to how you communicate your findings. One important ethical concern is getting informed consent. Informed consent provides participants (and parents/caregivers if necessary) with information necessary for them to decide if they want to participate. In youth programs with people under age 18, parent/caregivers must give consent, which can be active (i.e., signing a form of consent) or passive (i.e., only signing a form if they do not wish their child to participate). Regardless, in all cases, youth must also provide their assent to participate in the evaluation.

> While engaging staff in the evaluation plan during staff training, the Camp Sunshine evaluation team asked staff to consider the logistics of administering the survey to campers. Through this discussion, they practiced their instructions and planned accommodations for campers who might need help. They also decided to keep the surveys anonymous and include in their instructions to campers that no one could match their answers to their identity because no personal information was being collected. If campers did not want to complete the survey, they could work on a word puzzle staff would have available.

Evaluators should write the consent and assent forms using friendly, nonacademic language to explain the evaluation. Information about an evaluation for consent and assent purposes should include the following. We will consider some of these topics in greater detail next.

- How people are selected to participate in the evaluation (e.g., were they selected for a specific reason or were they randomly selected from a larger pool of people)
- Explanation of evaluation procedures and what participants will be asked to do
- A statement that consent is an ongoing process and that participants can decide at any time to stop or decide not to answer specific questions on the evaluation, without penalty

Evaluators should especially consider potential emotional, mental, or physical harm that could arise from participation in the evaluation.

- A statement about what will be done with the data when they are collected
- A statement about who will have access to the data
- A statement about how long the data will be kept
- Assurance that parents/caregivers of youth do not personally gain from their children's evaluation participation and that the decision to whether to participate will not affect the relationship between youth or parents/caregivers and the organization or agency
- Benefits and risks to participation, and any steps that will be taken to reduce the risks

Evaluators should especially consider potential emotional, mental, or physical harm that could arise from participation in the evaluation. Steps to manage these risks include the following:

- Providing easily accessible support to participants in the event of discomfort or harm
- Weighing benefits (potential social value and knowledge) against risks to participants
- Taking precautions and engaging in careful planning when evaluators visit study participants in the field or at their homes to ensure physical and emotional safety of the data collectors and study participant
- Fairly selecting participants so that risks are distributed among various groups
- Ensuring that vulnerable populations are not made to bear all risks of participation, and their participation must be accompanied by benefits
- Ensuring that risks are reasonable and evaluation must respond to the needs of the population in which the evaluation is conducted
- Avoiding coercion when requesting consent and assent

> Evaluations should safeguard participants' privacy in terms of what will be done with the data and who will see it.

Finally, evaluations should safeguard participants' privacy in terms of what will be done with the data and who will see it. Note that evaluation data can be either confidential or anonymous. If the evaluation team needs to match a youth's identity with his or her responses (e.g., for a pre- and post-test), the data are considered confidential but not anonymous. If the evaluation team collects data with no identifying information (e.g., name, age, date of birth, home address, etc.), data are anonymous and no one could ever match youths' responses to their identities. The following are promising practices for assuring the privacy of the data.

- Do not ask for identifying information unless it is essential to answer the evaluation question. Identifying information could be necessary if the evaluator is collecting pre- and post-test data.
- Balance the level of confidentiality with the level of the risk involved.
- Protect identifying information if it is collected.
- Encrypt files when sharing personally identifying information.
- Shred hard copies after the time specified to retain documents or delete permanently data stored in electronic form after an agreed to and specified length of time (e.g., one year after data are collected and stored).
- Keep hard copies of consent and assent forms in secure locations.

Sometimes research or evaluation projects must be approved by an outside group, such as a research advisory committee or an institutional review board. The purpose is to provide assurance that the project meets ethical standards. Check with your organization or agency director for guidance about whether or not you need to gain formal ethical approval.

Participatory research. Consider involving youth in evaluation as partners, rather than, or in addition to, participants. Participatory evaluation is an especially good strategy when working with youth from vulnerable groups. In participatory evaluation, youth help plan evaluation questions and methods, collect and analyze data, and present findings and recommendations for changes. Following are a few resources with advice on how to engage youth as evaluators:

- Act For Youth (http://www.actforyouth.net/youth_development/evaluation/ype. cfm)
- Youth Participatory Evaluation: Strategies for Engaging Young People by Kim Sabo Flores (ISBN: 978-0-7879-8392-5)
- Case studies and tips from the American Evaluation Association (http://aea365. org/blog/tag/youth-participatory-evaluation/)

Step 5: Collect Data

When collecting data, it is important to work with frontline staff to determine a good time and place to collect data. Down time, waiting time, or after a meal can be good times for youth to complete surveys or participate in interviews because they won't miss any fun activities, can be more focused, and can easily transition to other activities. Data collection can also be integrated into program activities. For example, at The Hole in the Wall Gang Camp, participants in the Hero's Journey wilderness program completed a survey with open-ended questions about their identities at the beginning and again at the end of the session. Both times, staff had planned a reflection activity as part of the program. Immediately after the first survey, staff asked participants to consider what they had written in the reflection activity and share anything that surprised them about what they had written or that they wanted the group to know about them. After the second survey, staff gave the participants their responses from their first survey and the group reflected on and discussed how their identities changed over the session. Tying data collection to program activities helped further the goals of the program while providing evaluators with valuable pre-post program data and keeping participants focused on the program.

Data collection at Camp Sunshine goes as planned…with a few exceptions. The entire staff—evaluation team and cabin staff responsible for administering the surveys—spent time during a brief meeting discussing the process and noting what worked and what did not work for the future. All surveys were stored in a locked cabinet in the staff office until they were entered into the computer, at which point they will be shredded.

Note that this is an example of data that were neither confidential nor anonymous. Consider in this case what confidential means. How do you think the camp participants felt about sharing their deep reflections about themselves with others? Do you think that they trusted the other campers as well as the staff to not talk about what they revealed? Perhaps campers only shared surface-level reflections for fear of another camper or staff telling someone else what they said. This is a good example of the type of evaluation that raises numerous ethical and data collection issues that must be taken into account when planning and conducting an evaluation.

Be sure to provide participants with something to do while they are waiting to be interviewed or after they finish, such as games or activities they can do on their own. Consider incentives or thank you gifts for participating, such as gift certificates or snacks. After data are collected, make sure the data set is secured in a safe location and backed up electronically.

Step 6: Analyze Data

Finally, you have data! Now what? First, "clean" and organize your data. Check for any outliers or errors, such as youth who report their age as 1,000. For recorded qualitative data, transcribe them yourself or use a transcription service. You will want to make sure you write down every word and every "um" or indicate when there was a significant pause in the dialogue. Be sure also to include the questions and prompts from the interviewer so the transcript reflects the exact dialog that took place.

> First, "clean" and organize your data.

For quantitative data not collected electronically, enter data from written forms (e.g., questionnaires or survey instruments) into a spreadsheet (e.g., Excel) and conduct basic descriptive statistics on each question, such as finding out the mean or average, range, and frequency of each response. It is also very useful to calculate the percent of respondents who have a certain characteristic (e.g., age range) on a variable of interest. For example, maybe you want to look at whether there is a difference in satisfaction given one's age. In this case, you would calculate the percent of youth aged 12 to 14 who were very satisfied compared to youth aged 15 or 16. This type of analysis can be done in Excel and there are many free tutorials online to show you how to do descriptive statistics.

Remember to reverse-score any questions that are negatively worded. Sometimes evaluators will write a question worded in a different manner to the rest of the questions to determine whether a respondent is reading the items carefully. For example, in a scale developed to measure happiness, three items may be similar in structure to this: "I am always happy." The negatively worded item would like something like this: "Lots of things make me unhappy." If the response scale was 1 = totally disagree to 5 = totally agree, you can see that if someone answered "5," it would mean something different in terms of degree of happiness.

For qualitative data, evaluators will assign a code (term or phrase) to a sentence or few words that indicate the general idea of that phrase or sentence. The idea is to come up with underlying themes from what the respondents said or wrote. One way to do this is to color-code similar ideas using a marker or stickie notes. Other people use a computer program such as Microsoft Excel or Word. Consider inviting someone else to look at your data to see if they also come up with the same codes. Using two or more people for interpretation makes your results more trustworthy because if multiple people come to the same conclusion about the meaning of something, the meaning is more credible.

> The Camp Sunshine evaluation team commits to looking at their data the very week it is collected—they know that if they leave it until the end of summer, they might forget about it completely. They use a computer program to run basic statistics on the survey scores, and engage a team that involves two cabin counselors to analyze the qualitative data from the open-ended questions. Throughout the process, they discussed their biases—both in terms of their impact on the survey design, and on the results.

For all types of data, make sure you answer each evaluation question when you run analyses so that you do not get lost in numbers. Take the previous logic model discussion that identified possible evaluation questions based on each level of outcome. Suppose your question was: "Did campers' teamwork scores improve from pre- to post-test?" Note that this would have been based on a short-term outcome identified by the developers of the program. To answer that question, for example, you might calculate the percentage of youth who showed improved scores in knowledge and compare them to those who showed no improvement or a negative change. Alternatively, you could calculate the average score of the outcome for all participants for the pre-test and post-test and compare the averages. You could then examine the scores of different groups in your sample and report averages, such as by gender, months in the program, family type, or other demographic variables and look for any notable difference between groups of participants on their scores. This information can help you better understand differences in outcomes for different groups of youth and help generate questions with your staff about what staff attitudes or practices or organizational procedures might be related to those differences.

In all analyses, consider biases that might have occurred because of the way questions were worded, or your understanding of the meaning conveyed in responses to open-ended questions, or your own desires for the program to show positive changes for youth. Also, consider situational factors that might have affected results, such as post-tests or retrospective pre-tests conducted at the end of a program when participants might be particularly happy (or sad). Finally, note any problems or lessons learned that could be fixed for future data collection.

Step 7: Visualize Data

Plan time toward the end of your analysis to visualize your data in different ways. As humans, we are visual people and can gain insights quickly when information is presented in a chart or graph, rather than as a row of numbers. Bar charts will work for most basic data from youth program evaluations. Line charts are good to show changes over time and are also frequently used. If you serve youth over a certain geographic area, maps are good ways to show what types of youth you serve, where they come from, and how many are served.

When planning how to best present your data there are a few things to consider. These include the following:

- Who is the audience? How much knowledge do they have?
- What is the purpose of your visualization? To tell a story to convince or persuade? Describe results of an evaluation or needs assessment?
- What format will you use? Printed brochure, PowerPoint presentation, video, website?

Camp Sunshine does not have a lot of resources to dedicate to a fancy report, so they decide to focus on a few effective visualizations of their results. Their audience is primarily the funder who is interested in 21st century learning, so the purpose of their visualizations is to convey a story about how Camp Sunshine promotes 21st century learning skills. Ultimately, this story will help secure grant funding for the program, so the team decides to format the visualizations in a way that will fit within the grant application template.

Typically, visualizations have a catchy headline and clearly stated purpose, perhaps with the research questions included. Include a few words of related literature to justify why you did the evaluation, a brief mention of the methods, and then the presentation of data, followed by an interpretation and conclusion. Ideas for future evaluation may also be included.

Numerous data visualization tools have come to market from software services such as Tableau, Fusion Charts, Google Charts, and Visual.ly to help better display quantitative data (see, for example https://google-developers.appspot.com/chart/ and https://google-developers.appspot.com/chart/interactive/docs/gallery). For qualitative data, some online options include Wordle, Tagxedo, TagCroud, and WordMosaic. Refer to http://betterevaluation.org/evaluation-options/wordcloud for ideas, guides, and tips for using word clouds. For any of these tools, make sure you understand the pitfalls of using the particular method for data display!

Other resources about visualizing data include those listed below:

- Stephanie Evergreen (http://stephanieevergreen.com)
- Ann K. Emery (http://annkemery.com)
- Chris Lysy (http://diydatadesign.com)
- Jon Schwabish (https://policyviz.com)

Step 8: Report to Stakeholders

Ideally you identified what your stakeholders wanted to know before you conducted your evaluation, so in this step you will decide how best to present this information in a way that it is useful. Evaluators often present findings to internal audiences, such as staff or youth, who then work to improve the program through program modifications or training. Evaluators also present findings to external audiences, such as current or potential funders, policymakers, or parents/caregivers of future participants, with the purpose of providing information to make funding and resource allocation decisions about the worthiness of a program for youth or to market to future participants.

As you embark on evaluation efforts, remember that every setting is different.

For example, a health-care related funder will want to know about evaluation results related to program participants' health, such as physical activity or nutrition. People who read a newsletter about the program would want to know how many participants were served or what programs were provided, and will want to see easy-to-read charts and graphs highlighting the outcomes gained by participants. Parents and caregivers will want to know how youth improved and what that might mean for their futures. Board or program owners will want to know if the program is achieving its mission. Prospective funders or supporters will want to know that programmers engaged in a formal process of evaluation, the results, and needed improvements. Youth and both new and experienced frontline staff who are intimately involved in the program want to see the bigger picture of their engagement. However, as you embark on evaluation efforts, remember that every setting is different, so consider reaching out to a few members of your different stakeholder groups to talk about what they value and want to see from your program evaluation. Doing this before you begin the evaluation will help you decide what outcomes to focus on and what data to collect.

In addition to their grant application, Camp Sunshine staff decide to present their evaluation findings to their board in the form of a report. As a team, they discuss the story they want to tell, and discuss ways to present this story in a concise, yet compelling format. Board members are busy, so a short (1–2 page) report, with effective visuals, seems like an effective way to engage their board in the results. They craft a report and share it with a member of the evaluation team to ensure the story is accurate and reflects what actually happened in the program.

There are many ways to report to stakeholders, and we have already touched on the need for good data visualization. Reports can be written as a document or executive summary, or even an infographic. Written reports can be sent to stakeholders or posted on a website. Sometimes evaluators or programmers hold in-person meetings and present the findings more conversationally. These presentations can be especially effective if there are negative or potentially confusing findings that need a deeper explanation. Depending on the audience and the purpose of the evaluation report, evaluators can make meetings visually interesting and interactive, and gameify results, such as doing "quizzes" or placing key findings in fortune cookies or Hershey's kisses. Some evaluators have hosted a data party (see, for example, https://www.acacamps. org/news-publications/blogs/research-360/have-data-party-share-evaluation-results). However you choose to share your findings, be sure to ask stakeholders what they learned and what they still want to know.

In your reporting, craft the story or narrative about what happened to your program participants. Explain how the findings were interpreted and the conclusions that emerged from the evaluation. Evaluators should always remember to acknowledge the limitations of the evaluation and recommendations for future evaluations. Include implications for program decisions such as deciding to start, stop, or continue program resources or activities.

Caution! Choose your words carefully and be precise. Be careful about using the following words in sharing about your evaluation.

- **"Cause."** As in, this program *caused* improvements in self-worth. Hedge your attribution of the program to improvements in participants by using phrases such as "this program seems to have influenced campers' friendship skills" or "Youth reported greater academic confidence, thus there is some evidence for the value of the program."
- **"Impact."** As in, this program had major *impacts* on youth. "Impact" is a precise word in science and is used when conducing long-term outcome studies, which are usually done by researchers and not youth program staff. Instead, use "associate with" or "showed signs of improvement."
- **"Prove."** Evaluators or researchers cannot *prove* anything; they can only disprove.
- **"Most."** As in, *most* of the program participants improved. What is meant by most? That is a vague term; is it more than half, or three-quarters, or over 90%? Be precise.

Step 9: Plan Program Improvements

Internally oriented evaluation for program improvement can be very different from evaluation for external stakeholders. Figure 14.2 depicts the relationship between these types of evaluations and factors associated with the evaluations. For example, often these stakeholders are funders, parents, or community members, so there might be pressure to provide evaluation results that show your program achieves its outcomes and approaches perfection. Evaluation done to demonstrate positive outcomes is stressful and feels like "high stakes" because of the money or support often tied to it. Evaluations that demonstrate program improvement (although still focused on achieving stated outcomes), on the other hand, are equally important, but not as stressful because internal program staff use it to make changes to the program over time. For this reason, program improvement tends to feel low-stakes because the goal is to understand how the program works and why, not to secure critical funding or partnerships.

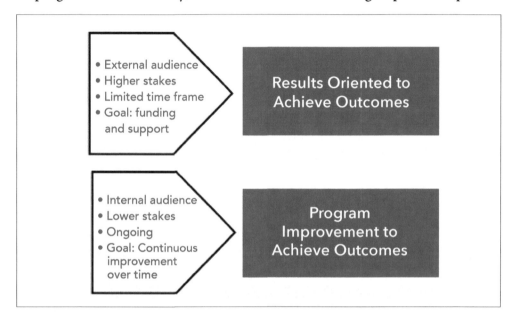

Figure 14.2. Different Uses of Evaluation Findings

Camp Sunshine staff are excited to celebrate their first evaluation project, but know their work is not done until they have a plan for using what they learned in the future. They decide to host an informal planning meeting—including pizza—so everyone feels comfortable discussing the results and sharing ideas for how to promote 21st century learning in their programs, as well as how they can improve their evaluations in the future. The group is careful to document their thinking, and makes a plan to share their recommendations with the board and the administrative team.

Once the results of the evaluation are complete and the evaluation team has debriefed and processed the information, the next step is to convene key leadership to discuss the evaluation implications for future programming and decision-making, as well as to discuss the evaluation process itself. These discussions will reflect on the findings and implications of the evaluation, and perhaps feedback from external stakeholders. Discussions will also focus on the evaluation process and possible changes to get better information next time. Next steps include brainstorming with frontline staff on the meanings of the findings and how staff members can use evaluation findings in their work, such as to better understand youth needs and experiences, and identify realistic improvements and priorities in program, policy, and/or administrative practices.

These types of meetings require preparation, especially when meeting with frontline staff who might be sensitive to being evaluated. Therefore, prior to any evaluation being conducted, establish a culture of learning so staff members can feel comfortable evaluating and being evaluated. Use challenges or low-scoring areas as learning opportunities to improve.

In the end, you will want to get the following from your evaluation:

- Ideas on how to better intentionally plan programs to achieve specific outcomes for participants
- What policy decisions to make or modify
- Areas for staff training
- Evidence for you to advocate for your program
- Material to build communications about program improvements to stakeholders

Conclusion

The journey to evaluation starts with cultivating a culture of inquiry. Ask yourself questions such as: What does my program do for participants? What changes do I expect to see after people participate in my program? What is the meaning and worth of what we do? Once you identify meaningful questions, you can find many avenues for answering them. Once you answer your questions, you get to share the story of your program with all of your stakeholders. Doing so will lead to more support and involvement in your program and ultimately better experiences for youth.

Discussion Questions

If you work or volunteer in a youth-serving organization, consider your organization as the setting for these questions. If not, choose an organization in which you are interested or would like to work or volunteer for.

1. What fears might you or your coworkers have about evaluation?
2. What do people familiar with your program want to know more about?
3. How could youth in your program get involved in evaluation?
4. What youth outcomes would you most like to know more about?
5. Which methods would resonate most with your program's youth? (e.g., survey, observation, participatory, etc.).
6. What are evaluation-related ethical concerns specific to your youth program?

Assignments

1. Which youth outcomes are most important to your organization or an organization you admire? Find a survey online that addresses one of the outcomes or develop one yourself.
2. Write five outcome survey questions for parents of youth in a youth program.
3. Find a youth program logic model (do a Google Image search for "youth program logic model") and write (a) a process evaluation plan and (b) an outcome evaluation plan.

Evaluation Resources

1. American Evaluation Association (http://eval.org). The American Evaluation Association offers free and members-only resources to learn about evaluation, such as community forums, videos, journal articles, blog posts, and much more. AEA offers "topical interest groups" such as Youth-Focused Evaluation, Disabilities and Underrepresented Populations, Nonprofits and Foundations, and many more.
2. Better Evaluation (http://www.betterevaluation.org/en). An international collaboration to improve evaluation practice and theory by sharing and generating information about options (methods or processes) and approaches.
3. American Camp Association (https://www.acacamps.org/about/who-we-are/research). ACA research efforts center on a two-fold approach that 1) advances the knowledge about the value of the camp experience and 2) enhances the business acumen of professionals involved in the camp industry. These approaches allow for the development of tools, information, and resources that address current societal issues such as positive youth development in camp and other out-of-school time settings, youth outcomes, workforce development, as well as business issues around industry benchmarks, staff training, and quality program improvement. ACA research efforts result in a variety of tested evaluation and research tools, training resources, trend reports, and scholarly as well as practical application publications.
4. Henderson, K. A., Bialeschki, M. D., & Browne, L. P. (2017). *Evaluating recreation services: Making enlightened decisions* (4th ed.). Urbana, IL: Sagamore–Venture Publishing.
5. Patton, M. Q. (2008). *Utilization-focused evaluation* (4th ed.). Thousand Oaks, CA: Sage.
6. Finding evaluation instruments
   a) Children, Youth, and Families (https://cyfar.org/search_evaluation_instruments) and common measures (https://cyfar.org/ilm_common_measures)
   b) The Forum for Youth Investment: From Soft Skills to Hard Data: Measuring Youth Program Outcomes (http://forumfyi.org/content/soft-skills-hard-data-) and Measuring Youth Program Quality: A Guide to Assessment Tools (http://forumfyi.org/files/MeasuringYouthProgramQuality_2ndEd.pdf)

c) Social-Emotional Learning Assessment Measures for Middle School Youth (http://www.casel.org/wp-content/uploads/2016/01/DAP-Raikes-Foundation-Review-1.pdf)

d) Guide Star Platinum's Common Results Catalog (https://learn.guidestar.org/hubfs/Platinum/GuideStar_Common_Results_Catalog_April_20161.pdf?t=1461000269486&utm_source=August+2016+Point+K+newsletter&utm_campaign=Newsletter+2016-8&utm_medium=email)

e) Instrumental Research (https://instrumentalresearch.com/)

f) Assessments and rubrics for observations (http://www.schrockguide.net/assessment-and-rubrics.html)

g) Resilience Research Centre Evaluation Tool Basket (http://www.resilienceproject.org/evaluation/toolbasket)

h) Tools for Evaluating Youth Programs (https://www.childwelfare.gov/topics/systemwide/youth/outcomes/tools/)

i) Informal Science (http://www.informalscience.org/evaluation/evaluation-tools-instruments)

j) Harvard Family Research Project (http://www.hfrp.org/out-of-school-time/publications-resources/measurement-tools-for-evaluating-out-of-school-time-programs-an-evaluation-resource2)

References

American Camp Association. (2011). American Camp Association Youth Outcomes Battery. Retrieved from https://www.acacamps.org/resource-library/research/aca-youth-outcomes-battery

Sabatelli, R. M., Anderson, S. A., & LaMonte, V. A. (2005). *Assessing outcomes in child and youth programs: A practical handbook.* Hartford, CT: State of Connecticut, Office of Policy and Management. Retrieved from http://www.unitedwaymatsu.org/docs/AssessingOutcomesChildYouthPrograms.pdf

Chapter 15

Reducing Attrition from Youth Programs

Through Structuring Deep, Valued, and Impactful Experiences for Youth

Gary D. Ellis, Andrew Lacanienta, and Patti A. Freeman

Prologue

A lanky 12-year-old boy strode to the back of the queue of his basketball teammates, just inside mid-court. He began waiting for his turn to get the basketball, dribble to the goal and shoot a lay-up. His team, the Sammy City Sharks, had been practicing once per week for two weeks, and was now warming up for its first competition of the season.

As the boy waited, he glanced at his teammates. He was starting to get to know them. One was a talented athlete who had excelled in other sports and was eager to learn basketball skills. Another was a very timid youth.

His parents had enrolled him in the program even though he did not want to play. Yet another had the habit of picking on others, berating them for mistakes, and making fun of failed efforts to dribble, pass, shoot, and defend. However, even though he knew none of his teammates well, he had learned that most were much like him.

Over the past few seasons, each of their parents had enrolled them in an array of structured experiences: football, soccer, swimming, piano, band, chorus, and dance. Some attended after-school programs and others were involved in 4-H clubs and camps. Almost all members of the Sharks were relatively new to basketball; they were giving the sport a try. The league was sponsored by the local parks and recreation department, and the director of youth sports had organized this particular group of participants into the Sharks. Under the direction of a patient and passionate volunteer coach (a parent), the kids were beginning to learn the fundamental skills of basketball. It had been fun so far.

A loud "whoop" from the opposite end of the court seized the volunteers' attention. The opposing team had arrived. Instead of being assembled by the youth sports director, this opposing team had signed up as an intact team. They played in multiple leagues across three different cities. They used games such as this one as practice sessions for the highly competitive league that most significantly challenged their abilities. The "whoop" was part of the team's pre-game ritual. Soon, those players were involved in a series of elaborately choreographed passing, running, defending, and shooting drills that not only served to stretch their muscles and increase their blood flow, but also to impress anyone watching and intimidate opponents. This team was obviously extremely experienced and very talented. Everyone in the gym knew this was going to be a blow out. The novice and intermediate players that comprised the Sammy City Sharks had little chance for success.

Our lanky 12-year-old cast his eyes to the floor. "This isn't fun," he thought. "I would much rather be surfing the web or exchanging text messages with my friends."

Forty-five minutes later, the game was over. The Sharks lost by a score of 68-12. The winning team completed their celebration ritual, and then, showing no enthusiasm, and according to league policy, they shook hands with each member of the team they had so thoroughly defeated. The Sharks were humiliated. The 12-year-old boy's father tried to console him. He reminded his son that the opposing team was more experienced, and then he offered yet another set of suggestions about ways to improve. However, the boy never set foot in that gym again. Instead, he became a statistic, one of the 70% of youth who drop out of organized sports before age 13 (Miner, 2016).

Introduction

While the specific people and setting of the preceding story is fabricated, the fundamental elements of the story are strikingly real. Youth enroll in structured experiences in impressive numbers, but their dropout rate is disheartening. A 2014 study by the United States Census Bureau (U.S. Census Bureau, 2014) revealed that 57% of all youth—almost six in every 10—participate in at least one after-school extracurricular program. Collectively, these programs are offered by a broad array of providers, including 4H, Boys & Girls clubs, scout groups, nature and sport camps, universities, public park and recreation departments, YMCA, YWCA, camps, and school systems. The "experiencescape," or "the spaces in which experiences are staged and consumed" (O'Dell & Billing, 2005, p. 16) across these programs is vast. Depending on the design of the program, youth may be engaged, immersed, or absorbed in these programs. On the other hand, they may be bored, anxious, alienated, shamed, or fearful. And, as a result of their participation in positive experiences, a variety of development outcomes may occur, including decreased school failure and dropout rates, reduced school absenteeism, increased academic achievement,

Unfortunately, little is known about the fate of dropouts, and attrition is a significant problem for providers of many OST programs.

increased rates of postsecondary education involvement, reduced problem behaviors, heightened psychosocial competencies, and increased social competence and emotional adjustment (e.g., Mahoney, Larson, Eccles, & Lord, 2005).

Yet, youth must sustain participation in out-of-school time (OST) programs that yield positive experiences in order to receive the "dosage" levels of participation (e.g., Hansen & Larson, 2007) necessary to achieve desired developmental outcomes. Unfortunately, little is known about the fate of dropouts, and attrition is a significant problem for providers of many OST programs. For example, a retrospective study of youth sport showed that between Grades 1 and 10, 94% of youth in the sample withdrew from at least one sport, and attrition increased as youth got older (Butcher, Lindner, & Johns, 2002). Attrition was largely attributed to lack of enjoyment. Additionally, 4-H programs in Kansas (Astroth, 1985) and West Virginia (Hartley, 1983) have reported attrition levels of 40% to 50% and 45%, respectively. Thus, a critical challenge for OST program providers is to develop strategies to attract youth to quality programs and ensure that positive benefits occur. This chapter integrates existing research and theory about youth development to propose a Youth Development Programming Process (YDPP) that has potential to reduce attrition and promote program success. Using the YDPP helps one become an experience designer.

Youth Development Programming Process

The YDPP is depicted in Figure 15.1. In the following paragraphs, we will walk you through various parts of this figure; refer to the figure as we go along. Five shapes are used in the figure (i.e., oval, rectangle with solid lines, rectangle with broken lines, diamond, and pentagon). Each shape has a precise meaning.

- The *ovals* represent starting and ending points.
- *Rectangles defined by solid lines* represent multi-step processes and use of cause and effect strategies within those processes. Each process has a definite ending point, and the occasion of reaching that point can be thought of as an "event."
- The multi-step processes yield specific outcomes, which are represented by the *rectangles with the broken lines* and the bidirectional arrows.
- *Diamonds* represent a decision option.
- The *lines with arrowheads* indicate the sequential flow of progress through the process, over time.
- The *pentagon* indicates a transfer: representation of the process continues across more than one page.

The YDPP includes three processes that yield explicit plans: (1) establishing a positive youth development culture, (2) structuring each session or meeting for "deep" experiences that participants will value, and (3) applying intentional programming principles, as appropriate to the purpose of the program and the mission of the sponsoring organization. Each of these processes yields a specific written plan for implementation of either an intentional program or an hedonic program. An intentional program seeks to produce specific developmental outcomes, while an hedonic program targets immediate enjoyment, while recognizing that a number of positive, serendipitous outcomes may also result.

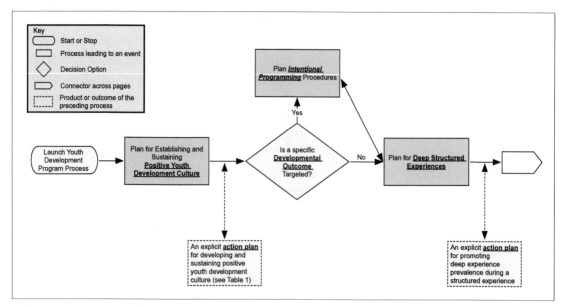

Figure 15.1. Youth Development Program Process: Beginning through "Plan for Deep Structured Experiences"

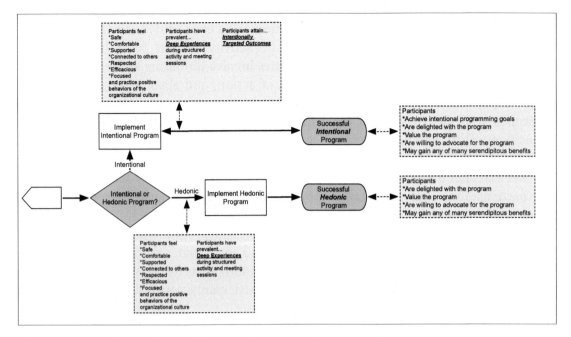

Figure 15.1. (cont.). Youth Development Program Process

Read the YDPP diagram in Figure 15.1 from left to right to follow the temporal order of the planning process. To launch the YDPP, the experience designer first develops a plan for establishing and maintaining a positive organizational culture for the program. Strategies must be in place for all point-of-service encounters with participants over the entire duration of the program. If the strategies are successful, participants feel safe, comfortable, supported, connected, respected, efficacious, and focused during all sessions or meetings (e.g., Eccles & Gootman, 2002). As a result, they may be more likely to remain in the program.

The next major process in the system is development of an "experience plan" for each program session. These plans identify strategies for structuring each session in ways that facilitate the prevalence of *deep structured experience* during that session (Ellis, Freeman, Jamal, & Jiang, 2017). The deep structured experience concept is akin to what other researchers have called flow (Csikszentmihalyi, 1975), deep play (Ackerman, 2011) peak experience (Maslow, 1962) and the "System 2" attentional state (Kahneman, 2001). Deep structured experience is thus a heightened state of attention, interest, and motivation. Participants' sense of time passage is altered and actions seem to occur automatically. The percentage of time during the activity that deep structured experience occurs for a given participant is called *prevalence of deep structured experience* (Ellis et al., 2017). Research has shown that greater prevalence yields greater perceived value; that is, the more prevalent deep structured experience is, the more participants value their participation (Ellis et al., 2017). To facilitate high prevalence of deep structured experience, the activity session must be engaging, immersive, and/or absorbing. Engaging activities involve unfolding stories, immersive activities are those that involve performance of action, and absorption activities are sensory experiences.

Explicit strategies for each of these three experience types have been advanced as propositions of the *Theory of Structured Experience* (Ellis et al., 2017) and are summarized in a subsequent section of this chapter. The Theory of Structured Experience also proposes that after a well-structured activity session, participants feel delight and value their participation. They are pleased they committed time to participation. After an intentional program experience, participants may report that they are "still thinking about" something they encountered or learned. Successful programs also yield advocacy. Participants are eager to "talk up" the program and encourage others to participate as future opportunities become available. Word-of-mouth advertising is deeply valued by any organization that strives to attract and retain participants, consumers, or supporters of a cause.

The third major process in the YDPP, planning for implementation of intentional programming principles (e.g., Duerden & Gillard, 2007), is relevant to situations in which a specific developmental outcome is targeted. This process requires explicit, sequenced, focused, and targeted actions designed to facilitate attainment of the goal (Duerden & Gillard, 2007; Durlak & Weissberg, 2007). Swim lessons, for example, should be taught using teaching techniques known to be best practices for teaching that activity. The same is true for programs directed at more complex and interconnected systems of knowledge, beliefs, attitudes, and behaviors. Programs directed at character development (e.g., Belnap, 2009) should use the specialized teaching strategies known to most reliably yield that targeted outcome.

Successful implementation of the YDPP yields outcomes within one or both of two sets: positive youth development program outcomes or hedonic program outcomes. A successful intentional program achieves its developmental goal in addition to hedonic outcomes. Readers are cautioned to not associate negative connotations with this use of the term *hedonic*. In popular usage, hedonic connotes excesses in immediate sensory experiences and a lack of achievement orientation. Thus, an individual leading a hedonic lifestyle is thought to be concerned primarily with immediate pleasures to the detriment of her or his well-being and responsibilities to self and others. To philosophers, though, hedonic does not carry those negative connotations. Hedonic simply refers to the immediate experience of pleasure, apart from any greater context. Thus, in the YDPP, the term hedonic simply designates that a program

A successful intentional program achieves its developmental goal in addition to hedonic outcomes.

is intended to yield pleasant outcomes; the program is not intended to explicitly target one or more developmental outcomes. However, unplanned developmental outcomes may certainly result from participation in hedonic activities.

For example, teens gathering at the recreation center after school to rehearse for a theatrical performance may yield new or strengthened friendships and heightened self-worth. In the YDPP, we consider such outcomes to be *serendipitous outcomes*. Serendipitous outcomes are the many ways that people learn and grow by simply enjoying activities and settings. The range of serendipitous outcomes is virtually limitless, but examples include strengthening friendships, creating shared memories, building family cohesiveness, learning new recreation activities, discovering intellectual and professional passions, developing empathy, embracing human diversity, developing a health-promoting habit, or becoming a better student or citizen.

With this overview of the YDPP in place, we turn our attention to the details of the three basic component processes: building a positive youth development culture, providing effective structured experiences, and intentionally programming youth experiences. Each process will be discussed in a subsequent section of this chapter.

Building a Positive Youth Development Organizational Culture

Youth Programs as Organizations

An organization may be defined as "a social unit of people that is structured and managed to meet or to pursue collective goals" (BusinessDictionary, 2017a). Thus, any youth development program is a type of organization. Like businesses organizations, government organizations, and nonprofit organizations, youth development programs are comprised of a group of people who gather for a defined purpose. Within the YDPP, the purpose is often hedonic activity that has potential to yield positive youth development outcomes. One or more people are formal leaders and are thus responsible for the activities and initiatives of the program. Formal and informal rules and procedures exist for becoming a member and taking ones place within the organization.

> Any youth development program is a type of organization.

The culture of an organization is the set "values and behaviors that contribute to the unique social and psychological environment" of the organization (BusinessDictionary, 2017b. These values and behaviors profoundly affect the productivity and performance of the organization. Culture impacts the quality of products and services of the organization, the quality of customer experiences, and the safety of both employees and customers. The BusinessDictionary (2017b) explains that organizational culture is manifest in four major ways:

1. "the way the organization proceeds about its affairs, treats its members, and interacts with the communities of which it is a part;
2. the extent to which freedom is present in decision-making, development and innovation, and personal expression;

3. how power and information flow through the hierarchy; and
4. how committed members are toward shared objectives of the organization."

The success of youth development programs depends heavily on its organizational culture. Providers of youth services are poised for success when they have knowledge of the features (e.g., values and behaviors; Eccles & Gootman, 2002) of organizational culture that yield positive intentional, hedonic, and/or serendipitous outcomes.

But what are these features? Leading youth development scholars have addressed this question and have advanced well-founded lists of features of organizational culture. Among the more notable are initiatives by the National Research Council and Institute of Medicine (Eccles & Gootman, 2002), and the HighScope Educational Research Foundation (Smith, Akiva, Arrieux, & Jones, 2006; Smith & Hohmann, 2005). A summary of these initiatives and respective features of culture for youth organizations follows.

National Research Council and Institute of Medicine Perspective

In 2002, Eccles and Gootman edited a seminal book outlining key features of youth program contexts. Their work was based on the deliberations of an elite panel of youth development authorities who integrated research about quality features of youth development programs and identified eight key features:

1. Safety, both physical and psychological
2. Structure appropriate to the program and its context
3. Supportive relationships among participants and leaders
4. A shared sense of belonging that appreciates individual differences and diversity
5. Social norms that are a foundation for actions reflecting accepted values and morals
6. Support for efficacy and mattering, with focus on improvement rather than absolute performance, and escalating responsibilities commensurate with growth in ability to lead
7. Opportunity for skill building, including physical, intellectual, psychological, emotional, and social skills
8. Integration of family, school, and community efforts

Eccles and Gootman emphasized that empirical research on these features was limited and that no single feature would ensure positive development. They also noted that little was known about possible moderating or mediating effects among the individual features. Some features may be effective only in the presence or absence of others. Thus, the committee emphasized the need for further research to help deal with these issues.

Program Quality Assessment Project Perspective

Another initiative that yielded a set of values and behaviors that are pivotal elements of organizational culture of youth programs is the Program Quality Assessment (PQA) initiative by the HighScope Educational Research Foundation (Smith & Hohmann, 2005; Smith et al., 2006). The PQA project was directed at identifying and validating a set of standards for best practices in OST programs. The validation study was thorough and extensive. The identified standards were evaluated through direct observation of 59 youth programs serving 1,635 youth in 116 different programs.

> The set of organization standards include youth-centered policies and practices, high expectations by students and staff, and access.

The PQA project identified five key features of program offerings and an additional three features of organizations that offer those programs. The five program offerings were communicated in the form of a "Pyramid of Program Quality" (Figure 15.2). That pyramid is organized from base to apex as follows:

- Youth voice and governance/professional learning community
- Safe environment
- Supportive environment
- Interaction
- Engagement

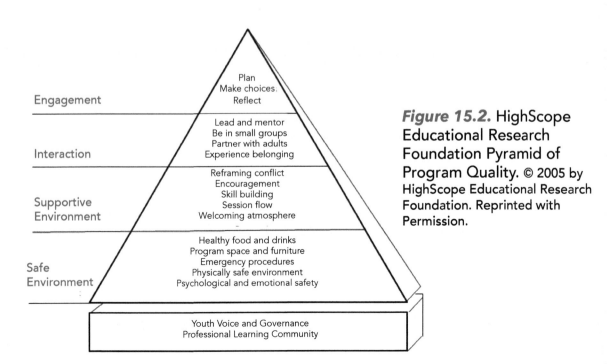

Figure 15.2. HighScope Educational Research Foundation Pyramid of Program Quality. © 2005 by HighScope Educational Research Foundation. Reprinted with Permission.

The set of organization standards include youth-centered policies and practices, high expectations by students and staff, and access.

The direct observation approach of the PQA project required specification of precisely defined indicators for each of the seven features. Indicators of interaction, for example included (but were not limited to) youth have opportunity to participate in small groups and youth have opportunity for adult-youth partnership. That level of detail allowed observers to make reliable judgments about whether each program met a specific standard.

The PQA standards and indicators align exceptionally well with the features reported by Eccles and Gootman (2002). Both lists emphasize the importance of safety and support. Eccles and Gootman highlight the need for supportive relationships between participants and leaders and the PQA list includes supportive environment. The shared sense of belonging feature of Eccles and Gootman's list is embedded within the Interaction feature of the Program Quality Assessment list. Opportunity for skill building from Eccles and Gootman's list is embedded in both supportive environment and engagement of the PQA.

An integrated list of the two sets of features is presented in Table 15.1. The table includes cultural elements (values), the desired participant experience of those cultural elements, and specific actions providers and participants can take to establish and sustain those cultural elements as part of the culture of the organization. To help you digest the information in the table, let's discuss two examples. First, psychological safety for a sport league can be promoted, in part, by requiring all participants to sign a petition against bullying (or perhaps in favor of good sportsmanship) and posting that petition in a conspicuous location for all sessions of the program (Ellis, Henderson, Paisley, Silverberg, & Wells, 2004; Wells, Ellis, Paisley, & Arthur-Banning, 2005). Additionally, use of a sociogram (i.e., a graphical representation of relationships in a group to show who is connected with whom) can help to identify participants who are without friends or in special need of psychological safety (Amidon, 1961).

Connectedness and acceptance among youth participants can also be facilitated by simply allowing youth to spend more time with one another.

Connectedness and acceptance among youth participants can also be facilitated by simply allowing youth to spend more time with one another. Positive affect between participants can increase simply through mere exposure to one another (Zajonc, 1968). As social cognitive theory (Bandura, 1986; 2011) suggests, the element *efficacious* can be promoted by ensuring success in simpler skills before introducing more complex skills (performance accomplishment) and through using peer role models to demonstrate task performance (vicarious experience).

Table 15.1

Establishing a Positive Youth Program Organizational Culture

Cultural Element (Values)	Participant Experience	Provider Behaviors	Participant Behaviors
Ambient Comfort	Participants are free of distress relative to maintaining homeostasis. They are not too hot, cold, cramped, hungry, thirsty, or distracted by unpleasant sounds or aromas irrelevant to the activity.	Optimize the meeting site for comfort in advance of arrival of participants to each session. Sample actions follow: • Adjust temperature of meeting space to comfortable levels. • Provide (healthy) snacks and food service, as appropriate. • Ensure access to water, fluids, sunscreen, insect repellant, sun protection. • Eliminate potentially distracting noises and unpleasant aromas. • Ensure access to clean and functional restroom facilities. • Monitor ambient comfort during the session. • Ensure that needed equipment and props are in place and ready for use. • Encourage participants to actively participate in establishing and maintaining ambient comfort.	Participants actively assist in monitoring comfort and take appropriate action to ensure that it is sustained.

(cont.)

Table 15.1 (cont.)

Cultural Element (Values)	Participant Experience	Provider Behaviors	Participant Behaviors
Safety, Physical	Participants are not at risk of injury due to tangible hazards in the activity setting.	Develop and maintain a "living" risk management plan of physical hazards (e.g., Spengler & Hronek, 2011). Sample actions indicated by the plan are as follows: • Monitor and mitigate or eliminate hazards that could give rise to tripping, choking, falling, cuts, or other injuries. • Provide adequate lighting in and around the activity setting. • Maximize visual penetration of areas around the activity setting. • Minimize encounters with biting and stinging animals. • Inform participants to be aware of possible encounters with harmful animals and insects. • Ensure that an adult present has first-aid training. • Ensure that communication devices are present for emergencies. • Systematically communicate safety rules and expectations. • Ensure that staff fully understand risk management protocols.	Participants actively assist in monitoring physical safety and take appropriate action to ensure that it is sustained. Participants assist in finalizing the risk management plan.

(cont.)

Table 15.1 (cont.)

Cultural Element (Values)	Participant Experience	Provider Behaviors	Participant Behaviors
Safety, Psychological	Participants do not feel more than transitory shame, embarrassment, fear, ridicule, or humiliation during any structured experience, nor do they perceive a high level of risk of these emotions.	Develop, maintain, and involve participants in finalizing a "living" risk management plan for psychological hazards. Sample actions within the plan are as follows: • Frequently remind participants to positively affirm and support other participants. • Require all participants sign a poster petition against bullying. Display the poster at every session. • Create a no tolerance policy with respect to bullying. • Create and maintain an anonymous "tell someone" system. • Ensure an appropriate ratio of adult leaders to participants. • Train leaders in managing bullies. • In residential programs, monitor homesickness. • Create and monitor socio-grams to identify and assist isolates and minimize unhealthy cliques.	Participants regularly encourage and celebrate successes of other participants. Participants actively assist in monitoring psychological safety and take appropriate action to ensure that it is sustained. Participants assist in finalizing and implementing the psychological risk management plan.
Support	Participants are confident that adult leaders and other group members care about their safety, success, and enjoyment during each activity session and are eager to help them succeed.	Promote feelings of support by… • Strategically using nonverbal communication with individual participants, including eye contact, touch on shoulder, smiling, orienting body directly toward participant. • Routinely telling participants you care about them and how they are enjoying and learning from the experience. • Periodically conducting "start, stop, continue" assessments, sharing results of those assessments with participants, and making changes, as appropriate.	Participants are consistently and invariably respectful to other participants and to leaders. Participants politely and tactfully correct others who engage in behaviors that would exclude others of make others feel unsupported.

(cont.)

Table 15.1 (cont.)

Cultural Element (Values)	Participant Experience	Provider Behaviors	Participant Behaviors
Accepted/ Connected	Participants feel valued and respected members of the group. They believe the group is better in specific ways because they are present.	Promote development of friendships by… • Crafting repeated opportunities for participants who have similar interests to work together and have shared, enjoyable experiences. • Modeling and encouraging openness of communication. Talk about your enjoyment, enthusiasm, hopes, and thoughts and encouraging others to do so as well.	Participants often share ideas and feelings. Participants collaborate effectively to have shared, enjoyable experiences. Participants gain affinity for one another through "mere exposure."
Effica-cious	Participants have a sense of self-efficacy. They experience success (either intra-personal or normative) during every structured experience. They believe their actions during the sessions will lead to predictable outcomes (self-efficacy expectancies) and desired outcomes (outcome expectancies).	Use instructional strategies that facilitate learning and communication strategies that facilitate self-efficacy. Examples of specific actions are as follows: • Using "scaffolding" approaches for teaching skills. Progress from simple to complex actions and activities. • Using theory-based principles for promoting self-efficacy: vicarious experience by similar role model, performance accomplishment, regulate situational arousal. • Maintaining orientation on intra-individual progress rather than absolute, fixed standards of performance. • Providing performance feedback messages that encourage attributions to ability and effort (e.g., "You are good at this!" and "You are a very hard worker!") instead of fate, luck, ease of task, or ambiguity (e.g., "Good job" and "Lucky that happened"). • Verbally praising participants when they encourage others and celebrate successes of others.	Participants exert effort. Participants show pleasure following success. Participants evaluate their performance using intra-personal standards, learning, and growth rather than normative standards. Participants attribute their successes to ability and effort. Participants encourage others Participants celebrate successes of others.

(cont.)

Table 15.1 (cont.)

Cultural Element (Values)	Participant Experience	Provider Behaviors	Participant Behaviors
Focused	Participants have sustained interest in and attention to the flow of activities and interactions during the session. They remain behaviorally engaged; their attention does not wander.	• Establish a precise and detailed agenda for each session, designating the time periods in which each component of the session will occur. • Prepare a narrative story board for each structured experience and implement the plan. • Start every session on time and also end at the designated time. • Constantly monitor the interest level of participants. Take action if members seem to be bored or distracted. Increase or decrease complexity, Change the novelty and complexity of the activity to maintain interest, or change the activity itself. • Encourage youth input on changes as the structured experience unfolds. • Design active (rather than passive) learning experiences.	Participants' behavior is on task. Participants make periodic suggestions for how structured experiences might unfold.

Importance of Formal Action Plans

By now you probably recognize the complex challenge of providing a quality youth development program and its individual structured experiences. The task of establishing and maintaining a positive youth development culture alone involves scrutiny and rigorous, continuous monitoring of the physical, interpersonal, and intrapersonal environment. Formal or informal indicators of safety, comfort, connectedness, efficacy, and being supported by leaders and co-participants must not only be monitored, but also managed. The YDPP phases of structuring for deep experience and intentional outcomes are at least as complex as establishing a positive culture. A youth development professional contemplating this complexity for the first time might be inclined to dismiss the process as unrealistic, and proceed with business as usual. "After all," the leader might conclude, "serendipitous benefits likely result for some participants, even in marginal programs. Let's just roll out the balls and have fun."

Luckily, however, just as organizations have cultures, they also have tools for managing complexity. Planning is one of these tools. Explicit plans are like maps to backcountry hikers; they help guide managers through complex environments and circumstances. Thus, in the following sections, we share ideas for planning each of the three phases of the YDPP. However, full development of ideas for planning is beyond the scope of this chapter. Our goal is to illustrate structures through which effective and impactful planning can be accomplished.

Action Plans for Establishing Organizational Culture

Figure 15.3 illustrates one (among many) approaches that might be used to develop a plan for establishing and maintaining a positive youth development culture for a hypothetical youth program. A cause-and-effect diagram is used. The ovals represent the cultural values/features of a positive youth development program, based on Eccles and Gootman (2002) and the Program Quality Assessment Project (Smith & Hohmann, 2005; Smith et al., 2006). The text not enclosed in a shape indicates specific actions (positive culture behaviors) taken by program leaders and participants to create and sustain the culture.

A few examples of specific actions may be helpful. For the element physical and psychological safety, we advocate development of written risk management plans highlighting the probability and severity of both physical and psychological risks (e.g., Spengler & Hronek, 2011). A good risk management plan will specify actions necessary to minimize each risk as well as appropriate response and recovery actions.

As another example, feelings of efficacy during structured experiences can be enhanced through careful scripting of point-of-service interactions and learning activities. For example, certain verbal persuasion messages are more effective than others in encouraging participants to feel efficacious. Thus, feelings of efficacy result when people attribute successes they experience to their own ability and effort instead of luck or ease of task (Ellis, Maughan-Pritchett, Ruddell, 1993; Weiner, 1986), and successes can be defined using intra-individual goals instead of absolute performance

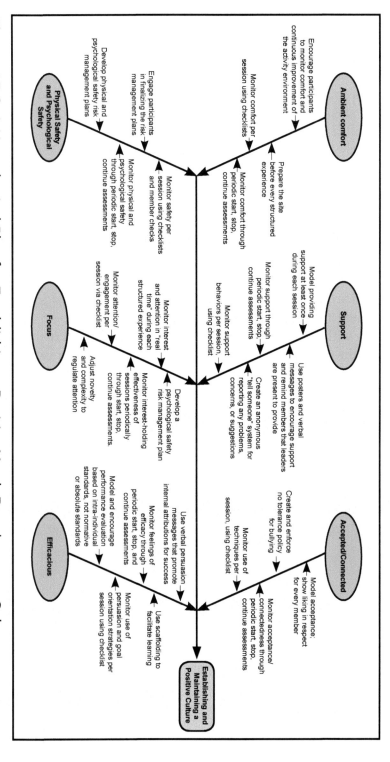

Figure 15.3. A Hypothetical Plan for Establishing a Positive Youth Development Culture

strategies (Wells, 2005). Imagine, for example, a youth is playing softball in a formal league for the first time. She walks to the plate, nervous about her first at-bat. A pitch is hurled toward the plate, and our new softball player succeeds in making contact with the ball. However, the swing is a fraction of a second late, and the ball goes foul. To enhance a feeling of efficacy, the first-base coach might comment, "What a swing! You are going to be a great hitter!" That comment encourages the youth to attribute success to her own ability and determination. The coach should avoid comments such as "good job" (e.g., an ambiguous phrase, which could be attributed to luck) or "almost!" (which implies failure).

Similarly, social cognitive theory suggests specific mechanisms that can be used to promote feeling *efficacious* (Bandura, 2011). These include actual performance accomplishments, positive verbal persuasion, vicarious experience (such as peer modeling), and adjusting situational arousal (stress) to optimal levels. The most potent of these is performance accomplishments, which can be facilitated through sequencing tasks (i.e., beginning with easier tasks and progressing to tasks that are more difficult).

> Social cognitive theory suggests specific mechanisms that can be used to promote feeling "efficacious."

From the examples and detail just provided, the reader can see that attention to the details of a structured experience can be very impactful in advancing elements of positive youth development culture. Even such small details as the wording of encouragement provided can have a significant impact on the quality of a participant's experience. A diligent leader will attend to those details, both through planning and through habits of working directly with youth in structured experiences.

One final comment on planning for a positive youth development culture is important before we explore an option for planning a structured experience. Consistent with quality management principles and practices (e.g., Evans & Lindsay, 2014), we strongly advocate that actual implementation of strategies specified in a plan be formally monitored. As text in Figure 15.1 suggests, monitoring can be accomplished using simple tools such as a brief checklist. Immediately following a structured experience, a leader can check whether an intended technique was used, perhaps count the number of occasions, and even write specific notes about what worked and did not work.

Another very simple and powerful way of monitoring quality of sessions is periodic "start, stop, continue" surveys. To conduct such a survey, a program leader simply asks participants to list things they want to start doing, stop doing, and continue doing during the sessions. Individually constructed written lists avoid dilution of ideas due to the presence of influential members or normative pressures to comply. The important point is to use assessment techniques to continuously monitor the pulse of the program. As leaders of the quality management movement explain, if outcomes of processes are not being measured, the actions and processes are not being effectively managed. (However, as authorities in quality management principles agree, just because an outcome can be measured does not mean it should be measured! The point is to focus measurement on the critical few outcomes and ignore the trivial many).

Providing Effective Structured Experiences

Theory of Structured Experience

With a positive youth development organizational culture in place, we now turn to another set of processes depicted in Figure 15.1, Plan for Deep Structured Experiences. For this section, we draw on the Theory of Structured Experience (Ellis et al., 2017). This theory provides guidance enabling an activity leader to plan structured experiences such that the participants experience a heightened state of attention, motivation, and emotion, referred to in the theory as Deep Structured Experience. Deep structured experiences vary moment to moment. When someone reports having been "in" such a state, she or he reports something like the following:

> I was in a state of effortless concentration so deep that I lost a) my sense of time, b) my thoughts about myself, and c) my thoughts about my problems. I wanted very much to keep doing this activity. (Ellis et al., 2017, p. 9)

Deep structured experience is a binary phenomenon; it is either present or absent at any given moment. When deep structured experiences are highly prevalent over the duration of an activity session, youth will report greater value in having chosen to do the activity, and in turn desire more such experiences. Youth will also feel more positive emotions and delight with the deep structured experience. The theory recognizes three very broad types of activities that give rise to deep structured experience: immersion, absorption, and engagement.

Immersion. Immersion activities require performance of physical action. Demand for action is constantly flowing during the activity, and the participant receives immediate feedback on the efficacy of her or his responses to those demands. Examples of activities that give rise to immersion are competitive and noncompetitive sports, creative arts (e.g., painting, sketching, sculpture), and performing arts (e.g., acting, singing, playing a musical instrument). When an individual is highly immersed in performance, her or his attention is deeply focused on the demands of the activity. Her or his responses are unfolding automatically, apart from deliberate thought. She or he perceives a high degree of control over the immediate outcomes of actions.

As an example of an immersion experience, imagine a teenage girl who is an experienced tennis player. She is playing tennis with an opponent who has a very similar level of skill and experience. It is our tennis player's turn to serve. She tosses the ball high into the air. Seemingly effortlessly, but with impressive force, she drives a ball downward into her opponent's court. Her attention follows the path of the ball while it also monitors the reactions of her opponent. The serve is well placed, but her opponent steps to one side and executes a beautiful backhand, sending the ball toward mid-court at a high rate of speed. Our tennis player maintains full focus on the ball. She automatically turns her body, brings her racquet back, and delivers a powerful forehand. She notices that the ball is headed directly toward the point on the court that she intended. She feels a rush of control, but that rush is not so intense that it causes her to lose her focus. She is loving this! She is fully immersed in this structured experience.

Absorption. While immersion experiences involve challenge and skill, actions, immediate feedback on the efficacy of those actions, and then reactions, absorption experiences are exactly the opposite. Absorption may result from activities that focus attention on immediate sensory experiences. Demand for action and reaction is not inherent to the experience. Specifically, a high level of absorption is a transitory condition of heightened attention, motivation, and emotion characterized by (a) high levels of relaxation and pleasure; (b) absence of demand for behavioral or mental action in response to stimuli; (c) absence of active thinking; and (d) loss of self-consciousness (awareness of problems, plans, challenges, and opportunities). Like immersion, absorption varies along a continuum from very low to very high.

> Absorption may result from activities that focus attention on immediate sensory experiences.

Imagine a youth at a swimming pool on a hot summer day. He has been sunbathing, resting on a towel not far from the edge of the pool. He has relished the contrast of the warmth of the sun on his back with the coolness of the concrete radiating through his thin towel. A cooling breeze occasionally passes, bringing occasional moments of delight. Then, he notices that the heat on his back has become excessive. He rises, walks to the edge of the pool, and dives into the water. The coolness of the water brings a transitory sense of ecstasy and he relishes his effortless motion through the water and the thrill of near weightlessness. Sounds of the world disappear under the water, and he notices the colors of the bottom of the pool and the legs of people around him. This youth is absorbed in a swimming experience.

Absorption can also occur in activities that involve movement, as long as those activities do not require focusing attention on action and reaction. Such activities as hiking easy trails, viewing landscapes, walking, cycling for pleasure, noncompetitive sailing, and listening to instrumental music have potential to be highly absorbing.

Engagement. Engagement activities are those that focus the participants' attention on a story or "unfolding narrative." Specifically, engagement is a transitory condition of heightened attention, emotion, and motivation, characterized by (a) extraordinarily high focus of attention on an unfolding narrative or story told in words, actions, and/ or music; (b) heightened emotions; and (c) agentic inclinations. Agentic elements stimulate an individual toward action (Reeve, 2013). Examples of engagement experiences include watching movies, attending dramatic performances, lectures, interpretive talks, sporting events, and musical theatre performances.

> Engagement activities are those that focus the participants' attention on a story or "unfolding narrative."

A structured engagement experience at the World War II Memorial in Washington D.C., for example, might be a story told by an interpretive ranger about a heroic soldier whose selfless actions accomplished a particularly difficult mission and saved the lives of fellow soldiers. Such a story might yield inclinations for greater empathy toward those who paid the ultimate sacrifice to secure the freedoms enjoyed in the United States today. Spectator events tend to afford opportunities for engagement. Like absorption and immersion, engagement varies along a continuum from very low to very high.

To gain a deeper understanding of engagement, reflect for a moment on how you felt as a spectator during a particularly good movie, sporting event, play or musical. Try to imagine how you would describe that experience to others. You would likely report that your attention was fully focused on the story as it unfolded. Your thoughts were flowing fluidly. What is happening? What will happen next? What would I be doing if faced with these circumstances? How does what I am watching fit with or conflict with things I believe, things I value, and things I trust? What, if anything, will I think more about when this story is over? If the story is good, your attention is so focused that you block out everything else that is happening in your environment. You do not notice sounds, lights, or actions of other people. You are "in" the story.

Please join us in an engagement experience. The following short story was posted on Facebook by "Inspiring Stories" on June 11, 2017. Facebook can be a wonderful source of engagement experiences. Please read the story and then reflect on the nature of your "engagement" during that structured experience.

Potatoes, Eggs, and Coffee Beans

Once upon a time, a daughter complained to her father that her life was miserable and that she didn't know how she was going to make it. She was tired of fighting and struggling all the time. It seemed just as one problem was solved, another one soon followed.

Her father, a chef, took her to the kitchen. He filled three pots with water and placed each on a high fire. Once the three pots began to boil, he placed potatoes in one pot, eggs in the second pot, and ground coffee beans in the third pot. He then let them sit and boil, without saying a word to his daughter. The daughter moaned and impatiently waited, wondering what he was doing.

After 20 minutes, he turned off the burners. He took the potatoes out of the pot and placed them in a bowl. He pulled the eggs out and placed them in a bowl. He then ladled the coffee out and placed it in a cup. Turning to her, he asked. "Daughter, what do you see?"

"Potatoes, eggs, and coffee," she hastily replied.

"Look closer," he said, "and touch the potatoes." She did and noted that they were soft. He then asked her to take an egg and break it. After pulling off the shell, she observed the hard-boiled egg. Finally, he asked her to sip the coffee. Its rich aroma brought a smile to her face.

"Father, what does this mean?" she asked.

He then explained that the potatoes, the eggs and coffee beans had each faced the same adversity—the boiling water. However, each one reacted differently.

The potato went in strong, hard, and unrelenting, but in boiling water, it became soft and weak.

The egg was fragile, with the thin outer shell protecting its liquid interior until it was put in the boiling water. Then the inside of the egg became hard.

However, the ground coffee beans were unique. After they were exposed to the boiling water, they changed the water and created something new.

"Which are you," he asked his daughter. "When adversity knocks on your door, how do you respond? Are you a potato, an egg, or a coffee bean?"

This story reflects the key elements of engagement. It is coherent (logically sequenced), self-relevant (relevant to all of us, as we contemplate how we negotiate adversity), and provocative (as you read, you probably were thinking, "Which one am I most like?").

It is important to note that immersion, absorption, and engagement do not occur in isolation, even though a given activity may be structured to emphasize only one of these. An evening campfire activity at a youth camp, for example, may combine engagement in conversation about the next day's agenda with absorption in rich sensory experiences, such as the warmth of the fire, the beauty and intrigue of the dancing flames, food and drink. In another setting, a youth on a fishing outing may choose to enjoy basking in the sun (absorption) for a few minutes before attending to the relatively complex task of casting a lure to a specific spot to try to catch a fish (immersion). Importantly, different youth may have different types of experiences during the same activity. Youth development leaders may design structured experiences that result in multiple types of subjective states.

How to Structure Experiences

So, what does this construction of immersion, absorption, engagement and deep structured experience mean to designers of youth experiences? We have suggested that a high prevalence of deep structured experience creates a perception of value: the time the participant devoted to the activity was well spent. Participants are pleased they chose to do the activity and they want to participate again in the future. Thus, the potential for attrition is reduced following each session characterized by a high prevalence of deep structured experience.

We have also suggested that three broad types of activity give rise to deep structured experience: immersion, absorption, and engagement. So, what can our experience designer do to promote immersion, absorption, or engagement, beyond simply making participation in such activities available? The Theory of Structured Experience proposes answers to this question. These answers are in the form of testable propositions, which are much like hypotheses you may have learned about in your science or research methods classes.

The most fundamental of these propositions is that, for deep structured experiences to occur at all, the structured experience must be delivered at a level of performance of customer service that exceeds a certain threshold. Customer service performance is complex.

> Three broad types of activity give rise to deep structured experience: immersion, absorption, and engagement.

Countless opportunities for success and failure exist. Think about the last time you had a bad experience at a restaurant, movie theatre, recreation center, or tourist attraction. Maybe a service provider was rude. Perhaps the restrooms were filthy. Equipment could have been broken or failed. Maybe you had to stand in a queue (line) far too long. Maybe umpires were poor judges of your athletic performance during a competition. Food that should have been hot might have been served too cold or food that should have been served cold was served too hot. You could have been the victim of deceptive pricing. A provider could have overpromised and underperformed.

An influential line of research by marketing professors showed that these service encounters (both successes and failures) can be classified into five types: (1) reliability of the service provided, (2) assurance of commitment to quality by the provider, (3) tangible features of the environment, (4) empathy shown by providers, and (5) responsiveness to the needs of customers (Parasuraman, Berry, & Zeithaml, 1991). If participants are angry, disappointed, frustrated, frightened, disillusioned, shamed, humiliated, or

cheated due to a service failure, they will not experience a high prevalence of deep structured experience. The probability of youth dropping out of the program is also certain to increase. Thus, it is critical that providers of youth services provide good customer service.

Further comment on negative emotions is important at this point. Customer service failures may indeed result in anger, disappointment, frustration, fear, disillusionment, shame, humiliation, and feeling cheated. Negative emotions due to customer service failures should certainly be minimized, if not eliminated entirely. Note also, however, that negative emotions are inherent to some structured experiences, particularly those that involve task performance. Not every moment of an athletic competition, artistic performance, practice session, and rehearsal is positive. Losing an important game is almost never pleasing, nor is failure to achieve an expected level of performance in art, writing, public speaking, livestock showing, or any other performance activity. Performance tasks that are too simple quickly lose their appeal. The experience of winning loses its appeal when one never loses. Unpleasant emotions naturally follow. Losing, failure, and their accompanying emotions are growth opportunities, when they are transitory and integrated into learning and personal improvement. Imagine, for example, that in the last second of a key basketball game, Sue misses an easy shot. If Sue had scored, her team would have won the game. She is deeply embarrassed. Her teammates, though, are quick to reassure her. They remind her of her value to the team and tell her how glad they are that she is a teammate. They are disappointed, but they also celebrate the excitement of the very close game. A bit later, her coach pulls Sue aside and points out that making a shot from directly in front of the rim can be deceptively complex. She shows Sue an effective strategy for taking such shots. Sue feels better and has learned. The negative emotions are inherent to her experience, success, and growth. Despite the disappointment and embarrassment she experienced, Sue begins to prepare for her next game.

Immersion, absorption, and engagement also have propositions. One of the key propositions for immersion (remember that those are the activities that involve task performance), is that providers should structure the experience such that the challenge of the tasks are roughly equivalent to the skills of the participant. In his classic work on the flow phenomenon, Csikszentmihalyi (1975) observed that participants become highly anxious when their skills are not sufficient to meet the demands of an activity. When skills are much greater than the activity, boredom and apathy result.

Think about our teenage tennis player from our discussion of immersion. If she glances across the net at a superbly talented opponent (imagine a professional tennis player, maybe even Serena Williams!), she will quickly realize that her skills are not sufficient and she will experience anxiety. In contrast, if her opponent is a young child barely able to hold a tennis racquet, the game will be very boring to our teen due the extraordinary superiority of her skill level compared to that of the toddler. These are, of course, extreme examples that would rarely occur. However, significant mismatches between skill and challenge are very common.

Deep structured experiences become possible in immersion activities if (a) the participant is genuinely interested because she or he likes the activity (her or his motivation is intrinsic) and (b) the challenge is commensurate with her or his skill. A youth sports coach teaching skills would thus do well to arrange practice sessions in which groups of youth at similar skill levels participate together. Authors of this chapter have more than once witnessed youth sport leagues in which intact highly skilled club-sport teams enroll in league competitions with teams comprised of individuals who have significantly less skill and experience (recall the story in the prologue to this chapter). The highly skilled teams enroll in such leagues as part of their plan for practicing new skills and plays. Games with huge final score disparities result, and members of the lesser-skilled teams are embarrassed and humiliated. Situations of

> Deep structured experiences become possible in immersion activities if (a) the participant is genuinely interested because she or he likes the activity (her or his motivation is "intrinsic") and (b) the challenge is commensurate with her or his skill.

extreme disparities in skill levels also, of course, occur in programs in all other types of immersion activities, such as dance, creative arts, drama and musical performance. Programs that do not account for such disparities do not promote immersion and are contraindicative to youth development.

Propositions about how to facilitate engagement are also part of the Theory of Structured Experience. Engagement results from stories that are coherent, provocative, and self-relevant. A coherent story is a story that follows the classic sequence identified in Freytag's (1898) pyramid (Harmon & Holman, 1996): exposition, rising action, climax, falling action, and dénouement. A very useful tool that can be used to create that sequence in a structured experience is to introduce a theme. A theme is comprised of a story line (sometimes called a narrative) and props that suggest an imaginary place, situation, or set of circumstances. During the summer of 2017, for example, the Texas 4-H youth camp in Brownwood created a special theme for its challenge course program. Campers became gold miners. The miners had succeeded in securing a sizeable quantity of gold. However, bandits were in hot pursuit. Thus, the miners needed to climb an imaginary peak (a cargo net) and then slide down a long bluff (zip line) to reach a town in which they could safety deposit their gold.

Like immersion and engagement, specific techniques can be used to enhance absorption (immediate sensory experiences). Positive psychology scientists (Bryant & Veroff, 2007; Quoidbach, Berry, Hansenne, & Mikolajczak, 2010) describe four techniques people can use to enhance their sensory (absorption) experiences: (1) being mentally present, (2) mental time travel, (3) behavioral expression of emotion, and (4) verbal expression of emotion (capitalizing).

Let us try out these techniques. Become mentally present by casting any problems or issues you may be thinking about away from you, fully out of your stream of thoughts. You can deal with those later. Then, become a mental time traveler. Close your eyes (or maybe not, because then you cannot read what we want you to think about). It is difficult to travel through time with your eyes open. Focus your thoughts on a future meal you intend to enjoy. Craft in your mind's eye a mental picture of the specific food item of that meal that is your favorite. Maybe that item is a steak, a hot piece of bread, a delicious salad, or maybe it is ice cream. Imagine its colors and shape as it rests on your plate. Now, imagine that you have lifted a portion of it to your lips and can enjoy its aroma. Take an imaginary bite. Try to experience its taste and its texture as you chew. Smile or lick your lips to show you like the imaginary taste and texture, and imagine a comment you might make to a friend or relative who is enjoying the meal with you. If you engaged in this exercise, you have used all of the savoring techniques. Not only did you have an absorption experience during the exercise, but when you actually eat that food later today, your experience will likely be enhanced.

In summary, well-structured (by self or others) immersion, engagement, and absorption activities yield deep structured experiences. As the prevalence of deep structured experience increases during an activity, value of participation in the activity increases. Value yields commitment, and commitment reduces attrition (dropping out). Prevalent deep structured experiences may be facilitated by carefully structuring immersion, absorption, and engagement activities using principles stated in the propositions in the preceding paragraphs.

Planning Structured Experiences

Planning and implementing these strategies is not an easy task. We acknowledge that it is much easier to follow the dominant practice of simply planning the logistics of activity sessions and then letting the experiences of the activity take care of themselves. "Just roll out the balls," is the mantra for such programs. However, problematic attrition rates in many programs demonstrate that simply rolling out the balls does not work.

A well-structured experience requires creativity, time, and energy. However, in our research with youth organizations, we have consistently found the investment to be well worth the effort. Not only have we witnessed significant improvements in participant engagement, immersion, and absorption, but we have also witnessed a heightened degree of pride youth development professionals have in the services they provide. Most activity specialists are highly creative, energetic people who care deeply about the quality of experiences of the youth they serve. Most leaders thus embrace the opportunity to elevate the quality of experience, and the act of creation can become a deep structured experience (an immersion task) in itself. Thus, quality quickly becomes a part of the culture of the youth organization.

In Table 15.2, we share a planning tool that we have found to be useful in planning structured experiences. We refer to our approach as a *narrative storyboard*. To construct a narrative storyboard, you essentially write a script as if you were writing a play for the event. Your script includes a summary of the plot or story line, a list of characters in the story, and any tangible props you will need. The narrative storyboard also includes dialogue for each phase of the experience. We recommend using some variation of the following phases of a planned session: arrival, decompression, reception, orientation, participation, and dénouement (ending or departure). Dénouement may work out best if it includes a surprise value-added item that participants can take away with them from the structured experience.

Two additional comments about the narrative storyboard are important. First, note that Table 15.2 illustrates the narrative for only one of these phases (decompression). In actual practice, narratives should be written for all of the stages of the experience. Also, note that although precise narrative may be written in the plan, in practice, the sessions will be conducted using improvisation instead of the scripted dialogue. Themed structured experiences are ordinarily best when participants actively engage by co-creating the story in real time and contributing to the ways in which it unfolds.

Intentionally Programming Youth Experiences

A vast body of research argues that youth experience a variety of benefits when they spend time in structured experiences. These experiences may facilitate healthy relationships, competence, and autonomy and contain engaging tasks that allow for skill development (Durlak & Weissberg, 2007). It is important to note that skill development

Table 15.2
Narrative Storyboard Script: Decompression Phase

Theme	Scouts of Sam Houston's Army: In Pursuit of Santa Anna
Plot/Story Line/Conflict	After a resounding victory at the Alamo, Santa Anna and his army have marched to the Southeast corner of Texas. Sam Houston's army is in hot pursuit. We are an advance reconnaissance team. With great stealth, we are following Santa Anna, watching the movements of his army. Our goal is to choose the best place for our army to attack. But we must continue to stay in the shadows, undetected by Santa Anna's scouts. We have arrived at an imposing bluff towering above the San Jacinto river, which we have just crossed. We know that Santa Anna's scouts will not be watching the bluff. It is steep and treacherous. His soldiers will think it unclimbable. But we are the Navy Seals of Sam Houston's army. We know that if we can succeed in climbing the bluff, we will have an extraordinary view of Santa Anna and his army. Climbing the bluff is the key to our victory.
Characters	Colonel (activity specialist, leads the story, teaches technique, ensures safety) Captain (assists Colonel as requested) Scouts, Lead Climbers (first wave of climbers) Sharpshooters (second wave of climbers) Navigator (carries compass and map, reads bearing to enemy following descent and reports to the captain) Medic
Props	Military hat with bars, designating the leader is a captain. Field glasses, telescope Water guns. Pistols for scouts, rifles for sharpshooters Frontier hats (newspaper hats) Possibles bags (sandwich bags) Canteens (water bottles) Knives (tongue depressors) Climbing equipment Compass (carabineer compass, big compass for the navigator) Map (paper, burned edges) Medic equipment: First aid kit, band-aids, aspirin (candy) Targets: tin cans
Sample Dialogue (Dialogue will be improvised in practice)	"Howdy! I am Colonel Lacanienta of the Texican Army. You must be the special forces reconnaissance team I have been waiting for! I am very glad to see you!" "Who is your captain?" (Choose a member of the group to be captain. Give him or her a captain's hat, bars, or other symbol designating captain rank). "I have the equipment you requested." • Captain, who is our navigator? (Choose one and have him retrieve the compass, map, weapon, and possibles bag). • Captain, who are our scouts and lead climbers? (Choose them and instruct them to retrieve field glasses, a weapon, a possibles bag, and confirm that each has a canteen [water bottle]). • Who are our lead climbers? (Choose lead climbers, and give them an arm band or something to indicate lead climbers. Instruct them to retrieve their weapons and possibles bags). • Who are our sharpshooters? (Choose sharpshooters and instruct them to retrieve their water rifles and possibles bags). "All of you, take five practice shots at those tin cans to get used to your weapons, then fall in line in front of me for an important briefing."

and other positive outcomes are more likely to occur when intentional programming is implemented (Durlak & Weissberg, 2007). Many programs are designed well and executed meticulously, but relatively few have explicit goals and are designed using principles of intentional programming (Sibthorp, Paisley, & Hill, 2003). In other words, while many programs are fun, enjoyable, and meet hedonic needs, few are designed and implemented in ways that intentionally facilitate developmental outcomes. In the paragraphs following, we define intentional programming and provide an overview of some of its key elements. Since intentional programming is the focus of Chapter 13 of this book. Thus, our attention to the topic in this chapter will be brief.

What is Intentional Programming?

The previous section described procedures for facilitating deep structured experiences for youth. As we discussed, such experiences have great potential to yield a variety of serendipitous outcomes, or unanticipated benefits. However, what about programs that have explicit goals? Such programs are intended and designed to yield specific, pre-determined benefits (e.g., improving math skills, strengthening social skills, or learning skills needed to pursue a specific hobby). Some programs seek to achieve very complex outcomes, such as character development, moral reasoning, or enhancing the spirituality. Youth sport programs are implicitly directed at teaching skills in their respective sports. As Figure 15.1 implies, in these instances, experience designers can apply principles of intentional programming.

As Chapter 13 reports, intentional programming is often guided by a logic model. Logic models date to the 1970s (Weiss, 1972) and have been used in a many different human services professions. Although many formats are used, the most fundamental elements of a logic model are inputs, activities, outputs, and outcomes/impacts. Inputs are the resources invested in the program, including human, physical, and fiscal. Activities are the specific actions taken by program providers to achieve desired results. Outputs are units of productivity yielded by the activities (e.g., number of sessions of structured experience,

> The most fundamental elements of a logic model are inputs, activities, outputs, and outcomes/impacts.

number of participants served), and outcomes/impacts are the targeted changes that result from the program. Outcomes/impacts are often divided into short-term, medium-term, and long-term changes.

Specification of linkages among inputs, actions, outputs, and impacts is helpful in many ways. Attention to inputs reveals the scope and nature of resources needed for the project and position a manager to evaluate the feasibility of a planned program. Outputs indicate the overall productivity of the program and are an important part of justifying future investments in the program. Outcomes keep programs focused on the problem or opportunity they are intended to address. Achieving success in targeted program outcomes is the overall goal of an intentional program. As noted in Chapter 13, a logic model is actually created by beginning with a specification of desired program outcomes, and works backwards through outputs, activities and inputs.

Pivotal to the success of an intentional program is the fit between the activities selected and the outcomes/impacts. Program managers must structure activities in ways that maximize the probability of the targeted outcome occurring. As an example of the importance of this fit, consider the class you are taking that required you to read this chapter. What teaching methods should be used to help you learn this content? Should the class primarily use lecture and discussion methods? Should the content be taught online? Should case study or role-play exercises be required? Should students be expected to demonstrate that they can apply concepts, principles, and procedures, or are they only responsible for an introductory level of understanding? With intentional programming, not "just any" approach to structuring experiences is acceptable. The person responsible for the program must know best practices for teaching the targeted knowledge, skills, attitudes, or values and implement those effectively. Theory often provides insight into best practices and is thus of central importance to successful intentional programming. Theory provides precision and a guiding framework that helps increase program success (Duerden & Gillard, 2007; Elias et al., 1997).

Ultimately, the success of an intentionally planned program depends on the quality of implementation of theory-based best practices principles. Leaders are both artists and scientists. They must orchestrate structured experiences using theory-based strategies that support the organizational culture, facilitate deep structured experiences, and meet the intended outcomes of the intentional program. The challenge is complex. To add to the complexity, leaders might try to facilitate an activity context in which co-creation occurs; participants must play a significant role in the way the activity unfolds. (Many youth development scholars refer to this co-creation process as youth voice; See Chapter 18).

S.A.F.E Protocols and Intentional Programming

S.A.F.E Protocols are a framework for designing intentional programs. According to that model, effective intentional youth programs are Sequential, Active, Focused, and Explicit (S.A.F.E; Durlak & Weissberg, 2007). These four elements are further grouped into process and content.

Process
- *Sequential:* Activities should take place in a sequence in order to facilitate skill development. For example, first a leader will explain and discuss the importance of a greenhouse. Second, he or she will lead a plant potting demonstration. Third, youth will practice their own plant potting. Fourth, the group will evaluate its progress.
- *Active:* Active and participatory learning help youth learn new skills as they learn by doing. For example, as opposed to dispensing information in front of a group of youth, ask questions, facilitate discussion, and provide opportunities for hands-on projects.

Content

- *Focused:* Elements of the program are focused on developing specific personal or social skills (e.g., developmental outcomes). For example, a basketball camp is bound to be a fun, hedonic experience for many youth, but a more focused basketball camp will use elements of practice or specific activities to develop specific basketball, teamwork, or leadership skills, thereby adding intentional programming to the already fun, hedonic experience.
- *Explicit:* Goals and desired outcomes are specific and clear as opposed to general. It is important youth know what they are expected to learn. For example, if the main goal of the program is to help youth do hard things, make sure to tell them that and repeatedly remind them of this goal.

A research experiment found programs that intentionally structured their programs using S.A.F.E. protocols produced positive results related to self-confidence, self-esteem, positive attitudes toward school, positive social behaviors, school grades, and achievement test scores. They also reduced problem behaviors such as aggression, noncompliance, conduct problems and drug use. On the other hand, groups who did not intentionally use S.A.F.E. protocols did not produce a single positive result for any of the previously stated categories (Durlak & Weissberg, 2007).

S.A.F.E protocols serve as an additional guide to intentional programming. When assessing the intentionality of your program use of S.A.F.E. can help ensure programs have a proper and orderly sequence and encourage active, engaged, and participatory learning. S.A.F.E. also provides insight into focusing program elements towards explicit goals and ensuring youth are aware of goals and why they are important to becoming a fully functioning adult (Bialeschki, Henderson, & James, 2007; Durlak & Weissberg, 2007).

Dosage: Attendance, Participation, and Engagement

Another important consideration is *dosage* (i.e., the amount of a program in which the youth participates). The potential benefits of intentional youth programming will not come to pass if youth do not receive a sufficient dosage of program elements in order for the program to yield positive outcomes (Durlak & Weissberg, 2007; Weiss, Little, & Bouffard, 2005). Clearly, youth dropping out of a program after a few sessions will not have the opportunity to participate in the same number of structured experiences as a youth who participates for let us say, 90% of the program sessions.

Dosage has been operationalized in a variety of ways, including days spent attending a program, participation in planned activities (participate vs. not participate), and time spent engaged in activities (Hansen & Larson, 2007; Simpkins, Little, Weiss, & Simpkins-Chaput, 2004; Weiss et al., 2005). Although there is more work to do to fully understand what is an optimal dosage level, current research on attendance, participation, and engagement help us to begin to understand if more is better and when enough is enough. As a general rule, however, youth who attend programs more frequently experience greater benefits (Simpkins et al., 2004).

Although *attendance* and *participation* are often used interchangeably, it is possible that youth will attend a program and choose not to participate (Weiss et al., 2005). Participation is often measured by assessing whether youth participated or not, but Weiss et al. (2005) extended this idea by conceptualizing participation as "participation = enrollment + attendance + engagement" (p. 19). Thus, they recommend that participation and dosage data also include an assessment of engagement since intentional youth programming are not a function of attendance alone, but rather result from the active engagement of youth in structured experiences.

In addition to dosage per program, youth are impacted by critical incidents that occur during participation and by repeated participation across multiple seasons or years. The impact of participation in multiple activities, versus only one, is not currently known. Effort exerted in participation is also a potentially important component, yet little is known about its impact (Weiss et al., 2005). Learning more about these indicators can help programs better understand how to manage and implement dosage.

As a general rule, however, youth who attend programs more frequently experience greater benefits.

Although research has consistently shown a positive linear relationship between dosage (e.g., attendance, time participating, engagement) and positive youth outcomes, it is possible dosage could have a curvilinear relationship with outcomes in certain situations (e.g., sports, art, team-building; Hansen & Larson, 2007). That is, at some point, too much time in structured youth experiences may yield negative side effects. For example, if a program is intentionally designed to provide help with homework in an effort to increase academic performance, then dosage in terms of amount of time participating and engagement will need to be consistently high. On the other hand, if a program's goals include developing leadership skills, youth may not need the same level of dosage as the academic program. In fact, a lighter dosage of any given program may be adequate for older youth, while younger youth may need a higher level (Weiss et al., 2005). Although there is no universally accepted measure for dosage, programs and organizations can collect and analyze their own participant dosage data in an effort to improve program elements and prescribe proper dosage levels to different youth populations in different program settings (Weiss et al., 2005).

Intentional Programming, Concluding Thoughts

Intentional programming practices are essential to achieving developmental outcomes through youth programs (Bialeschki et al., 2007). Youth programs are meant to be fun and enjoyable, but a purely hedonic experience is not often the purpose or goal. When discussing youth programming, transformative experiences come about by organizations implementing programs intentionally based on a theory of change (Duerden & Gillard, 2011). Youth-serving programs can accomplish this by using the previously discussed theories, frameworks, and models to intentionally design, stage, and evaluate their program offerings. Tightening the focus of programs should increase program quality (Sibthorp, Paisley, & Hill, 2003). As quality increases, youth will not only attend, but also engage and participate. Attrition levels should be lowered as well.

Conclusion

Youth development programs have long shown positive benefits (e.g., Mahoney et al., 2005) but programs still struggle to develop strategies to design programs with intentional developmental outcomes, attract youth to programs, and retain their participation. This chapter has presented a proposed framework to guide youth programming, the Youth Development Programming System (YDPP). The YDPP is a useful guide for establishing a positive youth development culture, structuring deep experiences, and applying intentional programming. The YDPP can be tailored to meet the needs of a variety of programs and organizations. If successfully implemented, the YDPP can facilitate feelings of safety and relatedness within a positive youth development culture, serve as a guide to structure immersion, absorption, and/or engagement experiences, and intentionally design desired programmatic outcomes. If appropriately applied, the YDPP should be a way to decrease program attrition.

It is important to note, however, that the model we have proposed is only one among many possible approaches to quality youth development programming. Other approaches are certainly possible. We believe, however, that the YDPP can help improve culture, experiences, and programing within any youth organization.

Discussion Questions

1. Reflect on one of your own structured experiences as a youth. What elements of the positive youth development culture were present? Which ones were absent? What could managers have done to improve the culture? What are some actions leaders took to structure positive experiences? How effective were those actions?

2. The chapter argues that serendipitous benefits are likely to occur from a youth development program that (a) has a positive organizational culture and (b) is comprised of structured experiences that promote engagement, immersion, absorption, and deep structured experience. However, the chapter ignores costs. Many youth programs are led by volunteers who have full-time occupations elsewhere, and many programs lack resources that might be used to create themes and use techniques discussed in the chapter. One might argue that implementation of these YDPP is unrealistic given these resource constraints. Do you agree or disagree? Defend your answer.

3. Make a list of 20 things you like to do. Then classify each of these according to the primary nature of the activity: engagement, immersion, or absorption. Organize your results in a bar chart showing number of activities of each type.

Compare your chart with that of other students. What are the similarities and differences in your results? What might be the implications of the differences?

4. Make a list of the structuring strategies described for each of the following: engagement, immersion, absorption, and deep structured experience. Try to identify at least one additional strategy for each of these that might be effective.

5. Find a friend. Recall three very memorable structured experiences you have had recently. Without telling your friend what you were doing, try to describe how you were feeling during each experience. Then ask your friend if she or he can correctly classify your activity as primarily engagement, immersion, or absorption.

Assignments

1. Rewrite the prologue to this chapter, imagining that the YDPP had been used to plan and manage the basketball league. Be sure to write a few sentences about organizational culture, structuring immersion experiences, deep structured experiences, and intentional programming.

2. Using the strategy given in Figure 15.3, develop a plan for establishing a positive organizational culture for a class in youth development.

3. Table 15.2 is incomplete. It provides an example of a narrative storyboard for introducing a theme/story into an activity. However, it includes narrative for only one phase of the activity, which we named *decompression*. Write or describe the narrative for one of the other sequential phases of that activity: arrival, orientation, participation, denouement, and departure. Be sure to use the activity structuring strategies discussed in the chapter.

References

Ackerman, D. (2011). *Deep play*. New York, NY: Vintage.

Amidon, E. (1961). The isolate in children's groups: Changing his stoichiometric position. *Journal of Teacher Education, 12*(4), 412–416.

Astroth, K. A. (1985). The challenge of retaining 4-H members. *Journal of Extension, 23,* 14–15.

Bandura, A. (1986). *Social foundations of thought and action: A social cognitive theory.* Englewood Cliffs, NJ: Prentice-Hall.

Bandura, A. (2011). Social cognitive theory. *Handbook of social psychological theories, 2012,* 349–373.

Belnap, R. D. (2009). Effects of a youth sport camp on individual character and fun of 11-to 14-year-old youth sport participants. Unpublished doctoral dissertation, University of Utah, Salt Lake City.

Bialeschki, M. D., Henderson, K. A., & James, P. A. (2007). Camp experiences and developmental outcomes for youth. *Child and Adolescent Psychiatric Clinics of North America, 16*(4), 769–788.

Bryant, F., & Veroff, J. (2007). *Savoring: A new model of positive experience.* Mahwah, NJ: Erlbaum.

BusinessDictionary. (2017a). Organizational culture. Retrieved from http://www.businessdictionary.com/definition/organizational-culture.html.

BusinessDictionary. (2017b). Retrieved from http://www.businessdictionary.com/definition/organizational-culture.html.

Butcher, J., Lindner, K. J., & Johns, D. P. (2002). Withdrawal from competitive youth sport: A retrospective ten-year study. *Journal of Sport Behavior, 25*(2), 145.

Csikszentmihalyi, M. (1975). *Beyond boredom and anxiety.* San Francisco, CA: Jossey-Bass.

Duerden, M. D., & Gillard, A. (2011). An approach to theory-based youth programming. *New Directions for Student Leadership, 2011*(S1), 39–53.

Durlak, J. A., & Weissberg, R. P. (2007). *The impact of after-school programs that promote personal and social skills.* Chicago, IL: Collaborative for academic, social, and emotional learning (NJ1).

Eccles, J. S., & Gootman, J. A. (Eds.). (2002). *Community programs to promote youth development. Committee on community-level programs for youth.* Board on Children, Youth, and Families, Commission on Behavioral and Social Sciences and Education, National Research Council and Institute of Medicine. Washington, DC: National Academy Press.

Elias, M. J., Zinia, J. E., Weissbert, R. P., Frey, K. S., Greenberg, M. T...Shriver, T. P. (1997). *Promoting social and emotional learning: Guidelines for educators.* Alexandria, VA: Association for Supervision and Curriculum Development.

Ellis, G. D., Freeman, P. A., Jamal, T., & Jiang, J. (2017). A theory of structured experience. *Annals of Leisure Research*, 1–22. Retrieved from http://dx.doi.org/10.1080/11745398.2017.1312468

Ellis, G., Henderson, H., Paisley, K., Silverberg, K., & Wells, M. (2004). Bringing sportsmanship back to your youth sports leagues. *Parks & Recreation, 39*, 6, 46–51.

Ellis, G. D., Maughan-Pritchett, M., & Ruddell, E. J. (1993). Effects of attribution based verbal persuasion and imagery on self-efficacy of adolescents diagnosed with major depression. *Therapeutic Recreation Journal, 27*(2), 83–97.

Evans, J., & Lindsay, W. (2014). *Managing for quality and performance excellence* (9th ed.). Mason, OH: South-Western, Cengage Learning.

Freytag, G. (1898). *Technique of the drama* (2nd ed.). Chicago, IL: Scott, Foresman.

Hansen, D. M., & Larson, R. W. (2007). Amplifiers of developmental and negative experiences in organized activities: Dosage, motivation, lead roles, and adult-youth ratios. *Journal of Applied Developmental Psychology, 28*(4), 360–374.

Harmon, W., & Holman, C. H. (1996). *A handbook to literature.* Upper Saddle River, NJ: Prentice Hall.

Hartley, R. S. (1983). Keeping 4-H members. *Journal of Extension, 21*, 19–24.

Kahneman, D. (2011). *Thinking fast and slow*. New York, NY: Farrar, Straus, and Giroux.

Mahoney, J. L., Larson, R. W., Eccles, J. S., & Lord, H. (2005). Organized activities as development contexts for children and adolescents. In J. Mahoney, R. Larson, & J. Eccles (Eds.), *Organized activities as contexts of development: Extracurricular activities, after-school and community programs* (pp. 3–22). Mahwah, NJ: Lawrence Erlbaum Associates.

Maslow, A. H. (1962). Lessons from the peak-experiences. *Journal of Humanistic Psychology, 2*(1), 9–18.

Miner, J. W. (2016) Why 70 percent of kids quit sports by age 14. *Washington Post*. Retrieved from https://www.washingtonpost.com/news/parenting/wp/2016/06/01/why-70-percent-of-kids-quit-sports-by-age-13/?utm_term=.d504a82b3e27.

O'Dell, T., & Billing, P. (Eds.). (2005). *Experiencescapes: Tourism, culture, and economy*. Chicago, IL: Copenhagen Business School Press.

Parasuraman, A., Berry, L. L., & Zeithaml, V. A. (1991). Understanding customer expectations of service. *MIT Sloan Management Review, 32*(3), 39.

Quoidbach, J., Berry, E., Hansenne, M., & Mikolajczak, M. (2010). Positive emotion regulation and well-being: Comparing the impact of eight savoring and dampening strategies. *Personality and Individual Differences, 49*(5), 368–373. doi:10.1016/j.paid.2010.03.048

Reeve, J. (2013). A self-determination theory perspective on student engagement. In S. Christenson, S., A. Reschly, & C. Wylie (Eds.), *Handbook of research on student engagement* (pp. 149–172). New York, NY: Springer.

Sibthorp, J., Paisley, K., & Hill, E. (2003). Intentional programming in wilderness education revisiting its roots. *Journal of Physical Education, Recreation & Dance, 74*(8), 21–24.

Simpkins, S., Little, P. M. D., Weiss, H. B., & Simpkins-Chaput, S. (2004). Understanding and measuring attendance in out-of-school programs. *Issues and opportunities in out-of-school time evaluation briefs, 7*.

Smith, C., Akiva, T., Arrieux, D., & Jones, M. M. (2006). Improving quality at the point of service. *New Directions for Student Leadership, 112*, 93–108.

Smith, C., & Hohmann, C. (2005). *Full findings from the Youth PQA validation study*. Ypsilanti, MI: High/Scope Educational Research Foundation.

Spengler, J. O., & Hronek, B. B. (2011). *Legal liability in recreation, sports, and tourism*. Urbana, IL: Sagamore.

U.S. Census Bureau. (2014). Nearly 6 out of 10 children participate in extracurricular activities, census bureau reports. Retrieved from https://www.census.gov/newsroom/press-releases/2014/cb14-224.html

Weiner, B. (1986). *An attributional theory of motivation and emotion*. New York, NY: Springer.

Weiss, C. H. (1972). *Evaluation research. Methods for assessing program effectiveness*. Englewood Cliffs, NJ: Prentice-Hall.

Weiss, H. B., Little, P., & Bouffard, S. M. (2005). More than just being there: Balancing the participation equation. *New Directions for Student Leadership, 105*, 15–31.

Wells, M. (2005). The effect of goal orientation on sportsmanship in youth sport experiences. Unpublished doctoral dissertation, University of Utah: Salt Lake City.

Wells, M., Ellis, G., Paisley, K., & Arthur-Banning, S. (2005). Development and evaluation of a program to promote sportsmanship in youth sports. *Journal of Park and Recreation Administration, 23*, 1, 1–17.

Zajonc, R. B. (1968). Attitudinal effects of mere exposure. *Journal of Personality and Social Psychology, 9*(2p2), 1.

Chapter 16

The Power of People
The Importance of Relationship-Based Programming

Jason N. Bocarro and Peter A. Witt

Faith Evans, an educator from Colorado, recounted a story about an experience she had while waiting to register at an outdoor education conference. A woman started calling out across the room, "Mary Faith, Mary Faith!" Faith knew that this was someone from a long, long time ago since she hadn't been called Mary Faith in probably 30 years. She turned around to see a woman in her 30s with a little girl of about 8 or 9 years old. "Mary Faith, I knew it was you." She ran up to Faith and put her arms round her. Faith was embarrassed by the woman's show of affection, especially because she had no idea who this woman was. Faith did what most of us would do….she pretended she did, telling her it was great to see her. Still she had no idea who she was, hoping the mystery woman would give her clues to their former relationship. After a few moments, the woman exclaimed that Mary Faith was her favorite camp counselor and had an amazing impact on her life. Through their former relationship, the woman explained, Faith taught her many lessons she lived by. Gosh, thought Faith, that was all those years ago and I was just a camp counselor…you just don't think about having that much of an impact on a child's life over a couple of summers. She turned to the little girl (this woman's daughter) and asked the little girl her name. The little girl looked up and replied, "Mary Faith…I was named after you." (Faith Evans, 2003)

Faith Evans' story provides evidence of the power of relationships established through out-of-school (OST) youth development programs. Relationships with youth take many forms, but the long-term impact of these relationships may be profound and last well beyond involvement in a particular program. In this chapter, we will discuss the importance of relationships established between youth and adults as a critical component of successful youth development programs. Crucial factors necessary for making these relationships successful will also be discussed.

Creating meaningful and productive relationships between young people and adults is a significant element of every model that addresses the factors necessary for enabling young people to grow to be successful and thriving adults. Furthermore, understanding why and how relationships contribute to youth development has been the focus of a number of research studies. Some findings from these efforts include the following:

- Studies of mentoring programs, such as Big Brothers, Big Sisters, have recognized the importance of relationships established between adults and young people, with youth development settings often serving as the environment for developing and sustaining these relationships (e.g., Eddy et al., 2017).
- Herrera, Sipe, and McClanahan (2000) found that over 90% of mentors felt "close" to their mentees, a bond that provided mentees with evidence of the mentors' commitment and strong support.
- Strong relationships between mentor and mentee are more likely to positively influence youths' lives (Rhodes & DuBois, 2008), and are a critical component of the success of any mentoring program.
- Strong relationships with teachers also result in stronger connections to school and increased academic performance.
- Positive relationships with non-family adults are increasingly critical, particularly given the increase in single-family households (Pew Research Center, 2015). Children from lower income families are disproportionately more likely to live with a single mother (Mather, 2010).
- In a meta-analysis of mentoring programs and adolescent health, mentoring relationships were a strong predictor of youth avoiding high-risk behaviors (Tolan, Henry, Schoeny, Lovegrove, & Nichols, 2014). This study supported previous research that found that children who formed a bond with at least one adult were more likely to exhibit healthy behaviors at 18 years old (Werner, 1989). In both of these cases, the adult was not necessarily a parent but also included adults from a school, the community, or a religious institution.

Relationship-Based Programming

Relationship-based programming (RBP) encompasses more than teaching skills and involves more than constructing settings in which young people can have a good time. Staff demeanor, a positive attitude toward youth, and the quality of relationships between participants and staff are critical for creating a successful programmatic atmosphere. This is important because atmosphere, rather than the activities themselves, helps to differentiate successful from unsuccessful OST youth development programs (Roth & Brooks Gunn, 2003). Moreover, a wide array of programmatic offerings and good facilities are usually less important than how well the participants and staff interact. When staff establishes good relationships with youth, more opportunities exist for positively influencing youth attitudes and behavior. For example, Roth and Brooks Gunn (2003) illustrate how important it is for program staff to give youth individual attention, act in culturally appropriate ways, and be willing to give youth both choice and responsibility. These programming essentials create an environment that resembles "a caring family where knowledge and supportive adults empower adolescents to develop their competencies" (p. 172).

Atmosphere, rather than the activities themselves, helps to differentiate successful from unsuccessful OST youth development programs.

Relationship-based programming differs from traditional activity-based programming in several ways. In particular, relationship-based programs move beyond just keeping youth involved in activities, entertained, and off the streets by intentionally creating additional objectives such as building strong ties between youth workers and youth. Relationships such as these may be the catalyst both for attracting youth to programs and for keeping them involved once they have joined.

Youth programs can follow this model by deliberately focusing on developing nurturing adult-youth relationships. This is certainly true of community-based OST programs that provide a rich context for developing supportive and caring relationships, something particularly important for youth living without a strong family support system, but critical to all youth regardless of their family situation. Research highlights the importance of programs that are embedded within a community context. For example, McDaniel and Yarbrough's (2016) recent review showed that mentor/mentee relationships were stronger in Community-Based Mentoring (CBM) programs as opposed to School-Based Mentoring (SBM) programs.

Adopting a Relationship-Based Programming Framework

Three main elements are critical to adopting a RBP framework within youth programming:

1. Encouraging involvement in programs
2, Implementing programs that address other facets of a child's life
3. Establishing relationships with members of the extended family

Each of these will be described in the following sections.

Encouraging Involvement in Programs

Previous discussion in this chapter has noted that it is important to move beyond a focus on activity provision to one that also includes cultivating relationships among youth and staff. Although activities are important, youth can be turned off or on to a program or activity based on their interactions with program staff. For example, some children drop out of sports because of a bad relationship with a coach or teacher. Indeed, there is a growing recognition that coaches of youth sports programs need better training that goes beyond the technical aspects of the game and includes information about youth development and how to build effective relationships with children (Agans, Ettekal, Erickson, & Lerner, 2016). Following are two examples illustrating the success of the Austin (Texas) Park and Recreation Department's initiative to establish relationships between youth workers and young people in order to increase their involvement in sport and recreation programs (Bocarro, 2001). As part of this initiative, staff assigned youth workers to roles as outreach workers (Roving Leaders) across the city.

Robert is one of the youth workers assigned to work in a predominately Hispanic community where many of the females did not participate in sports. Robert was determined to promote female athletics, and thus set up different female-only sports teams. His philosophy was straightforward:

> I don't want to knock the kids or anything, but our teams are always made up of scrubs, the kids who are never going to win a league, they may never even win a game, but we make sure that when we lose a game our kids aren't mad. They are just happy that they got to play. It's about teaching them teamwork, good spirit and having fun and getting a chance to participate. And we achieved that. (Bocarro, 2001)

Because of Robert's efforts, participation by girls increased dramatically in various sports, predominately because their disappointment with losing was offset by the fun many of the girls had and the supportive atmosphere that Robert had created within that program.

In another instance, a youth worker described how a 15-year-old female participant signed up for an outdoor fishing trip despite insisting she had no interest in fishing. Once on the trip she admitted that her involvement was motivated through being able to spend quality time with this particular youth worker.

Implementing Programs that Address Other Facets of a Child's Life

Successfully building relationships may be time consuming and require youth workers to become involved in a child's life beyond their participation in programs. This may mean responding to opportunities to help young people deal with school, personal, and family-related issues. Some of Bocarro's (2001) research illustrates how a youth worker might form a partnership with school counselors and teachers and act as a liaison between youth who have already dropped out or are about to drop out of school, as was the case with Jose.

Jose is an intelligent 17-year-old Hispanic male, living at home with his mom, dad, and younger brother. Jose had lived in several different public housing complexes, and had attended three different high schools in less than 18 months. Both he and his sister eventually dropped out of high school, and Jose began working full-time at a computer company. Jose spent a year enrolled in a charter school while working, but that did not work out either, and he dropped out again. According to Jose:

> I hated it there…It was hard, because I thought it was gonna be good but I went there for like one year, the first year, it was totally different. The kids that enlisted were fighting and cussing and the teachers never could teach so you couldn't never learn nothing and so I dropped out of there. (Bocarro, 2001)

Jose resumed working at the computer company, which offered a full-time night job with benefits. However, before the beginning of the next school year, he recognized the importance of obtaining his high school diploma. He stated,

> I figured that I needed to hurry up and get my high school diploma 'cause I'm going to be 18 already in October and so I want to graduate this year. And basically I feel like I just need to get it over with. I understand that a high school diploma is an important thing. (Bocarro, 2001)

Negotiating the high school system can be very confusing, particularly for a family with little experience with the education system, such as Jose's. Once Jose made the decision to go back to school, Robert, a youth worker who had developed a relationship with Jose as part of his outreach work, took Jose and his mother to the high school and helped him enroll. Jose found the traditional school setting difficult, and despite a lot of support from Robert, he quit again after three months. A few weeks after dropping out, the courts decided to fine him for not going to school. Robert testified on Jose's behalf in court and stopped the situation from becoming worse by clearly explaining all the circumstances. The court decided the best path for Jose would be to attend a GED program on the other side of town. With Robert's help, Jose saved enough money to buy a car and was able to get himself to the program.

> Youth workers' relationships with youth can contribute to youth development by helping to prevent situations from reaching extreme proportions.

This example illustrates the importance of relationships that provide a context for youth workers to have major impacts on various facets of youths' lives. As Jose's story shows, youth workers' relationships with youth can contribute to youth development by helping to prevent situations from reaching extreme proportions, reminding youth of the importance of education, and facilitating action (e.g., making regular school visits, talking to teachers, and sitting in on classes). Because it is easier to develop long-term and trusting relationships with youth in OST, recreation, and leisure programs than in most other contexts in a youth's life (e.g., school or work), youth workers have many opportunities.

Building Relationships with Members of the Extended Family

Developing rapport with members of a child's immediate and extended family facilitates successful relationship-based programming. Building meaningful relationships with family members as well as youth may aid a youth worker in helping a young person navigate difficult personal and family issues. These relationships may also help youth workers to understand why a particular youth may be acting in a certain positive or negative way.

The knowledge gained through contacts with family members may help guide a youth worker's approach to working with a youth who seems to be having difficulties, or developing programmatic activities for a particular child. Further, when youth workers successfully develop relationships with parents, they are then able to act as resources for a family and subsequently help solve problems that may be affecting all of the family members.

Despite the desirability of building relationships with parents, this process is difficult, time consuming, and requires a considerable amount of face-to-face contact.

Additionally, not all parents want to engage in a relationship with a youth worker. In activity-based programs, which are common in recreation departments and other OST programs, contact with the family is often minimal, and most of the communication is through letters taken home by the child or via telephone calls. This common approach to parental involvement presents a challenge to youth workers who wish to build relationships with family members, especially when time is limited. When dealing with difficult issues, face-to-face contact is more effective and, in certain cases, the only way to build relationships with extended family members.

The following example from Bocarro's (2001) research demonstrates some possible implications of relationship building:

> Loretta, a 13-year-old child enrolled in a park and recreation program, was often distraught by her mother's serious drug problem. Loretta's feelings often affected her mood, behavior at school, and interactions with her peers. One of the city's youth workers was able to pick up on this problem during informal conversations with Loretta, and due to the positive relationship that he had built with the child's mother over the past year, was able to refer the mother to agencies that could help her address her drug problem. The mother subsequently improved, which in turn made a difference in Loretta's situation and in her subsequent behavior.

Although many of the examples provided thus far have been about youth who lived in problematic environments (e.g., a mother with drug addiction) or who were experiencing problems (e.g., dropping out of school) it should be stressed that all youth benefit from relationship-based programming. Indeed, this fact is one of the major principles of youth development presented in Chapter 1; all youth, no matter how involved or uninvolved their parents are, need relationships with other caring adults. As we mentioned, recreation and leisure experiences and activities are contexts where relationships can be built and maintained with youth and in most cases, with family members. Next, we describe ways to build these strong relationships.

Relationship-Based Programming in Practice: Building Relationships

Let us begin by looking at the types of relationships that can be developed between youth and adults in recreation and other OST activity settings. Researchers have identified three types of relationships: counterproductive, prescriptive, and developmental (e.g., Morrow & Styles, 1995; Walker & White, 1998).

Counterproductive Relationships

It may be destructive to a young person's development when youth workers allow their personal biases to influence their relationships. Remember Jose from a previous example? An example of a counterproductive relationship would be if Jose's youth worker had a personal belief that most Hispanic boys who dropped out of school were no good and did not possess the cognitive skills to complete the requirements for a high school diploma. Youth workers who do not manage their personal biases are often seen as judgmental and belittling authority figures who do not take into account youths' needs and desires.

Prescriptive Relationships

These relationships develop when youth workers have preconceived goals that frame the context of the relationship. Often youth workers see themselves in the role of the rescuer and view their task as improving and re-educating youth, a perspective we discussed in Chapter 1 as not only "old school" but also detrimental to a fully prepared and engaged youth. Although this approach may be well intentioned, it leaves little room for youth input. Imagine if Faith had "pushed" her camper (instead of using encouragement and support) into taking swimming lessons because swimming was "good for her." It is doubtful Faith would have had the lasting impression and influence that she had if that had been her approach. In this mode of operation, any reluctance and reticence on the part of youth is seen as a challenge to the youth workers' authority and evidence that there is something wrong with the young person's attitude.

Developmental Relationships

This type of relationship occurs when youth workers devote themselves to establishing a strong connection to youth before addressing other goals. They work with youth in a respectful manner, concentrating on developing trust while being careful not to impose their own ideas and values as a condition of the relationship. These types of relationships often transcend ordinary day-to-day interactions. All of the examples provided so far in this chapter illustrate this type of relationship.

While youth workers at one time or another probably exhibit each of these relationship types, the goal of most youth workers is to build relationships with youth that are developmental in nature. That is why they are in a people profession.

What are the characteristics of individuals who are skilled at developing relationships? There is no question that developing relationships comes naturally to some people, but for most people, it is a skill to be developed. A couple of studies, in particular, help to answer that question. In their landmark study of neighborhood-based organizations, McLaughlin, Irby, and Langman (1994) identified talented youth

While youth workers at one time or another probably exhibit each of these relationship types, the goal of most youth workers is to build relationships with youth that are developmental in nature.

workers, termed *wizards,* who were successful in developing relationships and making a difference with youth. In all cases, positive outcomes were due to the relationships between youth and these wizards, and, in almost every instance, relationships were developed and sustained through recreation experiences. These wizards all shared five broad characteristics:

- Saw genuine potential in youth, not pathology
- Were youth-centered
- Were confident in their own abilities to make a difference
- Felt an obligation to give back to their community or society
- Displayed unyielding authenticity in all their interactions (i.e., they keep it "real")

Other research has suggested an addition set of important characteristics essential to helping youth workers develop effective relationships with youth (e.g., Bocarro, 2001; Bocarro & Witt, 2003; Kupersmidt & Rhodes, 2014). These are as follows:

- Be multifaceted and flexible
- Be hands-on
- Exhibit commitment and consistency
- Be patient and empathetic
- Establish mutual caring and respect

Multifaceted and Flexible

As discussed in Chapter 9, OST programs and activities are excellent contexts for development to occur. However, youth workers need to be flexible and multifaceted in how they interact with young people in order to implement successful programs and activities.

For example, youth may use an OST context to experiment with gender roles, work on their identity (e.g., who am I?), or practice emotional and social self-regulation. Because these developmental processes take work, youth workers have to react to the developmental issues that surface. This means that a relationship-based youth worker may have to play a number of different roles ranging from coach, to mentor, to teacher, to friend, depending on the circumstances of the young people with whom they are working, and the developmental needs at hand. Being dogmatic in approach and thinking there is only one way for a situation to be handled goes against relationship-based programming and does not contribute to youth development.

Being Hands-On

Successful youth workers are those who interact with youth and participate in activities, while those who are less successful often remain on the periphery and take on the role of disciplinarian. (However, successful youth workers also recognize the necessity of establishing appropriate disciplinary boundaries as well as not undermining the opportunity for youth voice.)

Being hands-on in this context does not necessarily entail being good at activities, just a willingness to be involved. Thus, one of the keys to developing relationships is the ability and willingness to facilitate interactions with kids. To accomplish this outcome, youth workers need to be playful, young at heart, energetic, and demonstrate enthusiasm. They must rely more on personal resources than physical or extrinsic resources (such as good facilities), and know when to "get their hands dirty" by playing and interacting with youth.

> Successful youth workers are those who interact with youth and participate in activities, while those who are less successful often remain on the periphery and take on the role of disciplinarian.

Commitment and Consistency

Being committed to making a difference is another critical aspect of relationship-based programming. Full youth worker commitment means that no matter how challenging the situation, the youth worker takes necessary steps to figure out a solution.

Several common conditions exist that may threaten commitment and consistency in relationship-based programming. These include budgetary constraints, lack of equipment, and lack of supervisory support. Youth behavior may also present a challenge…that is, often when staff perceive that youth are troublemakers who need too much individual attention, they are dropped from programs because it is easier than dealing with the problem, or because other parents or other youth complain. However, being committed means understanding circumstances in children's lives and the underlying reasons for their negative or inappropriate behavior. It also means developing a strategic plan for addressing the issue and finding ways to maintain commitment to the program.

For example, Vanessa was a child who had experienced a number of adults coming into and going out of her life. Thus, she mistrusted everyone who said they were there to help her or be her friend. She consistently used bad language and was aggressive with new staff. Vanessa explained that this was her way of testing them. Successfully working with Vanessa required commitment and consistency for a sustained period on the part of her youth worker.

Being consistent is critical because it allows workers to earn and maintain a child's trust and respect. An aspect of consistency includes certain commitments by youth worker staff; for example, it is essential that youth workers avoid breaking appointments or promises they have made to young people. Many youth who have experienced broken promises from other adults in their lives may perceive that a youth worker may only be around for a short time, making it difficult for children to forge healthy relationships. Providing consistency, therefore, establishes a platform on which a trusting relationship can be built.

One youth worker renowned for his consistency described why commitment and consistency were so important in particular to the teenage boys with whom he worked. He was critical of youth workers who were consistent and committed when things went well in a child's life, but who, when circumstances became more demanding, pulled away. His philosophy was that commitment demanded a youth worker to be present through both good and bad times. As he pointed out, "A good youth worker is when the kids see your presence, and you can hang out at the park and talk about what happened at school, but either way they know you'll be committed to them."

Patient and Empathetic

Being patient and empathetic is critical to building relationships with youth. Part of being patient and empathetic includes learning to be nonjudgmental, forgiving, and willing to deal with problems, even when changes take longer than desired. They must also subjugate their own needs and put youths' needs in focus. Relationships that are developmental rather than prescriptive tend to adhere to the philosophy of *meeting youth where they are at* rather than expecting them to be where the youth worker wants them to be in the end. Movement toward a goal (e.g., school attendance) requires both parties to be on the same page initially. Youth workers facilitate movement toward the goal by a relationship characterized by patience and empathy. For example, one youth worker discussed how he worked on building relationships with his group of boys, rather than simply worrying about how badly they were doing at school. He was particularly adept at recognizing the issues youth were facing, and discussed the need to take things slowly, however frustrating this might become.

> I think of myself as a positive influence, but hopefully I'm not necessarily another person in their face trying to beat it over their head that this is the way it's supposed to be or that type of thing, but just to approach things with a little more patience. Not to just hit them with, "this is how it is, this is what you're going to do, and this is how it's best." I mean just more of the approach of just being able to come down to their level and let them take it as slow as they need to or at a pace that they think is comfortable. (Bocarro, 2001)

This approach may require youth workers to be less judgmental. For example, one outreach worker pointed out that when he started working with a group of youth using inappropriate and foul language was common. If he had tried to reduce their use of foul language too quickly, and before he established rapport with the group, it would not have worked.

> My kids really have bad mouths. The way I deal with that is that when that kid respects you, he or she is going to catch themselves and say, "Oh, I'm sorry, Mister or I'm sorry, Miss" or something. That's what you want. You don't want to be so much about rules that they are like, "Oh you're just another one of those guys out there trying to change me." You want them to come on their own terms to respect you and to respect what you are trying to do for them and that's the point that I'm at with a lot of the kids. (Bocarro, 2001)

Mutuality

Recognizing that relationships are a two-way street is important. Children mold us as much as we try to mold them, and interactions with young people influence our own development. This means that mutual respect, trust, and liking need to occur. A healthy relationship may be difficult to maintain when one person cares about the relationship more than the other does.

For example, two university students, Amanda and Katy, worked at an after-school enrichment program serving predominately low-income youth aged 8–18. The program was situated next to some low-income housing. One day, Amanda noticed a 16-year-old girl from the housing projects, Rochelle, hanging around. She invited her to come along to help her work with some of the younger children. Rochelle explained that she was not interested, as she did not like "school stuff." However, both Amanda and Katy persisted and began sharing some of their personal stories with Rochelle in order to build up a degree of trust. In return, Rochelle began opening up and coming to the program on a regular basis. Rochelle felt that her relationship with Katy and Amanda was a two-way connection, and therefore she felt comfortable sharing some of the issues she was facing in school which included being written off by teachers and teased by other students about her weight.

We would like to share a couple of caveats here. First, it is important to recognize that in reality, relationships may be one-sided, if not only at first but over the long-term. Therefore, it is part of one's professional outlook to expect that not every child will want a relationship at that time. It is, however, one's professional obligation to persist. Second, it is also important to realize that although a professional's needs may be met as a secondary outcome to a relationship (e.g., a youth worker feels needed or competent), one's needs are always subordinate to youths' needs.

Challenges to Adopting a Relationship-Based Programming Perspective

Several challenges exist for programs wishing to adopt a relationship-based programming perspective. One challenge, noted in Chapter 1, is that many programs are not sustainable and fizzle out after a year or two. Another challenge is high staff burn-out rates. Maintaining the funding to sustain programs is also a debilitating issue faced by a number of youth development experts (e.g., Deutsch et al., 2017; Dryfoos, 1990; Lerner, 1995), and too often insufficient attention is given to developing a long-term plan for maintaining program funding and staffing (Pittman, Irby, & Ferber, 2000).

Lerner (1995) described some of the consequences of short-term programs that parachute in and out of communities. He pointed out that when programs shut down, communities often feel less hopeful and empowered than before the program existed. Thus, although there may be improvement in the lives of children and families, the inability to sustain program may result in residents' feelings of loss, disappointment, or even exploitation and anger.

Another related challenge is one of sufficient dosage (see also Chapters 13 and 15). Just as the right amount of penicillin taken over the right amount of time is needed to cure an infection, the amount of time and length of duration youth spend with youth workers is critical. Programs that last for only a short period of time probably have less impact than those that are able to sustain involvement over a longer time period. Too often policy makers like to see relationship-based initiatives as a quick fix rather than a commitment to long-term involvements (Deutsch et al., 2017).

> Too often policy makers like to see relationship-based initiatives as a quick fix rather than a commitment to long-term involvements.

However, little research exists that determines the correct dosage of relationships for different youth in different contexts. That implies that what might be a good dosage for some youth may not be the correct dosage for others, depending on life circumstances and personal characteristics. Thus, programmers must carefully take account of individual differences when designing programs.

A final challenge is that often staff do not receive adequate training, ongoing support and supervision, or public recognition. All three of these components are important to maintaining staff morale. Huebner et al. (2003) observed there is an unspoken assumption that anyone can work with youth. Instead, practitioners need to think more systematically about ways in which programs can better train their staff to work with youth by embracing the important principles of a positive youth development framework. Understanding how relationships with youth are formed and developed is critical, as the intentionality of building relationships with youth will be lost if all programmers are not on the same page. Therefore, pre-service and in-service training would make a significant contribution to relationship-based programming efforts.

Conclusions

There is a growing recognition that people are the most critical aspect of any youth program. A report by the Carnegie Council on Adolescent Development (1992) stated that:

> Youth-serving agencies, religious youth groups, sports programs, and parks and recreation services and libraries all report that the adults who work with young people in their systems, whether serving on a paid or voluntary basis, are the most critical factor in whether a program succeeds. (p. 87)

Thus, creating meaningful relationships between program staff and participants is more important than the particular activities in which young people are involved. Developing close relationships with an unrelated adult through out-of-school time programs is a significant factor in youth development. However, this happens too rarely, and when it does, relationships may not be sufficiently close or positive.

Youth workers are in a prime position to develop relationships due to the contextual and experiential elements of OST programs. Being intentional about developing relationships will make facilitating youth development through OST programs easier and more effective. This requires skill development through practice and training as well as adopting a perspective that simply focuses on the activity.

Discussion Questions

1. In the chapter, three types of relationship styles that adults typically employ when working with children were described. Give examples of adult leaders you have had contact with who have demonstrated each of these styles.
2. There a growing recognition that relationship-based programming is a critical component of youth development programming. Why do you think that is the case? Again, give examples from your own work with youth programs.
3. What does it mean to say that relationships within programs are more important to development that the specifics activities within which these relationships occur?

Assignments

1. This chapter describes how adults who work with youth have different relationship styles. Think about what style most defines you. Are there times when your style changes or when one style might be more applicable/appropriate than another? Is there one style that is more effective than another?

2. Think about organizations and experiences you've been a part of where an adult role model (teacher, coach, or camp counselor) made a tremendous impact on you. What was it about them that enabled them to build those relationships and why was it so effective? Trace back some of the qualities you have just described to the material from the chapter. What was different and what aligned with your own experiences?

References

Agans, J. P., Ettekal, A. V., Erickson, K., & Lerner, R. M. (2016). In N. L. Holt (Ed.), *Positive youth development through sport* (pp. 34–44). New York, NY: Routledge.

Bocarro, J. N. (2001). Mobile beacons: Roving leaders and the communities they serve. Unpublished doctoral dissertation, Texas A&M University, College Station.

Bocarro, J. N., & Witt, P. A. (2003). Relationship-based programming: The key to successful youth development in recreation settings. *Journal of Park and Recreation Administration, 21*(3), 75–96.

Carnegie Council on Adolescent Development. (1992). *A matter of time: Risk and opportunity in the out of school hours.* New York, NY: Carnegie Cooperation of New York.

Deutsch, N. L., Blyth, D. A., Kelley, J., Tolan, P. H., & Lerner, R. M. (2017). Let's talk after-school: The promises and challenges of positive youth development for after-school research, policy, and practice. In N. L. Deutsch (Ed.), *After-school programs to promote positive youth development: Integrating research into practice and policy* (pp. 45–68). Charlottesville, VA: Springer International Publishing.

Dryfoos, J. G. (1990). *Adolescents at risk: Prevalence and prevention.* New York, NY: Oxford University Press.

Eddy, J. M., Martinez Jr, C. R., Grossman, J. B., Cearley, J. J., Herrera, D., Wheeler, A. C., & Harachi, T. W. (2017). A randomized controlled trial of a long-term professional mentoring program for children at risk: Outcomes across the first 5 years. *Prevention Science.* doi: 10.1007/s11121-017-0795-z

Evans, F. (2003). Kurt Hahn Address 2001 AEE International Conference. *Journal for Experiential Education, 25*(3), 357–362.

Herrera, C., Sipe, C. L., & McClanahan, W. S. (2000). *Mentoring school-age children: Relationship development in community-based and school-based programs.* Philadelphia, PA: Public/Private Ventures.

Huebner, A. J., Walker, J. A., & McFarland, M. (2003). Staff development for the youth development professionalism: A critical framework for understanding the work. *Youth & Society, 35*(2), 204–225.

Kupersmidt, J. B., & Rhodes, J. E. (2014). Mentor training. In D. L. DuBois & M. J. Karcher (Eds.), *Handbook of youth mentoring* (pp. 439–456, 2nd ed.). Los Angeles, CA: Sage Publications.

Lerner, R. M. (1995). *America's youth in crisis: Challenges and options for programs and policies.* London, UK: Sage Publications.

Mather, M. (2010). U.S. Children in single-mother families. Population Reference Bureau. Retrieved from http://www.prb.org/pdf10/single-motherfamilies.pdf

McDaniel, S., & Yarbrough, A. M. (2016). A literature review of afterschool mentoring programs for children at risk. *Journal of At-Risk Issues, 19*(1), 1–9.

McLaughlin, M.W., Irby, M. A., & Langman, J. (1994). *Urban sanctuaries: Neighborhood organizations in the lives and futures of inner-city youth.* San Francisco, CA: Jossey-Bass.

Morrow, K.V., & Styles, M. B. (1995). *Building relationships with youth in program settings: A study of Big Brothers/Big Sisters.* Philadelphia, PA: Public/Private Ventures.

Pew Research Center. (2015). The American family today. Retrieved from http://www.pewsocialtrends.org/2015/12/17/1-the-american-family-today/

Pittman, K., Irby, M., & Ferber, T. (2000). Unfinished business: Further reflections on a decade of promoting youth development. Takoma Park, MD: The Forum for Youth Development. Retrieved from http://forumfyi.org/files/UnfinishedBusiness.pdf

Rhodes, J. E., & DuBois, D. L. (2008). Mentoring relationships and programs for youth. *Current Directions in Psychological Science, 17*(4), 254–258.

Roth, J. L., & Brooks-Gunn, J. (2003). Youth development programs: Risk, prevention & policy. *Journal of Adolescent Health, 32*(3), 170–182.

Tolan, P. H., Henry, D. B., Schoeny, M. S., Lovegrove, P., & Nichols, E. (2014). Mentoring programs to affect delinquency and associated outcomes of youth at-risk: a comprehensive meta-analytic review. *Journal of Experimental Criminology, 10*(2), 179–206.

Walker, J., & White, L. (1998). *Caring adults support the healthy development of youth.* 4H Cooperative extension, University of Minnesota.

Werner, E. E. (1989). High-risk children in young adulthood: A longitudinal study from birth to 32 years. *American Journal of Orthopsychiatry, 59*(1), 72–81.

Chapter 17

Family Matters

Supporting Positive Youth Development through Family Programming

Karen K. Melton, Camilla J. Hodge,
Nicole McAninch, and Ericka J. Olschewski

Adolescents' development is primarily shaped by their families (Bronfenbrenner, 1979). Therefore, if we care about adolescents, then we must also care about their families. While issues regarding family dynamics have received substantial attention, greater attention to family is needed in positive youth development (PYD) programming. Although most youth programs focus on direct programs and services for adolescents, it is also imperative to consider the role that youth programs have in supporting and collaborating with adolescents' families.

Although other chapters of this book provide examples of adolescent-centered programs, in this chapter we provide examples of family-centered or, at the very least, family-inclusive approaches to PYD programming. We begin by reviewing the role that thriving families play in PYD, and three indicators often used in assessing the quality of family life: family relationships, family functioning, and family experiences. These sections will provide the reader with a basic understanding of family life to appreciate why the family matters. In the second part of the chapter, we provide the reader with family-centered approaches and family-inclusive principles to consider when designing PYD programs to include families.

The Role of Families in PYD

Other things may change us, but we start and end with family.
—Anthony Brandt

Let's begin by defining the term *family*. Because of your own personal knowledge and experience with family, it may seem unnecessary to define such a common word. However, the word family brings to mind potentially different images for each person. These images may vary based on personal knowledge and experiences but also by culture and historical periods. For example, consider variations in *family structure* present in families today, including two-parent, one-parent, heterosexual couples, homosexual couples, stepfamilies, extended families, blended families, and many other family structures. Thus, the term family applies to a diverse set of circumstances and relationships.

Additionally, perspectives and definitions of families throughout history have largely depended on complex social perspectives on marriage, childhood, work, and adolescence. Legal proceedings and policies also have shaped the way families are classified. For example, same-sex marriages were considered illegal in parts of the United States until June 26, 2015, when the United States Supreme Court ruled in *Obergefell v. Hodges* that state-level bans on same-sex marriage were unconstitutional. For these reasons, it becomes necessary to define family. In this chapter, family represents the social relationships between at least two people related by birth, marriage, adoption, or long-standing ties of affection. This definition includes many diverse types of families beyond what may be considered historically traditional views of family structure.

In understanding families, we must also consider *family functions*, or the expectations of family. Families are often thought of as the "building blocks" of a society. This is because families are expected to complete many functions (or tasks) that build, maintain, and advance the workforce of a society. By understanding these expectations, you are better positioned to appreciate and support families. These expectations have varied across cultures and history. For example, in Colonial America, families functioned as little commonwealths, or highly independent systems, and were expected to provide education, vocational training, and manufactured goods that supported the growth and development of children (Mintz & Kellogg, 1988). In modern society, however, families serve five primary functions: (a) family formation and membership, (b) partnership relationships, (c) economic support, (d) childrearing, and (e) caregiving (see Table 17.1 for a description; Bogenschneider, Little, Ooms, Benning, & Cadigan, 2012). When families are not able to achieve these expectations on their own, government and human services often provide assistance.

Table 17.1
Family Functions: Societal Expectations of Families

Function	Responsibility
Family Formation and Membership	Families bring new individuals into the world and provide individuals with their basic personal identity and sense of belonging.
Partner Relationships	Families serve to strengthen and nurture healthy communication, cooperation, intimacy, and conflict management skills in their members.
Economic Support	Families provide everyday needs of food, shelter, and clothing.
Childrearing	Families raise, nurture, and socialize the next generation to be productive members of society.
Caregiving	Families provide care to one another across the life cycle, and special care is given when family members experience disease, diagnosis, and disaster.

Beyond understanding the structure and function of a family, it is also important to understand variations in quality of family life (e.g., healthy vs. dysfunctional families). Quality of family life is known to influence adolescents in all dimensions of development. For example, adolescents coming from unhealthy families are more at risk of mental health issues, drug use, unhealthy relationships, and poor academic performance (Van Ryzin, Kumpfer, Fosco, & Greenberg, 2016). In the following sections, we provide three indicators that have been used to determine the quality of family life: (a) family relationships, (b) family functioning, and (c) family experiences.

Family Relationships

When we consider the health of a family, we often first look at family relationships. Healthy parent-child relationships are vital to positive development, and much attention has been given to the relationship between parents and adolescents. However, sibling relationships are also important to adolescent development. Youth programs that consider family relationships tend to focus on parent-adolescent relationships but rarely address sibling relationships. This oversight in research and programming is increasingly problematic as demographic trends suggest children in the United States are more likely to share a household with a sibling than a father (Feinberg, Sakuma, Hostetler, McHale, 2013; McHale, Kim, Whiteman, & Crouter, 2007). Even as the average family size declines in the United States, most people have at least one sibling (Feinberg et al., 2013). Therefore, it is important to discuss both parent-child and sibling relationships because both contribute to adolescents' development and each should be considered during PYD programming.

Parent-child relationships. The parent-child relationship can significantly affect adolescents' identity development. Developmental psychologist Erik Erikson (1968) suggested adolescents' primary task is to develop their identity. During adolescence, young persons are trying to understand who they are as individuals. As such, it is natural for adolescents to separate from their families and begin to exhibit *autonomy,* which is the task of exercising control over their decision-making and gaining a sense of independence. Although some separation from parents is necessary, parents often mistake adolescents' desire and need for increasing autonomy as an opportunity to release responsibility and reduce conflict. However, families function best when parents remain connected and identify and enforce clear expectations for family members. Similarly, parents create healthy environments for adolescent identity development when they balance family closeness with adolescent individuality (Cooper & Grotevant, & Condon 1983).

Over time, researchers have identified four parenting styles: authoritative, authoritarian, permissive, and uninvolved (Baumrind, 1991). Parents who are warm and responsive to their children, set clear rules and realistic expectations for their behavior, and have high levels of involvement in their children's lives are known as authoritative parents. Authoritative parenting tends to be associated with the best outcomes for adolescents, including higher levels of self-esteem, social skills, and school performance (Steinberg & Morris, 2001). Adolescents also are less likely to engage in risky behaviors, including drug and alcohol abuse (Broman, Reckase, & Freedman-Doan, 2006). Authoritative parents tend to create an environment that informs and encourages adolescents to develop a healthy sense of self and healthy relationships with others (Mounts, Valentiner, Anderson, & Boswell, 2006).

> Families function best when parents remain connected and identify and enforce clear expectations for family members.

The other three parenting styles are associated with less desirable outcomes for most adolescents. *Authoritarian parents* have high expectations with strict rules for their children, but little warmth and responsiveness to their children's needs and individuality.

This parenting style tends to affect negatively an adolescent's sense of self-worth and school performance (Steinberg, Lamborn, Dornbusch, & Darling, 1992). *Permissive parents* are warm and engaging with their adolescents, but set few rules and expectations for their behavior. As a result, these adolescents tend to struggle with impulsivity, self-centered behaviors, and poor social skills (Lamborn, Mounts, Steinberg, & Dornbusch, 1991). *Uninvolved parents* show little warmth and interest in their adolescents, setting no rules or expectations for them. As a result, adolescents of uninvolved parents often engage in risky behaviors, including substance abuse and delinquency (Lamborn et al., 1991). Adolescents who come from families with unhealthy parenting styles often exhibit an unhealthy sense of self and relationship with others, including friends, family, teachers, and romantic partners (Schwartz, Hage, Bush, & Burns, 2006).

Sibling relationships. Like parents, sibling relationships can indirectly and directly affect adolescent development (McHale, Updegraff, & Whiteman, 2012). Direct sibling effects on development are derived from siblings' day-to-day interactions and involvement with each other (McHale et al., 2012). For example, children learn perspective-taking and problem-solving skills as they experience sibling conflict (McHale et al., 2012). Siblings also exert indirect effects on adolescent development. For example, parents' expectations about the behavior in adolescence are different for later-born siblings when they have already had a child transition from childhood to adolescence (Shanahan, McHale, Osgood, & Crouter, 2007; Whiteman & Buchanan, 2002). Table 17.2 provides a summary of siblings' direct and indirect effects on adolescent development.

Various theories can also help us understand why and how siblings can affect development. For example, *attachment theory* describes how a strong emotional connection to a caregiver is necessary for successful development. For some children, healthy sibling relationships can provide the emotional connection needed for positive development (Yeh & Lempers, 2004). *Social learning theory* describes how siblings act as models of prosocial behavior for each other and how adolescents can learn from one another via observation, imitation, and modeling (East, 2009; Whiteman, McHale, & Soli, 2011). The likelihood that siblings will acquire the prosocial behavior increases as siblings spend more time together and have higher quality relationships. Overall, these theories suggest programs should encourage positive sibling interactions while reducing negative interactions to support healthy sibling relationships and overall quality of family life (McHale et al., 2012).

Family Functioning

In addition to family relationships, another way to consider the quality of family life is by evaluating a family's level of functioning. *Family functioning* is (a) the family's ability to bond—known as *family cohesion* and (b) the family's ability to handle change—known as *family adaptability*. Healthy families can strike the balance of cohesion and adaptability through open communication between family members (Barnes & Olson, 1985; Olson & Gorall, 2003). *Open communication* occurs when family members can speak and listen in a way that allows members to express their true thoughts and feelings to one another.

Table 17.2

Siblings' Direct and Indirect Effects on Development

Direct Effects Siblings can directly support positive (or negative) social and cognitive developmental outcomes		Indirect Effects Siblings can indirectly affect positive (or negative) social and cognitive developmental outcomes	
Direct Effect	**Outcome**	**Indirect Effect**	**Outcome**
Siblings' daily interactions	• Problem-solving • Conflict resolution • Social competence & socialization • Companionship & emotional support • Social support • Altruism • Empathy	Older siblings shape parents' expectations of younger siblings	• Lower conflict with parents • Higher levels of warmth
Social learning (i.e., siblings acting as models for behaviors)	• Adjustment problems • Externalizing & antisocial behaviors • Development of family norms • Improvement in cognitive tasks	Parents' differential treatment (i.e., parents treating one sibling differently than the other)	• Poorer adjustment for less favored sibling
Sibling differentiation (i.e., identifying & emphasizing differences between siblings)	• Identity development • Social competence	Resource dilution (i.e., reduced resources available to younger siblings)	• Intellectual development • Academic achievement • Cognitive skills

*For more in-depth reading on these effects, see McHale et al. (2012), Downey (2001), and Cicirelli (1995).

Families with balanced adaptability and cohesion provide a healthy context for adolescent development, because adaptable families can create an environment where adolescents learn to make better decisions and improve their self-esteem (Brown & Mann, 1990; 1991). Cohesive families can recognize adolescents' need for separation and togetherness, which provide adolescents with the appropriate space to create their own identities. In contrast, families that live at the extremes of adaptability and cohesion may provide a dysfunctional context for adolescent development. Extremes of adaptability tend to lead to chaotic or rigid families, whereas extremes of cohesion tend to lead to enmeshed or disengaged families. Table 17.3 provides an overview of balanced and extreme (i.e., high and low) levels of family cohesion and family adaptability.

Table 17.3
Family Functioning

Family Functioning Component	Classification	Description
Adaptability the ability to handle change or stress	High—*Chaotic*	These dysfunctional families have none or few rules, roles, or routines that direct their family life, thus creating a chaotic home environment because expectations are ever changing.
	Balanced—*Adaptable*	These healthy families maintain clear expectations for their rules, roles, and routines of family life but adapt expectations when special circumstances arise.
	Low—*Rigid*	These dysfunctional families refuse to alter their expectations of rules, roles, or routines of family life to accommodate changing needs.
Cohesion the ability of family members to connect with one another	High—*Enmeshed*	These dysfunctional families rely exclusively on each other for support, reliance, and interaction; often characterized by an inability to allow for individuality and space between family members.
	Balanced—*Cohesive*	These healthy families recognize and balance family members' needs for separation and togetherness.
	Low—*Disengaged*	These dysfunctional families may share a home space or family name, but there is little interaction and reliance between family members.

Categories based on Olson & Gorrall (2003)

Family Experiences

A third indicator that can be used in determining the quality of family life is family experiences. Childhood and adolescent family experiences are powerful predictors of later development. Typically, childhood family experiences are classified as either adverse or positive. Adverse family experiences constitute such events as maltreatment, parental separation, parental alcoholism, parental loss, divorce, or financial hardships during the first two decades of life. These adverse experiences are often associated with unhealthy outcomes and risky behaviors during adolescence that persist into adulthood (Chashwell & Vacc, 1996; Matherne & Thomas, 2001). Findings from a longitudinal study suggest the number of adverse experiences during childhood has a profound effect on the ability of youth to have a successful life course (CDC, 2015). Therefore, it is imperative to mitigate or eliminate adverse experiences during childhood. Protective factors or assets that contribute to resiliency in youth can help mitigate adverse experiences (see Chapter 8).

Using a strengths-based approach to family life, the Search Institute has identified five types of positive family experiences, including (1) nurturing relationships, (2) establishing routines, (3) maintaining expectations, (4) adapting to challenges, and (5) connecting to community (Syvertsen, Roehlkepartain, & Scales, 2012). These positive family experiences can be strong predictors of quality of family life and resiliency. More specifically, the Search Institute has provided a list of 22 positive family experiences (i.e., assets) that are associated with adolescents becoming healthy and contributing members of society (see Table 17.4). This list of positive family experiences can inform the behaviors of parents in developing a healthy family culture. Considering the current demands and functions of family life, these positive family experiences are most likely to result when families have established roles, rules, rituals, routines, and recreation patterns. Research on family life has consistently indicated positive family activities promote family well-being (Hodge, Duerden, Layland, Lacanienta, Goates, & Niu, 2017).

Table 17.4
Family Assets (Source: Syversten, Roehlkepartain, & Scales, 2012)

Nurturing Relationships
- *Positive communication.* Family members listen attentively and speak in respectful ways.
- *Affections.* Family members regularly show warmth to each other.
- *Emotional openness.* Family members can be themselves and are comfortable sharing their feelings.
- *Support for sparks.* Family members encourage each other in pursuing their talents and interests.

Establishing Routines
- *Family meals.* Family members eat meals together most days in a typical week.
- *Shared activities.* Family members regularly spend time doing everyday activities together.
- *Meaningful traditions.* Holidays, rituals, and celebrations are part of family life.
- *Dependability.* Family members know what to expect from one another day to day.

Maintaining Expectations
- *Openness about tough topics.* Family members openly discuss sensitive issues, such as sex and substance abuse.
- *Fair rule.* Family rules and consequences are reasonable.
- *Defined boundaries.* The family sets limits on what young people can do and how they spend their time.
- *Clear expectations.* The family openly articulates its expectations for young people.
- *Contributions to family.* Family members help meet each other's needs and share in getting things done.

Adapting to Challenges
- *Management of daily commitments.* Family members effectively navigate competing activities and expectations at home, school, and work.
- *Adaptability.* The family adapts well when faced with challenges.
- *Problem-solving.* Family members work together to solve problems and deal with challenges.
- *Democratic decision-making.* Family members have a say in decisions that affect the family.

Connecting to the Community
- *Neighborhood cohesion.* Neighbors look out for each other.
- *Relationships with others.* Family members feel close to teachers, coaches, and others in the community.
- *Enriching activities.* Family members participate in programs and activities that deepen their lives.
- *Supportive resources.* Family members have people and places in the community they can turn to for help.

So, after reading the first part of the chapter, you should be able to recall the different ways that we have discussed the family: family structure, family functions, and quality of family life. We gave more attention to the quality of family life because healthy families provide the crucial element to positive adolescent development. Together, these sections indicate practitioners who care about adolescents must strive to support and empower families to thrive. Because today's families spend more time apart than together, there is a critical need for PYD practitioners to promote positive family experiences. In the next part of this chapter, we will focus on practical ways to support and empower adolescents' families.

Including Families in PYD Programs

(Family) Involvement alone will not heal the scars of malfunctioning families, but involvement which is informed by ways of making human relationships more satisfying, positive ways rather than merely therapeutic interventions after the damage has been done, is what is needed. This could be the business of leisure specialists. (Rapoport, Rapoport, & Strelitz, 1975, pp. 362)

An adolescent's involvement in a PYD program largely depends on his or her parents. This is because parents play a critical role in determining which activities are appropriate for their children (Beyer et al., 2015). While youth programs often position themselves as opportunities for youth, youth programs also offer a service to parents. Specifically, youth programs partner with parents in achieving the family function of childrearing (for a reminder see Table 17.1). Thus, it is important for youth program providers to understand their role as parental partners in adolescent development.

Two options for including families in PYD programming are discussed in the remainder of this chapter: *family-centered programs* and *family-inclusive programs*. Family-centered programs focus on improving the life of the adolescent and include program elements designed to actively engage adolescents' family members. In contrast, family-inclusive programs work primarily with the adolescent and include organizational policies designed to strengthen and partner with the family. Programs that are based on a family-centered or family-inclusive approach will be more effective in achieving program goals than programs that do not involve families (Dunst & Dempsey, 2007). This is because adolescents often need to hear a message multiple times and in various forms before it becomes part of their knowledge and, ultimately, guides their decision-making process. When practitioners make family members aware of program messages family members are positioned to reinforce these messages.

> While youth programs often position themselves as opportunities for youth, youth programs also offer a service to parents.

In the following sections, we provide practical approaches and principles to help PYD practitioners design family-centered and family-inclusive programs. But first, let's share a vignette based on the experiences of one author (Karen Melton) with an adolescent-centered program that highlighted the need for family-centered programming.

Vignette: Family Day

At one time, I was program director at an adolescent residential program serving teens with behavioral and substance use issues. For over a year, I had been successfully designing and implementing after-school and summer programs that combined recreation and life skills to promote positive youth development. I was feeling confident in my professional insight and the difference these programs were surely making in my adolescents' lives.

Then, one of the youth—who had returned to his family only a few weeks earlier—was suddenly back again in our facility. He had successfully completed our seven-week program, shown great strides in his personal growth and development, and yet, the individual who returned to the program was not the graduate we had celebrated six weeks earlier. His behaviors had worsened, he had returned to substance use, and our staff was tasked with beginning the program anew in hopes of making a more permanent impact.

This was a critical moment for me as a programmer. I realized no matter how well constructed, theory-driven, or fun our programs were, they would not be as influential as the child's immediate family environment. I realized if I wanted to create lasting change in a child's life, I had to include the family in the treatment process.

Based on this need and building on my training, I developed and implemented a new program, Family Day, to better involve the family. The family members (parents or guardians, siblings, grandparents) of the adolescents in our program were invited to come to the facility for a day. For the first half of the day, adolescents' parents or guardians attended classes with social workers covering topics such as guidance, boundary setting, logical consequences, and positive parenting while the adolescent and their siblings engaged in team-building activities. For the second half of the day, family members jointly participated in recreation activities such as horseback rides, kayaking, ropes course adventures, fishing, and eating tasty food. I remember watching parents laugh and talk with their children. I remember watching families trying new things together. I remember watching families try on new roles as the children—our youth who were already well versed in our recreation activities—led their parents through the activities and demonstrated their skills.

When the program ended, I was fearful the evaluation of Family Day would reveal low parental ratings for the education sessions. However, parents loved the entire day, including the education sessions. One hundred percent of the parents rated the program as highly satisfactory and said they would return for the next Family Day. In the subsequent Family Days, I saw healthier families who were motivated and trying to implement the tools they were taught. It also became apparent that the families who were not motivated (yet) to use the tools were stuck in a cycle of unhealthy family life.

Although this story comes from one of our authors, each of the authors has had similar experiences of seeing their programmatic work with adolescents either undone or magnified by family life issues. In fact, for two of us, practitioners-turned-researchers, it was those experiences that motivated us to become family researchers who now seek to understand and promote optimal family experiences to support positive youth development. In the following sections, we provide a discussion of two approaches to designing family-centered programming and five principles for family-inclusive programming.

Family-Centered Approaches in PYD Programs

A prevailing social assumption is that parents, by virtue of being parents, know how to build safe, stable, and nurturing relationships and environments for their children. However, this assumption may be false, as parents often rely on previously developed internal scripts of parenting. Internal scripts are the attitudes, phrases, and behaviors we learn from our own parents. Consider the following realizations: "Oh no! I sound just like my mom!" or "I just did what my dad always does!" In other words, some of the attitudes and behaviors exhibited by our parents may become part of the scripts we follow in dealing with our own children. At times, these scripts may not align with the behaviors of healthy and thriving families, and some families may need help rewriting their scripts of family life. Family-centered approaches to PYD programs work directly with adolescents and their family members to help them learn appropriate patterns of attitudes and behaviors for interacting within their own families.

> Family-centered programs focus on improving the life of the adolescent and include program elements designed to actively engage adolescents' family members.

Family-centered approaches are based on family systems theory. This theory suggests families are comprised of interconnected family members who interact and influence one another (Whitchurch & Webster-Stratton, 1991). Because families are interconnected systems, a change experienced by one family member has the potential to have wide-reaching impacts on the rest of the family. For example, consider a middle child who has learned and internalized an anti-bullying perspective. Before this attitude change, a younger sibling might describe how she and her friends bullied another girl in their program and the middle child would have just laughed. After the attitude change, the middle child might help his sister learn the lessons he learned, thereby mitigating further bullying by her and her friends. Family-centered programs are often designed to improve adolescent health and well-being by improving the overall health and functioning of the adolescent's family. In the following sections, we discuss two types of family-centered approaches used in PYD programs: *relationship promotion* and *behavioral training* (Van Ryzin, Kumpfer, Fosco, & Greenberg, 2016).

Approach 1: Relationship promotion. Relationship promotion programs focus on improving the quality of family bonds by promoting awareness of family members' needs, increasing sensitivity to family members' needs, and practicing appropriate affection. These programs are based on attachment theory, which suggests that a child's secure or insecure relationship with his or her primary caregivers will lead to the development of a cognitive framework used to understand the world, self, and others (Bowlby, 1969). Thus, relationship promotion programs focus on building healthy relationships by teaching family members healthy responses to and methods for supporting each other's needs for attention.

For decades, family leisure has been considered a vital context for family members to improve family (Orthner, Barnett-Morris, & Mancini, 1994). Yet, few, if any, formal guidelines or recommendations regarding families' shared leisure exist. Mantras such as "The family that plays together, stays together," while memorable, can reinforce misconceptions about the reality of family leisure (Melton, 2016). One misconception conveyed by the mantra is that all family leisure is equal. However, research demonstrates that the quality of family leisure experiences can vary widely by activity type. For example, consider the differences between watching television and eating dinner as a family. One activity creates an experience focused on a passive activity that may not support family interaction, while the other can be designed to be an engaging activity that elicits meaningful family interaction, communication, affective expression, and bonding.

Melton (2017) proposed the Family Activity Model (FAM) as a tool to help families understand the levels of interaction inherent in four distinct types of family activities: core-joint, core-parallel, balance-joint, and balance-parallel. Figure 17.1 illustrates this model. The FAM helps families and practitioners assess their family activities in terms of (a) family interactions and (b) activity environments. Both activity environment and family interaction factors can influence the quality of the leisure experience, and the expected relationship outcomes.

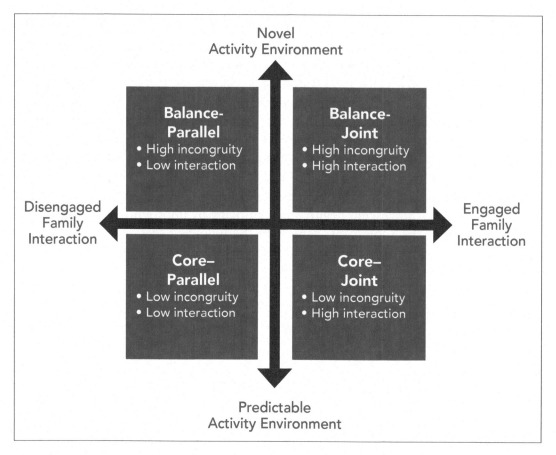

Figure 17.1. Family Activity Model (from Melton, 2017). Illustrates the four distinct categories of family activities based on family interactions (i.e., joint and parallel) and the activity environment (i.e., core and balance).

Each activity type can provide different benefits to the adolescent's development and family relations. For example, core-joint family activities seem to be a key to strengthening family relationships (Orthner, 1975; Zabriskie & McCormick, 2001), while balance-joint activities may provide opportunities for problem-solving and family memories (Orthner, Barnett-Morris, & Mancini, 1994; Shaw, Havitz, & Delemere, 2008). So what activities are best for families? The best advice is for families to diversify their family activity profile by including activities from all four categories of the FAM in their family leisure repertoire.

Using the FAM to construct family recreation experiences may be especially beneficial within relationship promotion programs. Recreation-based programs are uniquely positioned to provide accessible, low-risk situations through which parents and adolescents can develop positive relationships (Hodge, Zabriskie, Townsend, Eggett, & Poff, 2016). Specifically, family leisure education programs can be used to teach families healthy ways to play together. Moreover, family recreation should be considered as a programming element to promote relationships and as a mechanism for supporting healthy adolescent development.

Approach 2: Behavioral training. Behavioral training approaches teach parents and adolescents behavior management skills. The Family Day vignette included a behavioral training approach. To be skilled at conducting behavioral training may require additional education in family education or counseling. For example, in the vignette, the recreation practitioner partnered with social workers. The social workers conducted parenting workshops using tools to instruct parents on positive and productive family interactions. Most of the work on behavioral training tools stems from the work of Patterson and associates (e.g., Wiltz & Patterson, 1974), who found that family members may try to use coercive processes—threats, yelling, and harsh punishments—to control other family members during family conflicts. Frequently, one family member will start with a coercive behavior that is then reciprocated by another family member. This pattern continues escalating the hostility until one family member terminates the coercive behavior and the other family member "wins" the conflict. This type of family behavior can be detrimental to family relationships. Reducing coercive or other negative behaviors in family relationships through behavioral training can directly support positive development in adolescents by improving the quality of relationships. Consistency is key in behavioral training to increase long-term change. Behavioral trainings can range from learning healthy communication skills to tools that help families navigate potential parent-adolescent conflicts.

Because behavioral training can often require additional education, we have provided an example of a simple behavior training tool that can be useful when working with adolescents and their parents. One common source of conflict in parent-adolescent relationships is when an adolescent begins to exhibit more autonomy than he/she has earned from his/her parents. The Ball of Control is a behavioral training session used to help adolescents and parents communicate the appropriate level of autonomy for adolescents (Olschewski, 2017). An illustration and a brief set of instructions for using the Ball of Control are presented in Figure 17.2.

In the Ball of Control training session, the facilitator will draw a ball on a white board. The ball illustrates the adolescent's current level of autonomy. The facilitator will then draw two more balls, a larger ball on the left side and a smaller ball on the right side; these balls illustrate the continuum of autonomy. The facilitator explains that the adolescent has control over his/her behaviors such as making good or bad choices, but the size of the ball fluctuates, and the speed at which it moves is determined by the parents (e.g., privileges given or taken), dependent on the adolescent's compliance with family rules and degree of cooperation with family expectations. As the adolescent increases compliance, he/she builds trust and respect, and as a result, parents should enlarge the adolescent's social space for autonomy by giving more privileges, responsibility, and freedom. The reverse should occur if the adolescent rejects the rules and expectations, thus losing privileges, etc. The Ball of Control is further explained and discussed to connect abstract concepts of choices, control, consequences, and autonomy to specific behaviors of adolescents and parents. This teaching tool helps families understand a process that provides the adolescent opportunities to earn more autonomy.

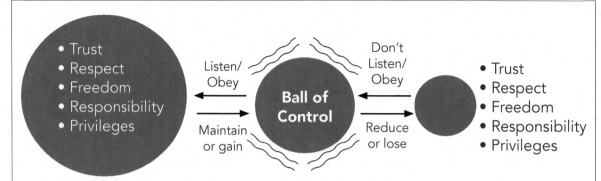

YOU control your choices; you **DO NOT** control the consequences.

Instructions for Practitioners:

Step 1: Draw the differently sized balls and write Ball of Control in middle ball.

Step 2: Draw arrow from middle ball to outer balls.

Step 3: Ask why the ball gets bigger and write the five answers in the ball (i.e., trust, respect, privileges…).

Step 4 Ask if that's why the ball gets bigger, why does it get smaller and write answers next to ball.

Step 5: Write "Listen/Obey" and "Don't Listen/Obey" above arrows.

Step 6: Add arrows going the opposite direction below previous arrows and discuss how it can get bigger or smaller.

Step 7: Share personal story of having a large ball of control based on following directions.

Step 8: Share a personal story of losing control based on not following directions.

Step 9: Write the phrase at the bottom "You control…"

Step 10: Talk about how this is not just when you are a child but when you are an adult too and share an example of what would happen if you didn't complete your job requirements.

Step 11: Ripple effects—talk about how a person's choices can have a ripple effect for others similar to someone choosing to throw a rock in a still lake and the lake rippling from it and give an example.

Figure 17.2. Ball of Control (Olschewski, 2017)

These types of tools are used within the behavioral training approach to moderate appropriate family behaviors, responses, and reactions. When parents use controlling behaviors or engage in poor supervision (such as reflected in the authoritarian, permissive, or uninvolved parenting styles), their adolescent is more at risk for social, emotional, and behavioral problems. The behavioral training approach empowers parents to generate positive and productive family interactions while also establishing clear rules and effective discipline. Behavioral trainings can improve consistency, communication, and compassion among family members. Other examples of behavioral training approaches include the following:

- The *Family Check-Up Model*, an intervention for adolescent drug abuse using the behavioral training strategies to modify family environments and parental practices (Dishion & Stormshak, 2007)
- The *Parent Training Management—Oregon Model* (PTMO), an evidence-based practice using behavioral training strategies designed to promote healthy development and reduce problem behaviors such as defiance and poor communication (Forgatch & Patterson, 2010)

Family-Inclusive Policies for PYD Programs

We now transition to discussing five family-inclusive principles that can be used to develop family-inclusive program policies. Family-inclusive policies are designed to strengthen a program's partnership with the family when working directly with adolescents and indirectly with parents and other family members. These policies are evident in programs that enhance a family's capacity to fulfill its functions. Karen Bogenschneider and colleagues (2012, 2014) outlined five principles critical to developing family-inclusive policies: (1) family engagement, (2) family responsibility, (3) family stability, (4) family relationships, and (5) family diversity.

Practitioners will not be able to incorporate all five principles into every program; instead, these principles can guide and direct conversations about how to indirectly support and partner with families when developing PYD programs. We strongly recommend being proactive in creating formal family-inclusive policies that represent a culture of empowerment, inclusion, and support of the family. In addition, as described in Chapters 13 and 14, logic models and good program evaluation practices will serve to identify where improvements are needed, what works from a process perspective, and whether identified outcomes are achieved.

> ... family-inclusive programs work primarily with the adolescent and include organizational policies designed to strengthen and partner with the family.

Principle 1: Family engagement. Family engagement is based on the belief that families should be incorporated into the philosophy, culture, and practice of the organization. Organizations should develop relational practices such as communicating with families with respect and dignity. Forms of communication (e.g., newsletters, text messages, emails, blogs) are ways to engage families in the culture and values of the program. When families know what children are learning, they are equipped to ask questions and reiterate the values of the program in the home (Dunst & Dempsey, 2007; (Hodge, Kanters, Bocarro, Forneris, & Sayre-McCord, 2017). Organizations may even involve families in a way that provides them with choices and input into programming decisions. In general, organizations that engage families recognize their role as a partner to families in adolescent development.

> When families know what children are learning, they are equipped to ask questions and reiterate the values of the program in the home.

In today's technology-dependent culture, facilitating family engagement may require a balance between too little and too much engagement, or too little or too much information. Organizations that establish appropriate family engagement outlets can offset emerging trends of extreme parental-involvement during out-of-school (OST) programs. Extreme parental-involvement trends have been nicknamed *over-parenting, helicopter parenting*, and even *bulldozer parenting* to suggest parents intervene to save their

adolescent from any potential inconvenience, problem, or discomfort. This type of parenting can be problematic as it reduces the adolescent's opportunity to gain autonomy, self-confidence, and problem-solving skills that are acquired through handling personal challenges such as a conflict with a peer or talking to an authority figure when there is conflict.

Overly involved parents may also disrupt adolescents' participation in program activities. Parents are becoming accustomed to hour-by-hour check-ins with children throughout the day and may expect their child to text them during the program. As a response, many youth programs establish cellphone-free spaces to protect adolescents' involvement from parental and peer distractions. However, parents may still want to be kept informed, especially in all-day or multiple-day programs such as camps. Some programs have begun the practice of hiring a social media staff member who is responsible for managing parent messaging and updating family members by way of a text message, Twitter, or blog. As technology continues to provide new and easier methods of communication, youth programs will face additional issues regarding family engagement. Programs should be proactive in considering which family engagement strategies will best aid the development of the adolescent while at the same time keeping family members appropriately engaged.

Principle 2: Family responsibility. Organizations should support the family as it completes its functions—family formation, partner relationships, economic support, childrearing, and caregiving—rather than unnecessarily displacing the family's role. When a well-intentioned organization oversteps its role as a partner to the parent and takes over parental responsibilities, the organization may end up doing more harm than good (Corbett & Fikkert, 2009). Therefore, organizations should aim to empower parents in ways that build the family's capacity to fulfill its functions and responsibilities.

Consider one community organization, Mission Waco, that serves low-income children, adolescents, and families. Mission Waco has multiple theater- and music-based out-of-school programs for youth. One special service it provides to parents is called Christmas Toy Store. The organization receives donated toys and provides parents the opportunity to purchase toys at 20% below the original cost. You may wonder, "Why not just give the toys to the families?" Mission Waco has found that parents feel it is their responsibility to be Santa to their children and these parents desire to provide the Christmas presents for their children. When parents are able to purchase the toys, even at a reduced cost, they maintain their sense of providing for and contributing to their family's holiday celebration. Thus, PYD programs can consider the feelings of parents and develop strategies to *assist* rather than *replace* parents.

Principle 3: Family stability. The principle of family stability is based on the understanding that family instability exposes adolescents to an array of negative developmental outcomes. Fragile families, or families experiencing high levels of instability, are disadvantaged both emotionally and economically, and as a result, adolescents tend to have less access to opportunities. When possible, programs should reinforce stability in family life. For example, youth programs can promote regular Friday or Saturday night events for youth, which are meant to provide parents with a date night to reconnect. Similarly, some faith communities promote family game nights that allow families to develop stable patterns of engaging in rituals, routines, and recreation (Mitchell & Mitchell, 1992). Constancy in family rituals and routines across life stages and other transitions can support healthy adolescent development and structure in family life, which may enhance family stability (Fiese et al., 2002).

The family stability principle also suggests that programs should recognize and provide extra support to families who are facing transitions, such as births, adoptions, divorce, and parental incarceration. These periods of transition are often marked by conflict and stress (Boss, Bryant, & Mancini, 2016). Staff working with adolescents may provide emotional support by listening and offering advice to them. In some cases, it may be appropriate to provide physical support. For example, some OST programs have a philanthropy closet full of donated items such as clothing, toiletries, and nonperishable food, providing a child the opportunity to shower, change clothes, and receive food. One such program, Care Counts, is a partnership between schools and Whirlpool. Whirlpool donates washers and dryers to low-income area schools in order to allow children to get their clothes laundered during the school day. Participating schools have seen a reduction in student absences from 12 to 3 missed school days per school year. Programs such as these may be supporting family stability by filling the gaps during times of transition and hardship.

Principle 4: Family relationships. We have already identified relationship-promotion as a family-centered strategy approach to PYD programming. Enhancing family relationships is another important principle for adolescent-centered programs and organizational level policies. For example, adolescent-centered youth development programs may be uniquely situated to support *sibling* relationships. Supporting sibling relationships in adolescent-centered programming may be as straightforward as co-enrolling siblings in the same youth development program. Co-enrollment of siblings allows the focus to remain on the individual adolescent but may also naturally create opportunities for shared experiences that support sibling relationships. Practitioners should consider scaled fee structures (e.g., reduction in registration fees) for multiple children co-enrolled in one program as a way to reduce costs for families with multiple children. However, it is also important to remember that healthy families are able to recognize and balance family members' needs for separateness and togetherness. Therefore, co-enrollment may not be an appropriate strategy for all families at all times.

Organizational-level policies should be implemented that support a variety of family relationships in addition to parent-child relationships. For example, programs could be designed so that adolescents take what they learn from the program (i.e., an activity or skill) and share, teach, or practice with a parent, sibling, or other family member. In this way, the program, while still centered on the adolescent, may create opportunities for adolescents to develop their family relationships. Using the principle of *family engagement* may help these types of programs be successful by clearly communicating with families the expectations and opportunities of the program. We caution, however, that increasing shared experiences or interaction in families where relationships are already in distress could prove problematic. Practitioners must familiarize themselves with the family climate of their participants when designing family-inclusive elements in their adolescent-centered programs.

Principle 5: Family diversity. This principle acknowledges and respects the diversity of family life. Programs should not discriminate against specific families based on structure, race, religion, or other factors. At times, practitioners may determine participants' eligibility for programs based on specific characteristics. For example, religious organizations may require some type of belief system for eligibility, while other programs may be for individuals from a specific race or ethnicity. However, organizations should consider if their eligibility criteria are a necessary part of the program and best serve the organization's mission or the adolescent's best interests.

> **Programmers should make concerted efforts to be mindful of who may be inadvertently disqualified from a program based on its design.**

Another potential concern is that programs may inadvertently discriminate against different family types, family relationships, or families in different life stages based on times and locations of the program offerings. For example, programs that start at 10 a.m. during the summer months may make it more difficult for certain families (e.g., dual-earner or single wage-earner families) to participate when parents are expected to be at work at 8 a.m. Similarly, programs taking place in faith-based locations may inadvertently exclude members of other faiths, religions, or those who do not practice a specific religion. Additionally, programs may discriminate inadvertently when trying to aid a specific population. For example, a community center with a single-mother discounted membership, or a mother-child yoga class, may inadvertently discriminate against single fathers and children who do not live with their mothers. This type of program should instead consider single-parent households as a whole. This consideration should inform not only the program design but also the marketing and promotion of the program, as well as the training and communication guidelines for staff who will interact with single parents.

One caveat: it is difficult to develop programs that fit *all* family types and situations. Programmers should make concerted efforts to be mindful of who may be inadvertently disqualified from a program based on its design. Programmers should also be mindful of the make-up of the community they serve, and in the unfortunate instance that a family feels excluded, programmers should hear and respond to such concerns with empathy and compassion, and when possible, make appropriate accommodations.

Summary

In this chapter, we have outlined the need for family-centered and family-inclusive approaches to PYD programming. We reviewed three indicators of quality of family life that explain *why* programming centered on and/or including families is crucial to healthy adolescent development. First, family relationships, such as parent and sibling relationships, are foundational to healthy developmental trajectories throughout the lifespan, including during adolescence. Second, we defined family cohesion, adaptability, and communication as the pillars of healthy family functioning to support positive youth development. Third, we described shared family experiences as a context for developing positive family relationships and functioning that support adolescent development. Building on this material, the heart of this chapter lies in our description of ways in which PYD practitioners and programmers can design, create, and implement programs that intentionally and thoughtfully include adolescents' families. Through consideration of adolescents' families, programmers can experience greater success with their PYD programs.

Discussion Questions

Successful PYD programs must incorporate families either directly through family-centered approaches to programming *or* indirectly through family-inclusive principles. The following questions invite you to apply, challenge, and critique this notion.

1. Name and describe youth programs you are familiar with that use a family-centered approach or family-inclusive principles.
2. Think of a youth program you were involved in that *did not* support families. What small changes could this program have made to support families?
3. With the advancement of technology, what are new ways to bring families together in youth programs that promote positive family relationships?
4. Do you agree or disagree PYD programs must *always* incorporate (or at least consider) their influence, support, and partnership with families? Discuss: Are there times when PYD programs should not incorporate or consider families?
5. Is it ever appropriate to disregard families' functions or roles in support of a program goal? Can you think of programs that have done so? How might this *hurt* or *weaken* families?

6. Can you think of programs that have inadvertently excluded families based on their structure and/or policies? In answering this question, consider issues of family structure, race, ethnicity, income, religion, and/or political views.

Scenarios

The following two scenarios are drawn from the lived experiences of families and the authors' observations of existing PYD programs. Read each scenario and consider what you would do if you were the service provider in each situation. Think of three potential solutions or plans of actions, and then for each of these solutions consider and list three potential consequences of each solution (e.g., feeling left out, undermining the family, etc.).

- A single father wants to purchase the family membership with the local city recreation center for himself and his son. He is informed that he and his son do not qualify for the family package because they are only two people, and by the program's definition, a family consists of three or more people. The cost of their memberships (a family of two) ends up exceeding the cost of their neighbors' membership (a family of five).
- A camp staff member was once invited into the home of a potential camper. The staff member knew that the parents held different values and beliefs from the camp mission statement, but the adolescent desperately wanted to attend this camp to be with his friends. To facilitate the adolescent being able to attend camp, the staff member lied about the program through omission of some information about the camp's mission and values. Instead, the staff member focused on the fun activities like archery, camping, ropes courses, and blobs. The parents allowed the child to attend the camp.

References

Baumrind, D. (1991). Effective parenting during the early adolescent transition. In P. Cowan & E. Hetherington (Eds.), *Advances in family research series. Family transitions* (pp. 111–163). Hillsdale, NJ: Lawrence Erlbaum Associates.

Barnes, H. L., & Olson, D. H. (1985). Parent-adolescent communication and the circumplex model. *Child Development*, 438–447.

Beyer, K. M., Heller, E. F., Bizub, J. M., Kistner, A. J., Szabo, A., Shawgo, E. E., & Zetts, C. J. (2015). More than a pretty place: Assessing the impact of environmental education on children's knowledge and attitudes about outdoor play in nature. *International Journal of Environmental Research and Public Health, 12*(2), 2054–2070.

Bogenschneider, K. (2014). *Family policy matters: How policymaking affects families and what professionals can do.* New York, NY: Routledge.

Bogenschneider, K., Little, O., Ooms, T., Benning, S., & Cadigan, K. (2012). *The family impact handbook: How to view policy and practice through the family impact lens.* Retrieved from http://familyimpactseminars.org/doc.asp

Bogenschneider, K., Little, O. M., Ooms, T., Benning, S., Cadigan, K., & Corbett, T. (2012). The family impact lens: A family-focused, evidence-informed approach to policy and practice. *Family Relations, 61*(3), 514–531.

Boss, P., Bryant, C. M., & Mancini, J. A. (2016). *Family stress management: A contextual approach.* Thousand Oaks, CA: Sage Publications.

Bowlby, J. (1969). *Attachment and loss: Attachment.* New York, NY: Basic Books.

Broman, C. L., Reckase, M. D., & Freedman-Doan, C. R. (2006). The role of parenting in drug use among black, Latino and white adolescents. *Journal of Ethnicity in Substance Abuse, 5*(1), 39–50.

Bronfenbrenner, U. (1979). *The ecology of human development: Experiments by nature and design.* Cambridge, MA: Harvard University Press.

Brown, J. E., & Mann, L. (1990). The relationship between family structure and process variables and adolescent decision making. *Journal of Adolescence, 13*(1), 25–37.

Brown, J. E., & Mann, L. (1991). Decision-making competence and self-esteem: A comparison of parents and adolescents. *Journal of Adolescence, 14*(4), 363–371.

Centers for Disease Control and Prevention (CDC). (2015). *Behavioral Risk Factor Surveillance System Survey ACE Data, 2009-2014.* Atlanta, Georgia: U.S. Department of Health and Human Services, Centers for Disease Control and Prevention.

Cicirelli, V. G. (1995). *Sibling relationships across the life span.* New York, NY: Plenum Press.

Cooper, C. R., Grotevant, H. D., & Condon, S. M. (1983). Individuality and connectedness in the family as a context for adolescent identity formation and role-taking skill. *New Directions for Child and Adolescent Development, 1983*(22), 43–59.

Corbett, S., & Fikkert, B. (2009). *When helping hurts: How to alleviate poverty without hurting the poor.* Chicago, IL: Moody Publishers.

Dishion, T. J., & Stormshak, E. A. (2007). *Intervening in children's lives: An ecological, family-centered approach to mental health care.* Washington DC: APA Books.

Downey, D. B. (2001). Number of siblings and intellectual development: The resource dilution explanation. *American Psychologist, 56*(6–7), 497–504.

Dunst, C. J., & Dempsey, I. (2007). Family–professional partnerships and parenting competence, confidence, and enjoyment. *International Journal of Disability, Development and Education, 54*(3), 305–318.

East, P. L. (2009). Adolescents' relationships with siblings. In R. M. Lerner & L. Steinberg (Eds.), *Handbook of adolescent psychology: Contextual influences on adolescent development* (3rd ed., pp. 43–73). Hoboken, NJ: John Wiley & Sons, Inc.

Erikson, E. H. (1968). *Identity: Youth and crisis.* New York, NY: Norton.

Feinberg, M. E., Sakuma, K. L., Hostetler, M., & McHale, S. M. (2013). Enhancing sibling relationships to prevent adolescent problem behaviors: Theory, design and feasibility of Siblings Are Special. *Evaluation and Program Planning, 36*(1), 97–106. doi: 10.1016/j.evalprogplan.2012.08.003

Fiese, B. H., Tomcho, T. J., Douglas, M., Josephs, K., Poltrock, S., & Baker, T. (2002). A review of 50 years of research on naturally occurring family routines and rituals: Cause for celebration? *Journal of Family Psychology, 16*(4), 381.

Forgatch, M. S., & Patterson, G. R. (2010). Parent Management Training-Oregon Model: An intervention for antisocial behavior in children and adolescents. In J. R. Weisz & A. E. Kazdin (Eds.), *Evidence-based psychotherapies for children and adolescents* (2nd ed., pp. 159–178). New York, NY: Guilford.

Hodge, C. J., Duerden, M. D., Layland, E. K., Lacanienta, A., Goates, M. C., & Niu, X. M. (2017). The association between family leisure and family quality of life: A meta-analysis of data from parents and adolescents. *Journal of Family Theory & Review, 9*(3), 328–346.

Hodge, C. J., Kanters, M. K., Forneris, T., Bocarro, J. N., & Sayre-McCord, R. (2017). A family thing: Positive youth development outcomes of a sport-based life skills program. *Journal of Park and Recreation Administration, 35*(1), 34–50.

Hodge, C., Zabriskie, R., Townsend, J., Eggett, D., & Poff, R. (2016). Family leisure functioning: A cross-national study. *Leisure Sciences,* doi: 10.1080/01490400.2016.1203847

Lamborn, S. D., Mounts, N. S., Steinberg, L., & Dornbusch, S. M. (1991). Patterns of competence and adjustment among adolescents from authoritative, authoritarian, indulgent, and neglectful families. *Child Development, 62*(5), 1049–1065.

Matherne, M. M., & Thomas, A. (2001). Family environment as a predictor of adolescent delinquency. *Adolescence, 36*(144), 655–664.

McHale, S. M., Kim J. Y., Whiteman S. D., & Crouter A. C. (2007) Sibling relationships in two-parent African American families. *Journal of Family Psychology, 21,* 227–235.

McHale, S. M., Updegraff, K. A., & Whiteman, S. D. (2012). Sibling relationships and influences in childhood and adolescence. *Journal of Marriage and Family, 74*(5), 913s–930.

Melton, K. K. (2016). *Empowering families to diversify their family activity profile.* CFLE Network. Minneapolis, MN: National Council on Family Relations.

Melton, K. K. (2017). *Creation of family experiences: Bridging the family leisure scholarship.* Indianapolis, IN: The Academy for Leisure Sciences.

Mintz, S., & Kellogg, S. (1988). *Domestic revolutions: A social history of American family life.* New York, NY: The Free Press.

Mitchell, J. P., & Mitchell, T. T. (1992). Family home evening. In *Encyclopedia of Mormonism.* Retrieved from http://eom.byu.edu/index.php/Family_Home_Evening

Mounts, N. S., Valentiner, D. P., Anderson, K. L., & Boswell, M. K. (2006). Shyness, sociability, and parental support for the college transition: Relation to adolescents' adjustment. *Journal of Youth and Adolescence, 35*(1), 68–77.

Olschewski, E. (2017). The ball's in your court: Positive parenting techniques for difficult children. Presented at Critical Issues Facing Children & Adolescents Conference, Salt Lake City, UT.

Olson D. H., & Gorall D. M. (2003). Circumplex model of marital and family systems. In F. Walsh (Ed.), *Normal family processes* (3rd ed., pp. 514–547). New York, NY: Guilford Press.

Orthner, D. K. (1975). Leisure activity patterns and marital satisfaction over the marital career. *Journal of Marriage and the Family, 37,* 91–102.

Orthner, D. K., Barnett-Morris, L., & Mancini, J. A. (1994). Leisure and family over the life cycle. In L. L'Abate (Ed.), *Handbook of developmental family psychology and psychopathology* (pp. 176–201). New York, NY: John Wiley & Sons.

Rapoport, R., Rapoport, R. N., & Strelitz, Z. (1975). *Leisure and the family life cycle.* Boston, MA: Routledge & Kegan Paul.

Schwartz, J. P., Hage, S. M., Bush, I., & Burns, L. K. (2006). Unhealthy parenting and potential mediators as contributing factors to future intimate violence: A review of the literature. *Trauma, Violence, & Abuse, 7*(3), 206–221.

Shanahan, L., McHale, S. M., Osgood, D. W., & Crouter, A. C. (2007). Conflict with mothers and fathers from middle childhood through adolescence: Within- and between-family comparisons. *Developmental Psychology, 43*, 539–550.

Shaw, S. M., Havitz, M. E., & Delemere, F. M. (2008). "I decided to invest in my kids' memories": Family vacations, memories, and the social construction of the family. *Tourism Culture and Communication, 8*(1), 13–26.

Steinberg, L., Lamborn, S. D., Dornbusch, S. M., & Darling, N. (1992). Impact of parenting practices on adolescent achievement: Authoritative parenting, school involvement, and encouragement to succeed. *Child Development, 63*(5), 1266–1281.

Steinberg, L., & Morris, A. S. (2001). Adolescent development. *Annual Review of Psychology, 52*, 83–110.

Syvertsen, A. K., Roehlkepartain, E. C., & Scales, P. C. (2012). *The American Family Assets Study.* Minneapolis, MN: Search Institute.

Van Ryzin, M. J., Kumpfer, K. L., Fosco, G. M., & Greenberg, M. T. (Eds.). (2016). *Family-based prevention programs for children and adolescents: Theory, research, and large-scale dissemination.* Hove, UK: Psychology Press.

Whitchurch, G. G., & Webster-Stratton, C. (1991). Systems theory. In P. G. Boss, W. J. Doherty, R. LaRossa, W. R. Schumm, & S. K. Steinmetz (Eds.), *Sourcebook of family theories and methods: A contextual approach* (pp. 325–355). New York, NY: Plenum.

Whiteman, S. D., & Buchanan, C. M. (2002). Mothers' and children's expectations for adolescence: The impact of perceptions of an older sibling's experience. *Journal of Family Psychology, 16*, 157–171.

Whiteman, S. D., McHale, S. M., & Crouter, A. C. (2007). Explaining sibling similarities: Perceptions of sibling influences. *Journal of Youth and Adolescence, 36*(7), 963–972.

Wiltz, N. A., & Patterson, G. R. (1974). An evaluation of parent training procedures designed to alter inappropriate aggressive behavior of boys. *Behavior Therapy, 5*(2), 215–221.

Yeh, H. C., & Lempers, J. D. (2004). Perceived sibling relationships and adolescent development. *Journal of Youth and Adolescence, 33*(2), 133–147.

Zabriskie, R. B., & McCormick, B. P. (2001). The influences of family leisure patterns on perceptions of family functioning. *Family Relations, 50*(3), 281–189.

Chapter 18

Youth Engagement, Voice, and Opportunities for Decision-Making

Theresa K. Sullivan, Rebecca N. Saito, and Rachel Chamberlain

Youth engagement is a commonly used phrase in the field of youth work. However, the term can mean different things to different people. For some, youth engagement refers to young people's involvement in youth programs; for others, to be *highly engaged* is a state of being. In more recent years, youth engagement has come to include youth having input into youth-related policies and working in partnership with adults toward social change. In this chapter, we provide a framework for thinking about the different types of youth engagement, the benefits associated with youth engagement, and ways to build engagement through youth programs.

Youth engagement describes experiences in which youth are "actively involved in cognitive and social endeavors that promote [their own] growth" (Weiss, Little,

& Bouffard, 2005, p. 24). However, such a broad definition does not highlight the diverse forms youth engagement takes and the multiplicity of benefits engagement has to offer youth and the programs in which they participate. In addition to enhancing general program outcomes, such as academic success, social and emotional skill development, and physical well-being (Brady, Dolan, & Canavan, 2017; Chapman, Deane, Harré, Courtney, & Moore, 2017; Mitra, 2003), some types of engagement also provide unique, direct benefits of their own. These benefits include problem-solving, planning, a sense of purpose, agency, identity and cultural connection, and commitment to a community beyond oneself. Each of these is a critical outcome for leading a successful life and undertaking leadership in the 21st century.

Rings of Engagement

This chapter introduces the Rings of Engagement framework (Figure 18.1), which delineates four distinct kinds of youth engagement: participation, passion, voice, and collective action.[1] Each ring is associated with a specific feature of engagement. Thus, *participation* is strengthened through opportunities for connection to positive people and places. Tapping into youth *passion* builds youth commitment to ongoing growth and development in and beyond a specific area of pursuit. Youth having a *voice* in programs requires opportunities not just to speak their mind, but also to be heard and taken seriously, to truly have input into decisions that affect them. In *collective action*, young people and adults share power and decision-making authority as they work together to achieve shared goals.

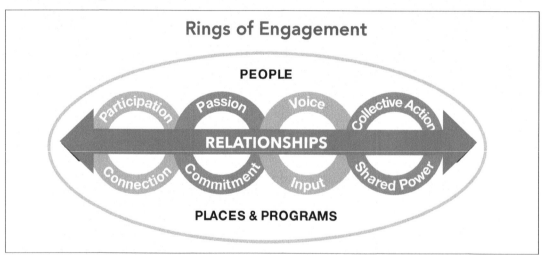

Figure 18.1. Rings of Engagement (Source: Theresa Sullivan, Rebecca N. Saito, August 2008, University of Minnesota, Center for Youth Development)

[1]The Rings of Engagement framework is based on a review of the youth engagement literature and an iterative process that included input and feedback from experienced practitioners and youth throughout Minnesota (Sullivan, 2011).

Note that the framework has a two-way arrow running through the rings. This represents two important ideas about youth engagement. First is the idea that building bidirectional, developmental relationships among youth and adults is critical for all four types of engagement. While youth engagement is often conceptualized as adults engaging youth, each of the rings in our framework involves youth and adults engaging with each other. It assumes a strengths-based approach in which young people as well as adults are viewed as having valuable skills, perspectives, and expertise.

The bidirectional arrow also signals that the four types of engagement are not hierarchical, with one form of engagement being more important or more mature than another, or one type necessarily preceding another. Rather, each form of engagement is equally important, with each fueling all the others. Participation in a youth program can lead to finding a passion that motivates stronger youth voice and more decision-making roles. Similarly, a young person might become engaged in a collective action project that leads to a passion about a particular issue (e.g., youth violence or health), and participation in other programs that address that issue. In addition to the benefits being additive, the four types of engagement in our framework are also interdependent. Expanding and deepening opportunities in one ring can help to further development of the others.

The youth engagement literature supports the notion that a flourishing community needs all four types of engagement opportunities to meet the needs of diverse youth and ensure they have opportunities to engage in ways that fit their current circumstances, interests, and capacities (Blyth, 2006; Eccles et al., 1993; Mekinda & Hirsch, 2014; Saito, 2006; Schwartz & Rhodes, 2016; Sullivan, 2011). The more types of engagement opportunities youth experience, the better off they will be. For example, a study of 15-year-olds found a cumulative effect when young people experience the following: strong relationships and opportunities for participation; an activity, issue, or ideal about which they are passionate; opportunities to build a sense of efficacy and plans to voice their ideas; and leadership roles and opportunities to solve community problems (Scales, Roehlkepartain, & Benson, 2010). Youth who scored high in all these areas fared better than other youth on every academic, psychological, social-emotional, and behavioral outcome studied.

> A flourishing community needs all four types of engagement opportunities to meet the needs of diverse youth and ensure they have opportunities to engage in ways that fit their current circumstances, interests, and capacities.

Although the study by Scales, Roehlkepartain, and Benson (2010) highlights the promise of providing a wide array of engagement opportunities, it also highlights the challenge of realizing that vision. Only 7% of 15-year-olds in this study experienced high levels of all these types of engagement; 38% did not score high on any of the three youth engagement indexes.

While it is clear from the literature that youth engagement is important and beneficial for all young people, this chapter pays particular attention to the needs of older youth, aged 14 and above. Developmentally, adolescents are particularly eager and ready for opportunities to expand their horizons and experience autonomy, challenge, voice, and decision-making (Nagaoka, Farrington, Ehrlich, & Heath, 2015; Roehlkepartain et al., 2017).

This chapter elaborates on the specific characteristics of each of the four elements of the Rings of Engagement framework, benefits of that element for youth, and what it takes to make sure each element is represented in youth programs. Key ideas are summarized in Table 18.1.

Table 18.1
Definitions and Ways to Strengthen Youth Engagement

	Definition	Benefits/Outcomes	Boosting Youth Engagement Within Programs
Participation	*Young people participate in formal, informal, and non-formal activities offering opportunities to connect with positive people and places, and challenges/supports that promote growth and development.*	• Psychosocial development • Academic achievement • Physical fitness • Mastery of skills • Reduced risk-taking • Positive identity • Civic trust/participation • Gateway to other kinds of engagement	• Remove barriers (e.g., location, scheduling, cost, transportation, childcare, feeling unwelcome/uncomfortable) • Understand needs/wants of youth (e.g., have fun, time with friends, develop skills, build resume, accomplish something that matters) and parents (e.g., keeping children safe, building positive skills, positive relationships) • Effective marketing to youth/parents
Passion	*Young people become engrossed in or passionate about something that matters. Marked by high levels of attention, enthusiasm, effort, persistence, and pride in success.*	• Life satisfaction • Motivation for continued learning, practice, growth, and development • Social approval, gateway to a supportive community • Contributions to social good • Academic achievement	• Social opportunities with peers • Authentic relationships with adults • Personal connection/cultural relevance • Clear goals, winnable challenges, immediate feedback • Identify, build on strengths • Opportunities for mastery, leadership, real-world contribution • Opportunities for personal reflection • Choice re: types/depth of participation

(cont.)

Table 18.1 (cont.)

	Definition	Benefits/Outcomes	Boosting Youth Engagement Within Programs

Voice	*Young people have opportunities to voice their ideas and have input into programs, policies, and practices that affect them.*	• Enhanced sense of efficacy/agency
		• Problem-solving, communication, and advocacy skills
		• Academic achievement
		• Improved programs that get others participating, passionate
		• Fulfills a fundamental human right
			• Authentic opportunities to be heard, have an impact
			• Avoid tokenism
			• Report back with impact of youth ideas on policy, practice
			• Build new perspectives/skills for youth and adults
			  - Active listening
			  - Appreciating diverse strengths
			  - Facilitating active conversations

Collective Action	*Youth and adults share decision-making authority as they work together to a) achieve shared goals within systems; and/or b) change or create new systems.*	• Positive civic identity • Sense of collective efficacy • Collaborative planning, decision-making, implementation skills • Critical social consciousness, analysis • Social/political change skills • Ongoing civic engagement • Organization/community change	• Identify shared passions • Broaden perspectives re: youth/adult roles, relationships • Transparency about roles, authority, responsibilities • Develop and utilize collaborative processes, skills • Develop knowledge/skills re: target issues and change processes • Identify and develop individual strengths within the collective • Stay flexible as issues/dynamics change

Two-Way Relationships

Search Institute (Roehlkepartain et al., 2017) and others define developmental relationships as close, bidirectional connections youth experience with adults and peers through which young people get what they need to thrive. Relationships are a main conduit through which programs engage youth. As such, they are a gateway through which youth garner all the benefits outlined in each of the Rings of Engagement. While the focus of this chapter is on youth-adult relationships, peer relationships are also important.

Benefits of Two-Way Relationships

Developmental relationships promote social-emotional strengths and other indicators of well-being and thriving (Li & Julian, 2012; Nagaoka, et al., 2015). In particular, developmental relationships build resiliency among youth facing stress and trauma (Roehlkepartain et al., 2017).

As youth and adults build relationships, they develop the trust required to take new risks with each other, opening doors to learn and achieve things that neither could have accomplished on their own (Innovation Center, 2008; Scales et al., 2010). Along the way, these trusting relationships broaden young people's access to ideas and resources beyond the relationship. For example, even when they are aware of an available health service, young people are far more likely to access that service if they learned about it from someone they trust.

> Along the way, these trusting relationships broaden young people's access to ideas and resources beyond the relationship.

At a more fundamental level, ideas about who we are and who we can and want to be are informed by conversations with people we trust. In this way, a constellation of trusting relationships broadens the range of roles we can envision ourselves playing and the resources we can access to help realize our goals (Eckersley, Wierenga, & Wyn, 2006; Griffith & Larson, 2016; Roehlkepartain et al., 2017).

How to Build Two-Way Relationships

Search Institute (2017) has published a framework that depicts five strategies for building developmental relationships: express care, challenge growth, provide support, share power, and expand possibilities. Youth, parents, teachers, and youth workers participating in Search Institute's research identified specific actions individuals take to bring the five core strategies to life. Table 18.2 synthesizes these actions and core strategies. The actions and strategies are applicable across the four Rings of Engagement.

A few actions under *share power* in Table 18.2 apply specifically to voice and collective action in our framework. However, the first action under share power, *respect me*, is critical for all forms of youth engagement. Another action, *let me lead*, was identified by the youth and practitioners who offered feedback on the framework as critical to all four forms of youth engagement. For example, youth described opportunities from leading peers in learning a hip-hop dance to organizing youth and adults to advocate for school policy changes (Sullivan, 2011). At the same time, *express care, challenge growth,* and *provide support* are critical to the relational core that fuels all four of the Rings of Engagement.

Table 18.2
The Developmental Relationships Framework

Young people are more likely to grow up successfully when they experience developmental relationships with important people in their lives. Developmental relationships are close connections through which young people discover who they are, cultivate abilities to shape their own lives, and learn how to engage with and contribute to the world around them. Search Institute identified five elements—expressed in 20 specific actions—that make relationships powerful in young people's lives.

Elements	Actions	Definitions
1. Express Care Show me that I matter to you.	• Be dependable • Listen • Believe in me • Be warm	Be someone I can trust. Really pay attention when we are together. Make me feel known and valued. Show me you enjoy being with me.
2. Challenge Growth Push me to keep getting better.	• Expect my best • Stretch • Hold me accountable • Reflect on failures	Expect me to live up to my potential. Push me to go further. Insist I take responsibility for my actions. Help me learn from mistakes and setbacks.
3. Provide Support Help me complete tasks and achieve goals.	• Navigate • Empower • Advocate • Set boundaries	Guide me through hard situations and systems. Build my confidence to take charge of my life. Stand up for me when I need it. Put in place limits that keep me on track.
4. Share Power Treat me with respect and give me a say.	• Respect me • Include me • Collaborate • Let me lead	Take me seriously and treat me fairly. Involve me in decisions that affect me. Work with me to solve problems and reach goals. Create opportunities for me to take action and lead.
5. Expand Possibilities Connect me with people and places that broaden my world.	• Inspire • Broaden horizons • Connect	Inspire me to see possibilities for my future. Expose me to new ideas, experiences, and places. Introduce me to people who can help me grow.

Note: Relationships are, by definition, bidirectional, with each person giving and receiving. Each person in a strong relationship both engages in and experiences each of these actions. However, for the purpose of clarity, this framework is expressed from the perspective of one young person. © 2017 Search Institute, Minneapolis, MN. www.search-institute.org. Used by permission.

When asked specifically about relationships with adults in youth programs, adolescents said they experienced some elements of the Developmental Relationships Framework more than others (Roehlkepartain et al., 2017). Sixty-seven percent said that leaders of youth programs challenged them in constructive ways. By contrast, 40% said these leaders helped them expand possibilities, and around half said program leaders showed care, provided support, and shared power (Roehlkepartain et al., 2017).

Search Institute (Sullivan, 2015) found that developmental relationships with adults in youth programs offer youth some experiences unique to this setting. For example, participants in their study said youth often interpret care and support from these adults differently than they interpret the same actions from parents and teachers. They feel special because these adults do not *have* to pay attention to them or love them. That paves the way for these adults to challenge growth and share power in ways that might be more difficult for parents and teachers. Study participants

Young people are more likely to grow up successfully when they experience developmental relationships with important people in their lives.

also said adults in youth programs have unique opportunities to expand possibilities by connecting youth to people and opportunities to which they might not otherwise be exposed.

Youth workers in the study talked about the importance of being *real, honest, transparent, telling the good and the bad, the hard truth, and not giving false praise*. One said, "They know when you're fake. They're probably better at it than anyone." Youth workers also saw the importance of recognizing young people's strengths, while also helping them be realistic about the abilities and the challenges they will face in achieving their goals, so they prepare themselves in ways that will help them succeed.

Youth workers were clear that challenging youth is effective only when other key aspects of the relationship are in place. "The more you care, the more they're gonna care to listen," one youth worker said.

Participation

It is important that young people participate in a range of programs and opportunities that enable them to connect with positive people and experiences, through which they learn and develop new skills. This includes after-school, evening, and weekend youth programs in nonprofit youth or community organizations, public parks, schools, libraries, and faith-based organizations.

Benefits of Participation

Research studies suggest that participation is associated with a wide range of positive developmental outcomes for youth, including physical health, positive psychosocial development, enhanced academic achievement, mastery of specific skills, reduction in violence and risk-taking behavior, and positive identity development (Eccles & Gootman, 2002; Scales & Leffert, 1998). For many young people, youth programs offer *a second home* (Hirsch, 2005, p. 41), a safe place in which young people develop supportive relationships with peers and adults that help them cope with a variety of life stressors and allow them to explore ideas about who they can be and who they want to be as a member of the broader community.

Participation, especially in diverse groups, can build a sense of belonging and social trust, and a belief that "most people are fair, helpful, and trustworthy" (Flanagan, 2003, p. 167). This breeds ongoing participation in community organizations and institutions throughout adolescence and adulthood (Hart, Donnelly, Youniss, & Atkins, 2007; Youniss & Hart, 2005) and widens one's sphere of others to whom one feels a sense of connection and responsibility (Beam, Chen, & Greenberger, 2002; Flanagan, 2003).

How to Build Participation

For youth to participate actively over time, youth workers must provide experiences youth value. This requires knowing what they value, and using what is known to inform the experiences offered. It also requires marketing programs in ways that allow prospective participants to effectively identify programs that offer experiences they value. Young people commonly say they join activities for the following reasons:

- To do something other than hanging out by themselves at home
- To meet and spend time with friends
- To develop specific skills
- To fulfill school requirements (e.g., community service hours)
- To improve their community
- To build a resume for college admission (Sullivan, 2011; Weiss, Little, & Bouffard, 2005)

They keep coming back when they have fun, develop positive relationships, and feel like they are growing or accomplishing something that matters to them (Hirsch, 2005).

Young people generally have more autonomy to choose activities in which they will participate as they enter adolescence. Participation rates for out-of-school programs drop overall after early adolescence, and remain low as youth get older (Bouffard et al., 2006). This is troubling given that this is an age at which young people are developing important knowledge, attitudes, skills, and habits that will impact their opportunities, choices, and experiences throughout youth and adulthood. Older youth tend to be attracted to opportunities for leadership, multiple options for participating, and opportunities to increase their academic success and workforce readiness (Harris, Valorose, Martin, & Ishizaki, 2007).

A Safe Place for Youth to Be Themselves Builds Participation

Now in its eighth year, Camp L.E.A.D. is a week-long YMCA Camp in rural north California, where soon-to-be high school freshmen develop leadership skills each summer. The camp does formal recruiting through area schools: distributing flyers, doing classroom presentations, and working with school counselors who promote the opportunity to students. The camp is free to youth who qualify, but entrance is competitive, with 55 youth chosen from among 85 applicants in the most recent season. Nearly all campers attend a reunion the following winter, and most of the camp counselors and staff are alumni of the program. While the camp features river rafting, that does not seem to be the biggest draw for campers. When asked what keeps them coming back, alumni talked about the camp as a safe place to be themselves, connect with others, and try new things they were not sure they could do. One said, "The counselors . . . they're a big, big aspect of it all. They are trying to work to get you more comfortable, and that's a hard thing." They said the counselors and activities helped them in "knowing my strengths, encouraging me, like, 'You can do that. Go get it.'"

Passion

Passionate engagement involves becoming engrossed in some activity. Doing the activity becomes rewarding in its own right, regardless of the outcome or external rewards such as social approval, money, or power (Esteban-Millat, Martinez-López, Huertas-Garcia, Meseguer, & Rodriguez-Ardura, 2014; Nakamura, 2001; Weiss et al., 2005). This kind of engagement is marked by high levels of attention, concentration, enthusiasm, and commitment. The latter can be seen in high levels of effort and persistence, as well as pride in success. When youth find an activity with which they engage in this way, Benson and Scales (2007) call it their *spark*. Nakamura (2001) calls it *vital engagement*. Csikszentmihalyi (1997) calls it *flow*, a state he and others assert we can find through any activity we find enjoyable, worth doing, and at which we can improve over time (Damon, 2008). However, many individuals struggle to find their passion, even into adulthood. The degree to which youth successfully seek and find what they are passionate about has important implications for youth being able to thrive (Mariano & Going, 2011). In a Search Institute study of young people and parents, the most commonly reported youth sparks, in order of the frequency with which they were reported, were creative arts; athletics; learning an academic subject (e.g., math, science, or history); reading; helping others/volunteering; spirituality/religion; a commitment to living in a specific way (e.g., with joy, passion, caring); animal welfare; and leading (Benson, 2008).

Benefits of Passion

New interests sparked through youth programs provide opportunities to master new challenges, which, in turn, motivate and facilitate ongoing learning and practice (Csikszentmihalyi, 1975; Denault & Poulin, 2016). People who are more psychologically engaged in an activity tend to learn more (Pearce & Larson, 2006), and not just in the activity about which they are passionate. Research has shown that young people who have identified a spark are more likely than others to do well in school. Youth say that pursuing their spark(s) enhances their learning outside of school as well, including building skills that could help them in a career. They also report higher levels of initiative, sense of purpose, desire to make a difference, and tend to be less driven by external rewards such as fame, power, comfort, and money (Csikszentmihalyi, 1975; Esteban-Millat et al., 2014; Scales, Roehlkepartain, & Benson, 2009, 2010).

> Research has shown that young people who have identified a spark are more likely than others to do well in school.

Passions that benefit other people or a broader community have been found to be the most satisfying, because they help people feel part of something greater than themselves (Damon, 2008). A sense of purpose beyond one's own self-interest has been found to build resilience in hard times and to help young people control destructive impulses (Damon, 2008).

How to Build Passion

Csikszentmihalyi (1975, 1997) found that experiences are more likely to elicit passionate engagement when they offer clear goals, immediate feedback, and challenges for which success is within one's grasp, but at the same time when one's capacities are stretched. Passive activities are needed for rest, and certainly can bring pleasure; yet they need to be balanced with experiences of growth and achievement that are valued.

It often takes a while for activities to produce enjoyment, making it difficult to get started and to sustain commitment, even when one is passionate about an activity. External structures (e.g., set practice times, nudges from trusted others) can help get youth started. While emotions are most positive when youth are doing something they want to do, they are generally happier doing something that moves them toward their goals. Sometimes incentives or low-commitment trial periods can encourage people to try out an activity. This is akin to a coupon or a "free trial offer" at the grocery store. For example, a church youth choir offered potential members an opportunity to attend three practices and sing at Easter. This allowed those not ready to commit to a full year of participation to make a small commitment through which they could experience the benefits that might lead to a longer-term commitment. Once on board, youth workers can prime intrinsic motivation by asking young people why an activity is enjoyable for them or brainstorming with them ways to increase their enjoyment. This reflection can help youth uncover elements of the activity that give it meaning (e.g., a sense of accomplishment, purpose, growth, connection), making those benefits more salient and motivating. Moreover, adults sharing what they find enjoyable and meaningful about their own passions can help young people uncover theirs.

> Adults sharing what they find enjoyable and meaningful about their own passions can help young people uncover theirs.

Scales et al. (2010) highlight the importance of authentic relationships for helping young people identify and develop their passions, and vice versa. They found that 15-year-olds who have meaningful relationships with caring adults are more likely to have a strong passion or spark. Yet, they found that fewer than half of 15-year-olds who had identified a spark said that someone outside their family had helped them identify and develop their passion (Scales et al., 2009, 2010). This suggests an opportunity for those beyond the family who work with youth to provide this support. Scales and colleagues suggest introducing youth to new interests and issues, while helping them prioritize and focus. This helps young people keep their options open, giving them a chance to find passions they care about most, without getting overwhelmed or discouraged at trying to do too many things. Youth say the most common way adults help them nurture their sparks is through support and encouragement (Scales et al., 2009).

In addition to simply providing exposure to potential new interests, program features identified as critical to creating passion, spark and flow overlap substantially with program features found to produce general positive youth development outcomes (Connell, Gambone, & Smith, 2000; Eccles & Gootman, 2002). Program features that create passion, spark, and flow include the following:

- Balance of freedom and structure
- Opportunities to socialize with peers
- Opportunities to choose specific activities as well as modes and levels of participation
- Cultural relevance, a personal connection to a shared ideal or cause
- Interactive/experiential learning
- Opportunities to identify and create individualized plans to develop one's own strengths and interests
- Opportunities to experience autonomy, mastery, empowerment, and leadership
- Opportunities to make meaningful contributions in the real world
- Opportunities to experiment with and reflect upon one's sense of who I am and who I want to be as an individual, as a member of a group, and as a member of the community at large (Pearce & Larson, 2006; Weiss et al., 2005)

A Focus on Passion Builds Participation

A high school Nordic ski team in northern Minnesota has won nine state championships in the past 12 years (boys and girls teams combined). What is their secret? According to participants, they win because the coaches do not focus on winning. Instead, they focus on developing a love for skiing and help skiers achieve individual goals. The satisfaction of getting better at doing something difficult builds passion and commitment, which ultimately helps them win. Participants said, "The coaching staff [is] . . . really good with . . . making sure everyone enjoys it. . . . They'll make you a training plan that you can follow. . . . It is incredibly hard, but then there's a great satisfaction that you get from doing that incredibly hard task. . . . You know the coaches are going to do their best to help you do well. . . . That keeps me coming back."

Voice

Voice refers to opportunities for youth to express their ideas and have input into programs, policies, and practices that affect them. Although youth do not have sole decision-making authority in this type of engagement, they have authentic input. This means they have the power to influence programs and policies by sharing new perspectives, information, and/or making a persuasive case to adults who truly consider their ideas as they make decisions.

Youth find opportunities to voice their ideas and have input into programs and policies in a variety of ways, including youth media (e.g., print, broadcast, Internet, film); advisory boards; political advocacy; and participating in surveys, interviews, and focus groups.

Benefits of Voice

When youth have a voice in the development of programs and activities, they help create programs in which they and other youth like them are more likely to participate (Pittman, Martin, & Williams 2007; Serido, Borden, & Perkins, 2011). In addition, youth voice presents opportunities for youth to gain new knowledge and skills. For example, youth learn about the structure and politics of organizations and institutions as they figure out how to effectively promote their interests within them. They can also develop problem-solving, communication (including public speaking, writing, artistic expression), and advocacy skills. Youth who make their voices heard also tend to exhibit stronger academic achievement (Kahn & Westheimer, 2004; Zeldin, Camino, & Calvert, 2007).

When youth have a voice in the development of programs and activities, they help create programs in which they and other youth like them are more likely to participate.

Having a voice helps youth develop a sense of efficacy and agency, coming to see themselves as people who can and do make organizations and communities better places. Youth understand that their voice matters and makes a difference. This, in turn, can motivate them to continue to try to make organizations and communities better places for all (Kahn & Westheimer, 2004; Zimmerman & Campillo, 2003). Flanagan, Stoppa, Syvertsen, and Stout (2010) found that when they were encouraged to voice their views in schools, students were more likely to act on behalf of a greater good beyond their direct self-interest. For example, they were more likely to speak up if a peer was talking about doing something dangerous at school. In addition, they felt a sense of solidarity and a personal sense of acceptance in their schools.

When youth have authentic opportunities to share their ideas, adults begin to appreciate their insights, wisdom, and commitment, countering common adult perceptions that today's youth are academically lazy, prone to crime and violence, and uninterested in anything beyond themselves (Noguera & Cannella, 2006). This makes it more likely that adults will continue to create new opportunities for youth to engage in this way.

The United Nations Convention on the Rights of the Child asserts that youth have a fundamental right to a voice in policies, programs, and practices that affect them and their communities (Ginwright & Cammarota, 2006; Hart, 1992; Sullivan, 2011).[2]

How to Build Youth Voice

Opportunities to voice their ideas must be authentic for youth to be motivated to continue to offer input. It is important that programs not engage just a few token youth in this way, but rather engage enough diverse youth to meaningfully represent the perspectives and needs of the many youth they serve. At the same time, adults must truly listen to and value the wisdom that young people bring, integrating it into their own thinking and using it to guide their decisions (Hazel, 2016; Serido, Borden, & Perkins, 2011; Zeldin et al., 2007).

Reporting back to young people how their ideas were incorporated into policies and programs helps them see their voice had an impact. If youth ideas were not used, reporting back is equally important to make sure they know why they were not used. As a teenager on staff at one youth program said,

> [When] people can express themselves and just be part of something, it's a really big deal. . .There's plenty of places where they ask your opinion, but when it comes right down to it, they might not use it, they might not really care. They just want you to think they are listening. . . . When people see a cause and effect, something happening with their idea, it gives them a lot of passion for it. (Sullivan, 2011, p. 23)

This is one way young people learn about things such as budget constraints and political ramifications that impact organizational decisions (Sullivan, 2011). It is also important for youth to know that one can still feel valued even if one's opinions are not used "at the end of the day." Having youth understand that their voices were definitely heard, but the final decision went in another direction and why, helps youth learn to collaborate with others without feeling that they have to be "right" every time.

Again, Scales et al. (2010) highlight the importance of authentic youth/adult relationships to foster youth voice. They found that teens who had a strong web of relationships with adults were more likely to feel comfortable expressing their ideas to adults.

Adults need to develop unique perspectives and capacities to provide impactful opportunities for youth voice. They include the following:

- Active listening, instead of immediately rejecting an idea and citing all the reasons it won't work
- Appreciating the unique perspectives, knowledge, and skills each participant brings to the table
- Facilitating effective dialogue to ensure full participation from all

---

[2]At the time of publication (2018), the United States had not signed on to the Convention on the Rights of the Child.

- An ability to apply new learning to improve programs and practices (Noguera & Cannella, 2006; Wheeler, 2007a)

To ensure that young people have an ongoing, consistent voice in programs and policies requires creating systems to support voice and a culture that invites constructive critique and new ideas. Supporting systems include formal advisory boards, regularly scheduled informal gatherings through which a broad base of participants can share their ideas, and a culture that invites open, informal conversations among youth and adults about ways to improve the organization (Sullivan, 2011).

Youth Appreciate Adults Who Support and Challenge Them to Voice Their Own Ideas

A peer leadership program in an urban public high school in California focuses on youth identifying issues they care about and voicing their ideas to affect change in their school. One cohort started by surveying students about their views of student/teacher relationships, as one student said, "because I know there's a lot of people [who] don't come to class because they don't get along with the teacher." They also did focus groups with students and teachers. Then, as one student described, "after school, we stayed and showed all the data that we had from the students to the teachers, to see what they can do better for the students." When asked how teachers responded, s/he said, "They were impressed by what we were doing, and a lot of teachers changed their ways in class." When asked about the role of program leaders, a student said, "It's really intimidating, but it really makes a difference to be an adult that's not doing for you, but an adult that's supporting you in your own ideas."

Collective Action

Collective action happens when youth and adults collaborate to achieve common goals, sharing power and authority to make decisions along the way. Watts and Flanagan (2007) distinguish between two distinct types of youth/adult partnerships for collective action, based on the breadth of decision-making power shared by youth and adults. In the first type of collective action, young people have clearly defined authority to shape policy and make decisions within current systems (e.g., setting editorial guidelines and making editorial decisions for a youth magazine; or identifying goals, setting criteria, and awarding a subset of a foundation's grants to youth programs). In the second, youth and adults share power to change or create new systems. This happens when youth and adults share decision-making authority for overall governance of an organization. Sometimes youth and adults within an organization work together to change things beyond the organization. Youth and adults partner in this way to achieve a wide range of goals, for example: creating and running new programs to attract previously disengaged youth (Sullivan, 2011; Walker, 2011), reducing youth violence (Wheeler, Sullivan, & Saito, 2011), strengthening the power of student councils (Kirshner, 2009), and advocating for increased funding to youth programs in underserved areas (Ginwright & Cammarota, 2006).

Benefits of Collective Action

Shared decision-making has been shown to increase youth and adults' commitment to and learning from a program (Innovation Center & National 4-H, 2003; Riemer, Lynes, & Hickman, 2014). This can lead to increased commitment to school and college (Larson, Walker, & Pierce, 2005). Perhaps its greatest benefit, however, comes from a shift in focus away from individual outcomes to developing a group's capacity to reach shared goals, what Watts and Flanagan (2007) call "collective human development" (p. 784).

Participants develop skills for collaborative goal setting, decision-making, planning and implementation, competencies they often carry into other parts of their lives (Larson et al., 2005; Zeldin et al., 2007). They learn to co-construct ideas through research, dialogue, and critical thinking, negotiating the development of individual beliefs and values within, and yet still independent from those of the group (Noguera & Cannella, 2006). Youth and adults build relationships of mutual respect as they work in partnership. In addition to offering emotional support, these relationships can open other doors in the community for young people, as adults offer to write college recommendations, connect them with jobs and internships, and scholarships (Zeldin, 2004) and other actions that Search Institute calls "expanding possibilities" (Roehlkepartain et al., 2017 p. 15).

As youth and adults affect tangible change together, they develop a collective identity, collective efficacy, and collective agency (Futch, 2016; Kirshner, 2009). They come to see their own self-interest as tied to the common good and recognize that together we can accomplish more than any of us can accomplish on our own (Kirshner, 2009; Larson et al., 2005). Collaborative attitudes and skills like those outlined above have been touted as particularly important for citizens, workers, and leaders to achieve their goals in the rapidly changing, multicultural world of the 21st century (Heifetz & Laurie, 1999; Levine, 2007).

Scales et al. (2010) found that African American and Hispanic/Latino 15-year-olds were more likely than their white peers to think it is important to correct social inequalities, be a community leader, help the poor, and improve race relations. As noted earlier, participation builds social trust, and social trust is also a precursor to participation (Flanagan, 2003). Collective action may provide a way for disengaged youth and adults to build trusting relationships within a group while helping to create programs in which they want to participate (Watts & Flanagan, 2007; Wheeler, 2007a&b). Putnam, Feldstein, and Cohen (2003) assert that the social capital built through such endeavors represents "not a comfortable alternative to social conflict, but a way of making controversy productive" (p. 3).

As people of all ages, cultural, and socioeconomic groups come to believe they can help shape programs aiming to serve them, and actually have opportunities to do so, these programs will come to more closely reflect the values and meet the needs of participants (Riemer, Lynes, & Hickman, 2014; Verba, Scholozman, & Brady, 1995).

How to Build Collective Action

Collective action requires youth and adults to be open to new ideas about their roles and relationships in order to collaborate in ways that fully capitalize on the strengths of each individual to achieve shared goals (Griffith & Larson, 2016; Search Institute, 2005; Watts & Flanagan, 2007; Wheeler, 2007a&b). It requires participants to develop skills for facilitating collective goal setting, planning, evaluation and decision-making to ensure that collective decisions and actions in fact reflect the values, desires, and needs of all participants (Larson et al., 2005; Noguera & Cannella, 2006; W. K. Kellogg Foundation, 2007). A critical aspect of this process is openly discussing and coming to a shared agreement about who has authority and responsibility to make which decisions and what to get done, with youth and adults holding each other accountable for commitments (Pittman et al., 2007; Sullivan, 2011; W. K. Kellogg Foundation, 2007).

To achieve the sustained commitment this kind of engagement requires, youth and adults must identify goals about which they have a deep, shared interest and passion. Each brings unique knowledge and connections to the partnership, making the whole greater than the sum of its parts. It is important to help individuals identify their own strengths, interests, and needs in order to connect them with opportunities to continually grow and develop in ways that are important to them, which also contribute to their value in the group (Sullivan, 2011; W. K. Kellogg Foundation, 2007).

Youth and Adults Partner in Collective Action to Impact Tobacco Legislation

The Minneapolis Youth Congress (MYC) is a vehicle for youth to inform and influence decisions and policies that affect them. In partnership with the Minneapolis Department of Health, the MYC passed local legislation to 1) keep cigarillos and flavored tobacco out of grocery corner stores and gas stations and limit their sale to tobacco stores, 2) increase the minimum selling price, 3) eliminate coupons or discounts, and 4) limit the pack size so no single cigars can be sold. This was accomplished over a multi-year partnership, with MYC members learning background information on tobacco targeted advertising, facilitating a youth survey of tobacco purchasing habits, presenting findings to multiple audiences including city council, and defending their opinions in conversations with tobacco lobbyists.

The Same Activity Can Engage Youth in Different Ways

Search Institute (2005) provides a helpful model delineating the types of activities through which organizations and communities engage youth. They include service/service learning; leadership (in which young people influence or organize others to accomplish a mission, task or objectives); decision-making; philanthropy; civic and political engagement (contributing to charities, electoral activities, political voice); organizing (altering power relations and creating meaningful institutional change); and research and evaluation. We incorporated many of these category distinctions into the Rings of Engagement framework. At the same time, we found that young people could engage in some of these activities in ways that fit within more than one of the rings. For example, Search Institute outlines many ways young people can engage in philanthropy, which includes youth giving of their own time, talents and/or financial resources for the common good (participation), helping to make grant recommendations (voice), or sharing in the funding decisions of a foundation, government agency or other grant-making institution (collective action).

Engaging Youth to Increase Youth Engagement

Participatory Action Research (PAR) engages those directly affected by an issue as co-researchers to study that issue, reflect on learning and then take action, building participants' capacity to change conditions in their own lives (Brown & Rodriguez, 2009; Freiri, 1970).

Youth Participatory Action Research (YPAR) can be a powerful tool for exploring and addressing barriers to youth engagement. For example, youth in Minnesota helped increase awareness of and participation in after-school youth programs through a program called Youth Action Crew (Walker & Saito, 2011). They reviewed existing program lists and interviewed youth and program staff. They then used this information to create colorful maps of their neighborhood, identifying program sites and other youth-friendly places. Youth distributed the maps door to door and at places where families gather (e.g., grocery stores, faith institutions, bus stops).

Youth-involved research and evaluation can be implemented in many different ways, reflecting each of the rings of engagement. Youth can have input into or co-create research goals, design, and methods. They can participate, offer input and/or partner with adults in data collection, analysis, interpretation and reporting results to stakeholders. Table 18.3 describes varying levels of youth involvement in research and evaluation.

Table 18.3
A Continuum of Youth Involvement in Evaluation and Research (Flores, 2008)

Youth Involvement	Process
Highest	Youth-led research/evaluation is part of organizational planning cycle; experienced youth act as peer trainers and are paid
High	Youth participate in research design, data collection, and analysis; youth report findings, implement change
Medium-High	Youth design and administer research instruments; adults analyze results, develop findings, implement changes
Medium-Low	Youth give input on process
Low	Youth collect data
Very Low	Information is collected from youth
None	Outside adult conducts research without collecting information directly from youth

Some argue youth have a right to participate in research that impacts them. Yet even for those who do not see it as a right, it is important to recognize ways in which, when done well, engaging youth participants in research about their experience of engagement will enhance the quality of the research. Based on their own participation in the programs and other experiences we seek to understand, youth have the following:

- Unique insight into how researchers can best study those experiences
- Trusting relationships that help them elicit valid data from other youth
- A unique perspective from which to critically analyze and interpret data
- An opportunity to recognize their own lived experiences and personal knowledge as valid sources of data

This insider knowledge helps to ensure the validity of the research and ultimately the relevance of programs to the youth they aim to serve (Rodriguez & Brown, 2009). Although helping programs become more relevant to other youth like them, involving youth in the change process provides a greater opportunity for them to develop a personal connection to activities and outcomes of a program, which can directly impact their own engagement (Dawes & Larson, 2011).

Overcoming Barriers to Participation

Although participation was the most commonly practiced form of engagement, there are known barriers to it. For example:

- Parents and young people do not know about programs that exist.
- Programs are inaccessible due to times, locations, or associated costs.
- Programs are perceived as disorganized, chaotic, or unproductive.
- Families and young people themselves have competing priorities, including work and care of other siblings at home.
- Young people prefer having unstructured time to just hang out with friends.
- Young people feel unwelcome by staff or uncomfortable with other participants.
- Programs do not offer the kinds of activities that interest them.

These barriers to do not impact all youth equally. Rates of participation in youth development programs and opportunities drop around age 12 or 13 and remain low through the rest of adolescence (Bouffard et al., 2006). Participation rates are especially low for youth who come from families and communities with lower incomes and opportunities (Littel & Wynn, 1989; Pittman, Wilson-Ahlstrom, & Yohalem, 2003).

Youth of color may experience harmful stereotypes and unequal balances of power in traditional youth programs, causing reluctance to participate (Delpit, 1988; Ladson-Billings, 2011). Lakind, Atkins, & Eddy (2015) describe, for example, a tendency for mentors to attribute environmental factors, such as home life or economic status, as causes for the challenges youth face. These associations can be rooted in negative racial stereotypes and alter the way youth of color are treated

> Youth of color may experience harmful stereotypes and unequal balances of power in traditional youth programs, causing reluctance to participate.

in youth programs. Youth workers can unknowingly treat youth of color differently due to these perceptions, even to the point of reacting unfairly to their behavior or expecting trouble to occur from them and not from others (Ladson-Billings, 2011).

For youth of color to feel comfortable participating, it is necessary for program leaders to proactively examine inequality in their organizations and create systems that promote equity in programs and practices (Powell, Branscombe, & Schmitt, 2005; Lakind, Atkins, & Eddy, 2015). Development for youth of color is maximized when program leaders attend to the intellectual, personal, and spiritual growth of students of all backgrounds and cultures, recognize and celebrate differences, and develop culturally responsive programs and practices (Delpit, 2003; Duncan-Andrade, 2007; Gay, 2000).

Overcoming these barriers requires listening to and working with disconnected youth and their parents to create programs in which they can and want to participate. Youth say they will participate and remain engaged in the program if they enjoy spending time with the staff and the other youth participants (Fritz Fogel & Saito, 2017). It also requires effectively marketing those opportunities so parents and young people know they exist and know how they can get involved (Saito, 2006; Weiss et al., 2005).

Overcoming Barriers to Passion, Voice, and Collective Action

Engaging youth participants to develop a passion, voice their ideas, and work together in collective action can present a different set of obstacles. For example, these forms of engagement are not always understood or lived as a value in youth programs. As such, it can be difficult to focus on these kinds of engagement that take additional time and effort.

Program delivery is often the core criteria on which youth worker performance is evaluated, reinforcing the notion that their job is to deliver programming rather than building relationships and engaging youth beyond participation. A seasoned youth worker said, "We have programs we can send [young people] to that start at 5 and end at 6:30, but a lot of young people are going to come because they want to sit at your desk and just talk about what's going on in their lives, families, a problem they have. We have to make sure our staff values that time. That's quality program time in my eyes" (Sullivan, 2011, p. 13).

At the same time, youth voice and sharing power are interpreted differently in different cultures. We may create conflict in families if the norms are different in programs than they are at home. For example, a youth program director said, "In African American culture, kids have their roles. 'This is grownup talk, y'all get to the back room.' ... So voice to me has got to mean something different than just saying 'talk back' or argue with them." S/he asserts that there is a common value at the heart of most cultures that can support these kinds of engagement. S/he said, "We all agree that voice means [youth] are valued; that they're worthwhile; they have opinions; they have a right to be here" (Sullivan, 2011, p. 37).

Another obstacle can be maintaining a culture of youth voice and shared power through changes in leadership. The executive director of a program intentional about engaging youth in decision-making embedded opportunities for youth voice into the program structure, to make it more likely that it would continue beyond his tenure there. For example, they have a monthly pizza party to get broad input from youth participants, and a volunteer team to address issues that come up there.

These barriers can be overcome by working with stakeholders to find common ground upon which this kind of engagement can be built, and integrating a shared vision for engagement into systems and the culture of an organization or program. This takes a willingness to practice what one program leader called the *dance* of youth engagement. S/he said, "When [a staff person or volunteer of any age] is newer to a role, you maybe have to lead a little bit more, teach them basic parameters, try a dip here and there. Then, as they mature in the program and get practice, they can become more of the leader in the dance."

It's More Than a Method

As we have demonstrated in this chapter, youth engagement can mean many different things. When some people talk about youth engagement, they are talking about the need to get more youth engaged in quality youth programs or other constructive activities; others think of youth finding something they work hard at and care deeply about. For others, youth engagement refers to youth giving input into decisions that affect them and/or having actual decision-making power and authority. The Rings of Engagement framework was designed to reflect these multiple meanings, and to support practitioners to be intentional about integrating all these kinds of engagement into youth programs.

All types of engagement are important and valuable, and although they are not sequential, one could argue that if youth do not get involved in a youth program, they cannot receive the benefits and outcomes associated with participation in high-quality youth programs. It may be, however, that a particular interest or concern about a specific issue brings young people into a program or organized activity. Or, as mentioned earlier, one program can incorporate participation, passion, voice, and collective action in multiple ways. Whatever the type of engagement, there is strong evidence that all types of engagement can result in better outcomes for youth, and, in the long term, our society.

Whatever the type of engagement, there is strong evidence that all types of engagement can result in better outcomes for youth, and, in the long term, our society.

One particularly wise elder reminds us that youth engagement is more than a set of techniques to practice. He argues that youth engagement is a lifestyle in which formal and informal relationships with young people are the ultimate goal of youth engagement. This highlights the importance of an implied fifth Ring of Engagement in the framework introduced here. It is the ring around the other four rings, representing the community of people and organizations surrounding young people who need to be intentional about and prepared to build reciprocal, authentic, developmental, engaging relationships.

Youth and adults engaging together in the ways described in this chapter will require people recognizing enough benefit in such endeavors to open their hearts and minds to see each other in a new light and to consider new ways of thinking about youth/adult roles in a variety of settings. (Noguera & Cannella, 2006; Zeldin et al., 2007).

A seasoned youth worker said, "When we talk about youth engagement, it's not just a method. . . It's a value commitment, it's a way of life . . . that includes young people in our community and in our life's journey" (Sullivan, 2011, p. 5).

Discussion Questions

1. Think back to when you were a teenager. Which types of engagement did you experience?
   -Where, how, and with whom did you experience them?
   -Which types were missing?
2. Think about a particular program in which you participated as a teenager. How could that program have enhanced engagement?
3. How did you see participation, passion, voice, and collective action fueling each other in those programs?

Assignments: Youth Engagement Program Dilemmas

In a group, review and discuss each of the following scenarios and reflection questions. Alternatively, make up your own program dilemmas and questions based on your own experiences.

SCENARIO #1: "Well, I ask them what they want to do, but..."

Venita is a youth worker who is trying to incorporate youth voice into her summer program. The first thing she does is ask the youth what they would like to do this summer in the program. They give her a list of activities including such things as "go to the amusement park," "go on field trips," and "go to Hawaii."

Venita is disheartened because she has no budget to take them to Valley Fair, let alone Hawaii, and she desperately wants to engage and empower them with some voice and input into the program.

1. What is the issue from Venita's perspective? What is the issue from the young people's perspective? Do they understand what the issue is from each other's perspective?

2. What could Venita do to figure out some compromise that gets at some of what the young people are hoping to get out of these experiences?
3. What suggestions would you have for Venita? How could Venita have introduced the discussion that might have been helpful?
4. What might Venita and the group do with their list of brainstormed ideas?

SCENARIO #2: "I'm afraid if I give them decision-making power, they're going to screw it up."

Frankie runs a well-known youth program that is very popular and has been around for years. At a youth engagement training he said, "You know, I know youth engagement is a good thing—smart people that I trust think it's a good thing, the research says it's a good thing—but I've worked so hard to make this program be really good, and I'm afraid that if I turn it over to the young people they're going to screw it all up."

OR

Frankie has noticed one young man, Lamont, who shows a lot of leadership—when he is there, he really listens and speaks up a lot. Frankie decides to turn the next meeting over to Lamont, emails him copies of her agenda template and tells him what they need to accomplish at the next meeting.

Frankie does not want Lamont to think he is not trusted so does not contact him between meetings. People gather for the next meeting and Lamont does not show up.

1. What is the issue from Frankie's perspective? How might have Lamont interpreted the situation?
2. What suggestions would you have for Frankie and/or Lamont?
3 How does this relate to your work?

SCENARIO #3: "He said it was youth-led!"

Jerri loved working at the radio station. From Jerri's perspective, it was a dream project where all the youth got to be in charge and talk and play music on a radio station for half an hour every Saturday night. They said it was a youth-led program.

Jerri wanted to play a favorite song, but for a variety of reasons, the youth worker vetoed the song. After lots of arguing, Jerri went on the air and accused the program staff of lying, proclaiming that this was not a youth-led program.

- What is the issue from Jerri's perspective? What is the issue from the youth worker's perspective?
- What suggestions would you have for Jerri and the youth worker?
- How does this relate to your work?

SCENARIO #4: "No–you don't understand; I'm the adult and I know better."

You are facilitating a group of youth and adults who have joined in a youth-adult partnership to work on a project together. They have been meeting for a while to plan an event. One of the adults disagrees with some of the youth and tells them that he knows what he's talking about and that they need to listen to him because he is in charge.

1. What is the issue from the young people's perspective? What about from the adult? What about from the facilitator's perspective?
2. What would you do in this situation? How would you handle this?
3. How does this relate to your work?

References

Beam, M., Chen, R., & Greenberger, C. (2002). The nature of adolescents' relationships with their "very important" nonparental adults. *American Journal of Community Psychology, 30*(2), 305–325.

Benson, P. (2008). *Sparks: How parents can help ignite the hidden strengths of teenagers.* San Francisco, CA: Jossey-Bass.

Benson, P., & Scales, P. (2007). Search Institute's ongoing development of the theory of thriving. Presentation at the Healthy Communities Healthy Youth Conference in Rochester, NY.

Blyth, D. (2006). Toward a new paradigm for youth development. *New Directions for Youth Development, 112*, 25–43.

Bouffard, S. M., Wimer, C., Caronongan, P., Little, P. M. D., Dearing, E., & Simpkins, S. D. (2006). Demographic differences in patterns of youth out-of-school time activity participation. *Harvard Family Research Project. Journal of Youth Development, 1*(1), 24–40.

Brady, B., Dolan, P., & Canavan, J. (2017). "He told me to calm down and all that": A qualitative study of forms of social support in youth mentoring relationships. *Child & Family Social Work, 22*(1), 266–274.

Brown, T. M., & Rodriguez, L. F. (2009). Youth in participatory action research. *New Directions for Youth Development, 123*, 1–9.

Chapman, C., Deane, M., Harré, K., Courtney, L., & Moore, N. (2017). Engagement and mentor support as drivers of social development in the Project K youth development program. *Journal of Youth and Adolescence, 46*(3), 644–655.

Connell, J., Gambone, M. A., & Smith, T. (2000). *Youth development in community settings in youth development: Issues, challenges, and directions.* Philadelphia, PA: Public/Private Ventures.

Csikszentmihalyi, M. (1975). *Beyond boredom and anxiety.* San Francisco, CA: Jossey-Bass.

Csikszentmihalyi, M. (1997). *Finding flow: The psychology of engagement with everyday life.* New York, NY: Basic Books.

Damon, W. (2008). *The path to purpose.* New York, NY: Free Press.

Dawes, N. P., & Larson, R. (2011). How youth get engaged: Grounded-theory research on motivational development in organized youth programs. *Developmental Psychology, 47*(1), 259–269. doi:10.1037/a0020729

Delpit, L. D. (1988). The silenced dialogue: Power and pedagogy in educating other people's children. *Harvard Educational Review, 58*(3), 280–298.

Delpit, L. (2003). Educators as "Seed People:" Growing a new future. *Educational Researcher, 32*(7), 14–21.

Denault, A. S., & Poulin, F. (2016). What adolescents experience in organized activities: Profiles of individual and social experiences. *Journal of Applied Developmental Psychology, 42*, 40–48.

Duncan-Andrade, J. (2007). Gangstas, Wankstas, and Ridas: Defining, developing, and supporting effective teachers in urban schools. *International Journal of Qualitative Studies in Education (QSE), 20*(6), 617–638.

Eccles, J. S., & Gootman, J. A. (Eds.). (2002). *Community programs to promote youth development: Committee on community-level programs for youth.* Washington, DC: National Academy Press.

Eccles, J., Midgley, C., Wigfield, A., Miller Buchanan, C., Reuman, D., & Flanagan, C. (1993). Development during adolescence. *American Psychologist, 48*(2), 90–101.

Eckersley, R., Wierenga, A., & Wyn, J. (2006). Flashpoints & Signposts: Pathways to success and well-being for Australia's young people. Australia 21and the Australian Youth Research Center. Retrieved from http://www.australia21.org.au/pdf/HPreport.pdf.

Esteban-Millat, I., Martínez-López, F. J., Huertas-García, R., Meseguer, A., & Rodríguez-Ardura, I. (2014). Modelling students' flow experiences in an online learning environment. *Computers & Education, 71*, 111–123.

Flanagan, C. (2003). Trust, identity, and civic hope. *Applied Developmental Science, 7*(3), 165–171.

Flanagan, C., Stoppa, T., Syvertsen, A. K., & Stout, M. (2010). Schools and social trust. In L. R. Sherrod, J. Torney-Purta, & C. A. Flanagan (Eds.), *Handbook of research on civic engagement in youth* (pp. 307–330). Hoboken, NJ: John Wiley & Sons.

Fritz Fogel, K., & Saito, R. (2017). *Minneapolis Youth Congress Evaluation.* Youth Coordinating Board.

Futch, V. (2016). Utilizing the theoretical framework of collective identity to understand processes in youth programs. *Youth & Society, 48*(5), 673–694.

Gay, G. (2000). *Culturally responsive teaching: Theory, research, and practice* (Multicultural education series). New York, NY: Teachers College Press.

Ginwright, S., & Cammarota, J. (2006). Introduction. In S. Ginwright, P. Noguera, & J. Cammarota (Eds.), *Beyond resistance! youth activism and community change: New democratic possibilities for practice and policy for America's youth* (xiii–xxii). New York, NY: Routledge, Taylor & Francis Group.

Griffith, A., & Larson, R. (2016). Why trust matters: How confidence in leaders transforms what adolescents gain from youth programs. *Journal of Research on Adolescence, 26*(4), 790–804.

Harris, L. Valorose, J., Martin, & A. Ishizaki, A. (2007). *Youth action crew: Formative evaluation.* Minneapolis, MN: Rainbow Research.

Hart, D., Donnelly, T. M., Youniss, J., & Atkins, R. (2007). High school community service as a predictor of adult voting and volunteering. *American Educational Research Journal, 44*(1), 197–219.

Hart, R. (1992). *Children's participation: From tokenism to citizenship.* New Florence, Italy: UNICEF.

Hazel, C. (2016). *Empowered learning in secondary schools: Promoting positive youth development through a multi-tiered system of supports* (First ed., Applying psychology in the schools book series). Washington, DC: American Psychological Association.

Heifetz, R., & Laurie, D. (1999). Mobilizing adaptive work: beyond visionary leadership. In E. A. Conger (Ed.), *The leader's change handbook* (pp. 55–86). Thousand Oaks, CA: Jossey-Bass.

Hirsch, B. J. (2005). *A place to call home: After-school programs for urban youth.* New York, NY: Teachers College Press.

Innovation Center for Community and Youth Development & Kellogg Leadership for Community Change. (2008). Collective leadership works: Preparing youth and adults for community change. Retrieved from www.theinnovationcenter.org

Innovation Center for Community and Youth Development & National 4-H Council (2003). *Youth in decision-making: Research highlights from a study on the impacts of youth and adults and organizations.* Takoma Park, MD: Innovation Center.

Kahn, J., & Westheimer, J. (2004). What kind of citizen? The politics of educating for democracy. *American Educational Research Journal, 41*(2), 237–269.

Kirshner, B. (2009). Power in numbers: Youth organizing as a context for exploring civic identity. *Journal of Research on Adolescence, 19*(3), 414–440.

Ladson Billings, G. (2011). Boyz to men? Teaching to restore Black boys' childhood. *Race, Ethnicity and Education, 14*(1), 7–15.

Lakind, D., Atkins, M., & Eddy, J. M. (2015). Youth mentoring relationships in context: Mentor perceptions of youth, environment, and the mentor role. *Children and Youth Services Review, 53*, 52–60.

Levine, P. (2007). *The future of democracy: Developing the next generation of American citizens.* Medford, MA: Tufts University Press.

Li, J., & Julian, M. M. (2012). Developmental relationships as the active ingredient: a unifying working hypothesis of "what works" across intervention settings. *The American Journal of Orthopsychiatry, 82*(2), 157–166.

Littel, J., & Wynn, J. (1989). *The availability and use of community resources for young adolescents in an inner-city and a suburban community.* Chicago, IL: The Chapin Hall Center for Children.

Mariano, J., & Going, J. (2011). Youth purpose and positive youth development. *Advances in Child Development and Behavior, 41*, 39–68.

Mekinda, M., & Hirsch, B. J. (2014). After-school programs. In D. DuBois & M. Karcher (Eds.), *Handbook of youth mentoring* (2nd ed., pp. 221–232). Thousand Oaks, CA: Sage.

Mitra, D. L. (2003). Student voice in school reform: Reframing student-teacher relationships. *McGill Journal of Education, 38,* 289–304.

Nagaoka, J., Farrington, C. A., Ehrlich, S. B., & Heath, R. D. (2015). *Foundations for young adult success: A developmental framework.* Chicago, IL: University of Chicago Consortium on Chicago School Research.

Nakamura, J. (2001). The nature of vital engagement in adulthood. In M. Michaelson & J. Nakamura (Eds.), *Supportive frameworks for youth engagement: New directions for child and adolescent development* (p. 93). New York, NY: Jossey-Bass.

Noguera, P., & Cannella, C. (2006). Youth agency, resistance, and civic activism. In S. Ginwright, P. Noguera, & J. Cammarota, J. (Eds.), *Beyond resistance! Youth activism and community change* (pp. 222–347). New York, NY: Routledge.

Pearce, N. J., & Larson, R. W. (2006). How teens become engaged in youth development programs: The process of motivational change in a civic activism organization. *Applied Developmental Science 10*(3), 121–131.

Pittman, K., Martin, S., & Williams, A. (2007). *Core principles for engaging young people in community change.* Washington, DC: The Forum for Youth Investment, Impact Strategies, Inc.

Pittman, K., Wilson-Ahlstrom, A., & Yohalem, N. (2003). *After-school for all? Exploring access and equity in after-school programs.* Out-of-School Time Policy Commentary. Washington, DC: The Forum for Youth Investment.

Powell, A., Branscombe, N., & Schmitt, M. (2005). Inequality as ingroup privilege or outgroup disadvantage: The impact of group focus on collective guilt and interracial attitudes. *Personality and Social Psychology Bulletin, 31*(4), 508–521.

Putnam, R. D., Feldstein, L. M., & Cohen, D. (2003). *Better together: Restoring the American community.* New York, NY: Simon & Schuster.

Riemer, M., Lynes, J., & Hickman, G. (2014). A model for developing and assessing youth-based environmental engagement programmes. *Environmental Education Research, 20*(4), 552–574.

Roehlkepartain, E. C., Pekel, K., Syversten, A. K., Sethi, J., Sullivan, T. K., & Scales, P. C. (2017). *Relationships first: Creating connections that help young people thrive.* Minneapolis, MN: Search Institute.

Saito, R. N. (2006). Beyond access and supply: Youth-led strategies to captivate young people's interest in and demand for youth programs and opportunities. *New Directions for Youth Development, 112,* 57–74.

Scales, P. C., & Leffert, N. (1998). *Developmental assets: A synthesis of the scientific research on adolescent development.* Minneapolis, MN: Search Institute.

Scales, P. C., Roehlkepartain, E. C., & Benson, P. L. (2009). *Teen voice 2009: The untapped strength of 15-year-olds.* Minneapolis and Richfield, MN: Search Institute and Best Buy Children's Foundation.

Scales, P. C., Roehlkepartain, E. C., & Benson, P. L. (2010). *Teen voice 2010: Relationships that matter to America's teens.* Minneapolis and Richfield, MN: Search Institute and Best Buy Children's Foundation.

Schwartz, S. E. O., & Rhodes, J. E. (2016). From treatment to empowerment: New approaches to youth mentoring. *American Journal of Community Psychology, 58*(1–2), 150–157.

Search Institute. (2005). *The power of youth and adult partnerships and change pathways for youth work.* Battle Creek, MI: WK Kellogg Foundation.

Serido, J., Borden, L. M., & Perkins, D. F. (2011). Moving beyond youth voice. *Youth & Society, 43*(1), 44–63.

Sullivan, T. K. (2011). Youth engagement: More than a method. A way of life for healthy youth and community development. Unpublished manuscript for the Extension Center for Youth Development, Minneapolis, MN.

Sullivan, T. K. (2015). A report of learning: Developmental relationships with non-teacher, non-parent caring adults. Unpublished manuscript for the Thrive Foundation, Menlo Park, CA.

Verba, S., Scholozman, K. L., & Brady, H. E. (1995). *Voice and equality: Civic voluntarism in American politics.* Cambridge, MA: Harvard University Press.

Walker, K. (2011). *The Youth Action Crew Project: A retrospective case study evaluation.* Minneapolis, MN: University of Minnesota Extension Center for Youth Development.

Walker, K. C., & Saito, R. N. (2011) Youth are here: Promoting youth spaces through community mapping. *Afterschool Matters,* Number 14, Fall 2011. National Institute for Out-of-School Time.

Watts, R., & Flanagan, C. (2007). Pushing the envelope on youth civic engagement: A developmental and liberation psychology perspective. *Journal of Community Psychology, 35*(6), 779–792.

Weiss, H. B., Little, P. M., & Bouffard, S. M. (2005). More than just being there: Balancing the participation equation. *New Directions for Youth Development, 105,* 15–31.

Wheeler, W. (2007a). *Youth engagement: A celebration across time and culture, framing the issue.* Battle Creek, MI: W.K. Kellogg Foundation.

Wheeler, W. (2007b). *Youth engagement: A celebration across time and culture.* Proceedings Summary. Battle Creek, MI: W.K. Kellogg Foundation.

Wheeler, W., Sullivan, T., & Saito, R. (2011). *Community power against violence: A case study of youth and adults partnering to impact community change.* University of Minnesota Center for Youth Development.

W. K. Kellogg Foundation. (2007). The collective leadership framework: A workbook for cultivating and sustaining community change. Retrieved from http://www.wkkf.org/default.aspx?tabid=101&CID=276&CatID=276&ItemID=500033&NID=20&LanguageID=0

Youniss, J., & Hart, D. (2005). The intersection of social institutions with civic development. In L. A. Jensen & R. W. Larson (Eds.), *New Directions in Child Development: New Horizons in Developmental Theory and Research, 109,* 73–81.

Zeldin, S. (2004). Youth as agents of adult and community development: Mapping the processes and outcomes of youth engaged in organizational governance. *Applied Developmental Science, 8*(2), 75–90.

Zeldin, S., Camino, L., & Calvert, M. (2007). Toward an understanding of youth in community governance: Policy priorities and research directions. *Analise Psicologica, 1* (XXV): 77–95.

Zimmerman, B. J., & Campillo, M. (2003). Motivating self-regulated problem solvers. In. J. E. Davidson & R. J. Sternberg (Eds.), *The psychology of problem solving* (pp. 233–262). Cambridge, UK: Cambridge University Press.

Chapter 19

The Role of Culture in Out-of-School Time Settings

Corliss Outley, Aishia Brown, M. Gayle Gabriel, and Alex Sullins

A walk through an old growth forest reveals a multitude of plants and trees. Each of these floras will vary in form, blossoms, leaves, and size; yet all share the same basic needs of good soil, adequate water, and sunlight. However, the type of soil, amount of water, and degree of sunlight required for continued growth varies, plant by plant. In addition, the same species may grow differently in different environmental contexts.

Like flora, youth are diverse and possess common and unique needs. Young people also grow up in diverse cultural contexts, interacting with their surroundings through processes that may enhance or diminish their development in unique ways. In this chapter we discuss the importance of culture as an aspect of youth diversity and address the ways culture impacts youth development.

Following our discussion of the role of culture in youth development, we will use this information to discuss the role of out-of-school time (OST) programs in the lives of youth of color. Youth development professionals should be aware of the similarities and differences between and across cultural groups; there is no such thing as a one-size-fits-all program! Like the forest, youth within the community share basic needs, but cultural differences may mean that they differ in the types of programs that best meet those needs. Thus, program providers should be aware, knowledgeable, and understanding of the varying cultural practices that enhance the positive development of diverse groups of youth. In addition, programs should be consciously tailored to focus on the concerns, priorities, needs, and resources of each cultural group that is served.

Key Concepts and Terms

There are many ways of defining culture, albeit often with subtle differences. In this section, we provide working definitions of various terms related to the cultural, racial, and ethnic differences ascribed to the U.S. youth population.

Culture

Culture has been defined as the following:

- "An integrated pattern of human beliefs, values, behaviors, and institutions shared by a distinct group, the inhabitants of a region, or the citizens of a nation" (Glossary – Living with the Future in Mind, n.d.)
- "Shared knowledge, behavior, ideas, and customs of a group or groups of people" (Illinois State Museum Society, 2000)
- Concerned with the production and exchange of shared meanings; "the 'giving and taking of meaning' between the members of a society or group that organize and regulate social practices, influence conduct and result in real practical effects" (Hall, 1997, p. 2)

Given the variety of definitions, culture is not a rigid set of behaviors, but rather it is a framework and world view through which people's behaviors and individual characteristics are filtered.

Additionally, culture is not reborn with each generation, but instead consists of shared knowledge that is learned and passed on from one generation to the next. In other words, culture is everything that comprises who we believe we are. It is a complex system, and a culture can have several subcultures within it (e.g., gender, religion, ethnicity, and race). People can also belong to several different subcultures at the same time (e.g., Filipino American and Buddhist). In the U.S., it is common to use the terms *dominant culture* or *majority group culture* to refer to the primary or predominant culture of a geographic region. However, these terms do not connote superiority of one group over another.

Race and Ethnicity

For many people, *race* refers to an individual's physical characteristics. However, race is a social construct developed by the dominant culture to categorize people based on socially defined physical characteristics such as skin color, hair texture, or facial features. In the U. S., the concept of race has been used (knowingly or unknowingly) to elevate the ideology that one particular race is superior to others. Based on this definition, people believe that they can walk into a room and identify the different racial groups that are present based on their physical appearance. Despite beliefs that a biological difference exists, there is no one characteristic, trait, or gene that distinguishes all members of one so-called race from all members of another race. So, why is race important? Race plays an important role in society's social, economic, cultural, political, legal, and ideological systems. Race has become an institutionalized concept that guides U.S. policies, laws, and procedures within our society.

A term that is often used interchangeably, but is distinctly different in meaning is *ethnicity*. Ethnicity refers to a group of people that share common characteristics such as history, national origin, religious belief, language, clothing, and traditions. Race and ethnicity are both socially constructed terms that carry significant meaning in U.S. culture. So how does ethnicity differ from race? As noted, race is a socially constructed concept based on socially defined physical characteristics and historical ideological understandings, whereas ethnicity is based on shared social and cultural identities. As an example of how these concepts are not mutually exclusive, consider an African American whose ancestors have lived in the U.S. for centuries, a Somali American immigrant, and a Black Colombian; all have different ethnicities, yet in the U.S., each of these individuals is classified as Black.

Next, we will look at how the U.S. defines the terms race and ethnicity. The U.S. Census includes questions that relate to ethnicity and race when it conducts the decennial Census of residents as mandated by the U.S. Constitution. These questions follow federal guidelines, and responses are based upon citizens' self-identification. As a result, Census data are collected in two separate and distinct categories: race and ethnicity. The first question asks about one's ethnicity, and individuals can choose whether one identifies (yes or no) as "Hispanic or Latin origin," which is defined as the "heritage, nationality, lineage, or country of birth of the person or the person's parent or ancestors before arriving in the United States" (U.S. Census Bureau, n.d., para 1). People of Hispanic or Latino/a origin can be from Cuba, Mexico, Puerto Rico, South or Central America, or from another Hispanic, Latino, or Spanish-descended group. People who identify as Hispanic or Latin origin may be of any race. Next, individuals identify their race. Racial categories used in the 2010 Census include the following:

- *White* refers to a person having origins in any of the original peoples of Europe, the Middle East, or North Africa. It includes people who indicated their race(s) as "White" or reported entries such as Irish, German, Italian, Lebanese, Arab, Moroccan, or Caucasian.
- *Black or African American* refers to a person having origins in any of the Black racial groups of Africa. It includes people who indicated their race(s) as "Black, African American, or Negro" or reported entries such as African American, Kenyan, Nigerian, or Haitian.

- *American Indian or Alaska Native* refers to a person having origins in any of the original peoples of North and South America (including Central America) and maintains tribal affiliation or community attachment. This category includes people who indicate their race(s) as "American Indian or Alaska Native" or report their enrolled or principal tribe, such as Navajo, Blackfeet, Inupiat, Yup'ik, Central American Indian groups, or South American Indian groups.
- *Asian* refers to a person having origins in any of the original peoples of the Far East, Southeast Asia, or the Indian subcontinent, including, Cambodia, China, India, Japan, Korea, Malaysia, Pakistan, the Philippine Islands, Thailand, and Vietnam. It includes people who indicated their race(s) as "Asian" or report entries such as "Asian Indian," "Chinese," "Filipino," "Korean," "Japanese," "Vietnamese," and "Other Asian," or provide other detailed Asian responses.
- *Native Hawaiian or Other Pacific Islander* refers to a person having origins in any of the original peoples of Hawaii, Guam, Samoa, or other Pacific Islands. It includes people who indicated their race(s) as "Pacific Islander" or reported entries such as "Native Hawaiian," "Guamanian or Chamorro," "Samoan," and "Other Pacific Islander," or provided other detailed Pacific Islander responses.
- *Some Other Race* includes all other responses not included in the five racial categories described above. Respondents reporting entries such as multiracial, mixed, interracial, or a Hispanic or Latino group (for example, Mexican, Puerto Rican, Cuban, or Spanish) in response to the race question are included in this category.

The U. S. Census categories were developed to reflect a social definition of race as the term is recognized in the U.S. However, you will notice that there is great variation within each of the racial categories. For example, the definition of race includes both racial classifications and some identifiers that reflect national origin or cultural groups. These categories are not an effort to define race biologically, anthropologically, or genetically. The definitions presented for each category and how we use them are important for creating policy solutions that are equitable and not driven by stereotypes.

> The definitions presented for each category and how we use them are important for creating policy solutions that are equitable and not driven by stereotypes.

Throughout this text, the authors will use the term *racial/ethnic* to indicate the social construction of both terms and the overlap that exists in U.S. culture. In addition, the terminology *youth of color* (rather than minority or nonwhite) will be used to refer to racial/ethnic groups that have been subjected to historical racism and discrimination in the U.S. The authors believe that using the terms *minority* or *nonwhite* reinforces the ideology of white as the norm or dominant group to which all other groups are compared and defined. Minority refers to a group that is cumulatively disadvantaged, especially in relationship to the distribution of society's power and resources, in proportion to their population size.

Other Key Terms

There are a number of other terms that are important when discussing race and ethnicity. Each of these terms will be defined below based on the works of Fitzgerald (2014) and Cashmore (1994).

Stereotypes. Stereotypes are overgeneralizations about a specific group of people. Stereotyping people based on distorted and inaccurate information that is accepted as fact can foster prejudice, racism, and discrimination. Many times, stereotypes are based on race, ethnicity, age, gender, sexual orientation (and potentially many other characteristics), and are learned through interactions with parents, peers, and mass media. Thus, stereotypes become part of our everyday lives. Some stereotypes may seem positive (e.g., Asians excel in math), but instead they create unrealistic and narrow expectations, and in most cases result in negative impressions about a group of people. Ultimately, stereotypes can be harmful by fostering prejudice, biases, and discrimination.

Prejudice. Prejudice is usually based on stereotypes, and refers to the thoughts, feelings, attitudes, and beliefs that someone holds about a particular group. Ultimately, having prejudicial thoughts and feelings are harmful because they can lead to biases and discrimination. However, note that people can have prejudicial thoughts without deliberate intent to take action on those thoughts. Stereotypes and prejudices are so ingrained in our society that they become very difficult to change because they are maintained and reinforced by our biases.

Biases. Biases cause a person to consciously or unconsciously filter out information that contradicts or challenges that person's pre-existing beliefs. Biases can influence a person's immediate response toward something or someone as either favorable or unfavorable. To find out what your level of bias is, you can take the Implicit Association Test (https://implicit.harvard.edu/implicit/), which measures an individual's level of unconscious racial bias. This test attempts to measure the strength of our associations between people and negative stereotypes. By discovering your subconscious biases and learning how to address them, you can be more impactful in your work with youth.

Discrimination. Discrimination occurs when people act on biased perceptions and prejudices and undertake differential treatment of people based on characteristics such as age, gender, disability, race, ethnicity, religion, national origin, and sexual orientation. Discrimination can take on many forms, for example, consciously not hiring an individual because she is Mexican American. In the U.S., we have legal protections against overt discrimination under the Equal Employment Opportunity Act. Unfortunately, many acts of discrimination can be covert as well (Pager & Shephard, 2008).

Racism. Racism is a system of beliefs, behaviors, and actions that combines stereotypes, prejudices, and discrimination to disproportionately disadvantage members of one racial/ethnic group. Racism can be used to justify the belief that one race is superior to another. It can be intentional or unintentional, and can be difficult to dismantle. Racism is embedded in the fabric of society and is reflected in disparities in our health, education, justice, economic, and employment institutions based on varying cultural dimensions of identity (e.g., age, race, gender).

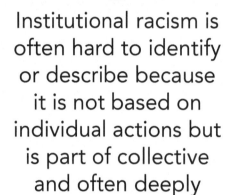

Institutional racism is often hard to identify or describe because it is not based on individual actions but is part of collective and often deeply rooted actions of U.S. society.

Institutional racism. Institutional racism is the differential access to services, goods, and opportunities for racial and ethnic groups of people that are built into the everyday practices, procedures, and policies of various sociopolitical systems. Institutional racism is often hard to identify or describe because it is not based on individual actions but is part of collective and often deeply rooted actions of U.S. society. For example, youth of color who come in contact with the juvenile justice system are more likely to be sentenced to harsher punishments in comparison to White youth (Alexander, 2010).

One of the greatest strengths of the U.S. has been the diversity of people living within its boundaries. Historically, waves of voluntary immigrants have come to the U.S. to pursue a better way of life. Immigrant culture (i.e., traditions, languages, religious beliefs, food, and clothing from places of origin) has contributed to the creation of a country that is increasingly diverse. Chapter 21 discusses immigrant youth in more detail. At the same time, cultural groups such as Native Americans, who were already in the U.S. when Europeans arrived and were violently removed from their lands, along with African Americans, who were violently enslaved and involuntarily brought to the U.S., have also contributed to the diverse landscape, despite historical imbalances in equality and opportunities.

The inclusion of voluntary immigrants, first-peoples, and involuntary immigrants have an impact on youth development approaches, given the demographic changes and inequalities that continue to exist and have impacted our society. For example, youth development professionals need to consider the degree of cultural adaptation experienced by youth and their families.

Cultural adaptation. Cultural adaptation refers to the degree to which a person or cultural community has adapted to the dominant culture and/or retained their traditional cultural practices. Attention also needs to be given to the distinct needs and experiences of *first-generation individuals* (those born outside the U.S.) who may identify more with their original cultural tradition; *second-generation individuals* (meaning they were born in the U.S., while one or both parents were born in their country of origin); and *third-generation individuals* (these children and their parents are born in the U.S.). This process has often been referred to as the *melting pot*. However, despite thinking of the U.S. as a melting pot, a majority of voluntary immigrants usually chose to maintain their traditional culture by living in their own communities and maintaining many familiar cultural practices. This has led to the cultural adaptation process being described as a *salad bowl*.

Acculturation. Acculturation refers to the degree of adaptation that takes place when members of a cultural group take on or adapt to the beliefs and behaviors of another group. This usually occurs when members of a minority group adapt to the cultural traits of the dominant group. Regardless of the process utilized, cultural adaptation and acculturation reflect the cultural interaction that has occurred in the U.S. over time. Each wave of immigrants has maintained many strengths of their own cultures, while adapting to their new social, political, and economic environments. However, these interactions have too often led to discriminatory responses (e.g., *No Irish Need Apply* in response to the late 19th century waves of Irish immigration; the implementation of the *Black Codes* after the Emancipation Proclamation of 1863); forced acculturation (e.g., Indian assimilation schools); and imprisonment (e.g., Japanese internment during World War II). With the changing demographics, this process, both good and bad, will continue to evolve as more people of different cultures continue to arrive in the U.S.

Racial/Ethnic and Cultural Identity and Youth Development

The process of adolescent identity development is addressed in other chapters in this book. In this chapter, we discuss the role of racial/ethnic and cultural identity in youth development. This topic should be under critical consideration for youth development professionals who work with youth from various ethnic, racial and/or cultural backgrounds. Understanding how young people develop perspectives of themselves in relation to others is important to understanding issues of diversity and intercultural understanding, and ultimately to promoting culturally relevant programming. These understandings are particularly important because youth who are members of racial/ethnic and cultural groups experience racism and discrimination, which is damaging to their sense of self (e.g., Priest et al., 2013; Titzmann, Brenick, & Silbereisen, 2015). Furthermore, a strong positive racial/ethnic identity is a protective factor that results in higher levels of adaptive functioning, including increased self-esteem, decreased depression, avoidance of drug use, commitment to education, less aggression, and more prosocial behaviors (e.g., Stein, Supple, Huq, Dunbar, & Prinstein, 2016).

During the process of identity development, adolescents learn who they are in relation to their parents, siblings, peers, teachers, community, nation, and the world. Developing a sense of self and possible selves (i.e., who I will be in the future) is far more complex today than in previous generations. For all youth, the process of identity development also means understanding who one is from a racial, ethnic, and cultural perspective. The term *racial/ethnic identity* refers to the connection people have to their cultural ancestry or ethnic group membership (Sue & Sue, 2016). Racial/ethnic and cultural identities are important because they provide a sense of belonging to a community and historical continuity with one's ancestors. Racial/ethnic identity formation takes place over time as youth explore, engage, and commit to the role or multiple roles they believe race/ethnicity plays in their lives. In addition, identity development may be a more pressing issue for youth of color as they are often confronted with the recognition at an early age that they are of a *different* racial/ethnic background than the people in the dominant culture and therefore must find unique ways to deal with this situation (Sue & Sue, 2016).

Exploration and identity formation, however, are complex. Today's youth wrestle with overlapping and conflicting identities (Burke, 1991; Hall, 1990, 1992; Stryker & Serpe, 1994). For example, a young person's home life may be associated with very traditional values based on parents' and family members' ethnic or cultural heritage, while at school or in other public places, youth may be faced with other societal influences. Furthermore, for some youth, understanding the self in relation to others happens in a more constricted environment, meaning their world consists of a small and/or homogeneous neighborhood or community. Other youth establish their identities and self-concept in more global or heterogeneous environments that expose them to a wide variety of outside influences.

In addition, racial/ethnic identity will not develop in the same way within or even across different groups of people. For example, the ethnic identity formation process will be different for a Latino/a American youth growing up in a barrio near the Mexico-U.S. border, who is being raised by a single mother who works as a migrant farmworker, compared to a Latino/a American growing up in the suburbs in a middle class two-parent household outside of a large Midwest city.

Other factors that can influence racial/ethnic and cultural identity include the following:

- Socioeconomic status
- Age
- Gender
- Language proficiency
- Time of arrival to the U.S.
- Sociopolitical climate
- Educational level
- Proximity to other members of their racial/ethnic group or community
- Proximity to racial/ethnic groups that are different from their own

Each of these factors influence their lives and can support or hinder the healthy development of a youth's racial/ethnic identity. However, remember that each youth and his or her family are unique, and culture-specific information may not apply to all youth in all situations. In other words, avoid the tendency to stereotype or make generalizations about one youth based on knowledge of other youth whom you might consider similar. Understanding the process of racial/ethnic identity development is important because it provides youth development professionals with a basic understanding that will enable them to ask questions and respond sensitively and effectively to the issues that racial/ethnic youth and their families may face.

Intersectionality

As noted, youth may wrestle with or embrace multiple racial/ethnic and cultural backgrounds. Using an intersectional lens when interacting with youth and developing programming for and with them is one way to recognize and support youth who identify with multiple racial/ethnic and cultural identities. *Intersectionality* is a term that describes the overlapping or interconnected identities of an individual or group (Crenshaw, 1991). These intersecting identities (e.g., race, gender, class, sexuality, geography, age, ability, migration status, religion, etc.) shape the way youth experience the world, and may be associated with different forms of prejudice or discrimination. Understanding intersectionality also helps one to identify how intersecting identities shape the levels of inequity individuals or groups experience.

A Brief Historical Perspective

In the following sections, we briefly describe common experiences, cultural practices, and beliefs of five distinct cultural groups: African Americans, Latino/a Americans, Asian Americans, Native Americans, and White Americans. While there are multiple racial/ethnic groups residing in the U.S., we chose to discuss these five groups based on their extensive U.S. history, commonly acknowledged racial/ethnic status by the U.S. government, and available U.S. Census data. This information will provide insight into contextual elements and forces that shape youth development and the provision of supports, opportunities, programs, and services. It is important to keep in mind that some youth are referred to as first, second, or third generation. These distinctions are important because a young person's degree of acculturation and cultural adaptation plays a major role in his or her world view and behaviors, and consequently in his or her development. To become a culturally competent youth development professional, you are encouraged to seek an understanding of key differences between each cultural group and respect those differences.

African Americans

Throughout history, racial identification of African Americans by the U.S. government has been controversial (Cohn, 2010). In 1790, during the early days of U.S. Census tracking, the Census designated this cultural group based on their status as *free persons* or as slaves. In addition, African Americans were counted as only three-fifths of a person for political representation purposes. This changed in the early 1850s, when the use of the terms *Black* and *Mulatto*, defined as "all persons having any trace of African blood," were used to indicate people of color. The U.S. also used the terms *quadroon* (one-fourth trace of black blood or one black grandparent) and *octoroon* (one-eighth trace of black blood or one black great-grandparent) during the 1890 and 1900 Census to identify African Americans. However, the definitions for these persons varied from Census to Census, and the use of *quadroon* and *octoroon* stopped altogether in 1910. Subsequently, the Census began using the "one-drop [of blood] rule," which continued for decades. The 1910 Census instructions continued to use the term Black ("all persons who are full-blooded Negros"), but also allowed the inclusion of Mulatto, ("all persons having some portion or perceptible

> Throughout history, racial identification of African Americans by the U.S. government has been controversial.

trace of Negro blood"). In addition, the 1910 Census included "any person that was mixed heritage of White and colored had to be designated as 'Colored', and any one mixed with another race or ethnicity was designated as the same racial identity of the father" (United States Bureau of the Census, 1975, para.3).

By the 1930 Census, the term *Negro* was introduced and was used to reflect any individual of African heritage regardless of the amount of "Negro blood" present. Most African Americans prior to the Civil Rights Movement in the 1960s were referred to as *Negros/Negroes* or *Coloreds*. During the late 1960s and early 1970s, African Americans began recognizing their Black identity in a celebratory way, which gave rise to the Black Power movement. People began encouraging the use of the term *Black* instead of *Negro*.

The 1970 Census was the first time individuals could self-identify their race. Before that time, Census takers filled out the forms and chose the category for each person based on their observed physical characteristics. In the 1980s, the term *Black* evolved into *Afro-American*, as many citizens attempted to trace their ancestral roots back to Africa after the 1976 publication of the novel, *Roots: The Saga of an American Family* by Alex Haley and its subsequent 1977 television miniseries. As a result, the 1980 Census provided several different terms to reflect the growing awareness of self-identification among Blacks.

It was not until 1988 that Jesse Jackson, in a press conference, announced that *African American* was the new preferred term for *Black* Americans due to the term's focus on an ancestral home country and a cultural heritage (Martin, 1991). Today there is disagreement on which specific term, *Black* or *African American*, should be used for this cultural group. The terms *Negro* and *Colored* are considered derogatory and should no longer be used. However, the 2010 U.S. Census still used "Negro" as a racial category; whether it will be used in the 2020 Census has yet to be determined.

For many years, African Americans were the largest minority group in the U.S., with a total 2016 estimated population of over 42 million adults and a youth population of around 10 million (U.S. Census Bureau, 2017). Between 2000 and 2010, African American citizens accounted for approximately 13% of the U.S. population. Currently, Latino/as have replaced African Americans as the largest minority group. Although African Americans continue to rise in total population, their rate of growth has slowed when compared to Asian and Latino/a American populations.

Latino/a Americans

The term *Hispanic* was officially designated during the 1970s by the U.S. Census and served as an umbrella term for over 20 different Spanish-speaking nationalities. However, many people view the use of the term *Hispanic* in a monolithic manner, implying that all Spanish-speaking peoples have a uniform cultural, social, and political heritage. In fact, the people categorized under this term come from diverse backgrounds and have different educational patterns, religious views, socioeconomic statuses, and languages. *Latino/a* is often preferred by members of this cultural group rather than Hispanic for describing people of Spanish descent in the U.S. Another term is *Chicano*, which was created during the Brown Power/Chicano movement by Mexican American activists in the late 1960s and early 1970s. This term became popularized during the farmworker strikes and youth movement led by Cesar Chavez. During this time, Chicano was used to demonstrate political consciousness and to reflect pride in the shared identity of Mexican and American cultures.

The use of identity terms for Latino/a groups is also regionally based. The preference for particular terms may vary by region within the U.S. and by country of origin. For example, the terms *Chicano* and *Mexican American* are used primarily in California, *Latin American* or *Latino/a* in Texas, Mexican in Arizona, *Cuban* and *Puerto Rican* in Florida, and *Spanish America*n in New Mexico. Terminology used to identify individuals of Latino/a descent may be further complicated by imposed racial categories (e.g., Black Puerto Rican) and the different racial designations used in other countries (e.g., someone who is Black in the U.S. may be White in Brazil, since variations in skin tone are interpreted differently in different countries). Finally, the term *Latinx* emerged in 2016 to reflect a more gender-neutral terminology for inclusiveness within the Spanish language.

The Latino/a community is now the largest minority group in the U.S. comprising about 17.1% of the total U.S. population (U.S. Census Bureau, 2017). Due to high birth rates and increased immigration patterns, the Latino/a population contributed to more than half of the growth from 2000 to 2010 of the U.S. population. Of the 54.6 million Latino/as in the U.S., nearly two-thirds (64%) are of Mexican origin, with 9.4% of Puerto Rican origin, 3.7% Cuban, 3.6% Salvadorans, 3.0% Dominicans, and from 1.2% to 2.2% each for Guatemalans, Colombians, Hondurans, Ecuadorians, and Peruvians. The remainder originated from other Central and South American countries.

Asian Americans

The term *Asian American* is an umbrella term that refers to all the Asian ethnic groups currently in the U.S. (e.g., Chinese, Japanese, Vietnamese, Filipino, Samoan, etc.). One of the first terms used to describe this cultural group was *Oriental*, and reflected the people and all goods and services that were derived from Asia. Similar to the terms *Negro* and *Colored*, the term *Oriental* was deemed inappropriate during the 1970s due to its negative and discriminatory historical use. In 2016, President Barack Obama signed legislation outlawing the term *Oriental* (as well as *Negro*) from all federal laws (Fabian, 2016).

In 2016, President Barack Obama signed legislation outlawing the term *Oriental* (as well as *Negro*) from all federal laws.

Recently, the term *Asian American* was also considered a monolithic term that assumes all Asian Americans are homogeneous, much like the term *Hispanic* is used for Latino/a Americans. Another term that is used in conjunction with Asian Americans is *model minority*, which assumes that Asian Americans are all high-achieving, economically sound, and the least likely to be in poverty or commit crimes of all the minority groups (Lee, 1996). However, the term *model minority* should not be used due to its potential for masking issues within specific Asian ethnic communities. For example, 14.3% of the Vietnamese American population live in poverty, while 7.5% of Filipino Americans and 12.1% of all Asians live in poverty (Lopez, Ruiz, & Patten, 2017).

According to the U.S. Census (2017), the Asian American population is the fastest growing racial group in the U.S., growing 2.2% between July 2014 and 2015, and with an overall population increase of 43% since 2000 (Hoeffel, Rastogi, Kim, & Shahid, 2012). The Census also projects the Asian American population will reach 40 million people by the year 2050 and that immigration from Asian countries will account for nearly 75% of the U.S. population growth (Pew Research Center, 2015). The Asian American population includes people with origins in the Far East (China, Japan, and Korea), Southeast Asia (Burma, Cambodia, Indonesia, Laos, Malaysia, the Philippines, Singapore, Thailand, and Vietnam), and South Asia (India, Pakistan, Sri Lanka, Bangladesh, Bhutan, and Nepal). Unique cultural characteristics and languages, as well as the historical, sociopolitical and economic conditions of their native countries, shape the experiences of people with different Asian ethnic backgrounds (e.g., Chinese, Korean, Vietnamese, Nepalese, etc.)

Native Americans and Alaskan Natives

Preferred terms for the indigenous people of the Americas have been controversial, changed over time, and vary by region, tribal designation, and age of individual. Terms

such as *Native American, Indian, Indian Americans, American Indian, Aboriginals*, and *AmerIndian* as well as *Eskimo* and *Alaskans* have been interchangeable throughout history (Jobe, 2004). The arrival of Christopher Columbus to this hemisphere while searching for a passage to India has perpetuated the designation of the indigenous people of the Americas as *Indians*. Objection to this term has arisen not only due to its historical and geographical error and its negative and demeaning connotations, but also because it does not adequately reflect the distinct cultural tribes that exist in the U.S.

The 1860 U.S. Census was the first time that Native Americans living in areas near White colonizers were counted and were referred to as *Indian*. Native Americans were counted by U.S. marshals as part of a special Indian Census, with the condition that Native Americans renounce their tribal affiliation; many refused (Jobe, 2004). This led the U.S. to begin federally recognizing tribes and their members in order to establish land agreements. By 1900, the U.S. had begun focusing on the distinction between full- and mixed-blood Native Americans to determine purity for tribal membership and the degree to which they had adopted a European immigrant lifestyle. As a result, Native Americans living on reservations and Native Americans living in the general population were separately identified in the Census. Those living on the reservation were typically viewed as still identifying with tribal affiliations and were noted as full blooded "Native American." However, those considered "pure blood" (i.e., full-blooded Native American) or "mixed breed" (of a mixed tribal or racial origin) who lived in local towns or cities among Whites were identified based on blood purity and their degree of assimilation. For example, people of mixed heritage, such as White and Native American, were designated as *Indians* on the Census. Exceptions occurred if a Native American had become integrated into the local European immigrant community and was viewed and accepted as being White by the residents (Jobe, 2004). The Indian Citizenship Act of 1924 declared all Native Americans born in U.S. territories as citizens, granting them the right to vote. This act was the first time the U.S. government recognized this cultural group's right to citizenship. In addition, Native American tribes and villages could also grant citizenship to its enrolled tribal members.

By 1950, the Census changed the racial designation to *American Indian* and *Alaskan Native/Eskimos*. During the American Indian Movement in the late 1960s, the term *American Indian* was encouraged by varying tribal groups in order to promote a pan-Indian identification. Today the terms *Native American, First Nations,* and/or *First People* are more common.

Approximately 6.7 million people self-identify as *Native American* and *Alaskan Native* alone or in combination with some other race. This represents 2% of the U.S. population (U.S. Census Bureau, 2017b). Some of these individuals belong to federally recognized tribes, while others belong to state recognized tribes, or are not enrolled in any tribe. Over two million are members and descendants of federally recognized tribes and qualify for access to certain federal benefits and services such as health care through the U.S. Indian Health Service. There are currently 567 federally recognized sovereign tribal groups across 36 states, of which 229 are Alaskan Native tribes (Indian Entities Recognized and Eligible to Receive Services, 2017). A federally recognized tribe is a tribal entity that is recognized as having a government-to-government relationship with the

U.S. through binding treaties, acts of Congress, and executive orders. Therefore, these tribes possess certain inherent rights of self-government and are eligible for funding, services and protection from the U.S. There are also 200 non-federally recognized tribes in the U.S. that are in the process of applying for federal recognition. Nevertheless, Native Americans and Alaskan Natives remain a mostly invisible group within U.S. society.

Whites

Caucasian refers to people of European origin. The term draws its origins based on the name used for people from the Caucasus Mountain region, which runs from Russia to North Africa, that were deemed as an ideal form of humanity. The term was introduced during the 18th century by Johann Blumenach, a German anatomist as part of a racial classification system and was adopted in the U.S. to justify the use of scientific racism—research used to scientifically justify racist ideology, in our legal system (Mukhopadhyay, 2008). The term *Caucasian* was never used officially in the U.S. Census categorizations but can be found in official government documents during the 18th and 19th century.

Beginning in 1790, Whites were categorized based on being "free white males" and "free white females." The term *White* was used in all subsequent Census enumerations. However, the meaning of *Whiteness* and who is or is not included in the White racial category has changed throughout U.S. history. The vast majority of early settlers emigrated from White European countries such as England, Sweden, France, and The Netherlands. These groups all became part of the U.S. when it gained its independence in 1776 and began to blend together into a distinct unique culture. The Naturalization Act of 1790 restricted U.S. citizenship to any free White person living in the country for two years. This left out White indentured servants, slaves, and women, which prevented them from becoming U.S. citizens. The early 1800s saw increased immigration from European countries and led to distinctions between people who were immigrants with citizenship (early settlers) and foreigners (new immigrants). These distinctions were further highlighted during a subsequent wave of mass immigration that occurred in the late 1800s and early 1900s. Groups like the Irish, Italians, and Poles were not considered White during this time period. In addition, non-foreign born Whites did not readily accept these new groups into their businesses or communities and viewed them as inferior, ignorant, and criminals (Alba, 1990; Hochschild & Powell, 2008). As time passed, each new immigrant group found ways to assimilate into U.S. mainstream culture and began to take on the label of *White* based on societal acceptance, historical events, and legislation.

As more "less desirable" European immigrants (e.g., Polish and Irish) arrived during the early 1900s, a resurgence of the belief in racial hierarchies emerged as nationality groups (i.e., Irish) began to challenge their non-White status and faced discrimination. In 1920, the White majority political leadership passed the Johnson-Reed Act, which established quotas for immigrants based on population proportions that existed in the 1890 Census. This led to segregation, job discrimination, and in some cases, even lynching of the new White immigrants (Pfeifer, 2005).

However, with the emergence of the Jim Crow era (from the mid-1800s to the 1960s), a time period where Whites used institutional policies and practices to distance themselves from African Americans and other racial/ethnic groups, many of the immigrants who had just arrived in the U.S. found it much easier to assimilate, and by the 1930 Census, many citizens from European nationalities were considered White. In addition, country of origin among the new immigrants lost its importance due to the negative connotations that were strongly tied to socioeconomic status of immigrants arriving from Eastern European countries. In other words, a social and legal process took place that allowed immigrants to cut their ties to past cultural specific traditions, and an emphasis was placed on becoming more American (i.e., speaking only English instead of their native language; Alba, 1990; Hochschild & Powell, 2008). This led to a rejection of past connections and a reinvention of the White race in a way that is viewed as a more generalized identity (i.e., White American).

Whites (non-Hispanic or Latino/a) currently represent the largest ethnic and racial group in the U.S. at 256 million, comprising 72% of the U.S. population. However, the proportion of Whites in the total U.S. population has decreased due to significant growth in Latino/a American and Asian American populations. By 2065, it is predicted that White Americans will constitute only 46% of the total U.S. population, and technically while still the largest racial group, will constitute a minority of the overall population (Pew Research Center, 2015).

Youth Population and Its Changing Demographics

The racial and ethnic diversity of the U.S. population has grown dramatically over the past decades and is expected to change further in the future. These changes have implications for the U.S., particularly if racial/ethnic disparities in education, health, employment, wealth, and other socioeconomic indicators continue to widen. In order to move forward, we have to understand the demographic changes and how data can assist us in ensuring the success of all youth.

As you read this and the following sections, consider how data may be used by others (and possibly yourself) to reinforce stereotypes and/or biases people have about various cultural groups. Consider ways as a youth development specialist you can help others interpret these types of data to mitigate their stereotypes and biases and how data can be appropriately used to promote social justice.

Table 19.1 provides the population of youth living in the U.S. from 2010 through 2016 categorized by race. In 2016, the U.S. had over 73 million youth under 18 years of age; 51% were White, non-Hispanic; 25% Latino/as; 14% were African American; 5% Asian; and less than 2% Native American. By 2020, over half of all children and youth under the age of 18 are expected to be Latino/as, non-White, and this percentage is expected to increase significantly by 2050 (Pew Research Center, 2015). By 2060, only 32% of the youth population will be White, non-Hispanic, based on projections that populations will continue to become more diverse.

Table 19.1
Youth Population by Race

	2010	2013	2016
All Youth	74,123,332	73,579,424	73,642,285
Native American/Alaskan Native	1%	1%	1%
Asian/Native Hawaiian/Pacific Islander	4%	5%	5%
African American	14%	14%	14%
Latino/a	23%	24%	25%
White	54%	52%	51%

Due to categories not shown, columns do not sum to 100% (Kids Count Data Center, 2017).

The White youth population (under the age of 18) decreased from 61% to 51% of the total youth population between 2000 and 2016. In the same time period, the percentage of Whites aged 18–24 years (college age population) decreased from 62% to 54% of the total 18–24 population, while the percentages of Latino/as and multiracial youth increased. By 2020, the White population growth is expected to slow with a decrease projected by 2050 due to the projected number of deaths among Baby Boomers exceeding the number of births. Since 2010, 46 states have recorded significant losses in their White youth populations, and 37 states have showed declines in youth overall.

By 2050, it is also projected that the African American youth population will continue to decrease from 14% of the total youth population to 13.1% (Pew Research Center, 2015). Currently, Texas, Georgia, Florida, New York, and North Carolina are the states that represent the largest populations of African American youth under the age of 18 (Kids Count, 2017a).

The Latino/a youth population comprises 25% of the total youth population in the U.S. Approximately 18 million Latino/as are younger than 18 years of age, with the median age being 28 years old. The states with the largest population of Latino/a youth are California, Texas, Florida, New York, and Illinois. Latino/a Americans are concentrated in three metro areas: Los Angeles, New York City, and Miami-Dade (Motel & Patten, 2012).

The Asian youth population is growing rapidly and at a faster rate than all other racial/ethnic groups in the U.S. Its total share of the youth population increased by 43% from 2000 to 2010. Since 2010, Asian, non-Hispanic children have increased from 3.5% of all U.S. children to 5% in 2016. By 2020, they are projected to represent 5% of all U.S. children and increase to 9.3% by 2060.

Similar to the White youth population, the percentage of Native American youth (currently about 400,000) is expected to decrease to 0.8% percent by 2020 and 0.7% by 2050. While Native American youth represent a very small population, Native American youth are amongst the most negatively affected in terms of poverty, family structure, and educational attainment.

Poverty among Racial and Ethnic Youth Populations

The U.S. Census uses a series of income thresholds, determined by the size of the family including the number of children under 18, as well as total family income, to determine who can be classified as living in "poverty." The 2018 federal definition of the poverty threshold for a family of two adults and two children (living in the contiguous U.S.) is an annual household income at or below $25,100. The current poverty rate for an average family of four would equal $2,092 a month, $483 a week or $69 a day.

Poverty, especially youth poverty, can negatively affect youth well-being. Poverty negatively affects children's educational attainment, impedes development, and is associated with increases in youth crime rates. These negative impacts contribute to lower social mobility, which makes it increasingly difficult for them to move upward toward a higher social or economic class. In addition, lowered social mobility exacerbates disparities and can exist across all race/ethnicities and even every family structure type (Evans & Kim, 2013).

Figure 19.1 provides statistics on the percentage of youth living in poverty by race. In 2016, over 14 million youth (19%) in the U.S. lived in poverty. The U.S. youth poverty rate has shown slight improvement; the percentage of youth classified as in poverty each year since 2012 has decreased. In 2016, African American (34%) and Native American (34%) children under the age of 18 years made up the two largest racial groups in terms of percentage living in poverty, although the raw number of African Americans is much higher compared to Native Americans (Musu-Gillette, de Brey, McFarland, Hussar, Sonnenberg, & Wilkinson-Flicker, 2017). The 2016 poverty rate of Latino/as (28%) is just slightly less than for African Americans and Native Americans. Asian American and White youth have the lowest poverty rates of all racial groups (12% each).

Family Structure by Race and Ethnic Youth Populations

Similar to poverty, the characteristics of a young person's family structure can influence educational attainment, poverty status, and overall well-being (Evans & Kim, 2013). In 2016, the majority (69%) of children in the U.S. lived in households headed by two parents (biological, step, or adoptive). Children living with unmarried parents accounted for 3 million children under 18 years of age. However, the number of all U.S. children living in single-headed households has almost tripled since the 1960s, and currently is at 27%. In single-parent households, 23% live in mother-led households, compared to 4% in father-led households. Figure 19.2 displays the breakdown of children and youth under the age of 18 based on family structure type. Since the 2010 Census, there has been little change in the percentage of children living with relatives (3%) and non-relatives (1%).

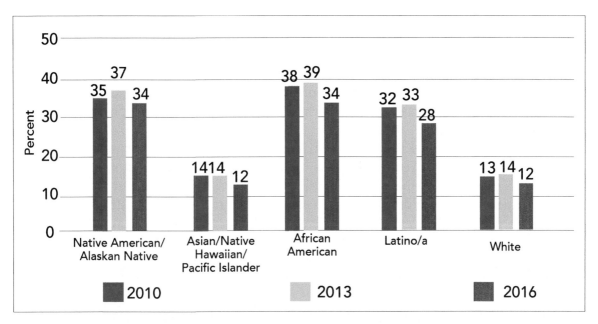

Figure 19.1. Percentage of Youth in Poverty by Race. Source: Kids Count Data Center (2017a). *Note:* A more accurate way to view population tables is to look at the proportion of each racial/ethnic group. Comparing gross numbers can lead to a misleading picture of social issues. For example, if the total African American youth population is 10.3M and the poverty rate for African Americans is 34%, then approximately 3.6M African American youth would be living in poverty. For Whites, if the total White youth population is 37.5M with a poverty rate of 12% for Whites, then approximately 4.5M White youth would be living in poverty. Thus, the percentages by themselves would be misleading with regard to the actual number of youth of each race who are impacted.

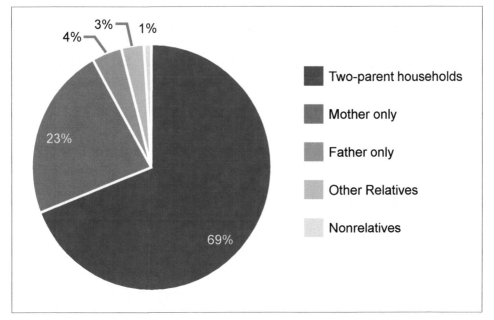

Figure 19.2. Breakdown of Family Structure by Type. Source: U.S. Census Bureau (2017c).

Single-parent families can result from children being born to a single female, because of a divorce or death within a married couple, or due to parents never being married. Such scenarios can create significant strain on the single parent to fulfill both parental roles, including providing the entire family income. Although the primary role of youth development workers is to support the growth and development of the youth they serve, it is also important to consider how their efforts may help support single and dual parent households.

Based on data from Kids Count (2017b), Figure 19.3 displays the percentage of youth living in single-parent households by race/ethnicity. As you can see, there are vast differences between these groups, with only 16% of Asian American youth living in single-parent households compared to 66% of African American youth. For Native American youth, 52% live in single-parent households, with Latino/a youth at 42%. White youth (25%) have the lowest rate of children and youth living in single-parent households.

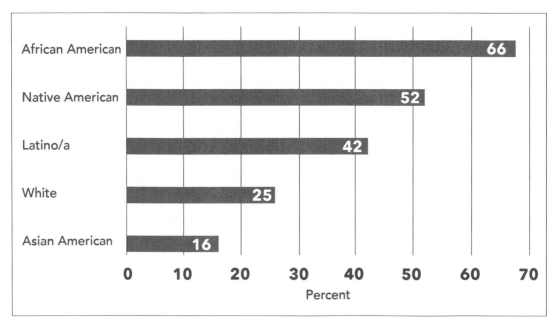

Figure 19.3. Percent of Youth Living in Single-Parent Households Source: Kids Count Data Center (2017)

Educational Attainment by Race and Ethnic Youth Populations

Educational completion and advancement are considered key components of youth development. As of 2015, the high school and GED graduation rates ranged from 82% for Native Americans, 88% for Latino/a, 92% for African Americans, 95% for Whites, to 97% for Asian Americans (Table 19.2).

Each racial group has made substantial improvements since 1990. For example, between 1990 and 2015, graduation rates of African American youth increased from 84% to the current level of 92%. For Latino/a youth the graduation rate rose from 59% in 1990 to 88% in 2015 (Musu-Gillette et al., 2017).

In addition, the graduation rate for Latino/a youth was 88% for those born in the U.S. and proficient in English, but only 70% for Latino/a children born outside of the U.S. For comparisons, the dropout rates have decreased since 2000, when Latino/a youth had the highest dropout rate (28%) among all cultural groups in the U.S., followed by African Americans (13%), and Whites (7%). By 2015, the gap in dropout rates between Latinos/as and Whites had closed from 9.2% to 4.6% (Musu-Gillette et al., 2017).

Following high school graduation, each cultural group (beside American Indian/Alaskan Native due to lack of information) has shown increases in higher education enrollment since 2000. In Table 19.2, 2015 data regarding graduation diploma or equivalent credential completion rates are provided along with 2016 higher education enrollment rates separated by race/ethnicity. Asian American youth (62%) have the highest rate of college enrollment among all cultural groups.

Table 19.2

Percentage of High School Graduation and College Enrollment Among 18- to 24-Year-Olds by Race

	2015 High School* Graduation or Equivalency Completion by Race, Aged 18-24	2016 College Enrollment Rate by Race, Aged 18–24
American Indian/Alaskan Native	82%	N/A**
Asian/Native Hawaiian/Pacific Islander	97%	62%
African American/Black	92%	43%
Latino/a	88%	47%
White	95%	47%

*Data provided by Musu-Gillette et al. (2017)

**Data not available for racial group. Source: U.S. Census Bureau, Current Population Survey (2017)

Becoming Culturally Competent in Youth Development Practice

Recognition and respect for variations in the characteristics among various ethnic and cultural groups are fundamental to developing strategies for developing quality youth development supports, opportunities, programs, and services (SOPS) in a culturally competent manner. *Cultural competence* is a set of behaviors, attitudes, structures, and policies that need to be applied in intercultural situations (Isaacs & Benjamin, 1991; Purnell, 2013). Cultural competence can be achieved by individuals and organizations through the development of (a) an increased understanding and appreciation of cultural differences and (b) the skills necessary to work with and serve diverse youth, their families, and communities.

Further, the implementation of culturally appropriate SOPS requires an understanding of culturally based strengths, assets, resources, and desires of specific groups rather than basing SOPS on stereotypes, biases, and myths. This process may prove difficult, as some professionals may not be open to considering cultural beliefs and practices or lack the training necessary to achieve the level of cultural competence needed to undertake effective programs and services. In some cases, they might not recognize the value and necessity of such training. Attaining cultural competency is complicated further by the lack of cultural diversity among professionals, academics, and advocates in the youth development field.

Individuals and organizations that are conducive to creating culturally competent programs and services adhere to certain values and principles. These values and principles include the following:

- Acknowledging culture as a prevailing factor in shaping behaviors, values, and institutions
- Understanding when the values of the dominant culture are in conflict with those of diverse cultural groups
- Respecting the culturally defined needs of a particular community
- Conducting cultural self-assessment and acknowledging and accepting that cultural differences exist and have an impact on how services are delivered and received
- Recognizing that the concepts of individual, family, and community often differ across cultural groups
- Adapting services to fit the cultural diversity of the youth, families, and communities served
- Institutionalizing cultural knowledge in self, organizations, and systems

Cultural competence is an ongoing process that requires dedication. The process or ability to be culturally competent is on a continuum, with cultural destructiveness on one end and cultural proficiency at the other end of the continuum as illustrated in Table 19.3 (Cross, Bazron, Dennis, & Isaacs, 1989). Recognizing this continuum does not mean that you need to know everything about every cultural group. It means that individuals are respectful and sensitive and understand their own world views. Being culturally competent is a process that youth development professionals should strive to accomplish and only through ongoing education and training will cultural competence be nurtured and implemented in actual programs and services.

Cultural Competency Principles for Youth Development

In order for youth development professionals to develop cultural competence, behavioral and institutional changes are needed to transform program design and implementation processes. These changes are necessary to give *voice* to diverse youth and provide services and programs that meet their developmental needs. Three principles are critical to implementing culturally relevant youth programs and services.

Table 19.3
Cultural Competence Continuum

Cultural Proficiency	Systems and organizations hold culture in high esteem, as a foundation to guide all of their endeavors
Cultural Competence	Systems and organizations demonstrate an acceptance and respect for cultural differences
Cultural Pre-competence	Awareness within systems or organizations of their strengths and areas for growth to respond effectively to culturally and linguistically diverse groups
Cultural Incapacity	Lack of capacity of systems and organizations to respond effectively to the needs, interests, and preferences of culturally and linguistically diverse groups
Cultural Destructiveness	Attitudes, policies, structures, and practices with a system or organization that are destructive to a cultural group

Principle 1: Awareness of bias. The first principle focuses on the cultural awareness of youth development professionals by asking them to examine their own biases regarding racial/ethnic youth, especially as they relate to prejudice, racism, and discrimination. Everyone has a unique life experience based on the influence of family, friends, school, work, and community. As a starting point, these positive and negative life experiences need to be discussed, shared, and examined. For example, are there stereotypes, perceptions, and/or beliefs that you as a youth development professional hold about a particular cultural group that would create a an intentional or unintentional barrier to how you serve and/or work on behalf of youth, their families, or their communities? To be culturally competent means "that you have dealt with these questions and have worked through the biases, feelings, fears, and guilt associated with them" (Sue, Rasheed, & Rasheed, 2016, p. 63).

Principle 2: Knowledge acquisition and understanding. Principle two involves the acquisition of knowledge connected to theories, models, and concepts dealing with demographic changes related to race and ethnicity in American society that are essential to cultural competency. It is important to understand youths' world view by acquiring knowledge related to their racial/ethnic background, daily lived experiences, family background, and personal fears and aspirations. Of particular importance is understanding the social, political, and historical factors in local communities that have led to conditions of oppression, marginalization and social inequality, and how these oppressive factors affect the lives of youth and their families. Finally, youth development professionals should acquire knowledge about the collective values, beliefs, history, family systems, religious and/or spiritual practices, and communication patterns associated with the racial/ethnic groups being served.

Principle 3: Fostering cultural responsiveness. This principle focuses on the professional application of knowledge to empower youth, their families, and their communities. The focus is on the delivery of programs and services that recognize and honor the cultural needs of the youth and their families. The use

> It is important to understand youths' world view by acquiring knowledge related to their racial/ethnic background, daily lived experiences, family background, and personal fears and aspirations.

of one-size-fits-all programming by youth development professionals is never warranted. The effectiveness of youth programs and services are enhanced when they are consistent with the world views, experiences, and cultural values of the youth.

Cultural Competency, Youth Development, and Social Justice

The goal of helping youth development professionals develop cultural competency is to ensure culturally based empowerment and advocacy. Through the proper use of methods and approaches that assist in facilitating youth empowerment, youth development professionals will be able to incorporate social justice principles into their work. Social justice involves providing access and opportunity to all groups by ensuring the removal of individual and systemic barriers to the provision of youth-based programs and services provided at the micro (individual), meso (family and neighborhood), and macro (society, region, state) ecological levels. In other words, for youth development professionals to be effective in their cultural competency efforts, they must put social justice at the center of their professional philosophy and practice. Social justice "includes a vision of society in which the distribution of resources is equitable, and all members are physically and psychologically safe and secure" (Bell, 1997, p. 3).

Why is having a just society important to the field of youth development? The goal of youth development programs and services is to enable youth to thrive and successfully navigate pathways to adulthood. Ginwright and Cammarota (2002) assert that youth development professionals must not only work to change the lives of youth, but also engage in changing the institutional, systemic, and cultural practices that prevent equal access and opportunity for youth throughout society. Therefore, a social justice youth development approach to cultural competency is warranted. Based on Ginwright and Cammarota's foundational work, the authors of this chapter propose a definition of social justice youth development as:

an approach focused on the development of equitable access and opportunities for all youth by actively reducing or eliminating disparities in education, health, employment, justice, and any other system that hinders the development of young people.

This active approach has the following four goals:

1. To produce equitable access and opportunity for all youth regardless of circumstances through the recognition of power imbalances in our communities
2. To reduce or eliminate societal systems and structures (e.g., in health and education programs and services) that perpetuate practices and policies that not only produce disparities, but also decrease quality of life
3. To encourage youth development professionals to consider cultural relevancy in the design, implementation, and evaluation of programs and services for youth, their families, and communities
4. To broaden the scope of youth development to include all sectors of a community in order to be inclusive of and responsive to the needs of all youth in a way that promotes social, economic and political change

Social justice youth development is ultimately concerned with putting an end to the injustices and obstacles that harm individuals in our society. The development of cultural competency serves as the foundation to guide the field in this direction. Additional information about cultural competency can be found in Chapters 20 and 21.

Conclusion

Enabling youth development professionals to develop cultural competency and practice social justice presents many challenges, as well as many opportunities. Each cultural group in the U.S. has unique strengths, assets, and needs. By acknowledging these differences, we can provide better services to youth from diverse racial/ethnic backgrounds. Youth development professionals should be proactive in developing culturally responsive programs and services. In order to optimize positive opportunities for human development, contextually and culturally responsive environments must be constructed and specific attention directed toward developing programs that are relevant to the lives of diverse youth.

Discussion Questions

Key Terms and Concepts

1. Select four group identities you possess (e.g., race, age). Of the four you have chosen, which one is most important to you? Why? Does its significance change in different settings? Why?
2. What are the differences between the concepts of race and ethnicity? Why do these differences matter?
3. Bella is a young person who identifies as a girl and describes herself as deaf, Latina, and lesbian. Bella is also overweight for her age and dark-skinned. These characteristics all contribute to her identity. What forms of discrimination might Bella face in her school, community, and OST activities? Would she face stronger or more types of discrimination given the intersectional nature of her identity? Would her disability, race/ethnicity, gender or sexual orientation, or a combination thereof, contribute to forms of discrimination, social injustice, or cultural identity?
4. In terms of race/ethnicity, do you believe someone can be colorblind? Why is it so difficult to acknowledge differences, especially cultural differences? In what ways does a colorblind approach hinder youth-adult relationships when working with youth?

Diverse Profiles

1. Were any of the historical racial/ethnic categorizations terms new to you? If yes, which ones? Would you consider yourself someone that has avoided interactions with other racial/ethnic groups because you were unsure "what to call them?" If yes, having read this chapter, how might you behave in the future?
2. What changes do you believe will occur in U.S. Census racial and ethnic categories over the next 50 years?

Cultural Competency

1. How do organizational policies and processes serve as barriers to the development of cultural competence by youth development professionals?
2. How do some youth development practitioners, despite their best intentions, cause inequality in their programs?

Class Assignments

1. Cultural Observation

- Historically, racial segregation has been a sociopolitical problem in the United States. Despite various social, political, legal, and economic policies to desegregate our schools, churches, businesses, parks, beaches, and neighborhoods, the U.S. continues to be segregated along racial and economic lines. Look around your campus (e.g., dormitories, recreation centers, classes) or your community (e.g., a local park, church). Take a minimum of 15 minutes to observe the people interacting. Answer the following questions:
  - Is there evidence of racial/ethnic segregation?
  - Why do you think people segregate along racial/ethnic lines?
  - What does it tell us about society? Is it harmful or beneficial for the development of youth?
  - Should we eradicate the ability of people to segregate? If yes, how would you accomplish this? If no, why not? Be prepared to justify your answer.

2. My Cultural Identity

- Your belief system was shaped to a large degree by primary caregivers and peers. You were taught what you now hold as "truth" through participation in religion, educational institutions, and life experiences. These socializing influences have contributed to your racial/ethnic identity. The purpose of this assignment is to encourage you to examine who you are by identifying your own values and beliefs and to begin to think critically about their impact on your ability to function effectively in a diverse environment.
  - Describe your family's racial, ethnic, and/or national background. What particular aspect of your culture explains your beliefs and attitudes about racial/ethnic differences (e.g., family practices, gender, race/ethnicity, religion, holidays, and traditions)?
  - What can you recall about events and conversations related to race/ethnicity that may have impacted your current perspectives and/or experiences? What did these experiences teach you about people who are racially/ethnically different from you?
  - Identify and discuss biases, prejudices, and stereotypes you have regarding racial/ethnic groups different from yourself. How do those experiences influence the ways in which you interact with members of those groups?
  - Were you particularly interested in or surprised by any of the information/ feelings you may have uncovered while completing this assignment?

References

Alba, R. (1990). *Ethnic identity: The transformation of White America.* New Haven, CT: Yale University Press.

Alexander, M. (2010). *The new Jim Crow: Mass incarceration in the age of colorblindness.* New York, NY: New Press.

Bell, L. A. (1997). Theoretical foundations for social justice education. In M. Adams, L. A. Bell, & P. Griffin (Eds.), *Teaching for diversity and social justice: A sourcebook* (pp. 3–15). New York, NY: Routledge.

Burke, P. J. (1991). Identity processes and social stress. *American Sociological Review,* 836–849.

Cashmore, E. (1994). *Dictionary of race and ethnic relations.* London, UK: Routledge & Kegan Paul.

Cohn, D. (2010, January 21). Race and the Census: The Negro controversy. Pew Research Center. Retrieved from http://www.pewsocialtrends.org/2010/01/21/race-and-the-census-the-%E2%80%9Cnegro%E2%80%9D-controversy/

Crenshaw, K. (1991). Mapping the margins: Intersectionality, identity politics, and violence against women of color. *Stanford Law Review, 43*(6), 1241–1299.

Cross, T., Bazron, B., Dennis, K., & Isaacs, M. (1989). *Towards a culturally competent system of care, Vol. I.* Washington, DC: Georgetown University Child Development Center, CASSP Technical Assistance Center. Retrieved from http://nccccurricula.info/culturalcompetence.html

Evans, G. W., & Kim, P. (2013). Childhood poverty, chronic stress, self-regulation, and coping. *Child Development Perspectives, 7*: 43–48.

Fabian, J. (2016, May 20). Obama signs measure striking 'Oriental' and 'Negro' from federal law. The Hill. Retrieved from http://thehill.com/blogs/blog-briefing-room/news/280751-obama-signs-measure-striking-oriental-and-negro-from-federal

Fitzgerald, K. J. (2014). *Recognizing race and ethnicity: Power, privilege, and inequality.* Boulder, CO: Westview Press.

Ginwright, S., & Cammarota, J. (2002). New terrain in youth development: The promise of a social justice approach. *Social Justice, 29*(4), 82–95.

Glossary–Living with the future in mind. (n.d.). Retrieved from http://www.state.nj.us/dep/dsr/sustainable-state/glossary.htm

Hall, S. (1990). Cultural identity and diaspora. In J. Rutherford (Ed.), *Identity: Community, culture, difference* (pp. 222–223). London, UK: Lawrence and Wishart.

Hall, S. (1992). The question of cultural identity. In S. Hall, D. Held, & T. McGrew (Eds.), *Modernity and its Futures* (pp. 274–316). Cambridge, MA: Polity Press.

Hall, S. (1997). *Representation: Cultural representations and signifying practices.* London, UK: Sage Publications.

Hochschild, J., & Powell, B. (2008). Racial reorganization and the United States Census 1850-1930: Mulattoes, half-breeds, mixed parentage, Hindoos, and the Mexican race. *Studies in American Political Development, 22*(1), 59–96.

Hoeffel, E. M., Rastogi, S., Kim, M. O., & Shahid, H. (2012). *The Asian population: 2010*. Washington, DC: U.S. Census Bureau.

Illinois State Museum Society. (2000). Glossary. Retrieved from http://www.museum. state.il.us/muslink/behind/htmls/gloss.html

Indian Entities Recognized and Eligible to Receive Services from the United States Bureau of Indian Affairs, 82 Federal Register 4915 (January 17, 2017), pp. 4915-4920.

Isaacs, M., & Benjamin, M. (1991). *Toward a culturally competent system of care, Volume II, Programs which utilize culturally competent principles.* Washington, DC: Georgetown University Child Development Center, CASSP Technical Assistance Center.

Jobe, M. (2004). Native Americans and the U.S. Census: A brief historical survey. *University Library Faculty and Staff Contributions, 28.* Retrieved from http:// scholar.colorado.edu/libr_facpapers/28

Kids Count Data Center. (2017a). Child population by race. Retrieved from http:// datacenter.kidscount.org/data/tables/103-child-population-by-race?loc=1&loct= 1#detailed/2/2-52/false/870/67,72/423,424

Kids Count Data Center. (2017b). Children in single-parent families by race. Retrieved from http://datacenter.kidscount.org/data/tables/107-children-in-single-parent-families-by-race?loc=1&loct=1#detailed/1/any/fal se/573/10,11,9,12,1,185,13/432,431

Lee, S. J. (1996). *Unraveling the "model minority" stereotype: Listening to Asian American youth.* New York, NY: Teachers College Press.

Lopez, G., Ruiz, N. G., & Patten, E. (2017). Key facts about Asian Americans, a diverse and growing population. Retrieved from http://www.pewresearch.org/fact-tank/2017/09/08/key-facts-about-asian-americans/

Martin, B. L. (1991). From Negro to Black to African American: The power of names and naming. *Political Science Quarterly, 106*(1), 83–107.

Motel, S., & Patten, E. (2012). Hispanics of Mexican origin in the United States, 2010. Retrieved from http://www.pewhispanic.org/2012/06/27/hispanics-of-mexican-origin-in-the-united-states-2010/

Mukhopadhyay, C. C. (2008).) Getting rid of the word "Caucasian." In M. Pollack (Ed.), *Everyday antiracism: Getting real about race in school* (pp. 12–16). New York, NY: The New Press.

Musu-Gillette, L., de Brey, C., McFarland, J., Hussar, W., Sonnenberg, W., & Wilkinson-Flicker, S. (2017). *Status and trends in the education of racial and ethnic groups 2017* (NCES 2017-051). Washington, DC: Department of Education, National Center for Education Statistics. Retrieved from http://nces.ed.gov/pubsearch

Pager, D., & Shepherd, H. (2008). The sociology of discrimination: Racial discrimination in employment, housing, credit, and consumer markets. *Annual Review of Sociology, 34*, 181–209.

Pew Research Center. (2015). Projected U.S. population by race and Hispanic origin, 2015-2065, with and without immigrants entering 2015-2065. Retrieved from http://www.pewhispanic.org/2015/09/28/modern-immigration-wave-brings-59-

million-to-u-s-driving-population-growth-and-change-through-2065/ph_2015-09-28_immigration-through-2065-a2-06/

Pfeifer, M. J. (2005). Wisconsin's last decade of lynching, 1881–91: Law and violence in the postbellum midwest. *American Nineteenth Century History, 6*(3), 227–239.

Priest, N., Paradies, Y., Trenerry, B., Truong, M., Karlsen, S., & Kelly, Y. (2013). A systematic review of studies examining the relationship between reported racism and health and well-being for children and young people. *Social Science and Medicine, 95,* 115–127.

Purnell, L. (2013). *Transcultural health care: A culturally competent approach.* Philadelphia, PA: F. A. Davis.

Stein, G. L., Supple, A. J., Huq, N., Dunbar, A. S., & Prinstein, M. J. (2016). A longitudinal examination of perceived discrimination and depressive symptoms in ethnic minority youth: The roles of attributional style, positive ethnic/racial affect, and emotional reactivity. *Developmental Psychology, 52,* 259–272.

Stryker, S., & Serpe, R. T. (1994). Identity salience and psychological centrality: Equivalent, overlapping, or complementary concepts? *Social Psychology Quarterly,* 16–35.

Sue, D. W., Rasheed, M. N., & Rasheed, J. M. (2016). *Multicultural social work practice: A competency-based approach to diversity and social justice* (2nd ed.). Hoboken, NJ: John Wiley & Sons.

Sue, D., & Sue, D. (2016). *Counseling the culturally diverse: Theory and practice* (7th ed.). Hoboken, NJ: John Wiley & Sons.

Titzmann, P. F., Brenick, A., & Silbereisen, R. K. (2015). Friendships fighting prejudice: A longitudinal perspective on adolescents' cross-group friendships with immigrants. *Journal of Youth and Adolescence, 44*(6), 1318–1331.

U.S. Bureau of the Census. (1975). *Historical statistics of the United States, Colonial times to 1970, Bicentennial edition. Part 1.* (No. 93). Washington, DC: Government Printing Office.

U.S. Census Bureau. (n.d.). Hispanic origin. Retrieved from https://www.census.gov/topics/population/hispanic-origin.html

U.S. Census Bureau. (2017a). Quickfacts. Retrieved from https://www.census.gov/quickfacts/fact/table/US/PST045216

U.S. Census Bureau. (2017b). FFF: American Indian and Alaska Native Heritage Month: November 2017. Retrieved from https://www.census.gov/newsroom/facts-for-features/2017/aian-month.html

U.S. Census Bureau. (2017c). Current Population Survey (CPS). Retrieved from https://www.census.gov/data/tables/time-series/demo/families/children.html

Chapter 20

Culturally Responsive Organized Activities

Lessons Learned from Latinx Families in the U.S.

Andrea Vest Ettekal and Sandra D. Simpkins

Think back to your own adolescence. Can you remember the most satisfying activities you participated in and during which you felt most like yourself? You probably felt as though you *fit* into the setting, that you felt physically and/or psychologically *safe*, and that you had a *voice*. You probably also felt that you had positive experiences in your environment. Maybe, however, you had times when you did not feel that you fit into your activity environment, when you felt unsafe, or that you did not have a voice. Unfortunately, this latter situation too often occurs for many youth who come from diverse or nontraditional backgrounds. That is not to say that youth from these backgrounds do not derive positive developmental benefits through their involvements in organized out-of-school time (OST) activities, because they do. However, emerging evidence suggests that activities may not be equally beneficial for all youth.

Evidence suggests that ethnic minority youth are less likely to participate in organized activities than their White peers (Fredricks & Simpkins, 2012), and some ethnic minority youth report negative experiences in activities, including ethnic discrimination (e.g., Gutierrez, Larson, Raffaelli, Fernandez, & Guzman, 2017; Lin et al., 2016). Given that organized activities can promote positive social, psychological, and physical outcomes for diverse youth (Fredricks & Simpkins, 2012), not participating or having potentially negative experiences needs to be addressed. Thus, it is important to consider how to help make organized activity settings accessible and meaningful so that they are available to support positive and healthy development among all youth.

We believe one way to improve activities for all youth is to enhance the *cultural responsiveness* of organized activities. Culturally responsive organized activities move away from one-size-fits-all programming to better fit the lives of the specific youth served (Lopez, Hofer, Bumgarner, & Taylor, 2017; Simpkins, Riggs, Ngo, Ettekal, & Okamoto, 2016; Williams & Deutsch, 2016). Though discussions about cultural responsiveness have evolved for some time in areas such as physician-patient and teacher-student interactions, the application of cultural responsiveness principles is relatively new in the field of organized activities. Thus, the purpose of this chapter is to provide an overview of the rationale for and principles of culturally responsive organized activities.

The following is a quick overview of what we will cover in the chapter. First, we provide a brief history of the underlying framework for culturally responsive organized activities. When applying or adapting a new framework to a field of study, in this case organized activities, it is helpful to know how the framework came to be. Next, we begin a journey into the lives of two Latinx families living in the southwest of the U.S. These two families provide real-life examples of the opportunities and challenges for immigrant Latinx youth in the U.S. Drawing from the stories of these exemplar families, we describe three specific areas for consideration in designing and supporting culturally responsive organized activities: (1) How does being an ethnic minority matter in organized activities?, (2) What happens when organized activities incorporate (or do not incorporate) youths' ethnic cultural backgrounds?, and (3) How should thinking about ethnic minorities' experiences and incorporating their ethnic cultural backgrounds be prioritized in organized activities? Finally, we offer practical guidance for activity staff working with diverse youth. Note that we use the term *Latinx* (pronounced *lateen-ex*) throughout (rather than Latino/a) because the term is gender neutral and inclusive of the multiple intersecting gender and cultural identities of Latin American descendants.

Culturally Responsive Organized Activities: A Brief History and Overview

What makes something a good activity? This question has concerned researchers and practitioners in the field of organized activities for decades—and for good reason —we need to know *what works* in organized activities. Although there are now many answers to this question, one of the most prominent frameworks came from a convening of the National Academies of Sciences (NAS), in which researchers and practitioners described the universal features of *what works* in organized activities (Eccles & Gootman, 2002). You have read about this work in previous chapters, but let's quickly review the list of high quality program features, which include the following:

- A physical and psychologically safe environment
- Appropriate structure
- Supportive relationships
- Opportunities to belong
- Positive social norms
- Support for efficacy and mattering
- Opportunities for skill-building
- The integration of family, school, and community efforts

Though the authors of this list argued that these are universal quality features that are applicable to all youth, they also stated that activities and these features need to take into account the local context.

Luckily, three frameworks have emerged to facilitate the process of designing and implementing organized activities in a culturally responsive way for ethnic minority youth. The first framework focused on a concept called *cultural competency* (Lopez et al., 2017) and was published by the National Research Center on Hispanic Children and Families (NRCHCF). Cultural competency means teaching service providers the skills and knowledge needed to be able to work effectively with culturally diverse individuals. Cultural competency assumes a set of skills can be learned once and then someone is ready to work with everyone from a certain group. However, this ignores the fact that there is great variability among individuals who identify with the same demographic groups, and that individuals change over time. Thus, cultural competency oversimplifies the dynamics between people, within and across ethnic groups.

Atmosphere, rather than the activities themselves, helps to differentiate when OST programs successfully or unsuccessfully promote positive youth development.

A second framework on *culturally responsive organized activities* highlighted the dynamic relationships between youth and their activity settings (Simpkins et al., 2016). The culturally responsive organized activity framework considered each of the eight NAS features and how they mattered specifically for ethnic minority youth—including how activity leaders and youth shape experiences in the activity, as well as how the activity content shapes the behaviors and knowledge of activity leaders and youth. The authors described how ethnicity and culture matter for each of the eight features in terms of program structure and staff practices. For example, the culturally responsive organized activities framework discusses how building positive social norms in ethnically diverse activities means establishing norms that are acceptable to all groups and do not privilege certain ethnic groups. As another example, providing skill-building activities in a culturally responsive way means that activity leaders should be aware of potential cultural differences in valued skills (e.g., assertiveness is valued in some cultures and not others). Table 20.1 describes how to adapt each of the universal features of high-quality programs identified by the NAS in ethnically diverse activities (Simpkins et al., 2016).

Table 20.1

Indicators of Cultural Responsive Staff and Program Structure

Categories	Staff	Program Structure
Physical and Psychological Safety	• Be aware of potential culturally based contributors to interpersonal conflict • Avoid use of language that is discriminatory, teases, or makes fun of a particular group or furthers stereotypes • Promote constructive culturally based conflict resolution among youth and staff • Positively counter practices degrading to particular groups, biases, stereotypes, discrimination, and microaggressions • Handle specific safety concerns of youth who are marginalized, victimized, or have other safety concerns (e.g., lack citizenship documentation)	• Provide clear structure and procedures for all youth to address safety concerns (e.g., victimization, bullying) with staff and to feel comfortable in doing so • Have written policies and procedures specifying how the activity is welcoming to all youth and families • Provide a physical environment that is safe, accessible, and welcoming to youth and families of all ethnic and cultural backgrounds • Ensure all groups have equal status
Appropriate Structure	• Use behavior management strategies that are based on cultural norms concerning limit setting, rules, and monitoring • Be flexible and adapt demands to align with youths' cultural backgrounds • Co-construct rules and decision-making processes with youth	• Actively seek input from all families and youth concerning culturally appropriate structure in the program • Ensure that all families and youth understand the program expectations and procedures • Balance autonomy and structure that are consistent with youths' cultural norms • Adapt rules to recognize youths' responsibilities outside of the activity so that a particular group is not unduly penalized

(cont.)

Table 20.1 (cont.)

Categories	Staff	Program Structure
Supportive Relationships	• Have positive attitudes about all cultural groups • Focus and build on individuals' assets and strengths • Foster partnerships with youth where both culturally diverse youth and staff are viewed as skilled, knowledgeable individuals • Engage in culturally sensitive interactions with youth and families (e.g., culturally sensitive displays of emotions) • When appropriate, highlight similarities among cultures	• Make all communication available in the languages and communication styles (e.g., email, level of eye contact) youth and families prefer • Have team-building activities for staff and youth to get to know one another
Opportunities to Belong	• Foster positive interactions among youth from diverse cultural groups • Actively include diverse youth in all group-based activities • Assist youth in bridging cultural differences • Cultivate a shared activity identity while honoring youths' unique group identities	• Provide opportunities, including leadership roles, for youth regardless of background • Structure activities to foster collaboration toward a common goal rather than competition across groups • Structure the activities and groups to minimize marginalization or segregation
Positive Social Norms	• Encourage prosocial cultural norms and behavior among staff and youth • Treat all participants, staff, and families with equal respect and consideration • Promote youths' respect and value of diversity • Have similar expectations for youth of all ethnic and cultural backgrounds	• Program norms should integrate norms of all cultures to develop a set of activity norms • Have written expectations and discussions with staff and youth on positive social norms around cultural differences, diversity, and integration
Support for Efficacy and Meaning	• Encourage youth to express their opinions and provide respectful feedback • Do not avoid or dismiss youths' questions about their cultures or others' cultures • Support youth as they explore their cultural identity and resolve issues concerning culture	• Include youth voice in identifying ways to make the program culturally meaningful (e.g., relevant issue they can address, materials, physical space, family events, how they are taught/how the group is structured) • Provide opportunities to connect programmatic content to their daily lives or the lives of those in their community in a culturally meaningful way so that they better understand the relevance of the activity

(cont.)

Table 20.1 (cont.)

Categories	Staff	Program Structure
Opportunities for Skill Building	• Seek teachable moments to discuss with youth their culture and others' cultures, teach youth strategies to bridge cultural differences in a positive manner, and about cultural capital to succeed in U.S. schools • Be aware of potential cultural differences in valued skills (e.g., assertiveness)	• Provide content that is responsive to youths' and families' cultures such that skills valued by those cultures are taught, cultural holidays are celebrated, and culturally relevant material is taught (e.g., cultural songs) • Teach youth about the history, traditions, and beliefs of other cultures
Integration of Family, School, and Community Efforts	• Know about the diversity and lives of youth and families in the area • Be sensitive to families' cultural values and work with families to bridge any cultural differences or conflicts with families • Actively seek out and communicate with all families and other important people (e.g., teachers, religious leaders, promotoras) about youths' overall well-being	• Provide opportunities for all parents to be involved, get to know one another, and provide feedback on the program in ways that accommodate parents' schedules and ways of gathering • Consider youths' cultural events and familial obligations in the requirements and schedule • Capitalize on culturally diverse community resources (e.g., Asian-American History Museum)

Reprinted from Simpkins et al. (2016), *Journal of Adolescent Research, 32*, pp. 5–7, with permission of Sage Publications, Inc.

Finally, a third framework broadened the existing *programs—activities—relationships—culture* (PARC) model to describe how race and ethnicity matter in youth programs (Williams & Deutsch, 2016). The extension of the PARC model highlights the idea that youth bring into the activity a background and history of experiences related to their race/ethnicity. This background and history has been shaped by their immediate experiences as well as by the larger society. Race and ethnicity are not simply grouping variables that describe youth experiences (e.g., discrimination against a racial or ethnic minority youth in a majority White setting), but are linked to youths' cultural beliefs and attitudes (e.g., youth are socialized within their racial or ethnic group to believe and act in certain ways). The PARC model highlights the importance of considering the variability among youth both within and across groups by emphasizing that each youth brings a unique cultural background and history into the activity and each youth has a unique cultural experience even within the same activity.

Across the frameworks, there are three common messages for serving diverse youth in organized activities.

1. Individuals and their environments are part of an integrated system. Thus, the role of ethnicity and culture cannot be examined without simultaneous consideration of the characteristics of the youth and the features of the activity setting.

2. Race, ethnicity, and culture are frequently used interchangeably, but are in fact distinct constructs. Culture encompasses a wide array of beliefs, values, behaviors, and traditions; individuals' ethnicity and race are cultural contexts themselves and can encompass multiple cultures within them. (See Chapter 20 for a fuller discussion of these terms).

3. Youth have unique experiences in activities that are in part informed by their race, ethnicity, and culture. Thus, for each youth in each activity, we need to consider (a) how race, ethnicity, and culture matter, in that specific activity; (b) for which specific youth outcomes; (c) at that specific time in their lives; and (d) during that specific historical period.

Exemplar Cases of Latino Youth Living in the Southwest of the U.S.

Next, let's consider examples of Latinx families' real-life experiences with organized activities. These examples come from Project Reach. The project focused on Latinx families because they are the largest and fastest growing ethnic group in the U.S. (Pew Hispanic Center, 2013), yet have the lowest participation in activities among ethnic minority youth (Fredricks & Simpkins, 2012). Studying differences among Latinx families allows us to better understand diversity among youth of the same Latinx ethnic cultural background. Understanding the differences within an ethnic group also helps to highlight the dangers of stereotyping and treating all youth from one ethnic group in the same way. Though Project Reach focused on many dimensions of diversity among Latinx families (including immigration, generational status and social class), we focus here on experiences related to ethnicity and ethnic culture because they are central to the culturally responsive organized activity framework we are discussing.

To illustrate principles of culturally responsive organized activities, we draw on interview data from two families of Mexican origin (youth and their parents). The two families we highlight serve as examples of the types of challenges and opportunities many families discussed with regard to their Mexican ethnicity and ethnic culture. Although the two families share many similarities, including their Mexican ethnic background and respect for their ethnic cultural heritage, they offer different experiences with organized activities.

Jose, the "White Mexican Boy"

Jose is a 14-year-old Mexican American born in Arizona. He lives with his single mother, a second-generation Mexican American who was born in a border town in Texas. He has one brother and lives in a mostly White, relatively affluent neighborhood. His mother works from home as a human services consultant with Spanish- and English-speaking families. Although Jose recently started visitations with his father, his relationship with his father has been largely estranged (we obtained little information about Jose's father, but know that he lived in Mexico at the time of the interview). Jose's mother makes a decent living as a consultant and is able to support Jose and his brother's organized activity choices. Is it very important to Jose's mother to provide supervision and structure during her son's after-school hours. As a young child, Jose participated in soccer, karate, summer camps, and music lessons, but as a seventh grader, he has narrowed his focus to piano and voice lessons. Jose's older brother is also musically inclined and takes guitar lessons.

Jose's family is not highly engaged with Mexican culture, though Jose's mother believes they should know about and respect their heritage. They are not highly engaged with Mexican culture, in part because the Mexican culture they experience in America is not what they perceive to be authentic. For instance, Jose's mom said, "Mexico doesn't celebrate Cinco de Mayo. Even the Mexican food [in the U.S.] is not the food that we eat [in Mexico]. The Mexican culture you experience outside is the American-Mexican culture, not the real Mexican culture." Jose's mother would like her sons to engage in organized activities that teach them about their Mexican heritage because "it reinforces what's happening in the house already." However, they have not found organized activities that incorporate Mexican culture in a way that Jose and his brother enjoy.

The Mexican culture Jose and his brother have experienced in their music lessons does not seem to interest them. For instance, Jose's brother took guitar lessons and his teacher tried to get him to play Mexican cultural songs. However, he did not enjoy playing Mexican songs because he was more interested in rock songs from mainstream American culture. As his mother said, "[his teacher] wanted to focus on Mexican songs… to do 'La Bamba,'" and her son "wanted rock. He was just like, 'No, that's not me!'" Jose's mother even said, "it was the exact same cords she was using, but she was tying them to Mexican songs and he wasn't interested, so he quit." Thus, Jose and his family enjoy cultural activities, but not necessarily in their particular organized activities.

Jose's mother thinks activities that incorporate Mexican culture would be great because they are "trying to reconnect people back to their roots." However, she thinks her son's organized activities have not incorporated Mexican culture well because they have English-only policies. She says that "part of the problem is that when you lose the language, you lose culture. In America, we're so English-only, the backlash has been that in losing the language, a lot of the culture has been lost in following generations." Jose's mother thinks speaking Spanish is very important.

> "We're not you, [mom], we're not Mexican, we're American."

Spanish was both of her sons' first language, and they both take Spanish classes at school. However, both Jose and his brother have gone "through periods of thinking 'We're not you, [mom], we're not Mexican, we're American.'" Jose's mother thinks some of the struggle for her sons is that at home "they're surrounded by Spanish, there is Spanish music going all the time, I have lots of Mexican friends." However, Jose and his brother leave home and then go to their school, which is comprised largely of White, English-speaking American youth. The challenge for Jose and his brother is navigating whether, when, and how to engage with their American and Mexican cultural backgrounds. For now, the boys seem to divide their lives into being Mexican at home and American at school.

Jose and his brother have different skin colors, which has affected their ability to navigate between their mostly White school setting and their Mexican family setting. Jose has lighter colored skin, and his mother describes Jose as "just a white boy…he's just a white Mexican boy." On the other hand, Jose's brother has darker colored skin. The boys' skin colors have led to different challenges in their school.

Each son has spent some time wanting to be his brother's skin color. For instance, Jose's mother described how Jose had "self-esteem issues galore because of his [lighter] coloring," and actually wanted to go to a tanning salon so that he could fit in with Mexicans and "show them that he's Mexican." Jose's brother wanted lighter skin so he could fit in with his White American peers at school. Jose's mother says that "If you're Mexican and you're brown, it's an issue. [Jose] is fair, so he gets by with anything. [Jose's brother] is dark, so he doesn't." In one instance, a teacher at school even questioned whether Jose and his brother were related because they had different skin colors.

Issues with skin color may also be a reason Jose has been more interested in engaging with mainstream American culture than traditional Mexican culture in his organized activities. Jose's mother describes some experiences where Jose "was in these environments with all of these White kids and they wouldn't let him participate." His adult leaders told Jose that "the other kids had more talent." Jose and his mother perceived this as discrimination against Jose because he was Mexican. Jose began to develop "stereotypes in his head about what Mexicans are—they're landscapers or cleaning people." Consequently, Jose has "very few Latino friends and seeks out the White kids and doesn't participate in anything that has to do with a lot of Mexicans." Jose's mother suggests that being a Mexican boy or the only boy of color in an all-White school is so difficult that "the toll on his self-esteem was just horrific." Thus, it may come as no surprise that Jose was not interested in highlighting his native Mexican culture in his mostly White school or in his organized activities with his White, mainstream American peers.

As Jose's experiences suggest, his family faced challenges navigating between native Mexican and mainstream American cultures. Jose's family was proud of its Mexican heritage but found few opportunities to engage with and express its Mexican culture authentically, including organized activities. On the one hand, Jose and his mother disliked the Mexican culture they experienced in America, felt culturally diminished by widespread English-only policies, and Jose's brother struggled to fit in with his peers in mostly White settings. On the other hand, Jose and his family accepted that they were living in America and must engage with and learn about mainstream American culture, but as Jose began to fit in more with his American schoolmates, he then struggled to be "Mexican enough" to fit in with Mexican family members who "looked" more Mexican.

In the next section, you will meet Aubrey, a Mexican American youth in a neighborhood less than 30 miles away from Jose. She has similar struggles navigating between her native Mexican culture and mainstream American culture. However, Aubrey's struggles differ from Jose's, as her activities are comprised of mostly Hispanic peers.

Aubrey, the "American, not Mexican" Girl

Aubrey is a 13-year-old Mexican American who lives with her mother, father, and several older and younger siblings. Aubrey's mother was born in Mexico and moved to the U.S. when she was 17 years old. Her mother has a high school diploma from Mexico and works full time as a custodian. Aubrey's father was born in Mexico and moved to the U.S. when he was 35. He attended college in Mexico but did not graduate with a degree. He works seven days a week as a roofer. With both of Aubrey's parents working, the family makes a decent living and does not experience severe financial hardships. Aubrey's needs are met, and she has the resources to participate in the organized activities she wants.

Aubrey's mother provides strict supervision over her children. One of her primary rules is that her children cannot have substantial free time hanging out with friends in unfamiliar places. She actively monitors her children's activities and always likes to know where her kids are. The primary benefit of organized activities, according to Aubrey's mother, is that they provide a safe place, with adult supervision, where parents always know what is happening and the location of their children.

Aubrey has participated primarily in sports during her childhood and adolescence. As a seventh grader, she participates in volleyball and softball. Aubrey likes to participate in sports because she is good at them and her friends also participate. Similar to her parents' perspective, Aubrey thinks that sports are good for her because they keep her out of trouble. In recent years, Aubrey would hang out on the streets and get into fights. After Aubrey started getting into trouble in the neighborhood, her mother became nervous about letting her hang out "on the streets." Aubrey's family lives in a lower income neighborhood comprised of mostly Latinx and African American families; the neighborhood has a history of racial tensions between the two groups. Aubrey and her mother agree that organized activities are a safe place for Aubrey to spend her out-of-school time.

Aubrey's mother wants her children to learn about their Mexican cultural heritage and respect Mexican traditions. She says that they are "Mexicans, not Americans, and they need to always remember that." Aubrey's mother also wants her to speak Spanish so they can communicate with their family in Mexico when they go back to visit. Aubrey is bilingual and speaks Spanish at home with her family and English when she is at school or with her friends. Aubrey's mother thinks being bilingual is important to foster communication across cultures and because "being bilingual opens more doors" in terms of career opportunities. However, Aubrey's mother is not concerned with her speaking Spanish outside of the family. She says that Aubrey "speaks English [in her activities], and [at home] we speak just Spanish. The Spanish they speak is because we speak to them in Spanish. That's why I don't care if she speaks just English on the outside, she has to speak English."

Aubrey's mother believes that she does not have decision-making power when her daughter is outside the home and that she can only control what happens in the home. For example, she does not care if Aubrey's coaches are Mexican because "we are in an American nation, and I can't pick who is going to be her coach. I can't say I want it to be a Mexican so that she learns Mexican things. They have to learn the story of [America] first and then later, little by little, of Mexico." Aubrey's family's approach to culture is that Mexican heritage can be taught at home and they can learn about mainstream America on the outside.

One exception Aubrey's mother has to leaving Mexican culture "in the family" is with regard to Aubrey's peers. Aubrey's mother thinks it is important to "interact with Mexican kids because there are things that can be learned about their beliefs" and they can join each other in Mexican cultural celebrations, such as "the Day of the Dead." When Aubrey is with her peers, she shares her mother's ethnic pride. Otherwise, Aubrey does not care much about Mexican culture and often calls herself "American, not Mexican" and refuses to speak Spanish. However, when she is with her softball team, comprised of mostly Mexican American girls, she calls herself Mexican and says that "being Mexican helps me feel accepted there. Some people don't work well with other races, and we work well together because we're all mostly Mexican." Even though Aubrey's mother says that her teammates are "American, just the same as [Aubrey], born [in America], they did not come directly from Mexico and they don't know about the Mexican culture either," Aubrey gives a different perspective. When Aubrey and her teammates come together and jointly represent their softball team, they seem to display greater Mexican ethnic pride than when they are independently elsewhere.

Despite Aubrey being persistent about being "American, not Mexican," she says she is "protective about being Mexican and likes to represent it." Aubrey admits, "I don't really necessarily care if I learn about the culture. My mom basically, she tries to force me into this because it's Mexican beliefs. But I really do enjoy doing it because it's where I come from and what I need to represent." However, Aubrey thinks that learning about Mexican culture in softball would be "a little bit weird because it has nothing do with it." As you can see, Aubrey thinks there are times to be proud to be American and times to be proud to be Mexican. Similarly, there are times to engage or not engage in the cultures. If you are confused about Aubrey's orientation toward Mexican and/or American cultures, what you are experiencing is the natural bicultural identity fluctuations of immigrant youth in America. Aubrey wants to represent her native Mexican heritage but does not necessarily enjoy engaging in the culture or speaking Spanish. She has found a home with Mexican American peers in her sports and together, they find pride in representing their native culture, but ultimately, they just want to "play ball."

Ethnicity and Ethnic Culture in Latinx Adolescents' Organized Activities

As you can see from the experiences of Jose and Aubrey as Mexican American youth, ethnicity and ethnic culture are major parts of their lives. Ethnicity and ethnic culture clearly matter, but in different ways to each youth. Both youth expressed indecision about whether and how to engage with their native Mexican cultural heritage. Jose and Aubrey had different experiences being Mexican American teenagers in their schools. Their parents had different approaches to whether and how to teach their kids about their native Mexican heritage. Among the parents and youth, each had different goals for organized activities, different reasons for joining, and different experiences in their activity settings. Next, we provide some concrete examples, based on the stories of Jose and Aubrey, of the roles of ethnicity and ethnic culture in ethnic minority youths' organized activities.

Ethnicity in Latinx Adolescents' Organized Activities

When people think about the role ethnicity plays in any setting, some of the first things that come to mind are discrimination, prejudice, and stereotyping. Before we confront these issues as they relate to ethnicity, it is important to understand the broader context in Arizona at the time of these interviews. In 2010, Senate Bill 1070, an immigration bill in Arizona, was developed, debated, and passed. The bill required all residents of Arizona over the age of 14 who were not U.S. citizens to register with the U.S. government and carry their registration documents with them at all times. Thus, ethnic discrimination and ethnic-based stereotypes were hot topics in the local community at the time we spoke with these families. Although negative experiences related to being Mexican American were not spontaneously mentioned often among many of the Latinx families we interviewed, the discriminatory experiences families spoke of may have been in the front of their minds because of the daily tension they experienced within the local community.

Jose's mother described her son's experiences with race (skin color) and with ethnicity (native heritage). Although race and ethnicity are distinct constructs, they are intertwined. Jose, with lighter colored skin, had to defend his Mexican heritage because he did not "look" Mexican. Jose's brother, with darker colored skin, felt like he could not fit in within White American peers because he "looked" so different. Jose's mother described how, for her sons, being the ethnic minority in a mostly White school or activity was "horrific" for their self-esteem. Jose developed stereotypes about Mexicans that generated low self-beliefs about what he could be or could do with his life. He experienced discrimination; for example, he thought the reason a coach did not play him on a sport team was because he was Mexican and all of the other boys were White.

We heard from some of the other Mexican American teenagers from Jose's school that they experienced ethnic teasing. For example, one of Jose's schoolmates said that his peers on his cross-country team told him that he could "run fast because you are Mexican, you just jump the border wall." Jose's schoolmate went on to say that he thought "a lot of people think soccer is just for Mexican people," indicating that he may want to drop cross-country and join soccer (Lin et al., 2016, p. 572).

> Unfortunately, ethnic teasing and related forms of discrimination can often be viewed as normative jokes, but may involve potentially offensive language and ethnic-based humor that is received negatively by youth.

Unfortunately, ethnic teasing and related forms of discrimination can often be viewed as normative jokes, but may involve potentially offensive language and ethnic-based humor that is received negatively by youth. For example, Jose's schoolmates were probably naively joking when they told a Mexican peer "you just jump the border wall." However, the statement caused the schoolmate to consider quitting cross-country. There are three potential ways the leader could have responded to this cultural incident (Gutierrez et al., 2016). First, the leader could ignore the incident; however, youth perceive leader inactivity as confirmation that the leader supports such stereotypes and marginalization. Second, the leader could address the incident by talking only with the ethnic minority youth who was targeted by the offensive language. However, talking only with the targeted youth can cause him/her to feel alienated and at fault. Third, the leader could engage constructively with the incident and facilitate a discussion among all youth in the activity. Constructive engagement with all youth following cultural incidences represents best practices, in which leaders should intervene immediately, assess the situation by listening to the youth involved, and involve all youth in a reflective discussion about the incident that honors their voices and viewpoints.

Although incidences of race, ethnicity, and/or culture occur in diverse settings and in ethnically homogeneous activities, Aubrey described positive experiences being a Mexican American on a softball team comprised mostly of Mexican American youth. Aubrey described how being Mexican helped her feel accepted and fostered a sense of belonging on her team. Aubrey's mother liked that she was able to spend her time with other Mexican-origin peers, but neither Aubrey nor her mother cared whether the leader was of Mexican origin. Their lack of concern about the leader's ethnicity seemed to stem from not having a choice in the matter. Being aware of her embeddedness in "White America," Aubrey's mother understood why her kids would want to "act and behave White on the outside" and supported that they reserved their engagement with Mexican culture for family settings. Interestingly, although Aubrey's mother used the word *White* to describe their experiences in America, neither Aubrey nor her mother described issues related to skin color. This may be because she was using the term *White* to refer to American culture (that is, she was not referring to race) or because skin color was never described as an issue in Aubrey's life.

These examples highlight the importance of considering dynamics at play in the local communities and schools in which organized activities take place. Experiences related to ethnicity may differ for youth who are the numerical minority compared to youth in ethnic enclaves. For example, Aubrey lived in a neighborhood with a history of tension between Mexican Americans and African Americans, but did not describe experiences with ethnic discrimination perhaps because she found a peer network of other Mexican-origin peers. Jose lived in a mostly White neighborhood where dark-skinned Mexican-origin youth "stood out." Activity leaders should be aware of the history of the neighborhood by engaging with community members and having open conversations with youth about potential issues related to ethnic or racial discrimination. Contextual knowledge, as well as a deep understanding of the youth who are participating, may help prepare activity leaders to resolve ethnic-based tensions that occur within a single ethnic group, as well as between different ethnic groups.

> Experiences related to ethnicity may differ for youth who are the numerical minority compared to youth in ethnic enclaves.

Ethnic Culture in Activities

Learning about ethnic culture in organized activities is complex. The story may seem fairly straightforward based on Jose's and Aubrey's stories; they were not interested in Mexican cultural content in their activities, so on the surface there appeared to be no reason for the leader to teach about it. Jose's brother wanted to play mainstream American rock in his guitar lessons, and Aubrey just wanted to play softball. However, teaching about ethnic culture is much more complex and is certainly not an all-or-nothing choice. There are multiple ways to teach ethnic culture in organized activities.

Jose's story described an experience with a leader who explicitly taught Mexican culture in the activity (e.g., teaching native Mexican songs in guitar lessons). However, explicitly teaching about Mexican culture in activities does not work when youth have other interests, such as learning about mainstream American culture or just hanging out with friends. This may sound perplexing because Jose and Aubrey both said that they care about their native Mexican heritage. For program leaders, the key is learning whether and how to teach about ethnic culture in activities.

Why is it that some Latinx youth who believe in and engage in their Latinx culture would not want to learn about Latinx culture as part of their activities? Part of the answer is youths' interests. For example, Aubrey just wanted to play softball and was not interested in learning about Mexican culture on the softball team. Another part of the answer may have to do with the type of cultural content included in the activity. For example, Jose's brother was taught traditional Mexican songs in his guitar lessons, such as "La Bamba," but he wanted to play mainstream American music. His guitar teacher may have had better luck teaching about Mexican culture if he had tried exposing Jose's brother to modern Mexican rock songs. Jose's mother even suggested that the Mexican culture they experienced is not "the real" Mexican culture. Thus, the cultural content Jose's brother was exposed to may have been too traditional, too narrow, and inauthentic.

Aubrey did not care about including Mexican culture as part of her softball experience because she was primarily there to stay out of trouble, have fun, be good at something, and hang out with her friends. She could not even come up with examples of how Mexican culture could be incorporated in her activities and just thought it would be "weird." However, in situations like Aubrey's softball team, when the context and experience has little to do with ethnic culture, cultural content could be taught in the activity in implicit ways. Both Jose and Aubrey discussed implicit ways that they learned about their Mexican culture in their activities. For example, an implicit approach to incorporating ethnic culture could involve the language policies within the activity. As Jose's mother suggested, the Spanish language can be a cultural tool for youth to engage with their native Mexican heritage. Aubrey's mother had a slightly different perspective on speaking Spanish, describing the language as more of an instrumental tool to foster future job prospects and "open more doors." Either way, allowing youth to speak their native language may help some youth retain their Mexican identity in their American activities without deviating from their interests in the content of a specific activity, which in itself may have little to do with ethnic culture.

Aubrey discussed hanging out with her Mexican American teammates as another way that she implicitly learned about and engaged with her native Mexican culture during softball. Aubrey's mother described Aubrey's engagement with culture as "Mexican in the family" and "American on the outside." However, being around Mexican peers was an exception to the approach that Aubrey's mother took to learning about culture. She thought it was important to be around Mexican peers because youth can talk informally "about what your families do to celebrate" Mexican culture or "the culture in your family." Indeed, Aubrey described how she had Mexican pride when she was with her Mexican teammates and how they shared stories about their Mexican families.

Of course, teaching about ethnic culture, whether in explicit or implicit ways, is only part of the approach of culturally responsive programming. Organized activities concern *what* youth do, but also *how* they do it. Regardless of activity content, respect for ethnic and cultural diversity is crucial. Thus, one of the key components of high quality programs is having a respectful and inclusive environment. Aubrey described how she felt a sense of belonging with her Mexican-origin peers and, thus, felt respected for being Mexican American. Aubrey's softball team is an example of the potential for team-building activities to bring diverse youth

> Allowing youth to speak their native language may help some youth retain their Mexican identity in their American activities without deviating from their interests in the content of a specific activity, which in itself may have little to do with ethnic culture.

together to offer opportunities for youth to share similar cultural experiences and to feel respected about their ethnic culture heritage.

In sum, the key to culturally responsive programming is learning when and how to appropriately teach about ethnic culture. One choice is whether activities should teach about ethnic culture explicitly, implicitly, or not at all. Regardless of the choice for ethnic culture as part of the activity content, high-quality activities are facilitated to be respectful and inclusive of youth's multiple, diverse ethnic cultural backgrounds. Some considerations for how youth learn ethnic culture in their activities are described below:

- Consider the activity purpose. Some activities are more amenable than others to explicitly teach about ethnic culture. For example, the purpose of sport is an athletic competition or game, the purpose of many arts activities could have indirect connections to ethnic culture (such as, teaching ethnic dances or songs), and the purpose of school clubs could be directly related to ethnic culture (e.g., a migrant student association).
- If youth are interested, all activities could consider implicit ways of learning about and engaging with youths' ethnic or cultural backgrounds. For example, fostering informal social opportunities in activities with several youth who share an ethnic heritage can allow youth to share stories about their families and cultural traditions.
- If youth are interested in learning about their ethnic heritage through explicit activity content about their ethnic culture, the type of content should align with the interests of the youth participating in the activity. Youth should have a strong voice in what they want to learn about and have multiple options for explicit activity content about ethnic culture that support a range of youths' preferences for traditional or modern culture.
- Activity leaders should avoid making broad generalizations about specific ethnic groups. For example, youth may share the same Mexican heritage, but have different preferences for whether they engage with explicit or implicit content about their ethnic culture. Moreover, youth may share the Mexican heritage but differ in their pride for their ethnic culture.
- All youth do not experience all activities similarly. Listening to the voices of the youth participants in an activity is important in order to design activities that are enjoyable, challenging, and engaging for the specific youth in the activity. Only the specific youth in the activity can voice what they prefer, what skill level is appropriate for them, and how they are engaged in psychological and behavioral ways.

The experiences described by Jose and Aubrey underscore the importance of being *responsive* in creating activity programming. Leaders' good intentions to connect with youth may prove to be counterproductive if these intentions are executed without being aware of the participants' cultural backgrounds and checking in with youth regarding their preferences about their ethnic culture.

Prioritizing Ethnicity and Ethnic Culture in Activities

The shifting Mexican and American identities of Aubrey and Jose are natural for immigrant youth. According to Erickson (1994), early adolescence (about ages 10–13) is characterized by a focus on skill and competency development. Identity exploration occurs during the middle adolescent years (about ages 14–17). Youths' identities often do not solidify until their older adolescent years. As 13-year-olds transition from early to middle adolescence, developmental experiences are important to consider when deciding whether and when to prioritize ethnicity or ethnic culture in organized activities.

Whereas the experiences of Aubrey and Jose showed their efforts to grapple with identity exploration, the main focus of their activity experiences was skill development. One of the primary reasons Aubrey liked playing sports was because she was good at it. Moreover, Aubrey's mother liked that she played sports because they were safe places where her daughter could learn new things and stay out of trouble on the streets. Similarly, Jose and his brother just wanted to learn to play the music they enjoyed on their instruments. Although Jose's mother would have liked for her sons to take more interest in Mexican culture in their music lessons, she admitted that Mexican culture was not a priority "on the outside." These examples demonstrate how it may be important to prioritize skill development related to the specific activities (e.g., learning sport skills, learning a new song) over teaching explicitly about ethnicity or ethnic culture in the activity. For example, parents may be looking for leaders who have the ability to competently run the activity, as opposed to same-ethnicity leaders who engage with the participants' ethnic cultural heritages. Although Jose's and Aubrey's stories revealed how they grappled with their Mexican identity and explored how central Mexican culture was to their identity, it may not be until later that their cultural identity becomes more explicit in their organized activities.

Deciding whether to prioritize ethnicity or ethnic culture in activities may be particularly tricky when youth and parents disagree.

Deciding whether to prioritize ethnicity or ethnic culture in activities may be particularly tricky when youth and parents disagree. Both Aubrey and Jose's parents had strong beliefs about their Mexican cultural heritage and emphasized Mexican cultural practices in their families. However, if the only factor considered in this scenario was how important Mexican culture was to these parents, we would have drawn the wrong conclusions about whether to prioritize ethnicity or ethnic culture in these youths' organized activities. On the one hand, Aubrey's mother raised her children in a way that engaged them with Mexican culture in the family and with American culture at school. Thus, Aubrey's family wanted organized activities to complement her family setting, not strictly match what they did in the family. Aubrey's mother thought she got enough Mexican culture at home. On the other hand, Jose's mother would like her boys to engage in Mexican cultural activities, but they were not interested. Nevertheless, she wanted activities that reinforced what they did at home or more closely matched their Mexican cultural heritage. Activity leaders could cultivate relationships across activity and family settings so that leaders understand to what degree youth and families want to incorporate their ethnic culture.

Whereas attention to ethnicity and ethnic culture may not be deciding factors for some Mexican-origin families, there was one clear exception. Bilingual activity leaders are essential to foster communication and connection for Spanish-speaking families. The families showcased here were bilingual, where the parents and the youth could speak Spanish and English. However, there are many immigrant families in the U.S. who are still learning to speak English. Language use is a logistical concern that could prevent youth from participating simply because parents are unable to communicate with activity leaders. Thus, the ability of leaders to speak the native language may still be necessary to attract and retain some youth in activities.

Culturally Responsive Organized Activities: Lessons for Practice

At the outset, we presented frameworks addressing cultural competency in organized activities (Lopez et al., 2017); designing culturally responsive organized activities (Simpkins et al., 2016); and the complexities of race, ethnicity, and culture (Williams & Deutsch, 2016). Across these frameworks, there are three common messages that provide a basis for practice:

1. Youth and activities are part of an integrated system.
2. Race, ethnicity, and culture are distinct constructs.
3. Development is unique for each individual, so practitioners should tailor programs to the specific youth in their specific program.

Let's review each of these messages and consider some concrete suggestions for promoting culturally responsive organized activities.

Youth and Activities are Part of an Integrated System

First, youth and activities are part of an integrated system. That is, activity settings should not be designed independent of the youth who participate in them. The experiences of Jose and Aubrey underscore the importance of ensuring that activities are responsive to the backgrounds and interests of the participants and that well-intentioned ways of incorporating ethnic culture may go awry when they do not reflect the perspectives of youth and their families. While it may seem appropriate to align the content of the activity with youths' characteristics without their input, Jose's story provides an example of how incorporating native Mexican culture into his brother's guitar lessons caused him to eventually quit. The negative reactions to the Mexican cultural content were explained, in part, by families' perspectives that the Mexican ethnic culture experienced in activities was inauthentic, too narrow, or too traditional. Over the various interviews conducted during Project Reach, it was clear that there were potentially negative repercussions when ethnic culture was superficially incorporated or when it was simply a quick add-on, such as incorporating ethnic culture without considering the specific youth in the activity. Thus, activity leaders should incorporate the opinions of the youth and families served, as well as consider youths' lives beyond the activity. Some families may want activities that serve as extensions of the ethnic culture in their homes (like Jose's mother who wanted to reinforce what was done at home), whereas other families prefer to prioritize learning about ethnic culture at home (e.g., Aubrey's mother who wanted to complement her family's Mexican cultural practices with mainstream American culture outside of the family).

Race, Ethnicity, and Culture are Distinct Constructs

Second, ethnicity and culture offer only arbitrary boundaries for categorizing youth and families. Ethnic minority youth vary on several dimensions, such that they are different from other ethnic groups, but also have differences within their own ethnic group. The two stories we presented demonstrated that Mexican American youth could have very different experiences based on their ethnicity and their beliefs about their ethnic culture. Same-ethnic individuals can represent different cultures; likewise, individuals can share similar cultural values and be from different ethnic groups. Considering the differences within groups may be helpful to avoid artificial classifications that may impede individual preferences for ethnic culture.

The differences between the experiences of Jose and Aubrey while attending different schools (a mostly Hispanic school versus a mostly White school) suggest that the broader context is an important consideration for whether and how to incorporate ethnic culture. Like Jose, ethnic minorities in mostly White schools may prefer not to highlight their ethnic culture because they are trying to fit in with their White American peers. Like Aubrey, highlighting ethnicity can help some youth feel accepted and that they belong when they are surrounded by peers who are the same ethnicity. Activity leaders might benefit from being knowledgeable in issues of local diversity and ethnic or cultural tensions specific to their area.

> Same-ethnic individuals can represent different cultures; likewise, individuals can share similar cultural values and be from different ethnic groups.

Training may be necessary to ensure that activity leaders are adequately equipped to handle conflict effectively as ignoring ethnic or cultural conflicts may have negative implications (Gutierrez et al., 2016).

Development is Unique for Each Individual

Third, youth have unique experiences in any given activity (e.g., Williams & Deutsch, 2016). That is, how ethnicity and ethnic culture matter in organized activities varies depending on the specific activity and the specific youth. The stories of Jose and Aubrey exposed differences based on their own individual characteristics, features of their activities, as well as the broader context. Culturally responsive programming may be tailored to the specific youth, in the specific activity, embedded in the specific neighborhood, and at a specific time in history. While it is impossible and impractical to tailor each specific activity for each youth, it is possible to develop common strategies to tailor universal programming for specific youth, which include incorporating youth and family voice, as well as being flexible and adaptive in one's practices. Culturally responsive activities are youth-led and incorporate youths' and families' preferences for content about their ethnic cultures. Youth and families may also benefit from contributing to designing the rules and regulations that govern the activity, such that the activity design is sensitive to potential barriers to participation among ethnic minority youth and complementary to families' normative approaches to issues related to ethnicity and ethnic culture.

American youth represent diverse ethnic and cultural heritages. Ethnic- or culture-based conflicts will inevitably arise in programs, but key will be the professional training to develop leaders who can positively and effectively address interpersonal tensions surrounding ethnic or cultural issues. All youth bring into activities unique backgrounds and histories. Principles of culturally responsive organized activities should be implemented authentically and address the unique ethnic or cultural needs of the specific youth they serve. Culturally responsive organized activity systems are vital for activities to attract and retain youth from diverse ethnic and cultural backgrounds and, subsequently, promote positive developmental outcomes.

Discussion Questions and Class Activities

Using the framework of culturally responsive organized activity systems, the experiences of Jose and Aubrey, and the implications for practice, consider the following questions as starting points to think critically about organized activities as settings that are accessible to all youth, provide positive experiences for all youth, work in synergy with youths' multiple facets of life, and promote positive developmental outcomes among all youth.

1. Imagine you are an activity leader in an area where there is a history of tension between various ethnic groups. Should you proactively pursue discussions with youth about ethnic or cultural issues, or should you wait to react to ethnic or cultural tensions that arise? Consider ethnic or cultural issues specific to the youth your activity serves and what strategies you might use to ensure that ethnic or cultural conflicts do not arise and to resolve conflicts positively and effectively.

2. Think about the various types of activities that are offered, such as sports, arts, clubs, service, or religious activities. How might programming be responsive to youths' ethnic or cultural backgrounds in different types of activities? If you were the activity leader, how would you decide whether and how to incorporate content related to youths' ethnic or cultural backgrounds? What aspects of youths' families, neighborhoods, or schools might you consider when deciding whether and how to incorporate content related to youths' ethnic or cultural backgrounds? How does the type of activity (e.g., sports versus arts) matter for your decision to incorporate cultural content? Try to come up with different ways to incorporate culture into different types of activities.

3. Think about the responsibilities and expectations of the adult leaders who run youth activities. How might the ethnic or cultural backgrounds of the youth shape the role of the adult leaders? What special training might staff need to work positively and effectively with the specific youth they serve? Consider scenarios in which the activity leader is similar and different from the youth in terms of ethnic and cultural backgrounds. Also, consider scenarios in which the activity is comprised of mostly White youth, one ethnic minority group, or youth from many different ethnic backgrounds.

4. Incorporating participant voice is essential to providing activities that empower and engage youth and families. Think about various strategies to incorporate youths' and families' perspectives about the program offerings. How might an activity leader gain perspective of families' preferences for activities and how to work effectively with the specific families served? Should the leader talk to each family individually? Host a discussion session with multiple families? Hire a family liaison? How might the strategies of activity leaders differ depending on youths' ethnic or cultural backgrounds and/or how many ethnic minority youth are in the activity?

References

Eccles, J. S., & Gootman, J. A. (Eds.). (2002). *Community programs to promote youth development.* Washington, DC: National Academy Press.

Erickson, E. H. (1994). *Identity and the life cycle.* New York, NY: WW Norton & Company.

Fredricks, J. A., & Simpkins, S. D. (2012). Promoting positive youth development through organized after-school activities: Taking a closer look at participation of ethnic minority youth. *Child Development Perspectives, 6,* 280–287. doi: 10.1111/j.1750-8606.2011.00206.x

Gutierrez, V., Larson, R. W., Raffaelli, M., Fernandez, M., & Guzman, S. (2017). How staff of youth programs respond to culture-related incidents: Nonengagement versus going "full-right-in." *Journal of Adolescent Research, 32,* 64–93.

Lin, A. R., Menjívar, C., Ettekal, A., Simpkins, S. D., Gaskin, E. R., & Pesch, A. (2016). "They will post a law about playing soccer" and other ethnic/racial microaggressions in organized activities experienced by Mexican-origin families. *Journal of Adolescent Research, 31*, 557–581.

Lopez, M., Hofer, K., Bumgarner, E., & Taylor, D. (2017). *Developing culturally responsive approach to serving diverse populations: A resource guide for community-based organizations.* Bethesda, MD: National Research Center for Hispanic Children & Families.

Pew Hispanic Center. (2013). *A demographic portrait of Mexican-origin Hispanics in the United States.* Washington, DC: Pew Hispanic Center.

Simpkins, S. D., Riggs, N., Ngo, B., Ettekal, A. V., & Okamoto, D. (2016). Designing culturally responsive organized after-school activities. *Journal of Adolescent Research, 32*, 11–36.

Williams, J. L., & Deutsch, N. L. (2016). Beyond between-group differences: Considering race, ethnicity, and culture in research on positive youth development programs. *Applied Developmental Science, 20*, 203–213.

Chapter 21

Leisure and Recreational Sport Among Immigrant Youth

Monika Stodolska and Leslie N. Camarillo

Immigration has shaped American society for centuries to the point where the United States is one of the most diverse countries in the world. Today, immigration continues to have a significant influence on the development of the U.S. with immigration issues at the forefront of current political, social, and cultural debates. Immigrants who seek entry into the U.S. are attracted by the prospects of improved economic opportunities, safety, and life conditions. In fact, the U.S. is the number one destination in the world, attracting one-fifth of the world's international immigrants (Lopez & Bialik, 2017). Future immigration flows into the U.S. will likely depend on the possible changes to the immigration policies, refugee quotas, and border enforcement measures.

Let's look at some of the statistics. In 2015, more than 43.2 million people in the U.S. were foreign-born (i.e., born outside of the United States), accounting for 13.4% of the U.S. population (Lopez & Bialik, 2017). Approximately 11.6 million (27%) of all U.S. immigrants came from Mexico, making Mexicans the largest population of immigrants in the U.S. China (6%), India (6%), the Philippines (5%), and El Salvador (3%) comprise the other four major groups (Lopez &

Bialik, 2017). Children of immigrant parents constitute 26% of the population of people younger than 18, and by 2050 are expected to make up one-third of all U.S. children (Cowden & Kreisler, 2016; Zong & Batalova, 2017). Assuming current trends continue, immigrants and their children are projected to account for the great majority (88%) of U.S. population growth through 2065 (Lopez & Bialik, 2017).

Immigrants, however, face some significant issues once they are in the U.S. For example, immigrant children born outside of the U.S. are less likely than their native-born counterparts to be covered by health insurance, to use public benefits such as the Supplemental Nutrition Assistance Program (SNAP) or Medicaid, and are more likely to have health that is "poor" or "fair" (Immigrant Children, 2014). Parents of many immigrant children are also more likely to have a low level of education and struggle with communicating in English. These factors, combined with the undocumented status of many immigrant parents, restrict out-of-school time (OST) and other opportunities available to immigrant youth. Working with immigrant populations brings challenges and opportunities for OST professionals. Thus, this chapter will focus on helping you understand unique factors that affect the out-of-school time behavior of immigrant youth and how OST settings can provide important cultural and developmental opportunities to ease the immigration and acculturation process.

We will first examine demographic patterns of immigrant youth, and then explore how the between-country journey, transition to a new life, and cultural changes affect their OST patterns, opportunities, and constraints. Before we proceed, however, let's explore some key terms related to immigration (i.e., who are the first-generation, one-and-a-half, and second-generation immigrant children, and what is the difference between immigrants and refugees). The box below lists these terms and their definitions.

Key Immigration Terms

First-generation child. A child born outside the country to which he or she immigrated.

One-and-a-half generation child. A child who was born abroad but was raised in the United States (e.g., a child who was born in Mexico but was brought to the United States at a young age and was raised in the United States).

Second-generation child. A child who was born in a country to which a family has immigrated and who has at least one foreign-born parent.

Children with immigrant parents; children of immigrants; or immigrant children. First, one-and-a-half, and second-generation immigrant children.

Refugee/asylum-seeker. Any person who—owing to a well-founded fear of being persecuted for reasons of race, religion, nationality, membership of a particular social group, or political opinion—is outside the country of his/her nationality, and is unable to or, owing to such fear, is unwilling to avail himself/herself of the protection of that country.

(Cowden & Kreisler, 2016; Rojas, 2011; United Nations High Commissioner for Refugees, 1951; Zong & Batalova, 2017)

For the majority of this chapter, unless specified otherwise, we will use the terms *immigrant children* or *immigrant youth* when referring to first-generation, one-and-a-half, and second-generation immigrants.

Demographic Profile of U.S. Immigrant Youth

Generational Status and Country of Origin

In 2015, 17.9 million children in the U.S. under the age of 18 had at least one immigrant parent (Zong & Batalova, 2017). The majority (88% or 1.8 million) were second-generation immigrants, and only 12% (or 2.1 million) were born abroad (Zong & Batalova, 2017). Close to 6 million (5,760,000) of the youngest children (0–5 years of age) and over 12 million (12,106,000) of youth 6–17 years of age had at least one immigrant parent (Migration Policy Institute, 2016).

These numbers provide interesting insights into the potential needs, preferences, and constraints of young immigrants when it comes to OST activities. They are also indicative of which activities (e.g., soccer, family-oriented activities) may gain popularity in the future when the children of immigrants grow up and have children of their own (third generation).

Relatively few immigrant children who reside in the U.S. were born abroad. While the lives of the first-generation and one-and-a-half generation children are shaped by their experiences in the home country (e.g., Mexico, China, India) and their immigration journey, the second-generation youth have no memory of their homelands. Second-generation children are also often bicultural (i.e., they are equally proficient in the culture and language of their parents' country of origin and of the United States) (Keefe & Padilla, 1967). Despite the fact that most immigrant children were born in the U.S., growing up in first-generation immigrant families presents a number of challenges and opportunities that we will discuss in this chapter.

> Second-generation children are also often bicultural (i.e., they are equally proficient in the culture and language of their parents' country of origin and of the United States).

The Location of Residence

Immigrant youth can be found across the United States, but over half (58%) of them live in just five states: California, Texas, New York, Florida, and Illinois (see Figure 21.1; Zong & Batalova, 2017). The location where immigrant children reside affects their access to OST opportunities and services. For instance, schools, nonprofit OST providers, and recreation centers in areas that traditionally received a large share of immigrant population may have a long history of working with a particular segment of immigrant youth and thus be better prepared to serve the needs of immigrant children than the new immigrant destinations (Harinen, Honkasalo, Ronkainen, & Suurpää, 2012). Their staff may be already trained in how to provide culturally sensitive services and how to communicate with newcomers. Agencies in "new" destinations may lack staff with appropriate language skills and knowledge of how to serve immigrant youth.

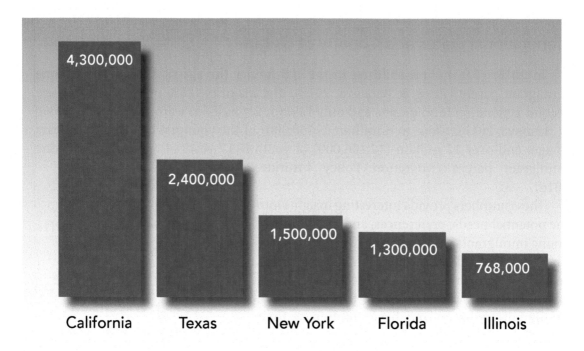

Figure 21.1. The top five states by the total number of children under age 18 living with immigrant parents

Additionally, the size of the ethnic community where children settle affects how fast they assimilate versus how much they will retain their culture of origin. For instance, in areas that are predominantly Latino, such as some counties in California, New Mexico, and Texas, children who are born in the U.S. primarily speak Spanish until they are immersed in the U.S. school environment. Moreover, they maintain many customs and traditions of their parents' home country (e.g., preference for music, sport, and food, coming of age traditions such as quinceañeras). In contrast, children in families who settle in diverse or predominantly Anglo communities at a young age socialize with English-speaking peers and quickly pick up mainstream American sports and other OST activities.

Socioeconomic Background

Census data show that although educational attainment among immigrant groups varies, immigrants in the U.S. as a whole have lower levels of education than the U.S.-born population (Lopez & Bialik, 2017). For instance, immigrants are three times as likely as people who were born in the U.S. to have failed to complete high school (29% vs. 9%). Among all immigrants, those from South and East Asia (51%) and the Middle East (48%) are the most likely to have a bachelor's degree or higher, while immigrants from Mexico (6%) and Central America (9%) are the least likely to have graduated from college (Lopez & Bialik, 2017).

Immigrants work in a variety of occupations. Lawful immigrants are most likely to hold professional, management, or business and finance jobs (37%) or service jobs (22%), while undocumented immigrants are most likely to work in service (32%) or construction occupations (16%; Lopez & Bialik, 2017).

In general, poverty levels among immigrants are much higher than among the general U.S. population. Currently, more than a quarter (26%) of children of immigrant families live below the poverty level, compared with 19% of children whose parents were native born. Recreation and other OST activities for immigrant children who live in families below the poverty level are often restricted due to lack of quality facilities and program offerings. Furthermore, they have few resources to sign up for extracurricular programs, buy sports equipment, or travel. In addition, parents in low-income families often have to hold more than one job just to make ends meet. Overworked and tired parents often have little time or energy to attend their children's activities. Safety is also an issue in lower-income communities.

Legal Status

It is difficult to approximate how many undocumented immigrants live in the U.S., but some estimates put this number at 11 million (Lopez & Bialik, 2017). It is estimated that in 2010, 1.1 million undocumented children resided in the U.S. (Gleeson & Gonzales, 2012). However, the great majority of immigrant children are U.S. citizens as they either were born in the U.S. or entered this country legally (Woods, Hanson, Saxton, & Simms, 2016).

> Parent education, occupation, and poverty influence how much time and energy parents can devote to children's OST activities.

Before they turn 18, undocumented children have access to K-12 education and the same benefits as their documented peers. Some of them only become aware of their undocumented status when they try to obtain a driver's license, find a job, or apply for federal or state financial aid or a scholarship when they go to college (Abrego, 2006). Other children are aware of their undocumented status early in their lives and often live in fear of deportation or separation from their parents who are themselves facing deportation prospects.

In summary, the demographic characteristics of young immigrants greatly affect available OST resources and opportunities. Parent education, occupation, and poverty influence how much time and energy parents can devote to children's OST activities.

Where young immigrants reside as well as their legal status also affect OST activities. We will explore some of these issues in greater detail subsequently.

Migration, Settlement, and Transition Among First-Generation Youth

The migration process (including whether the migration is voluntary or forced, and what occurs during the migration journey) influences the general well-being of young immigrants after arrival, their attitudes toward their new country and their country of origin, and their future ethnic identification (Cowden & Kreisler, 2016). The vast majority of youth arrive in the U.S. with their parents as voluntary economic migrants. Their parents enter the country legally, seeking better lives for themselves and their children. Other youth come as refugees escaping wars, persecution, and poverty in their home countries (Whitley, Coble, & Jewell, 2016), while others arrive as undocumented migrants, crossing the borders illegally either with their parents or on their own with the hope of reuniting with their family members who are already living in the host country.

An increasing number of youth come to the U.S. from East Asian countries such as China, Korea, and Japan, as *parachute* children or as part of *astronaut* family arrangements (Waters, 2002; Zhou, 1998). *Parachute* children arrive in the U.S. without

their parents. Some live with their extended family members or family friends; others reside in boarding schools or sometimes on their own. In *astronaut* family arrangements, it is usually the mother who brings the child to the U.S. while the father remains in the home country and supports his family abroad. The common thread linking these two migration streams is the goal of affording children a chance to develop their English language skills and gain a coveted American education. *Parachute* and *astronaut* children either permanently settle in the U.S. or return to their home country with the skills and experiences that put them ahead in the competitive job market of the East Asian economies.

Young newcomers, particularly those coming with undocumented status, face unique challenges after arrival to the U.S. They not only are in the midst of experiencing the normal identity development typical of adolescence, but they also have to adjust to a new environment, culture, language, school, and friends. Moreover, they have to deal with the stresses of family separation, parent-child role reversals, cultural conflicts between home and school, parental unemployment, and often the unwelcoming climate of the host country (Campbell, Glover, & Laryea, 2016; Doherty & Taylor, 2007). As Doherty and Taylor (2007) described, "Fitting in to a new school, getting along with teachers and peers, peer rejection, anxiety, and feelings of isolation are of immediate relevance, yet they are also important predictors of later outcomes of the settlement, adaptation, and integration process" (p. 32). For young immigrants who struggle with the questions of belonging, ethnic identification, and cultural change, OST activities may be an important arena to develop, express, and negotiate their personal, social and cultural identities, and to adjust to life in the new society (Mata-Codesal, Peperkamp, & Tiesler, 2015).

> Min-Suk, a Korean interviewee commented, "Compared to Korean students, I think I do have more leisure time because I don't have private tutoring after school. But here everything is so expensive, so I cannot go to PC rooms or play pool as much as I could in Korea. So, we more often hang around the lakes or at friends' houses" (Stodolska & Yi, 2003, p. 72).

New Structures in OST

After relocating to a new country, young immigrants have to adjust to a new school, leisure, and sometimes work schedules. Free time is often structured differently in North America than in their home countries. Some young newcomers, such as those from Korea, who often had to spend their free time in after-school tutoring programs, find leisure time in the U.S. to be abundant (see quote from Min-Suk). Others consider leisure environments in the U.S. to be more structured, less spontaneous, and filled with organized extracurricular activities than their home countries.

Many immigrant youth also believe that leisure in the U.S. is more commodified than in their home countries. For instance, in Stodolska and Yi's (2003) study, Mexican and Polish teenage immigrants revealed that they were able to purchase leisure-related items previously unavailable even to their parents (e.g., cars, computers). The young immigrants became immersed in a more materialistic culture and realized that one needed financial resources to be able to afford leisure and to fit in within the American teenage culture (see quote by Michał).

Michał, a Polish interviewee revealed, "Who at our age in Poland could afford a car? Here, a kid arrives, particularly if he comes from a working-class family, he'll spend all his money on a car, on clothes, on gadgets, you know, so he can show off in front of people, 'Look at me, what I have, I can afford it.' (…) The truth is that in America a lot of girls will fall for a guy with a car. I can tell you from my own experience; I had a girlfriend, an American, and she told me, 'If I fall in love with somebody it's OK, but I will marry the guy who has the money, because then I will have an easier life'"
(Stodolska & Yi, 2003, p. 67).

Constraints to OST Activities Among Immigrant Youth

Settling in a new country exposes youth to new OST opportunities. Their lives, however, are also affected by a number of constraints that limit what pastimes they can engage in or that make their leisure less enjoyable. Lack of familiarity with leisure activities, sports, and games typical of North America and lack of proficiency in the English language are two such constraints (Doherty & Taylor, 2007; Whitley et al., 2016). These constraints lead to fear, confusion, lack of confidence, and feelings of isolation and marginalization. Lack of language proficiency also prevents children from effectively communicating with their teachers, forming new friendships, and being able to fit in. For example, in Campbell et al.'s (2016) study, newcomer youth socialized mainly with other immigrants in their school and found developing contacts with mainstream kids problematic. They spent their unstructured time at school in their ESL home room and after-school time at home. Immigrant youths' meaningful interactions with domestic students were few and far between, and few listed their domestic counterparts as close friends.

Lack of language proficiency among parents also constrains OST opportunities of their children. For instance, in 2013, 41% of immigrant children in the U.S. had at least one parent who was not proficient in the English language, and 22% lived in "linguistically isolated households," in which none of the parents could communicate in English (Woods et al., 2016). Parents who struggle with English have problems accessing information about recreation and other OST opportunities, available resources that can foster children's participation (e.g., scholarships), as well as communicating with their teachers, coaches, and OST personnel. As Vignette 1 illustrates, even within one family, parents and children of different ages can have a different proficiency in English and their home country language, which will affect their ability to access recreation resources.

Vignette 1

Yolanda and Cristian are immigrants from Mexico who settled in California over 26 years ago. They have five children who speak English and Spanish with different levels of proficiency. For instance, the two eldest children, Vanessa and Nicole, are bilingual in Spanish and English (speaking, writing, and reading). Jasmine is proficient in English and is fairly proficient in speaking Spanish, but not reading and writing. On the other hand, Natasha and Francisco, the two youngest children, are proficient in English but have very limited proficiency in reading, writing, and speaking Spanish.

Thinking exercise: *Why do you think that a single family can have children with various levels of language proficiency?*

Although all families are different and although there might be different factors affecting children's language proficiency, in this specific scenario we would like you to focus on the order of the children's birth and the length of time their parents spent in the U.S. at the time when each child was born. For instance, when Vanessa and Nicole were born, their parents had just immigrated to the United States and knew no English; therefore Vanessa's and Nicole's first language was Spanish. When Jasmine was born, Yolanda and Cristian (her parents) had acquired some English proficiency, which although limited, allowed Jasmine to continue to speak Spanish to her parents but not practice it to the extent that Vanessa and Nicole did. Jasmine grew up understanding and speaking Spanish but not learning how to write it and read it like Vanessa and Nicole did. At this time, the siblings' main language of communication was Spanish. By the time Natasha and Francisco were born, Yolanda and Cristian understood English fairly well. Moreover, Vanessa, Nicole, and Jasmine were already fluent in English; therefore, the primary language of conversation among the siblings was English. Natasha and Francisco were exposed to English at a younger age than were Vanessa, Nicole, and Jasmine. Also, since Yolanda and Cristian had become more proficient in English, the children could speak to their parents in "Spanglish" (i.e., a combination of English and Spanish). Natasha and Francisco became fluent in English, but not in Spanish; they understand Spanish but have difficulty sustaining a proper Spanish conversation.

As the parents became more proficient in speaking and understanding English, the children were no longer "forced" to only speak Spanish to their parents, which led to the children having less exposure to the Spanish language. This, in turn, became a factor that impeded the middle and younger children from becoming fully proficient in Spanish.

Many immigrant youth experience less freedom after immigration in terms of how, when, and with whom they spend their OST activities. They attribute this change to different social standards in the U.S. (e.g., children are not allowed to play unsupervised), to the geographic layout of the city (majority of leisure-related places in the U.S. require driving), the decreased role of community in supervising children and adolescents, and safety and security issues (Stodolska & Yi, 2003). Furthermore, in the initial period after arrival, parents are often concerned for their children's safety, and thus strictly monitor their OST activities (see quote from Maria).

Maria, a Mexican interviewee revealed, "Here I need to ask my father to let me go out. [In México] I was like 'ahorita vengo...' [informal way of saying 'I'll be back soon...'] (...) Here it is totally different, 100% different. In here it is, 'Where are you going? Why? With whom? What will you do? What time will you come back?'" (Stodolska & Yi, 2003, p. 72).

Family dynamics are often disturbed by the process of migration. Youth who are separated from their families in the process known as *chain migration* experience particularly severe struggles. In many cases, separation from immediate family members is relatively short, lasting from several months to a couple of years. Some youth, however, are separated from one or both of their parents for more than a decade. Once reunited with their families, adolescents who were raised in their home countries by their relatives or grandparents have to go through a difficult readjustment period. They often question their parents' authority and have to deal with the mental anguish of being separated from their "real" families back home (e.g., grandparents, cousins). Comments from a 17-year-old Korean teen, Doohyun, who was separated from his father since he was seven years old reveal this phenomenon (see quote).

Comment from Doohyun, 17-year-old Korean teen: "My sister and I grew up here, in America. At first we struggled because the money that my father was sending us was not enough, but then things got better. My father came to live with us two years ago. I knew my mother was happy to see him, but then he couldn't find a good job, and he would come home angry, and he was telling us what to do. And what right does he have to run our lives?" (Stodolska, 2008, p. 11).

Discrimination experienced from peers, teachers, school personnel, and recreation youth leaders is an additional obstacle to immigrant youths' adjustment and their ability to take part in and enjoy leisure activities (Doherty & Taylor, 2007; Tirone, 1999). For instance, South Asian teens interviewed by Tirone (1999) in Canada experienced name-calling and taunting, which they believed was a result of their wearing distinctive clothing and head coverings. Some of these incidents occurred in schools, while others at community recreation programs, YMCAs, summer camps, and sport activities. Teens also believed some of the physical education teachers and coaches were insensitive to Muslim students who had to fast during the month of Ramadan, which constrained their ability to participate and compete in sports. Racist incidents were particularly pronounced among younger teens and tended to subside somewhat as the youth entered their late teens and early adulthood. Mexican and Polish teenage immigrants in the U.S. also mentioned frequent fights, being ridiculed, teased, and name-called by students of other racial and ethnic groups (Stodolska & Yi, 2003).

One of the reasons why people acquire prejudicial attitudes and engage in discrimination is stereotyping. The process of stereotyping includes three stages: "(a) the identification of a category, (b) the attribution of traits to the category, and (c) the application of the traits to anyone belonging to the category" (Fleming, 1997, p. 172). Stereotyping can lead to channeling immigrant youth into some sports (e.g., African Americans to football) and away from others. For example, some people hold the perception that Asian teens will not excel in contact sports or that they may be physically weaker than their Caucasian and African American counterparts, which may lead to them being offered fewer opportunities to play (Harrison & Bimper, 2014; Lee & Stodolska, 2017). Such stereotyping on the part of OST professionals, coaches, and PE teachers may lead to immigrant youth being offered fewer opportunities to engage in their preferred OST activities. Lack of role models with whom immigrant youth can identify additionally shapes perceptions of sporting behaviors "appropriate" to people from their ethnic group and may dissuade immigrant youth from engaging in some sports and recreation activities (Fleming, 1994).

Lack of information about available opportunities also constrains OST behavior among many immigrant youth. "Information on local leisure opportunities often spreads through the grapevine (i.e., the word gets round only among the local youth, and in many localities, there is no comprehensive multilingual information available)" (Harinen et al., 2012, p. 185). Such obstacles are particularly pronounced among youth who reside in smaller towns that lack bilingual resources and staff, and among children of temporary immigrants such as seasonal workers or university visiting scholars who reside in the local communities only for a short time.

Lower socioeconomic status also restricts OST options among a significant portion of immigrant youth. For instance, in the U.S., the share of children in low-income families (those with income below 200% of the federal poverty level) increased from 51% in 2006 to almost 55% in 2013 (Woods et al., 2016). Lack of financial resources affects families' ability to sign their children up for recreation and sport programs and camps, pay for their recreation or arts equipment and entrance to facilities, or afford transportation. Moreover, families of lower socioeconomic status often reside in central-city neighborhoods that suffer from high levels of crime, and that afford little access to quality recreation resources, parks, and facilities. Immigrant youth who reside in high crime neighborhoods often show lower participation rates in physical activity and outdoor recreation (Shinew, Stodolska, Roman, & Yahner, 2013).

Socioeconomic constraints are particularly pronounced among children of undocumented immigrants. In addition to struggling with the lack of resources, fear of deportation makes their parents less willing to interact with coaches and recreation personnel or to travel with their children to away games. Undocumented first- and one-and-a-half generation youth are also at risk of deportation from the U.S. Fear of deportation restricts activities undocumented youth can join and the locations they can travel to. For instance, youth cannot travel to away games if the travel requires going through immigration checkpoints. Although second-generation children have the benefit of being U.S. citizens, they are not exempt from facing travel restrictions either. This is especially the case when the youth have undocumented parents and/or undocumented siblings.

As the two stories in Vignette 2 illustrate, immigrant youths' participation in recreation activities can be constrained both by their and their parents' and siblings' undocumented status, low socioeconomic resources, lack of English language fluency, and lack of knowledge of how to access recreation opportunities. Such constraints lead to youth who could otherwise excel in sport to participate at a lower level or not being able to participate at all, miss opportunities for college athletic scholarships, and be channeled into participation in ethnically run sport leagues (e.g., all Latino soccer clubs). Hence, opportunities for youth are shaped not only by their preferences, skills, and talents, but by the structure and resources of their families. While it is true of all North American youth, regardless of their ethnic background and immigration status, family-related constraints can play a particularly detrimental role in restricting OST opportunities among immigrant youth.

Vignette 2

Family #1: Francisca and Juan are undocumented immigrants from El Salvador who have a 12-year-old child, Edgar, who was also born in El Salvador, but brought to the U.S. when he was only one year old (i.e., 1.5 generation). Edgar is an exceptional soccer player and was offered a collegiate scholarship to play for a competitive soccer team. Due to the traveling requirements of competitive soccer, his parents decided to opt out of receiving the competitive soccer scholarship and enrolled him in a recreational soccer league, which only travels locally and is not as sought out by college recruiters. Edgar and his parents live in Orange County, California, but have never traveled outside of the county out of fear of getting stopped at a checkpoint and deported. Travel limitations create unique constraints that limit leisure activities and opportunities (e.g., receiving competitive scholarships) available to undocumented children.

Family #2: Brian and Cynthia are undocumented immigrants from Mexico. They have three children, aged 5–13 years old, who were born in the U.S. The eldest, Joshua, plays recreation soccer with a Latino-majority league. Although Joshua is a U.S. citizen and can legally travel anywhere in the country, Joshua has never left San Diego County. Joshua is bound to play with an unofficial soccer league run by Latino immigrants because his parents are unaware of the requirements to enter the city's official soccer league due to their language barrier. Although Joshua's circumstances are different than Edgar's (Joshua has U.S. citizenship), his travels are limited due to his parents' undocumented status. Similar to Edgar, Joshua has limited access to leisure due to the constraints experienced by his parents (e.g., lack of awareness of resources, limited English, undocumented status).

Benefits of Sport and Recreation Activities for Immigrant Youth

Participation in OST activities can have a number of benefits for immigrant youth who struggle with resettlement to a new country. Recreation and other OST programs offer immigrant youth fun, safe, and supportive environments (Doherty & Taylor, 2007). Sport, recreation, and other OST programs teach immigrant youth transferable life skills, increase their feelings of competence, foster social inclusion, help learn a new language, provide orientation to the mainstream culture, and ease their adjustment to life in a new country (Doherty & Taylor, 2007; Whitley et al., 2016). Participation in sport and recreation also helps immigrant youth develop a sense of mastery, positive self-identity, self-concept, and self-esteem. It gives them a positive challenge and an opportunity to be good at something and feel they have control over things that happen in their lives (Doherty & Taylor, 2007). Read the quote in the sidebar to see how a young African immigrant described the role of sport in helping him learn the new language.

"First year I had problems with the language, but now I know basically every word. The coach yells out 'Tuck your shirt in!' or 'Shoot the ball!' Okay—you have to know all the words"
(Campbell et al., 2016, pp. 222–223).

Participation in recreation and sports is often a way for young immigrants to develop social relationships and make new friends (Doherty & Taylor, 2007), which can minimize their feelings of social exclusion in schools and make them more comfortable in PE classes (Whitley et al., 2016). Being proficient in sports can be a way in to school in-groups in cultures where the sport is an important component of social prestige (Spaaij, 2015). Read the quote below to see how skating helped an 18-year-old Iranian girl who had immigrated to Finland make new friends. Young African immigrants to Canada even revealed that the activities in which they participated were relatively unimportant; they primarily valued the activities for helping them connect with peers (Campbell et al., 2016).

Studies have shown that leisure can also contribute to ethnic identity development among immigrant youth. As early as in preadolescence, immigrant children begin to struggle with questions related to their personal (who am I?) and social (to what groups do I belong?) identities (Cowden & Kreisler, 2016). Having a strong ethnic identity has a number of benefits for young immigrants. It serves as a protective factor against anxiety, depression, substance abuse, and conduct problems (Cowden & Kreisler, 2016). In particular, children who are considered bicultural and bilingual are able to capitalize on the benefits of both cultures and show greater academic achievement and increased likelihood of attending college (Dinovitzer, Hagan, & Parker,

"It's terribly difficult to make good friends in cafés. But hobbies are different. I still have contacts with the skaters, my former hobby friends. We are talking, sending messages. So, in different hobbies friends can be made"
(Harinen et al., 2012, p. 186).

2003). To take advantage of these benefits of ethnic identity, a number of ethnic and religious organizations in North America, Europe, and Australia developed recreation and sport programs whose goals are to instill strong ethnic pride in minority youth. For instance, mosques in Norway offer sport programs to attract immigrant Muslim youth and help them develop "Norwegian Muslim" identity (Walseth, 2016). Both religious and lay organizations, in addition to sport associations and clubs, use sport and recreation to attract new members, to teach them about their culture, and to instill in them pride in their heritage (e.g., Somali soccer clubs in Australia; Jewish Maccabi Games in the U.S.; Maccabi USA, n.d.; Spracklen, Long, & Hylton, 2015).

Sport and recreation can have particularly important benefits for refugee youth who have to deal with forced relocation and often struggle with the horrors of war they had witnessed, being child soldiers, and/or losing their parents to HIV/AIDS (Whitley et al.,

2016). In their previous lives, they also had minimal financial resources, food, or access to medical services and educational opportunities. After stays in refugee camps and relocating to a new country, youth struggle with feelings of isolation and marginality. They often feel like they are excluded from both their old homeland and their new host country. Participation in recreation and other OST programs helps them feel like valued members of the team, relax, enjoy themselves, develop relationships with the adult leaders, learn to trust again, and acquire important life skills such as teamwork and leadership (Whitley et al., 2016).

Sport and recreation, however, can also lead to some negative consequences. Spaaij (2015), for instance, argued that:

> ...any generalised claim that sport is a mechanism for "good settlement" is contentious because sport is not necessarily inclusive, but is also used to differentiate and exclude. The social and cultural norms that organised sports embody may potentially lead newcomers or minorities to feel alienated or marginalised. While playing sport can in some cases contribute to a sense of social integration... it can also have the opposite effect of exposing participants to social exclusion, racism, and cultural resistance, which may lead them to abandon sport or to segregate themselves into separate clubs or leagues. (p. 304)

Sport is also often associated with "winning at any price, top-down domination, exclusion, sexism, racism, homophobia, [and] xenophobia" (Spraklen et al., 2015, p. 117). Sport participation in the context of physical education (PE) classes at schools has been shown to lead to alienation and marginalization of immigrant youth (Doherty & Taylor, 2007). For example, immigrant students in school PE classes are sometimes excluded from games due to their unfamiliarity with their rules and inability to communicate with their peers and teachers in English. Contacts with mainstream peers developed through recreation and sport are also often weak and shallow, and tend to be confined to particular leisure settings and activities (Kivijärvi, 2015; Lee & Scott, 2013). Immigrant teenagers are more likely to form friendship ties with other immigrant youth with whom they share similar experiences as "foreigners" in the host country than with their mainstream peers (Kivijärvi, 2015).

Culture, Cultural Preservation, and OST Activities: Mutually Influencing Roles

Cultural background and identity influence leisure time activities of immigrant youth. Additionally, through involvement in recreation and sport, youth can learn about their culture, preserve cultural traditions, and assert their place in the destination communities.

To a large extent, leisure activities popular among immigrant youth do not differ much from their mainstream counterparts. Immigrant teenagers spend much of their time watching TV, playing video games, socializing on social media, and spending time in malls, cafés, and fast food restaurants (Harinen et al., 2012). There are, however, certain important differences in preferences for leisure activities and in the styles of participation based on youths' cultural backgrounds. For instance, Latino(a) immigrants in the U.S. show a preference for sedentary activities (such as family picnics and events), usually spend time in large, multigenerational (e.g., grandparents, aunts, cousins), family-oriented groups, and play soccer more often than other sports (Cronan, Shinew, & Stodolska, 2008). In general, there is a strong family orientation in leisure among Latino(a) immigrants. *Familismo* or familism, which refers to feelings of solidarity, loyalty, and reciprocity, is a cultural value that is considered central to many Latino cultures (Calzada, 2010; Cruz-Santiago & Ramirez Garcia, 2011; Villarreal, Blozis, & Widaman, 2005).

Different preferences for leisure activities and styles of leisure engagements are often passed through generations and largely shape leisure patterns of immigrant youth. For instance, young Latino(a) immigrants are expected to stay closely connected to their extended families. Immigrant children are also socialized early in their lives into which activities are popular and acceptable within their ethnic group; they learn sports by watching their family and peers play and are influenced by the expectations of their family members. Parents may expect youth to engage in certain sports because "this is what our people do" or conversely, channel them away from participation in others (Harrison & Bimper, 2014). Families may also have reservations as to their children's participation in leisure activities that are not in accordance with their cultural beliefs. For instance, some Muslim parents restrict their daughters' sport and leisure activities (e.g., swimming and skating) that involve wearing clothes considered inappropriate by their faith (Carrington, Chivers, & Williams, 1987). Muslim teens' religious background may also constrain their participation in any activity that involves alcohol, smoking, dancing, or socializing in mixed-gender groups (Stodolska & Livengood, 2006; Tirone & Pedlar, 2000).

Following immigration, most children and youth are caught between the cultures of their home and host countries. While adopting the culture of the new country helps them fit in within the local peer group, maintaining their culture of origin allows them to retain close connection to their families and ethnic communities, instills pride in their heritage, serves as a buffer from the experiences of discrimination, and provides an array of other important benefits. Family often plays a central role in immigrant youth's leisure. Previous studies have shown that in the period immediately following immigration, African, Chinese, South Asian, Mexican, Korean, and Polish adolescent immigrants spent most of their time at home and that the connection to family allowed them to retain a sense of cultural identity (Stodolska & Yi, 2003; Tirone & Pedlar, 2000). Read the quote above about African immigrant youth.

African immigrant youth often: "Hunker[ed] down in their homes to cope with the adjustment and relied on their family to buffer the overwhelming novelty of and anxiety induced by their new surroundings" (Campbell et al., 2016, p. 222).

Youth may preserve their ethnic culture by maintaining fluency in their native language, wearing traditional clothing, celebrating traditional holidays, eating ethnic food, listening to traditional music, continuing to perform religious ceremonies, and socializing with teens from the same ethnic group (Tirone & Pedlar, 2000). Events celebrated with extended family members and friends from the same ethnic community are often central to the leisure engagements of immigrant youth of South Asian and Latino origin. Many young immigrants are also members of ethnic clubs that provide activities for children and teens such as sports, dances, and festivals, and play an important role in the preservation of their ethnic traditions. They allow youth to interact with their peers from the same ethnic group, form friendships, and participate in recreation activities and sports within the limits prescribed by their religion and cultural tradition (Amara & Henry, 2010; Tirone, 1999; Tirone & Pedlar, 2000; Walseth, 2016).

For many immigrant youth, the "ideal leisure" often incorporates elements of their traditional culture and community and the new opportunities provided by the host society (Tirone & Pedlar, 2000). They frequently desire to strike a balance between preserving their ethnic traditions and being open to the new ways of spending free time. Immigrant teens' attitudes toward the importance of cultural preservation seem to be also influenced by their gender and age. For instance, South Asian girls and young women show stronger commitment to their family life and other aspects of their culture, and are more likely than boys to "perceive 'izzat' (the need to uphold the family's status and honor) as 'very important'" (Carrington et al., 1987, p. 273). Younger teens are also more likely to succumb to the assimilationist pressures, put more weight on fitting in with their North American peers, and thus, be more self-conscious about the aspects of their heritage (e.g., clothing, head covering) that set them apart from others. Older teens tend to show more pride in their heritage and are less concerned about visible displays of their ethnic identity (Tirone, 1999). Chapter 20 provides a closer look at how OST professionals can provide culturally responsive activities.

Cultural Change and OST Activities

As young immigrants adapt to the new environment of the host country, their culture begins to change. Cultural change is observed not only among the first-generation immigrant youth, but also among one-and-a-half and second-generation children who, as they enter mainstream schools and develop friendships with peers from other ethnic groups, begin to be exposed to values, norms, and behavior styles of the broader North American society. There are different theoretical models that explain how culture changes among immigrants. Although reviewing them is beyond the scope of this chapter, it is important that you know how different concepts such as assimilation, acculturation, and selective acculturation are defined (see the box on the following page).

Perspectives on Culture Change Among Immigrants

- **Acculturation** has been defined as "those phenomena which result when groups of individuals having different cultures come into continuous first-hand contact, with subsequent changes in the original culture patterns of either or both groups" (Sam & Berry, 2006, p. 11). The following are strategies a person may use during acculturation:
  - **Assimilation:** Internalization of the social and cultural aspects of the new culture
  - **Integration:** Acceptance of the new culture while maintaining the culture of origin
  - **Separation:** Rejection of the new culture while maintaining the original culture
  - **Marginalization:** Rejection or denial of access to the new culture along with loss of the original culture (Cowden & Kreisler, 2016; Sam & Berry, 2006)
- In the process called **selective acculturation,** immigrants "adopt strategic traits (especially those, such as learning English, which will improve their economic status), while retaining other traditional cultural values and patterns, including child-rearing practices, family organization, native foods, and music preferences" (Keefy & Padilla, 1987, p. 18). Unique leisure and sport patterns would be such traits minority members could retain for several generations.

Cultural change plays an important role in shaping leisure time activities of immigrant youth. We have learned from past studies that employed the concepts of assimilation and acculturation that there are some marked differences in recreation and sport behavior among young immigrants of different acculturation levels. For instance, highly acculturated Chinese immigrant youth participate more often in out-of-home recreation activities, especially sports, and more frequently join recreation organizations than their less acculturated counterparts (Yu & Berryman, 1996). Bicultural Mexican-American youth are more likely to participate in family leisure activities that are common, spontaneous, and inexpensive than highly acculturated youth (Christenson, Zabriskie, Eggett, & Freeman, 2006). On the other hand, more acculturated Mexican-American youth are more likely to take part in activities that are new, challenging, often outdoors, and require more interaction with mainstream Americans.

Changes that occur in youths' leisure as a result of a cultural shift often lead to conflict between youth and their family members. Conflicts can arise when parents pressure their children to retain cultural traditions and beliefs while youth wish to follow the ways of living of the mainstream society (Doherty & Taylor, 2007). For instance, some of the South Asian youth who desire to participate in the same leisure activities as their mainstream peers—such as dances, sports, and going to clubs—are met with strong objections of their less acculturated parents (Tirone & Pedlar, 2000). Establishing friendships with people of the opposite sex and dating can be particularly hard for some South and East Asian parents to accept.

Differences in children's and parents' experiences in the host country and the rate of language acquisition can lead to acculturation gaps, which are defined as the parent-child discrepancies (i.e., lack of compatibility or similarity) in the levels of acculturation (Kwak, 2003). Children are usually more strongly tied to the new culture, while parents strive to maintain connections to their former ways of life (Cowden & Kreisler, 2016).

Differences in language proficiency and the growing acculturation gap can make communication between immigrant youth and their parents more difficult. Children who acculturate faster than their parents also often have to serve as cultural and linguistic bridges between their families and the new society. For instance, parents who cannot speak English depend on their children to help them translate and navigate the English-speaking institutions such as schools, health care, and recreation agencies (Portes & Rumbaut, 1996). Serving as mediators between parents and the mainstream environment of the host country allows children to gain more power in families, liberate themselves from their parents' control, and become less dependent on their support and direction (Chao, 2006; Portes & Rumbaut, 2001; Schofield, 2012; Umaña-Taylor, 2003). Such role reversals and power shifts are quite common in immigrant families. A role reversal occurs "when children's familiarity with English and the host culture (i.e., U.S.) has moved so far ahead of their parents' familiarity that key family decisions become dependent on the children's knowledge" (Schofield et al., 2012, p. 871). Role reversals and power shifts can play an important role in recreation decision making in immigrant families (see Vignette 3).

Vignette 3

Sofia is the daughter of Chinese immigrants. Although her parents have lived in the U.S. for over 14 years, they have not become proficient English speakers and do not feel confident speaking English with native speakers. The only one in the household who is a fluent English speaker is Sofia; therefore her parents depend on her to help them navigate English-speaking institutions. Sofia wants to join a lacrosse team, which is not a sport that is common in Asian cultures, so her parents are hesitant. They do not know anything about the sport, what is required to participate, or how to register Sofia for a team. Sofia agrees to find out all the information, fill out paperwork, and translate everything for them. Although hesitant, her parents agree to let Sofia join a team.

In this scenario, you can see that Sofia was able to convince her parents to allow her to join a sport unconventional in Asian cultures. Sofia was able to do this because, although her parents did not have the proper skills to communicate, she knew how to "navigate" the system. Ability to speak the English language and the knowledge of recreation programs gave her an upper hand and allowed her to gain more autonomy.

In some families, children may be embarrassed by their family's status as immigrants and by their ethnic culture (Stodolska & Yi, 2003). Such feelings are particularly pronounced among younger teens who feel the need to fit in within their mainstream peer groups. As a result, some teens try to distance themselves from their less acculturated parents, siblings, and members of their ethnic community. For example, read what Kasia, a 16-year-old Polish immigrant revealed (see quote at left).

Kasia, a Polish immigrant stated: "I was ashamed of … being different… Because, you know, people don't understand that there are those Polish people who came here, who got jobs, and who are assimilating and living as everyone else and there are those… Polish people [with disapproval] who think that they are still living in Poland. They…they are not assimilating. They refuse to speak English, they speak Polish all the time, they look different, they behave different. But people don't know that, they think we are all like that" (Stodolska & Yi, 2003, p. 63).

Some immigrant youth also perceive their parents to be weak role models in the new environment of the host country. They witness their parents' struggles, disappointments, frustrations, confusion, and feelings of loss after leaving their home country (Doherty & Taylor, 2007). Not being able to fully rely on the emotional support from their parents makes immigrant children's adjustment more difficult. Considering the struggles experienced by immigrant youth, it is important that OST professionals provide recreation and sport opportunities to mitigate some of the difficulties they experience adjusting to the new society.

Principles and Suggestions for Working with Immigrant Youth in OST Settings

Rodriguez, Larsen, Látková, and Mertel (2012) argued with respect to recreation programs targeting Latino youth that their leaders should be "flexible, consistent, compassionate, empathetic, and patient," and that "efforts to implement programs should focus not only on the proper implementation of an activity, but also on the deeper experiences and outcomes obtained from these activities" (pp. 97–98). Certainly, the same principles apply to programs targeting all young newcomers. The following are some other suggestions you should consider when working with immigrant youth in OST settings.

Know Your Constituents

In order to provide better recreational services for immigrant youth, it is essential to understand their needs, preferences, and constraints. Recreation preferences and/ or constraints might vary depending on the state where the youth reside. For instance Latinos in California might have different preferences or constraints then Latinos in

Texas or New York. In order to better understand the minority population in your area, recreational and other OST staff might benefit from conducting surveys and focus groups to get a sense of what their local community needs. Additionally, it is of great importance to gather information from users and nonusers; feedback from both groups will be essential to understanding why some individuals use the recreational facilities while others do not.

Work With Your Community Leaders

The immigrant population is unique in that it faces constraints that the native-born population generally does not face. With the current political climate, undocumented immigrants have begun to seek more anonymity in order to avoid deportation and look for support and information from immigrant advocate groups. One way to establish a connection and build trust within this population is through local leaders, churches, and support groups. Working alongside immigrant advocate groups might be a great first step to gain access and possibly the trust of the undocumented community. From our experience of working alongside organizations that cater to the undocumented communities' needs, we have observed that once undocumented individuals establish a trust with an organization, they are more likely to trust staff at facilities or organizations recommended to them by that organization. Establishing a connection with trusted leaders and organizations might be vital to reaching a community that is becoming harder to access.

Be Flexible

Although the majority of children of immigrants are American citizens, they are still bound by some of the same constraints as undocumented individuals. Most of the time, children rely on their parents to give them rides to and from their games or to recreational facilities. This can become a problem when, for example, a child has a game outside of the city limits or a place that requires them to go past immigration checkpoints. When this is the case, these children are subject to their parents' traveling restrictions. A suggestion for facility owners and managers is to be flexible—be willing to provide transportation for children who need it, schedule activities locally rather than outside of city limits or places that require you to go past immigration checkpoints, and be willing to offer new activities that are popular among different immigrant populations. Furthermore, program facilities should be willing to be flexible with requirements, rules, and regulations. As suggested above, some undocumented immigrants are hesitant to give certain information to facilities out of fear of being tracked by immigration services or might not have some of the required documents to sign up (e.g., check stubs, credit/debit card, identification card). Therefore, being flexible is essential.

Bilingual Staff and Materials

A prevalent constraint among immigrant communities is a language barrier. Language limitations not only affect adult immigrants, but they also affect their children.

On many occasions, parents who do not speak English rely on their children to help them navigate English-speaking institutions (e.g., health care system, school system, recreation providers). The problem arises when the children are unwilling or unable to translate for their parents. When this happens, the opportunities that parents and children have to access recreational facilities are greatly diminished. In situations like this, parents are faced with the decision to either keep their children out of recreation activities/sports or seek programs and facilities that are more culturally friendly. For this reason and many more, it is vital to have websites, information pamphlets, and program applications in multiple languages. Also, it is important to have diverse staff that understand the culture, the language, and the needs of the immigrant population. This can be achieved by hiring bilingual personnel who should be required to undertake diversity training.

Diversity Training

It is important to hire staff members who are equipped to work with immigrant youth. Diversity training is a program designed to increase participants' cultural knowledge, awareness, and communication and minimize stereotyping. It is essential to provide diversity training to staff in order to increase inclusion, promote tolerance, avoid civil rights violations, and create a positive work environment. With a changing society and current political tensions, it is crucial to promote a welcoming environment for youth from immigrant populations.

Avoid Homogenizing Immigrant Populations

It is essential to understand the differences between immigrants and refugees/asylum seekers as both groups can be affected by different constraints, and can have different immigration experiences and legal status. Additionally, it is important for owners, managers, and other OST staff to understand the differences between first-generation, one-and-a-half, and second-generation immigrant youth. Similar to immigrants and refugees, these groups can have a wide range of leisure constraints and experiences. Staff at recreational facilities should understand that immigrant groups are not homogeneous and target their services and recruitment efforts to youth based on their unique characteristics.

Concluding Thoughts

OST activities provide a number of benefits for immigrant youth. In particular, they foster inclusion and help young newcomers develop friendships with peers from other ethnic groups. OST activities can also serve as a good introduction to the culture of American society—they can expose children to a new set of opportunities and activities and provide an array of psychological benefits for youth who struggle with establishment-related problems. Considering current population dynamics, children of immigrants are the future of American society. Thus, it is incumbent upon recreation professionals to provide immigrant youth with programs and activities that will help them realize their full potential.

Discussion Questions

1. You are a gymnastics coach. You coach a very talented young athlete who, in observance of his religion, must fast during the day during the month of Ramadan. Fasting makes him weak and tired and unable to perform at his full potential. The competition, however, is fast approaching, and you are concerned that lack of vigorous training will decrease his chances of winning the competition. How do you approach this situation?
2. You run an aquatics facility in a town with a large Muslim immigrant population. You have noticed that parents are reluctant to allow their daughters to use your facility as the Muslim religion does not allow girls to wear revealing swimsuits and to swim in the company of boys. How do you resolve this situation and foster participation in aquatic activities among local Muslim girls?
3. You are a high school PE teacher. You have noticed that two immigrant teenagers from Spain do not get along and the tension in the class is growing. After confronting them, you find out that one of the teens is from Madrid, the other is Catalan. Prior to immigrating to the U.S., the Catalan youth lived in a region which seeks independence from Spain. The teens are adamant that they do not want to play on the same team. How do you approach this situation? Do you try to convince them to play on the same team or do you keep them apart to avoid potential conflict?

Assignments

Assignment 1

Choose one sport, recreation or other OST activity (e.g., picnicking, computer gaming, exercise, basketball, baseball, soccer, hockey, drama, music) and conduct research on how immigrant youth of a specific ethnicity/race in the U.S. (e.g., Latino, Asian, European) participate in this activity. In your assignment:

1. Describe history of this leisure or sport activity.
2. Describe unique styles of participation in this activity among immigrant youth from your chosen ethnic/racial group. It is preferable that you use published sources of information to answer this question. However, if no published data are available, you can answer this question based on your own observations or discussions with professionals.

3. What constraints may prevent immigrant youth from your chosen ethnic/racial group from participation in this leisure or sport activity?
4. Provide suggestions for how sport/leisure organizations may try to help immigrant youth overcome those constraints to participation.

Assignment 2

Please conduct an interview, lasting at least five minutes, with a young immigrant on the topic of his/her leisure and sport participation. Your interview should include the following questions:

1. What is the race/ethnicity of your interviewee?
2. How old is your interviewee?
3. How old was the interviewee when he/she immigrated to the U.S.?
4. How long has the interviewee resided in the U.S.?
5. What are your interviewee's favorite leisure and sport pursuits?
6. How has the interviewee's ethnic/racial background affected his/her leisure and sport preferences and opportunities?
7. How has the interviewee's ethnic/racial background affected his/her leisure and sport constraints?

In your assignment, describe your interviewee's answers to questions 1–4. In questions 5, 6, and 7, provide your own description and analysis and use direct quotations from the interviewee to support the story.

References

Abrego, L. J. (2008). Legitimacy, social identity, and the mobilization of law: The effects of Assembly Bill 540 on undocumented students. *California Law & Social Inquiry 33*(3), 709–734.

Amara, M., & Henry, I. (2010). Sport, Muslim identities, and cultures in the UK, an emerging policy issue: Case studies of Leicester and Birmingham. *European Sport Management Quarterly, 10,* 419–443.

Campbell, G. T., Glover, T. D., & Laryea, E. (2016). Recreation, settlement, and the welcoming community: Mapping community with African-Canadian youth newcomers. *Leisure Sciences, 38*(3), 215–231.

Carrington, B., Chivers, T., & Williams, T. (1987). Gender, leisure and sport: A case study of young people of South Asian descent. *Leisure Studies, 6*(3), 265–279.

Chao, R. K. (2006). The prevalence and consequences of adolescents' language brokering for their immigrant parents. In M. H. Bornstein & L. R. Cote (Eds.), *Acculturation and parent-child relationships: Measurement and development* (p. 271–296). Mahwah, NJ: Erlbaum.

Children of Immigrants. (2014). Immigrant children. Retrieved from https://www.childtrends.org/wp-content/uploads/2013/07/110_Immigrant_Children.pdf

Christenson, O. D., Zabriskie, R. B., Eggett, D. L., Freeman, P. A. (2006). Family acculturation, family leisure involvement, and family functioning among Mexican-Americans. *Journal of Leisure Research, 38*(4), 475–495.

Cowden, J. D., & Kreisler, K. (2016). Development of children in immigrant families. *Pediatric Clinics in North America, 63*, 775–793.

Cronan, M. K., Shinew, K. J., & Stodolska, M. (2008). Trail use among Latinos: Recognizing diverse uses among a specific population. *Journal of Park and Recreation Administration, 26*(4), 62–86.

Cruz-Santiago, M., & Ramirez García, J. I. (2011). *"Hay Que Ponerse en los Zapatos del Joven"*: Adaptive parenting of adolescent children among Mexican-American parents residing in a dangerous neighborhood. *Family Process, 50*(1), 92–114.

Dinovitzer, R., Hagan, J., & Parker, P. (2003). Choice and circumstance: Social capital and planful competence in the attainments of immigrant youth. *Canadian Journal of Sociology, 28*, 463–488.

Doherty, A., & Taylor, T. (2007). Sport and physical recreation in the settlement of immigrant youth. *Leisure/Loisir, 31*(1), 27–55.

Fleming, S. (1994). Sport and South Asian youth: The perils of false universalism and stereotyping. *Leisure Studies, 13*, 159–177.

Gleeson, S., & Gonzales, R. G. (2012). When do papers matter? An institutional analysis of undocumented life in the United States. *International Migration, 50*(4), 1–19.

Harinen, P. M., Honkasalo, M. V., Ronkainen, J. K., & Suurpää, L. E. (2012). Multiculturalism and young people's leisure spaces in Finland: Perspectives of multicultural youth. *Leisure Studies, 31*(2), 177–191.

Harrison, L., & Bimper, A. Y. (2014). Race, ethnicity, and sport. In M. Stodolska, K. J. Shinew, M. Floyd, & G. J. Walker (Eds.), *Race, ethnicity, and leisure: Perspectives on research, theory, and practice* (pp. 215–227). Champaign, IL: Human Kinetics.

Keefy, S. E., & Padilla, A. M. (1987). *Chicano ethnicity*. Albuquerque, NM: University of New Mexico Press.

Kivijärvi, A. (2015). Fragility of leisure ties between ethnic minority and majority youth: An empirical case from Finland. *Leisure Studies, 34*(2), 150–165.

Lee, K. J., & Scott, D. (2013). Interracial contact experience during recreational basketball and soccer: Korean American male's perspectives. *Journal of Leisure Research, 45*(3), 267–294.

Lee, K. J., & Stodolska, M. (2017). Asian North Americans' leisure: A critical examination of theoretical frameworks used in research and suggestions for future study. *Leisure Sciences, 39*(6), 524–542.

Lopez, G., & Bialik, K. (2017). Key findings about U.S. immigrants. Retrieved from http://www.pewresearch.org/fact-tank/2017/05/03/key-findings-about-u-s-immigrants/

Maccabi USA (n.d.). Competitions. Retrieved from https://www.maccabiusa.com/events/categories/competitions/

Mata-Codesal, D., & Peperkamp, E., & Tiesler, N.C. (2015). Migration, migrants and leisure: Meaningful leisure? *Leisure Studies, 34*(1), 1–4.

Portes, A., & Rumbaut, R. (1996). *Immigrant America: A portrait.* Berkeley, CA: University of California Press.

Portes, A., & Rumbaut, R. G. (2001). *Legacies: The story of the immigrant second generation.* Berkeley, CA: University of California Press.

Rodriguez, A., Larsen, D., Látková, P., & Mertel, S. J. (2012). Development of Latino youth: Implications for park and recreation programs and services. *Journal of Park and Recreation Administration, 30*(1), 85–106.

Rojas, L. B. (2011). 1.5 generation definition. Retrieved from http://www.scpr.org/blogs/multiamerican/2011/04/07/7099/introducing-the-cultural-mashup-dictionary-our-fir/

Sam, D. L., & Berry, J. W. (2006). *The Cambridge handbook of acculturation psychology.* Cambridge, UK: Cambridge University Press.

Schofield, T., Beaumont, K., Widaman, K., Jochem, R., Robins, R., & Conger, R. (2012). Parent and child fluency in a common language: Implications for the parent–child relationship and later academic success in Mexican-American families. *Journal of Family Psychology, 26*(6), 869–879.

Shinew, K. J., Stodolska, M., Roman, C. G., & Yahner, J. (2013). Crime, physical activity and outdoor recreation among Latino adolescents in Chicago. *Preventive Medicine, 57,* 541–544.

Spaaij, R. (2015). Refugee youth, belonging, and community sport. *Leisure Studies, 34*(3), 303–318.

Spracklen, K., Long, J., & Hylton, K. (2015). Leisure opportunities and new migrant communities: Challenging the contribution of sport. *Leisure Studies, 34*(1), 114–129.

Stodolska, M. (2008). Adaptation problems among adolescent immigrants from Korea, Mexico, and Poland. *Journal of Immigrant & Refugee Studies, 6*(2), 197–229.

Stodolska, M., & Livengood, J. S. (2006). The effects of religion on the leisure behavior of American Muslim immigrants. *Journal of Leisure Research, 38,* 293–320.

Stodolska, M., & Yi, J. (2003). Impacts of immigration on ethnic identity and leisure behavior of adolescent immigrants from Korea, Mexico and Poland. *Journal of Leisure Research, 35*(1), 49–79.

Tirone, S. (1999). Racism, indifference, and the leisure experiences of South Asian Canadian teens. *Leisure/Loisir, 24*(1–2), 89–114.

Tirone, S., & Pedlar, A. (2000). Understanding the leisure experiences of a minority ethnic group: South Asian teens and young adults in Canada. *Loisir et Societe, 23*(1), 145–169.

Umaña-Taylor, A. J. (2003). *Language brokering as a stressor for immigrant children and their families.* Los Angeles, CA: Roxbury Publishing Company.

United Nations High Commissioner for Refugees. (1951). The 1951 UN Refugee Convention. Retrieved from http://www.unrefugees.org/what-is-a-refugee/

Villarreal, R., & Blozis, S., & Widaman, K. (2005). Factorial invariance of the Pan-Hispanic Familism Scale. *Hispanic Journal of Behavioral Sciences, 27,* 409–425.

Walseth, K. (2016). Sport within Muslim organizations in Norway: Ethnic segregated activities as arena for integration. *Leisure Studies, 35*(1), 78–99.

Waters, J. (2002). Flexible families? "Astronaut" households and the experience of lone mothers in Vancouver, British Columbia. *Social and Cultural Geography, 3*, 117–134.

Whitley, M. A., Coble, C., & Jewell, G. S. (2016). Evaluation of a sport-based youth development programme for refugees. *Leisure/Loisir, 40*(2), 175–199.

Woods, T., Hanson, D., Saxton, S., & Simms, M. (2016). Children of Immigrants: 2013 State Trends Update. Washington, DC: Urban Institute. Retrieved from https://www.urban.org/sites/default/files/publication/77911/2000616-Children-of-Immigrants-2013-State-Trends-Update.pdf

Yu, P., & Berryman, D. L. (1996). The relationship among self-esteem, acculturation, and recreation participation of recently arrived Chinese immigrant adolescents. *Journal of Leisure Research, 28*(4), 251–273.

Zhou, M. (1998). "Parachute kids" in Southern California: The education experience of Chinese children in transnational families. *Educational Policy, 12*(6), 682–704.

Zong, J., & Batalova, J. (2017). Frequently requested statistics on immigrants and immigration in the United States. Migration Policy Institute. Retrieved from http://www.migrationpolicy.org/article/frequently-requested-statistics-immigrants-and-immigration-united-states#Children

Chapter 22

Out-of-School Time Programs and Resistance to LGBT Oppression

Daniel Theriault

It is estimated that in the United States at least nine million individuals identify as lesbian, gay, bisexual, or transgender (LGBT; Gates, 2011). Thus, out-of-school time (OST) practitioners will likely be called upon to serve both LGBT adolescents and family members. The goal of this chapter is to prepare OST professionals to serve effectively LGBT adolescents, first through an introduction of two characteristics common within the LGBT community: oppression and resistance. After that, I will introduce strategies OST professionals can employ to resist LGBT oppression. I close the chapter with an overview of opportunities and challenges that may arise for professionals who seek to work with LGBT individuals to resist oppression.

Most traditional youth development knowledge is relevant to work with LGBT youth (Theriault & Witt, 2014). Like their heterosexual peers, LGBT young people stand to benefit from developmentally appropriate supports, opportunities, programs, and services to build relevant life skills. Moreover, the process of youth development shares common characteristics regardless of sexual identity (Savin-Williams, 2009). Most young people who identify as LGBT navigate the road through adolescence and successfully transition into adulthood. LGBT youth also face similar challenges and benefit from similar developmental assets in comparison with their heterosexual counterparts (Savin-Williams, 2009).

It is important to discuss issues of sexual identity because we live in a society that structurally privileges heterosexuality and oppresses non-heterosexuals (Blumenfeld, 2010a). This oppression is connected to a set of "beliefs about gender morality, and danger by which homosexuality and sexual minorities are viewed as deviant, sinful, and threatening. Hostility, discrimination, and violence are thereby justified as appropriate and even necessary" (Herek, 2004, p. 15). As a result, LGBT youth often confront harassment in traditional developmental contexts, including OST programs. Moreover, this harassment is embedded in norms, habits, stereotypes, and other everyday practices (Young, 2010) that may cause oppressive behavior to be viewed as normal or natural to some. Interventions are therefore required to enhance the developmental appropriateness of OST programs and to disrupt oppressive everyday practices with LGBT youth. Effective interventions begin with youth practitioners seeking to gain a basic familiarity with the everyday experiences of LGBT youth in order to promote empathy and facilitate the design of responsive services.

Oppression

Meet Sarah. Sarah shares much in common with other 12-year-olds. She loves sports, pop music, and spending time with her friends. For several years, Sarah has suspected that she is different from most of her friends, but it wasn't until considerable self-reflection and Internet research that she concluded she is a lesbian. After hiding the news from friends and family for months, she decided to tell her friends that she is a lesbian. Lindsay, her friend since kindergarten, responds that she does not want to be Sarah's friend anymore. Crushed, Sarah turns to her mother for comfort, who yells at Sarah, claiming, "This is just a phase."

Examples of oppression can be defined as the inhibition of people's "ability to develop and exercise their capacities and express their needs, thoughts, and feelings" (Young, 2010, p. 35). Although oppression shapes many aspects of the lives of LGBT individuals, this section provides examples of the operation and consequences of oppression in two contexts: schools and OST programs.

Payne and Smith (2012) argued that schools often support cultures that perpetuate oppression. In schools, cultural scripts for normal gender and sexual behavior (e.g., males are sexually attracted exclusively to females) are reinforced. Conformity to these scripts grants access to social acceptance and popularity while deviation invites teasing and harassment. Moreover, restrictive gender and sex behavior norms are also embedded in school policies, practices, and programming (Griffin & Ouellett, 2003). For example, policies may include only allowing students to take individuals of different genders to a prom or do not include sexual or gender identity in anti-discrimination statements. School climate research has indicated that teachers often make unsupportive comments (e.g., using "That's gay!" as an insult) or fail to intervene in LGBT harassment when it occurs (GLSEN, 2015). Rigid gender/sex roles are further reinforced through the school curriculum, such as avoiding stories that feature LGBT characters in English courses (Blackburn & Smith, 2010).

Because oppression operates as an interconnected system, LGBT youth are likely to be oppressed in OST contexts as well. For example, Oakleaf (2013) found that oppressive aspects of society and summer camp more specifically prompted camp staff members to manage their sexual identity to avoid potential harassment. LGBT staff who engaged in romantic relationships with each other were viewed as controversial. Other camps in that study had policies that stated that LGBT staff could not be employed, while still others forbade staff from acknowledging their sexual identity to campers. Participants reported carefully managing their sexual identity in order to avoid being "outed" as LGBT and exposed to harassment. Notably, staff members' prior experience with heterosexism and homophobia magnified their concerns about negotiating an LGBT identity (Oakleaf, 2013).

Research in recreation contexts has generally indicated that LGBT persons either report negative experiences during participation with heterosexuals or prefer to participate with other members of the LGBT community for safety reasons.

Oppressions, such as those identified by Oakleaf (2013), also negatively impact OST program participants. Research in recreation contexts has generally indicated that LGBT persons either report negative experiences during participation with heterosexuals or prefer to participate with other members of the LGBT community for safety reasons (Kivel & Kleiber, 2000; Lewis & Johnson, 2011). Future OST professionals must therefore consider the extent to which their programs perpetuate LGBT discrimination (Russell & Van Campen, 2011) so that the consequences of oppression may be minimized.

Consequences of Oppression

The consequences of LGBT oppression are far reaching. The Gay, Lesbian, and Straight Education Network's (2015) school climate survey, which was administered to over 10,000 students between the ages of 13 and 21, indicated the following:

- Approximately two-thirds of respondents avoided extracurricular activities and school functions for safety reasons
- 85% of respondents experienced verbal harassment
- 27% of respondents experienced physical harassment
- 66% of respondents experienced discriminatory school policies

In order to avoid these negative consequences of publicly acknowledging a LGBT sexual identity, some LGBT individuals attempt to "pass" as heterosexual by, for example, lying, concealing information, or avoiding questions that might reveal their LGBT status (Lasser & Wicker, 2008). Passing requires constant, careful regulation of speech, clothing, and behavior, as well as planning whom to disclose one's sexual identity to and how (Seidman, 2002). Passing may compel some LGBT youth to believe that their authentic sexual or gender identity is something to be hidden and managed rather than openly celebrated. The need to pass has been linked with increased use of alcohol and drugs to manage the associated emotional pain among individuals who identify as transgender (Gagné, Tewksbury, & McGaughey, 1997). Oppression has also been linked with depression, a decreased sense of belonging (Poteat & Espelage, 2007), more suicidal thoughts (Russell, Ryan, Toomey, Diaz, & Sanchez, 2011), and increased use of drugs and alcohol (Collier, van Beusekom, Bos, & Sandfort, 2013). The financial costs of oppression associated with OST programs include losing talented employees, failing to connect with a specific target market for programs or services, rehiring costs, retraining, and staff missing days due to a hostile work environment, and potential lawsuits (Robinson & Dechant, 1997).

Heterosexuals are not immune from the consequences of LGBT oppression. For example, oppression encourages conformity to more rigid gender roles (e.g., males are unemotional, physically tough, and courageous) and discourages creativity and alternate expressions of gender identity (Blumenfeld, 2010b). Wendell Berry (1999) opined that oppression stains our humanity, "the language [of racism] thus involves a sort of schizophrenia, a curious ability to confront the most horrible facts and then to look away from them, as if they did not exist…" (p. 10). Though the consequences of oppression are far reaching, youth such as Sarah often do not passively accept its consequences.

Acts of Resistance

After her experiences with her mother and Lindsay, Sarah learned that she must carefully assess to whom she discloses her lesbian identity and when she should share that information. She continued her Internet research after her parents went to sleep to learn more about her identity. One evening, she came across an OST program called Pulse, which supports LGBT youth that was near her parents' house. Pulse offers recreation activities, discussion groups, and most important, an opportunity to meet new friends who also identified as LGBT. Sarah immediately decided to skip her next swim team practice to attend Pulse.

Although LGBT youth face a variety of injustices in their everyday lives that require immediate remediation, most LGBT young people are able to successfully negotiate these challenges and thrive as adults (Savin-Williams, 2008). One of the core reasons for the resiliency of LGBT youth is that a variety of programs and services facilitate LGBT youths' resistance to oppression. The term *resistance* refers to the ways that LGBT youth confront, subvert, mock, and otherwise respond to the oppressive forces in their lives. For example, recreation programs might provide LGBT adolescents with a safe space to engage in activities, which might be unsafe in other contexts such as dating, celebrating LGBT culture, or dressing in unconventional fashions (Theriault, 2014). Programs that offer dances, for example, might support the attendance of same-sex or gender-atypical couples. Similarly, summer camps and other OST programs may provide an environment to achieve developmental tasks. For example, summer camps may be a beneficial context to support the development of healthy, same-sex romantic relationships due to the significant amount of time spent with others, the emotional nature of the experience, and the fact that camp attendance often coincides with adolescence, when romantic relationships begin (Davis-Delano & Gillard, 2015). OST programs have also resisted oppression by offering services that LGBT youth are denied elsewhere, such as health education, sexual and gender identity discussion groups, HIV prevention meetings, or support groups related to overcoming homophobia (Kivel & Johnson, 2008).

OST programs might also resist oppression by developing separate spaces for LGBT youth to acquire support and resources (Kumashiro, 2000). A good example is gay-straight alliance (GSAs) clubs. GSAs are middle and high school extracurricular clubs in which LGBT students and their heterosexual allies come together to engage in recreation in a safe space, support one another, and advocate for social change. The Genders & Sexualities Alliance Network (2016) estimated that there are over 4,000 such clubs today. For example, the Mill Creek High School GSA in Hoschton, Georgia (2017) seeks to create a safe and welcoming environment for anyone who would like to discuss sexual or gender identity issues. Members of the Mill Creek GSA also seek to "increase awareness, decrease prejudices, and create a safe school atmosphere for all" (Mill Creek High School, 2017, n.p.).

The mere existence of a separate space for support may be an act of resistance against school policies that silence and demean LGBT voices. GSAs also resist oppression by providing opportunities for members to discuss personally relevant issues (Mayberry, 2013; Russell, Muraco, Subramaniam, & Laub, 2009). The opportunity for discussion is significant because both sex education and school curricula in general often do not address LGBT issues (Blackburn & Smith, 2010). LGBT-serving organizations may provide members with an opportunity to support one another and develop social support within the LGBT community (Singh, 2013). Members also have opportunities to educate faculty and peers on LGBT issues and confront oppressive school policies (e.g., lobbying for additional LGBT resources in the library; Mayberry, 2013). GSAs have also been linked with benefits for all students on campus, such as lower levels of fear about safety, and verbal and physical harassment (Marx & Kettrey, 2016). However, employee knowledge, skills, and attitudes are needed to resist successfully LGBT oppression through OST programs.

Strategies for Resistance

As Sarah walked through Pulse's front door, she met Tom, a bubbly, hyper-friendly employee who showed her around and introduced her to the other youth. She joined a group of youth playing *Guitar Hero* and was relieved to find that she was already having fun. About an hour later, Tom pulled Sarah aside and began giving Sarah advice that she never asked for. He explains how he disclosed his gay identity at school and the harassment that followed (even though Sarah is not ready to share her identity at school). He explained how he found support through his church even though Sarah is not religious. She thanked Tom for the advice, but began to wonder as she was walking home if Pulse was the right place for her after all.

In that moment, Tom lacked an awareness of his biases and how his experiences differed from Sarah's. These issues made it difficult for Tom to connect with Sarah and understand her unique needs. This section expands on these and other concrete strategies practitioners can employ to frame OST programs as potential sites of resistance to LGBT oppression. These strategies have been culled from the writing and speeches of LGBT activist Urvashi Vaid. Each subsection below is organized around a goal for practitioners who wish to develop their program into a site for resistance to oppression of LGBT individuals.

Are your employees self-aware? For employees to resist oppression, they must not only acknowledge that oppression exists but also understand how it impacts their lives. Many may be hesitant to accept the existence of oppression because (a) they fear it implies their complicity in committing (inadvertently or not) acts of oppression or injustice themselves, or (b) because it is not immediately obvious to them how their actions have contributed to LGBT oppression, or (c) because discussing LGBT issues in general makes them uncomfortable. However, national data are unequivocal: LGBT youth face deleterious consequences due to oppression. Hesitance to confront oppression will not change the fact that LGBT youth are being oppressed; it will only deepen the problem and the consequences (Kumashiro, 2000).

In addition, it is important for you, as a potential OST practitioner, to understand that privilege and oppression matter within your everyday life. OST practitioners may believe that oppression is not an issue within their program because LGBT identities are not visually obvious. As such, it may be unclear the extent to which the program serves or has served young people who identify as LGBT. Practitioners may also suggest that they have never heard of injustices committed against LGBT youth in their programs. However, LGBT youth may be less likely to make instances of injustice known because (a) adult leaders are often complicit in their oppression, (b) they are used to adult leaders not acting on their concerns, and (c) youth and staff are hesitant to disclose their LGBT status. Therefore, just because you are not immediately aware of the ways oppression influences your program does not mean that there are no oppressive forces present.

> OST practitioners may believe that oppression is not an issue within their program because LGBT identities are not visually obvious.

A variety of methods is available for OST practitioners who are interested in developing employee self-awareness. For example, one study reported that college students who watched a 10-minute video in which individuals gave testimonials about the impact of heterosexual privilege in their lives (e.g., being unable to get married) was linked with increased awareness of heterosexual privilege and internal motivation to not act or speak in prejudiced ways (Case, Hensely, & Anderson, 2014). OST professionals might also consult LGBT professors, lawyers, counselors, educators, or youth workers to discuss the consequences of LGBT oppression (Case & Meier, 2014).

These training sessions should also feature opportunities for staff members to connect with their personal experiences of oppression and opportunities to reflect on how those experiences are aligned with their personal values (Duhigg, Rostosky, Gray, & Wimsatt, 2010). Professionals might also consider connecting around a common vision of what a youth development program is designed to accomplish, as opposed to awareness of oppression. Particularly among staff with little direct experience with oppression, connecting around common program ideals (e.g., safety, welcoming to all) may open up discussion of how a diverse staff can make these visions a reality (Pless & Maak, 2004).

Although being aware of one's own bias and privilege is an important step toward working for change (Kivel & Johnson, 2008), attitudes are not always connected to action (Vaid, 2010). Instead, personal experience with being "othered" may be more directly connected to action (LaPointe, 2015).

Do your employees believe that change is possible? Are they prepared to resist oppression? Vaid (1998) suggested that faith in the possibility of social change arises through personal experiences with oppression. Accordingly, simply bringing in a cultural representative for a one-hour seminar may be insufficient for employees to connect personally with the importance of resistance (Chapter 19). Instead, practitioners might promote extended engagement with LGBT groups through coalition building, particularly among those employees with less experience with oppression. Practitioners might also consider incorporating interview questions relating to experiences with oppression or empathy toward the LGBT community into the hiring process (Gillard, Buzuvis, & Bialeschki, 2014).

Even when employees have a personal connection to LGBT individuals or a general understanding of oppression, they must also feel that they can effectively respond to LGBT-related instances of injustice. For example, employees must feel that they are able to intervene in anti-LGBT comments made by both staff and other youth. Trainings that provide mock scenarios of name-calling have been shown to be effective in increasing teachers' self-efficacy in responding to LGBT harassment (Greytak, Kosciw, & Boesen, 2013). Additional mock scenarios might include separating teams by boys and girls, creating activities based around traditional gender assumptions, responding to parent questions (e.g., isn't this just a phase?), responding to individuals who believe that non-dominant sexuality identities conflict with their religious beliefs, and responding to a young person's question about which bathroom a transgender student should use. The more staff are prepared for tough situations that relate to LGBT oppression, the more

Although being aware of one's own bias and privilege is an important step toward working for change, attitudes are not always connected to action.

likely they will be to respond effectively to that issue when it arises in practice (Case & Meier, 2014).

Training should also be infused with the recognition that LGBT youth share much in common with their heterosexual peers (Savin-Williams, 2014). Many of the same programmatic features that OST practitioners have sought for generations (e.g., physical and psychological safety, age-appropriate structure, opportunities to belong, and supportive relationships with adult leaders) are highly relevant to LGBT youth. Many of the same developmental assets that staff have provided youth with for generations are again highly relevant to LGBT youth (Theriault & Witt, 2014). Effective service with LGBT youth may not be a matter of abandoning traditional youth development knowledge but of amplifying that knowledge through acknowledgment of and reaction to oppression. OST practitioners who demonstrate a commitment to resistance may amplify the effectiveness of existing program features and goals. For instance, practitioners who stop transphobic bullying may enhance feelings of physical and psychological safety among transgender participants. Such behavior may also enhance the belongingness of transgender populations.

The Process of Resistance

Tom left Pulse that evening frustrated with how he had interacted with Sarah. He knew better than to give advice unless it was asked for or to assume that his experience was the same as Sarah's, but sometimes he is so eager to help that he forgets the mentorship training he received at Pulse. He resolved to talk less and listen more if Sarah returned. Just then, Linda, Pulse's director, called to ask if Tom was ready to take a call from Sarah's mother. Wanting to redeem himself, Tom agreed. He quickly learned that Sarah's mother was upset that Sarah skipped swim practice, lied to her, and spent the afternoon at an LGBT-supportive program. After listening to Sarah's mother vent her frustrations for nearly 20 minutes, Tom is so overwhelmed he does not know what to say.

Before implementing specific strategies, professionals should be familiar with how the process of resistance might unfold within an OST program. Familiarity with resistance processes may be useful in selecting strategies that best meet the needs of a given program. For example, organizational diagnosis might reveal specific targets for resistance. Familiarity with the process of resistance may also encourage setting up initiatives for success, by preparing for a long-term focus and strategically accumulating stakeholder support. More generally, OST workers who engage with resistance should not expect a simple, one-time intervention to erase permanently all vestiges of oppression. Instead, effectively working toward a more just program involves negotiating resistance and support for initiatives, preparing to focus on oppression over the long term, and seeking system-level change.

Expect Stakeholder Opposition

Practitioners should expect to encounter stakeholder opposition to their efforts to support LGBT adolescents (Doherty, Fink, Inglis, & Pastore, 2010; Watson, Varjas, Meyers, & Graybill, 2010). For example, some employees may disagree with initiatives that are specifically tailored to the LGBT community, while others may believe that as heterosexuals, it is not their responsibility to serve LGBT participants (Allison & Hibbler, 2004). Practitioners are also likely to encounter varying levels of opposition for inclusion initiatives from donors, parents, staff, and participants.

Wasserman, Gallegos, and Ferdman (2008) recommended that professionals should routinely expect to encounter resistance to diversity programs and then seek to understand the reasons why specific individuals are resistant. For example, some might be hesitant to support a diversity program due to a lack of information, such as not understanding why LGBT youth require unique consideration in OST programs. In this case, simply providing that information may be sufficient to garner support. Other forms of resistance are more entrenched, such as dealing with individuals who believe that because they do not discriminate, they should not have to participate in trainings or discussions. One way of responding to this attitude might be to honor the behavior of these individuals but work to expand their ability to intervene in group-level patterns of discrimination (Wasserman, Gallegos, & Ferdman, 2008).

Build Coalitions

Coalitions are essential for the success of resistance work within OST programs as well as the broader goal of reducing LGBT oppression. However, best practices often limit coalition building to LGBT-specific organizations such as gay-straight alliance clubs (e.g., Theriault & Edwards, 2014). If practitioners focus solely on LGBT-specific organizations, the resulting coalitions may exclude the needs of LGBT people of color (Vaid, 2012). Coalitions built with groups outside of the LGBT umbrella also yield access to increased power for social change work (Vaid, 1997). Therefore, practitioners can seek partnerships with any institution that is affected by sexual identity oppression, whether families, other OST programs, religious institutions, or schools. Such coalition building offers the advantage of a coordinated approach to reducing oppression in multiple sectors of youth lives (Craig, Dentato, & Iacovino, 2015). Coalitions that strategically accumulate support around a shared vision of youth development may be more successful than programs that try to resist oppression alone (Eccles & Gootman, 2002). Coalitions also offer enhanced access to resources, such as knowledge for staff training or allies for advocacy work.

> Coalitions that strategically accumulate support around a shared vision of youth development may be more successful than programs that try to resist oppression alone.

Resistance is a Long-Term Process

Resistance may be characterized by stops and starts, delays, reversals, accelerations, and decelerations (Gonzalez, 2010; Vaid, 2009). Therefore, OST program managers might create structures in order to attend to diversity issues over the long term. For example, practitioners might strategically mobilize a group of committed staff into a diversity committee that is responsible for regularly assessing the diversity climate within and outside the program and developing recommendations for change. For example, practitioners might evaluate who is being excluded from current resistance efforts (Kumashiro, 2000). Similarly, practitioners might seek support from top management. Such understanding may be critical if resistance initiatives encounter barriers. Finally, if inclusion is an ongoing process, the capacity to reflect on and learn from that process is an essential skill for OST practitioners. Professionals of all backgrounds may make insensitive comments and assumptions about young people on the road to developing programs that are more inclusive. OST professionals who view these errors as opportunities for growth will continue to enhance their inclusion knowledge and skills. Ongoing training in LGBT knowledge, attitudes, skills, and contemporary issues may further support the efforts of professionals to grow from their interactions with diverse populations (Crisp & McCave, 2007).

Seek System-Level Change

Practitioners who employ single best practices for inclusion may be undermined by other exclusionary practices within the organization (Allen & Montgomery, 2001). For example, employees who are trained to stop instances of discrimination during a recreation program may be undermined by the absence of wording related to sexual or gender identity in anti-discrimination statements. Likewise, marketing schemes aimed at LGBT populations can be undermined if OST practitioners do not create welcoming experiences for LGBT groups. Regardless of how effective a marketing program is initially, consistent mistreatment of LGBT participants may spread a message within the community or across social media that a program is unwelcoming to LGBT youth. Therefore, disrupting institutional practices that sustain oppression may be a more effective long-term solution than simply focusing on the safety of individual members. For example, individual students and staff come and go. Thus, it is essential that changes be institutionalized so that short-term gains are not lost over time (Griffin, Lee, Waugh, & Beyer, 2004).

To achieve system-level change, OST practitioners must undertake a thorough organizational diagnosis to determine areas of LGBT oppression, such as the following:

- **Structural:** Does your organization have nondiscrimination or anti-bullying policies that explicitly enumerate protection of LGBT populations? Policies that specifically mention gender or sexual identity signal current and future stakeholders that a program is intended to be inclusive. Moreover, such policies also provide staff with the administrative support needed to intervene in instances of harassment (Russell, Kosciw, Horn, & Saewyc, 2010).
- **Marketing:** What messages do your marketing materials send to LGBT participants? LGBT participants often research programs to determine potential safety issues before they join. Websites that do not explicitly mention LGBT or include gender nonconforming individuals may send an unintended message that a program is not welcoming (Gillard, Buzuvis, & Bialeschki, 2014).
- **Programming:** Do you offer programs that explicitly or exclusively cater to LGBT youth? Programs that explicitly or exclusively cater to LGBT youth offer not only safety but also the prospect of connecting with other members of the LGBT community as well—opportunities they are frequently denied in other contexts (Kivel & Johnson, 2008).
- **Social climate:** Does your organizational climate support or discourage the discussion of non-dominant sexual identity issues? OST programs have an opportunity to support LGBT youth in their development of healthy sexual identities (Oakleaf, 2013). In order to achieve this goal, professionals must begin to work toward developing a program climate where adolescents feel safe discussing gender and sexual identity issues. Hiring LGBT role models, including LGBT information in program libraries, and supporting youth who acknowledge their sexual identity to program staff may be important first steps toward developing a more welcoming organizational climate.

- **Training:** Do staff have the opportunity to reflect on their experiences with privilege and oppression? As noted, providing staff with an opportunity to reflect on their experiences with privilege and oppression during staff training may solidify the importance of staff responding to LGBT oppression during OST programs.
- **Hiring:** Do you ask questions to help identify potential advocates during the interview process? OST professionals might ask about a candidate's prior experience with LGBT youth or consider their responses to mock situations that relate to sexual identity issues. These questions communicate the importance of the LGBT community during the hiring process and may assist with identifying training needs for incoming staff (Gillard, Buzuvis, & Bialeschki, 2014).
- **Social interaction:** Do staff stop instances of bullying and harassment? All instances of using gender or sexual identity as an insult must immediately be stopped, including using the words "That's gay," "You play like a girl," and "Fag." Such actions communicate to everyone that LGBT harassment will not be tolerated and highlight to LGBT participants that their identity is respected.

Although the number of potential areas of LGBT oppression and acts of resistance may appear overwhelming, OST professionals should start small when seeking to disrupt oppression (Johnson, 2010). For example, begin with your behavior. The next time you hear a homophobic joke at work, respond that you do not think it is funny. The next time activities are offered around traditional gender lines, participate in an activity with a different gender. Train staff not to create teams around assumed gender identity. While changes may appear small, each action disrupts oppression and models an alternative path for staff and youth alike (Johnson, 2010), thus providing the basis for undertaking future actions.

> While changes may appear small, each action disrupts oppression and models an alternative path for staff and youth alike, thus providing the basis for undertaking future actions.

Conclusions

Sarah and her mother had their biggest fight that evening over Sarah's sexual identity and her program choices, but that did not stop Sarah from attending Pulse. Over time, Sarah developed a group of supportive friends at Pulse and learned to have a frank discussion with her mother about her lesbian identity. Sarah also rediscovered her interest in art at Pulse. While not a great artist, she nonetheless found relief in the ability to express herself through drawing and painting. Oppression followed Sarah throughout her life, but she left Pulse seven years later with the support and skills she needed to better confront societal attitudes and barriers. Whatever came her way, Sarah knew she was ready.

I wish this chapter was not necessary. Many of us dream of a world where sexual and gender identity will not matter in the context of OST programs and individuals' daily lives. In a perfect world, young people would be free to express their sexual and gender identity however they see fit and without fear of intimidation, abuse, or harassment. However, most LGBT individuals experience verbal and physical harassment simply because they are LGBT. Headlines featuring stories of LGBT persons who are terrorized are all too common (Kivel & Johnson, 2008). The only acceptable response to the oppression of LGBT youth is action (Kumashiro, 2000). Indeed, advocates throughout the United States have demonstrated that individual and collective actions make a difference in the everyday lives of LGBT youth. Adults have created GSAs with LGBT youth. Youth and educators have protested oppressive school policies. New York City residents responded creatively to chaining of a wooden cross to an apartment gate on Gay Street in Greenwich Village. Residents removed and replaced the lock so that the owner could not move it and then painted the cross with the colors of the LGBT rainbow flag (Nichols, 2017). Demonstrating courage, creativity, and love—as those individuals did—may help bring about the reality that one day, sexual and gender identity will not matter.

Discussion Questions

1. Have you or anyone you know experienced some form of oppression? Describe. How did those experiences make you or other individuals feel?
2. How are the everyday experiences of LGBT youth similar to and different from other marginalized populations discussed in this book?
3. What are the implications of those similarities and differences for OST practice?
4. Do you think OST programs can effectively resist oppression? Why or why not?
5. Do you think OST practitioners have traditionally engaged in resistance? Why or why not?
6. What are some specific examples of opposition programs that are framed as "sites for resistance to oppression" might face?"
7. Do you think engaging in resistance in OST practice is right for you? Why or why not?

Activity

Pull up a website for a local OST program. After reviewing the program website, put yourself in the shoes of a young person who identifies as a lesbian. Then answer the following questions:

1. Is she likely to view that program, based solely on the information on the website, as a safe space? Why or why not? Be sure to use specific examples in your response.
2. Using specific examples, explain how you might modify this program's website in order to send a clearer message that it is a welcoming space for LGBT youth.

References

Allen, R. S., & Montgomery, K. A. (2001). Applying an organization development approach to creating diversity. *Organizational Dynamics, 30*, 149–161.

Allison, M. T., & Hibbler, D. K. (2004). Organizational barriers to inclusion: Perspectives from the recreation professional. *Leisure Sciences, 26*(3), 261–280.

Berry, W. (1999). *The hidden wound* (5th ed.). New York, NY: North Point Press.

Blackburn, M. V., & Smith, J. M. (2010). Moving beyond the inclusion of LGBT-themed literature in English language arts classrooms: Interrogating heteronormativity and exploring intersectionality. *Journal of Adolescent & Adult Literacy, 53*(8), 625–634.

Blumenfield, W. J. (2010a). Introduction. In M. Adams, W. J. Blumenfeld, C. Castañeda, H. W. Hackman, M. L. Peters, & X. Zúñiga (Eds.), *Readings for diversity and social justice* (2nd ed., pp. 373–375). New York, NY: Routledge.

Blumenfield, W. J. (2010b). How homophobia hurts everyone. In M. Adams, W. J. Blumenfeld, C. Castañeda, H. W. Hackman, M. L. Peters, & X. Zúñiga (Eds.), *Readings for diversity and social justice* (2nd ed., pp. 376–384). New York, NY: Routledge.

Case, K. A., Hensley, R., & Anderson, A. (2014). Reflecting on heterosexual and male privilege: Interventions to raise awareness. *Journal of Social Issues, 70*(4), 722–740.

Case, K. A., & Meier, S. C. (2014). Developing allies to transgender and gender-nonconforming youth: Training for counselors and educators. *Journal of LGBT Youth, 11*(1), 62–82. doi: 10.1080/19361653.2014.840764

Collier, K. L., van Beusekom, G., Bos, H. M. W., & Sandfort, T. G. M. (2013). Sexual orientation and gender identity/expression related peer victimization in adolescence: A systematic review of associated psychosocial and health outcomes. *Journal of Sex Research, 50*(3–4), 299–317. Retrieved from http://doi.org/10.1080/00224499.2012.750639.

Craig, S. L., Dentato, M. P., & Iacovino, G. E. (2015). Patching holes and integrating community: A strengths-based continuum of care for lesbian, gay, bisexual, transgender, and questioning youth. *Journal of Gay and Lesbian Social Services, 27*(1), 100–115. doi: 10.1080/10538720.2015.988317.

Crisp, C., & McCave, E. L. (2007). Gay affirmative practice: A model for social work practice with gay, lesbian, and bisexual youth. *Child and Adolescent Social Work Journal, 24*(4), 403–421.

Davis-Delano, L. R., & Gillard, A. (2015). Summer camp as context for girls' and women's same-sex attractions and relationships. *Leisure/Loisir, 39*(1), 1–36. doi:10.1080/14927713.2015.1074400

Doherty, A., Fink, J., Inglis, S., & Pastore, D. (2010). Understanding a culture of diversity through frameworks of power and change. *Sport Management Review, 13*(4), 368–381.

Duhigg, J. M., Rostosky, S. S., Gray, B. E., & Wimsatt, M. K. (2010). Development of heterosexuals into allies: A qualitative exploration. *Sexuality Research and Social Policy, 7*, 2–14.

Gagné, P., Tewksbury, R., McGaughey, D. (1997). Coming out and crossing over: Identity formation and proclamation in a transgender community. *Gender & Society, 11*(4), 478–508.

Gates, G. J. (2011). How many people are lesbian, gay, bisexual, and transgender? Retrieved from http://williamsinstitute.law.ucla.edu/wp-content/uploads/Gates-How-Many-People-LGBT-Apr-2011.pdf

Genders and Sexualities Alliance Network. (2016). History and accomplishments. Retrieved from https://gsanetwork.org/about-us/history

Gillard, A., Buzuvis, E. E., & Bialeschki, M. D. (2014). Supporting transgender and gender nonconforming youth at summer camp. *Journal of Park and Recreation Administration, 32*(3), 92–105.

Gonzalez, J.A. (2010). Diversity change in organizations: A systemic, multilevel, and nonlinear process. *The Journal of Applied Behavioral Science, 46*(2), 197–219.

Greytak, E. A., Kosciw, J. G., & Boesen, M. J. (2013). Educating the educator: Creating supportive school personnel through professional development. *Journal of School Violence, 12*(1), 80–97. doi: 10.1080/15388220.2012.731586

Griffin, P., Lee, C., Waugh, J., & Beyer, C. (2004). Describing roles that gay-straight Alliances play in schools. *Journal of Gay & Lesbian Issues in Education, 1*(3), 7–22. doi: 10.1300/J367v01n03_03

Herek, G. M. (2004). Beyond "homophobia": Thinking about sexual prejudice and stigma in the twenty-first century. *Sexuality Research and Social Policy, 1*(2), 6–24.

GLSEN. (2015). The 2015 School Climate Survey Executive Summary. Retrieved from https://www.glsen.org/sites/default/files/GLSEN%202015%20National%20School%20Climate%20Survey%20%28NSCS%29%20-%20Executive%20Summary.pdf

Griffin, P., & Ouellett, M. (2003). From silence to safety and beyond: Historical trends in addressing lesbian, gay, bisexual, transgender issues in K-12 schools. *Equity & Excellence in Education, 36*(2), 106–114. doi: 10.1080/10665680303508

Johnson, A. G. (2010). What can we do? In M. Adams, W. J. Blumenfeld, C. Castañeda, H. W. Hackman, M. L. Peters, & X. Zúñiga (Eds.), *Readings for diversity and social justice* (2nd ed., pp. 610–615). New York, NY: Routledge.

Kivel, B. D., & Johnson, C. W. (2008). (De)constructing the "other": Fostering leisure and the development of sexual identities. In M. T. Allison & I. E. Schneider (Eds.), *Diversity and the recreation profession: Organizational Perspectives* (pp. 163–188). State College, PA: Venture.

Kivel, B. D., & Kleiber, D. A. (2000). Leisure in the identity formation of lesbian/gay youth: Personal, but not social. *Leisure Sciences, 22*(4), 215–232.

Kumashiro, K. K. (2000). Toward a theory of anti-oppressive education. *Review of Educational Research, 70*(1), 25–53.

Lapointe, A. A. (2015). Standing "straight" up to homophobia: Straight allies' involvement in GSAs. *Journal of LGBT Youth, 12*(2), 144–169. doi: 10.1080/19361653.2014.969867.

Lasser, J., & Wicker, N. (2008) Visibility management and the body. *Journal of LGBT Youth, 5*(1), 103–117.

Lewis, S. T., & Johnson, C. W. (2011) "But it's not that easy": Negotiating (trans)gender expressions in leisure spaces. *Leisure/Loisir, 35*(2), 115–132. doi:10.1080/1492771 3.2011.567062

Marx, R. A., & Kettrey, H. H. (2016). Gay-straight alliances are associated with lower levels of school-based victimization of LGBTQ+ Youth: A systematic review and meta-analysis. *Journal of Youth and Adolescence, 45*(7), 1269–1282. doi: 10.1007/ s10964-016-0501-7

Mayberry, M. (2013). Gay-straight alliances: Youth empowerment and working toward reducing stigma of LGBT youth. *Humanity & Society, 37*, 35–54. doi: 10.1177/0160597612454358

Mayberry, N., Chenneville, T., & Currie, S. (2013). Challenging the sounds of silence: A qualitative study of gay-straight alliances and school reform efforts. *Education and Urban Society, 45*(3), 307–339.

Mill Creek High School. (2017). Mill Creek High School chapter of the Gay-Straight Alliance (GSA). Retrieved from http://www.millcreekhs.com/index.php/gsa

Montgomery, S. A., & Stewart, A. J. (2012). Privileged allies in lesbian and gay rights activism: Gender, generation, and resistance to heteronomatity. *Journal of Social Issues, 68*(1), 162–177.

Nichols, J. M. (2017). Someone chained a cross to Gay Street in NY. What happened next was beautiful. *The Huffington Post*. Retrieved from http://www.huffingtonpost. com/entry/love-cross-nyc_us_58ff5447e4b0b6f6014ac24e

Oakleaf, L. (2013). "Having to think about it all the time": Factors affecting the identity management strategies of residential summer camp staff who self-identify as lesbian, gay, bisexual or transgender. *Leisure/Loisir, 37*(3), 251–266. doi: 10.1080/14927713.2013.856100

Payne, E., & Smith, M. (2012). Rethinking safe schools approaches for LGBTQ students: Changing the questions we ask. *Multicultural Perspectives 14*(4), 187–193. doi: 10.1080/15210960.2012.725293

Pless, N., & Maak, T. (2004). Building an inclusive diversity culture: Principles, processes, and practice. *Journal of Business Ethics, 54*(2), 129–147.

Poteat, V. P., Calzo, J. P., & Yoshikawa, H. J. (2016). Promoting youth agency through dimensions of gay-straight alliance involvement and conditions that maximize associations. *Journal of Youth & Adolescence, 45*(7), 1438–1451. doi:10.1007/ s10964-016-0421-6

Poteat, V. P., & Espeleage, D. L. (2007). Predicting psychological consequences of homophobic victimization in middle school students. *The Journal of Early Adolescence, 27*(2), 175–191.

Robinson, G., & Dechant, K. (1997). Building a business case for diversity. *The Academy of Management Executive, 11*(3), 21–31.

Russell, S. T., Kosciw, J., Horn, S., & Saewyc, E. (2010). Safe schools policy for LGBTQ students. *Social Policy Report, 24*(4), 1–17.

Russell, S. T., Muraco, A., Subramaniam, A., & Laub, C. (2009). Youth empowerment and high school gay-straight alliances. *Journal of Youth and Adolescence, 38*(7), 891–903. Retrieved from http://doi.org/10.1007/s10964-008-9382-8

Russell, S. T., Ryan, C., Toomey, R. B., Diaz, R. M., & Sanchez, J. (2011). Lesbian, gay, bisexual, and transgender adolescent school victimization: Implications for young adult health adjustment. *Journal of School Health, 81*(5), 223–230.

Russell, S. T., & Van Campen, K. (2011). Diversity and inclusion in youth development: What can we learn from marginalized young people? *Journal of Youth Development, 6*(3), 96–108.

Savin-Williams, R. C. (2008). Then and now: Recruitment, definition, diversity, and positive attributes of same-sex populations. *Developmental Psychology, 44*(1), 135–138. doi:10.1037/0012-1649.44.1.135

Savin-Williams, R. C. (2014). The new sexual-minority teenager: Freedom from traditional notions of sexual identity. In J. S. Kaufman & D. A. Powell (Eds.), *The meaning of sexual identity in the twenty-first century* (pp. 5–20). Newcastle upon Tyne, UK: Cambridge Scholars Publishing.

Seidman, S. (2002). *Beyond the closet: The transformation of gay and lesbian life.* New York, NY: Routledge.

Singh, A. A. (2013). Transgender youth of color and resilience: Negotiating oppression and finding support. *Sex Roles, 68,* 690–702. doi: 10.1007/s11199-012-0149-z

Theriault, D. (2014). Organized leisure experiences of LGBTQ youth: Resistance and Oppression. *Journal of Leisure Research, 46*(4), 448–461.

Theriault, D., & Edwards, M. B. (2014). Limiting sexual identity discrimination in parks and recreation programs. *Parks & Recreation Magazine, 49*(8), 14–16.

Theriault, D., & Witt, P. A. (2014). Features of positive developmental leisure settings for LGBTQ youth. *Journal of Park and Recreation Administration, 32*(2), 83–97.

Vaid, U. (1997). Coalition as a goal not a process. *Gay Community News, 22*(4), 6–9.

Vaid, U. (1998). A shared politics of social justice. In the South End Press Collective (Ed.), *Talking about a revolution* (pp. 95–112). Cambridge, MA: South End Press.

Vaid, U. (2009). Ten lessons from LGBT activism. Retrieved from http://urvashivaid.net/wp/?cat=4&paged=2

Vaid, U. (2010). Looking forward: The future of GLBT activism. Retrieved from http://urvashivaid.net/wp/?cat=4&paged=2

Vaid, U. (2012). *Irresistible revolution: Confronting race, class, and the assumptions of LGBT Politics.* New York, NY: Magnus Books.

Wasserman, I. C., Gallegos, P. V., & Ferdman, B. M. (2012). Dancing with resistance: Leadership challenges in fostering a culture of inclusion. In K. M. Thomas (Ed.), *Diversity resistance in organizations* (pp. 175–206). New York, NY: Lawrence Erlbaum.

Watson, L. B., Varjas, K., Meyers, J., & Graybill, E. C. (2010). Gay–straight alliance advisors: Negotiating multiple ecological systems when advocating for LGBTQ youth. *Journal of LGBT Youth, 7*(2), 100–128.

Young, I. M. (2010). Five faces of oppression. In M. Adams, W. J. Blumenfeld, C. Castañeda, H. W. Hackman, M. L. Peters, & X. Zúñiga. (Eds.), *Readings for diversity and social justice* (2nd ed., pp. 35–44). New York, NY: Routledge.

Chapter 23

Including Youth of All Abilities

Lynn S. Anderson and Mary Ann Devine

Adolescence is a time of searching for belonging. Peers become more important than family to identity formation and well-being. Youth put great effort into fitting in, being accepted, and finding friendships. However, imagine having a difference that makes fitting in difficult, makes acceptance by one's peers challenging, and makes building friendships daunting. Many youth with disabilities experience a sense of segregation and isolation from their peers. All youth need support and confirmation from those around them; this need may be amplified for youth with disabilities. Out-of-school time (OST) practitioners in youth and recreation services can play an instrumental role in facilitating inclusion and a sense of belonging for youth of all ability levels in programs, services, and settings.

The purpose of this chapter is to help OST practitioners gain the knowledge and tools necessary to ensure that all youth, regardless of ability, have the opportunity to belong, to grow, and to develop into healthy adults. This chapter explores what inclusion means, particularly in relation to youth with disabilities, and provides a new way to think about ability level that is functional and useful for professionals in youth and OST services. We will look at why inclusion is important and how to best facilitate physical, administrative, and programmatic inclusion. The goal of this chapter is to enable OST practitioners to have a clearer sense of what inclusion is, why it matters, and what tools can be used to ensure inclusion for all youth in programs and services.

What is Inclusion?

Inclusion is defined by Webster's dictionary as "being a member of a larger whole; to encompass or embrace as part of a whole." This definition reflects the philosophy of including youth with disabilities into OST opportunities in our communities. It also reflects the broader spirit of inclusion: It is the duty of all to make changes or adjustments in a situation so that all people can be fully engaged in OST pursuits. In addition, youth with disabilities can enrich the OST experience of others and add healthy diversity to a program. It is important to understand that inclusion means not only physical inclusion but social inclusion as well. Adolescents with disabilities, like all adolescents, want to meet new friends, have opportunities for social interaction, and be fully engaged participants in OST activities. Physical and social inclusion must be fostered for these needs to be met.

Anderson and Kress (2003) provide an expanded perspective on inclusion. They stress six principles:

- **Having the same choices and opportunities in OST settings that other youth have.** Just because a participant may learn slowly or use a wheelchair does not mean he or she should not be able to participate in the same activities as everyone else. An accommodation may be needed to allow for inclusive participation, but the accommodation itself should not deter the opportunity to participate. If an activity is of interest to the participant, then the opportunity needs to exist. The idea of inclusion is to be able to choose what we want to do based on interest.

- **Being accepted and appreciated for who you are.** Many youth with disabilities have many strengths to add to an OST program. We often tend to overlook those strengths. Youth with disabilities will tell you what they can and cannot do, and it is often more than people expect.

- **Being with friends who share your interests, not your disability.** Inclusion is participating in programs where you share the same interests as your friends. The common bond is the OST activity, not the disability.

- **Being a valued member and a welcomed participant in youth programs, regardless of ability level.** Inclusion is an opportunity to open doors to serve more youth, regardless of ability level. Youth with disabilities need to be seen as valued members and welcomed participants, not as special cases or charity work.

- **OST facilities and areas that are accessible and easy to use by everyone.** Inclusion is providing facilities and areas that are accessible. Accessibility benefits not only youth with disabilities, but also parents, grandparents, family members, and even staff who may have a functional difference. Accessibility makes everyone's life easier.
- **Providing the necessary individual adaptations, accommodations, and supports so every young person can benefit equally from an OST experience with friends.** Inclusion is a process that begins with a young person who may need supports. Providing the individualized supports and accommodations needed by each person is key to successful inclusion.

To have a clear understanding of inclusion, it is helpful to understand what inclusion is not. According to Anderson and Kress (2003), inclusion is *not* the following:

- **Putting large groups of youth with disabilities in one program.** Putting youth with disabilities in large groups makes it harder for them to get to know peers without disabilities, as well as for youth without disabilities to get to know them.
- **Disrupting the natural proportion of individuals with and without disabilities in the community.** Programs that are developed and implemented at your agency should reflect the composition and culture of your community. For example, communities are not only made up of people with disabilities; they are made up of people of all ability levels. Your agency should offer a variety of youth programs to meet the needs of your diverse community in an inclusive manner.
- **Special, labeled programs such as "Autistic Arts Program" or "Teen Special Needs Program."** Segregated programs may limit opportunities for inclusion, especially if community members view segregated programs as the only choice for out-of-school time activities for youth with disabilities. It is important to offer an array of choices in recreation activities (Mayer & Anderson, 2014).
- **"Caring for" or "looking after" youth with disabilities instead of facilitating equal opportunities for equal participation that include risk and challenge.** Youth with disabilities should have the opportunity to take risks and face challenges like everyone else. Challenge is important to a quality leisure experience and youth with disabilities have the same right to quality leisure as anyone else.

Inclusion is a far-reaching concept with profound implications for how people relate to each other. By welcoming and including youth of all abilities into out-of-school time programs and services, inclusion can help create a richer life for all youth.

Why Is Inclusion Important?

Inclusion not only benefits youth with disabilities, it also benefits youth without disabilities, provides enriched environments, leads to careful and well-conceptualized programming strategies, and enhanced developmental assets. Here we explore the benefits of inclusion, how inclusion enriches a focus on developmental assets, what barriers and facilitators exist to inclusive services, and the theoretical underpinnings of inclusion.

Benefits of Inclusion

The benefits of participation in inclusive OST activities for youth have been explored from many perspectives. Overall, studies have demonstrated that both youth with and without disabilities experience benefits from engagement in inclusive recreation. All youth, including those with disabilities, benefit by increasing self-determined behaviors (Devine, Malley, Sheldon, Dattilo, & Gast, 1997), developing friendships (Schleien, Fahnestock, Green, & Rynders, 1990), and developing socially appropriate behaviors (Modell, 1997). For youth with disabilities in particular, inclusive environments build important life skills (e.g., age-appropriate social skills), improve physical functioning, such as cardiovascular endurance (Green & DeCoux, 1994), and reduce social isolation (Devine, 2015). Another benefit of OST program participation unique to youth with disabilities is that inclusive environments are a forum to dispel myths and stereotypes about their limitations (Anderson, Schleien, McAvoy, & Lais, 1997; Devine & Wilhite, 2000).

For youth with disabilities in particular, inclusive environments build important life skills (e.g., age-appropriate social skills), improve physical functioning, such as cardiovascular endurance, and reduce social isolation.

Other researchers have noted additional benefits of inclusive OST participation. Youth with disabilities expressed a heightened freedom of choice when inclusive programs were options in their leisure repertoire (Mayer & Anderson, 2014). Finally, research has found increased social acceptance of youth with disabilities involved in inclusive recreation programs (Devine, 2004; Devine, Piatt, & Dawson, 2015).

In the early years of inclusive programming, some stakeholders (e.g., parents, participants, and staff) were concerned that youth without disabilities would be negatively impacted by including youth with disabilities in youth services. Studies examining inclusive recreation contexts have found this sentiment to be unsubstantiated (Mayer & Anderson, 2014; Schleien, Hornfeldt, & McAvoy, 1994). Research has found improved communication, physical fitness, problem-solving skills, and social skills for youth with and without disabilities as the result of participation in inclusive leisure programs. As well, inclusive recreation participation increased an appreciation for similarities and differences between youth with and without disabilities (Devine & O'Brien, 2007). In sum, all youth experience benefits from an inclusive environment.

Developmental Assets and Inclusion

Research consistently shows that inclusion has benefits that extend well beyond the child or youth with a disability. In fact, when analyzed in relation to the 40 developmental assets, defined by the Search Institute (2006), inclusion can be viewed as key in helping to support youth in their positive development, regardless of disability.

The 40 developmental assets, grouped as external or internal assets, are defined as building blocks that help youth grow into responsible and caring adults (Search Institute, 2006). Inclusion contributes to almost every building block or asset. Table 23.1 shows each group of developmental assets and how inclusion can contribute to developing and strengthening each of them (Anderson, 2008).

Table 23.1
How Inclusion Contributes to Developmental Assets

EXTERNAL ASSETS	ROLE OF INCLUSION
SUPPORT	
1. **Family support**—Family life provides high levels of love and support. 2. **Positive family communication**—Young person and her or his parent(s) communicate positively, and young person is willing to seek advice and counsel from parents. 3. **Other adult relationships**—Young person receives support from three or more non-parent adults. 4. **Caring neighborhood**—Young person experiences caring neighbors. 5. **Caring school climate**—School provides a caring, encouraging environment. 6. **Parent involvement in schooling**—Parent(s) are actively involved in helping young person succeed in school.	**Inclusion** is about providing support to others. Through engagement in the inclusion process in recreation activities, youth learn not only how to receive support, but how to create and sustain it. Youth experience caring "micro-communities" in inclusive recreation activities that model what it means to be valued and supported, regardless of ability level. The lessons learned in supportive, inclusive recreation environments can carry over to all aspects of a youth's life.
EMPOWERMENT	
7. **Community values youth**—Young person perceives that adults in the community value youth. 8. **Youth as resources**—Young people are given useful roles in the community. 9. **Service to others**—Young person serves in the community one hour or more per week. 10. **Safety**—Young person feels safe at home, school, and in the neighborhood.	**Inclusion** provides a multitude of opportunities for youth to provide valued service to others and to fulfill a valued role. Research shows consistently that youth assisting other youth with disabilities in being included in recreation activities is one of the most effective strategies for successful inclusion. Inclusion helps youth feel safe, as they see some of society's more vulnerable members being supported and respected.

(cont.)

Table 23.1 (cont.)

EXTERNAL ASSETS	ROLE OF INCLUSION
BOUNDARIES AND EXPECTATIONS	
11. **Family boundaries**—Family has clear rules and consequences and monitors the young person's whereabouts. 12. **School boundaries**—School provides clear rules and consequences. 13. **Neighborhood boundaries**—Neighbors take responsibility for monitoring young people's behavior. 14. **Adult role models**—Parent(s) and other adults model positive, responsible behavior. 15. **Positive peer influence**—Young person's best friends model responsible behavior. 16. **High expectations**—Both parent(s) and teachers encourage the young person to do well.	**Inclusion** is about helping everyone learn how to meet high expectations and how to respect the boundaries of others. Inclusion, when it is implemented well, even with youth with behavioral challenges, provides clear and consistent structures for all youth, even though the youth who need behavioral support may benefit most. Youth see adults model respect and acceptance of youth with differences in inclusive recreation programs, and they learn to help each other be caring and supportive. Inclusion is about "doing programs well," and that includes setting clear boundaries and high expectations.
CONSTRUCTIVE USE OF TIME	
17. **Creative activities**—Young person spends three or more hours per week in lessons or practice in music, theater, or other arts. 18. **Youth programs**—Young person spends three or more hours per week in sports, clubs, or organizations at school and/or in the community. 19. **Religious community**—Young person spends one or more hours per week in activities in a religious institution. 20. **Time at home**—Young person is out with friends "with nothing special to do" two or fewer nights per week.	**Inclusion** is a creative process. It happens one person at a time. Across programming areas, and in one's "hanging out" time, learning how to include someone with obvious challenges and differences makes youths' use of time even more constructive.

(cont.)

Table 23.1 (cont.)

INTERNAL ASSETS	ROLE OF INCLUSION
COMMITMENT TO LEARNING	
21. **Achievement motivation**—Young person is motivated to do well in school. 22. **School engagement**—Young person is actively engaged in learning. 23. **Homework**—Young person reports doing at least one hour of homework every school day. 24. **Bonding to school**—Young person cares about her or his school. 25. **Reading for pleasure**—Young person reads for pleasure three or more hours per week	**Inclusion** is a learning process. When youth observe a peer with a disability meet a challenge to learn something new, even against all odds, they can be inspired and uplifted. When youth are a part of helping that peer with a disability learn, the bonding that occurs is strong, deep, and meaningful.
POSITIVE VALUES	
26. **Caring**—Young person places high value on helping other people. 27. **Equality and social justice**—Young person places high value on promoting equality and reducing hunger and poverty. 28. **Integrity**—Young person acts on convictions and stands up for her or his beliefs. 29. **Honesty**—Young person "tells the truth even when it is not easy." 30. **Responsibility**—Young person accepts and takes personal responsibility.	**Inclusion** perhaps contributes most to building this group of developmental assets. Inclusion is about caring, equality, and social justice. By being a part of including a peer with a disability in a recreation experience, youth can experience integrity, honesty, and responsibility.
SOCIAL COMPETENCIES	
31. **Restraint**—Young person believes it is important not to be sexually active or to use alcohol or other drugs. 32. **Planning and decision-making**—Young person knows how to plan and make choices. 33. **Interpersonal competence**—Young person has empathy, sensitivity, and friendship skills. 34. **Cultural competence**—Young person has knowledge of and comfort with people of different cultural/racial/ethnic backgrounds. 35. **Resistance skills**—Young person can resist negative peer pressure and dangerous situations. 36. **Peaceful conflict resolution**—Young person seeks to resolve conflict nonviolently.	**Inclusion** helps build social competencies in youth with and without disabilities. Youth become comfortable with differences in intellectual ability, speaking ability, physical ability, and emotional control. They learn to resist pressure to bully and tease, and to resolve conflicts within groups of varying abilities. Youth use empathy and sensitivity and develop friendships with people who are different than themselves in recreation experiences that include individuals with disabilities.

(cont.)

Table 23.1 (cont.)

INTERNAL ASSETS	ROLE OF INCLUSION
POSITIVE IDENTITY	
37. **Personal power**—Young person feels he or she has control over "things that happen to me." 38. **Self-esteem**—Young person reports having a high self-esteem. 39. **Sense of purpose**—Young person reports that "my life has a purpose." 40. **Positive view of personal future**—Young person is optimistic about her or his personal future.	**Inclusion** builds a sense of purpose and meaning for all youth. When a young person without a disability is able to make a positive difference for a peer with a disability in a recreation experience, self-esteem can improve, and a sense of control is heightened. Inclusion can build positive identity in all youth.

Constraints and Facilitators to Inclusion

Constraints to inclusive programming. What prevents youth from being able to play wherever they choose, regardless of ability level? What constraints must an adolescent negotiate to be included in OST spaces? Barriers to inclusive OST programming include attitudes; the pervasiveness of the medical model with its long history of segregated services; the continuum approach; characteristics of the built, natural, and social environment; and lastly, an overreliance on the compliance approach (Anderson, Wilkins, & Penney McGee, 2014; Devine, 2012).

Perhaps the most significant barrier to inclusive OST services is that of *attitudes*. Research has shown that attitudes can range from negative and discriminatory to fear and uncertainty based on lack of skills and knowledge (Anderson & Heyne, 2000; Scholl, Smith, & Davison, 2005). Attitudinal barriers reflect assumptions and myths that result in stereotypes about youth with disabilities (Oliver, 1996). For instance, when OST professionals plan and organize a recreation program for youth under the assumption that youth with disabilities will not be participants, they are a product of an attitudinal barrier (see quote at left).

The pervasiveness and overapplication of the *medical model* also creates a barrier for people with disabilities to experience full inclusion in OST settings (Anderson & Heyne, 2012; Sylvester, 2011). In the medical model, people with disabilities

George Covington, former White House adviser on disability, said it best: "The first barrier to universal design is the human mind. If we could put a ramp into the mind, the first thing down the ramp would be the understanding that all barriers are the result of narrow thinking .... You have to ramp the human mind or the rest of the ramps won't work" (Szenasy, 2010, para. 2).

are viewed as a diagnosis or problem, and experts are needed to help "fix" the disability. This in turn creates the need for specialists and special services different from those offered to typical community members. Over time, therefore, communities have created many separate, but not equal, recreation programs for youth with disabilities, ranging from Special Olympics to "Saturday Morning Gym and Swim for the Handicapped." The segregated services are often offered as "skill-building" to prepare people with disabilities for "real recreation" once they have become more acceptable for inclusion.

The *continuum approach*, though based on good intentions, was designed to help move young people to the "least restrictive environment." This approach has several pitfalls and making these explicit helps us truly understand the limitations of this method of providing inclusive services. Taylor (2004) described three major pitfalls:

1. **The "readiness" assumption.** Readiness is when youth with disabilities have to show some functional or other improvement within a more specialized or segregated service environment before they can move to or "graduate" to more inclusive services. Readiness is determined by expert specialists, not the individuals themselves. Often this means that individuals are stuck at one level of service and experience lack of personal control.
2. **Fostering a lack of self-determination.** The lack of personal control leads to a vicious cycle of lack of self-determination, which leads to further entrapment in the continuum. The cycle leads to a further erosion of freedom and self-determination essential to meaningful recreation and other OST experiences.

Taylor (2004) emphasizes the irony of this trap, as the most restrictive services meant to prepare youth for a least restrictive environment do not prepare, and in fact disempower, them for self-determined community living that is needed for a high quality of life.

3. **Change must happen in the individual.** The continuum approach makes the false assumption that change must happen in the participant in order to move up the continuum toward more freedom and choice. The approach lacks attention to the environmental changes, supports, and accommodations that may need to take place for a participant to achieve quality of life.

The continuum approach also puts all the duty to change or fit in on the youth with the disability and none of the responsibility for change on youth without disabilities or OST practitioners. This approach actually runs counter to the inclusion principle, which states that it is the responsibility of all to make changes in a recreation environment so youth with and without disabilities can engage together in activities (Devine, 2015).

The built, natural, and social environments can also present major constraints to inclusion in recreation for youth with disabilities. Lack of accessibility, poor design, narrowly interpreted policies, and rigid programming practices can all prevent inclusion. The idea that "one size fits all" permeates recreation services and disenfranchises not only young people with disabilities but also many youth who do not fit into a narrow "norm."

Lastly, the *compliance approach* to moving OST services from inaccessible to inclusive has created at the least a sense of disempowerment and perhaps worse, resentment toward making changes to be more inclusive. Disability advocates have historically needed to resort to litigation to get the changes needed to access recreation services (Lewkowicz, 2006). Under litigation, OST providers, from businesses to public services, often see the cost of forced accessibility without seeing the benefits to a broad range of users. The compliance approach not only builds resentment, but also has been less than effective. The Americans with Disabilities Act has been in force since 1990, yet according to a recent national survey, large gaps still exist between people without and with disabilities in many areas of life, including recreation and socialization (National Organization on Disability, 2010).

> Deegan (1996), a self-advocate with a disability, once stated, "We say let the mainstream become a wide stream that has room for all of us and leaves no one stranded on the fringes ....The goal is not to become normal. The goal is to embrace our human vocation of becoming more deeply, more fully human. The goal is not normalization. The goal is to become the unique, awesome, never to be repeated human being that we are called to be" (p. 92).

Though numerous constraints to inclusive services persist, we have learned much about what facilitates inclusion and accessibility (Anderson, 2015). Focusing on facilitators has allowed us to develop models, strategies, and tools that bring about positive change.

Facilitators to inclusive programming. The *social model* of disability has helped foster inclusion in community OST services and is built on a strengths-based and ecological approach. Situating the person in the environment and focusing on strengths helps foster well-being and inclusion in OST programs (Anderson & Heyne, 2012). The World Health Organization (WHO) acknowledges the vital role of *activities and participation* in well-being. WHO embraces a social model of disability and recognizes the importance of the environment and a strengths approach in its conceptualization of the International Classification of Functioning (ICF) (2003). The ICF looks not only at how a person functions, it considers the *environmental factors* in which that functioning occurs. Therefore, inclusion is designed not around deficits and diagnoses, but around ability and functionality. The WHO conceptualizes ability and functionality at three levels: (a) body function and structures (e.g., physical functioning related to cognition, speech, cardiovascular health, and related systems); (b) the person (e.g., age, lifestyle, education, assets); and (c) social and environmental contexts (e.g., physical environment, social attitudes, interpersonal relationships). As such, well-being is a holistic concept incorporating the body, the individual, and society.

Based on a social model of disability, we now have an increased understanding of strategies that facilitate inclusion. Research has helped us understand what concrete actions we can take to ensure accessible facilities, programs, and practices (Miller, Schleien, & Lausier, 2009). With evidence-based tools at our disposal, we are able to modify normative programs, services, and environments to fully accommodate a broader range of youth, including those with disabilities. OST providers are able to see positive outcomes from the changes made for accessibility and inclusion. New and modified facilities, policies, program practices, and partnerships result in inclusion of many diverse community members, shifting the "main stream" to a "wide stream" in OST services.

Theoretical Foundations of Inclusion

Theory helps elucidate deeper meanings and provides guidance to practice. This section will describe four theories that are useful in understanding inclusion: *contact theory, social construction theory, ecological theory,* and *self-determination theory.* Each of these theories facilitates generalizations and predicts future events concerning psychological, sociological, and environmental phenomena related to inclusion of youth in recreation services.

Contact theory. Contact theory asserts that the quality of interactions between people with differences tends to influence changes in attitudes toward one another (Allport, 1954). Specifically, the theory suggests that prejudice, stereotyping, and discrimination may be reduced by creating a context in which contact and interactions are positive (Allport, 1954). Thus, contact theory suggests that it is possible to change one group's perceptions or attitudes toward another group, although contact alone is not enough to result in positive attitudinal changes. Contact also could be a source of embarrassment, irritation, and escalation of conflict (Wilhite, Devine, & Goldenberg, 1999).

The type of change depends primarily on the conditions under which contact has taken place. The form of contact and experiences that occurs determines its success or failure (Roper, 1990). For example, Allport (1954) suggested that favorable conditions tend to improve attitudes, whereas unfavorable conditions tend to foster harmful attitudes. Minimal or infrequent contact tends to reinforce negative perceptions people with and without disabilities have of each other (Allport, 1954). Favorable conditions that tend to foster positive attitude changes involve contacts that do the following:

- Produce equal status as well as promote contact
- Are mutually rewarding to those with and without disabilities
- Are personal rather than casual, allowing individuals to get to know each other well
- Persist over time
- Focus on establishing common rather than individual goals
- Receive strong support from relevant authorities (Allport, 1954)

Contact theory suggests that to set the stage for positive contact, no one person should be more or less important than another, contact should be on-going, everyone should gain something from the experience, and everyone should be working toward a similar goal. In inclusive recreation environments, contact theory can be applied by designing programs that promote meaningful interdependence across time. Programmers should also facilitate youth getting to know each other on a personal level. This requires creating an atmosphere where youth can communicate interests, needs, and concerns. Personal contact can also be promoted by focusing on shared interests between youth.

Social construction theory. Social construction theory asserts that people construct meaning through social interactions, and that the behaviors, objects, and language associated with social interaction contribute to how one creates meaning (Devine, 1997). That is, behaviors, objects, or language in the specific context help one to understand "what is going on" and create a perception of the reality of the situation (Douglas, 1970). For example, if youth associate the use of a wheelchair by someone with cerebral palsy to reflect "independence in participation," then the behaviors toward, objects used in relation to, and language about the wheelchair will reflect independence. In a dance class, for instance, the use of a wheelchair might then be viewed as a tool to create freedom of expression. On the other hand, if youth associate another youth who uses a wheelchair to be someone who is "wheelchair bound," their perception of the person using the wheelchair will likely be one of

> Behaviors, objects, or language in the specific context help one to understand "what is going on" and create a perception of the reality of the situation.

sympathy and lack of ability, and they might view the youth as struggling during the dance class. Context is an important component in understanding social construction theory because context establishes meaning. In different contexts, meanings associated with the same behavior, objects, and language may change.

The social construction theory also addresses the meaning of disability. The social construction of disability refers to the meaning ascribed by society to physical, mental, cognitive, and emotional impairments (Oliver, 1996). In certain contexts, disability may have a positive meaning; however, traditionally disability has been associated with a negative meaning (Bogdan & Taylor, 1992). For example, often youth with disabilities are perceived as being incapable of meeting societal standards, which tends to emphasize physical attractiveness, reciprocity in relationships, capabilities, and independence. By not meeting these standards, youth with disabilities are perceived to be inferior and disadvantaged (Taylor & Bogdan, 1993). They are often stereotyped as not being capable of functioning as independently, accomplishing as much, or having relationships that are as reciprocal as people without disabilities (Devine & Lashua, 2002).

The application of social construction theory to inclusive OST participation suggests that we should try to promote positive meanings associated with behaviors, objects, and language associated with disability, thereby reducing the negative meanings and stereotypes about disability. For example, OST professionals could create opportunities for individuals with disabilities to challenge the notion that they cannot participate in high-adventure types of recreation activities (e.g., whitewater rafting, rock climbing) by presenting wheelchairs as vehicles for movement and adventure, not as something constraining.

Ecological theory. Ecological theory suggests that people and their environments are interconnected. That is, there is a reciprocity and interaction among systems within which we live (Anderson & Heyne, 2012). Systems are social organizations (e.g., family, schools, religious affiliations, society) that people interact with directly as well as indirectly. Bronfenbrenner (1979) stated that an individual is nested in a complex web of interconnected systems where each system and each component within a system is related to, and influences, the other. Ecological theory asserts that if a change occurs within the community, not only will the change impact that system, but also will directly or indirectly influence individuals. In addition, if something occurs to an individual, there will be a reciprocal influence on another system (e.g., family). For instance, when the ADA was written into federal law, that change affected state and local governments, communities, families, and individuals with disabilities. Conversely, when individuals with disabilities began to demand full inclusion in society, it affected families, local communities, and state and federal systems.

> Ecological theory asserts that if a change occurs within the community, not only will the change impact that system, but also will directly or indirectly influence individuals.

Examining constraints to inclusion for youth with disabilities from an ecological perspective suggests that OST professionals should explore individuals' needs in relation to the context of their social and physical environment (Scholl, Dieser, & Davison, 2005). They should also view barriers to inclusive services as stemming from not one causal factor, but from multiple directions.

Self-determination theory. Self-determination theory suggests that one is healthier and happier when one is in control of one's actions (Ryan & Deci, 2000). Another word often used to describe this phenomenon is *autonomy*. External influence or interference in making choices or decisions would be considered contrary to promoting self-determination, unless those external influences have been internalized (i.e., accepted as one's own) and valued by the individual. Therefore, if one is unable to or chooses not to make decisions, as long as one endorses the decisions of others and perceives decisions or choices as being consistent with one's values, one is self-determined. Being self-determined is intrinsically motivating, while externally motivated behaviors often create apathy and boredom.

Inclusive recreation programmers should provide multiple OST opportunities for youth so meaningful choices appropriate to their age and developmental stage can be made. To provide meaningful opportunities for self-determined behavior, programmers need to understand youths' interests and preferences. Increasing youth voice, promoting communication, asking for input and ideas from all participants, and responding to ideas are all important ways to increase self-determination and empower youth with disabilities. Active participation and engaging in decision-making promotes feelings of competence and can further one's sense of freedom from constraints.

In summary, we have reviewed benefits, constraints, facilitators, and theories that further elucidate what inclusion means and provide guidance on how successful inclusion might occur. At the heart of successful inclusion, and consistent across the information we have presented, is the idea that young people with disabilities are more than their labels. We have a new way to think about ability level: ability level is another variation in the human condition.

A New Way of Thinking about Ability Level

Historically, people have tended to think about individuals with disabilities categorically as their diagnosis or label. That is, one has an intellectual disability or not, mental illness or not, quadriplegia or not, and so on. The new way of thinking about human beings is less categorical and more fluid. We know that people vary on a continuum in ability level. We all have more or less physical ability or intellectual ability than others, for example. Some of us are Olympic athletes, but most of us are not; some of us are geniuses, but most of us are not. Some of us are Olympic athletes but not geniuses. In other words, people do not fit into a "yes" or "no" box on any characteristic associated with being human and having a disability. Categorical labels become less meaningful and even misleading. If OST practitioners conceptualize ability level as a composite of variations on a continuum across dimensions, then they are better able to create an environment where inclusion works.

Viewing Disability as a Functional Variation in the Human Condition: All the Ways We Vary

People have historically viewed disability as something being "wrong" with the person. We previously described the medical model that focuses on changing the individual with a disability to help him or her function better in the social world. We take a different approach to understanding disability, one that is functional and social. Ability is *not* an inherent attribute of the individual but results from interactions with the physical and social environment. It results, in part, from choices society makes about our environment (Institute of Medicine, 2007).

Ability is how one is able to function in the world. All people function in many ways to accomplish daily activities. People vary in their functioning across the following domains: *physical, sensory, communication, intellectual, social,* and *emotional.* These variations could be due to a variety of disabilities, illnesses, injuries, poverty, and more. What matters is not the cause of the variation, but how functioning is impacted and how that interacts with the environment. Viewing disability as part of being a human being helps us to better understand that we are all different, have something to offer to a situation, and being different from one another is a positive part of the recreation experience (Anderson, Wilkins, & Penney McGee, 2015; Devine, 2015).

Thus, we offer you an approach to understanding disability that is both functional and social. For each functional domain, we offer general guidelines to assist you in accommodating a young person who may have that particular difference. Most of the guidelines focus on changing the environment (both the physical and social environment) to assist an individual with a disability to be fully included in OST services, programs, areas, and facilities (Anderson, Wilkins, & Penney McGee, 2015).

Physical functioning. Physical functioning includes things such as walking, lifting, moving, balancing, grasping, muscular control, fine motor skills, endurance, strength, and cardiovascular fitness. Differences in physical functioning could be due to things such as spinal cord injury, amputation, stroke, obesity, muscular dystrophy, spina bifida, or cerebral palsy. Common ways to adapt environments and activities to allow fuller physical participation include ramps, elevators, wide doors, doors that open easily or automatically, lighter objects, level ground or slight grades, rest stops, grab bars, firm surfaces, or service dogs/animals. Guidelines for interacting with a person with a physical difference include the following:

- Be aware of what is accessible and what is not accessible to youth who use wheelchairs.
- Try to put yourself at eye level when talking with someone using a wheelchair.
- Assist only when asked, but make it comfortable for someone to ask for assistance.
- Do not push, lean on, or hold on to a person's wheelchair unless the person asks you to. The wheelchair is part of his or her personal space.
- Rearrange furniture or objects to accommodate a person using a wheelchair before the person arrives.
- Offer to tell where accessible rest rooms, telephones, and water fountains are located.
- Do not make assumptions about the youth's physical abilities or capabilities.
- Provide accurate descriptions of an inclusive environment or service.

Sensory functioning. Sensory functioning includes things such as hearing, seeing, touching, and integrating sensations. Differences in sensory functioning could be due to blindness, deafness, hearing impairment, vision impairment, color blindness, or autism. Common ways to adapt environments and activities to allow fuller sensory participation include alternate forms of communication, sounds, audible signals, written communication, sensory strips (e.g., sidewalks, trails), quiet areas, closed captioning, assisted listening devices, pictorial cues, sign language interpreters, use of scent (e.g., gardens), or service dogs/animals. Guidelines for interacting with a person with a sensory difference include the following:

Hearing difference:
- Let the person take the lead in establishing the communication mode, such as lip-reading, sign language, or writing notes.
- Talk directly to the person, even when a sign language interpreter is present.
- If the person lip-reads, face him or her directly, speak clearly, and with a moderate pace.
- With some people, it may help to simplify your sentences and use more facial expressions and body language.
- Pay close attention to communication barriers that may socially isolate youth with hearing differences and model inclusive communication.

Vision difference:
- When greeting the person, identify yourself and introduce others who may be present.
- Do not leave the person without verbally excusing yourself first.
- When asked to guide someone with a visual impairment, never push or pull the person. Allow him or her to take your arm or shoulder, then walk slightly ahead. Verbally note the location of doors, stairs, curbs, and different areas of a building as you approach or leave them.
- As you enter a room with the person, describe the layout and location of furniture and other objects.
- Be specific when describing the location of objects using a familiar method such as the clock method. (Example: "There is a chair three feet from you at 11 o'clock.")
- Do not pet or distract a guide dog. The dog is responsible for its owner's safety and is always working. It is not a pet. Do not greet a guide dog before you greet the person who is using the guide dog.

Communication functioning. Communication functioning includes things such as verbal, nonverbal, expressive, or receptive communication. Differences in communication functioning could be due to things such as cerebral palsy, stroke, intellectual disability, hearing or vision impairment, or autism. Common ways to adapt environments and activities to allow fuller communication participation include alternate forms of communication, written communication, quiet areas, pictorial cues, sign language interpreters, or use of mobile devices or computers. Guidelines for interacting with a person with a communication difference include those listed below:

- Pay attention, be patient, and wait for the person to complete a word or thought. Do not finish it for the person.
- Ask the person to repeat what is said if you do not understand. Tell the person what you heard, and see if it is close to what he or she is saying.
- Be aware that some youth with hearing impairments or autism may not understand slang phrases or words.
- Be prepared for various devices or techniques used to enhance or augment speech.

- Do not be afraid to communicate with someone who uses an alphabet board, iPad, or a computer with synthesized speech.

Intellectual functioning. Intellectual functioning includes things such as learning, processing information, memory, problem-solving, paying attention, reading, writing, and following directions. Differences in intellectual functioning could be due to things such as intellectual disability, autism, learning disability, other developmental disabilities, attention deficit disorder, or traumatic brain injury. Common ways to adapt environments and activities to allow fuller intellectual participation include alternate forms of communication, simplified directions, breaking down activities into small, sequential parts or steps, quiet areas, pictorial cues, positive behavioral supports, staff/volunteer assistance, or peer support. Guidelines for interacting with a person with an intellectual difference include the following:

- Keep your communication simple. Rephrase comments or questions for better clarity.
- Stay focused on the person as he or she responds to you.
- Allow the person time to tell or show you what he or she wants.
- Be patient and allow the person to complete his/her communication.
- When communicating with youth who are on the autism spectrum, be aware that you may have to communicate using concrete rather than slang words or phrases.
- Treat youth as you would anyone else of the same age. Do not patronize or talk down to people with disabilities.

Social and emotional functioning. Social and emotional functioning includes things such as experiencing enjoyment, coping with stress, feeling good about oneself, being able to interact with others, forming friendships, understanding social norms, and communicating effectively. Differences in social and emotional functioning could be due to things such as mental illness, attention deficit disorder, autism, other developmental disabilities, or traumatic brain injury. Common ways to adapt environments and activities to allow fuller social and emotional participation include positive behavioral supports, structured social interaction opportunities, staff/volunteer assistance, peer support, simplified directions, clear rules, quiet areas, or positive role models. Guidelines for interacting with a person with an emotional or social difference include the following:

- Always interact with individuals based on your experience with that person, not on assumptions about a particular diagnosis or label.
- Use clear and straightforward language.
- Do not rush the person; have patience and respect for what the person has to say.
- Keep the pressure of the situation to a minimum.
- Check that the person understands you—just ask him or her.
- If a person becomes distressed, stay calm and be supportive as you would with anyone. Ask how you can help and find out if there is a support person who can help.

Remember, youth with disabilities are people first. Never assume you know about a young person with a disability based on a label or diagnosis. Find out what a person's abilities are and use them to facilitate full inclusion. Avoid labels and discover abilities. The person with a disability is your best source of information. Using a functional approach to understanding disability and ability gives OST practitioners a clear pathway to inclusion. Several strategies and tools are available to help the OST practitioner along that pathway.

How to Facilitate Inclusion: Tools for Positive Change

How can OST practitioners move their organizations to a higher level of inclusion for all youth? If an OST practitioner fosters inclusiveness at every level, from direct provision of programs and services, to the administrative level of the agency, then inclusion can flourish. Inclusion is a continuous process that invites, welcomes, and celebrates participation of all youth. OST practitioners then need skills and competencies to fuel that process at the physical, administrative, and program levels. Overarching all levels of leadership, and a powerful tool in its own right, is the language we use. To be an inclusive OST practitioner, language is critically important (Anderson & Heyne, 2012).

Language

Language bridges all levels, from informal conversations with co-workers to formal communication issued by an agency. Language is not only a means of communication, but it shapes the way people perceive and experience the world (Wilkins, 2012). It welcomes and invites, or it hurts and excludes. Language is powerful. Because of this, and because it is something we can learn, use, and practice, language is a powerful change agent. OST practitioners must be prepared to learn the language of inclusion, and because society is always evolving, relearn that language on a regular basis.

What words do you use to describe variations in ability? What words are inclusive and respectful? Which perpetuate stereotypes and negative views? In choosing words to describe other people, it is im-

"....we can assume that most people want to use the most respectful terms. Since we have inherited a system that routinely perpetuates prejudicial attitudes and beliefs about groups, we often hear well-intentioned people unconsciously reinforcing those beliefs through their use of words" (Castania, 2003, p. 1).

portant to be accurate, sensitive, and positive. Framing language in a positive way also conveys genuine respect. Negativity is often associated with many groups who have experienced historical prejudice and discrimination. Terms such as *confined to a wheelchair* or *crazy lunatic* are examples of negative word choices. *Handicapped* is a word that has long been used to describe people with disabilities, even though its root meaning is very negative—beggar, loser, or disadvantaged. Yet we see the word handicapped everywhere in relation to amenities or services meant to assist people with disabilities. Reframing language to be positive conveys respectfulness and helps erase stereotypes. *Handicapped parking* becomes *accessible parking*. *Confined to a wheelchair* becomes *uses a wheelchair*. And *crazy lunatic* becomes *a person with a psychosocial disability*. This is called *person-first language*. That is, in choosing words, keeping the person first is the best guideline, and then if needed at all, the label comes second (Snow, 2009). Table 23.2 provides examples of person-first language and other examples of accurate, sensitive, and positive word choices in relation to disability.

Table 23.2
Inclusive Language Guidelines

General Guideline	Instead of This....	Say This
Use person-first language. Put the person before the disability or difference, describe what the person *has*, not what the person *is*, and only use the label if it is necessary.	Autistic child Disabled person Mentally retarded She is bipolar	Child with autism Person with a disability Person with an intellectual disability She has bipolar disorder
Use positive, sensitive language. Examine your words to ensure you are not communicating or perpetuating negative images or stereotypes.	Handicapped parking Confined to a wheelchair Afflicted with CP Birth defect	Accessible parking Uses a wheelchair Has cerebral palsy Congenital disability
Be aware of language that perpetuates dominance. Some words reinforce what is considered normal, mainstream, or standard.	Normal people	People without disabilities

In addition to language, OST practitioners can also facilitate inclusion across their organization at the physical, administrative, and program levels. In this chapter, it is not possible to share the wealth of strategies available to leaders to put inclusion into practice. We provide here an introduction to some common strategies as well as a way to think about making changes for inclusive practice.

Physical Inclusion

Approach, enter, and use universal design. Who can approach, enter, and use the facilities and amenities at an agency? If an agency can answer, "All people!" then it has used universal design principles in its facilities, amenities, programs, and services. Universal design means that an OST environment is designed for all people and reflects an inclusive society. Environments, services, and products are usable by as many people as possible regardless of age, ability, culture, or circumstance. Though universal design is often associated with disability, it is a design approach that helps everyone.

The principles of universal design are equitable use, flexibility in use, simple and intuitive use, perceptible information, tolerance for error and safe, low physical effort, and size and space for approach and use by all (The Center for Universal Design, 2010). Universal design means that a person who is transgender will find an appropriate restroom to use, as will the person using a wheelchair and the mother with three toddlers in tow. It means there is a barrier-free, well-lit, well-marked route of travel from the parking area or bus stop to the entrance to the changing area to the activity area. Universal design allows all people to approach, enter, and use a facility or program area.

Administrative Inclusion

It is often said that inclusion happens one person at a time, from the top down as well as the bottom up. Administrative practices that focus on inclusion can change the culture of youth-serving agencies. Lack of these practices can unintentionally turn youth away. OST practitioners can readily implement the following sample strategies.

> It is often said that inclusion happens one person at a time, from the top down as well as the bottom up.

Communication and marketing. Who do you invite to your programs? What messages do the marketing strategies convey regarding appropriate participants for special events or sports programs? OST practitioners must take a critical look at an agency's marketing materials to be sure they include images of all kinds of youth. Marketing materials and other agency communications should reflect the diversity of the community and youth with all abilities should be represented. The materials should let people know what is available to help them participate. On the agency website, there should be an easily found page that provides detailed information about physical access, safety guidelines, available adaptive equipment, availability of quiet spaces, sliding fee scales and scholarships, policies that facilitate participation, an invitation to call ahead for individual consultation, and other information to help youth access and enjoy what the agency has to offer.

Communication needs can be met in a wide variety of ways, from providing alternative forms of communication to assistive listening devices to apps on a smart phone that facilitate interaction. Alternative forms of communication can include interpreters (sign language, other languages), computer devices, iPads, online translating programs, and the like. The key is to let the public know what forms of communication are available, how they can be accessed or arranged, and an openness to explore new ways to communicate.

Administrative structure, planning, and evaluation. When doing any new construction or renovations, or designing new programs or services, OST practitioners must include a wide variety of people in the planning to ensure inclusivity from the initial phases of the project. Youth who live with a disability or their family members, for example, will have great insights that can help leaders design projects that truly meet needs. Administrations that use a welcoming philosophy create an environment that is open and accepting of people of all abilities. When planning programs or events, leaders must take into consideration the location of the event, scheduling, transportation, cost, and other considerations. Leaders must be alert to unintentionally excluding segments of the community for any of these reasons.

Who does not yet feel invited?

As well, leaders must continually evaluate strategies for creating inclusive agencies. Satisfaction on the part of current users is important, but so, too, is determining who is still not coming. Who does not yet feel invited? These are important areas to monitor and to continually make changes to ensure equity and inclusion.

To ensure a formalized voice in administrative decision-making, including planning and evaluation, youth with disabilities or their family members should have representation on advisory boards or planning committees. This will ensure that inclusion is not forgotten as important decisions about services and facilities are made.

Staffing and staff training. All staff members, from permanent to seasonal, need to have an understanding of what inclusion is and how it can be facilitated. Research has found that staff are important role models in facilitating inclusion between youth with and without disabilities (Devine & O'Brien, 2007). In hiring staff, leaders must be mindful of inclusion and choose staff who are comfortable with people with disabilities and other differences and are positive about inclusion. Once hired, OST practitioners must provide routine staff training on making accommodations, increasing ability awareness and facilitating inclusion strategies.

Policies. Clear and well-communicated policies and procedures are critical for facilitating inclusion. A number of policies and procedures are especially important to foster inclusive environments. Policies and procedures for emergency evacuation of people with disabilities and other functional differences are essential for safety. An agency policy about personal care attendants (those who accompany a person who has a disability and is only there to help, not participate) is needed; many agencies allow personal care attendants to attend free, as the attendant is solely there to assist. Policies on how the agency will accommodate service dogs/animals, mobility devices, quiet times, and other policies must be in place, as well as shared with the public. All staff must know the policies, from custodial staff to the executive director, so that they can be fairly and equitably implemented.

Programmatic Inclusion

What can OST practitioners do to promote program and activity inclusion? At its most basic level, inclusion happens one person at a time. And, at the level of the program or activity, inclusion is more easily facilitated due to the level of control a leader has in the program environment. Abandoning an age-old assumption that youth with disabilities will not be participants in the activities we plan is the first step for creating inclusive programs. The following suggestions for programs and activities can be easily implemented. They do not require much in the way of resources but more a willingness and positive attitude toward inclusion and diversity. All suggestions are based on the Bridging the Gap Model, which gives leaders a clear and simple way to conceptualize and operationalize inclusion (Anderson, 2017).

Bridging the Gap Model. All young people want fun-filled recreation experiences in their lives. Differences in a young person's functional level may make it necessary to change the activity or the place where the activity is done. The Bridging the Gap Model (see Figure 23.1) provides a concrete and useful way to conceptualize needed changes to ensure full participation (Anderson, 2017). Find out a young person's skills and abilities in relation to the demands of the recreation activity or environment, and use that information to figure out how to bridge the gap between the two if needed.

"We welcome all youth to our event/program. If you have specific needs to participate, please call ahead to let us know how we can help you."

You can begin to learn about a young person's skills and abilities through your registration or check-in process. Whether it is a formal or informal check-in process, it is a chance to start a conversation about what will be needed for a successful experience. Asking if any additional assistance is needed on your registration or promotional materials is the first step. You are inviting youth with disabilities and their families to dialogue with you about what they need to successfully participate in the program or activity. For programs where preregistration is required, a section on the registration form should allow people to identify any specific needs they may have to participate in a program.

This request for information begins the individualized process needed to facilitate inclusion. In essence, the process is about bridging the gap between the requirements of the activity the participant would like to be involved in and the skills and abilities of the participant. The "gap," if there is one, is bridged with services, supports, accommodations, adaptations, training, and any other means to help with successful participation. The methods of bridging the gap are limitless as there are a wealth of strategies, resources, and practices available (Anderson, 2017). Figure 23.1 illustrates the Bridging the Gap model that can be used by OST practitioners, and Table 23.3 provides concrete steps to follow. There are numerous supports and accommodations that can be used to bridge the gap, depending on each individual youth with a functional difference. The next section highlights some of the more common and effective strategies.

Figure 23.1. Bridging the Gap Model

Bridging the Gap with Supports

Structure social inclusion based on contact theory. As noted earlier when discussing contact theory, people do not automatically or even naturally get to know each other in a group situation unless it is structured to encourage the development of positive interactions. This is especially true if some of the group members are noticeably different than the majority, such as youth with disabilities. Coupled with many people's fears of disability, the chances of really getting to know other people in a group setting, and possibly developing friendships, becomes remote. Contact theory provides guidance on how to facilitate positive interactions between group members that lead to improved relationships. Principles to structure group recreation activities,

Table 23.3
Bridging the Gap Components

Bridge the Gap Questions	Bridge the Gap Actions
What are the goals, ability level, and functioning of the youth?	Determine goals and ability level during registration or check-in. If needed, invite youth and family to a pre-orientation tour of your agency and conduct an interview to learn more.
What are the demands of the recreation activity or environment? What does it take to do this activity in this place?	Analyze the demands of the activities you offer and the places you offer them. What functional abilities are needed to participate? Physical? Social? Cognitive? Communication?
What is the match between what the youth can do and the demands? Is there a gap between the two?	Compare the demands of the activity to the abilities of the youth. Is participation possible without changing anything? Or do you need to bridge the gap?
What can we do to bridge the gap so the young person with a disability has a good experience?	• Adaptive equipment • Skill modification • Rule modification • Space modification • Goal structure • Team/group modifications • Structured social interaction • Partial participation • Staff training • Policy modifications • Facility changes • Others

Source: Anderson (2016)

based on contact theory, can help OST practitioners set up a situation that will foster positive group interaction, social inclusion, and friendship development (Anderson & Heyne, 2011; Devine & Wilhite, 1999). These principles, described in Table 23.4, will benefit all participants in the activity, not just youth with disabilities.

Table 23.4

Principles to Structure Positive Social Interaction

Principle	How to Implement—Example Activities
Provide frequent and consistent opportunities to get acquainted.	• Provide ice-breaker activities (e.g., introductions, share favorites) • Break into small groups; do activities in small groups • Arrange seating to promote social interaction • Use pairs or partners; have one partner introduce other partner to group • Mix up groups often • Wear name tags
Maintain equal status; work carefully to structure the recreation activity and situation so each participant has equal status in the group, including the participant with a disability. Equal status reduces negative stereotypes, communicates respect, and is fair.	• Include everyone in the decision-making process • Mix up groups and responsibilities • Change the format in which information is given; provide alternative formats • Ask different group members to demonstrate • Assign roles in activities—everyone gets to try a role • Break down activities and skills to enable everyone to try • Make sure all participants are paying participants—no "special" breaks, no "special" volunteers, and no "charity cases"
Set mutual goals.	• Accentuate teamwork to reinforce equal status • Clearly set mutual goals; set the tone for cooperation • Ask the group to set mutual goals • Verbalize and reinforce mutual goals • Allow everyone a chance to play; rotate positions • Instill a spirit of camaraderie • Give feedback to the whole group on progress toward goals

(cont.)

Table 23.4 (cont.)

Principle	How to Implement—Example Activities
Support cooperation and interdependence to enhance the feeling that each individual's successes depend on the successes of the other group members.	<ul><li>Assign duties or tasks, all of which are needed to successfully complete the activity</li><li>Have participants sit in a circle or around a table</li><li>Cultivate team spirit and group identity</li><li>Use team nicknames, t-shirts, or other group identifiers</li><li>Keep verbal communication clear</li><li>Use a cooperative structure, where each person completes a part of the whole task</li></ul>
Provide accurate information about the participant with a disability; structure the recreation activity so that all participants receive information about the participant with a disability that is accurate and that doesn't perpetuate stereotyped beliefs about the disability.	<ul><li>At the initial session, explain the disability or supports and accommodations the individual needs</li><li>Let the individual determine what should be shared with group</li><li>Have the individual demonstrate how to use a communication device or piece of adaptive equipment</li><li>Create an environment of open communication</li><li>Do ice breakers that focus on similarities and differences</li><li>Assume a "can-do" attitude</li><li>Draw attention to the participant with a disability when s/he is doing something very well</li></ul>
Create and reinforce fair and tolerant norms that promote caring behavior and celebration of diversity on the part of the leaders, participants, and spectators.	<ul><li>Don't patronize or "over help"</li><li>Model positive, accepting behavior</li><li>Rotate positions, roles, and tasks</li><li>Accent positive attributes and skills</li><li>Emphasize teamwork</li><li>Get diverse input from all group members</li><li>Reinforce rules and fairness</li><li>Equal out or balance skill levels among participants</li></ul>

Source: Anderson & Heyne (2011)

Peer orientation. Depending on the individual and the significance of her or his disability, it may be beneficial to orient other youth in a recreation program to disability awareness in general, and to specific needs of the individual being included. Peer orientations are not always desirable or necessary; it really depends on the individual and the group. If you conduct a peer orientation, it is always preferable to have the young person with the disability (along with parent/guardian, if desired or needed) share information with the group. Focusing the peer orientation on similarities, commonalities, and needed supports and accommodations allows peers to learn about the individual, ask questions, learn how they can help, and begin a positive relationship. Sometimes something as simple as teaching peers how to use a young person's communication device, for example, can break the ice to begin a friendship.

Staff, volunteer, and peer assistance and modeling. Research has shown modeling and assistance to be one of the most powerful ways to facilitate inclusion (Heyne, Wilkins, & Anderson, 2012; Miller, Schleien, & Bowen, 2010). Providing additional human support for the young person with a disability, whether staff, volunteer, or a peer, assists that person to participate more fully. Those providing support must be trained to be effective and to avoid "hovering," infantilizing, and isolating the young person with a disability. One technique that works well is when the support staff or volunteer assists the youth with the disability only when needed, and assists other participants when not. In this way, they provide a model for helpful and appropriate behavior. Other youth learn how to interact by observing and emulating staff, volunteers, and trained peer supports. Some examples of behaviors that demonstrate accepting and inclusive behavior are provided in the box at left.

> **Being an Inclusion Role Model**
> - Focuses on the person, not the disability
> - Emphasizes abilities, not limitations
> - Does not give excessive praise or excessive attention to the person with a disability
> - Does not patronize or speak in a condescending manner
> - Treats the person with a disability like other participants
> - Does not speak for the person with a disability, lets that person speak for him- or herself
> - Does not make decisions for the person with a disability, lets him or her make decisions
> - Pays attention to group dynamics and draws excluded participants into the group through words and actions
> - Gently corrects the behaviors of other group participants who may not be accepting or respectful

Positive behavioral supports. All behavior is a form of communication. The goal of positive behavioral supports in a program is to help participants use positive helpful behavior to communicate needs, versus behavior that alienates others. Actions an agency can implement to foster a positive approach to behavior in all young people, but that are especially helpful to those with functional differences, are provided in the list at right.

Quiet spaces and calming kits. A designated quiet space near program areas is a best practice in inclusion. OST environments are often noisy and distracting, and someone who has difficulty integrating stimuli or handling stress may need a quiet place to regroup or relax for a short period. The quiet space does not need to be special; it can be an unused room, a corner of a room with floor pillows and lower lighting, or even a tent or yurt set up outside the mainstream of an outdoor activity. OST practitioners must make sure that youth know about the availability, location, and rules of the quiet space, and that it is comfortable and inviting. You can also offer and advertise quiet times when the noise and activity level is calmer and less busy so that youth can choose to use the facility or join programs at those times.

Calming kits are another best practice, especially when paired with a quiet space. Calming kits contain several items in a backpack to aid youth with various sensory differences such as attention deficit disorder, PTSD, autism, or other intellectual or developmental disabilities. Items are specifically chosen based on research that has shown the benefit they can have for calming, de-escalating, communication, and/or refocusing youth who need additional support. Typical items in a calming kit include fidget spinners, fidget toys, stress balls, noise-canceling headphones, UV-blocking sunglasses, a small photo album with nature pictures, relaxation strategy cards, social stories, rubber wristbands to snap, hand sanitizer, and more.

Positive Behavioral Supports

- Program expectations and rules are clearly defined for all participants.
- Expectations are reviewed with all participants on a routine basis.
- When participants meet expectations, they are rewarded or praised frequently.
- Clearly defined consequences are in place if participants do not meet basic behavior expectations.
- Consequences are implemented consistently.
- Transitions are used between activities on a consistent basis.
- Attention is paid to distractions or disruptions in the environment, and actions are taken to minimize these.

Bridging the gap with accommodations. Where supports tend to focus on human resources and interactions, accommodations tend to focus on changing the activity or environment itself. The following accommodations are commonly used to facilitate inclusion in recreation.

Activity adaptations. OST practitioners often complete task or activity analysis on a routine basis. Staff identify all the steps and skills needed to successfully complete an activity. They then use this information to plan their teaching or leadership strategies. Generally, the task analysis is not written down, but a routine part of the program planning thought processes.

Activity adaptation is altering some aspect of a recreation activity or environment to allow for successful participation by all. Activity adaptation and partial participation are easily accomplished when activity and task analysis are completed. Activity adaptation and partial participation allow youth with disabilities to partake in the parts of the activity they can do, or can do in a different way. For example, allowing young persons with a significant disability to use a personal flotation device will allow them to participate with their peers at the waterpark slide. Modifying the skill level in a cycling program by using a tandem bicycle for a youth with blindness, having that youth pedal and participate on the back seat without having to steer, is another example. Activity adaptation can include activity space, length of the activity, skill level, cooperative versus competitive goal structure, rules, and more.

Partial participation can be facilitated more easily if task analysis is done. Partial participation allows a participant with a disability to participate in the portions or steps of the activity that will be successful. Often, this strategy is used with persons with significant disabilities. For example, when youth are playing a board game, a young person with a significant intellectual disability may not be able to participate in most of the game, but could roll the dice for everyone throughout the game, helping include that person fully in the activity by only doing a part of the activity.

Adapted equipment. Adapting equipment involves changing the characteristics of equipment or materials so that a young person with a functional difference may more fully participate in a recreation activity. Pieces of recreation equipment can be adapted by making them lighter or heavier, larger or smaller, lower or higher, changing sounds or method of use, and more. A variety of adapted equipment is available to assist people with functional differences achieve full participation in recreation. Adaptive equipment ranges from beach wheelchairs, to grasping cuffs, to assistive listening devices, and more. Adapted equipment can be purchased or homemade. For example, using a piece of foam to build up a paintbrush handle would allow someone with limited grasp to use that piece of equipment. Equipment should be adapted to provide independent participation by the young person with the disability.

Advocacy

These are just a few of the many strategies and approaches OST practitioners can use to encourage and promote successful participation by youth with disabilities in services, programs, and facilities. Just as important, OST practitioners must be ready to be willing and active advocates for youth with disabilities. When resources are scarce for the public good, those who most often suffer are youth who are marginalized and lack a collective voice. OST practitioners must be prepared to help give voice to the needs of all youth so that all people can play wherever they choose. Advocacy is speaking, writing, and/or acting on behalf of the sincerely perceived interests of a disadvantaged person or a group without conflict of interest.

Advocacy requires three things: (1) a passionate desire to see positive change, (2) a sound understanding of the issue or idea for which you are advocating, (3) and a willingness to go public to effect change (Anderson & Heyne, 2012). Advocacy can occur at the grassroots level, where you join with other community members in advocating for a particular change, through many different avenues, such as organized communication, media events, protests, rallies, attending and testifying at public meetings, providing public input on proposals, writing letters to the editor, and more. Alternatively, advocacy can be more formal, where you work with organizations to change laws, rules, and policies. Advocacy is an important skill for OST practitioners.

Assessing for Inclusion

OST practitioners can facilitate and advocate for inclusion across multiple levels of youth services. How do you start to make environments, programs, services, and communities more inclusive? One analytical tool to help begin and sustain the inclusion process is called the Inclusivity Assessment Tool (IAT; Anderson et al., 2015). The IAT is an assessment tool that provides a way of asking questions about what is done in everyday practice and gathers descriptive information about the physical and social inclusion at an agency. The IAT gathers information about necessary physical aspects of an agency using the framework of approach (transportation, parking, route of travel), entry (stairs, ramps, doors), and use (registration/ticket areas, restrooms, elevators, routes of travel). It gathers descriptive information about the amenities at the agency such as sports fields, fishing piers, campsites, fitness areas, playgrounds, pools, and more. The IAT gathers information on administrative practices that promote inclusion. It asks about things such as inclusive mission, staff training and awareness, planning, inclusive marketing, communication, accessible websites, specific policies and procedures that promote inclusion, evaluation, and partnerships. The IAT gathers information on programmatic inclusion such as registration, training and skills of program staff, supports available to assist in inclusion, modifications and accommodations, adapted equipment, and any specialized programs or services that are available for youth with disabilities.

> Advocacy requires three things: (1) a passionate desire to see positive change, (2) a sound understanding of the issue or idea for which you are advocating, and (3) a willingness to go public to effect change.

By completing an inclusivity assessment, OST practitioners have a clear idea of what they do well and where they want to make changes so that all youth can access and be fully included in programs, services, and facilities. Ideally, OST practitioners can complete an inclusivity assessment with the help of youth, particularly those with disabilities. From the inclusivity assessment, an inclusion action plan can be formulated to provide an ongoing road map to positive changes at the agency.

Summary

All youth want to be included. For some youth with disabilities, OST practitioners must be prepared to make changes to their activities, programs, services, and facilities to ensure successful inclusion. This chapter provided an overview of concepts of inclusion, benefits of inclusion, constraints and facilitators to inclusion, underlying theories, and a way of thinking about disability as a functional variation in the human condition. We examined several tools and strategies to help facilitate inclusion for all youth, from physical environments to administrative and programming practices. By thoughtfully and carefully assessing and addressing all aspects of service, OST practitioners can not only help inclusion flourish, but also improve the overall quality of their work. Youth with and without disabilities will benefit from that work, and their road to successful adulthood enhanced.

Discussion Questions

1. Given the benefits of inclusion to youth with and without disabilities, how will you facilitate inclusion in your work with youth?
2. Have you worked in an agency that has done a good job with inclusion? What principles and practices identified in this chapter were used to facilitate inclusion? If you worked in an agency that did not do a good job, or did not even promote inclusion, what suggestions would you give to administrators and program leaders based on this chapter to promote inclusion?
3. Think of someone you know who has a disability. What physical, administrative, or programming inclusion practices would most help that person pursue the recreation experiences of his or her choice?
4. What inclusion strategies do you plan to implement in your work with youth? Why?

Assignments

Watch the video "I'm Tyler" at this link: http://imtyler.org/index.php/video/ (video is 12 minutes long). As you view the video, make notes of your thoughts and reactions throughout. Think about these questions as you take notes:

- What did you think of Tyler? Was he what you consider a "normal" teen?
- What was your reaction as you learned more about Tyler? Did your attitude change?

- What helped Tyler have the life he wanted?
- What is your takeaway from watching this video?
- Discuss the video with others, sharing your thoughts, reactions, and lessons learned.

References

Allport, G. W. (1954). *The nature of prejudice.* New York, NY: Addison-Wesley.

Anderson, L. (2008). The 40 developmental assets of inclusion. *The Voice,* Winter, 30–31.

Anderson, L. (2015). Leadership, diversity, and inclusion. In T. O'Connell, B. Cuthberston, & T. Goins (Eds.), *Leadership in recreation and leisure services* (pp. 68–95). Champaign, IL: Human Kinetics.

Anderson, L. (2016). *Improving usability for all visitors.* Cortland, NY: Inclusive Recreation Resource Center/Adirondack North Country Association.

Anderson, L. (2017). Inclusion U Online. Cortland, NY: SUNY Cortland/Inclusive Recreation Resource Center. Retrieved from www.inclusiverec.org

Anderson, L., & Heyne, L. (2000). A statewide needs assessment using focus groups: Perceived challenges and goals in providing inclusive recreation services in rural communities. *Journal of Park and Recreation Administration, 18*(4), 17–37.

Anderson, L., & Heyne, L. (2011). Structuring recreation and youth programs to facilitate social inclusion. *Impact, 24*(1), 34–35.

Anderson, L., & Heyne, L. (2012). *Therapeutic recreation practice: A strengths approach.* Urbana, IL: Sagamore-Venture Publishing.

Anderson, L., & Kress, C. (2003). *Inclusion: Strategies for including people with disabilities in parks and recreation opportunities.* Urbana, IL: Sagamore-Venture Publishing.

Anderson, L., Schleien, S. J., McAvoy, L., & Lais, G. (1997). Creating positive change through an integrated outdoor adventure program. *Therapeutic Recreation Journal, 31*(4), 214–229.

Anderson, L., Wilkins, V., & Penney McGee, L. (2014). Eco-ability: Putting theory into action. In A. Nocella, A., J. Bentley, & J. Duncan (Eds.), *Earth, animal, and disability liberation: The rise of the eco-ability movement* (pp. 174–186). New York, NY: Peter Lang Publishing.

Anderson, L., Wilkins, V., & Penney McGee, L. (2015). *Inclusivity Assessment Tool user manual.* Cortland, NY: SUNY Cortland/Inclusive Recreation Resource Center. Retrieved from www.inclusiverec.org

Bogdan, R., & Taylor, S. J. (1992). The social construction of humanness. In P. M. Ferguson, D. M. Ferguson, & S. J. Taylor (Eds.), *Interpreting disability* (pp. 275–296). New York, NY: Teachers College Press.

Bronfenbrenner, U. (1979). *The ecology of human development.* Cambridge, MA: Harvard University Press.

Castania, K. (2003). *The evolving language of diversity.* Ithaca, NY: Cornell University.

Deegan, P. (1996). Recovery as a journey of the heart. *Psychiatric Rehabilitation Journal, 19*(3), 91–97.

Devine, M. A. (1997). Inclusive leisure services and research: Consideration of the use of social construction theory. *Journal of Leisurability, 24*(2), 3–11.

Devine, M. A. (2004). From connector to distancer: The role of inclusive leisure contexts in determining social acceptance for people with disabilities. *Journal of Leisure Research, 35*(2), 137–159.

Devine, M. A. (2012). A nationwide look at inclusion: Gains and gaps. *Journal of Park and Recreation Administration, 30*(2), 1–18.

Devine, M. A. (2015). Leveling the playing field: Perspectives of people with disabilities on the ADA, access to reasonable accommodation in public parks and recreation. *Disability Studies Quarterly, 35,* 125–151.

Devine, M. A., & Lashua B. (2002). Constructing social acceptance in inclusive leisure contexts: The role of individuals with disabilities. *Therapeutic Recreation Journal, 36*(1), 65–83.

Devine, M. A., Malley, S., Sheldon, K., Dattilo, J., & Gast, D. L. (1997). Promoting initiation of community leisure participation for adults with mental retardation. *Education and Training in Mental Retardation and Developmental Disabilities, 32*(3), 241–254.

Devine, M. A., & O'Brien, M. B. (2007). The mixed bag of inclusion: Conditions of an inclusive camp environment and perceptions of youth with and without disabilities. *Therapeutic Recreation Journal, 41*(3), 201–222.

Devine, M. A., Piatt, J., & Dawson, S. L. (2015) Social acceptance and quality of life: Camp experiences for youth with cochlear implants and hearing aids. *Therapeutic Recreation Journal, 49*(4), 293–309.

Devine, M. A., & Wilhite, B. (1999). Application of theory to inclusive leisure services. *Therapeutic Recreation Journal, 33,* 29–47.

Devine, M. A., & Wilhite, B. (2000). Meaning of disability: Implications for inclusive leisure services for youth with and without disabilities. *Journal of Park and Recreation Administration, 18*(3), 22–40.

Douglas, J. D. (1970). Understanding everyday life. In J. D. Douglas (Ed.), *Understanding everyday life: Toward the reconstruction of sociological knowledge* (pp. 3–43). Chicago, IL: Aldine.

Green, F. P., & DeCoux, V. (1994). A procedure for evaluating the effectiveness of a community recreation integration program. *Therapeutic Recreation Journal, 28*(1), 41–47.

Heyne, L., Wilkins, V., & Anderson, L. (2012). Social inclusion in the lunchroom and on the playground at school. *Social Advocacy and Systems Change Journal, 3*(1), 54–68.

Institute of Medicine. (2007). *The future of disability in America.* Washington, DC: National Academies of Sciences.

Lewkowicz, B. (2006). Opening the door to nature for people with disabilities. Bay Nature, October-December. Retrieved from http://baynature.org/articles/oct-dec-2006/accessible-outdoors/opening-the-door-to-nature

Mayer, W., & Anderson, L. (2014). Perceptions of people with disabilities and their families about segregated and inclusive recreation involvement. *Therapeutic Recreation Journal, 48*(2), 150–168.

Miller, K., Schleien, S., & Bowen, F. (2010). Support staff as an essential component of inclusive recreation services. *Therapeutic Recreation Journal, 44*(1), 35–49.

Miller, K., Schleien, S., & Lausier, J. (2009). Search for best practices in inclusive recreation: Programmatic findings. *Therapeutic Recreation Journal, 43*(1), 27–41.

Modell, S. J. (1997). An examination of inclusive recreation and leisure participation for children with trainable mental retardation. Unpublished doctoral dissertation, Florida State University, Tallahassee.

National Organization on Disability. (2010). *The ADA, 20 years later.* New York, NY: The Harris Interactive.

Oliver, M. (1996). *Understanding disability: From theory to practice.* London, UK: MacMillan Press Ltd.

Roper, P. (1990). Changing perceptions through contact. *Disability, Handicap & Society, 5*(3), 243–255.

Ryan, R. M., & Deci, E. L. (2000). Self-determination theory and the facilitation of intrinsic motivation, social development, and well-being. *American Psychologist, 55*, 68–78.

Schleien, S. J., Fahnestock, M., Green, R., & Rynders, J. E. (1990). Building positive social networks through environmental interventions in integrated recreation programs. *Therapeutic Recreation Journal, 24*(4), 42–52.

Schleien, S. J., Hornfeldt, D., & McAvoy, L. H. (1994). Integration and environmental outdoor education: The impact of integrating students with severe disabilities on the academic performance of peers without disabilities. *Therapeutic Recreation Journal, 28*, 25–34.

Scholl, K., Dieser, R., & Davison, A. (2005). Together we play: An ecological approach to inclusive recreation. *Therapeutic Recreation Journal, 39*(4), 299–311.

Scholl, K., Smith, J., & Davison, A. (2005). Agency readiness to provide inclusive recreation and after-school services for children with disabilities. *Therapeutic Recreation Journal, 39*(1), 47–62.

Search Institute. (2006). The 40 developmental assets. Retrieved from http://www.search-institute.org/assets/

Snow, K. (2009). A few words about people-first language. Disability is natural. Retrieved from http://www.disabilityisnatural.com

Sylvester, C. (2011). Therapeutic recreation, the International Classification of Functioning, Disability, and Health, and the capability approach. *Therapeutic Recreation Journal, 45*(2), 85–104.

Szenasy, S. (2010). Twenty years and counting. *Metropolis Magazine.* Retrieved from http://www.metropolismag.com/story/20100915/twenty-years-and-counting

Taylor, S. (2004). Caught in the continuum: A critical analysis of the least restrictive environment. *Research and Practice for Persons with Severe Disabilities, 29*(4), 218–230.

Taylor, S. J., & Bogdan, R. (1993). Promises made promises to be broken. In P. Wehman (Ed.), *The ADA mandate for a social change* (pp. 255–268). Baltimore, MD: Paul H. Brookes.

The Center for Universal Design. (2010). About UD. Retrieved from http://www.design.ncsu.edu/cud/about_ud/about_ud.htm

Wilhite, B., Devine, M. A., & Goldenberg, L. (1999). Self-perceptions of youth with and without disabilities: Implications for leisure programs and services. *Therapeutic Recreation Journal, 33*(3), 15–28.

Wilkins, V. (2012). Communicating humanness: Attitudes and language. *Social Advocacy and Systems Change Journal, 3*(1), 38–43.

World Health Organization. (2003). International Classification of Functioning, Disability, and Health Version 2.1a. Retrieved from http://www.who.int/classifications/icf/site/checklist/icf-checklist.pdf

Chapter 24

So, You Want to Be a Youth Professional

Peter A. Witt

You are probably reading this book because you are taking a course related to youth development, preparing to enter the youth development field, or already working in the youth development field. Whatever the reason, my experience teaching and interacting with youth development professionals suggests that as a young person you have probably had experiences working with youth through a summer job, internship, or volunteer activities, which influenced your interest in pursuing a career related to youth development. As an illustration, let me share with you my own journey.

My Journey

While I was growing up, I attended several different youth programs in my community. For example, early on my parents enrolled me in a youth theater program. They also enrolled me in programs at a local community center where I joined the swim team and took part in a club called the AquaTeens. I also attended summer camp for a number of years, including attendance at a private camp, a YMCA camp, and a camp sponsored by the Jewish community center. I was also on my high school track team, although the coaching left a lot to be desired.

Through these opportunities, I experienced some truly caring youth leaders but unfortunately also some folks who seemed to be providing "so-called" leadership just to supplement their incomes. I also attribute a lot of personal growth to the experiences I had during my out-of-school or informal activities. I gained confidence in myself, learned how to interact with others, and learned a set of life skills that I would not have gained through my formal school experiences.

My interest in youth work went beyond what I gained through my participation and extended to leading youth groups at the community center, working at several camps, and while I was getting my master's degree, working as a teacher at a private school for children with behavioral problems.

However, like many people who take up youth development work, I initially went to college with another career path in mind. My parents would not have understood if I had said I wanted to go to college to learn how to be a youth worker. So, political science was originally my undergraduate major, then business (accounting). I graduated with a B.S. in Business Administration.

However, during my senior year, I took a course from a professor who talked about recreation, recreation services, and youth programs, among other things. I dutifully completed my accounting courses, but my passion for working with young people was rekindled. I eventually worked with my mentor on a recreation master's degree, and then pursued a doctorate at the University of Illinois, with an emphasis on working with children and youth with disabilities. Then it was on to a career in university teaching, research, and interests that broadened to out-of-school time services for all youth.

My story is not atypical of many people who ultimately pursue a career path related to youth development. Many of us are deeply impacted by our own youth experiences. We have a strong desire to give back or influence the lives of others, but many of us start out pursuing other degrees or interests only to be called back to our fundamental interest in directly influencing the lives of young people.

What Is Your Journey?

So, stop and think a moment: What has been your journey up to now? What might it be in the future?

- What were your out-of-school time experiences while you were growing up? What organizations did you join? What types of activities, organized or unorganized, were you involved in?

- What was the impact of these experiences on you: socially, psychologically, educationally, and physically? What did you learn through your participation in these activities?
- Think about the leaders of the programs and activities in which you participated. How did they influence your life?
- Why are you reading this book? What are your goals for the future? If your goals are related to working in the youth development field, what are your aspirations? What kind of information, education, training, and experiences will you need to achieve those goals?

The Road Ahead

Whatever your path to date, you have an exciting journey ahead. Although in the past, many youth programs were more akin to babysitting with a heavy emphasis on simply providing fun and games, today blue-ribbon youth programs and services are built on the youth development principles discussed in Chapter 1, and throughout this book, in order to intentionally promote learning, development, and skill building of youth participants. Blue-ribbon programs also employ staff who are trained to provide these types of supports, opportunities, programs, and services (SOPS). Staff typically have backgrounds in psychology, social work, education, recreation and parks, or a combination thereof.

As noted by Borden, Scholomer, and Bracamonte Wiggs (2011): "Youth programs of the past were often seen exclusively as a place to play and have fun; however, today the expectations for youth workers and programs include the promotion of the overall positive development of the young people within the program" (p. 1).

The term *youth work* is "an umbrella term to refer to those working in the after-school, school-age care, out-of-school time, youth development, recreation, and youth services fields" (Starr, Yoholem, & Gannett, 2009, p. 3). In its simplest form, a youth worker is anyone who develops or implements supports, opportunities, programs, and services to promote positive development; designs settings to enable young people to use their out-of-school time to increase socialization and learning; provides opportunities to build life skills; and/or promotes the development of positive relationships with peers and adults (Eccles & Gootman, 2002; Lerner, 2004; Perkins & Borden, 2001).

To become a youth worker, one needs to understand what youth work is, how it works, and how it can be undertaken. Fusco and Baizerman (2013) pose some interesting questions that form the basis for outlining the types of issues that people in the youth work field must be able to answer. For example:

- What are the underlying social and political philosophies (e.g., responsibility, care, equity, justice) that form the basis of youth work?
- What images do youth workers have of youth? What is the pact with youth that society makes about how they will be raised and the type of society they will be raised in?
- What kind of knowledge and training do youth workers need to work effectively with young people, their families, and communities?

There have been ongoing efforts to identify the core competencies needed by youth workers to deliver high-quality, developmentally appropriate supports, opportunities, programs, and services. For example, Starr et al. (2009) reviewed 14 youth worker core competency frameworks developed by various states and organizations. The authors noted that the identification of core competencies is a way to bring related sub-fields such as school-age care, after-school, youth development, recreation, and summer learning together under a common umbrella. "By articulating what effective youth work practice looks like, core competencies can help those within and outside of our field(s) understand the unique role of youth work professionals and at the same time, the shared contributions that those working in a range of settings make to the lives of children and youth" (Starr et al., 2009, p. 4).

The following is an adapted listed of the competency areas that occurred most frequently across all of the frameworks reviewed by Starr and colleagues (2009):

- Curriculum, program planning, and design
- Connecting with youth and families
- Health, safety, and nutrition
- Child and adolescent development
- Cross-cultural competency
- Guidance, mentoring
- Program management, record keeping
- Connecting with communities
- Creating youth-friendly spaces
- Assessment of community, family, and youth needs
- Youth empowerment, building youth voice

Another useful list of youth worker competencies, referred to as *occupational standards*, has been developed in England and include the following:

- Working with people and others
  - Building relationships and engaging young people
  - Engaging with the local community
  - Building working relationships and networks
- Facilitating the person, social, and educational development of young people
  - Facilitating learning and development of young people through youth work
  - Planning and implementing learning activities in youth work

- – Promoting young people's self-awareness, confidence, and participation
- – Promoting access to information and support
- Promoting inclusion, equity, and young people's interests and well-being
  - – Engaging in critical dialogue and working with young people in promoting their rights
  - – Safeguarding the health and welfare of young people
  - – Promoting inclusion, equity, and the valuing of diversity (culturally responsive programming)
  - – Fulfilling regulatory and organizational requirements
- Developing youth work strategy and practice
  - – Establishing and prioritizing requirements for youth work
  - – Planning and implementing youth work strategy
  - – Monitoring and evaluating the effectiveness of youth work strategy and plans
- Developing, leading, and managing self and others
  - – Managing yourself
  - – Leading and managing others
  - – Developing colleagues
  - – Maintaining health and safety in the workplace (adapted from National Youth Work Agency, 2017)

Together these frameworks provide a useful way to envision the knowledge, attitudes, values, skills, and behaviors that individuals desiring to work with youth should strive to develop through some combination of university and pre- and in-service training. The frameworks make it clear that youth work is not just about spending time with young

people, but constructively developing and implementing the supports, opportunities, programs, and services that will enable young people to thrive.

Some Issues to Consider as You Pursue a Career in Youth Development

Although skilled youth workers are critical to developing and delivering quality supports, opportunities, programs, and services for young people, there are many barriers that are impeding the development of a stable pipeline of youth workers and quality youth services. These barriers include the following:

- **Limited infrastructure.** Often there is a lack of or inadequate facilities, a dearth of SOPS in an area of high need, and lack of funding to support development of needed SOPS.
- **Low compensation.** Too many youth development positions are part-time or full-time positions with low wages and lack adequate health and retirement benefits. It is often hard for people to maintain their commitment to a career in youth work while maintaining an adequate level of income.
- **Limited career pathways.** In some cases, organizations do not supply adequate opportunities for advancement, thus confining compensation and opportunities for organizational leadership.
- **Unstable funding.** A lot of funding for youth programs and services comes through nonprofit organizations that depend on fund-raising, government funding, and foundation grants. Political processes, the economy, and competing priorities can greatly impact the stability of these funding sources.
- **Insufficient pre-service and in-service training.** Youth organizations often spend too little time and resources on adequately training new hires and continuing the training process during employment. In some cases, after-school program workers miss the beginning of the school year training sessions because they are hired during the program year.

In many cases, a combination of these issues can lead to high staff turnover, which in turn can lead to difficulty in building relationships between youth and adults. When there is a high rate of staff turnover, this can lead to problems of continuity of services, and it is harder for young people to bond with staff (Starr et al., 2009). Caring relationships between youth and program staff are important, as youth are more likely to leave programs when

Caring relationships between youth and program staff are important, as youth are more likely to leave programs when they do not feel a strong connection with staff members.

they do not feel a strong connection with staff members (Borden et al., 2006; Rhodes, 2004).

It should be noted, however, that a number of organizations make considerable efforts to overcome the identified barriers and issues through the provision of quality work environments, reasonable pay and benefits, good supervision and mentoring, and opportunities for quality pre- and in-service training. Thus, when you are seeking employment in the youth development field, it would be good to carefully scrutinize organizational structure and practices in each of these areas.

At the same time, to help overcome some of the barriers and issues, there has been some discussion about how to professionalize the youth work field. Professionalization would involve efforts to (a) identify competencies needed by individuals seeking employment and advancement in the youth development field, (b) develop curricula and training methods for achieving the competencies, and (c) credential or certify that individuals have been trained and have developed the desired competencies (Fusco, 2011). Borden, Schlomer, and Bracamonte Wiggs (2011) argue that to improve compensation levels, achieve greater uniformity in training, and improve funding levels, it may be necessary to turn youth work into a profession. They argue that "One way to ameliorate this discrepancy is the professionalization of the field. Professionalization centers on increasing the compensation, status, and benefits of the youth worker as well as the structure of the youth worker field" (p. 134).

Fusco and Baizerman (2013) argue that professionalization could provide three beneficial outcomes: "(a) legitimacy to the field, helping it gain value and recognition in society; (b) improved wages and work conditions; and (c) better quality of the practice, thereby strengthening client outcomes" (p. 92).

Youth Work: An Honorable Undertaking

Despite some of the problems and issues related to the field of youth work, working with young people is an honorable and worthy calling for many individuals. Although for some, it may never progress past summer or part-time jobs while in school, for others it can become a life-long commitment to making a difference in the lives of others. For most people I know who are involved in youth work, it is indeed a calling...something they are passionate about, something they are driven to do because of their interest in helping youth thrive. The authors of the materials in this book are pleased you are exploring the youth work field and wish you well in your efforts to be a part of making a difference in the lives of young people.

> For most people I know who are involved in youth work, it is indeed a calling.

Discussion Questions

1. Was there a youth leader in your past who demonstrated the knowledge and skills outlined in this chapter? If yes, describe how the leader's behavior and interactions with you contributed to your development.
2. What are the key ideas from this book that will help you become a better youth leader in the future? How about parent? Citizen?

Assignment

Answer the questions posed in the chapter regarding "What is your journey?" In addition, identify how what you have learned from your experiences as a participant in or leader of youth programs will influence your interactions with young people in the future.

References

Borden, L. M., Schlomer, G. L., & Bracamonte Wiggs, C. (2011). The evolving role of youth workers. *Journal of Youth Development, 6*(4), 126–138. Retrieved from https://jyd.pitt.edu/ojs/jyd/article/view/179

Borden, L. M., Perkins, D. F., Villarruel, F. A., Carlton-Hug, A., Stone, M. R., & Keith, J. (2006). Challenges and opportunities to Latino youth development: Increasing meaningful participation in youth development programs. *Hispanic Journal of Behavioral Sciences, 28,* 187–208.

Eccles, J., & Gootman, J. A. (2002). *Community programs to promote youth development.* Committee on Community-Level Programs for Youth. Board on Children, Youth, and Families, Commission on Behavioral and Social Sciences Education, National Research Council and Institute of Medicine, Washington, DC.

Fusco, D. (2011). On becoming an academic profession. In D. Fusco (Ed.), *Advancing youth work: Current trends, critical questions* (pp. 111–126). New York, NY: Routledge.

Fusco, D., & Baizerman, M. (2013). Professionalization in youth work? Opening and deepening circles of Inquiry. *Child & Youth Services, 34*(2), 89–99.

Lerner, R. M. (2004). *Liberty: Thriving and civic engagement among America's youth.* Thousand Oaks, CA: Sage Publications.

National Youth Work Agency. (2017). LSI YW00 Youth Work National Occupational Standards Introduction. Retrieved from www.nya.org.uk/wp-content/.../National-Occupation-Standards-for-Youth-Work.pdf

Perkins, D. F., & Borden, L. M. (2001). Programs for adolescence. In R. M. Lerner & J. V. Lerner (Eds.), *Adolescence in America* (pp. 535–540). Santa Barbara, CA: ABC CLIO.

Perkins, D. F., & Borden, L. M. (2003). Risk factors, risk behaviors, and resiliency in adolescence. In R. M. Lerner, M. A. Easterbrooks, & J. Mistry (Eds.), *Handbook of psychology: Vol. 6, developmental psychology* (pp. 373–394). New York, NY: Wiley.

Rhodes, J. E. (2004). The critical ingredient: Caring youth-staff relationships in after-school settings. *New Directions for Youth Development, 101,* 145–191.

Starr, B., Yoholem, N., & Gannett, E. (2009). Youth work core competencies: A review of existing frameworks and purposes. Next Generation Youth Work Coalition. Retrieved from https://www.niost.org/pdf/Core_Competencies_Review_October_2009.pdf

Index

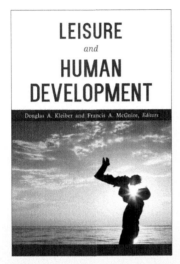
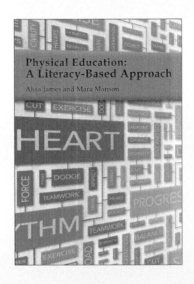